Empirical Political Analysis

PEARSON

At Pearson, we believe in learning – all kinds of learning for all kinds of people. Whether it's at home, in the classroom or in the workplace, learning is the key to improving our life chances.

That's why we're working with leading authors to bring you the latest thinking and the best practices, so you can get better at the things that are important to you. You can learn on the page or on the move, and with content that's always crafted to help you understand quickly and apply what you've learned.

If you want to upgrade your personal skills or accelerate your career, become a more effective leader or more powerful communicator, discover new opportunities or simply find more inspiration, we can help you make progress in your work and life.

Pearson is the world's leading learning company. Our portfolio includes the Financial Times, Penguin, Dorling Kindersley, and our educational business, Pearson International.

Every day our work helps learning flourish, and wherever learning flourishes, so do people.

To learn more please visit us at: www.pearson.com/uk

Empirical Political Analysis

James Babb

University of Newcastle

PEARSON

Harlow, England • London • New York • Boston • San Francisco • Toronto • Sydney
Auckland • Singapore • Hong Kong • Tokyo • Seoul • Taipei • New Delhi
Cape Town • São Paulo • Mexico City • Madrid • Amsterdam • Munich • Paris • Milan

Pearson Education Limited
Edinburgh Gate
Harlow
Essex CM20 2JE
England

and Associated Companies throughout the world

Visit us on the World Wide Web at:
www.pearson.com/uk

First published 2012

ISBN: 978-1-4082-0462-7

British Library Cataloguing-in-Publication Data
A catalogue record for this book is available from the British Library

Library of Congress Cataloging-in-Publication Data
A catalog record for this book is available from the Library of Congress

10 9 8 7 6 5 4 3 2 1
16 15 14 13 12

Typeset in 10/12 Times by 73
Printed and bound in Great Britain by 4edge Ltd, Hockley. www.4edge.co.uk

Contents

Chapter 3 Setting the foundation: techniques of systematic bibliographic search 36

Part II Research design 61

Chapter 4 From abstract to concrete: operationalisation and measurement 63

Chapter 5 Working from a plan: considerations in research design | 90

Chapter 6 Experimental research design | 103

Part III Quantitative data | 117

Chapter 7 Who, what, where, when: the problem of sampling | 119

Chapter 8 Survey research | 135

Chapter 9 Scaling techniques 159

Chapter 10 Sources and applications of aggregate data 171

Chapter 11 Data preparation and data processing 187

Part IV Quantitative analysis — **199**

Chapter 12 Content analysis — **201**

Chapter 13 Quantitative comparative research — **214**

Chapter 14 Social network analysis: finding structure in a complex world — **225**

Chapter 15 Describing the data: the construction of tables and charts — 237

Part V Statistical techniques — 249

Chapter 16 Statistics I: summarising distributions on one variable — 251

Chapter 17 Statistics II: examining relationships between two variables — 263

Chapter 18   Statistics III: examining relationships among several variables   283

Part VI   Qualitative methods   299

Chapter 19   Elite and specialised interviewing   301

Chapter 20   Focus group methodologies   312

Part VII Reporting the results 377

Chapter 24 Writing (and reading) the research report 379

Chapter 25 Overview 394

Appendix A: Statistical tables 401

Appendix B: Ethical standards in empirical research 410

Preface to the UK adaptation of *Empirical Political Analysis* (7th edition)

A few years ago I was asked to comment on the potential of the popular US textbook *Empirical Political Analysis* (7th edn) to be revised and adapted for the UK or international market. Along with several other reviewers I saw some potential in the down-to-earth style of the writing and the clear explanation of the quantitative material. When I was later asked if I wanted to try my hand at adapting the textbook for the British market, I replied I would only do it if no one else wanted to. Apparently no one did. At the time, writing or editing textbooks was not an activity which many academics felt was a good use of their time. I disagree.

The revisions can be broadly divided into three types:

1 *Softening the 'logical-positivist' or 'scientific' bias of the text.* A more nuanced epistemology was needed based on the latest thinking in the social sciences. The text still promotes rigour and high standards of conduct, but also supports a broader notion of what constitutes legitimate research.
2 *Modifying examples and terminology to broaden the appeal of the text.* The original text assumed US university student readership. In this revision, British, EU and other non-US examples are used though in some cases it is appropriate to retain the US-based examples.
3 *Suggestions of additions and deletions.* Additions are made only in those areas where the existing text overlooks key concepts related to the field. In particular, new material was required on case studies, discourse analysis and hermeneutics. Suggested deletions are focused on material that is not central to the mainstream study of politics or expendable for other reasons.

With the revisions and additional chapters, the textbook should now have broader appeal and support a wider variety of research projects.

The main epistemological problem with the original text was a false dichotomy between value and fact. With the addition of important new material, the text now deals more effectively with the problem of bias which seemed to have been the main concern of the authors. The original aim – to promote the pursuit of research based on rigorous procedures and clear standards – has been preserved. The mistake made in the original text was to assume 'science' easily allows us to do this. The problems involved in dealing with bias are much more slippery than a 'positivist' approach admits.

The chapter on research design also required substantial revision because the example given was largely quantitative and the original chapter seemed to have been an excuse to present material on experimental and quasi-experimental design. Experimental method is important, not because it is widely used in politics research but more because it is an example of the scientific approach, its potential and limitations. This discussion is located in a separate chapter. The new research design chapter now makes a more balanced distinction between quantitative and qualitative approaches.

The qualitative methods section of the textbook has also been substantially rewritten and important new chapters introduced. The original text displayed a very narrow understanding of qualitative research. The discussion over-emphasised the problem of bias as if it was exclusively a problem in qualitative research. The qualitative methods chapters now acknowledge more up-to-date social science literature on issues of objectivity and bias. The text also notes that transforming individuals into numerical data and creating inappropriate categories for numerical analysis are also forms of possible bias. Bias in both quantitative and qualitative research is now more equally and thoughtfully addressed.

The original textbook reflected the bias of US political science which tends to focus on 'American' politics. It was revealing that the universe of cases for quantitative analysis was often the 50 states of the United States or the committees or constituencies of the US Congress. Given the similarities between the cases within one country, it did allow for control of variables. No one should doubt the important contribution of US political science to the study of politics in the last 50 years. At the same time, the generalisability of the findings, given the limited universe of cases, can and should be questioned.

It was particularly problematic that the original tended to dismiss non-quantitative approaches, such as interviews or direct observation, as unusual or inferior. Even though the top US political science journals articles tend to publish quantitative research (usually on US cases), the most important political monographs (books) tend to use qualitative or mixed methods. The revisions now make the text supportive of such research, though at the same time recognises areas for improvement. Ironically, the original unduly undermined the value of qualitative methods for testing and refining existing theory, and even seemed to endorse a form of relativism. The significance of qualitative approaches and high standards required to undertake qualitative research successfully are now clearer in this revised version.

The new qualitative chapters are not without their problems, however. There is some overlap between the chapter on direct observation/ethnography and the two new chapters on discourse analysis and hermeneutics. In the conventional use of these terms, the approaches are more distinct. However, insights from more radical forms of hermeneutics have informed discourse analysis and ethnography. 'Critical' approaches to ethnography and discourse analysis raise challenging ideas drawn from epistemology and hermeneutics. An introductory text can only raise these issues in the most rudimentary form, but a careful reading and re-reading of the chapters together should enhance student understanding of these difficult issues at the cutting-edge of research in politics and the social sciences in general.

The revisions I have made are based on years of training and experience in 'political science'. My undergraduate degree in 'Political Science' was taken at an ordinary state university in the United States and teaching reflected the debates in US political science in the aftermath of the Vietnam War. My PhD is in 'Political Science' from Stanford University where many of the prominent scholars of postwar US political science were still teaching. Quantitative methods were increasingly emphasised, but there was a large range of approaches and methodological orientations. The behaviourialist approaches of Gabriel Almond and Heinz Eulau, were stressed just as much as the political sociology of Seymour Martin Lipset or the case study research of Alexander George. The more quantitative approaches of John Ferejohn were increasingly influential and I enjoyed working too with George Tsebelis, who was a postdoc in the department at the time. Terry Moe graciously led our doctoral cohort through two semesters of statistics and econometrics, and though I was happy and surprised to pass these courses, much more has 'stuck' than he or I would have imagined at the time. The sum of my experience at Stanford was that it is clear no one type of methodology is dominant in political research, even in the United States. I felt any revision of the textbook had to reflect this diversity.

Since I was training to be a specialist in a non-European 'area studies' context, I have also had extensive experience overseas and watched political research in action outside the US, particularly in Europe and east Asia. Since language is so important to area studies research, it was essential to remain sensitive to issues of discourse and hermeneutics. As a direct consequence of this interest and background I was for several years in charge of a module on 'The Nature of Enquiry and Explanation in the Social Sciences' on the Economic and Social Research Council-approved research student training programme for the Faculty of Humanities, Arts and Social Sciences at the University of Newcastle-upon-Tyne. This programme forced me to keep up-to-date with developments in the epistemology of the social sciences and interact with research students from a variety of fields. This background particularly informs the chapter on hermeneutics, but was an influence throughout the revision.

This is the core text for my Research Methods in Politics module. Of course, your reading should be aided by introductory lectures and practicals with a sympathetic teacher. I would not have had the confidence to use these methods and teach this material had it not been for a few outstanding teachers who gently guided me to a better understanding of the potential and limits of statistics. Be grateful if you find one. However, this book is an excellent guide in itself. I believe the information in this book will make you a better student, scholar, employee, activist, entrepreneur and thinker – whatever you want to be. Please enjoy it and make as much use of it as you can.

Acknowledgements

First of all, there are many people at Pearson who deserve appreciation. I cannot mention them all but the most important is Philip Langeskov, former Acquisitions Editor at Pearson, who originally approached me to review this textbook for adaptation and enthusiastically pursued the project. In fact, all the editorial staff at Pearson, past and present, have been outstanding. They are friendly and understanding despite being very busy. Sarah Turpie was particularly patient with me over cover design and other marketing issues.

Second I would also like to thank the anonymous reviewers for really helpful and useful feedback on various plans and drafts of the textbook.

Third I should thank the authors and copyright owners of the original textbook of which this is a radical adaptation. I was given a free hand to make changes as I saw fit. Of course, that also means that any remaining problems with the textbook are entirely my own.

Next I need to thank all of my students in Politics at Newcastle who have taken my various methods modules over the years. They have been a pleasure to teach and their feedback on various aspects of politics research methodology has been invaluable.

Last, but not least, I thank my family. I love my work, the teaching as much, if not more, than the research, but when academic life in England becomes bureaucratic and petty, my family is always there to give my efforts extra meaning and joy. Fumie is not just a fantastic wife but a great friend and supporter of all my projects over many years. My children have been more important to this project than one might imagine. They have a deep intuitive understanding of philosophy and enjoy maths (and I am glad that they seem not to have to struggle with maths as I did), so when I start to rant about topics such as research methods, they have given me surprisingly useful advice. That is why this book is dedicated to them—Emmy, Hannah, Rei and, especially, Kai.

Publisher's acknowledgements

We are grateful to the following for permission to reproduce copyright material:

Figures
Figure 2.2 adapted from *Empirical Political Analysis*, 8, Pearson Inc. (Brians, C.L., Willnat, L., Manheim, J.B., Rich, R. C. 2011); Figure 4.3a from *The Craft of Political Research*, Prentice Hall (Philips Shively, W. 2009) 59–60; Figure 7.3 from *Interviewer's Manual: Survey Research Center*, Institute of Social Research, University of Michigan (1969) p. 8–12; Figure 17.1 from Drug markets and homicide locations, Washington, DC, *Washington Post*, 13/01/1999, p. E1

Tables
Table A.1 from The RAND Corporation. A Million Random Digits with 100,000 Normal Deviates 1966, New *York Free Press*, p. 1, RAND Corporation; Table A.2 adapted from *Elementary Sampling Theory*, Prentice Hall (Yamane, T. 1967) p. 398; Table A.3 adapted from *Elementary Sampling Theory*, Prentice Hall (Yamane, T. 1967) P. 399; Table A.4 from *Statistical Tables for Biological Agricultural and*

Medical Research, 6th (Fisher, R.A. and Yates, F); Table A.5 from *Statistical Tables for Biological, Agricultural and Medical Research* 6th, Pearson Education Ltd (Fisher, R.A., Yates, F.); Table A.6 from *Fundamentals of Behavioural Statistics*, 3rd (Runyon, R. P., Haber, A. 1976) p. 378–79; Table 23.1 from Interpreting British Governance, *Journal of Politics and International Relations*, 6, 131 (R.A.W. Rhodes 2004).

In some instances we have been unable to trace the owners of copyright material, and we would appreciate any information that would enable us to do so.

Part I

Theory and research in politics

1 The research process

- Why research politics?
- What are the characteristics of politics research methods?
- Are qualitative and quantitative methods the only ways available to research politics?

Introduction

Curiosity and necessity drive human inquiry. We may seek to understand the world around us for the sake of knowledge, or we may seek to understand it so that we may protect or improve our lot in it. Whichever is the case, the more we learn about our social and physical environment, the better equipped we are to adapt to our conditions or to modify them. This is just as true of our knowledge of politics as it is of other fields. The key to understanding and dealing with politics is, simply, knowing more about it.

The quest for knowledge

However, this simple idea of knowing raises two far less simple questions: *How* do we know? *Why* do we want to know it? The first is a question of methods; the second, one of using knowledge. In the first instance we are interested in obtaining and structuring knowledge; in the second we are concerned with using knowledge to do what we think is right. Both questions require the exercise of judgement and both draw upon our experience, but each demands its own distinct kind of intellectual effort.

Obtaining knowledge

To decide how we know, we must set forth certain hard-and-fast rules for exploring political phenomena. For example, we might simply try to observe politics. That seems straightforward enough. But what is politics? What kind of observations are we speaking about? Have we witnessed all possible political events, or is our definition unduly limiting? Is politics a product of the observer, and if so will different observers, having had different experiences and perspectives, arrive not only at different understandings of politics but at different *ways of understanding* as well? The result might be a highly individualised body of knowledge with no mechanism for sharing it. The problem of deciding how we know, then, is a problem of arriving at a generally accepted way of obtaining knowledge, at a common language of inquiry, so that anyone who learns the rules or 'speaks the language' can communicate on the basis of shared understanding with all others who have been similarly trained. We can talk to each other intelligently and start to make sense of the world.

Using knowledge

Deciding how we should *use* what we know is a different process. The most common reason we are interested in political research is because we care about political issues. An interest in politics usually develops from a concern about issues such as war, climate change or world poverty. The political dimension of these issues can appear, contradictorily, to be both the solution to these problems and an obstacle to a solution. It is only by researching the politics of these issues and nature of problems that the feasibility of solutions becomes clearer.

It is a mistake, however, to mix one's opinions and one's research indiscriminately. In fact, a desire to take sides might undermine the ability of the researcher to focus on the problem accurately. A politics researcher can and perhaps should have political opinions, but should also try to be as open minded and methodical as possible when approaching a political research problem. By doing so, one can communicate more effectively with other researchers and engage in a dialogue with one's opponents. It will make the researcher a better advocate of their own political position when the research is completed.

Empirical analysis

Empirical analysis is concerned with developing and using a common language and set of methods to *describe* and *explain* politics. It can be **quantitative**, based on counting and examining statistically the properties of the numerous cases of political phenomena, or it can be **qualitative**, based on more detailed exploration of the characteristics of a smaller number of such cases.

The emphasis in this book is on empirical political analysis, but our goal is to develop – in addition to a familiarity with various aspects of empirical technique – an appreciation of the larger perspective within which knowledge is interpreted. The term used in this book for the logic of interpretation is **hermeneutics**. Empirical analysis in the absence of sensitivity to hermeneutics can lead to a collection of observations, data and analysis whose significance we are not able to understand fully. The object, then, in undertaking political inquiry is to draw upon both types of analysis – empirical and hermeneutic – so as to maximise not only our knowledge but also our understanding of politics.

Hermeneutics

Hermeneutics is just a fancy word for interpretation. As we shall see in the chapters that follow, even quantitative political research requires the investigator to engage in some degree of interpretation. For example, the quantitative researcher must first interpret the nature of the problem and the best categories for data collection. The results of quantitative research might be numerical, but one should not ignore the need for interpretation in making sense of the results. When the focus of research is comparative, qualitative or case study based, interpretation is even more important.

Hermeneutics is often contrasted with 'science' but for the purposes of this book, the complementary aspects of the two approaches are emphasised. Those who argue that empirical research on politics is a 'science' (as in 'political science') tend to overstate the ability of empirical methods to provide access to reality and 'the truth'. In fact, any understanding of politics is contingent on time, place and perspective. At the same time, there are aspects of scientific method which help provide a solid basis for discussion among a wider community of scholars and students of politics.

Scientific method

In this context, we can view science as a way of knowing and as a common language of inquiry. Science can be defined for our purposes as those procedures and methods which are rigorous, transparent and produce relatively consistent results. Empirical research fulfils these conditions because it is *explicit, systematic* and *controlled.* It is explicit in that all the rules for defining and examining political phenomena are clearly stated. Nothing is knowingly ignored and nothing is taken on faith. Such research is systematic in that each item of evidence is linked by logic or observation to other items of evidence. It is controlled in that the phenomena under analysis are, to the extent possible, observed in as rigorous a manner as the state of the art allows. Generalised conclusions are reached only after the most thorough and painstaking assessment, and caution (in the larger sense of exercising great care and attention to being consistent) is a watchword. Yet for all its constraints, or, indeed, precisely because of them, such research opens for those versed in its ways a set of abilities which are widely recognised in academia and business – because these approach methods are commonly understood by those trained in this way.

Empirical research, therefore, is a *means of testing theories and hypotheses by applying certain rules of analysis to the observation and interpretation of political phenomena under strictly delineated circumstances.* These are the rules and constraints that we must learn in order to gain and communicate knowledge of politics.

The research process

Political science research is best thought of as a *process* of gathering and interpreting information. This research process consists of six distinct but highly interrelated stages: (1) the formulation of theory; (2) the operationalisation of that theory; (3) the selection of appropriate research techniques; (4) the observation of behaviour; (5) the analysis of data; and (6) the interpretation of the results. These six stages provide the organising rationale for much of this book and for much of your research.

The formulation of theory

The first step in undertaking political research is the selection of an appropriate *research question,* and here we can readily see the importance of mixing hermeneutic with empirical considerations. What criteria make one research question more appropriate than another? Although a number of such criteria come to mind, ranging from the personal interests of the researcher to the collective interests of society, most fall into one of two major categories. A question is worthy of research either because it fulfils an academic interest – that is, because its answer will further our theoretical understanding of some phenomenon – or because it is believed to fulfil a societal need – that is, because its answer may help us to deal with one or another of the problems faced by our society.

Although these two types of research questions, frequently termed **basic research** and **applied research**, are not mutually exclusive (asking one does not *necessarily* mean you cannot ask the other), they do frequently compete with one another. For example, should we study the hypothetical determinants of aggression under conditions of stress in order to develop a sophisticated predictive model of human behaviour, or should we instead focus on the reasons riots occur and on ways to prevent them? Should we examine at length the decision-making processes of national leaders to help us understand leadership, or should we instead concentrate on identifying and avoiding the types of decisions that lead to war? Because too few resources (money, time and trained personnel) are available to study all potentially interesting or important research questions, there is often a conflict between the need to perform basic research – whose practical payoffs, however great, are almost always felt only indirectly and far in the future – and the need to use our empirical knowledge in the present for the immediate benefit of humanity, even though we may, in the process, delay or prevent the further development of our research. The choice must be made by individual researchers in accordance with their own values.

Once you have identified the problem you wish to tackle and the type of contribution you wish to make, then you need to frame a more specific *research question.* First, you should identify which aspect of the problem interests you most. Since research projects may be lengthy and no research question can be answered adequately without hard work, you should not take on a task in which you have little interest.

Second, you must sift through the various elements or components of the research topic to identify those that may be important to your research. Draw on your powers of observation, reasoning and on past research to identify the major factors that bear on the behaviour you are seeking to understand.

Third, you must place your approach to the problem in the context of past research on the topic. For every issue there is a relevant politics literature which will have addressed the same or similar questions. It is crucial to explain how your research builds upon or differs from previous research efforts. Few politics researchers create their own theoretical frameworks so must rely on testing and modifying the work of others. Even those who put forward a new theory do so by demonstrating how the new theory is better than older approaches. A relevant body of political research literature should be the starting point for your own research.

A research example

Let us imagine that in the middle of a valley there is a town called Littleton that consists of several miles of bars and restaurants stretching from the exit ramp of a motorway to the edge of the horizon. One can do nothing in Littleton except drink and eat.

Now, suppose we have decided to study the voting behaviour of Littleton in elections so that we may explain why one person votes Socialist while another votes Conservative. In this simplified example, the subjects of our analysis (voters in Littleton) differ from one another in only two ways besides their voting preferences: each is either an owner or a worker, and each is associated with either a bar or a restaurant. Each of these factors, which political scientists term *variables*, represents a characteristic of a particular individual. One citizen of Littleton might be (1) an employee of (2) a restaurant (3) who votes Socialist, whereas another is (1) an owner of (2) a bar (3) who votes Conservative. We wish to explain differences in voting behaviour in terms of other kinds of differences among the voters, so we must focus on all the factors that might bear on a person's electoral preference. In this instance, we have only two to choose from: employee or owner status and pub or restaurant affiliation. Let us refer to these respectively as *socioeconomic status (SES)* – with ownership representing higher status than employment – and business affiliation. Is there any reason to expect that knowing either characteristic of a particular person will help us to predict that person's voting preference?

To answer that question, we must do two things. First, we must *think.* We must ask ourselves: Is there any *logical reason* to expect either of these factors to influence voting behaviour? Second, we must consult the political science literature: Is there, in previous studies of this or related topics, any *empirical evidence* that one or the other of these factors influences voting behaviour? In reality, there is little reason to expect the business-affiliation variable to make much difference in voting behaviour in this instance. Differences may well exist between those associated with pubs and those with restaurants, but these differences are not likely to have much impact on voting preferences. Few parties run on a pro-bar, anti-restaurant platform (or vice versa), and, other things being equal, this variable is not likely to help us explain voting behaviour. The second variable, SES, however, is a different story. Socialist parties are popularly identified as the party of workers and conservative parties as the party of business, and since persons of higher SES are more likely than those of lower SES to vote Conservative, we might well expect that employees will be more likely to vote for the Socialist candidate and owners for the Conservative.

Indeed, the research literature is replete with examples of precisely this kind of relationship. Thus, logical reasoning and empirical evidence both point in the same direction. Our research question might then become, 'Does the SES of a voter in Littleton influence voting preference?'

In the real world, of course, people differ from one another on more than two or three characteristics, but the problem we face in framing a research question is essentially the same. Because no one has the resources to measure every possible variable, we must choose, from among the thousands of human (or institutional) characteristics, those few that we expect will help us to explain whatever pattern of behaviour interests us. With the aid of both logic and literature we try to anticipate and identify the factors that might be related to the behaviour of interest. In so doing, we are not prejudging our results, but rather refining our thinking about the research problem to identify those avenues of inquiry most likely to lead to successful explanation. This process of refining our research question through informed selection, based on the politics literature and logical inference, is what we mean by the term *formulation of theory*.

The operationalisation of theory

Once we have arrived at one or more research questions and the theory needed to direct our search for answers, we must progress to the next step, that of **operationalisation** – the conversion or redefinition of our relatively abstract theoretical notions into concrete terms that will allow us actually to measure what we are after. Operationalisation involves moving from the conceptual level (thinking about a problem) to the operational level (deciding how to solve it); it involves learning to think in *practical* terms.

Defining terms

Suppose, to continue our example, that we have a hypothesis – a statement of the answer we expect to find for our research question – that Littleton residents of higher SES (owners) are more likely than those of lower SES (employees) to vote Conservative in the next election. This is in line with the findings of countless other voting studies and is a reasonable expectation in the present instance as well. But how do we find out for sure? We cannot simply walk up to a voter in Littleton and say, 'Good evening. Are you of higher or lower socioeconomic status?' To begin with, the person we are interviewing probably will not understand what we are talking about, since *socioeconomic status* is a technical term with many variations of meaning. And second, even if we get an answer, we will probably not be able to interpret it. Suppose the respondent replied, 'Yes, I am of higher socioeconomic status.' Higher than whom? How high? How does that person define socioeconomic status? Does it mean the same thing to the respondent as it does to the researcher? Once we have an abstract concept in mind, we must find a way to define more explicitly what we mean by that concept and then we must form our definition into as clear a question or measure as possible.

The problem here is to make intelligent yet arbitrary choices among numerous shades of meaning. When we use the variable SES, are we thinking about respondents' level of income, occupation or perhaps even subjective notions of which social class they belong to? Each might be a component of SES, but each has a somewhat different meaning, and each must be measured differently: What was the total income of your family last year? What is your occupation? Would you say that you consider yourself to be a member of the working class, the middle class, or the upper class? We must also take care to consider how the terms are interpreted by ourselves as researcher as well as by those whom we are researching. Is 'higher' and 'upper' interpreted as better? Are there aspects of the terminology or categories we use that can reveal bias in our thinking and thus bias in our research?

In other words, once we arrive at some hypothesis or research question, we have to examine very closely just what it is that we mean by each phrase we use, and if there is the possibility of misinterpretation by the individuals who are asked the question and bias in the research design. Therefore it is essential to translate terminology into a more precise definition, into measurable indicators which make sense for a given context. We seek, in effect, the clear and widely acceptable meaning. (Although not everyone would, for example, assign the same meaning to the term *socioeconomic status*, almost everyone would understand *total annual income in their own local currency, such as euros or UK pounds.*) In the process our concepts are narrowed and shades of meaning are lost, but because of this our thinking becomes much more precise, and our ability to communicate in clear, unambiguous terms what we have done is greatly enhanced. This process of translation and simplification, which we term *operationalisation,* is *the single most important key to conducting meaningful research.*

The selection of appropriate research techniques

Once we have decided what we want to measure, we must decide how we will measure it. We must devise a research strategy, a plan of attack. Two considerations are of primary importance here.

First, we must select a technique or a combination of techniques that will enable us to ask the particular questions – to measure the particular variables – that interest us, and we must do so in ways that are consistent with our operationalisations. We cannot, for example, measure the attitudes of individual voters by analysing the content of newspaper coverage of a given election, because newspaper content may reflect the views of an editor or of those few people whose letters to that editor are published, without necessarily reflecting the views of most voters. Moreover, analysing news or editorial content does not permit us to differentiate among different types of voters, such as those of higher or lower SES. Thus, content analysis would not allow us to answer our research question – that is, to test our hypothesis; survey research or intensive interviews would be more useful. On the other hand, suppose that we wish to assess the coverage given by a newspaper to a political campaign. We might simply analyse the content of the newspaper itself, counting references to the candidates and so forth, or we might survey readers of the newspaper to measure what information they remember reading about the campaign. In the first instance, we would have a direct measure of content from which we are forced to infer impact; in the second instance, we would have a direct measure of impact from which we are forced to infer content. Depending on the precise formulation of our research question, one or the other or the combination of both strategies might be useful. The point is that the *appropriateness* of a given research technique is, in large part, determined by the particular problem we have selected for study.

The second consideration is *feasibility.* This is the stage of the research process at which we prepare to leave our ivory tower and actually go out into the real world. For that reason, we must assure ourselves that whatever method or technique we select can be employed properly under the particular set of conditions we are likely to face. For example, since there are no newspapers in our town of Littleton (only bars and restaurants), we cannot use content analysis even if we want to. Similarly, the most direct way to measure the level of tension between the leaders of Russia and those of one of its neighbouring states might be through a series of personal interviews with the leaders themselves, but such interviews are, to say the least, difficult to arrange. In each instance, we have to find less-than-ideal ways of measuring the key variables. A feasible technique, then, is one that will be maximally effective given the constraints of the research situation.

For student and professional researchers alike, feasibility is most often determined by time and resource constraints. The length of a given academic term or the years of funding for postgraduate research or the number years between research assessment exercises are time limits. Resources include money to fund original research or lengthy, direct observation fieldwork or personnel to hand code thousands of pages of text. Ultimately, then, researchers choose techniques that fit within their available time and resources.

To summarise, we must find a way to measure those variables we wish to measure that will be (1) consistent with our working definitions of the variables and (2) practicable. We must be as rigorous as possible, but we can only be as rigorous as the circumstances allow.

The observation of behaviour

The fourth stage of the research process involves actually carrying out the research strategy developed in stage 3. Many factors must be taken into account here, but two in particular are worthy of note. The first is the notion of generalisability; the second that of reactivity.

Generalisability refers to the ability to generalise or extend our conclusions with some confidence from the observed behaviour of a few cases to the presumed behaviour of an entire population. It is a concern we must take into account in selecting the particular cases (people, decisions, organisations or nations) that we wish to study. The problem here is basically one of scale. If there are only, say, four or five occurrences of an event or subjects in a group we wish to study, we can examine each of those occurrences or subjects individually and make various general statements about them, with reasonable confidence that our conclusions apply to all the cases. However, if we have so many hundreds or thousands or millions of cases that it is impossible to examine each firsthand, we will have much less confidence that a study of a relative few of these cases – perhaps fewer than 1 in 1,000 – will allow us to make accurate statements about the entire group. In such circumstances we must develop a strategy, often termed a *sampling procedure,* by which we can select from the many cases a few to study and come to conclusions that might apply to the entire population of cases. In doing so, we must decide how many cases to study and how these cases should be selected, and we must try to estimate the representativeness of these few cases. The key to generalisability lies in selecting for observation those cases that are likely to represent, or be most typical of, the larger population.

Once we have selected our cases for analysis, we must exercise great care in observing them. We must avoid measuring political phenomena or behaviour in ways that display **reactivity** – a situation in which either the person who is doing a study or the actual methods of the study somehow interfere with and alter the way those under observation would behave or think in the absence of the researcher. In other words, a danger exists that the act of observation may itself cause those being observed to change their behaviour so that the results of the observation are misleading.

Hawthorne Effect

The classic case of reactive observation was a 1939 study of the effects that changes in working conditions at a particular factory had on worker productivity. During the 1920s and early 1930s, such factors as hours of work, rest periods, lighting and methods of pay were varied for a small group of workers. Regardless of what conditions they worked under, whether long or short hours, few or frequent rest periods, or some other variant, this group of workers continually out-produced all other workers in the same factory. The most influential factor in their productivity, it turned out, was an unusually high level of morale associated with the fact that members of this group knew they were being observed and experimented upon (Roethlisberger and Dickson 1939). This so-called Hawthorne Effect, named for the factory where it was first observed, meant that no conclusion could be drawn regarding the relationship between working conditions and productivity because the act of observation created a false reality, a work environment unlike the normal one.

Sometimes in undertaking political research, we encounter similar, obvious examples of reactivity. An overbearing or unfriendly interviewer, a leading question or a meddlesome observer can so damage the research situation that no confidence can be vested in its outcomes. As often as not, however, the process is more subtle. We might, for example, properly train the perfect interviewer to ask a perfectly good question, yet still incur reactivity: *Q*: 'Do you favour or oppose the government's economic policy?' *A*: 'I'm in favour of it. I think it is a good idea.' But how do we know for sure that our respondent has really given any thought to the government's economic policy before being interviewed? Is it not possible that the interview itself acted as a catalyst, in effect crystallising the respondent's thoughts and creating an opinion where none had previously existed? This, too, is reactivity, but of a type that is much more difficult to detect and to avoid.

It is not enough simply to march into the field armed with a few questions and start looking around for answers. We must exercise great care in deciding how and where we shall enter the field and how and whom we shall observe. The best theory and the best plan of attack can be squandered if we are careless in our observation.

Reflexivity

The reactivity noted above involves the reaction of research subjects to the research, but what about the problem of how researchers themselves react with the research? One hermeneutically sensitive solution to the problem of potential bias caused by reactivity is called **reflexivity**. It is the conscious 'taking of a position' in relation to one's research. It means being aware of the relationship between the research and the research subject, including those individuals who make up the research subject. For example, if one holds strong socialist views, it might be difficult to be sympathetic to business owners or conservative politicians. How might such views have an impact on how the research is planned, conducted and interpreted? Even if one is focused on an area with which one has sympathy, such as environmental protest groups, such groups may be suspicious of outsiders. Does your academic agenda cause you to view them differently from the way they view themselves? No matter whether or not you like or dislike or even feel neutral about your subject, it is important to explicitly think through the possibilities for bias and how it might have an impact on your research. For this reason, reflexivity is discussed in more detail in Chapter 23.

The analysis of data

The bits of information about each case that we gather during our observations are called **data**, and once we have them in hand, the end is in sight. The object at this point is to ascertain what answers we have found to our research question. This may be done in many instances by answering three questions. First, is there some association between, on the one hand, the behaviour we are hoping to explain or to understand better and, on the other hand, the factors we think will help us to do so?

Is there a relationship?

Suppose, for example, that we expect to find that people who differ in their level of formal education will differ systematically in the likelihood that they will vote. Our first question must be, does this happen? Do people who differ from one another in one of these variables tend to differ consistently in the other as well? Are the more educated people consistently either more or less likely to vote than the less educated people? We might find in examining our data, for instance, that less educated people tend to vote about as often as more educated people and that knowing a person's level of education does not help us to predict or explain the difference between that person's likelihood of voting and someone else's. If this is the case, we say that one's level of education does not influence the likelihood of voting or, alternatively, that there is no association between the two variables. Our expectation is not supported by our analysis. If, on the other hand, we discover that six or seven times out of ten, knowing the level of education does allow us to predict accurately the likelihood of a person's voting, this constitutes evidence supporting our expectation that the two variables are related. It tells us that more educated people are *systematically different* from less educated people when it comes to voting and helps us understand our subjects' voting behaviour. The first thing to look for in assessing a hypothesis, then, is whether the two variables are *related*. There are at least two ways of examining the relationship: see if they are statistically associated in a large number of cases or examine the process by which education has an impact on voting through the detailed exploration of a smaller number of case studies.

What type of relationship?

How are the two variables related? Are more educated people more likely than less educated people to vote? Alternatively, are they less likely to vote? Or is the relationship between the variables even more complex? If we have thought through our hypothesis so that we have some reasons to expect the level of education to be related to voting, we probably have one or another of these possibilities in mind.

We might argue, for example, that having more formal education increases the likelihood of someone having the skills and information needed to support an interest in politics. Accordingly, a more educated person is more likely to vote than is a less skilled or less informed person. Thus, we might expect voting to be more frequent or more common among the more educated of the people we study. This type of relationship is illustrated in Figure 1.1(a), where points on the line represent corresponding values on the two variables.

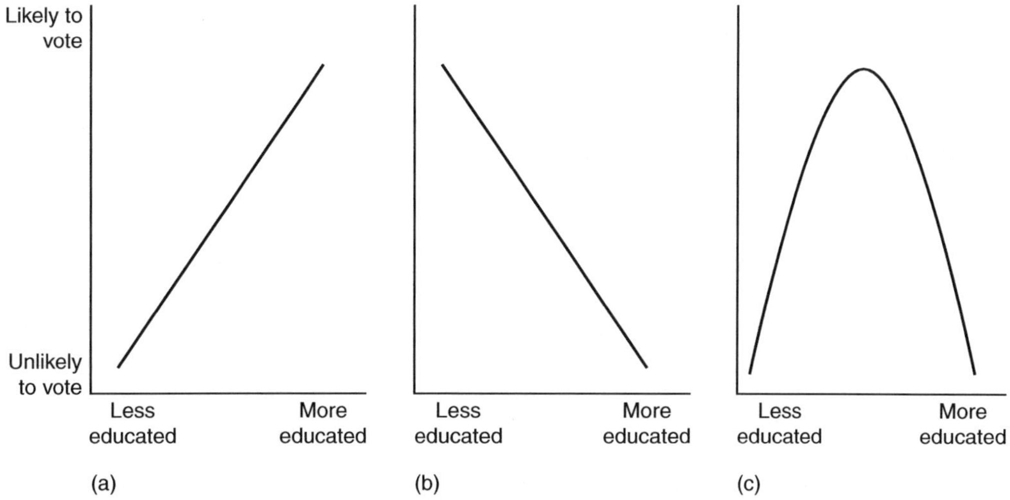

Figure 1.1 Possible relationships between individuals' level of education and their likelihood of voting

the data into inappropriate categories because they would seem to support our research? Is there more to the political phenomenon being studied than the theory and research design allows? These are difficult questions to answer, but good researchers will always try to do so, because only when they are answered can researchers know how much confidence to place in the product of the research.

Ethical considerations

At each stage of the research process, and in each chapter of this book, there are ethical choices to be confronted. As you conduct your research, you should keep the potential consequences of your actions in mind. Maintaining this awareness is acutely important for you as a budding politics researcher, because in social research people may be harmed. To be a good politics researcher is defined as adopting a specific ethical attitude to others and to the research process itself. Throughout this book, you will detect the tension that exists in the discipline of politics between an interest in learning about human behaviour, and the concern that we are affecting humans through our research. Sometimes your research may directly impact a human when you ask a survey subject about her attitude towards abortion policy, and she recalls a personal experience. Other times, your research may influence human lives more indirectly, such as when your findings are employed in debates among policy makers considering new legislation or by judges as they wrestle to interpret the law.

The foregoing examples noting the real human impact of political research should make it clear why you will find a section titled 'Ethical considerations' in each chapter. If you still have doubts, though, consider the weight that others in society and government give to the importance of ethical conduct. In university, unethical use of others' research in your writings is called plagiarism, and may cause you to receive a failing grade, or even cause you to be expelled from university. In academic research, failing to obtain prior permission to carry out research or not fully protecting human or animal research subjects will lead to sanctions against you, and may well cost you both your reputation and your livelihood. In business, using others' copyrighted material without permission may be punishable with a fine amounting to hundreds of thousands of pounds, and a decade in prison – per offense! Clearly, our society values ethical behaviour; in this text we will do our part to promote ethical standards at each stage of the research process by suggesting specific strategies you can use to foster and develop your ethical compass.

Conclusion

This chapter's brief overview of the six stages of the research process will give you a good idea of what empirical research into politics is like and what this book is about. We shall devote a good many of our pages to learning to perform and evaluate each of these tasks. We realise, of course, that most who read these pages will never become politics researchers. But we know, too, that the same skills that go into creating quality research may also be applied to developing more thorough and critical skills in reading and evaluating the research done by others. This is an ability that anyone with an interest in the study of politics will do well to possess. Social scientific research is increasingly used as a basis for both public policy and legal decisions. It is, therefore, increasingly important that citizens be able to judge the merits of research in order to discharge their responsibilities in a democratic society.

The body of knowledge that we call political science was not handed down on stone tablets in antiquity. It is constantly growing, changing and being refined. Every piece of research is a potential extension of our knowledge and understanding. But that potential can be met only if the research itself can withstand critical scrutiny – only if it comes up to accepted standards. Those standards are what this book is about, and learning them, whether for research of your own or for critical reading, will provide you with a basis both for understanding the literature of political science and for making a contribution to it.

Summary points

■ The politics research method is a progression of steps: building a theory, defining terms and operationalisation, choosing a research technique, observing behaviour, analysing data, and interpreting results.

■ Empirical research, using qualitative or quantitative methods, is but one of many ways to explore politics and explore our political environment.

■ Hermeneutic sensitivity and ethical awareness is required at each stage in the research process. The aim is to produce nuanced but rigorous research.

Suggested reading and examples

Research examples

Rarely is every part of the research process described in great detail in published work, because many authors reserve scarce printed space for their findings. However, explicitly identifying each of the components of a published research report may serve to guide the reader through the work and make it accessible to a wider audience. Throughout such articles, authors clearly explain each step in the development of the project, from building the theory from the existing literature, to data coding and merging, to interpreting the results.

Methodological reading

This textbook is focused on explaining basic research methods in politics so that you can conduct your own research. None the less, it is also useful to look at books which examine the larger issues in political research methodology. A basic introduction is *Research Methods in Politics* (Pierce 2008). An influential attempt to transform qualitative empirical political science research to the same level of quantitative research is found in *Designing Social Inquiry: Scientific Inference in Qualitative Research* (King, Keohane and Verba 1994). A more balanced approach to the problem of political research methods is *Rethinking Social Inquiry: Diverse Tools, Shared Standards* (Brady and Collier 2010). For even more advanced consideration of special methodological issues see *The Oxford Handbook of Political Methodology* (Box-Steffensmeier, Brady and Collier 2010).

Forming the basis for our modern understanding of study reactivity, the official company report on the experiments done by the Western Electric Company at its Hawthorne assembly plant in Illinois is documented in the book *Management and the Worker* (Roethlisberger and Dickson 1939).

References

Box-Steffensmeier, Janet M., Brady, Henry and Collier, David. 2010. *The Oxford Handbook of Political Methodology*. Oxford: Oxford University Press.

Brady, Henry and Collier, David. 2010. *Rethinking Social Inquiry: Diverse Tools, Shared Standards*, 2nd edn. New York: Rowman and Littlefield.

King, Gary, Keohane, Robert and Verba, Sidney. 1994. *Designing Social Inquiry: Scientific Inference in Qualitative Research*. Princeton, NJ: Princeton University Press.
Pierce, Roger. 2008. *Research Methods in Politics*. London: Sage.
Roethlisberger, Fritz and Dickson, William. 1939. *Management and the Worker*. Cambridge, MA: Harvard University Press.

Key terms

applied research	generalisability	quantitative
basic research	hermeneutics	reactivity
data	operationalisation	reflexivity
empirical research	qualitative	

2   The theoretical and conceptual context of political research

- Why develop a theory before beginning to research a relationship?
- What roles do induction and deduction play in developing theory?
- What are the characteristics of useful theories?
- How do covariation and causation differ?
- How are theories elaborated using hypotheses?

Introduction

The first chapter explained the overall context of political research: we want to understand the complex world around us, either for the satisfaction of knowing or because we want to be able to anticipate or even influence events. Research, then, starts with something we want to know. This is our **research question**. It is usually quite general. We might want to know, for example, why some people actively support environmental protection while others are opposed or indifferent to it. The most effective way to find an accurate (and therefore useful) answer to this question is to employ established methods of empirical research to investigate the relationships we see in the world. Before we can employ rigorous procedures in an attempt to find a generally acceptable answer to our question, we have to reduce this highly general question to one or more highly specific ones. Unless we do this, we will not know what to observe in order to seek an answer to the question, and we cannot understand how what we observe is related to our research question.

The purpose of theory

Transforming our general research question into one or several specific ones requires developing some plausible explanations for what we observe. We might, for instance, reason that people's position on environmental protection is influenced by the nature of their job. Some occupations, for example, benefit from environmental protection measures whereas others are hurt by them (at least in the short run). We might also think that age influences people's attitude towards environmental issues, because younger people have grown up with an awareness of the problems of pollution while older people grew up before these problems were understood.

This reasoning helps us to reduce the complexity of social life and puts us in a position to begin systematic inquiry. We can apply logic and information that we already have about empirical relationships to reason out a set of things we expect to be true if our tentative explanation is valid. Now we can ask questions like these: Do younger people support environmental legislation more often than older people? Do office workers and professional people support environmental measures more often than workers in manufacturing? We can devise ways to make observations that will allow us to answer these questions and, when we have explored enough small questions, to answer our initial research question.

When we attempt to create possible explanations for events, we are **theorising**, or developing a theory. Theories are created in our effort to gain understanding. They help direct the research to determine if our understanding of events is correct. This is why theory building is the first stage in the research process and why it is essential that we understand the relationship between theory and research.

Theories aid interpretation

Without a sound theory we will not be able to tell why our research 'findings' provide an answer to the research question. Suppose we begin research with only the general question posed earlier. If we ask a properly selected sample of 2,000 voters about their position on environmental protection and a series of questions about their personal characteristics, we can use our results to *describe* the kinds of people who support and oppose environmental legislation, but we cannot tell *why* they support or oppose it.

If, on the other hand, we start with a theory that offers an explanation of why people support or oppose environmental protection policies and ask questions to check on the accuracy of the expectations that logically follow from this theory, our results will contribute to our understanding of why people take the positions they do.

To illustrate, say that we theorise that people's first concern is their economic well-being and that their position on environmental protection is determined totally by their perception of how proposed legislation will affect their income. One expectation or prediction that logically follows from this line of reasoning is that people who expect to be financially hurt by environmental protection laws will oppose them, whereas those who expect to be helped by these laws will support them. If our theory is an adequate explanation of how people develop attitudes about environmental protection, then this prediction should be an accurate statement about real-world relationships. We can then get some idea of the usefulness of our theory by checking on the empirical accuracy of the prediction that logically follows from it. For example, we might ask people about their position on environmental protection and their perception of its effect on their income to find out whether the prediction is borne out by what we learn about actual relationships.

Regardless of the outcome, our research can then tell us something about why people feel as they do about this issue. If the research is correctly done and the prediction is supported, we are encouraged both to believe that we have developed a sound explanation for the behaviour in question and to search for further evidence of its utility. If the prediction is shown to be wrong, we at least have reason to believe that this is not likely to be a useful theory for understanding people's position on this matter, and we can begin to explore other possible explanations.

Whether we start our research with a theory or without a theory, it may produce the same facts. But the facts will contribute to our understanding *only* if we can tie them together through a theory. For example, knowing that office workers tend to support environmental protection more often than workers in manufacturing do will provide an explanation of why people take the positions they do only if we can give some reason why occupation and position on ecology should be related. Otherwise, the fact could be a coincidence, and knowing it will add nothing to our ability to explain people's attitudes. Theories provide sets of reasons why facts should be connected in given ways. Therefore, *theories make facts useful by providing us with a framework for interpreting them and seeing their relationships to one another.*

The political studies literature helps us think about theory. For example, we may find literature on environmental politics which includes research on groups, such as young people or ethnic minorities, which might suggest ways we can conduct research on the environmental views of manufacturing workers. Looking at these studies it is possible to investigate the books and articles that others have used as a starting point or background and how the researchers have formulated research questions and design. The existing politics literature will indicate the possibilities and problems with this type of research. Techniques for finding and utilising politics literature will be covered in Chapters 3 and 4.

This chapter is designed to help you understand how theories are developed and how they are used to guide research. We will discuss the nature of social science theorising, the elements of theories and the relationship of theory to the rest of the research process. When you have finished the chapter, you should be able to begin thinking about political questions that interest you in ways that will prepare you to undertake systematic empirical research in order to find valid answers to those questions.

The nature of social science theory

Usefulness of theories

First, theories help simplify reality so that we might understand it in order to influence it or adapt to it better. Second, once we have developed such an understanding, theories can guide us in testing its accuracy. Theories do this by providing a logical basis for expectations or predictions about the world that can be compared with reality through research. When our predictions are supported by evidence, the understanding that provides a basis for those predictions is also supported, and our confidence that we have a grasp of the way things work is increased. When our predictions are inaccurate, we begin to question our understanding of events and to look for ways to improve it.

Theories are *sets of logically related symbols that represent what we think happens in the world.* They are simply intellectual tools. Understanding this is important, because it helps us realise that theories are neither true nor false in any absolute sense, but only more or less *useful.* You cannot expect to discover a theory the way an explorer discovers a new island. Why? Because theories do not exist 'out there' to be discovered. They are the products of human imagination, hard work and sometimes good fortune.

If theories are essential to sound research but cannot be discovered by simply looking at accumulated data, how can we go about building a theory to guide our quest for an understanding of those aspects of political life that interest us? What processes are involved? The answer is neither neat nor simple, because theories are developed in a variety of ways. We cannot outline a set of procedures to produce a useful theory in the same way as we might describe how to build a table. We can, however, provide an explanation of the major ideas and stages commonly involved in theory construction. The first of these stages is the *conceptualisation of the problem.*

The logic of theory building

Beginning with the event or behaviour we want to understand, we must first ask ourselves what we know about the phenomenon that might help us explain it. Insights might be gained from personal experience, casual observation or creative thinking. More often we will find it useful to investigate systematically what others have found about the subject. Useful theories begin from a thorough knowledge of the events we want to explain. Without such knowledge, we might fail to understand what is to be explained or might not have a clue where to begin looking for relationships that can be used to explain the events. An example might highlight the importance of having a thorough knowledge of the facts to aid our research conceptualisation.

An example

The massive riots that took place in many cities in the late 1960s deeply worried many people. Political scientists and other social scientists were asked to investigate the causes of the riots. When the riots first occurred, many public officials said they were the acts of a group of poor citizens without stable ties to society. If we had accepted this interpretation and sought to understand the riots, we would have defined our task as one of explaining why so many of these 'riffraff' were concentrated in our cities at that time and how they were moved to riot. Many public officials turned to the alleged presence of 'outside agitators' as an explanation. As social scientists conducted interviews in the riot-torn cities, however, we learned that rioting was not restricted to riffraff. In fact, as a group, rioters differed very little from the general population of those cities (Fogelson and Hill 1986). This fact presents us with a very different research task from that suggested by the riffraff interpretation. We must now seek to understand how average citizens with jobs, families and other ties to society were motivated to riot. Subsequent explanations have focused on variables such as racism rather than 'outside agitators'.

In this case, an inadequate knowledge of the facts could have fundamentally misdirected our theory-building efforts. This is why **exploratory research**, which is designed to establish the facts in a given case, is important. It is also the reason why we must search the literature for information on the phenomena we seek to explain if we hope to develop sound theories.

But once we have as many facts as we can find, how do we construct a theory to explain these observations? We generally begin by searching the facts for patterns that can account for the observed events.

For example, we might want to know what causes political protests on university campuses. Answering this question involves explaining what leads students to take part in protests. Having been or having known protesters might provide us with some insights into their motivation, but to develop an explanation of why large numbers of students participate would require information on a much larger number of people. We would be wise to seek data on the characteristics and motives of student protesters *in general* in order to frame our explanation. If we found among protesters commonalities that set them apart from nonprotesters, we might reason that these characteristics led to their participation in demonstrations. The prominence of these characteristics among university students then becomes part of our explanation of why protests occur.

Induction

The process of generalising from what we have observed to what we have not or cannot observe is called **induction**. Theories built through inductions from observations are said to be *empirically grounded*.

In the process of induction, we reason from what we know to be the case in some situations to what might be the case in other, similar situations; we make a logical leap from what we have seen to a prediction about what we have not seen, based on the assumption that there is some constant underlying pattern to events in the world. We all use induction in our daily life. If we observe five consecutive times that the elevator door opens after our pushing a button on the wall, we will quickly draw the conclusion that pushing the button causes the door to open. This is an inductive generalisation from the few cases we have observed (pushing the button five times) to cases we have not (pushing the

We might also argue, however, that the more educated one becomes, the more one comes to believe that political activity is futile. Education, in this view, gives rise to disillusionment, which in turn reduces the inclination to vote. Here we expect voting to be more frequent among the less educated of our subjects. This type of relationship is illustrated in Figure 1.1(b).

Or, we might even argue that education contributes to skills and interests to a point, but that those who are educated beyond that point (for example, those who attend university) become increasingly disillusioned and less interested in politics. Here we expect voting to be most frequent among those of moderate educational attainment, with lower levels of voting at either extreme. This more complex relationship is illustrated in Figure 1.1(c).

In each instance, a relationship exists between a person's level of education and likelihood of voting, but clearly the implications of these varying relationships are vastly different. It is possible, then, to find a strong relationship between the two variables and yet fail to substantiate our hypothesis.

Of course, one could ask individuals in detail about their education and the ways in which educational experiences may have had an impact on their attitude towards voting, but this would be a time-consuming process if large numbers were involved. The best research would complement statistical research with qualitative analysis of the relationships by conducting interviews with a smaller representative sample of voters.

Confidence in findings?

How likely is it that the relationships we find in a sample also occur in the population from which those cases were drawn? This is simply a statistical way of asking how good a job we have done in ensuring that our small sample is representative, or typical, of the larger population. If we have properly selected a large enough sample of the cases to be studied, then we can say with confidence that our conclusions, though based on but a few cases, may be applied to all. If we have made errors, we may be less confident. Unfortunately, as will be emphasised in Chapter 7, when conclusions are based on a sample of the population, we can never be *totally* certain of them.

The same problem arises in qualitative research. One must always explain how the small number of cases to be examined intensively is adequately representative of the broader group of individuals being discussed. One cannot generalise about the views of the central bankers in advanced industrial countries on the basis of interviewing two or three of them, even if they share similar views. Similarly, if one interviews party activists in a particular party, the method of selection and the number contacted will have an impact on the confidence with which conclusions can be made.

Interpretation of the results

Finally, we reach a point where we must put all the pieces together. Have we succeeded in actually asking the research question that we set out to ask? What have we discovered? What is the substantive importance of our findings? How do these results square with our expectations? In essence, we have by this time reduced some aspect of political behaviour to a set of numbers, which may or may not reveal statistical relationships, or we will have a transcript of interviews with a lot of information on the individuals concerned. We must decide what any such relationships, as well as other things we have learned along the way, tell us about the answer to our research question.

But there is more, for we must also look back with a critical eye on our research itself. Have we made some fundamental error along the way that may invalidate our findings? Have we forced

Figure 2.1 Diagrammatic representation of inductive and deductive reasoning

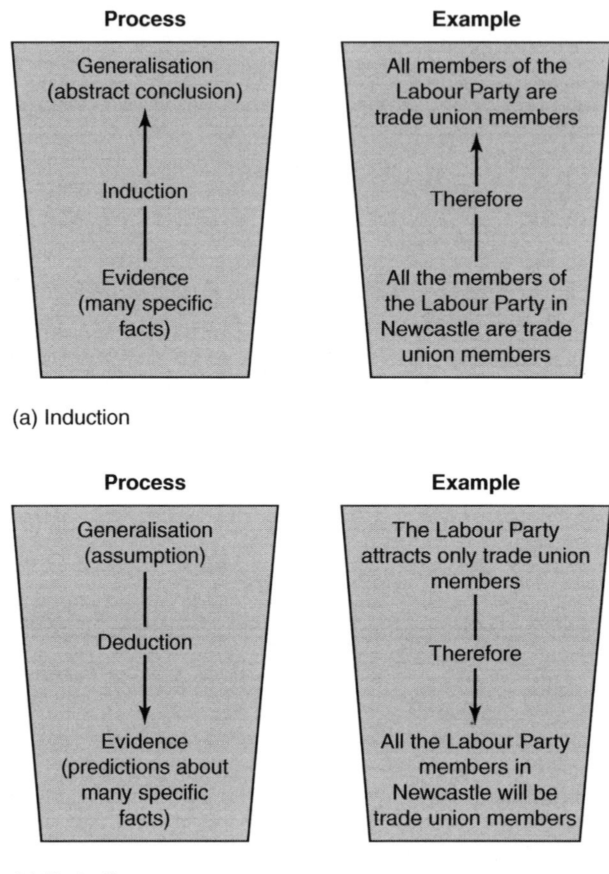

button more times or pushing elevator buttons in other buildings). The process of induction is presented diagrammatically in Figure 2.1(a). This diagram suggests how inductively constructed theories are grounded in facts.

There is more to theory building than induction, however, because pointing out facts does not provide an explanation unless we can show *why* those facts have led to the observed results. Let us return to the example of student protest. Suppose we find that protesters tend to be more dissatisfied with public policies than nonprotesters and that protesters also tend to have far less faith in the effectiveness of conventional politics in getting policies changed. Stating this fact constitutes an explanation of protest only if we are able to show why such attitudes should lead to protest behaviour. Showing this might involve making some *assumptions* about political behaviour. Specifically, it might involve assuming that people will act to change policies they strongly oppose and that they will resort to protest behaviour if they feel that conventional political participation (voting, letter writing etc.) will not alter the policies.

These **assumptions** (sometimes called *axioms* or *postulates*) then become part of our theory. Assumptions describe the conditions under which we expect the tentative explanation we have reached to be supported by evidence. They tell why we expect student protest from what we know about students on college campuses by making general statements about political behaviour under certain conditions. We can now explain specific behaviour (protest) by showing that it follows logically from a set of theoretical assumptions.

Deduction

This process is the reverse of inductive reasoning. Deductive reasoning moves from abstract statements about general relationships to concrete statements about specific behaviours. This process of reasoning *from the abstract and general to the concrete and specific* is known as **deduction**. We all use deductive logic in everyday life. If we assume that elevators work on a system of wall-mounted buttons and find ourselves confronted with an elevator, we will generally deduce that the way to enter the elevator is to push the appropriate button. We have moved from a generalisation to the prediction of a specific event by deduction. This process is illustrated in Figure 2.1(b).

Deduction is the process that enables us to use theories to explain specific events. If we can show by a process of deduction that some observed event can be logically predicted from the set of assumptions that constitute our theory, then the theory provides an explanation for the observed event. The theory helps us to understand the event by giving a reason why it is as it is. The role of deduction is to provide this link between the theory and our observations.

Theory construction

The process of theory construction involves the interaction of both inductive and deductive logic in the following stages: (1) we use induction to translate what we have observed into assumptions; (2) we employ deduction to derive predictions; (3) we test these predictions against new observations; and (4) we revise our assumptions to make them consistent with the results of our observations. Then we repeat the process in an effort to make the theory increasingly useful as a tool for understanding events.

Merely devising a theory, however, does not make it valid. We can generally come up with many theories to explain a given event. The question we must ask is, which of these theories is most useful in helping us understand the world? Answering this question will require that we test alternative theories against reality.

Before we can discuss theory testing, it is important to understand two things. First, we have to know what features make a theory useful so that we can know how to go about building theories. Second, we must know how the components of a theory are related to each other and to empirical research.

Characteristics of useful theories

For a theory to be useful in explaining observations, it must meet several standards:

1   It must be *testable*. Can we reason from the theory to expectations about reality that are concrete and specific enough for us to make observations that either support the expectations or fail to support them? Can the theory be related to the world in systematic ways, or is it only a set of abstractions?
2   It must be *logically sound*. Is the theory internally consistent? Are its assumptions compatible and the terms it contains unambiguous?
3   It must be *communicable*. Can other, properly trained people understand the theory in ways that allow them to use it to explain events and to test hypotheses derived from it?
4   It must be *general*. Is it possible to use it to explain a variety of events in different times and places? Can we deduce predictions from it that can be tested in different circumstances, or is it tied too closely to one set of observations?

5 It must be *parsimonious*. Is it simple enough to be readily applied and understood, or is it so complex, so filled with conditions and exceptions, that it is difficult to derive explicit expectations about real-world events from it?

Theories can have each of these desirable characteristics in different degrees, and sometimes we have to choose among them in developing a particular theory. We may have to sacrifice some parsimony in order to obtain more generality or testability, for instance. We have to keep all these desirable features in mind when formulating theories if the products of our labours are to be truly useful.

Components of social science theory

Theories are composed of sets of *concepts* that are related by propositions logically derived from a set of *assumptions*. This is the *logical structure* of a theory. It is this structure that allows us to use the theory to explain events, because it allows us to give reasons why we can logically expect things to be as they are.

Defining concepts

The quest for useful theory begins with the decisions we make about the building blocks of theories: concepts. A **concept** is merely a *word or symbol that represents some idea*. There is nothing mystical about concepts. We use them every day to help us cope with the complexity of reality by categorising the things we encounter according to some of their properties that are relevant to us. We classify the four-legged creatures we see into cows, cats, dogs and other species, and that classification alone provides a basis for some important expectations (for example, dogs are not a good source of milk). Assigning a name to something allows us to predict certain things about it, because the name is a symbol for particular combinations of properties.

Political research concepts serve the same purpose. They point to the properties of objects (people, political systems, elections) that are relevant to a particular inquiry. One observer might be interested in a person's personality structure, another is interested in partisan identification, and a third focuses on the person's level of political alienation. The person has all of these properties (a personality, a party identification and a degree of alienation) and many more, but only certain of the properties are relevant to any given piece of research. All three observers are dealing with the same reality; they simply choose to organise their perceptions of it differently. Concepts help us to decide which of many traits or attributes are important to our research.

Making concepts useful

Concepts, like theories, are tools that we create for specific purposes and that cannot be labelled true or false, but only more or less useful. What makes a concept useful? There are three major considerations.

First, since we are involved in *empirical* inquiry the concept must refer to phenomena that are at least potentially *observable*. In medieval times, the concept of divine will played an important role in explanations of events. We cannot verify such explanations, however, because we cannot observe divine will to tell whether it is present or absent in any given case. If it is to have any scientific value, a concept must refer to something that can be measured with our ordinary senses.

This does not mean that all concepts must refer to *directly* observable things. Some of the most useful concepts in the social sciences refer to properties we cannot observe directly. For example, people do not have a class status in the way that they have blue eyes, but if we know certain things about them (their income or their occupation, for example), we can infer what their class status is. Similarly, nations do not have authoritarian or democratic political systems in the way that they have mountains or deserts, but we can *infer* the degree of democracy that exists in a nation by observing certain things about its political life (the nature of elections and provisions for civil liberties, for instance).

The question is: Can we devise a set of procedures for using our senses to gather information that will allow us to judge the presence or absence or magnitude in the real world of the thing to which the concept refers? If we can do this for a concept, it is said to have **empirical referents**; it refers to something that is directly or indirectly observable.

Second, in addition to having empirical referents, concepts must be *precise*. They must refer to one and only one set of properties of some phenomenon. We must be able to know exactly what we are talking about when using a concept to describe an object. For instance, is the degree of inequality of distribution of wealth part of what we are referring to when describing a nation's political system as democratic or authoritarian, or is the nature of the political system determined exclusively by other factors? Precision is important because it tells us what to observe in order to see how a concept is manifested in any given case. Only if we can determine this can we use the concept in empirically grounded explanations.

Precision also helps us identify our empirical referents and make distinctions among observed phenomena. If democracy means *only* the presence or absence of popular elections for public officials, then the former Soviet Union and Great Britain both were democracies in the twentieth century since elections occurred in both nations. Do we want to treat these two nations as examples of the same kind of political system for purposes of our research despite radically different political systems? If not, then we need to refine the concept, making it more precise, so that we can draw a distinction in our study between the two nations.

Finally, useful concepts have **theoretical import**. A concept has *theoretical import* when it is related to enough other concepts in the theory that it plays an essential role in the explanation of observed events.

In our hypothetical explanation of student protest, we employed two concepts. One was *intensity of policy preferences*, and the other was *perception of the effectiveness of conventional political action in changing policies*. These two concepts were tied together by the assumptions that people will act to change policies with which they strongly disagree and that they will turn to protest when they feel that other means of influence will not bring results. Given these assumptions, finding the particular combination of attitudes we have referred to will lead us to expect protest behaviour. Each concept is essential to the explanation and is linked both to the theoretical assumptions and to the other concept. Each concept has theoretical import because it plays a necessary role in our explanation.

It is important to remember, however, that concepts are the human constructs. They are not set in stone. As with theories, they must be judged as more or less useful for making sense of the political phenomenon to be studied. No concept can cover all the nuances of the individual cases to be observed. In that sense, they are a simplification and crude categorisation of what we observe.

Relationships in social science theory

Now we can begin to see that theory makes concepts useful by tying them together so that they can be used in formulating explanations. Theory ties concepts to one another by stating relationships between them. These statements take the form of **propositions** derived from our assumptions. Propositions generally posit one of two major types of relationship among concepts. These are *covariation* and *causation.*

Covariational relationships indicate that two or more concepts tend to change together: as one increases (or decreases) the other increases (or decreases). Covariational relationships tell us nothing about what causes the two concepts to change together. For instance, we might predict that level of political information and likelihood of voting covary, so that as one increases so does the other. But are people more likely to vote because they have more information, or do they gain information because they intend to vote and want to make a sound decision, or are both information level and likelihood of voting the products of some third factor, such as interest in politics or perceived civic duty? The covariational proposition does not tell us.

Causal relationships exist when changes in one or more concepts lead to or cause changes in one or more other concepts. For example, the stronger one's party identification, we might argue, the more likely one is to vote. Feeling oneself to be a member of a party can lead one to vote, but the likelihood of voting does not create one's party identification.

We are accustomed to thinking in terms of cause and effect in our everyday life, and generally use these concepts loosely. In scientific research it is often very difficult to identify the causes or consequences of human behaviour; the more important the event, the more difficult isolation of its causes can be. What brings on a war, a social movement or the creation of a new political party?

Testing causation

Because of such complexities, we must be careful to postulate causal relationships only when four conditions are simultaneously met. First, the postulated cause and effect must change together, or covary. Second, the cause must precede the effect. Third, we must be able to identify a *causal linkage* between the supposed cause and effect (meaning, we must be able to identify the *process* by which changes in one factor cause changes in another). Fourth, the covariance of the cause-and-effect phenomena must not be due to their simultaneous relationship to some third factor – a condition we discuss next.

Spurious relationships occur when A and B vary together only because they are both caused by C. If they would not covary in the absence of C, the apparent relationship between A and B is termed *spurious.* We must carefully examine the assumptions we are making in an effort to uncover possible spuriousness in relationships before we build them into our theories as though they were the product of causal interaction. A classic instance of spuriousness is the case in which an investigator first finds that the price of imported rum and the salaries of ministers fluctuate together and then reasons that changes in the price of rum cause changes in ministers' salaries. It is more likely that both rum prices and ministers' salaries change in response to changes in general economic conditions and overall price level. The relationship between the first two variables is covariational, but it is not causal.

It is important to recognise two other features of social causation. First, one phenomenon may cause another either directly or indirectly. For example, A may cause B only in that it is the cause of C, which directly causes B. We must be alert to the role of **indirect causation** in attempting to make our theories as complete as possible. Second, we must be sensitive to the fact that human behaviour generally has more than one cause. In theorising, we should avoid oversimplifying and thus recognise the role of **multiple causation** in social life. This simply means that any one event may have several different causes, and that many events sometimes must come together to cause a given occurrence.

To cope with all of these complexities, it is generally a good idea to draw a **causal model** of the theory. This is simply a diagram that clearly specifies all the relationships posited in the theory so

Figure 2.2 Causal model of the hypothetical determinants of an MP's support for welfare legislation

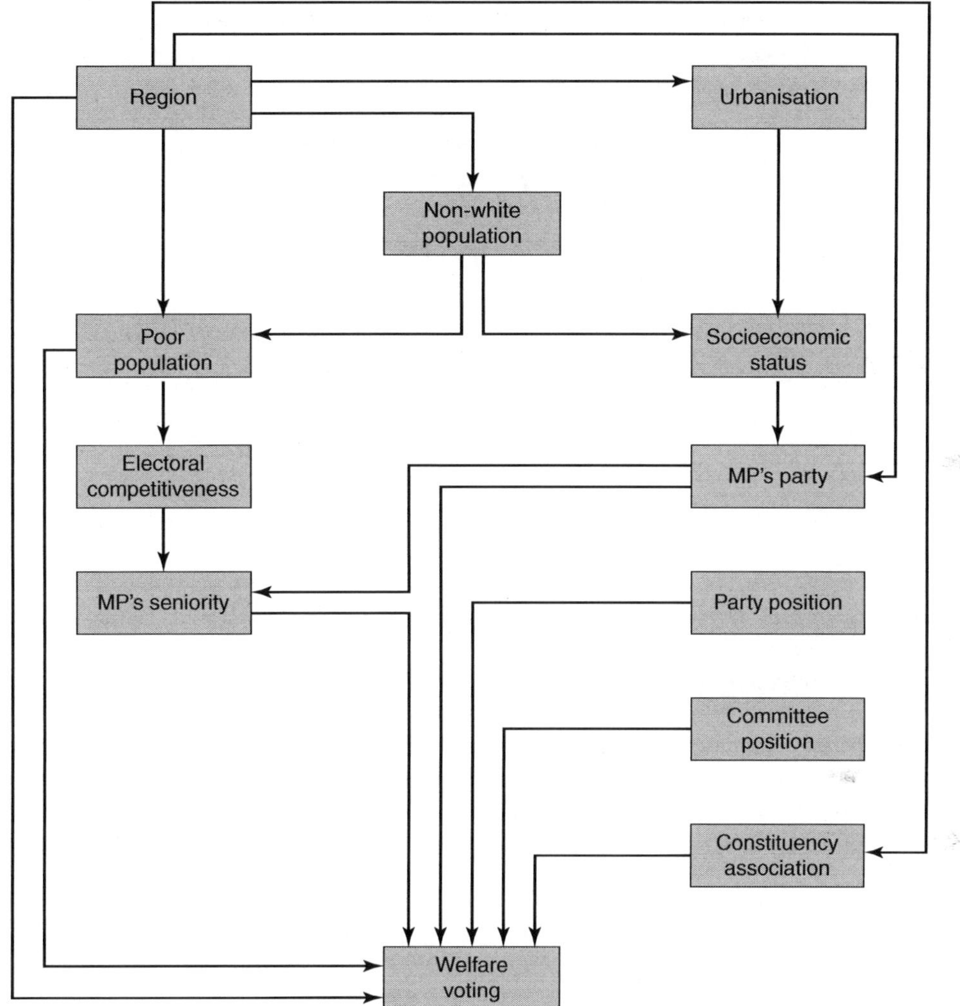

Source: Adapted from Rich (1984: 135). Reprinted with permission.

that it is easier to see the implications of our arguments. Figure 2.2 presents an example of such a model. Each arrow in the model represents a causal influence, and the direction in which it is pointing indicates which variable is theorised as dependent and which as independent. The theory illustrated in Figure 2.2 asserts that a variety of factors influence an MP's decision to rebel against the party whip and vote against their party over social welfare legislation in both direct and indirect ways. For instance, the size of the poor population in the MP's parliamentary constituency is depicted as influencing voting both directly (independently) and indirectly through the electoral competitiveness of the district and the seniority level of the representative (parliamentary minister or not).

At this point, we should note that although our theories typically specify a causal relationship between our concepts, we rarely encounter social science data that can establish definite causation. Later in this text, we will highlight the exceptional degree of control the experimental setting offers, which helps to identify causal relationships.

Positive and negative relationships

Both covariational and causal relationships can be either *positive* or *negative*. This means that the two concepts can change either in the same direction or in opposite directions, respectively. An example of a **positive relationship** is: the *higher* the relative deprivation of minority groups within a society, the higher the likelihood of political violence. A **negative relationship** may be posited as follows: the *higher* the degree of political alienation one feels, the *lower* the likelihood that one will take part in conventional political activities. Our theories must specify whether we expect positive or negative relationships among concepts. This information can be added to causal diagrams by placing a plus (1) or minus (2) sign on each path in order to indicate whether the relationship is thought to be positive or negative.

Theory testing and elaboration

Theories must never be regarded as finished products, but always as tools that should occasionally be inspected and can often be improved. We start with a research question that asks for an explanation of observed events, select concepts that promise to be useful in explaining those events, and relate the concepts through propositions logically derived from a set of assumptions we choose to make in order to secure an explanation. Now our backs are against the wall. Is this lovely structure any good? It seems to explain what we want to understand, but can we check it in some way? Can we test its utility so that we can know how much confidence to place in it and persuade others of its value?

Theory testing is at the centre of the research process. Because our theories are generally developed from bits of knowledge about actual relationships, the tasks of theory testing are essentially those of using the theory to formulate some expectations about other relationships we have not observed and then checking to see whether actual observations are consistent with what we expect to find. We cannot rely on relationships we have already observed, because showing that the theory leads us to expect the very relationships the theory was built to explain would be no test at all.

In our example of the elevator, after observing the elevators in one building, we will be quite confident that the elevators in that building operate in response to a system of wall-mounted buttons. We might even be willing to generalise from our observations to reach the conclusion that all elevators work this way. We can check the validity of that conclusion only by actually trying it out in other buildings. It does not help to double-check the elevators in the building we started in, because we already know that they respond to the buttons and showing that they do does not make us feel any more secure that other elevators do as well. We have to go to other buildings to see how their elevators operate.

We can never actually prove that our theory of elevator operation is correct because we can never observe all the elevators in the world. As we see more and more elevators that do work this way and we never encounter any that do not, our confidence in the validity of our generalisation will increase. If we cannot find any other elevators that work by buttons, however, we will quickly conclude that we have been mistaken in generalising from the initial observations to all other elevators.

Theory testing in the social sciences works by the same principle. We must move from what we have observed in devising the theory to what we have not observed, in order to discover whether or not the theory provides us with an accurate set of expectations about the world.

Suppose, for example, that we want to construct a theory to explain voting behaviour. We review previous research on the subject and discover that, for citizens of the United Kingdom, higher education is positively related to the propensity to vote. On the basis of these observations, we include in our theory an assumption that higher educational levels lead to a greater likelihood of voting. We know that these factors appear to be related in the United Kingdom, but what about in other nations? Could there be something unique to the educational system or the informational complexity of voting in the United Kingdom that causes this relationship? The only way we can find out is to observe people and the political systems in other nations, because, as political researchers, we are interested in finding *general* relationships in human behaviour.

From the assumption that education increases the likelihood of voting, we might deduce the prediction that people with some university education are more likely to vote than people who left school at the age of 18. We can test this prediction by seeing whether it accurately reflects relationships found in data from a variety of countries. The more often we find evidence consistent with the prediction, the more confident we will feel that our theory is useful in predicting human behaviour. We can never be absolutely certain that the theory is 'true', because we can neither observe all cases nor be sure how the empirical relationships might change with time. However, we can acquire more or less confidence in the utility of the theory by comparing the predictions derived from it with observations. If it allows us to accurately predict things we have not previously observed, then it is useful.

Theories, as sets of concepts, assumptions and propositions, are never finally proved or disproved. Rather, our confidence in the *usefulness* of a theory builds as we accumulate observations that are consistent with the expectations or hypotheses derived from it. Alternatively, our confidence diminishes as we accumulate observations that are inconsistent with theoretically derived hypotheses.

The role of hypotheses

The above section's **theory elaboration** is based largely on a process of comparing hypothesised conditions with reality and, once we have the results, modifying our theory so that the hypotheses that can be derived from it are more and more consistent with what we observe. Now we consider how our research questions are translated into hypotheses that can guide empirical investigations and provide us with clues to the adequacy of our theoretical explanations.

Hypotheses defined

A **hypothesis** is essentially a statement of what we believe to be factual. It tells what we expect to find when we make properly organised observations of reality. Hypotheses are declarative sentences stating expected relationships between the phenomena to which our concepts refer. They are usually stated in the following general form:

The higher (lower, greater, larger, slower etc.) the_______, the higher (lower, greater, larger, slower etc.) the _______.

The blanks are filled in with the names of the phenomena that we expect will change together. For example, Rich (1984) demonstrated that those US Congressional Representatives with a greater number of poor constituents tended to favour welfare legislation. Working from Rich's theory, we might hypothesise the following for those MPs who favoured reintroducing a lower threshold for taxation for poorer families in the UK:

The larger the proportion of a district's population that is composed of poor constituents, the more likely that the MP will favour lower taxes for poorer families.

This is a covariational hypothesis. It does not tell us how parliamentary voting is determined, but it does point us to something that we can observe in an effort to acquire some evidence on the fit between our theory and reality.

Acquiring that evidence through empirical observation requires that we move from the very general level of theory to a more specific level from which to organise observations. In doing this, we have to begin to think in terms of **variables**. A variable may be defined as an empirically observable characteristic of some phenomenon that can take on more than one value. Sex and nationality are two variables that can take on only a limited number of values and can be 'measured' only qualitatively by designations such as 'male' or 'British'. Age and gross national product are two variables that can take on a much wider range of values; they can be measured quantitatively by counting.

Concepts into variables

To facilitate empirical testing, abstract concepts must be translated into statements with more precisely defined variables. For instance, the concept of *pluralism* is important in political studies, but its empirical referents are not particularly clear. In order to test the empirical accuracy of any statement relating pluralism to anything else, we have to translate the concept into some variable or set of variables with clear empirical referents. We might want to use the number of organised interest groups in a nation as a variable to represent the concept of pluralism in our research. We can then reason backward from our observation of relationships among variables to evaluate the empirical validity of statements about relationships between concepts. If we are willing to assume that the variable *number of organised groups* captures the essential meaning of the concept *pluralism*, we will be willing to take evidence that this variable is related to some other variable (such as the level of government expenditures) as evidence that pluralism is also related to that other variable or the concept it represents.

Independent and dependent variables

Variables have a central place in the research process for two reasons. First, they help us identify what we will have to observe to test our theory by providing more precise empirical referents. Second, we can organise our observations by knowing the role variables play in hypotheses. Variables that are thought to change value in response to changes in the value of other variables are referred to as **dependent variables**. Their value depends on the value of other variables. Variables that influence the value of other variables through changes in their own values are referred to as **independent variables**.

An example

Whether a variable is dependent or independent is determined by the relationship asserted by the hypotheses containing it. The same variable might be dependent in one study and independent in another. For example, a theorist observing the lobbying efforts of interest groups might reason that the larger the number of organised interest groups in a nation is, the higher the level of government expenditures will be. In this case, the number of groups is the independent variable and the level of expenditure is the dependent variable. This relationship is illustrated in Figure 2.3.

Figure 2.3

Interest group activity (independent variable) leads to higher government spending levels (dependent variable)

An independent variable's change in value must precede changes in the dependent variable. For example, following the above hypothesised relationship, we might observe an increase in government spending between 1980 and 1990 and also see a positive change in the number of organised groups between 1990 and 2000. Logically, this subsequent surge in interest group formation cannot have been responsible for a level of expenditures that preceded it. In fact, these observed data should prompt a reconsideration and (perhaps) a theoretical reformulation that accounts for this phenomenon.

Intervening variables

A close look at Figure 2.3 alerts us to another type of variable important in social analysis. In the theory summarised by the diagram in Figure 2.3, lobbying activity is an intervening variable; it comes into play *between* the number of organised interest groups and the level of government spending. **Intervening variables** provide the link between independent and dependent variables. In this case, interest groups would not affect the level of government spending if they did not engage in lobbying to get funds appropriated to their cause.

Intervening variables *condition* the relationships between other variables. This means that the value attained by intervening variables can affect the strength and direction of relationships between other variables. If lobbying activity is slight in Figure 2.3, then the relationship of interest group organisation to public spending is weak. If lobbying is extensive, the relationship between the other variables will be strong.

Because intervening variables condition relationships between other variables, our knowledge of the role they play will affect our expectations about relationships between variables. If we are theorising that lobbying intervenes between group organisation and increases in spending, then we can make the following predictions:

Interest group organisation will be positively related to increases in government spending when lobbying activity is vigorous.

Interest group organisation will be related only weakly to increases in government spending when lobbying activity is highly limited.

We will not be satisfied to predict simply that interest group organisation will be related to increases in government spending, because we believe that whether the two variables are related depends on the value of the intervening variable – lobbying. For this reason, we must specify the order of relationships and the role played by each variable in our theories.

Antecedent variables

Whereas intervening variables come between independent and dependent variables, antecedent variables come into play before the independent variable does. For instance, we know that studies of voting behaviour in the United States show that people who identify strongly with a political party are more likely to vote than those who do not. We might then want to theorise that party identification leads to or causes voting frequency. But what causes some people to identify strongly with a party while others do not? We might reason that the strength of their parents' party identification plays an important role in people's development of such party identification. Parents' party identification then is an **antecedent variable** in the causal chain that produces voting frequency.

Using both intervening and antecedent variables in our theories helps to clarify the *causal chains* at work in creating the phenomena we want to explain. It gives us more of a basis for deriving hypotheses through which we can test the utility of our theories, because hypotheses are essentially *statements of relationships between variables*. Hypotheses provide a basis for collecting evidence about the empirical utility of our theoretical structure. The more numerous and the more detailed the relationships we postulate, the more predictions we can make about the world and therefore the more potential tests we have of our theory.

This leads to the question of how we decide what relationships to assert in the form of hypotheses around which to build research projects.

Formulating hypotheses

We arrive at hypotheses by either inductive or deductive reasoning. Which one we use depends on the stage we have reached in the research process. If we are still using trial and error to construct a theory, we might develop hypotheses by a process of *inductive generalisation.* For example, we might observe that the level of popular political participation varies directly with the extent of industrialisation in Europe, and we might generalise that this relationship between variables is also found when comparing nations. If we find evidence to support the hypothesis, we will be more confident in including industrialisation as a variable in a theory designed to explain political participation. Until we have a theory that shows *why* industrialisation and participation are related, however, we cannot use the fact of their relationship as an explanation of political participation.

Hypotheses arrived at inductively can be important in *exploratory research*, which helps us construct theories, but they do not help us explain phenomena. Once we have stated a theory relating our variables in a logically coherent system, we can derive hypotheses from that theory by *deductive reasoning.* Because these hypotheses are predictions about the world that are logically implied by the theory with which we are working, finding support for them does help us explain events, because such findings reflect the validity of the theoretical system from which the hypotheses have been derived.

We cannot learn anything new about relationships from deduction alone. Deductive logic is a process by which the information contained in a set of statements can be made explicit. We use deduction to *clarify the implications of our assumptions*, and it is that clarification that produces hypotheses.

The deduction contained in Figure 2.1(b) shows this. If the assumption stated there is correct, that is, if the Labour Party attracts *only* trade union members, then any subset of the members of that party will be trade union members also, and since the Labour Party members in Newcastle are members of that party, they too will be trade union members. This is the kind of reasoning referred to when we say that one conclusion 'logically follows' from another. The conclusion that all Labour Party members in Newcastle will be trade union members is logically implied in the assumption that the Labour Party attracts only trade union members.

Since hypotheses are derived from theories, testing hypotheses indirectly tests our theories. Returning to our example, if we interview a properly drawn sample of Newcastle Labour Party members and find that not all are trade union members, we will have good reason to question the validity of our assumption. Finding small business owners among Newcastle Labour Party members shows that the party does not attract *only* those in trade unions. We will then want to modify our assumption so that the theory can more closely reflect reality. We may want to change it to read, 'The Labour Party tends to attract more trade union members than small business owners.' From this assumption we can derive the hypothesis 'There will be more trade union members than small business owners in the Newcastle Labour Party.'

If we find a few small business owners and many trade union members in the Newcastle branch of the Labour Party, we can say that the evidence is consistent with the hypothesis and the modified assumption from which it has been drawn. We still cannot put much faith in the general accuracy of the assumption until it is supported by evidence about the trade union or small business character of a larger sample of the national Labour Party. After all, Newcastle may be unique in some way. Perhaps, for example, there are only ten small businesses in the entire city, and the fact that only a few of the Newcastle Labour Party's members are small business owners is a result of this more than of the relative attractiveness of the party to small business owners or trade union members.

Indirect theory testing

The important point here is that evidence about the accuracy of hypotheses represents evidence about the accuracy of a theory *only when the hypotheses are linked to the theory by deductive logic.* Only when this is the case can we safely reason backward from evidence of the validity of a hypothesis to any judgement about the parent theory. Theories are developed, expanded and improved by this process of logically deriving hypotheses, checking them against reality and evaluating the theory in light of the results.

One type of hypothesis that plays an especially crucial role in this process is the **alternative rival hypothesis**. There are many possible explanations for any event. Some of these explanations are fully consistent with one another; more than one may be correct. In some cases, however, the explanations are opposed to one another: if one is correct, the other cannot be. If we state our explanations as hypotheses, then those which are inconsistent with one another are termed *alternative rival hypotheses.* They are alternatives because they provide different ways of looking at or understanding the event to be explained. They are rivals because they cannot both be valid. If one is accurate, the other has to be inaccurate. We cannot test and compare all possible alternative hypotheses relating to any event, but if we are to have faith in the accuracy of any one hypothesis, we must attempt to test the major rival hypotheses to be sure that we are not being misled by our observations.

One common form of alternative rival hypothesis is that which states that the relationship between any two variables is spurious and that changes in both are in fact due to some third factor. This type of alternative rival hypothesis is especially useful in theory testing because it suggests a research finding that gives us a solid basis for judging which of the two hypotheses in question is more accurate.

An example

In our illustration inferring a causal relationship between rum prices and ministers' salaries, one major alternative rival hypothesis is that fluctuations in both measures are caused by changes in general economic conditions, as represented by general price levels. If this hypothesis is correct, then the relationship between rum prices and ministers' salaries will disappear when we 'control for' (that is, hold constant) the effect of the overall prices on each of these variables. If the statistical association between rum prices and ministers' salaries vanishes when we control for general price level, we will have a basis for rejecting the original hypothesis in favour of its rival. If the relationship between rum prices and salaries remains even after our imposition of controls for general price level, we have more confidence in the hypothesis that these variables are genuinely related.

Ethical considerations

The ways in which research questions are formulated can have a dramatic impact on how politics is viewed. For example, it is possible to divide individuals in society into two classes, workers and owners, and to make sense of political views based on that distinction, but does this polarisation enhance understanding or merely fuel division in society? Once a conceptual category is chosen, it is difficult to see the world in any other way. This does not mean that one cannot generalise at all. It simply means that concepts must be defined, refined and tested repeatedly to ensure they are valid and to tease out all their implications. No concepts or categories are going to fit all cases. Any concept does some violence to the reality it purports to represent. This does not mean that concepts and categories cannot be used, it simply means that a researcher must be open to thinking about the ways in which political relationships might be conceptualised and how the conceptual validity is demonstrated.

It is also important to remember that, implicitly or explicitly, politics research always involves humans. Thus, it is unrealistic to pretend that people's lives could never be affected by your research, whether it explores media messages, or interest groups or executive power. How would you feel if someone used your research to manipulate voters through the media during a political campaign? What if a government in a developing nation realised, through your research findings, that its environmental groups' voices may be silenced without popular backlash, as long as the government maintains economic development? Would you like it if, based upon your research findings that people are greatly comforted by a strong executive during times of popular fear, a democratic regime sharply limited judicial oversight in favour of concentrating power in the executive? Although these are intended to represent hypothetical examples, you should never assume that your own research cannot have consequences for real people's lives – for good or ill.

Often the political impact of conceptualisation is subtle but profound. A good example is 'realism', a prominent theory of international relations. Realist or more accurately 'neo-realist' theory suggests that much of what happens between nations is based on the relative power capabilities of countries and the distribution of power with the international system. Based on this theory, it was logical for some US decision makers to believe that as the US was by far the strongest of the countries of the world after the end of the Cold War in 1990, the US had the capacity and right to act unilaterally. The 'realist' school of international political studies certainly had an influence on US decision makers. Yet, other scholars have pointed out that a focus on power was self-fulfilling prophecy. Since the US acted unilaterally based on those areas in which the US had overwhelming strength in military and economic power, it made it appear that power was the most important factor in international relations. If relations between nations had been conceived of and acted upon in other ways, it is possible that power would have seemed less important. The question becomes: was the theory of 'realism' correct from the point of view of US decision makers because it reflected reality or did the theory influence events in such a ways as to reinforce belief in the theory?

Thinking critically about theory will aid your ability to understand the research of others and undertake your own research. If, as in the above example, one wanted to challenge the logic of realism, what should be the conceptualisation of international relations put in its place? How would one demonstrate that the new approach had validity and was a viable alternative? Do the alternatives merely express wishful thinking so that there is no empirical basis for believing in an alternative approach? These are the types of questions which a good critical politics researcher pursues.

Conclusion

Theories gain acceptance as useful intellectual tools as we find evidence consistent with predictions derived from them and eliminate alternative rival hypotheses. We must keep in mind, however, that no single piece of research provides sufficient evidence for accepting or rejecting any theory or part of a theory that pertains to phenomena beyond those included in the study. There is always the possibility that some future research will produce evidence against the theory's validity. We must always be open to contrary findings and willing to return to induction to build new evidence into more useful theories.

Theory building is a process of constant interaction between conjecture and evidence, and between reasoning and research. It calls for creative ingenuity, hermeneutic sensitivity and hardheaded empiricism. Although you must provide the creativity, we hope to provide a good dose of the latter in the chapters that follow.

Summary points

- Theories aid the research process by suggesting explanations of relationships.
- Theories guide testing through simplifying reality.
- Theories may be derived by inducing from specific observations and then tested using deductions.
- Theories may be more or less useful – not true or false.
- Useful theories are testable, logical, communicable, general and parsimonious.
- Covariates tend to change together, whereas causal factors lead to changes in other concepts.
- Hypotheses state expected relationships between concepts.
- Hypotheses are deduced from theories and indirectly test the source theory.

Suggested reading and examples

Research examples

Research in all fields of political science is built on a solid foundation of theory, grounded in the relevant literature. A study of the values held by the Iraqi citizenry is structured using the theories related to survival, regime instability and attitudes towards those in out-groups (Inglehart, Moaddel and Tessler 2006). Theories that look to the family for the roots of citizens' understanding of political power relations supply the basis for Barker and Tinnick's (2006) empirical study of humanitarianism versus individualism.

Methodological reading

Both newcomers and advanced researchers will find provocative and persuasive arguments on the nature of causation and logical reasoning in the late Wesley Salmon's (1998) collection of essays in *Causality and Explanation*. A broad-ranging and highly readable treatment of the role of theory in the research process is *The Elements of Social Scientific Thinking* (Hoover and Donovan 2004).

References

Barker, David C. and Tinnick, James D. 2006. 'Competing visions of parental roles and ideological constraint'. *American Political Science Review*, vol 100 (May), pp. 249–263.

Fogelson, R. M. and Hill, R. B. 1968. 'Who riots? A study of participation in the 1967 riots', in The National Advisory Commission on Civil Disorder, *Supplemental Studies for the National Advisory Commission on Civil Disorders*. Washington, DC: US Government Printing Office.

Hoover, Kenneth and Donovan, Todd. 2004. *The Elements of Social Scientific Thinking,* 8th edn. Belmont, CA: Thompson/Wadsworth.

Inglehart, Ronald, Moaddel, Mansoor and Tessler, Mark. 2006. 'Xenophobia and in-group solidarity in Iraq: A natural experiment on the impact of insecurity'. *Perspectives on Politics*, vol. 4, no. 3, pp. 495 – 505.

Rich, Richard. 1984. 'The representation of the poor in the policy process: Changes in congressional support for welfare' in Robert Eyestone, ed. *Public Policy Formation*. Greenwich. CT: JAI Press.

Salmon, Wesley. 1998. *Causality and Explanation.* New York: Oxford University Press.

Research exercises

1 Several concepts that might be used in political research are given in the following list. List one or more variables that might be used to represent each of them. Indicate how confident you are that the variables you select to represent each concept adequately capture all that you mean when you use the concept. Do you need several variables to capture the meaning of some of the concepts?

economic development	political representation
party competition	racial discrimination
international tensions	conservatism
political equality	terrorism

2 Select any four of the concepts listed in Exercise 1 and state a hypothesis that predicts a relationship between each of those concepts and some concept not on the list. Formulate two of the hypotheses so that they state positive relationships and two so that they state negative relationships.

3 Select a news article about some political trend or event in which you are interested. Devise at least two explanations for the trend or event, and state them as clearly as possible. List the concepts employed in each explanation. Pair each concept with a variable counterpart for it that you could use in a research project, and indicate the status (independent, dependent, intervening, antecedent) of each variable. Produce a diagram to illustrate the causal chain implied in each of your explanations.

4 Examine articles in political studies journals and find one that moves clearly through the stages of conceptualisation, theory building, hypothesis generation and hypothesis testing. Explain the research design using the stages above (including any stages which appear to have been missed!).

Key terms

alternative rival hypothesis
antecedent variable
assumptions
causal model
causal relationships
concept
covariational relationships
deduction
dependent variables
empirical referents

exploratory research
hypothesis
independent variables
indirect causation
induction
intervening variables
multiple causation
negative relationship
positive relationship
propositions

research question
spurious relationships
theoretical import
theories
theorising
theory elaboration
theory testing
variables

3 Setting the foundation: techniques of systematic bibliographic search

- Why should we seek previous research on our topic?
- How can we use the existing literature to help frame our research questions?
- How do we conduct a systematic search of the relevant literature?
- What is the advantage of using the library's resources versus searching the internet?
- How do we evaluate information found on the internet?
- Why take notes on the references found?

Introduction

One of the most important steps in theory-building is to familiarise yourself with the previous research or writing on your topic. The literature in the field of political studies and relevant subfields is enormous and, even in the best organised and most complete academic library, the relevant research may appear to be scattered to three of the four winds. It is found in hundreds of scholarly journals and thousands of books. Some of these are available in printed form, some in electronic form; some are available in most university libraries, some are in very few. This chapter offers a systematic strategy to maximise the effectiveness of your literature searching efforts.

Using the existing literature

We may learn a great deal from the successes and failures of those who have already tackled problems similar to our research. This may help us to refine our theories, to avoid pitfalls in our research, and to tighten our thinking. We must realise that our own work can contribute, even if only in a small way, to the intellectual development of the discipline. By placing our work in the context of, and building directly upon, the literature, we increase the potential value of our contribution many times over. Our own work becomes, in effect, part of the literature that researchers may draw upon later.

As with any mature discipline, the body of political studies knowledge has incrementally accumulated over a long period through a series of relatively small intellectual advances. Even major theoretical or methodological innovations can be seen, in the longer view, to have been logical next steps that built upon the state of the art. New bits of knowledge become known and these generate new insights. The insights themselves give rise to new research questions, which in turn give rise to still more new bits of knowledge. And so it goes on and on, the insights becoming ever more sophisticated, the bits of knowledge more complete and the questions more pointed.

It is in the context of this incremental process of developing our understanding of politics that the importance of the careful bibliographic grounding of our research becomes clear. Political enquiry has been around in one form or another since the days of Socrates, Plato and Aristotle. Empirical political science, which focuses on the systematic and objective description of political activity, has developed in large part since the 1940s, but its roots may be traced back as far as Machiavelli. Today, tens of thousands of individuals hold advanced degrees in the discipline around the world, some of whom work as political scientists of one type or another. Given these facts, it is extremely likely that any research question we might come up with has already been posed or partially explored by someone before us.

Positioning your research

The realisation that the existing literature may already speak to most questions you might develop does not mean that your research can make no contribution; rather, it means that your contribution will most likely represent an addition to an *existing* body of knowledge instead of the creation of a new one. This fact may cause you to feel that all the really interesting work has already been done, that the field is closed to innovation, and that no individual accomplishment can amount to much. Each of these perceptions is incorrect. The acquisition of knowledge is a cumulative and incremental process, and your knowledge of the existing research allows you to properly position your theory and findings. Contextualising your work helps others both to locate and to utilise your findings.

Thus, rather than erecting constraints, the research process offers opportunities. Familiarity with past politics research suggests the direction for future inquiry, and the value of individual effort is enhanced by the collective context. The value of a piece of research increases as that research builds upon the existing body of political research.

The interactive research process

Reading the literature that relates to your theory is an interactive process, so you should not be daunted by what you do not know when you begin your research. As you gain familiarity with the extant literature, your literature review plan will also evolve. You will want to read widely in the existing literature on topics related to your theory, but also approach this reading intelligently and efficiently. As you are reading, consider: (1) what research questions have already been asked (what theories have been posed); (2) how researchers have gone about answering those questions; and (3) what researchers have found. While gathering this information, keep in mind two specific questions. First, what substantive information about your theory can you glean from the literature? Second, what useful insights have previous researchers developed, what mistakes have they made and what might they have overlooked in answering their research questions? Or, to put it another way, what methodological lessons can you learn from the literature?

To identify the books and articles that are relevant to your theory, you might just head for the library, locate the politics books, and start reading book and article titles until you locate some of interest. Alternatively, you might just search Google or a similar site on the web. These approaches are inefficient in two ways. First, in undertaking unfocused searches, you waste a great deal of time. In order to find the few titles that might be of interest, you are forced to sift through hundreds of volumes and thousands of journal articles that have nothing whatsoever to do with the topic you are pursuing. Second, an unfocused search simply will not turn up the greater part of the literature you need. This is because politics is so diverse a discipline – it is not at all uncommon to find politics research published in journals of sociology, psychology, communication, geography and economics, to name only a few. Additionally, the titles of books or articles do not always offer solid guidance to their content, and even if they did, not all of a library's holdings may be on the shelves at a given time. In sum, random searching will yield too much that is somewhat related to your topic, but too little that is directly related to your theory. Clearly, you need a better strategy for identifying the items that interest you.

Developing a system

Systematic bibliographic search is simply a way of preparing and planning to ensure the most productive use of your institution's library resources. It involves (1) specifying your needs; (2) planning how you will allocate your efforts; (3) maximising your use of the resources available; and (4) recording what you find for later use. Each of these is explored in turn.

Listing keywords

The first step is to develop a list of terms from the three (at least) concepts in our theory. An example will best demonstrate this process (the concepts are italicised). Suppose we theorise that *pro-European Union voters* with British *Conservative Party* partisan identification who plan to vote for a local Conservative *anti-EU candidate* are more likely to think (incorrectly) that their preferred candidate shares their policy views on Europe, because to think otherwise could cause these voters to experience *cognitive dissonance*.

From the concepts mentioned in our example theory, we brainstorm a list of political terms: *pro-European Union, voters, Conservative (UK), anti-EU, candidate, European Union* and *cognitive dissonance*. Then, we can individually list the synonyms or words that are related to these concepts. For example, the term *Conservative* may suggest: Conservative voter, the Conservative Party, Tory, Tories, Conservative partisan identification, a UK political party, conservative ideology, right wing etc. Notice that few of the related words in our list are truly identical in meaning to the initial word. Some are broader (UK political party), some are more specific (Conservative Party) and some are related but fundamentally differ from the original term (right-wing ideology). Additionally, when thinking of related terms, remember the multiple meanings that many words have – British Conservative Party versus conservative parties elsewhere in the world. At this point, an important part of our brainstorming is to develop a fairly wide list of relevant keywords, because we do not know how the existing research may characterise our theory's concepts.

Filling in the grid

A **concept search grid** helps us keep track of our potential search terms and their possible relationships. Figure 3.1 illustrates the grid's use with our brainstormed concepts written in. The grid in Figure 3.1 is used by simply writing your initial concepts (from your theory) on the upper lines, and then listing the brainstormed terms below each concept. These 'Related terms' may be synonyms, narrower words, broader words or subject headings (sometimes called descriptors) from your library's catalogue, indexes or databases. The 'link' between the terms is printed in lighter type because it is optional. Initially, you may want to search for your related terms individually, and later narrow your focus by adding (or combining) terms to the search. Since your theory has at least three concepts and you will probably use several different library tools in your search, you will need to use multiple grids to include all of your concepts. Remember, the grid is simply a tool; use it as long as it facilitates your literature search, modifying it as your search progresses.

Developing the initial list of related words should not be too time consuming, and may provide enough terms to get your keyword search started. Remember, a literature search is interactive; thus, you will be adding words to the grid as your research progresses and crossing off words that you discover to be less useful.

Figure 3.1	Sample concept search grid

	Theoretical concept:		**Theoretical concept:**
	Conservative		EU
Search	**Related terms:**	Link (and/or)	**Related terms:**
1	Conservative voter		Lisbon Treaty
2	Conservative party		Euro-sceptic
3	Party identification		Out of EU
4	Right-wing		
5			
6			
7			

Note: Printable copies of this grid may be downloaded from Craig Leonard Brians' website: www.psci.vt.edu/cbrians.

The usefulness of the key terms on the grid is better tested using search tools that more closely represent the text of current research. Thus, we begin our search with periodicals, before moving to books listed in the library catalogue.

Periodical indexes and databases

Academic libraries typically offer two kinds of tools for article searching: full-text databases and indexes. Full-text databases contain complete articles. Oriented around keywords, searching full-text databases is similar to using a search engine (e.g., Google) on the free web. Indexes describe articles and provide citations. Thus, using indexes is like using the library catalogue, and includes the very powerful function of finding related items under a standardised list of subject headings. Online indexes generally include hyperlinks to the journals to which your library subscribes, as well as citations to many articles not available in your library. Print indexes, which are still available, provide citations to articles written before the digital era.

Once you have developed your list of search terms, you need to put these to use and learn what the political science literature has to say about your research topic. An excellent starting point is a **general periodical database**, such as 'EBSCO' or 'Web of Knowledge'. Widely available in most academic libraries, these databases include citations – and often the full text – of articles on topics related to a variety of academic disciplines, including the humanities, physical sciences and social sciences. The coverage is wide but seldom deep enough to be the sole source for thorough research.

Starting your search in a general database has two purposes. First, these resources generally offer a good sense of the background information related to your topic, quickly confirming whether your theory is plausible. Popular periodicals provide access to information on your topic, since you are not yet an expert on the jargon and techniques of a discipline. Second, although the scholarly content is worth evaluating separately (and we will do so below), general databases also contain research from many academic journals. Thus, in addition to a popular periodical overview, searching these databases may also give you a taste of the academic research on your topic.

Searching with keywords

Whether your library subscribes to *JSTOR* or another general periodical database, the **keyword** (the typical default search for library databases) searching process is quite similar. Keyword searches check the available records in the database for articles that contain the search term you enter. The database does not 'know' what you or the article's author(s) intend by a word. The search merely matches a string of characters. Therefore, if the author of an article that is relevant to your theory used a different set of words to describe the concepts, or even a different spelling, a keyword search will bypass the article. Keeping records on your search results on the concept grid may assist you in focusing your efforts on the most productive search terms.

Most indexes and databases permit the use of wildcard characters to expand your search; that is, you may substitute an '*' or similar character for several letters (e.g., 'Conserv*' finds Conservative, conservatives, conservatism, but also conservation). Since this type of search expands the terms being searched, wildcard searching yields far more results than any single root word.

Searching by keywords in *JSTOR* is straightforward. Returning to the words in the grid in Figure 3.1, we type the word 'Conservative Party' in the *JSTOR* search box (see Figure 3.2). Performing this keyword search yields tens of thousands of recent articles that apparently mention the Conservative Party. As we begin to read these articles (either online or in hard copy in the library), we will discover two things. First, many of the articles are only tangentially related to the Conservative Party in the United Kingdom. Second, it is exhausting to locate the few articles that even mention the European Union.

To address these challenges, we need to refine our search and become more efficient searchers. The next section describes a technique to sharpen our focus on articles that are most relevant to our

Figure 3.2   Typical search window for an online periodical index or database

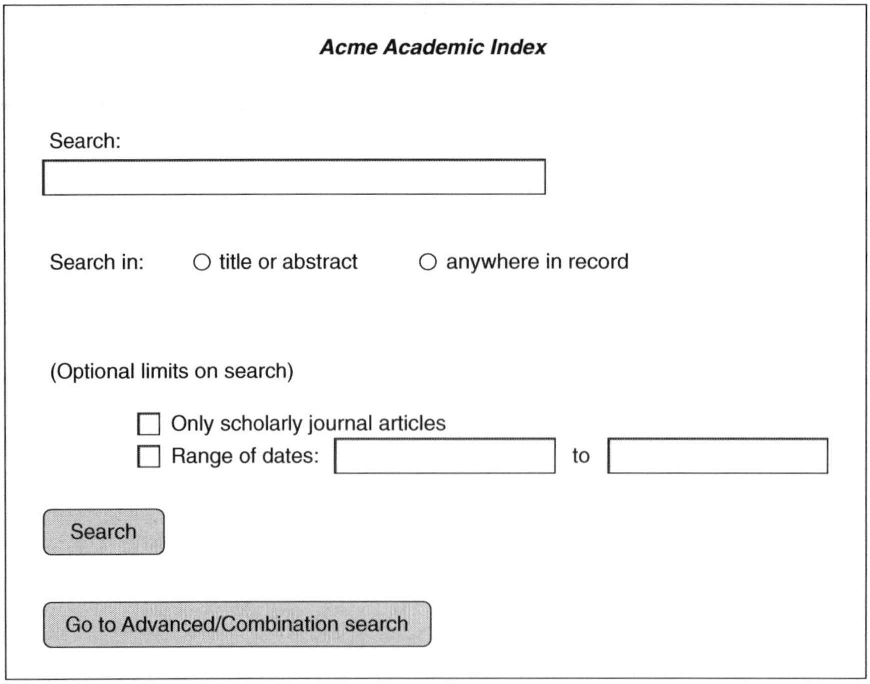

Acme Academic Index

Search:

Search in: ○ title or abstract   ○ anywhere in record

(Optional limits on search)

☐ Only scholarly journal articles

☐ Range of dates: ______ to ______

Search

Go to Advanced/Combination search

study of the Conservative Party. The same principles apply to the European Union policy side of our theory, as well. After mastering these tools, we will be ready to combine searches to locate literature that addresses both aspects of our theory.

Moving from keywords to subjects

Once you have located a few relevant (in some respect) articles using the keyword search, you will want to take advantage of librarians' work on your behalf to find related articles. Library indexes, many full-text databases and library catalogues are designed to get new users past several of the problems associated with keyword searching (e.g., word choice, ambiguity and spelling). One of the most common and powerful ways is by adding **subject headings** (sometimes called **descriptors**). These standardised headings link articles dealing with related topics by identifying the several fundamental issues or topics that the articles address.

Searching by subject in *JSTOR* is also straightforward. Simply click on the article title in the search results and you will find the *JSTOR* subject links to other articles at the bottom of the article record. Using subject headings benefits your search in two ways. First, they can help clarify your thinking about your theory. The list of subject headings for a given article can make you aware of connections between concepts in that piece of research; they give you a snapshot of how the discipline categorises the article. Second, subject headings help you to locate other articles that fall into those same disciplinary categories.

An example

An article from the search described previously has several subject headings, including 'Conservative Party (United Kingdom) – demographic aspects'. Clicking on any of these subject heading links will initiate a subject heading search, yielding more articles that are related to the subject. If we carefully choose which subject to search by, these new articles are more likely to have a sharper emphasis on the particular facet of the 'Conservative Party' that relates to our research.

As we find these subject headings, we must take down the information and note which database used them. Unfortunately, the subject headings used in one database will not necessarily be the same as those used in another database, index or library catalogue. In the electronic research environment, there are many ways to get to the same article. Using the grid to trace our search tactics will help us return to useful articles when we need them, as well as giving us potentially productive starting points for further research.

Refining your search

Electronic search tools (library catalogues and web search engines as well as library databases and online indexes) provide a number of ways to refine your searches by combining terms. The most common is by using 'Boolean operators', notably AND and OR. Connecting your search terms with the AND operator tells the computer to find items (bibliographic records or articles) that contain both of your search terms – that is, AND narrows your search. Connecting your terms with OR tells the computer to find items that contain either your first term or your second (or your third one etc.). Thus, OR broadens your search. Working from your concept grid, use OR searches to combine related terms within each concept column, such as synonyms, variant spellings and plurals. Once you have found the most effective searches for each concept, use AND searches to see what, if any, articles covered by your tools deal with more than one concept.

As you have probably noticed in web searching, Boolean operators are rather imprecise tools. In a general database, especially if it includes newspapers and news magazines, 'Conservative AND party' will find articles not only about the Conservative Party, but also about dinner parties attended by Conservative party officials.

Library tools deal with this problem in several ways:

1   By coverage: a specifically political science database like *Worldwide Political Science Abstracts* (*WPSA*) will include many more articles on political parties as organisations and fewer on festive events. *Infotrac Expanded Academic* and various other databases allow you to restrict your search to scholarly (i.e., 'peer-reviewed' or 'refereed' journals) material. Full-text databases such as *JSTOR* and *LexisNexis Academic* force you to select specific portions of their content before they will run a search.

2   By the structure of the data: indexes (like library catalogues) break down their descriptions of articles into many pieces (called 'fields') to which you can restrict your searches. The most familiar fields are: author (official writings by the Conservative Party), article title (pieces mentioning the Conservative Party), abstract (pieces noting the Conservative Party, in some context), and subject heading (pieces that cataloguers identify as being about the Conservative Party). Other useful fields include date of publication, title of the journal (often, confusingly, called 'source' or 'citation' in indexes and databases, but always 'title' in the library catalogue), and language, among others.

3   By search options: full-text databases usually provide fewer fields to search in; many do not provide subject headings. Explore a database to see if it offers some kind of 'proximity' searching: if your search terms occur near one another, it is likely that an article uses them as related terms. Depending on the database, proximity searching allows you to search for words within a given number of words (say, fifteen or twenty-five), words in the same sentence, or words occurring in the same paragraph.

Most online library indexes and some full-text databases make it simple to search large swathes of literature and then quickly explore various combinations. Look for a feature called 'search history', 'previous searches' or 'combine', which tracks every search. The terms vary by database. Simply mark checkboxes to tell the database to combine your most effective previous searches.

Experiment with search combinations that use a subject heading for one concept or variable in your theory with keywords for aspects of your other concepts or variables. A caveat: combining subject headings for all of your concepts is not likely to be beneficial to your research. It will either be too narrow to locate much literature, or if this search does produce results, your own research may not be adding much to the universe of political science knowledge.

Often, a database's default search screen is the least useful one. You may want to get into the habit of starting in an advanced search window, even if you seldom use more than one or two of its features in a search session. It will give you more options for selecting fields, combining terms, restricting your searches to particular publication dates or information types and otherwise making your search more precise.

Searching academic subject indexes

General periodical databases are broad but not necessarily deep enough for full-fledged literature reviews. **Academic subject indexes**, available for most disciplines, provide depth for specialists. For political science, *Worldwide Political Science Abstracts*, *International Political Science Abstracts* and *PAIS (Public Affairs Information Service) International* are probably the most comprehensive and widely available. As the titles of these databases suggest, their coverage is not restricted to US politics, the works they identify are not necessarily in English and your library will probably not subscribe to every periodical or other resource that they cover.

In addition to the tighter scope of their coverage, subject indexes are often easier to search than full-text databases. Indexes are heavily structured descriptions of information sources. They are designed to minimise ambiguities. Thus, you can target your searches more precisely, focusing on words in particular fields – paying particular attention to abstracts – and exploiting their systems of subject headings. The index records are shorter than the full text of the articles they describe, so they are easier for you to peruse to identify additional search terms, such as authors and technical vocabularies (also known as terms of art or jargon – the consistent shorthand insiders in a discipline use to communicate with one another).

For example, when you identify the author of one relevant article, you should search elsewhere in that index, other indexes and databases, the library catalogue, and the web for other articles and books by that author that might be relevant to your research. Another example relates to the use of the technical term *turnout*. Among political scientists, *turnout* denotes specific voting behaviour on Election Day, so it is an effective keyword in a political science index. However, in a general database or on the web, you would need to combine *turnout* with *voter* in order to exclude articles about fashion and firefighting, which use the word *turnout* in a rather different way.

The principles of searching in a subject index like *Worldwide Political Science Abstracts* are very similar to those already described for searching in *JSTOR*: start with keyword searches, look through the results lists for titles that seem relevant to your theory, examine the full records for subject headings (which *WPSA* labels 'descriptors') and other potentially useful information and run further searches with appropriate keywords, descriptors and combinations.

Summarising the literature search

Figure 3.3 highlights the key steps in searching for literature. These condensed steps apply equally whether you are searching for popular or academic articles or searching for books.

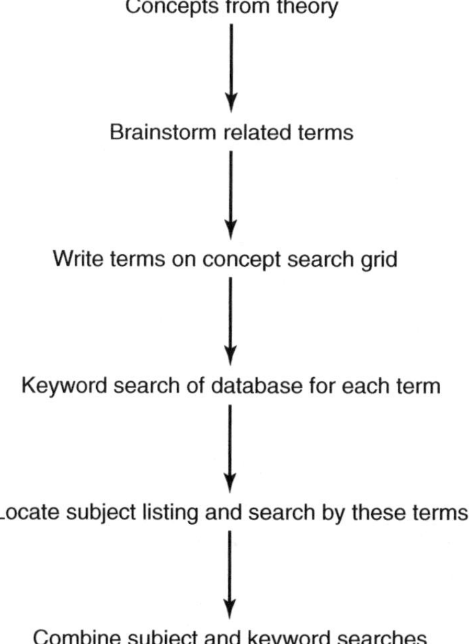

Figure 3.3 Steps of a systematic literature search

There is, of course, an additional step in literature searching: finding the articles. Depending on your library's subscriptions, contracts among information providers and technology, this access may be as simple as clicking on a link in a record to an electronic journal or as complicated as requesting that your library borrow a copy of the article for you from another institution via interlibrary loan. Generally, you will use your library catalogue to determine if your library has the journal issues containing the articles your searches identified, their format and where you can get them.

Library catalogues

In the course of your research you will need to visit the library physically for several reasons. First, not all of the relevant articles you have identified are available online. Second, if you limit your bibliography to those articles that are available online, you allow an external source of selection bias to distort your research (Chapter 7 will discuss proper sampling). Third, while doing periodical research, it is likely that your articles will reference books that you will want to review personally.

Library organisation

Once you have a citation for a book or journal from an index or bibliography, you need to locate a physical copy of that work. Finding materials in the library requires knowing something about the way that most libraries are organised, as well as the resources that they make available.

Libraries organise their collections using two different sets of organising principles that try to put related materials together. One principle has already been described: subject headings are elaborate, standardised sets of labels that describe aspects of the contents of books and the coverage of periodicals. Subject headings make *intellectual connections* among items in the library, even though the items may be physically separated or some of the items may be online. The other principle tries to put related items *physically* near one another, so that if you find one relevant book on the shelf, you can easily browse along the shelf to find others that address the same material.

The key tool for this physical arrangement is the call number, which the library affixes to the spines (or sometimes the covers or other containers) of the materials in its collection. Two call number systems are widely used: the Dewey Decimal Classification system, used mainly by schools, British universities and public libraries; the other is the Library of Congress Classification system, widely used by US universities and large research libraries. If the call numbers on a book's spine in your library begins with decimal numbers of the type 320.072, your library uses the Dewey Decimal system. If the call numbers begin with a combination of letters and numbers, such as JA86.M35, your library uses the Library of Congress system. (Both identifiers, incidentally, designate the same book.)

Library catalogue searching

Online catalogues allow us to perform searches by keyword, title, author, subject or call number. To locate the printed copies of a journal, we *title search* in the library's catalogue for the periodical's name – not the article title. Similarly, to find a book that has been cited in your research, search for the book's title. On the other hand, you may use the *author search* feature to locate all of the books written by a given author who does research in your field.

The library catalogue is the single best guide to the books, journals and other works held by a particular library, but from the perspective of the thorough researcher it suffers from two major limitations. First, the catalogue lists mainly books, even though much, if not most, of the important empirical research in political science or any other field is found not in books, but in articles in scholarly journals. Whereas journals themselves are listed in the catalogue, their content is not. Second, most library catalogues list only the holdings of the particular library you happen to be using. Fortunately, neither of these problems is insurmountable. As we have seen, databases and indexes offer access to journal article content. Additionally, union catalogues bring together the catalogue records of multiple libraries within a locality, a state or even around the world, as in the case of *WorldCat* and *RLG Union Catalogue* (also called *RLIN*). Increasingly, union catalogues are linked with interlibrary loan systems, whereby your library can borrow materials from other libraries on your behalf.

Internet research

The internet has dramatically changed the way political research is done. More and more public opinion polls, for example, are conducted with online questionnaires, thus eliminating costly telephone interviews and the need to interrupt respondents' dinners. Millions of informational web pages, online library catalogues and online databases allow those who have access to the internet to conduct research without ever leaving their home or office. The internet also brings together researchers who have to coordinate national or international projects by allowing them to exchange information quickly and cheaply through e-mail or other internet-based services.

Most of us who have surfed the web know that finding useful information online is a big challenge. Answers to simple questions such as 'Who is the current chancellor of Germany?' usually are found quickly thanks to search engines such as *Google* or *Yahoo!* More complicated research questions, however, such as 'What studies exist about political communication in Great Britain?' require more sophisticated research strategies and some knowledge about where and how information can be found on the internet.

There are particular problems with internet research and finding information online. Special emphasis will be placed on the research tools and the strategies that help to locate useful resources on the web.

The biggest problem with the internet is the fact that good and reliable information is often difficult to find. There are millions of web pages published by governments, organisations, businesses, academics and individuals. Most of those pages are scattered and not available through central directories. The trick is to find those pages that might be useful to a particular research project.

It is important to remember that the internet is a good source of current and frequently updated information, such as news, economic statistics or polling data for an ongoing election. The internet also allows easy access to electronic databases and information that otherwise might be difficult or time consuming to locate. Electronic versions of important public documents, such as political speeches or transcripts of press conferences, are usually accessible through the internet and can be scanned easily for relevant information with simple text searches.

The internet is less suited for research on information that might not be available in electronic form, such as older documents that are only available as hard copies. Even primary documents such as books, excerpts or quotes that are available online might not accurately reflect their original content because they might have changed slightly when they were transcribed or copied from one web page to another. Thus, it is usually safer to rely on published originals rather than online versions of such documents.

Searching for information

As you probably know, simply browsing the internet is fun, but it is unlikely to yield much useful information. Because information on the internet is so spread out and disorganised, you will need to use a set of search tools and strategies in order to find useful information.

There are three basic types of search tools that allow you to explore the internet: *search engines*, *meta-search engines* and *subject directories*. Which one of the three tools you should use for your search depends mainly on what kind of information you want to find.

A **search engine** is a searchable database of links to web pages collected by computer programs called crawlers robots or spiders. These programs routinely prowl the internet and index all web pages they come across. Users of these search engines are then able to search the index with keywords and are presented with links to those web pages that contain the particular keywords.

Currently, the two most popular search engines are *Google* (www.google.com) and *Yahoo!* (www.yahoo.com). *Google*'s simple interface and fast keyword searches have a well-deserved reputation for consistently retrieving the most relevant pages by ranking possible returns with a patented algorithm. This algorithm (called 'PageRank') ranks the importance of a website mainly by the number of external links referring to it. *Google* also offers specialised search services such as *Google Scholar* (scholar.google.com), which allows you to search specifically for scholarly literature, including peer-reviewed papers, theses, books and abstracts from broad areas of research.

Yahoo!, which started in 1994 as a human-compiled web directory, now offers both a subject directory and an excellent search engine that closely matches *Google*'s performance. Those using *Yahoo!* as their primary search tool should be aware that the directory only provides links to those websites that have been reviewed and included by *Yahoo!*'s employees. It therefore represents only a limited view at what is available on the internet. The regular *Yahoo!* search engine, on the other hand, features comprehensive crawler-based listings of links to web pages just like *Google*.

Since queries performed on different search engines produce different results, it is usually not a good idea to rely on one search engine only. The easiest way to make sure that you find all relevant web pages is to use a **meta-search engine** such as *Dogpile* (www.dogpile.com) or *MetaCrawler* (www.metacrawler.com). Meta-search engines do not search the web themselves, but send searches to several search engines at once. The results are then compiled and presented together on one page. *Dogpile*, for example, provides access to major search engines such as *Google*, *Yahoo!*, *Windows Live* and *Ask.com*. Those interested in search returns that differ from the relevance ranking system found in traditional search engines such as *Google* or *Yahoo!* should have a look at *Clusty* (clusty.com), which automatically groups similar search results into topics or 'clusters'.

Although meta-search engines offer a convenient way to hunt for information across various search engines at once, it is important to remember that the quality of the searches is highly dependent on the databases from which they are obtained. Moreover, meta-search engines might only retrieve the top-ranked results from other search engines because of processing time or other programming limitations. In general, it is safer to use meta-search engines only for a 'first look' at what might be available and then search each search engine directly.

One of the easiest methods of searching for relevant resources is using **subject directories** that have been compiled and organised by commercial, academic or professional organisations. Subject directories store and present links to websites submitted by web authors or reviewers, and are usually organised into subject or topic categories. Because the categorisation is subjective, the contents of even the most popular subject directories differ greatly and cannot be regarded as complete subject classifications. It is therefore a good idea to visit more than one directory in order to obtain a variety of possible subject classifications. The biggest advantage of subject directories is that they make it fairly easy to narrow searches (for example, 'government') to a specific topic by simply following links in the directory to selected subtopics (for example, 'political advertising').

Commercial subject directories, such as the one offered by *Yahoo!* (dir.yahoo.com), should be used with great caution in research because they cater to the general public and often mix scholarly internet resources with everything else. Academic and professional directories, on the other hand, are often maintained by subject experts, cater to the specific needs of researchers, and are less dependent on internet traffic for support. Good examples of academic subject directories are *INFOMINE* (infomine.ucr.edu), a large collection of scholarly internet resources maintained by several university libraries. One of the most useful professional subject directories is the *Librarians' Index to the Internet* (www.lii.org), which is a searchable, annotated subject directory of more than 20,000 internet resources selected and evaluated by librarians for their usefulness to users of public libraries.

Internet search strategies

Finding information on the internet usually requires more than simply inserting a few keywords into a search engine and then sifting through hundreds of hits. Although many of us probably do just that, a carefully planned search on the internet can yield more reliable information in a fraction of the time it takes to conduct a series of more or less random searches. Because information on the internet is highly decentralised, successful searches generally require a carefully planned search strategy. Depending on the complexity of your search, you should consider the following steps as part of your search strategy.

Determine what kind of information you need

Before you start a search, consider whether the internet is really the best place to find what you are looking for. Not all information is available on the internet (listings of older books, for example), which means that it is sometimes necessary to search other resources as well (such as your library's electronic catalogue). Next, think about what *type* of information you are looking for – this will allow you to narrow your search and focus on specific sources. If you are looking for a general news story, for example, you should start with searching news sites such as *CNN.com* or *Washingtonpost.com*. To find books, it is usually best to search the catalogues of online libraries rather than the web in general. If you are looking for information that originated within the government, on the other hand, you might want to limit your search to government web pages (those ending with .gov). You also might focus your search on specific *forms* of information such as images, videos or audio files. Most search engines allow you to search for these data separately.

Develop keywords for your search

This is probably the most crucial step and usually requires a bit of intuition. Before you start a search, try to develop a list of keywords that might produce the most relevant search results. Enter these keywords into a search engine and check the results. In most cases, you probably have to adjust or change the keywords in order to focus your search. Consider related terms, concepts, synonyms or other keywords that might be associated with the information you are searching for. If you have trouble coming up with new terms, it is often helpful to search for related keywords on web pages that come very close to what you are seeking.

Use more than one search engine

Remember that queries performed on different search engines usually produce different results. It is therefore not a good idea to rely on one search engine only – try the same search on different search engines or use meta-search engines such as *Dogpile*.

Learn about the advanced search functions

Many searches can be done more efficiently with advanced search operators that allow users to narrow or widen their searches. For example, in an advanced search window, *Google* and *Yahoo!* allow users to restrict their searches to specific websites or top-level domains such as .gov or .edu. Although many of the advanced functions found in search engines such as *Google* or *Yahoo!* are similar, there are some crucial differences that are important to know. Searches in *Google*, for example, are not case sensitive (this means that a search for 'United States' and 'uNiTeD StAtEs' will yield the same results), whereas queries in other search engines may be case sensitive. Thus, if you are interested in more efficient and precise searches, it usually pays to spend a few minutes learning the advanced search functions of one or two major search engines.

Consider using a subject directory

Sometimes it might be better to start your search with a subject directory instead of a keyword search. Subject directories can be useful, for example, when you are not very familiar with a particular topic and cannot think of good keywords to describe it. In such cases, you will be able to start with a broad topic like 'government', and scan the subcategories until you find what you are looking for. Subject directories are also helpful when keyword searches alone yield too many false hits (records that match the search criteria but are not relevant to your project). Under such circumstances, a combination of keyword and subject directory searches is likely to result in a more focused search.

Narrow your search results

Search engines use a number of different mechanisms to search for or limit information. The most common search mechanism is called **Boolean logic**. Boolean logic uses three primary search operators: AND, OR and NOT. The operator AND will narrow a search. For example, a search for 'public' AND 'opinion' will return only links to web pages that contain both keywords. Note that some search engines (such as *Google* and *Yahoo!*) automatically return results that contain all keywords (thus assuming the operator AND between all keywords). In most cases, adding keywords to a search is a very simple and effective way for narrowing searches. The operator OR, on the other hand, will broaden a search. For example, using the terms 'Spain' OR 'France' will return links to web pages that contain any or both keywords. Since only one of the two keywords needs to be found on a web page to be recognised as relevant, you will get many more hits compared to using the AND operator. The operator NOT, on the other hand, will narrow a search by dropping any links to web pages that contain the excluded keyword. For example, a search for 'virus' NOT 'computer' will exclude links to web pages that contain discussions of a computer virus – but it will be more likely to retrieve links to pages with discussions of a biological virus.

One of the most effective ways to narrow a search is to use entire phrases rather than keywords. For example, a search for 'political effects of the internet' which is placed between double quotation marks ("political effects of the internet") will retrieve only links to web pages that contain this particular phrase (1,080 *Google* hits). Obviously, a search using the separate keywords 'political' 'effects' and 'internet' would result in many more hits compared to the phrase search (18 million *Google* hits). Almost all search engines have additional 'advanced' search functions, which allow you, for example, to search for keywords in the title or in the text of web pages only. Make sure you are familiar with these functions, as they make searching for information much easier and more precise.

Maximise your search results

There are a variety of strategies to improve searches that do not retrieve the desired information. One way to maximise the number of possible search hits for a particular term is to use the **stem** of a word rather than the entire word. For example, a search for politic* will result in links to web pages containing the keywords politics, political, politician etc. (The wildcard symbol depends on the search engine. Some search engines, such as *Google* and *Yahoo!*, automatically use stems in keyword searches.) In cases where your search results in only a few but very relevant links, you might be able to find more information by tracing the URL of a relevant website to the root URL, which usually links to the home page of websites (for example, www.gwu.edu/~smpa can be reduced to www.gwu. edu). Another trick is to pursue the links to 'similar pages' (*Google*) or 'more from this site' (*Yahoo!*) that are offered as alternatives to the displayed results in most search engines.

Search the invisible web

Since not all information available on the internet can be retrieved with regular search engines (for example, password protected databases), for some projects it might be useful to search *database directories* that list those 'hidden' resources. The information available in databases and other resources that cannot be easily retrieved with search engines might be extremely valuable and should not be ignored in any research project.

Evaluate your search results

It is always important to check the quality of the information you find on the web. Remember that anybody can 'publish' on the internet and that there is no guarantee that the information you find is accurate or important. According to Alexander and Tate (1999), information obtained from websites should always be checked for its authority, objectivity, accuracy, currency and coverage. To do so, simply try to answer the following questions when encountering doubtful material on the internet:

- *Who made the information available? (Authority)* To answer this question, check the publisher or author of the website from which you obtained the information. In general, information published by academic and government institutions is more reliable than information from interest groups, businesses or individuals. Make sure you check the original source of the information you found, even if it is published on a website of a reputable organisation. Verify the legitimacy of any source with which you are not familiar.
- *What was the reason for making the information available? (Objectivity)* Always ask yourself whether the objectivity or quality of information you found on the internet might have been influenced by the goals or interests of the source. Make sure you understand potential ideological,

political or other biases of any website you use in your research. The US National Rifle Association, for example, is unlikely to publish data showing the negative consequences of gun ownership. Clues about the goals of such interest groups or other organisations usually can be found in the 'About Us' section of their home pages.

■ *How accurate is the information? (Accuracy)* As in any other research, you have to evaluate the quality and reliability of information you gather on the internet. Check whether the sources for any factual information are clearly listed and referenced. For example, if you read about the findings of a public opinion poll on the website of a political party, you should be able to find information about who conducted the poll on the same site. If you are not absolutely sure about the quality of the information you find, try to verify it by searching for the same information on other websites, or in books, journals etc.

■ *How old is the information? (Currency)* Although it is true that the internet is a great source for up-to-date information such as news or business data, many websites contain information that is not regularly updated. This might not be a problem with information that does not need frequent updating (historical reviews, for example). Other data, such as internet user statistics, on the other hand, have to be as recent as possible. If you need current information, check if there are any dates which might indicate when the information was compiled or when the source page was last revised. You also might want to verify whether there is any more recent information than what you found by searching for similar data in other resources.

■ *How complete is the information? (Coverage)* One of the most important steps in evaluating information gathered from the internet is to find out how complete or detailed it is. The best way to assess the potential breadth and depth of information found on the internet is to check the purpose of the source and what audience might be the target. If there is any indication that the information you found on a particular web page is incomplete or simplified, track down the original source. In addition, ask yourself whether it is reasonable to assume that all information is available online. It is, for example, quite likely that some materials are excluded because they are copyrighted or simply not available in digital format.

Save and organise your search results

If you do a lot of online research, keeping track of what you find can be difficult. The simplest way to save your search results is to bookmark each site you have visited or to save individual web pages from within your browser (*Internet Explorer* and *Mozilla Firefox*, for example, let you save complete web pages and store them on your computer). However, you will quickly learn that bookmarking or saving entire web pages is not the most efficient way to keep track of bits and pieces of information found on the internet. Too often, the content of web pages disappears or changes and is therefore impossible to retrieve at a later point. Information on web pages that have been saved on your computer, on the other hand, might be difficult to locate later.

Fortunately, there are a number of free software programs available that make web research more efficient. One of the best tools for collecting and organising the data you find online is called *Onfolio* (free add-on for Windows Live Toolbar: www.onfolio.com). The program works together with *Internet Explorer* and displays a separate window, where you can create and save research folders. Within each folder, you can collect and sort different types of data you gather from the web: entire websites, URLs of websites you visited, images, text snippets etc. The program will save the gathered information on your computer together with automatically collected information about where and when you found each item. Similar free add-ons are available for users of *Mozilla Firefox* (see *ScrapBook*) or *Google Gmail* (see *Google Notebook*). The biggest advantage of these research tools is that they allow you to gather and organise a lot of different pieces of information in a central location on your computer without the need to find and retrieve it later from the internet.

Cite your search results

It is easy to obtain and copy information from the internet, but it is important that you quote and cite your sources accurately and honestly. The most common citation styles used in political science are the *American Political Science Association* (APSA) style and the *American Psychological Association* (APA) style. Because there is a large variety of web sources you might be dealing with, it may be helpful to check for the most recent style information (details are available at www.apa.org). In general, though, references to documents found on the internet are formatted as follows: **APSA style**: Author, A. A. 2007. *Title of Work*. Date of internet publication (if available). Retrieved day, month, year, source URL. **APA style**: Author, A. A. (2007). *Title of Work*. Retrieved month day, year, from source URL.

Other web resources

The web includes more than just web pages. A large part of the most valuable information consists of databases from businesses, government agencies, universities, libraries and other organisations around the world. Most of these databases are only accessible through direct user queries (often requiring special logons or passwords).

Another large section of the internet is the thousands of *newsgroups, mailing lists, blogs* and *podcasts*. Although none of these information networks is particularly new, they have gained importance in recent years as alternative sources of news and information. The importance of these networks is based on the fact that they are free and easily accessible to every internet user – which means that they can link a large number of users with similar interests and provide them with the most recent information.

The various types of networks available on the internet can be good sources for information on issues that are difficult to research. **Newsgroups**, for example, offer public discussions of topics that might be difficult to find in more traditional resources. The origin of newsgroups can be traced back to a collection of e-mail-based bulletin boards (also called *Usenet*) that started in 1981. Since then, the popularity of newsgroups has increased enormously, and they now cover even the most obscure topics imaginable (in mid 2007, *Google* listed more than 10,000 newsgroups and about 270 of those related to 'politics'). It is possible to read and post messages in newsgroups with so-called newsreaders, which are included in most internet browsers. The easiest way to access and search newsgroups, however, is through *Google Groups*, which provides a searchable list of all *Usenet* and *Google* discussion groups and an archive of more than 1 billion newsgroup postings that date back to 1981.

Mailing lists are another good way to keep up with new developments on issues of interest to you. Mailing lists will connect you with people who share your interests and might be able to provide you with new insights or answers to any questions you may have. The main difference between newsgroups and mailing lists is that you can read the discussions in a newsgroup whenever you want, whereas discussions in a mailing list are sent to you via e-mail. To subscribe to a mailing list, usually all you have to do is send a 'subscribe' message to the mailing list program address. Since some of the more popular mailing lists might generate a large number of e-mails, you should carefully select the lists to which you subscribe – otherwise, you will end up with thousands of e-mails in your mailbox every day. To find interesting mailing lists, check the websites of organisations that you belong to or are interested in. The *American Political Science Association*, for example, offers a good selection of mailing lists related to political science at www.apsanet.org.

The surge in the number of internet users in recent years also has led to a proliferation of **blogs**. A blog is a personal journal that is frequently updated and intended for general public consumption. The content and purposes of blogs vary greatly – from personal diaries to news about sports, celebrities or political commentary. Many blogs also contain links and commentary about other websites the author favours. Similar to newsgroups and mailing lists, blogs bring together people of similar interests to share information, ideas and questions about those interests. Although it is difficult to determine the exact number of blogs that exist on the internet, according to *Nielsen Buzzmetrics* there were an estimated 49 million blogs in the United States alone in mid 2007 (check www.nielsenbuzzmetrics.com for the most recent estimates and a list of the top forty blogs). One of the most popular search engines for blogs is *Technorati* (technorati.com/blogs), which features a categorised directory of blogs (about 85 million political blogs were listed in mid 2007) and a list of the one hundred most popular blogs.

As the popularity of blogs has grown in recent years, various institutions have adopted them as a new form of communication. Media organisations such as *the New York Times* or *BBC News* (news.bbc.co.uk), for example, make their news stories available to blogs through automatic news feeds, podcasts or their own blogs. The political importance of blogs has been demonstrated by the fact that many politicians now maintain official blogs, which allow them to bypass the mainstream media and create a direct channel of communication between them and the voters. If you are interested in reading political blogs, you can find a comprehensive list at the website of the *Campaigns & Elections Magazine* (www.campaignline.com/blogs). Good information on how blogs and other new communication technologies are influencing politics and the media can be found at *CyberJournalist.net* (www.cyberjournalist.net).

Organising your findings

Research in the electronic environment, paradoxically, puts a premium on taking thorough notes at each step of the process. You should keep revising your concept grid. You will want to create a separate grid for each resource – catalogue, index, full-text database, web subject directory and web search engine – so you can relocate your information sources easily when you need to. Even if you have saved the full text of articles or citations on your computer, your notes will help you to locate these resources rapidly. Consistent note taking helps to prevent oversights, and including all of the pertinent information at the outset saves return trips to the library databases and catalogue.

Recording literature research

To facilitate taking thorough notes, you should have a sizeable stack of blank file cards or a word processing document open in your computer to record your citations' bibliographic information and your comments on each reference. Each time you find a potentially useful source listed, create a separate card or page that includes the complete bibliographic citation, recording – as appropriate – author, title, journal (including volume number, year of publication and pages), date and place of publication and publisher. For books, remember to record the library call number. Include notes about how you found each article or book, the database you used, your search terms and the book or articles that cited it. If an article database offers persistent or stable web links to individual articles, you will want to include these as well. Most article links, though, are specific to your online session, so you should not depend upon them for later access.

Decide in advance the format or style guide you will use for reference citations in the research report and remember to record in that format the appropriate information about each source. Check with your instructor to find out the preferred style for references. Your School or Departmental secretaries should have copies of the preferred style manual. Chapter 24 offers more guidance on the structure of research reports and citing literature.

Your notes should also include all of the main points of the book or article, any especially useful tips or facts, a summary of the method the author used and of the findings if research is reported, and any potentially useful quotations. Make frequent page references to the specific locations of the items you record. Figure 3.4 gives an illustration of a completed bibliography card made using this technique.

Writing your research report will be expedited if you obtain electronic copies of your reference citations and type your notes on each reference. For example, word processing software allows a quick search of the entire file for keywords using the 'Find' function, making it easier to find all references that address a given issue. You can also copy and paste citations and quotes from your bibliographic notes and insert them directly into the text rather than retyping them. Whether you obtain direct quotes electronically or paraphrase the reference's text, always include a citation to the original author's work.

Figure 3.4   Sample bibliography card

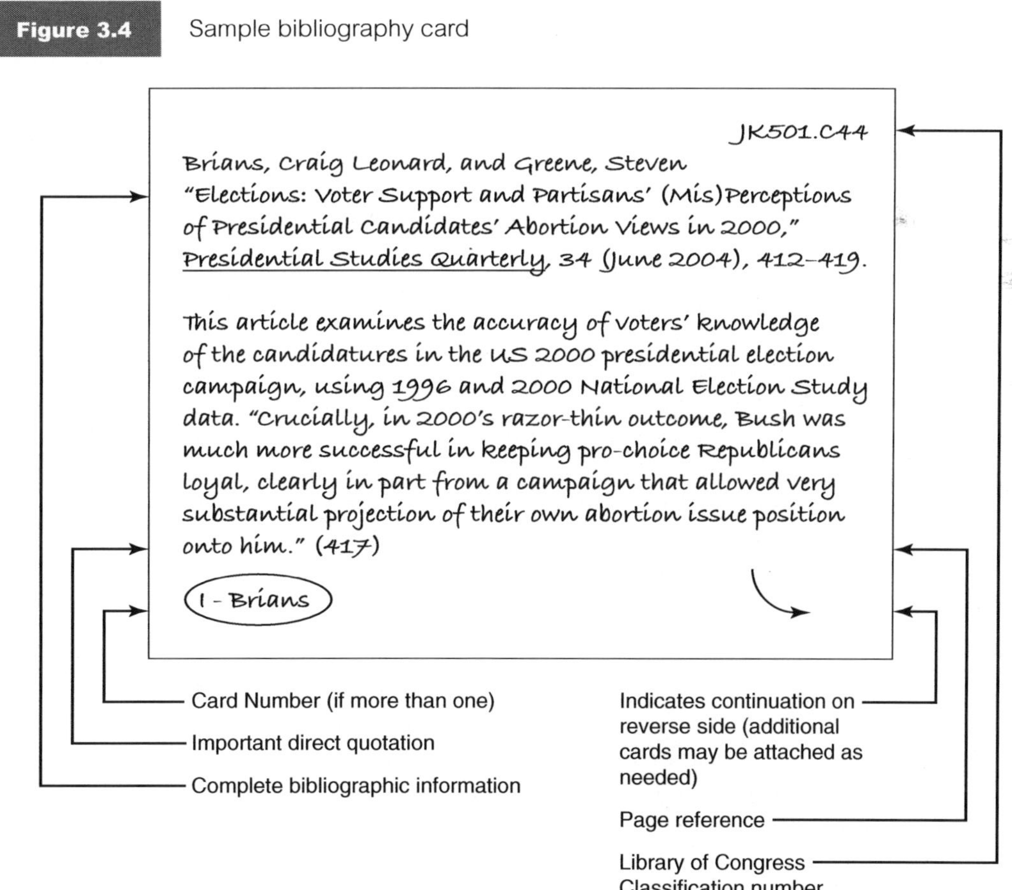

Why keep notes?

Whether you use note cards or a computer, the physical act of writing notes – which requires thinking about the material that you record – is a more effective way of understanding and applying information than merely highlighting your photocopied or printed articles, or copying and pasting chunks of text. The more you understand of the state of knowledge on your theory, the better able you will be to decide whether any additional piece of information is relevant to your project. Thus, you will want to take notes as you locate your literature resources.

A thorough job of note taking at each stage of your research saves time in two ways. First, it lets you use, cite and discuss any of your sources without necessitating a return to the library or rereading the source. Second, if for some reason you must reread a source, the page notations help to pinpoint the portion of the material that is of interest. An investment of a little time and care to document your literature research pays great dividends.

At the conclusion of this task, you will have accomplished two major objectives. First, you will have compiled a relatively complete listing of the literature in your area of interest. Second, you will have sufficiently familiarised yourself with that literature so you may better anticipate problems and, thus, improve your own work, properly placing that work in the larger context of which it is a part.

Reviewing and summarising the literature

The literature review places your research into a broader context, justifies the importance of your work, and serves to establish the plausibility of your theory. How much attention others will pay to your research findings may be determined by the quality of your review of the literature. A literature review that precisely identifies the body of literature within political science to which you are contributing allows others to incorporate your findings more easily into later research. The literature review establishes the distinct contribution that your research will make to the existing body of research. Since no research stands completely on its own authority, reviewing the literature related to your research establishes the initial plausibility of your theory.

Organising the literature

The easiest way to begin organising and writing a literature review is by outlining a chain of reasoning, based upon your theory. The chain of reasoning is simply a series of relationships (or hypotheses) that establish the plausibility of your theory, using the existing research. For example, the left column of Figure 3.5 shows summarisation of the chain of reasoning from the literature review in the sample article presented in Chapter 24. The right column in Figure 3.5 notes citations to the research literature that supports each assertion in the chain of reasoning. In the research described in Figure 3.5, the authors simply broke the theory down into its most basic components. Then the authors used the literature-search tools and strategies described earlier in this chapter to locate evidence supporting the ideas in the chain for reasoning.

Your theory and the chain of reasoning you initially write will undergo many refinements as you read the available literature, just as your outline and first draft only approximately resemble your final paper. In other words, you will start your literature search with a working theory and some idea of how to support it logically, but you also should be prepared to learn and adapt as you read the literature and let the new information you encounter shape the eventual form of your literature review.

Figure 3.5 A sample theory and chain of reasoning for a literature review, derived from the article in Chapter 24

Theory:
A presidential candidate who publicly obfuscates his policy position on a contentious issue can obtain the support of voters who hold opposing policy views, because many voters will project their own views onto the candidate.

Idea	Reference
The candidate actually opposes all abortions	(*Dallas Morning News* 1994)
↓	
The candidate contradictorily says he supports a party platform that proposes a no-exception Constitutional Amendment barring abortion, as well as allowing certain exceptions	(*Larry King Live* 2000)
↓	
This pattern continues in the Presidential Debates	(Commission on Presidential Debates 2000)
↓	
It would be advantageous for a presidential candidate to conceal his true positions, if it were unpopular with voters	(Gallup Organization and *USA Today* 2003)
↓	
Both parties have similar numbers of members who oppose their party's official position	(Greene and Brians 2001)
↓	
The importance given to the abortion issue is similar for both parties	(Greene and Brians 2001)
↓	
Voters who (mis)perceive that a candidate's views are close to their own are more likely to support that candidate	(Wilson and Gronke 2000; Krosnick 1990; Martinez 1988)
↓	
Voters frequently project their own views onto candidates to rationalise a vote choice	(Berelson, Lazarsfeld and McPhee 1954; Brody and Page 1972; Page and Brody 1972; Wattenberg 1991)

Ethical considerations

This chapter teaches techniques that are designed to uncover prior research on a given topic(s). Gathering and summarising this prior literature builds a foundation upon which new research rests, and positions research findings within the discipline. Whether earlier research is found in printed books, or online journal articles, or in a video documentary, it is crucial never to lose sight of the fact that these specific words and the ideas conveyed by those words belong to their authors. As such, any appropriation of this intellectual property by others violates federal copyright laws, which authorise both civil and criminal penalties.

In practice, you demonstrate the amount of effort you have expended researching others' findings and your mastery of the extant literature through a well-documented literature review. This means that (1) you may never paraphrase anyone else's ideas without attribution to the original source; (2) you will never quote any verbal or written text without placing the quote marks around the material that is in the original author's own words; and (3) you should use a standard bibliographic style that conveys your references clearly to your reader.

The internet has become central to the way we do research today. It allows students to access information from anywhere they can find an internet connection. Some see this as eliminating long trips to the library and sometimes tedious searches through journals or books for a particular reference. We hope that as you do research, you will weigh the resources and strategies presented in this chapter. The fact remains that although much is freely available online, free information is often poorly organised and may contain hidden bias.

With information so easily accessible in a digital format, some budding researchers simply 'copy and paste' material from the internet directly into research papers. However, if you use others' work without properly citing the source, you are committing plagiarism – something that academically and legally constitutes theft. It cannot be overstressed that you must properly attribute all ideas or material that comes from others. The growing number of digital sources makes keeping careful records of where you found your references even more important today than ever before.

Conclusion

This chapter offers a brief overview of the basic procedures associated with using online book and article databases to find literature illuminating your theory, and a strategy for organising the information you find. Because this textbook is used at colleges and universities in many other countries as well, it is not possible for us to present a comprehensive primer on the specific resources that your institution's library offers.

Electronic searching looks easier than it is. Still, armed with the basic understanding of literature searching techniques and the literature review organisation model this chapter provides, as well as some perseverance, you will be able to get started on building a literature review. To progress beyond our general treatment of literature searching, and to get the most from your library's resources, you should experiment with searches, utilise your search tool's help functions and contact a librarian with more involved questions that arise in the course of your research. With experience, you will develop your own repertoire of preferred resources and search techniques, but it is unnecessary for you to work completely solo. A reference librarian at your college will be your most authoritative source of information and guidance.

It should be obvious by now that internet research requires much more than simply plugging a few keywords into a search engine. It is true that more and more information is available online, but the rapid growth of the internet also makes it more difficult to find useful and reliable facts. Moreover, search engines such as *Google* or *Yahoo!* encourage somewhat random searches because of the way they index and display information. Thus, in order to become 'good' internet researchers, we need to learn how to use appropriate search tools and strategies that will efficiently retrieve the information we are seeking.

Summary points

- Identifying previous research findings will help you to position your research within the literature and help your work to contribute to the cumulative function of scientific learning.
- The existing literature can show us what has been learned and the research methods used, which help to frame our research question.
- A systematic search of the literature includes entering the concepts from our theory into the concept search grid, brainstorming for related terms, searching general periodical databases, searching academic subject indexes and going to the library.
- Your university's library's resources are preferable to those freely available on the Web because librarians have filtered this information to enable more efficient searching. If you have any doubt about how to find relevant information, ask a librarian.
- You begin developing your research report as you gather information from references, making note taking a crucial part of this process. Additionally, accurate notes enhance searching efficiency.
- The best way to search the internet is to develop a search strategy that will allow you to do a systematic search for relevant and high-quality information. It is generally useful to rely on more than one search engine and to be familiar with the advanced search functions these tools offer.
- The quality of information gathered from the internet should be evaluated by assessing its authority, objectivity, accuracy, currency and coverage.

Suggested reading and examples

Research examples

Noting that the research of 'academic giants is not generally composed of lengthy literature reviews', McMenamin (2006) nevertheless describes the key value and function of the cited literature as a source for ideas and material to critique in your own work. Periodically, the journal *Political Research Quarterly* publishes 'Field Essays', which summarise and evaluate the current research in a given subfield, for example, Gronke and Newman (2003) wrote on the assessment of presidential approval ratings. As with any literature review, these essays also suggest gaps and inconsistencies in the current research – useful research ideas for other scholars to pursue.

Academic studies that look specifically at the internet as a research tool are still the exception. However, there are numerous recent examples of studies that take advantage of the internet as a research topic. Krueger (2006), for example, investigates whether online mobilisation campaigns favour voters who have the political motivation and technical ability to use the internet. Best and Krueger (2005) observe that factors predicting online participation often differ from the factors that predict offline participation. Hardy and Scheufele (2005) examine the effects of face-to-face communication, computer-mediated interactions and internet news use on participatory political behaviour.

Methodological reading

A classic guide to synthesising the extant literature into a useful review is *Integrating Research* (Cooper 1989). For a comprehensive, descriptive listing of journals in political science, see *Getting Published in Political Science Journals: A Guide for Authors, Editors, and Librarians* (Martin and Goehlert 2001). Political science journals are ranked by subfield and for overall 'impact' in Garand and Giles (2003).

Good introductions to Internet-based research can be found in the following publications: *Internet Research* (Barker and Terry 2006); *Research Strategies for a Digital Age* (Tensen 2006); *Using the internet for Political Research* (Dawson 2004); *The Hidden Web: Finding Quality Information on the Net* (Henninger 2004); *Find*

It Online (Schlein 2004); and *Internet Research Methods: A Practical Guide for the Social and Behavioural Sciences* (Hewson *et al.* 2003). An excellent introduction to searching with *Google* is Nancy Blachman's *Google Guide*, which is available online at www.googleguide.com.

References

Alexander, Janet E. and Tate, Marsha Ann. 1999. *Web Wisdom: How to Evaluate and Create Information Quality on the Web*. Mahwah, NJ: Laurence Erlbaum.

Barker, Don and Terry, Carol D. 2006. *Internet Research*, 3rd edn. Boston, MA: Thomson Course Technology.

Best, Samuel J. and Krueger, Brian S. 2005. 'Analyzing the representativeness of internet political participation'. *Political Behaviour*, vol. 27, no. 2, pp. 183–216.

Blachman, Nancy. *Google Guide*. www.googleguide.com.

Cooper, Harris M. 1989. *Integrating Research: A Guide for Literature Reviews*, 2nd edn. Newbury Park, CA: Sage.

Dawson, Heather. 2004. *Using the internet for Political Research*. Oxford: Chandos.

Garand, James C. and Giles, Michael W. 2003. 'Journals in the discipline: A report on a new survey of American political scientists'. *PS: Political Science and Politics*, vol. 36 (April), pp. 293–308.

Gronke, Paul and Newman, Brian 2003. 'FDR to Clinton, Mueller to ?: A field essay on presidential approval'. *Political Research Quarterly*, vol. 56 (December), pp. 501–12.

Hardy, Bruce W. and Scheufele, Dietram A. 2005. 'Examining differential gains from internet use: Comparing the moderating role of talk and online interactions'. *Journal of Communication*, vol. 55 no. 1, pp. 71–84.

Henninger, Maureen. 2004. *The Hidden Web: Finding Quality Information on the Net*. Sydney, NSW: University of New South Wales Press.

Hewson, Claire, Yule, Peter, Laurent, Dianna and Vogel, Carl. 2003. *Internet Research Methods: A Practical Guide for the Social and Behavioural Sciences*. Thousand Oaks, CA: Sage.

Krueger, Brian S. 2006. 'A comparison of conventional and internet political mobilization'. *American Politics Research*, vol. 34, no. 6, pp. 759–76.

McMenamin, Iain. 2006. 'Process and text: teaching students to review the literature'. *PS: Political Science & Politics*, vol. 39 (January), pp. 133–35.

Martin, Fenton and Goehlert, Robert. 2001. *Getting Published in Political Science Journals: A Guide for Authors, Editors, and Librarians*, 5th edn. Washington, DC: American Political Science Association.

Schlein, Alan M. 2004. *Find it Online, Fourth Edition: The Complete Guide to Online Research*, 4th edn. Tempe, AZ: Facts on Demand Press.

Tensen, Bonnie L. 2006. *Research Strategies for a Digital Age*, 2nd edn. Boston, MA: Heinle.

Scholarly political science journals

This list of some of the major scholarly political science journals is not comprehensive; there are other scholarly journals that have been omitted due to limited space, but many of the key journals relevant to empirical political research appear here.

American Journal of Political Science

American Political Science Review

American Politics Research

British Journal of Political Science

British Journal of Politics and IR

Comparative Political Studies

Comparative Politics

European Journal of Political Research

Foreign Affairs

Foreign Policy

International Journal of Public Opinion Research

International Organisation

International Political Science Review

International Studies Quarterly

Journal of Commonwealth and Comparative Politics

Journal of Conflict Resolution

Journal of Politics
Millennium
Parliamentary Affairs
Party Politics
Political Communication
Political Psychology
Political Research Quarterly
Political Science Quarterly

Political Studies
Political Theory
Polity
Public Opinion Quarterly
World Politics

Political sources on the internet

The following list of selected websites offers information that might be of interest to students of politics. This list is by no means complete and should be seen only as a starting point for further searches.

- *British Library* (http://www.bl.uk) is one of the world's premier libraries and keeps a copy of every publication produced in the UK and Ireland. The collection includes over 150 million items in every known language. The Library works closely with higher education institutions in the UK and supplies much of its material directly through interlibrary loans.
- *Companies House* (www.companies-house.gov.uk) is the official organisation to which all companies registered in the UK must send their accounts. These can be ordered on-line for a fee, but the site also provides free access to a Companies Name and Address Index and a disqualified directors database. RBA (Rhodes-Blakeman Associates), a training and consultancy company, has a web page which lists similar sites for most of the countries of the world at www.rba.co.uk/sources/registers.htm.
- *Directgov* (www.direct.gov.uk/en/index.htm) is the UK government information portal designed to provide assess to all public services in one location online.
- *Documents Center* (www.lib.umich.edu/govdocs) is a central reference and referral point for US and foreign government information.
- *Electoral Commission* (www.electoralcommission.org.uk) is the organisation with which all UK parties must register so contains a comprehensive list of British political parties and records of their finances.
- *ElectionGuide* (www.electionguide.org) provides information on all national-level presidential, parliamentary and legislative elections in other countries. It also has links to each country's election authorities, summaries of election results and data on voter turnout.
- *Institute of Fiscal Studies* (www.ifs.org.uk) is an independent research institute which examines the impact of current and proposed government social and economic policies. It publishes a yearly assessment of UK government budgets and pre-budget reports as well as research on a variety of economic and social programmes of the UK government.
- *Office for National Statistics* (www.statistics.gov.uk) provides online access to the official Census data and statistical information on the economy. It is a non-ministerial agency which reports directly to the British parliament to produce timely statistical information to inform public debate and decision making.
- *The National Archives* (www.nationalarchives.gov.uk) is the official archive of the British government. The material it contains ranges from ancient documents to digital files. Most of the historical archives are from the Public Record Office and Historical Manuscripts Commission. However, it is also responsible for the publication of all UK legislation and advises upon and encourages the re-use of public sector information through the Office of Public Sector Information (www.opsi.gov.uk) and Her Majesty's Stationery Office.
- *Political Resources on the Net* (www.politicalresources.net) is a searchable directory of international political websites with links to parties, organisations, governments and the media in each country.
- *PollingReport.com* (www.pollingreport.com) compiles hundreds of national and state polls on important political issues and public officials. Since the polls are categorised by topic, comparisons of different polls on the same topic are possible. Access to state polls, however, is for subscribers only.
- *Richard Kimber's Political Science Resources* (www.politicsresources.net) maintains useful lists of politics related sites around the world but with a particular emphasis on British government and politics. It is not comprehensive but is extensive and easy to use.

- *UK Parliament* (www.parliament.uk) is the official site for the UK House of Commons and House of Lords including information on individual members and pending legislation. The site also provides online access to Hansard (www.parliament.the-stationery-office.co.uk/pa/cm/cmhansrd.htm), the official proceedings of the House of Commons.
- *WorldPublicOpinion.org* (www.worldpublicopinion.org) offers in-depth analyses of public opinion from around the world on international policy issues.

Research exercises

1 a State a theory.
  b Develop a keyword list for a search of the literature related to your research question.
  c Outline a search strategy, both for online and library searching.
  d Use at least two different search engines to search for information on your theory. Compare the results you retrieve from each search engine. When comparing your results, consider the following points: How many results did you retrieve in each search engine? What proportion of these results did you consider relevant to your search?
  e Next, use a meta-search engine, such as *Dogpile*, to search again for information on your theory. Compare your results with those you retrieved with individual search engines. Consider the same points as you did above.
  f Browse the *Yahoo!* subject categories related to your theory. Consider the following points: Which of the two methods – search engines or subject directories – do you consider more successful or more appropriate? Why? What are the advantages and disadvantages of each method?
  g Using your search strategy and at least two indexes, develop a bibliography of ten to fifteen items that appear to be of interest. Prepare a file card with all of the necessary information for each item.
  h Locate at least three items from your bibliography in the stacks of the library. At least one should be a book and one a journal article.
  i Read each item you have located. Take notes on what you read.
  j Consider the relationship between what you have read and your research question. How might each item help you to better frame or pursue documents related to your question?

Key terms

APA style	general periodical database	stem
APSA style	keyword	subject directories
academic subject indexes	mailing lists	subject headings (or
blogs	meta-search engine	descriptors)
Boolean logic	newsgroups	
concept search grid	search engine	

Part II
Research design

4 From abstract to concrete: operationalisation and measurement

- How are theories operationalised?
- What are the levels of measurement?
- How might error creep into measurements?
- Of what importance to accurate measurement is internal validity? External validity? Reliability?

Introduction

Empirical research is a means of obtaining answers to questions about our observable reality. Our questions may be primarily practical, or they may be principally of academic interest. In either case, they will probably be stated in abstract terms. Yet the answers we want are usually concrete and specific. One of the first challenges in research is to devise ways of getting from the abstract level of our questions to some concrete observation that will allow us to answer them.

To take a nonpolitical example, suppose we want to resolve a debate between flatmates about which of the supermarkets in their town is the best. Obviously we will need to compare the two in some way to settle the argument, but on what grounds shall we compare them? We want to determine which one exhibits more of the qualities of a great store, but *supermarket excellence* is an abstract concept. In order to evaluate each store in terms of this quality, we may choose to *quantify* the concept of supermarket excellence. We might agree to compare their prices on a fixed set of items, and to let the resulting quantity stand for supermarket excellence. Or, more likely, we might perform several such operations on different aspects of the stores' performance so that we can get a more complete picture of how well they perform, and then combine them in some way. Once we have these numbers, we will be ready to make concrete comparisons and attempt to resolve the dispute.

What we have just described is essentially the process by which we proceed from abstract concept to concrete observation in quantitative social science research. It is a crucial phase in the research process, for only if it is done correctly will the information we gather represent evidence about the utility of our theories or provide answers to our questions. The process of selecting observable phenomena to represent abstract concepts is known as **operationalisation**, and the specification of steps to take in making observations is called **instrumentation**. The application of an instrument to assign numerical values to cases results in a **measurement**, and it is this measurement that we finally use as evidence in making decisions and answering questions.

In this chapter we describe these processes in detail and discuss the problems you may encounter in attempting to operationalise and measure concepts. Upon completion of this chapter, you will be ready to state the explanations devised from your search of the literature in a form that will allow you to test them through actual observations.

It should be noted that this chapter primarily focuses on answering research questions using *quantitative* data rather than employing *qualitative* methods; the focus on numerical measurement in the chapter is intentional, but is not intended to exclude qualitative research. Techniques for qualitative

operationalisation are integrated directly into the chapters on interviewing, direct observations and focus groups, applying the distinct approaches to each method.

Operationalisation: the link between theory and observation

In Chapter 2 we stressed the importance of having a theory to guide observation. The research process was described principally as a matter of comparing actual observations with the expectations about reality that we derive from our theories in order to judge how much theories are relied on as explanations of political phenomena. These expectations are stated in the form of hypotheses, which predict relationships between variables that represent the concepts in the theory. The object of this chapter is to describe how we can devise observations that will make these comparisons possible. The question is how to quantify our concepts in order to make precise statements about whether or not our theoretically derived expectations are supported by what we observe. A simple example will help make some of the issues clear.

An example

Let us say that we want to test experimentally the hypothesis that a chemical fertiliser spread in one cornfield will stimulate more growth than the natural nutrients found in another field. Growth is an abstract concept; it is not seen directly. We need to translate *growth* into an empirically observable variable so that we can determine when one plant has shown more of it than another.

Variable *height attained* represents the concept *growth* because relative heights are empirically observable. But corn plants do not wear signs telling their height; we have to ascertain it for ourselves. How? We could use human judgement and have observers rate plants in the two fields as tall or short. Such a procedure would allow only crude comparisons between plants and would be subject to all kinds of errors, because people differ in their perceptions. We need a more precise and dependable means of determining heights to make meaningful comparisons.

Implementing instruments

To quantify our measurements, we must translate the variable height into terms of *an instrument* that can be used to yield precise, standardised indications of the extent to which the characteristic is embodied in individual corn plants. We can let height be represented by an **indicator**, such as *length in inches*, and measure the plants with a tape measure. The readings from the tape measure then become the **values** we assign to plants on the variable *height*, and these values are what we actually compare in attempting to assess the accuracy of our theoretical prediction of greater growth in one field than in another.

We have moved, then, from the abstract concept *growth* to the variable *height*, and then to the indicator *length in inches*. This transformation is known as *operationalisation*, because an abstract concept has been reduced to a set of values that can be obtained through specifiable operations.

Observing indicators

We finally make the comparisons on which we will judge the accuracy of our hypothesis about relative growth by comparing the values that result from the measurement process (in this example, the readings from the tape measure). When we speak of **observation** in research, we are referring to *the process of applying a measuring instrument in order to assign values for some characteristic or property of the phenomenon in question to the cases being studied.* In other words, observation means using an instrument to measure a trait or behaviour.

This is an important point to understand. It makes clear the significance of operationalisation and measurement in the research process. We can never actually compare concepts, even though our theories and our research questions will be stated in concepts; instead, we compare *indicators of concepts.* In our example, we cannot compare the growth of plants in the two cornfields in our example. We can compare only the readings we get from the tape measures – the measures produced by the indicator that represent the concept.

This means that our *comparisons can be accurate only to the extent that the indicators selected mirror the concept we intend them to measure.* If we have improperly operationalised our concepts, the relationship between our indicators may not be an accurate reflection of the relationship between the concepts they are supposed to represent. As a result, any conclusions drawn from our observations about the concepts or the theory of which they are a part will be faulty.

Figure 4.1 illustrates this situation. Our theory posits a relationship between two abstract concepts. Our hypothesis predicts a relationship between two empirically observable variables, which we reduce to measurable indicators, and our observations reveal a relationship (or lack of relationship) between two sets of values on these indicators. Obviously we can infer something about the reality of the theoretical relationship only if the variables accurately represent the concepts *and* the indicators accurately represent the variables.

Operationalisation almost inevitably involves some simplification or loss of meaning, since indicators seldom reflect all that we mean by a concept. Since we almost always have to accept some loss of meaning, we need to operationalise so as to minimise that loss. We have to seek indicators that encapsulate as much of the meaning of the concept as possible and that represent at least some aspects of our concepts as accurately as possible.

Figure 4.1   Operationalisation: the relationships of concept, variable and measure

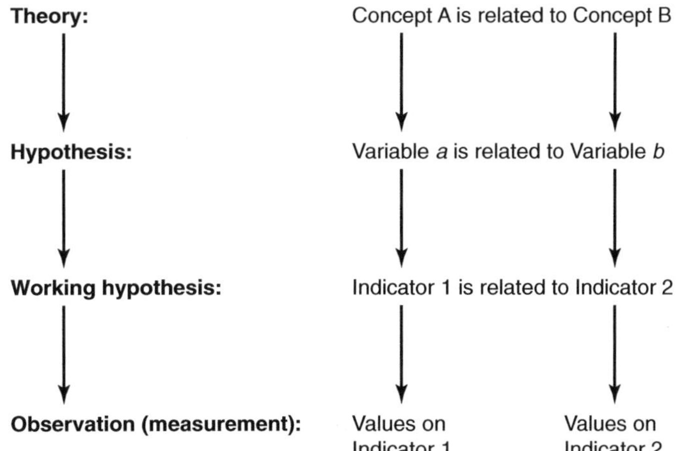

Note: This simplified example omits the theory's explanatory component.

Using multiple indicators

Our agricultural example illustrates the implications of a single indicator that fails to fully capture our concept. Once we have begun the research, we may realise that there is more to the concept *growth* than height and that the indicator *length in inches* does not fully capture what we want to measure. For instance, it may be that the amount of growth in the two fields is substantially different, but all the difference is in stalk diameter, width of leaves and weight of corn ears; the height of the plants in the two fields may not be noticeably different. In that case, if only the height is considered in evaluating the effects of the fertiliser, we will be seriously misled, because the link between the concept (growth) and the variable that represents it (height) is imperfect. The variable used here does not *fully operationalise* the concept it represents. It does not capture all the meaning in the concept, and using it misleads us about the relationship that exists in the real world.

This is an especially common situation in the social sciences since most important social science concepts are **multidimensional** in that they have more than one aspect or component. Our measures of these concepts must reflect their diversity if they are to be useful indicators of the concepts. For example, if we operationalised the concept of democracy only in terms of the holding of regular elections, we might classify dictatorial regimes that hold elections with only one candidate per office and do not allow freedom of expression as being just as democratic as the nations of western Europe. To obtain an accurate measure of the degree to which nations are democratic, we obviously need indicators that reflect the various dimensions of the concept.

The fact that even clearly undemocratic countries, such as Iraq under Saddam Hussein, can hold regular elections should help to clarify why operationalisation is crucial to theory testing and the research process in general. It is not as easy to explain how to ensure proper operationalisation. This is because selecting variables to represent concepts and devising indicators for the variables involve a good deal of creativity and cannot be reduced to a set of standardised steps that will unerringly produce good measures. What we do here is point out some of the pitfalls to be avoided in the process and to describe ways of evaluating the adequacy of operationalisations once they have been selected. We do this in the sections on measurement in this chapter.

Operational definitions

Before moving to a discussion of social science measurement, however, we should consider what is involved in operationalising a concept. This is done by specifying a set of procedures to be followed or operations to be performed in order to obtain an empirical indicator of the manifestation of a concept in any given case. These procedures then provide an **operational definition** of the concept and its variable counterpart. The process of operationalisation essentially reduces to a matter of selecting operational definitions for concepts.

To be useful – that is, to provide valid and reliable measures of our concepts – operational definitions must tell us precisely and explicitly what to do in order to determine what quantitative value should be associated with a variable in any given case. They should specify a complete set of steps to take in the process of measurement.

Importance of precise definitions

We need precise definitions for at least three reasons. First, we want to be able to tell others exactly what we have done to obtain our measures, so that they can evaluate our work and possibly repeat our study to verify its results in another setting. Second, if assistants are actually gathering the information, we will want our instructions for them to be detailed and precise enough to ensure that each one takes the measurements in exactly the same way as the others do. If our instructions are vague and our assistants go through slightly different sets of steps in obtaining measures, their results will not be comparable and we will be unable to draw valid conclusions from them. Finally, precise and detailed statements of how to operationalise a variable will help us in evaluating the results obtained and in eliminating rival explanations of those results that essentially claim that the 'findings' have been produced by flaws in the measurement process. (We will have more to say about this in subsequent sections of this chapter.)

When devising operational definitions for variables, you should routinely write out a description of the procedures you will use to obtain measurements. Every step should be detailed. This not only provides a record of your research and ensures standardisation of measuring procedures, but also gives you an opportunity to think through the act of obtaining a measurement in order to discover possible errors that can damage the reliability of the results.

An example

Suppose we want to measure the degree to which members of the main parties support their own party in parliament. We can operationalise the concept *party unity* as *voting together on parliamentary votes* and then use the percentage of the average member's votes that agree with those of the majority of their party as our indicator of *voting together*. Having decided to do this, however, we face a number of critical choices in actually operationalising our variable.

Before doing anything else, we must initially define both voting and unity. We might get information on how each legislator votes from the records of the legislature, but we will then have to decide which of the many recorded votes to include in our count. Some votes are unanimous (such as a vote to issue a proclamation of praise for some national hero) and do not reflect party unity because they do not involve partisan issues. Thus, including all votes reduces the extent to which our measure reflects our concept. We have to state criteria for selecting votes to include. In order to focus only on controversial issues, therefore, we might, for instance, choose to include only those parliamentary votes in which at least two-thirds of the members of parliament vote and in which the losing position gets no less than 30 per cent of the vote.

We also have to decide how to devise a procedure for determining how a majority of the party has voted in order to classify each member's votes as consistent or inconsistent with that majority position. We need to decide how to treat abstentions. Do they count as a failure to support the party, or do we exclude them from our count? In addition, we have to specify a procedure for first computing and then averaging the percentages of agreeing votes for each legislator.

With every operationalisation, we face similar decisions about exact procedures to follow in obtaining measures. A well-constructed, complete operational definition reveals how we have decided to handle such problems and leaves no ambiguity about what we actually did in taking our measures.

Developing instruments

Building an operational definition results in the development of an **instrument** for taking measurements. In the physical sciences, such instruments as scales, light meters and micrometers are used to obtain indicators of the degree to which things exhibit some property. In the social sciences, measuring instruments take different forms. Typical social science instruments include a series of questions on a survey form, instructions on how to make and record observations of certain events (such as a debate on the floor of the United Nations) and sets of numbers to be taken from a sourcebook and the rules for combining them into a measure.

Proper instrumentation is as important in the social sciences as it is in the physical sciences. Just as we would not attempt to measure weight with a ruler, we would hesitate to measure *political alienation* solely using demographic questions, such as age or family size. In discussing the validity and reliability of measures in the next section, we also suggest some ways to test the instruments developed in the process of operationalisation in order to increase our confidence that they measure what we want.

Measurement

We operationalise variables in order to have a way to concretise abstract concepts so that we can make meaningful comparisons between real-world phenomena in terms of the properties suggested by those concepts. This assigning of numerals to represent properties is known as measurement. The result of measuring is that we have a *value* to associate with some variable for a given case.[1]

This means simply that we can speak with more precision about the extent to which a given unit of observation (for example, a person, a city, a nation or an organisation) exhibits the property represented by the variable being measured. Rather than say that a city has a 'bad crime problem', we can speak of specific crime rates. Rather than say that a person is a 'devoted Conservative', we can say that one has scored a 7 out of 7 on our *strength of party identification* measure.

Levels of measurement

Measuring procedures provide a means of categorising and ordering phenomena. Some procedures, however, produce more precise and detailed distinctions between events than do others. When we say a procedure produces a given **level of measurement**, we are classifying it according to how much information it gives us about the phenomena being measured and their relationship to one another. The levels of measurement are referred to as *nominal*, *ordinal* and *interval/ratio*.

Nominal measurement provides the least information about phenomena; it gives only a set of discrete categories to use in distinguishing between cases. Nominal measurement is obtained by simply naming cases by some predetermined scheme of classification. Nationality is generally 'measured' at the nominal level by classifying people as Swiss, Brazilian and so on. However, that 'measurement' neither tells us how *much* of the characteristic 'nationality' different individuals have nor allows us to rank-order them. Using nominal measurement is simply a way of sorting cases into groups designated by the names used in a classificatory scheme.

To be useful, nominal measurement schemes must be based on sets of categories that are **mutually exclusive** and **collectively exhaustive**. This means (1) it must not be possible to assign any single case to more than one category and (2) the categories should be set up so that *all* cases can be assigned to some category. If we want to classify voters in the United Kingdom by use of a nominal measuring

---

[1]It is crucial that we appreciate the difference between a variable and its *values*. We recognise a variable because of its capacity to take on different values. The variable is a concept translated into empirical terms. A value is some magnitude or quality of the variable that individual cases can reflect. For example, Lutheran is a value for the variable *religious denomination*; upper class is a value for the variable *socioeconomic status*; and 23 years is a value for the variable *age*.

scheme, the categories *Labour, Liberal Democrat, Conservative, socialist, moderate* and *right-wing* cannot be used successfully, because these categories are not mutually exclusive. Since each UK political party appeals to a broad spectrum of voters so categories based on specific political views will not allow us to differentiate among voters in all cases. Similarly, if we try to categorise voters by party affiliation using only three categories – *Conservative, Labour* and *Liberal Democrat* – we will find that our categories are not collectively exhaustive, because some voters consider themselves independents or members of other parties.

In order to facilitate analysis, we will probably want to substitute a number for each category in a scheme of nominal measurement. It is important to recognise, however, that such numbers have no real meaning in this context; they are simply symbols. Just because we choose to substitute a 5 for the *Conservative* category and a 1 for the *Labour* category, it *cannot* be assumed that Conservatives have five times as much party affiliation as Labour supporters. Any number can be substituted for any category of a nominal measurement so long as each category has a unique number associated with it.

Ordinal measurement provides more information because it allows us both to categorise and to order, or rank, phenomena. Ordinal measurement allows us to associate a number with each case. That number tells us not only that the case is different from some other cases, and similar to still others, with respect to the variable being measured, but also how it relates to those other cases in terms of how much of a particular property it exhibits. With ordinal measurement we can say which cases have more (or less) of the measured quality than other cases, and we can rank cases in the order of *how much* of the quality they exhibit. That ranking gives us more detailed and precise information about the cases than we would get from a nominal measurement. The concept *social class* is often measured at the ordinal level, with individuals being ranked as lower, middle or upper class.

Interval/ratio measurement provides even more information. Not only can we classify and rank-order cases when they have been measured at the interval level, but we can also tell *how much* more (or less) of the measured property they contain than other cases. Ordinal measurement is not based on any standardised unit of the variable in question and does not allow us to tell how far cases are from one another in terms of that variable. It allows us only to say that some have more or less of it than others. Interval/ratio measurement is based on the idea that *there is some standard unit of the property being measured.*

Whereas ordinal measures give us only a rough idea of the relationship between cases with respect to a variable, interval measures provide information on the 'distance' between cases. The variable *income* is a clear example. Income is usually measured in units of currency (for instance, pounds in the United Kingdom). Because we use *standard units* in our measurement, the difference in income between £10,000 and £11,000 a year is exactly the same as the difference in income between £50,000 and £51,000 a year (i.e., £1,000). We cannot do that with ordinal measurement. If income is measured ordinally by dividing people into such income categories as *under £10,000* and *£10,000 to £19,999*, we can say that one person has more or less income than another, but we cannot say exactly how far apart they are in income because we cannot tell where an individual falls within the category. The income difference between a person in category 1 (under £10,000) and a person in category 2 (£10,000 to £19,999) can be as little as one pound (£10,000 minus £9,999) or as much as £10,000 (£19,999 minus £9,999), depending on their exact incomes, but we cannot make this distinction from an ordinal measure.

In addition to giving us precise information on the absolute differences between cases, interval measurement lets us make accurate statements about the *relative* differences between concepts. We can, for instance, agree that 50,000 people is twice as large a population as 25,000 people because we can speak meaningfully of a place that has no population. There is a *zero point* in true interval/ratio measures and it is at least conceivably possible for a case to score zero on such measures. Because there is no meaningful zero point on an ordinal scale, we cannot say, for example, that upper-class people have twice as much 'class' as lower-class people, because we do not know what it means to completely lack any standing in social class.

It should be noted that we have merged interval and ratio as a single level of measurement. They actually differ based upon the meaning of a variable's zero point, but this distinction is rarely a factor in political studies.

Distinguishing between levels

A handy tool to remember the levels of measurement in order uses the acronym NOIR (pronounced: no-ear). Simply recalling the names of each level, though, is insufficient to operationalise measurement in research. Still, knowing the names and a working definition of each level are the first steps towards employing appropriate analyses of your measures. Examples and definitions for each level of measurement are provided in Table 4.1.

Increased precision is advantageous

The benefit of increasing precision suggests an important point about levels of measurement. Nominal-level measurement is the least useful form of measurement when comparing phenomena. If we use it when we can use a 'higher' (more precise) level of measurement, we may be wasting potentially valuable information. If, in a study of voting behaviour, people are categorised only as Conservatives, Labour and Liberal Democratic when we can ask a different set of questions and produce a rank-ordering of them as strong to weak party identifiers, we may be giving up information that will help us understand the relationships observed. Ordinal-level measurement is more useful than nominal, but it too has limitations. Interval/ratio-level measurement is the most desirable form of measurement both because it provides the most detail and because of the mathematical procedures it allows us to perform on our data.

The point is that we should strive for operationalisations that allow interval-level measurement whenever possible and appropriate. But how do we decide which level of measurement is appropriate for the particular concepts we want to operationalise? This is a matter of both conceptualisation and measurement technology.

In the theory-building stage of research, we must first ask ourselves if there is a continuum underlying the differences seen in cases. If there is, we can devise ordinal and even interval measurements

Table 4.1   NOIR: Summarising levels of measurement

Level of measurement	Definition	Examples of variables
Nominal	Unable to rank-order	Race, Gender, City, Employed/Unemployed
Ordinal	May be rank-ordered	Support for increased taxation (1–6 scale), Approval of the president (1–4 scale)
Interval/Ratio	Known distance between ranks	Feeling thermometer rating of Republican Party, Age in years

for a concept that might otherwise be measured only by nominal classification. An historical example will help clarify the significance of this.

An example

Suppose we are studying the effects of immigrants' nationality on the degree of their support for big-city political machines in the early twentieth century in the United States. If we operationalise nationality at the nominal level and categorise city voting precincts' support for the machine, we might get a picture like that presented in Figure 4.2(a). There is no apparent relationship between nationality and voting behaviour, because knowing a precinct's dominant nationality does not help us rank it relative to the others.

When examining our reasoning, however, we might conclude that the reason we expect nationality to be related to support for the machine is that countries of origin differ in the opportunities they allow their citizens for political participation. When people have had little experience with democratic politics in their native land, we might reason they will be more willing to give up to a political boss their right to self-government. If we can follow this reasoning and rank-order the nations of origin by the extent of political participation they allow their citizens, we can construct a graph like that shown in Figure 4.2(b). In that graph, a relationship between nationality and support for the machine is apparent. The ordering of categories on our independent variable (IV) helps us discover a pattern in its relationship to the dependent variable (DV).

If we are bold enough, we may even upgrade our measurement of the independent variable to an interval/ratio level. For example, we might count the number of legal provisions for political

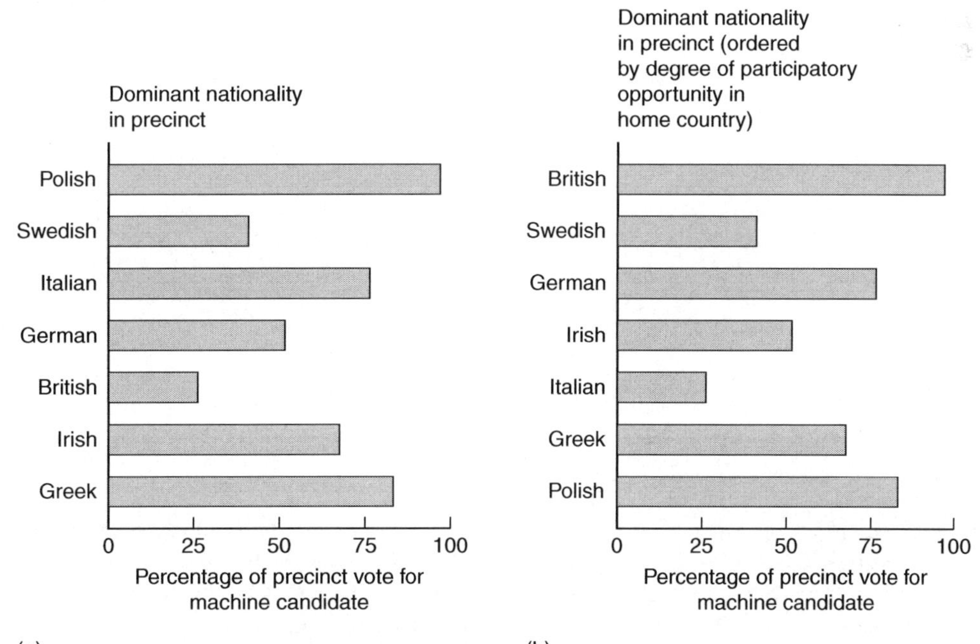

Figure 4.2 An example of how level of measurement can affect the interpretation of data

participation in the statutes of each country in question for the years just prior to the beginning of significant immigration to the United States. We can use the resulting numbers to rank nationalities along an interval scale and make even more precise comparisons of independent and dependent variables.

Whether or not upgrading of variables can be achieved from the nominal to the ordinal or interval/ratio level depends both on developing a theoretical rationale for doing so and on the technical possibility of applying the operational procedures that produce the higher-level measurements. Even if we can conceptualise *nationality* in interval terms in our example, we may not have access to the legal records necessary to place countries along the interval scale. In that case, *measurement technology* limits what we can do to strengthen our measures.

These situational factors make it difficult to set down rules about operationalising concepts to achieve certain levels of measurement. We do, though, suggest that you use the most precise measures possible, given the subject you are studying.

Excessive precision is disadvantageous

At this point, we need to add a qualification to our general interest in greater precision. There are cases in which too much precision in measurement is actually undesirable. In Figure 4.3 we see data on the relationship between age and presidential election voting is presented in two different ways. In Figure 4.3(a), age is measured in single years. Because there is greater volatility due to the few people in each age group (for example, 21–22, 35–36, 50–51) the chart reveals no clear pattern in the relationship between the two variables. In Figure 4.3(b) age is measured less precisely, in five-year groupings. With more cases in each group, we can see that there is a broad pattern to the relationship, with voting likelihood increasing to age 75 and then generally declining.

Giving up some precision in our measurements may provide clearer results, but if taken too far we may lose sight of relationships. Using twenty-year groupings to measure age will mask each age group's turnout differences, and we might falsely conclude that age is unrelated to the likelihood of voting. Because we generally do not know in advance of actual data analysis how much precision will be needed to discover relationships, we should follow the rule of operationalising our concepts as precisely as possible. We can always discard unnecessary precision by 'collapsing categories' (moving to larger units of differentiation), if necessary. If detailed information is not collected in the first place, though, we limit our future options.

Working hypotheses

Measurement assigns values to cases with respect to given variables. These values are what we use to represent concepts when comparing observations. Before we can understand the implications our observations have for our theories, we have to translate our hypotheses concerning relations between variables into working hypotheses, which state the expected relationships between measures or indicators. The penultimate line in Figure 4.1 suggests the form that **working hypotheses** take. These hypotheses force us to state explicitly the linkages between indicators and variables that are implied by the operationalisation of our theory.

Consider an example from the study of international relations. Suppose we are interested in a theory of dominance in the international sphere. We start with the theoretical proposition that *the more dominated a nation is, the more conformist its foreign policy will be because the nation economically depends upon its patron state.* From this theory we can hypothesise: *As a nation's economic dependency increases, its support for the international policies of its patron state will increase.* We

Figure 4.3 An example of how level of measurement can affect interpretation of data

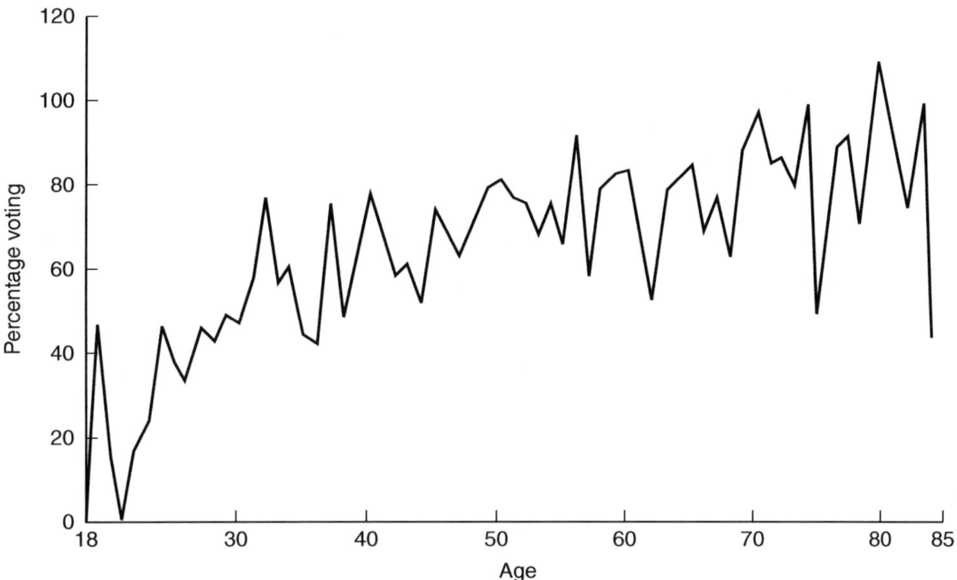

(a) Age and participation in 2002 election: age measured by years

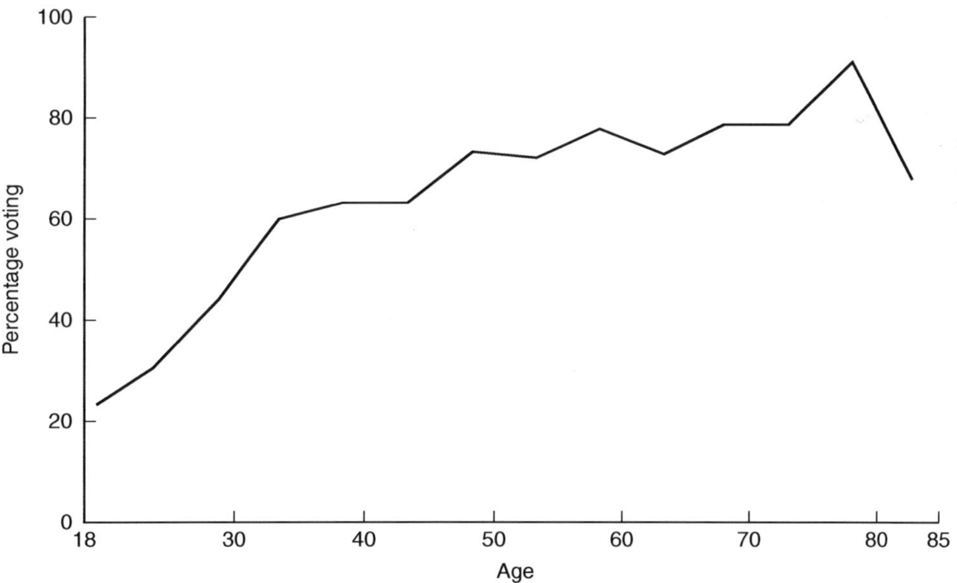

(b) Age and participation in 2002 election: age measured by half-decades
Source: Philips Shively (2009: 59–60). Reprinted with permission.

can operationalise *economic dependency* as the percentage of the nation's exports that go to the patron country. The percentage of exports becomes our indicator of the independent variable *dependency.* *Support* can be measured by the percentage of votes in the United Nations General Assembly in which the client nation's vote differs from that of the patron state. A percentage of votes in the United Nations becomes our indicator of the dependent variable *support for the patron state's policies.* We can now set out a working hypothesis that states the positive relationship expected between indicators: *The higher the percentage of exports going to the patron state, the higher the percentage of votes in the United Nations that agree with the votes of the patron state.*

This working hypothesis tells us what observations are consistent with our hypothesis and theory. It also suggests the relationship we envision between our variables and indicators. That relationship is illustrated in Figure 4.4.

When doing research, in addition to your theory about political phenomena, you should be able to state a **measurement theory** that sets out *why you expect your indicators to be related to your concepts.* In this example, why should we expect economic dependency to be related to concentration of exports? What is there about the distribution of exports that makes it a reflection of what is meant when we refer to dependency? These are the types of questions a well-developed measurement theory helps us answer. A measurement theory consists of the assumptions that explain why our indicators should change values as the degree to which cases manifest our concepts changes.

Indicators cannot be casually selected but must be chosen as a result of careful reasoning about the way things are related in the world. That reasoning is much like what we go through in constructing theories about political phenomena. This issue of whether or not there is any correspondence between our concept and variables on the one hand and our indicators or measures on the other is the central problem of measurement in science. The question of whether changes in our indicators are actually the result of changes in the concepts they represent gives rise to the problems of reliability and validity that are discussed in subsequent sections of this chapter.

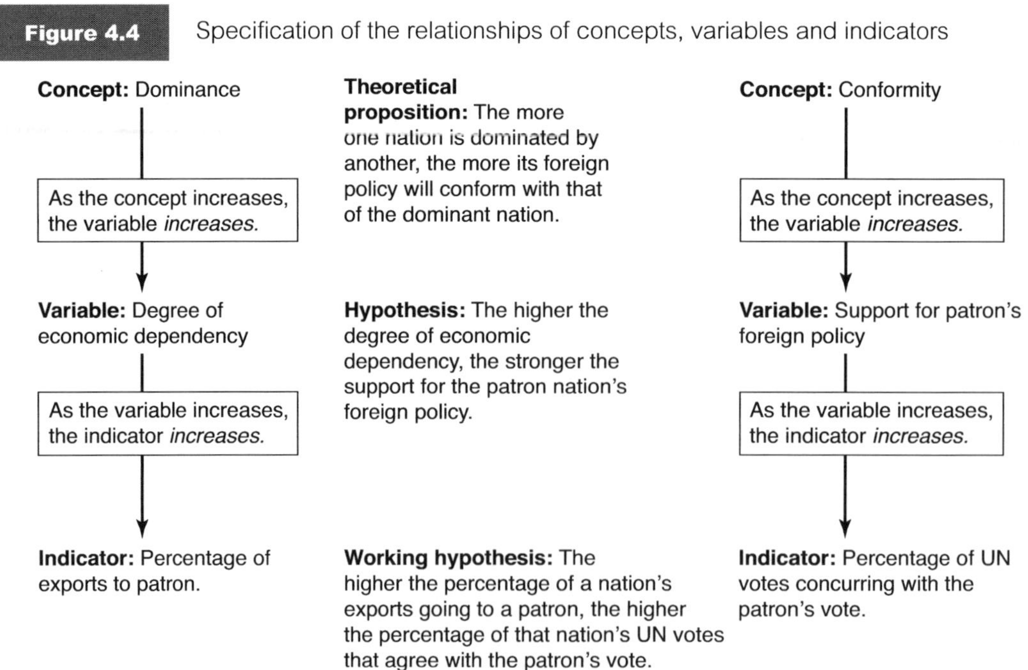

Figure 4.4 Specification of the relationships of concepts, variables and indicators

Note: This simplified example omits the theory's explanatory components.

Measurement error: the enemy

The process of measurement determines the values of cases depending upon how they score on our indicators. The differences in the scores can be entirely attributed to two basic sources. First, the cases really exhibit different degrees of the property in which we are interested. Different scores occur when our measures actually pick up those differences. In this case, *actual* differences in the concept are reflected in our measures. Second, something about the measure itself or the setting in which it is applied causes different cases to get different scores. In that instance, our measures are showing differences between cases that are *not* real – that is, the measurement difference is an artefact, rather than reflecting authentic differences in the concept we want to measure.

If our measures were perfect, they would reveal only the first kind of differences between cases, but our measures are rarely flawless. Differences in the values assigned to cases inevitably reflect not only real differences in the degree to which those cases manifest the concept, but also 'artificial' differences created by the measurement process. Any differences in the values assigned to cases that are attributable to anything other than real differences are known as **measurement error**. They are not real differences between cases, but differences that are erroneously recorded because of flaws in the measuring process.

An example

This distinction between true variations in scores and variations due to measurement error is similar to the distinction between differences in objects viewed directly and differences seen when we look only at their reflection in a mirror. The mirror used may be a precision-ground, optically correct mirror or a funhouse mirror, but we do not know through which we are observing our phenomena. To the extent that the mirror distorts the images, it either masks differences seen when viewing the images directly or creates an impression of differences we would not otherwise perceive. In the social sciences, we rarely can observe our key concepts directly and must rely on measurement procedures analogous to the mirror to reflect these concepts in any given case. Consequently, the accuracy of our impressions of the two depends on the precision with which our measures reflect reality.

What are some of the sources of distortion in the images our measures provide? The answer to this question is needed if we are to control measurement error or recognize it when it is present in our data. We can list several of the primary sources of measurement error by identifying common sources of differences in the scores assigned to cases *other than true differences in the characteristics we want to measure*.

1 *Differences in the distribution of other, relatively stable characteristics among the cases that are unintentionally revealed by our measures*: For example, the questions representing our measure of political ideology may require a given level of intelligence to interpret and answer. If this is the case, responses will reflect not only differences in people's political ideology, but also differences in their intelligence. When looking at the resulting data, the effects of intelligence and political ideology will be confused, and we will be unable to distinguish differences in scores that reflect ideological difference from those that reflect differences in intelligence. Similarly, other characteristics of our units of analysis (such as the regional location of cities, the cultural traits of nations or the sources of documents) can be inadvertently reflected in our measures and distort our perceptions of the manifestation of the target concepts. When these 'contaminating' influences can be identified and measured, we should check to see whether holding their values constant wipes out, reduces or increases differences in the scores that cases receive on our measures.

2 *Differences in the distribution of temporary characteristics among the cases that are reflected in our measures*: A person's mood or state of health can affect the way one responds to items on a questionnaire. The recent political history of cities (the revelation of corruption among public officials, for instance) can create systematic but temporary differences in the way those cities' citizens answer survey questions. A massive natural disaster can produce a drastic but temporary change in the statistics we are relying on to indicate the level of economic development. The effects of such temporary 'abnormalities' are more difficult to identify and control than the effects of the stable characteristics in our cases. The only approaches for guarding against them are being alert to signs that individual cases are subject to such transient influences (for example, studying the recent political history of the cities included in our sample or advising our interviewers not to attempt to interview a person who is temporarily bedridden) and following the procedures for checking the reliability of measures described in the section of this chapter discussing reliability.

3 *Differences in subjects' interpretation of the measuring instrument*: This is a problem only when people must respond directly to questions, as opposed to when the researcher constructs measures by observing behaviour. If questions are ambiguously worded, the different interpretations our respondents place on them can produce differences in their scores on the measures composed of those questions. Suppose, for instance, we are careless enough to ask the question *'Did you vote in the last election?'* in a study of voting behaviour. If some of the interviewees do not know that a local election has been held the prior week, they may answer that they *have* voted because they think the question refers to the last national election, even though they have not voted in the election to which our questions referred. We can guard against this source of unintended differences in scores by pretesting questions and testing our measures for reliability.

4 *Differences in the setting in which the measure is applied*: This is a source of measurement error principally in research that relies on individuals' responses to questions as its measures. One well-established fact in survey research, for example, is that the race, sex and age of interviewers can affect responses. Answers (and therefore scores on measures) can differ among interviews on the basis of the characteristics of the interviewer alone. Similar problems can arise outside survey research. For instance, we may make the mistake of doing a content analysis of one country's domestic newscasts and another's newscasts intended only for foreign nations. We will then be applying the same instrument in very different settings and can expect some differences in scores from this fact alone. This source of measurement error can be avoided only by making every effort to see that the situations in which we measure are standardised.

5 *Differences in the administration of the measuring instrument*: The scores assigned to cases can differ as a result of a variety of errors that occur in collecting and recording information. Interviewers may misunderstand instructions and ask questions in ways the researcher might not intend. Poor lighting may cause a respondent to mismark a questionnaire. Pencils can break and pens run out of ink at crucial moments so that observers fail to record key events in a group interaction. These kinds of variation in the administration of measuring instruments cause differences in scores independent of any differences in real values for the variable under investigation. Beyond employing only dependable assistants, the primary way to guard against such sources of measurement error is through *pretesting* our instruments. A trial run will help us discover potential 'mechanical' problems with the instrument (such as insufficient space for recording typical answers on a coding form) and human factors that may affect results (such as length of time observers can work without fatigue).

6 *Differences in the processing and analysis of data*: Information has to undergo a great deal of handling before it can be analysed; it often changes form several times. For example, interviewers may record responses by writing down every word an interviewee says in answer to a question. Those written passages may subsequently be reduced to a single number as responses get coded. The written number may be transferred to a computer file as an entry in the appropriate column of a spreadsheet. In each of these steps, data analysis has been made simpler, but with each step there is a chance of

errors that can cause cases to appear to differ on a variable when they do not. The possibility of such errors makes it a good idea to always double- and triple-check each transformation of data and to keep the original form for future reference.

7 *Differences in the way individuals respond to the form of the measuring instrument*: This is especially a problem when our units of analysis are people, rather than countries or news articles or the like. Measuring instruments can take such different forms as oral interviews, questionnaires to be filled out by the respondent and observation by a trained researcher. The different forms place different demands on the people under study. An interview requires ease of speaking, and a questionnaire requires an ability to read and write, for example. If people differ in these abilities, their scores may differ even when the people are actually alike on the variable being operationalised. The best guard against this source of measurement error is the use of more than one form of measure meant to operationalise each concept. We say more about this in the next section of this chapter, which discusses validity.

All of these factors can introduce measurement error into our research. The various errors that arise from these seven sources are generally categorised as either *systematic* or *random* errors.

Systematic errors are those that arise from a confusion of variables in the world (as discussed in item 1 in the preceding list) or from the nature of the instrument itself. They appear in each use of the instrument and are constant among cases and studies in which the same measure is used. Constant errors cause *invalid* results, in that the differences (or similarities) our measures seem to reveal are not accurate reflections of the differences we think we are measuring.

Random errors affect each application of the instrument differently. These errors occur as a matter of chance and are due to transient characteristics in our cases, situational variations in application of the instrument, mistakes in administration and processing, and other factors that vary from one use of the instrument to the next. They make our measures invalid in much the same way that systematic errors do. Random errors also make our measures *unreliable*, in that we cannot consistently get the same results when we use the measure if random errors are occurring.

How do we avoid having measurement error distort the results and render our research useless or misleading? To answer that question we must give careful attention to the issues of validity and reliability.

Validity

We can seldom obtain direct measures of the concepts used in social science theories. Such concepts as power, democracy and representation cannot be quantified as simply as the concepts of length and weight. We have to use indicators that correspond only indirectly to the concepts they represent. There is always a chance then that the indicators chosen will not adequately reflect the concepts we want to measure. **Validity** is the term used to refer to *the extent to which our measures and/or cases correspond to the concepts they are intended to reflect*.

To be valid, a measure must be both *appropriate* and *complete*. If, for example, we are interested in comparing the quality of public education in different Local Education Authorities (LEAs), we may be tempted to use the number of teachers in those LEA's schools as an indicator of the quality of educational services. This measure is *inappropriate* because the number of personnel in a school system is determined largely by the number of students and the size of the local authority and may have little to do with the quality of education. If the ratio of students to teachers is used as our indicator of educational services, we will have a more appropriate measure, in that differences caused by local authority size will be reduced or eliminated. The measure, however, will still be *incomplete*. Education involves more than teachers; it also involves school buildings, equipment, books and a variety of other factors. Looking at any one of these factors by itself might leave us with a false impression of the total quality of educational services. A school system may have a highly desirable student–teacher ratio but inadequate facilities and learning materials. It is a mistake to say that such a school system is equal to one with an identical student–teacher ratio *and* excellent facilities and learning materials. To achieve validity, we must strive to construct measures that are both appropriate and complete.

Internal versus external validity

There are two primary types of validity associated with empirical research: internal and external. **Internal validity** involves accurate measurement of our theoretical concepts. In other words, *are we measuring what we think we are measuring?* A later section in this chapter examines types of validation, which seek to answer this question. **External validity** pertains to the *generalisability of our results*. Can we reasonably expect to find the same causal influences at work in other settings? Does this study tell us anything about people, governments and situations *not* included in it? A field experiment on the effects on the public's driving habits of adding a pound-a-litre surcharge to the price of petrol, for example, has little external validity if it is conducted in a community where the average family's annual income is above £100,000, because we cannot expect middle- and low-income people to react to increased prices in the same way as wealthy people.

Factors that threaten validity

The major categories of threats to both internal and external validity include the following (Campbell 1969: 407–29):

Factors that threaten internal validity

1 *History*: Events other than the IV that can alter posttest scores and that occur between the pretest and posttest. For example, a well-publicised statement by a political leader can alter subjects' attitudes independently of some long-term experimental treatment they are undergoing.
2 *Maturation*: Natural changes in the subjects that alter scores on the DV over time independently of the IV (for example, human fatigue, population growth in geographically defined units of analysis, ageing of physical facilities).
3 *Instability*: Random changes in recorded values due to unreliable measures, inconsistent sampling of subjects or other causes.
4 *Testing*: The test effect described in this chapter.
5 *Instrumentation*: Differences in the measuring devices used that produce differences in scores independently of the effects of the IV (for example, different biases among interviewers, an improperly calibrated machine or inconsistent precision among coders).
6 *Regression artefacts*: Changes due to regression towards the mean, discussed in Chapter 16.
7 *Selection*: Differences in scores resulting from differential recruitment of test and control groups (for example, when members of a test group are forced by law to be exposed to the IV, whereas members of one of the control groups volunteer to be exposed).
8 *Experimental mortality*: Different rates of loss of subjects from test and control groups (for example, those cases that can make the control group as a whole respond to the IV in the same way as the test group may drop out of the experiment before posttest).

9   *Selection–maturation interaction*: Biases in selection processes that lead to different rates of maturation in test and control groups (for example, in a study involving juvenile delinquents in a deterrent study, test subjects may be older because they have volunteered for the programme only after a series of juvenile arrests, and they may thus outgrow juvenile delinquency faster than the younger control group).

Factors that threaten external validity

1   *Interaction effects of testing*: Posttest scores of the pretested subjects may be rendered unrepresentative of the unpretested population because of the way in which the pretest has sensitised the subjects to the IV.
2   *Interaction of selection and experimental treatment*: Biased selection processes may produce a test group that responds to the IV in ways atypical of the larger population.
3   *Reactive effects of experimental arrangements*: Conditions of the experimental setting may be unrepresentative of real-world conditions.
4   *Multiple-treatment interference*: The simultaneous application of more than one treatment may create changes that are different from what would occur if any one treatment or IV were used alone.
5   *Irrelevant responsiveness of measures*: All measures pick up multiple aspects of the environment, and some may include irrelevant components that give the appearance of change when none has occurred or that obscure actual changes.
6   *Irrelevant replicability of treatments*: When IVs are complex events (as is a college education), researchers may not be aware of what aspect causes the change in subjects, and they may fail to include the relevant aspect of the IV in all experimental exposures to it.

Types of validation (advanced tools)

Achieving appropriate and relatively complete operationalisations depends both on knowing a good deal about the subject of our study and on conducting a careful, logical analysis of alternative operationalisations. Unfortunately, we can check the validity of our measures in order to determine whether or not we have developed sound measures only *after* we have collected data. The process of evaluating the validity of our measures is referred to as **validation**. There are four basic approaches to validation summarised in Table 4.2.

Pragmatic validation

The degree to which a measure allows us to predict behaviour and events, establishes **pragmatic validation**. For example, say that we devise a measure of how appealing political parties are to voters. We can get some indication of the validity of this measure by applying it to all the parties in each of several election years and predicting their chances of gaining or losing seats on the basis of their relative scores on our 'voter appeal' measure. The more successful we are at predicting the political parties' electoral fate, the more confident we become that we have a valid measure, one that accurately reflects the intended concept. Measures that allow us to predict future events accurately are said to have **predictive validity**.

Pragmatic validation requires that there be some alternative indicator of variables that we feel fairly certain is a valid reflection of them. We check our measures against this alternative as we might

Table 4.2 Types of validation

Pragmatic validation	Construct validation	Discriminant validation	Face validation
Check results obtained from use of the indicator against results obtained from use of another indicator that is known to be a valid measure of the concept, or test the *predictive validity* of the indicator by using it to predict events that reflect the concept being measured.	*Internal (convergent) validation*: Infer validity of the indicator from its relationship to other indicators of the same concept using *multiple indicators*. *External validation*: Infer validity of the indicator from its relationship to indicators of *other* concepts to which the concept being measured should *theoretically* be related.	Infer validity of the indicator from the degree to which it is *un*related to indicators of other concepts that are theoretically distinct from the concept being measured.	Assume validity from the self-evident character of the indicator. (Can knowledgeable persons be persuaded that this is a valid indicator of the concept?)

check the accuracy of verbal reports of age against birth certificates. Unfortunately, there are seldom any clearly valid alternative indicators for the concepts used in social science research. As a result, we generally have to rely on the second type of validation – *construct validation*.

Construct validation

We *infer* the validity of a measure to develop **construct validation**. Essentially, we determine the extent to which a variety of measures are consistent with what our theory predicts. This involves two lines of reasoning.

First, we might say to ourselves, 'If concept X has a positive relationship to concept Y and a negative relationship to concept Z (as our theory says it does), then it will also be true that scores on a valid measure of X will have a positive relationship to scores on a valid measure of Y and a negative relationship to scores on a valid measure of Z.' The measure cannot be validated by comparing scores on it to scores on some other measure of the same variable that we know to be valid (as in the case of the birth certificate). We can, however, judge its validity by the extent to which using it as an indicator of our variable produces the kinds of relationships that our theory leads us to expect between that variable and other variables.

An example

To study international alliances, we might create a measure of the strength of an alliance based on a content analysis of newspaper articles from the countries involved. Is what the newspapers of one nation say about another nation a valid indicator of the strength of the alliance between the two countries? We might get an idea of whether it is by reasoning as follows: 'Our theory tells us that the stronger an alliance between two nations is, the more often they will vote together in the United Nations and the fewer restrictions they will place on trade with each other. Therefore, scores on a valid measure of *strength of alliance* will be positively related to scores on measures of *voting together in the United Nations* and negatively related to scores on measures of *number of trade barriers.*' We then proceed to do the data analysis necessary to see whether this expectation is supported by our observations. If the relationships are as expected, we will have greater confidence in the validity of our measure of *strength of alliance*. If they are not as we have expected, we will question whether we have a sound measure of this concept.

What we have just described is often referred to as **external validation**. It involves comparing scores on the measure being validated with scores on measures of *other* variables. To use this method of validation, of course, we have to include measures of the other variables in our research. This means that *we have to begin thinking about ways to validate our measures early in the research process*. Certainly by the time we are ready to develop a research design, we have to know how to check the validity of our measures so that we can be certain to gather any necessary information.

Our efforts at external validation will produce convincing evidence about the validity of our measure of one variable only if we can have a high degree of confidence in the validity of the measures used for the other variables. In the previous example, for instance, we could not conclude anything about the validity of our measure of *strength of alliance* from the relationships between scores on it and scores on the other two variables if we did not believe that our indicators of *voting together* and *trade barriers* were valid.

Because it is often difficult to find clearly valid indicators of variables to which our key variable should be related, external validation procedures must be used with caution. This is very much like testing a hypothesis. No single result guarantees the validity (or invalidity) of the measure. Rather, as instances of successful validation attempts accumulate, our confidence in the validity of our measure grows. For that reason, it is wise to seek out as many theoretically predictable relationships as possible to use in external validation. The more different tests of validity we have, the stronger our case will be.

This same logic applies to the second type of construct validation – **internal** or **convergent validation**. This type of validation involves devising several measures of the *same* variable and comparing scores on these various measures. We reason that if each of the indicators provides a valid measure of the concept in question, the scores individual cases receive on the measures should be closely related. If A, B and C are all valid measures of X, then any individual's scores on A, B and C should be highly similar.

An example

Suppose that we want an indicator of the quality of street lighting in residential neighbourhoods as part of a study of the distribution of public services. We might want to use citizens' perceptions of the adequacy of street lighting (as revealed in survey interviews) as that indicator. A sample of citizens in a neighbourhood can be asked how adequate they think the area's streetlights are and we can take the average evaluation as our measure of *quality of street lighting*. In order to perform an internal validation, we may also measure street lighting quality (1) by using a light meter to get a physical measure of the brightness and distribution of lighting; (2) by having trained observers rate the lighting; and (3) by having citizens compare their street lighting with that pictured in a series of photos showing streets with different qualities of lighting and then averaging their rankings to get a measure for the neighbourhood. This gives us four measures of the variable. If each is valid, all should be strongly related.

We can check this with appropriate statistics. If we find that scores on the measure based on responses to interview questions are weakly related to scores on the other three measures *and* that scores on those other measures are strongly related to one another, we will have reason to suspect that our first measure is not valid.

This is much like weighing the same object on three different scales. If each of the scales gives an accurate weight and we have no reason to assume that the object has changed weight in the course of the test, we expect the weights obtained from the three scales to be identical. If one gives a different weight, we suspect it of being out of adjustment.

Figure 4.5 suggests the differences between internal and external forms of construct validation. In Figure 4.5(a), we see that internal validation is achieved by checking the correspondence of scores on several different measures of the *same* concept. The more closely they correspond, the more justified we feel in claiming that any of the measures is valid. In Figure 4.5(b), we see that external validation involves determining whether our measure of one variable shows it to be related to *other* variables as we expect it to be from our theory. If the expected relationships do not appear, we have reason to suspect that the indicator we have selected does not provide valid measures of the concept.

The same caution that applies to the use of external validation procedures applies to the use of internal validation. We cannot always be certain that our measures of the key concept are valid and should, therefore, always be careful about concluding that a measure is valid or invalid from any one test of validity. We can significantly increase our confidence in the results of an internal validation if a simple rule is followed: *The alternative measures of the concept should be based on as many different types of operationalisation as possible.*

In the street lighting example, our measures come from four distinct types of operationalisation: citizens' verbal ratings, physical measurements, observers' judgements and citizens' selection of photographs. Each of these represents a different *mode of operationalisation*. The more different modes we can use and the more independent they are of each other, the more confidence we can place in our validation. Why? The logic is as follows:

The principal source of invalidity is systematic and random measurement error. Different measures are subject to different kinds of measurement error. The more indicators we have for any variable and the more they differ from one another, the less likely it is that all the indicators will be affected by the same measurement error. If this is true, we will have a better chance of both recognising measurement error as a source of differences in the scores on any one of our measures and getting an accurate measure of our variable if we use **multiple indicators**. These indicators may be combined into a scale; a topic discussed in great detail in Chapter 9.

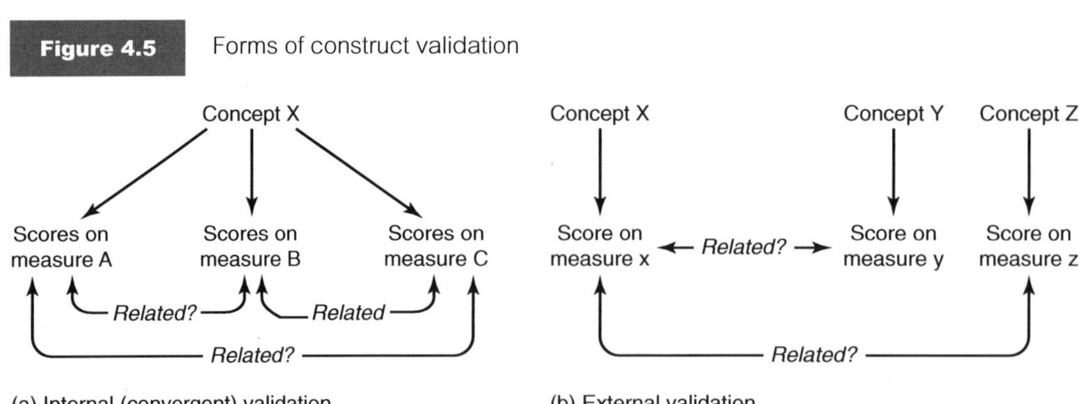

<table>
<tr><td>Figure 4.5</td><td>Forms of construct validation</td></tr>
</table>

An example

The factors that may invalidate our physical measure of street lighting quality (such as a faulty light meter) are likely to be quite unrelated to any factors that might introduce systematic errors into the measure based on citizens' evaluations (such as a tendency for people to claim, out of a sense of community pride, that public services in their neighbourhood are as good as those in other areas). If we use only one mode of measurement, any source of measurement error may affect the scores on each measure, giving us a consistently invalid indicator and not allowing meaningful comparisons among measures. If, for example, we rely only on the physical measure of lighting but take readings in several different ways (say, on the pavement, on the curb and in the street), then any flaw in the measuring instrument (the light meter, in this case) will affect all measures and none can be used to check another.

This logic suggests the great value of having multiple indicators for our variables. The availability of multiple measures not only gives us an opportunity to *test* the validity of our indicators, but also *improves our chances of obtaining a valid measure* of our variables in the first place. Multiple measures can actually increase the validity of measurement by allowing us to combine the results of several different measurement procedures so as to produce a *composite score* that is more likely to be a valid reflection of the actual value of our variable than any of the measures taken alone. This is because there is a chance that the errors that cause each measure to be invalid will cancel out when the results of several measurement procedures are combined. (In Chapter 9, the sections on scaling describe some possible methods of combining scores to produce a composite measure.)

Discriminant validation

A third approach to validation is referred to as **discriminant validation**. When we ask whether a measure exhibits *discriminant validity*, we are essentially asking whether using it as an indicator of a given concept allows us to distinguish that concept from other concepts. For example, we might want to measure the concept *trust in political officials* through a series of questions in a survey. If we also have on the questionnaire a series of questions designed to measure *trust in people* (in general), scores can be compared on the two measures to ask whether our first set of questions actually reflects simply another way of measuring trust in people. If scores are highly similar, we say that the political trust measure does not have discriminant validity because it does not permit us to distinguish the concept of *trust in political officials* from the concept of *trust in people*.

Face validation

A final approach to validation relies on the concept of **face validity**. Some measures are based on such direct observation of the behaviour in question that there seems to be no reason to question their validity; such a measure seems valid 'on the face of it'. For example, suppose we want to measure compliance with a state law, requiring each business establishment to display its operating licence on its front door. Having trained observers simply note the presence or absence of such licences seems to provide an obviously valid measure of compliance. Though we should always ask ourselves if the measures selected appear valid on their face, it is generally a mistake to rely on face validity alone to ensure accurate results from research. We should attempt to ascertain the validity of our measures through established procedures, such as those already described.

Reliability

Whereas validity considers how closely the measured values correspond to the true values of the variable, when we ask about the **reliability** of a measure, we are assessing how *stable* the values it yields are. Can we get the same value for any given case when we apply the measure several different times, or does each application result in the assignment of a different value to each case? If we do not get substantially the same value for any given case from successive applications of a measure, that measure is *unreliable* as an indicator of the concept. Rulers are made of inelastic materials in order to ensure reliability. If rulers were made of elastic materials, they might very well show different lengths for the same object – even when the object's true length has not changed – simply because the ruler stretches and contracts.

Reliability versus validity

If a measure is unreliable, it cannot be valid because at least some of the differences in the scores assigned to cases result from measurement errors rather than from true differences between cases. Recall our example of the study of street lighting. What if the light meter we use is so sensitive that, in addition to recording the light from the streetlights, it picks up light from the moon? Then the values assigned to each street on the variable *quality of street lighting* will depend both on the brightness of the street lights and on such random factors as the fullness of the moon and the density of the cloud cover. To the extent that these random factors influence our results, the measure will not be a valid reflection of actual differences in the quality of street lighting. In this case, unreliability produces invalidity.

A measure may be quite reliable and yet invalid. Recall our example of the study of the extent to which people in different nations agree with the policies of their government. We said that survey questions may give invalid measures because people in authoritarian countries are afraid to tell the truth about their opinions. Because this factor produces a systematic rather than a random error, the questions might produce very stable results. No matter how many times they are asked, people might give the same 'safe' responses. This does not, however, make the measure valid.

Thus, a measure may *be reliable without being valid, but it cannot be valid without being reliable.* Whereas validity is challenged by both systematic and random error, reliability is jeopardised only by random error. This means that if a measure has been convincingly validated in prior studies we can use it without being worried about its reliability; it has to be reliable if it is valid. But demonstrating reliability does not guarantee validity.

Testing reliability

How do we guard against unreliability? How do we determine whether or not a given measure is reliable? Preventing unreliability depends on our being aware of the various sources of random measurement error described earlier in this chapter and doing what we can to control them. This involves thinking through the actual measurement process and pretesting our measuring instruments to discover previously unrecognised causes of random error.

It is often quite difficult to determine whether or not we have devised a reliable measure in the social sciences. This is because the true value of the variables with which we are concerned can change dramatically with time and circumstance – people change their opinions in response to experience, nations alter the way they allocate resources between social services and defence efforts in response to perceived military threats and so on. When real values are changing, it is hard to distinguish the effects of random measurement error from genuine fluctuations in the concepts being measured. This means that tests of reliability should be conducted over as short a time span as possible.

There are essentially three broad methods of assessing the reliability of measures in the social sciences. The first is the *test–retest method*. Here the same measure is applied to the same set of cases again and again, over time. To the extent that cases get the same score each time, the measure is considered reliable. A difficulty with this technique arises when our measure involves interviewing people (as opposed to measuring inanimate objects or making concealed observations of people). If we repeat questions in a short time, interviewees may remember their first answer and, in an effort to be consistent, repeat that answer rather than respond truthfully in answering the question. If this happens, we cannot get an accurate picture of the questions' reliability as an indicator of the concept. In an effort to avoid this test effect, we might let a good deal of time pass before asking the questions a second time. In doing that, however, we will run into another problem: true values on the variable may have changed with the passage of time, and we may be unable to distinguish differences in scores caused by unreliability in the measure from actual changes in the variable.

Because of that difficulty, a second type of reliability test has been developed: the *alternative form method*. Different forms of the measure are applied to the same group of cases, or the same measure is applied to different groups *at the same time*. In this way there can be no reaction to being measured because no case will be measured more than once and, because no time will lapse between applications of the measure, actual changes in the variables under study cannot affect the results. The success of this strategy, however, depends on the alternative forms of the measure being perfectly comparable to each other as a measure of the concept, or on the two groups being virtually equivalent with respect to the distribution of the measured variable. If we can assume that these conditions are met, the more the scores on the two measures, or the scores of the two groups, are alike, the more confidence we have in the reliability of our measure. If we cannot come up with comparable measures or groups, however, the method cannot be used properly.

The final basic approach to testing the reliability of a measure is known as the *subsample method*. In it we draw one sample of cases and divide it into several subsamples in such a way that each is highly similar to the others in composition. Then, the same measure is applied to all subsamples and we use the similarity or difference of responses from subsample to subsample as an indicator of the reliability of the measure. Because the same measure is used, we do not have to be concerned about comparability, as in the alternative form method, and because we can rely on sampling theory to ensure the equivalence of our subsamples, we do not have to worry that the groups selected for measurement will not be sufficiently alike. Because no case is measured twice, we can discount reaction to testing as a threat to the accuracy of our reliability test, and because the measures are administered simultaneously, actual changes in the variable cannot create problems for this method as they can for the test–retest method. However, use of the subsample method depends on our being able to draw a large enough sample that we can divide it and still have subsamples large enough for our statistical tests to be meaningful. This is not always possible and can represent a barrier to the use of the subsample method in testing reliability.

There are many variations on these methods. Which one is most appropriate for any given research project will depend both on the time and resources available to complete the research and on the nature of the study. For instance, if we want to measure street lighting by having trained observers rate the lighting on various blocks, the test–retest method can easily be used without concern about a test effect. Street lighting will not change simply because it is measured by someone, and so we can have different observers independently rate the same street on the same night. We cannot have the same confidence in this method if our measure of street lighting quality is based on citizens' responses to interview questions.

Regardless of the reliability test we choose to use, it is important to establish the reliability of our measures *before* actually beginning research. This involves pretesting the measure by collecting the data necessary for the purpose of assessing the instruments we will use in the final study. Failing to do this, we may find only *after* the study is complete that our measures of key variables are unreliable (and therefore invalid). This means that we will not be able to place any faith in the results of the research and that our energies will have been partially or totally wasted. *Pretests of the validity and reliability of measures should be part of any research project that either uses measures that have not been convincingly validated elsewhere or relies on measures that have been validated only in settings very different from those in which they will be used.*

Ethical considerations

In the process of defining terms and choosing measurement types, researchers make decisions that fundamentally determine the (eventual) research interpretation. During operationalisation, an awareness of the limits and strengths of each level of measurement, as well as an appreciation of the measures' reliability and validity will maximise the interpretability of the research and its acceptance by others.

A good researcher should not forget that the operationalisation of concepts has implications for those being studied. When considering the relationship between education and political participation, for example, one might ask what exactly is to be examined. Education can be measured by the number of years of education, but some very clever individuals may have dropped out of school early and not all school leavers or university graduates are of equal intellectual capability. Is the focus of our research the intelligence of the individuals or the number of years they have spent in education? Of course, even if we had the funds to devise and administer a test for intelligence, what is being measured? We might define intelligent in a way that suits our own preconceptions of what it means to be a good citizen (open-minded, ability to cope with complex problems etc.) but would risk stigmatising those who do not fit this norm as unintelligent or even stupid. Is an individual with little education or a simple political philosophy a worse citizen than one with a higher level of education or a complex political philosophy? Research can have a dehumanising impact on those being studied by creating implicit standards and norms which are difficult for most people to attain (the ideal citizen, politician etc.).

Later, when writing your research report, you will need to articulate each choice made during operationalisation. Documenting each of the reasons for these choices as you are making them will streamline writing, and limit the likelihood that you will accidentally make excessive claims about the power of the measures. Instead of developing your own instrument, you may choose to employ measures tested and used by earlier researchers. Using measures with known reliability and validity may greatly simplify operationalisation, as long as you are fully aware of measurement levels, critique the possible pitfalls and fully attribute your use of others' measures.

Conclusion

At this point we have introduced all the basic elements of the research process. Figure 4.6 depicts their relationships to one another. The operationalisation of our concepts through the development of measurable indicators prepares us to enter the field to make the observations on which we will base our conclusions. Before we can make those observations, however, we need a 'plan of attack' – a scheme for making the observations in a way that will maximise the number of conclusions we can confidently draw from them. This plan, or *research design*, is the subject of the next chapter.

Figure 4.6 A model of the research process

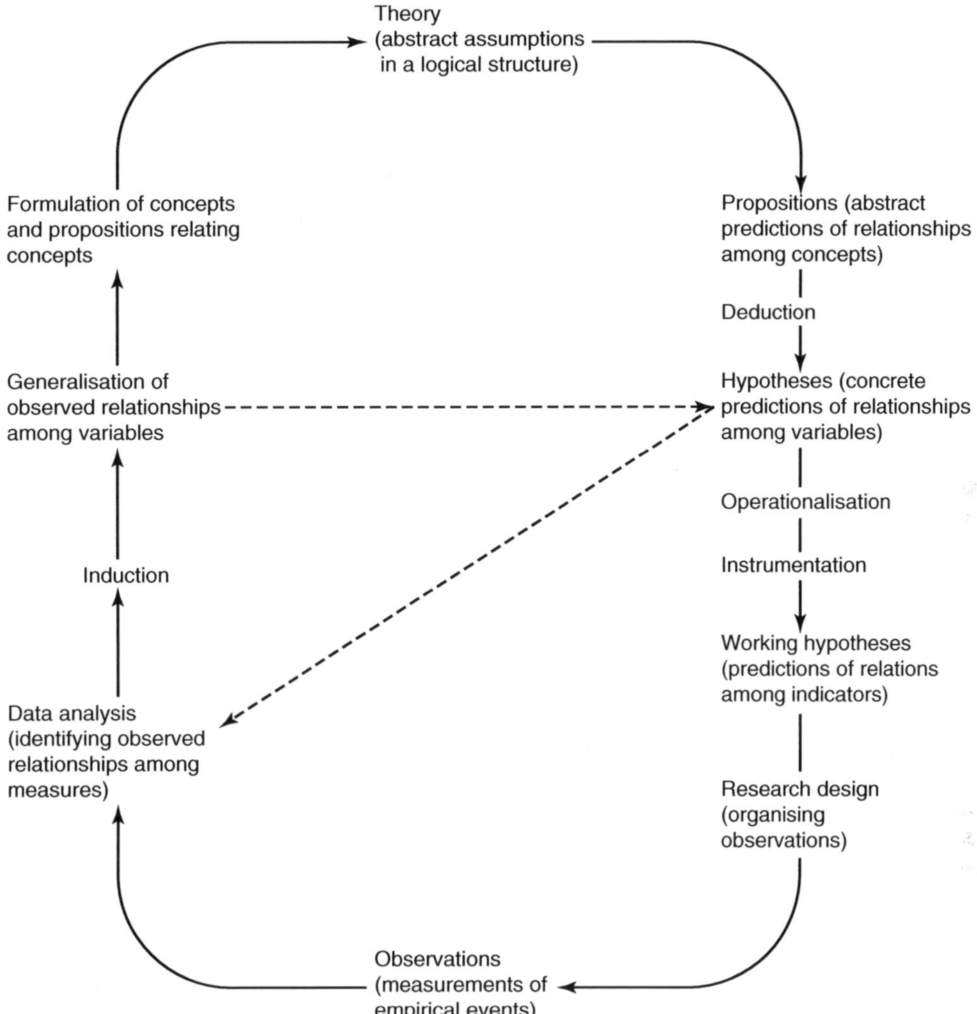

Summary points

- Theories are operationalised with instruments to measure their concepts.
- The levels of measurement are: nominal, ordinal and interval/ratio. These may be easily remembered using the acronym NOIR.
- Sources of measurement error include: instrument weakness, subjective interpretation and inaccurate or incomplete interpretation of results.
- Internal validity is strengthened if your measurements are appropriate and complete.
- Stronger external validity increases the generalisability of your results.
- Reliable measures enhance replication of your research.

Suggested reading and examples

Research examples

A controlled experiment studied the meaning of survey questions and how readers obtained inaccurate information during public policy debates about Social Security during the late 1990s. In Jerit and Barabas' (2006) experiment, subjects read excerpts of news stories and then answered survey questions about Social Security. This article explains its operationalisation of research concepts in considerable detail.

Methodological reading

Many explanations of measurement in the social sciences are found in literature that reports research results or develops sophisticated measurement techniques. An excellent general introduction to measurement strategies is in W. Philips Shively's *The Craft of Political Research* (2009). A more detailed discussion of measurement error, from the psychology research tradition, is found in *Research Methods in Social Relations* (Hoyle, Harris and Judd 2002).

References

Campbell, Donald T. 1969. 'Reforms as experiments'. *American Psychologist*, vol. 24 (April), pp. 407–29.

Hoyle, Rick H., Harris, Monica J. and Judd, Charles M. 2002. *Research Methods in Social Relations*, 7th edn. Pacific Grove, CA: Thompson Wadsworth.

Jerit, Jennifer and Barabas, Jason. 2006. 'Bankrupt rhetoric: How misleading information affects knowledge about social security'. *Public Opinion Quarterly*, vol. 70 (Fall), pp. 278–303.

Philips Shively, W. 2009. *The Craft of Political Research*, 7th edn. Upper Saddle River, NJ: Pearson Prentice Hall.

Research exercises

1 Using one of the political science periodicals given in Chapter 3, locate an article that reports the results of an empirical investigation. Identify at least two principal concepts from the article and write down how each concept was operationalised. If the article uses only one operationalisation for each concept, describe at least two more for each concept. If more than one operationalisation is used for each concept in the article, describe at least one alternative operationalisation for each. If possible, your operationalisations should rely on indicators that are in a different form from those used in the article.

2 Select another scholarly article reporting the results of empirical research. Identify at least two of the major concepts employed and describe how they were operationalised. Then state a line of reasoning that will lead us to expect the indicator selected for each variable to change when values of the variable change. In other words, state a *measurement theory* justifying the use of that indicator.

3 Using the variables from the article selected for Exercise 2, devise at least two alternative measurement theories showing how changes in each indicator employed in the article can result from changes in a variable *other* than the one it is used to represent. In other words, identify at least two possible sources of invalidity for each indicator.

Key terms

collectively exhaustive
construct validation
discriminant validation
external validation
external validity
face validity
indicator
instrument
instrumentation
internal (convergent) validation
internal validity

interval/ratio measurement
level of measurement
measurement
measurement error
measurement theory
multidimensional
multiple indicators
mutually exclusive
nominal measurement
observation
operational definition

operationalisation
ordinal measurement
pragmatic validation
predictive validity
random errors
reliability
systematic errors
working hypotheses
validation
validity
values

5 Working from a plan: considerations in research design

- Why is a research plan fundamental to a successful project?
- In explanatory research, what components comprise the research plan?
- What is qualitative methodology and why are qualitative methods necessary?
- How does one choose and design case studies in qualitative research?
- Are qualitative and quantitative methods compatible with each other?

Introduction

Just as experienced mountaineers would not attempt to climb Mount Everest without a great deal of planning designed to ensure that they had the right equipment, took the best route, and knew what to do if certain things went wrong, social scientists would not undertake a research project without carefully planning the steps that they would take. This plan of attack is referred to as a *research design.*

'A **research design** is the scheme that guides the process of collecting, analysing and interpreting data. It is a logical model of proof that allows the making of valid causal inferences' (Nachmias 1979: 21, emphasis added). Without an adequate and appropriate design for research, the best of measures will be useless, since their meaning cannot be determined. Before undertaking any serious study, you should write out a research design that not only tells exactly what you intend to do in the research process and how you intend to do it, but also tells *why* you are taking each step and why you are taking it in the way that you are, rather than in some other way.

Research purpose and research design

Research can have a variety of purposes, and the research design that is most appropriate for any given project depends on the project's purpose.

Types of research

Some research projects consist of **exploratory research**. They are intended only to provide greater familiarity with the phenomena to be investigated so that we can formulate more precise research questions and perhaps develop hypotheses. Such studies can be essential when investigating new phenomena or old phenomena that have not been studied before. Some projects involve **descriptive research**. These projects are intended to provide an accurate representation of some phenomenon so that we can better formulate research questions and hypotheses. We may, for example, need to know the frequency, geographic distribution and sequence of events of a phenomenon or need to know what other phenomena it tends to be associated with before beginning to theorise about what might have caused it. Finally, research can be intended to test causal hypotheses. If we can use the results of a study to argue that one thing causes another, we can begin to develop explanations of the second event. For that reason, hypothesis-testing research may be described as **explanatory research**. Such research is appropriate when we have enough knowledge about a phenomenon to begin to seek explanations for it.

The significance of this rough typology of research purposes is that research of each type requires different things of a research design. Exploratory research requires flexibility more than precision, because its purpose is to discover possible explanations rather than to test hypothetical explanations. Exploratory research designs need only provide an opportunity to observe the phenomenon in question. Descriptive research, however, requires accurate measurement of phenomena. In descriptive studies, the research design must ensure reliable observations if the studies are to produce accurate representations of the events of interest. Research designs must ensure both reliable observation and provide a basis for inferring the causal influence of one or more variables on others. A research design provides a basis for causal inferences when it allows us to rule out any plausible explanations for observed results that represent alternatives to the causal hypothesis being tested.

Regardless of the specific purpose of a study, its research design should include the following *basic elements*:

1   A statement of the purpose of the research.
2   A statement of the theory and hypotheses to be tested (if any).
3   A specification of the variables to be employed.
4   A statement of how each variable is to be operationalised and measured.
5   A detailed statement of how observations are to be organised and conducted.
6   A general discussion of how the data collected will be analysed.

It is this aspect of research design that provides a basis for ruling out alternative rival hypotheses and that most scholars have in mind when they refer to a research design.

Coping with alternative rival hypotheses through research design

We can demonstrate the impact of the way we structure or organise our observations on how useful the results of research are by considering a hypothetical research project.

An example

Imagine that the Home Office has implemented a new programme designed to reduce anti-social behaviour. The programme involves taking young offenders, as well as potential offenders who volunteer or are volunteered by their parents, into prisons for one-day visits. The programme is founded on the theory that glimpsing the horrors of prison life will discourage young people from committing crimes that might result in their being sent to prison, because the youths' exposure to incarceration will cause them to fear prison. Let us say that after the programme has been in operation for some months, the government wants to know whether it is having the desired effect, and it hires you, a skilled analyst, to evaluate its results. How will you go about this?

Because the programme, known as Operation Fright, is intended to reduce anti-social behaviour, anti-social behaviour will be your dependent variable. You might operationalise it as *being arrested for a criminal offence* and then, one year after their prison visit, simply check on the criminal records of the youths who went through Operation Fright. If they have been arrested during this time, you label them anti-social. If they have not been arrested during this time, you label them not anti-social.[1]

Let us say that you find that 70 per cent of those who have been in the programme have *not* been arrested during the following year. Can you then conclude that the programme has been 70 per cent effective in preventing anti-social behaviour? To do so with any confidence, you need to rule out other explanations of why 70 per cent of those youths have not been arrested.

Evaluating alternative rival hypotheses

Your *operating hypothesis* is that the Operation Fright experience prevents anti-social behaviour. Some possible alternative rival hypotheses that may explain your findings include the following:

1   No more than 30 per cent of the youths would have been arrested, even if they had not gone through Operation Fright.
2   The family background of those who were volunteered for Operation Fright is different from the background of those who were not, and it is that background that has prevented their anti-social behaviour, not the government programme.
3   Many of the youths have committed crimes but have not been caught.
4   Though there may be temporary effects from Operation Fright, they will wear off and the youths will revert to criminal behaviour. (The programme delays rather than prevents anti-social behaviour.)
5   The youths involved in the programme have been arrested more often than they would have been had they not taken part in Operation Fright, because participation labels them as potential criminals and subjects them to greater police scrutiny. (The programme causes more frequent arrests regardless of its effect on behaviour.)

Alternative rival hypothesis 1 essentially asserts that the programme has had no impact. With a single observation you cannot demonstrate that this is or is not true. You can never know how those who have gone through the programme would have acted had they not taken part in Operation Fright, but you can include in your research design a check of the criminal records of a group of youths who have *not* gone through Operation Fright, but who are otherwise similar in as many respects as possible to those who have. You can then compare the anti-social behaviour rate of those who have been in the programme with that of those who have not and argue that any difference in the two rates can be attributed to the programme, since we can assume that those in the programme would have acted essentially the same way as their peers in the absence of Operation Fright. Observing the control group (those not participating in the programme) allows us to assert a causal link between the programme and delinquent behaviour.

Rival hypothesis 2 is a claim that any apparent relationship between programme participation and anti-social behaviour is spurious. It holds that family background causes both programme involvement and subsequent non-involvement with anti-social behaviour. This reasoning suggests that there is a selection process in which those who have the family support to help them avoid criminal

---

[1]This simplified operationalisation of anti-social behaviour treats it as a dichotomous, nominal variable. In practice, you would probably want to use an operationalisation that provided more information and was more sensitive to differences between individuals. You might, for example, choose to develop a 'anti-social index' that combined the number of arrests in a year with some measure of the severity of the crimes for which the subjects were arrested in order to have an indicator of the *degree* of anti-social activity.

behaviour are also the ones most likely to have gone through the programme and that this creates an *apparent* relationship between Operation Fright and the absence of anti-social behaviour.

A single observation will not allow you to rule out this possibility, but having a control group including youths with family backgrounds similar to those who have gone through Operation Fright does, as in the case of rival hypothesis 1, allow you to determine whether this is the case. You can check to see whether programme participants and nonparticipants do in fact tend to have different family backgrounds, and whether those with similar family backgrounds tend to have the same offending rate regardless of participation in Operation Fright.

Ruling out rival hypothesis 2, like dealing with hypothesis 1, requires that you make a second observation (checking the criminal records of some youths not involved in the programme). In addition, however, coping with hypothesis 2 requires that you make a third observation, in which you collect data on the subjects' family backgrounds. You may be able to obtain some objective indicators of this variable (for example, presence of both parents, parents' educational level and occupation and family income) from public records, but you may also have to conduct interviews with family members or the youths themselves. Operationalising family background, to include attitudes and the character of personal interactions, will make such interviews necessary. You will therefore not only increase the amount of data you collect but also adopt another method of data collection – the personal interview.

Rival hypothesis 3 reinforces the need for this additional data collection method. It poses the possibility that Operation Fright has made its participants more cautious and perhaps even cleverer criminals rather than reducing the number of crimes they commit. It questions the adequacy of the operationalisation of the dependent variable. As long as official arrest records are the only measure of anti-social behaviour, you cannot have any confidence that this is not the case.

One way to cope with rival hypothesis 3 is to operationalise anti-social behaviour so as to include reports of criminal actions from the youths themselves and to conduct interviews both before and after they go through the programme. You will have to interview both participants and nonparticipants and include information on family background for each group to be sure that your results cannot be explained by hypotheses such as 1 and 2 phrased in terms of this new indicator of anti-social behaviour. With this action you have added not only another **observation point** (the preprogramme interview) but also another mode of operationalisation for the dependent variable.

Rival hypothesis 4 adds a time dimension to the study. To discount it, you will have to interview and check on the criminal records of both programme participants and the control group not just one year after the prison visit but also two and perhaps three years after. The reason for making subsequent observations of programme participants should be clear, since hypothesis 4 contends that participants will eventually become anti-social. You will also need to observe the control group in order to ensure that changes in delinquency rates for programme participants in later years are not the result of other factors, such as maturation, changes in family situation or worsening economic conditions. Only if programme participants have a subsequent anti-social behaviour rate similar to (or worse than) the anti-social behaviour for nonparticipants *at the same time* can you conclude that the programme has been ineffective (or that it has had a negative effect).

Unlike the others, rival hypothesis 5 argues that Operation Fright has been *more* effective than your results suggest. It raises the possibility that by using arrests as the measure of anti-social behaviour, you have introduced an additional independent variable (selective treatment from authorities) whose effects cover up the actual influence of Operation Fright on anti-social behaviour.

One way to cope with this possibility is to include yet another operationalisation of the dependent variable. Looking at *convictions* as well as arrests for both participants and nonparticipants, you will have some evidence of whether the cases brought against programme participants are any less valid than those brought against youths who have never gone through Operation Fright, and you may infer from this whether or not the police are any more likely to arrest those who volunteered for Operation

Fright. If participants are arrested without ultimately being indicted or convicted significantly more often than are nonparticipants, you will have reason to believe that rival hypothesis 5 is correct.

This brief examination of a few of the possible rival hypotheses that can challenge the value of your results has provided the basis for developing a much more elaborate research design than that first suggested. If you want to be able to rule out these five alternative interpretations (and you must do so if your study is to be of any value), you will have to move from a single operationalisation of the dependent variable and a single observation to a research design involving multiple modes of operationalisation, multiple methods of data collection and several observation points. The new research design might involve the following major steps:

1   Select a sample of youths who have been designated to take part in Operation Fright and a sample of youths who have the same mix of characteristics relevant to anti-social behaviour (e.g., sex; age; race; education; parents' occupation, education and income; living situation; and place of residence) but who are not to participate in the programme.
2   Interview those subjects designated to participate in the programme before they take part in Operation Fright, and at the same time interview the control group to obtain self-reports of anti-social activity and information on family background.
3   Interview members of all subjects' families to obtain information on family background.
4   One year after the subjects have visited the prison, interview both participants and nonparticipants to obtain self-reports of anti-social activity and to find out whether family circumstances have changed.
5   At the time you perform step 4, check the arrest and conviction records of both programme participants and nonparticipants.
6   Two years after the subjects have taken part in Operation Fright, repeat steps 4 and 5.
7   Three years after Operation Fright, repeat steps 4 and 5.

In analysing the data, you will want to compare the arrest rates, the conviction rates and the differences between arrest and conviction rates for the programme participants and the control group, being careful to eliminate any members of the control group who have taken part in Operation Fright after their initial selection for the study. By coding the information numerically, entering the data into a statistical programme and employing appropriate statistical procedures in the analysis of the data produced by these observations, you should be able to reach highly defensible conclusions about the value of Operation Fright as a deterrent to youth anti-social behaviour. Because of your ability to rule out major rival hypotheses, the Home Office may place a good deal of confidence in your conclusions – a confidence they could not have if those conclusions were based on the first research design.

Adequacy of design

Given the large amount of data generated by the study as outlined above, the design suggests a quantitative approach. The purpose of this exercise is not to argue that a quantitative research design is preferable to qualitative one. The important consideration is the *adequacy* of the design, not the type of data covered or the method analysis. If a research design provides a logical basis for the kinds of inferences the researcher wants to make, it is adequate.

The discussion of this hypothetical study provides an example of how adequate research designs are developed. In planning a research project, you will go through the same kind of reasoning that we have just laid out. *Research design is a process of formulating alternative rival hypotheses and reasoning through the kinds of observations that are needed to test those hypotheses so that they can be ruled out as explanations for potential findings.*

Alternative rival hypotheses are arrived at in the same manner as operating hypotheses. They result from logical analysis of our theories and from thorough knowledge of the facts that surround the events we are trying to explain. A true alternative rival hypothesis predicts the *same relationship* as our main hypothesis but explains it in terms of a different causal process.

Alternative rival versus 'other hypotheses'

It is important not to confuse true alternative rival hypotheses with what we can call *other hypotheses*. Due to the existence of multiple causation in social phenomena, it is usually possible to come up with a variety of equally valid explanations of any given event. Identifying another cause of the observed relationship simply produces another hypothesis that may not be a rival to the original. *A hypothesis is an alternative rival hypothesis only if it is logically impossible for both that hypothesis and the original hypothesis to be true at the same time.*

Identifying crucial rival hypotheses is principally a creative activity. There are no hard-and-fast rules to ensure that you will identify all the rival hypotheses that can challenge the value of your research. The process of designing a research project will differ with each study. You cannot simply select an appropriate research design from a limited set of alternatives as you might choose a pair of shoes from those that are your size in a shoe store. There are, however, several general types of research designs, each of which is suited to dealing with particular types of problems. The next chapter provides an overview of experimental research which forms an ideal for quantitative approaches to the study of politics and informs the logic of quantitative research design. Experimental design focuses on controlling aspects of problem to be studied to isolate the key variables to be considered. In the real world, this degree of control is usually impossible.

The value of qualitative approaches

The logic of research design outlined above is most appropriate for quantitative studies which produce numerical data that can be analysed statistically. However, there are limitations in using only **quantitative methods**. Critics of quantitative research typically raise four types of concerns.

First, some believe that since research methods were developed in the physical sciences, with their emphasis on treating all cases alike and reducing complex concepts to numeric representations, these methods can never fully capture important dimensions of human thought and interaction. To these critics, even the most carefully executed quantitative research does not provide an adequate understanding of the actions of humans who are each unique in many ways and may see very different meanings in the same phenomena.

Second, some critics argue that quantitative research methods require that we remove subjects from their natural setting and pay attention only to limited aspects of who or what they are. People, they argue, may not behave in real contexts in the same way as they behave in, for example, the artificial setting of a survey interview. Moreover, these critics contend that actions can only be fully understood by understanding the context in which they occur, for it is their context that gives them meaning.

Third, statistical techniques often mislead researchers into making a logical jump between correlation and causal linkages. Good statisticians know that correlation or association between two variables is not the same as causation or proving that there is a causal linkage between the two variables. None the less, many researchers are willing to accept the causal link if there is a plausible theoretical basis for the relationship. The problem is that the causal link is still assumed rather than demonstrated. Often more detail is needed to understand the nature of the relationship(s). This detail can be provided by tracing the process by which one factor is related to another. This level of detail is usually only provided by qualitative research.

Finally, some view quantitative methods as so inherently politically biased that they are inappropriate for the study of some subjects and populations. For example, these critics argue that applying the methods of the physical sciences can never capture crucial aspects of the lives and thinking of marginalised groups – people who, because of some personal characteristic, are excluded from political, social and economic power. They often argue that quantitative methods are a cultural artefact of the same processes that created the currently dominant social and political culture. Accordingly, they believe that we cannot employ quantitative research to gain a valid understanding of the deep cultural roots of contemporary political or social behaviour.

This indicates that there can be some fundamental differences between qualitative research and the type of inquiry we have described so far. There are, however, substantial similarities between the way many qualitative and quantitative researchers approach their studies. Indeed, **qualitative methods** are most self-evidently *empirical,* so it is important to emphasise the fact that *empirical research can be either quantitative or qualitative* so long as its purpose is to characterise accurately political phenomena.

Comparing qualitative and quantitative methods

It is useful to frame a comparison between qualitative and quantitative research by highlighting their differences in each of the major steps in the research process. In making this comparison, we will speak of qualitative and quantitative researchers as if they were two different groups. Please remember, however, that the same scholar may employ both types of methods – sometimes even within the same study. In addition, it is important to recognise that the distinctions discussed are generally more matters of degree than absolutes. The two types of methods often require only different *forms* of work, but are working towards similar objectives.

Empirical focus of research questions

Both qualitative and quantitative research begin with a research question. Although scholars using each of the approaches tend to pursue rather different research questions, both approaches are designed to produce knowledge of the empirical world. Both rely on concepts that are, at least in principle, observable with the ordinary human senses. Thus, qualitative researchers are just as obliged to represent accurately the reality that they observe as are those using strictly quantitative methods.

Research design

It is important for those using qualitative methods – just as it is for those using quantitative methods – to be clear about their research question and to know what they are seeking to learn from their study. A qualitative research design will generally focus on who or what is to be observed, in what settings they are to be observed, how observations are to be conducted, what methods will be used to secure the information needed and how data will be recorded. In some cases, there is even less concern with forcing the data collected into set categories and more concern with viewing the people or events as they 'naturally' occur. Only in this way, some qualitative researchers argue, can one fully and accurately describe and understand behaviour, beliefs, values, social interactions and the like.

Theorising

Qualitative researchers are often just as likely as those using quantitative methods to be interested in testing preformed theories. None the less, one of the advantages of some qualitative approaches is that they are more likely to attempt to gain insights into some phenomenon as they develop our conceptual understanding. Qualitative researchers sometimes seek to be 'taught by the world' to a far greater extent than quantitative researchers. They can look for evidence based on observation consistent with their theories, but they can also refine their theories as they make their observations.

Sampling

Qualitative researchers also differ from their quantitatively oriented colleagues in that they are less concerned with generalising conclusions to large populations and more concerned with gaining insights into specific cases from which they can construct an understanding (rather than a statistical explanation) of broad phenomena. As a result, they use very different sampling methods from those we describe in the quantitative methods chapters below.

In some forms of qualitative research, the sample of cases is allowed to 'emerge' as the study progresses. That is, researchers may select an initial case to observe and then let what they learn from those observations determine whom or what they observe next. This strategy reflects their belief that we can determine where to look for the answers we seek only after gaining a partial understanding of the subject by direct experience with it. This is consistent with qualitative researchers' view that each case is unique and should not be treated in a standardised way (as is done in quantitative research).

Case studies

Qualitative researchers can also use case studies to look at outliers or unrepresentative cases which can yield rich insights missed by conventional quantitative or qualitative approaches. To illustrate, a qualitatively oriented scholar might try to understand the fundamental assumptions that constitute 'political participation', not by surveying a representative sample of 'ordinary' citizens, but by conducting in-depth interviews with people who do not share these assumptions and reject the dominant approach to political participation. By understanding the political approach of those missed by traditional methods, the researcher would hope to see how assumptions of the prevailing ideas of political participation underlie the majority's thinking about politics.

In quantitative research, sampling is often based on the logic of probability and designed to produce statistical representativeness. In qualitative research, the **case study** is the most frequently used. This method is common in comparative politics and international relations research and is most often applied to areas of research in which there are small numbers of cases, the so-called, **small-'n'** (number) studies, with the smallest as n = 1. Case studies can be contrasted with quantitative research which is applied to issues involving large amounts of data such as votes in national elections, responses to public opinion polls, roll call votes in legislatures, parliamentary committee decisions and other settings in which either large numbers of individuals are involved or large numbers of decisions are made. This data can be counted and statistically analysed. The reason case studies are so important is that there are many issues in politics for which large numbers of cases do not exist and so are not amenable to statistical analysis.

The number of cases of postwar prime ministers, twentieth-century presidents, countries of the EU or acts of genocides are necessarily few. In some instances, a student or researcher will want to examine a single case in detail in order to understand the dynamics of the process. Most case studies, however, are seen as important as part of a larger universe of cases relevant to theories of politics. There are many types of case studies, but the two most important are *theory building* and *theory testing*. Theory building case studies are used when there is no existing literature or theory applicable to the case or cases. Often, similar cases are examined in detail to inductively define key similarities and differences. The second type of case study is theory testing – case studies can also be used to test theories. Individual cases can be examined in detail to determine whether the theory unfolds in the detail of the case as predicted by the theory, and if not, why not. Demanding tests are better for theory testing and development, so cases must be selected with these tests in mind.

The distinction between **'most-likely'** and **'least-likely' case studies** are useful in this context. For example, it can be helpful to examine cases that are 'most likely' to support the theory but do not. For example, a theory may state that big businesses with extensive political connections are able to influence government policy in their favour. However, you may find a number of cases where major businesses were unable to block or modify legislation that they strongly opposed. It was 'most likely' that these business would win, but they did not. The fact that such cases seem to contradict the theory makes them good candidates for intensive analysis. The question is: Why did the theory not match the case? Similarly, a 'least-likely' case study can help to test a theory because despite its being unlikely to fit the theoretical criteria, in fact it does. For example, a theory may state that politically inexperienced citizens have little success in overturning local council decisions. However, you may find a case where a group of politically inexperienced citizens do just that. It was 'least likely' for the citizens to succeed but they did. In such cases, the reasons need to be explored in some detail to understand the inability of the theory to explain or predict the outcome accurately.

One common problem with case studies is that a case is selected because it suits the interests of the investigator. It has already been noted that cases which already seem to support a theory are not good candidates for case study research as it is unlikely that new and interesting results will emerge. Investigators also often focus on a particular case because they are familiar with it from their own personal background. It is not uncommon for researchers to study a country they have visited or where they have a family connection. There is nothing inherently wrong with studying a case about which one has considerable personal knowledge, but there is a danger of the theory being selected because it fits the case rather than the case selected because it is a rigorous test of the theory. Care must be taken to think about the case and its relationship to a theory independently of one's desire to focus on that particular case.

Data collection

The most obvious differences between qualitative and quantitative methods appear during the data collection stage. On the surface, there is the fact that data in qualitative research usually consist of words (or sounds and images translated into words) rather than numbers. This data comes in the form of interview transcripts and documents, official and unofficial.

None the less, both quantitative and qualitative research methods require data to be collected. In quantitative research the data is numerical. It can be collected from existing statistics, such as income data, or it can be created by putting data into numerical categories, such as coding political party affiliations with a number and entering the number into a database. Quantitative data must also be categorised. The types of discourse about politics are put in categories, for example, such as confrontational or accommodating. All research requires some categorisation and simplification of the data in order to find patterns of political phenomena. Even if the uniqueness of each case underlying the data should not be ignored, the features it shares with similar cases should not be overlooked either.

Data analysis

In quantitative studies, data analysis is planned in advance so that data can be obtained in the necessary form. The analysis is then carried out after all the data are gathered. The data are then statistically tested to see if there are correlations between variables or significant differences between groups based on set numerical criteria.

In studies using qualitative methods, data collection and analysis generally proceed together. For those methods of qualitative research which consist primarily of observing and recording those observations, the very act of deciding what to pay attention to and how to record it involves some analysis.

To illustrate the interaction between observation and analysis, consider a qualitative researcher who seeks to understand the political power structure in a voluntary organisation by observing its meetings. This observer will see, hear and feel a great deal at each meeting – for example, the temperature in the room, noises from outside, whether or not people bring small children to the meeting – but may regard most of it as irrelevant to the research. However, some seemingly irrelevant things may be important in understanding the power structure. Deciding whether to record and how to describe such things as what clothes different people wear to the meeting, the order in which they arrive or the tone of voice they use in asking questions involves deciding what each of these things means in the context of the study. That requires on-the-spot analysis as well as when writing up the notes later.

Failing to recognise the importance of an event when it is observed or transcribed can lead to a failure to understand accurately the subject under study. Thus, some level of analysis must begin immediately. As a result, qualitative researchers often modify their data collection techniques in the course of the project as a result of new insights gained from this early analysis.

In qualitative analyis, however, the simple fact that one type of phenomena seems to be related to another is not taken at face value. Qualitative case studies usually engage in **process tracing**. This involves the use of evidence in a case study to make detailed links between independent and dependent variables in ways that statistical 'inference' cannot. In order to provide evidence that a chain of events is an accurate portrayal of the links between independent and dependent variables, detailed evidence supporting the logic of a relationship between the links in the causal chain must be considered and weighed against competing evidence to make the strongest argument for a particular sequence of events.

Another distinction between qualitative and quantitative research is the use of computerised data analysis. With large numeric datasets, computers are central to most quantitative analysis. Qualitative researchers are far less likely to make much or any use of them because the form of data they have (narratives) does not lend itself to computerised manipulation. A number of computer programs have been developed to assist in the analysis of qualitative data, so this distinction is not as stark as it was previously. However, it is highly unlikely that computerised analyses will ever be used as extensively in the interpretation of qualitative data as they are in quantitative research.

Standards of evidence

Quantitative researchers are usually able to employ some well-established rules of analysis in deciding what is valid evidence for or against their theory. These include such tools as measures of statistical significance and statistical tests of validity, as well as formal logic. Qualitative researchers generally lack this type of commonly agreed-to 'objective' tool. At the same time, qualitative researchers must persuade those assessing their research that the observations they have made are adequate to support the arguments they make. There must be a form of validity in the sense that the data collected are consistent with what the researcher says has happened. They must rely on their ability to present a clear description, offer a convincing analysis and make a strong argument for their interpretation to establish the value of their conclusions. Advocates of qualitative methods argue that this is an inevitable result of seeking to deal with the richness of complex realities rather than abstracting artificially constructed pieces of those realities for quantitative analysis. Critics of their approach contend that the vagueness and situational nature of their standards of evidence make it difficult (if not impossible) to achieve consensus on what really happened.

Reporting the results

Reports of quantitative research usually rely heavily on presentations of numerical data to make the case for the interpretations offered, whereas reports of qualitative research usually consist primarily or entirely of narratives describing and interpreting what was observed.

More substantively, reports of qualitative projects often include quotations from interviews or documents, or present the 'stories' they told the researcher about their 'lived experience'. This is necessary not only to capture the full complexity of the subject matter, but also to give readers a way to judge the validity of the researcher's interpretations (as explained in the discussion of rules of evidence above). Accordingly, the process of writing the report is even more crucial to qualitative projects than to quantitative ones. Qualitative researchers must be highly concerned with avoiding even unconscious bias in deciding what evidence (quotations, observations etc.) to include in the report if they are to give other scholars a chance to critically evaluate their conclusions.

Different methods for different questions?

There are disagreements about many aspects or applications of all types of research methods. In most cases, these disagreements arise from a sincere desire to make research as accurate and valuable as possible. Such debates usually have the positive effect of making all researchers examine their methods and conclusions very carefully, and thus produce better research.

Most empirical researchers work primarily with either qualitative or quantitative methods but recognise value in the other approach. The differences between the two traditions can often be resolved by using the insights provided by both to gain a more complete understanding of a subject, or by using results obtained with one type of method to generate questions to be explored using the other. In some cases, the two types of methods can even be used as complements to each other in a single study, with the results from each approach providing a form of validation for findings generated from the other. Scholars who take this position do not feel that qualitative and quantitative methods are fundamentally at odds.

In creating our research design, we choose from a wide variety of research options. Although external validity is emphasised in quantitative research, a deeper knowledge of our research observations' meaning (that is, internal validity) is emphasised in qualitative research. Rather than automatically choosing one over the other, our research benefits most from a design approach that incorporates multiple methods, where appropriate.

Summary points

- A clearly constructed research plan enables you to evaluate your project's feasibility and its measurement qualities.
- An explanatory research plan clearly states your theory, hypotheses, relevant literature, variable operationalisation and measurement, data source(s) and data analysis techniques.
- Qualitative methods differ from quantitative methods in the nature of the theories they examine; the ways they collect, record and analyse data; the standards of evidence they apply; and the ways they present their results.
- Qualitative and quantitative methods may be compatible with one another and can also complement one another to provide a more complete understanding of the political world.

Suggested reading and examples

Research examples

Rather than listing generic examples in the introduction to this section, each qualitative research chapter features examples related to its specific technique.

Methodological reading

Berg (2003) offers an entry-level text that provides a broad overview of qualitative methods. The handbook edited by Denzin and Lincoln (2000) provides a collection of readings that illustrate the various paradigms for doing qualitative work, the strategies developed for studying people in their natural setting, and a variety of techniques for collecting, analysing, interpreting and reporting qualitative findings. In *Interpreting Qualitative Data: Methods for Analysing Talk, Text and Interaction*, Silverman (2001) examines the challenges of analysing qualitative data. Merging qualitative and quantitative methods, Creswell (2002) makes the case for research designs that combine the best of both techniques.

Those interested in pursuing qualitative research will find like-minded individuals in the Organised Section on Qualitative Methods of the American Political Science Association (APSA). The Section publishes a semiannual newsletter (*Qualitative Methods*), which features discussion of current topics in the field as well as research notes utilising qualitative methods. Information on membership of the Section may be obtained from the APSA (www.apsanet.org).

Software

Arguably, two of the most popular programs among academics (and others) for the analysis of qualitative data are *Atlas.ti* developed by Scientific Software Development (www.atlasti.com) and *NVivo* developed by Qualitative Solutions and Research (www.qsrinternational.com). Each of these programs offers a platform for the transcription, viewing, grouping and analysis of textual or visual data gathered in the course of qualitative research. As an added bonus for prospective users of these programs, many colleges and universities teach short training courses on using the programs and offer discounted pricing for the software. The manufacturers typically also offer trial versions and tutorials for those considering a purchase.

References

Berg, Bruce L. 2003. *Qualitative Research Methods for the Social Sciences*, 5th edn. Boston, MA: Allyn & Bacon.
Creswell, John W. 2002. *Research Design: Qualitative, Quantitative, and Mixed Methods Approaches*, 2nd edn. Thousand Oaks, CA: Sage.

Denzin, Norman K. and Yvonna S. Lincoln, eds. 2000. *Handbook of Qualitative Research*, 2nd edn. Thousand Oaks, CA: Sage.

Nachmias, David. 1979. *Public Policy Evaluation*. New York: St Martin's Press.

Silverman, David. 2001. *Interpreting Qualitative Data: Methods for Analysing Talk, Text and Interaction*, 2nd edn. Thousand Oaks, CA: Sage.

Research exercises

1 Refer to the example of Operation Fright, used early in the chapter, and state one additional, plausible alternative explanation of why so few of those going through the programme are subsequently arrested. Explain in detail what modifications of the original research design described in that example would be needed to evaluate the accuracy of this hypothesised explanation using quantitative methods.

2 You are studying the relationship between inequality in the distribution of wealth and internal political violence in the nations of the world. You have operationalised inequality as the difference in the proportion of national income that goes to the top 20 per cent of income earners and the proportion that goes to the bottom 20 per cent of income earners. Political violence is operationalised as the number of incidents of politically motivated violence reported by the domestic press each year in each nation. Your operating hypothesis is: *The greater the inequality in the distribution of income, the larger the number of incidents of political violence.*

   List at least three hypotheses that represent rivals to this operating hypothesis. For each alternative you suggest, list each variable you will have to control in order to be able to rule it out as a valid explanation of observed events.

3 Using the examples in the two exercises above, create research designs using qualitative approaches to study the same problems. What are the benefits and drawbacks of both the quantitative and the qualitative approaches to the two problems?

Key terms

case study	most-likely/least-likely case studies	quantitative methods
descriptive research	observation point	research design
explanatory research	process tracing	small-n problem
exploratory research	qualitative methods	

6 Experimental research design

- How is experimental research design a 'model' of the scientific approach to politics?
- What design technique do experiments utilise to permit comparison and manipulation?
- In what way do the limitations of experimental design underline the difficulties of applying such a scientific approach to the study of politics?

Introduction

If the study of politics wanted to approach the scientific rigour of the natural sciences, it would have to rely on research designs which would more closely approximate the experimental methods in natural science. In reality, however, few of those who call themselves 'political scientists' use experiments to test the major theories of politics. None the less, experimental methods can and are used in political research and by understanding the benefits and limitations of experimental design, a better understanding of the ideals of research design can be gained. The purpose of any sound research design is to allow us to identify the effects of one variable on another with as much confidence as possible. Experimental research designs allow us to do this by providing an element of **control** over the conditions under which variables interact. This control is the key to experimental research design.

Control: An example

If several animals on a farm contract a disease after a new kind of feed is added to their diet, the farmer cannot feel sure that the new feed is the cause of the illness, because the animals may have been exposed to a variety of new substances (for example, insecticides in their water supply) at the same time. On the other hand, if an unusually large proportion of the test animals in a medical research laboratory contracts a disease after a new substance is added to their diet, the researcher is more likely to feel sure that the substance is the cause of the disease, because here it is possible to control the environment of the test animals and ensure that they are *not* exposed to any other new substances during the observations. The setting in which the researcher works permits an element of control, whereas the farm does not.

Research designs can be classified by the degree of control they allow. The basic distinction that is of interest to political scientists is that between *experimental* and *quasi-experimental designs*.

The *experiment* is the classic model of scientific proof. It is based on an assumption that changes in the value of one variable cause changes in the value of another variable (for example, *changes in temperature result in changes in the viscosity of oil*). The experiment allows us to test this assumption by exposing those cases or **subjects** manifesting the dependent variable to the independent variable under conditions that allow us to be relatively sure that any observed change in the dependent variable is a result of changes in the independent variable.

The basic **experimental design** involves an **experimental group** composed of subjects who will be exposed to the independent variable, or **stimulus**, and a **control group** of subjects, who are like the experimental group in all relevant respects but will not be exposed to the stimulus. The value of the dependent variable in each group is measured prior to introduction of the stimulus in what is called a **pretest**, and again after the experimental group has been exposed to the stimulus in what is called a **posttest**. The impact of the stimulus (independent variable) is inferred from a comparison of the pretest and posttest scores for each group. The greater the difference in values between pretest and posttest in each group, the greater the effect attributed to the independent variable. Table 6.1 shows the logic of the experimental research design. The advantage of this research design is that it allows us to achieve two conditions that facilitate valid causal inferences: *comparison* and *manipulation*.

The assertion that one thing has caused another is based on the concept of change. We must be able to show that some change has occurred before claiming that causal forces have been at work, and the idea of change implies comparisons. Also, we must be able to compare values of the dependent variable before the subjects have been exposed to the independent or causal variable with values of the dependent variable after such exposure, and if possible, compare values of the dependent variable after exposure with some indicator of what those values might be if exposure had never occurred. The experimental design, with its pretest–posttest procedure and its test and control groups, provides an opportunity for both types of comparison.

To feel confident that one variable has a causal influence on another, we must be able to know which subjects have been exposed to the independent variable and which have not in order to make the appropriate comparisons. The classic experiment provides this knowledge because it is the researcher who introduces the independent variable. The scientist manipulates the subjects' environment so that their exposure to the causal influence is not left to chance. In addition, the researcher manipulates the subjects' environment to ensure that all other possible causes of a change in the dependent variable are removed from the experiment at the time of the subjects' exposure to the independent variable.

A variety of other research designs build on the logic of the classic experiment, but add modifications that are especially relevant to social scientists. Social scientists' need for more elaborate research designs is largely due to the facts that (1) the objects of their research are often affected by the very act of studying them (for example, people's behaviour may change if they know they are being watched); and (2) the objects of their research are not static but ever-changing (for example, people's values may change as new situations arise). Two experimental designs developed by R. L. Solomon (1949) illustrate ways of dealing with these facts.

Illustrated in Table 6.2, Solomon's first design addresses a type of reactivity known as the **test effect**. When experimental subjects are pretested, it is always possible that their score on the posttest will be a result of both their reaction to the stimulus *and* a reaction to the pretest itself. Any difference between pretest and posttest scores that is due solely to reactions to the pretest is known as a

Table 6.1   The classic experimental design

Group	Time 1	Time 2	Time 3	Effect formula
Experimental	Pretest	Stimulus	Posttest	Effect (of experimental variable) = (posttest$_E$ – pretest$_E$) – (posttest$_C$ – pretest$_C$) where E refers to the
Control	Pretest	–	Posttest	experimental group and C to the control group

Table 6.2 The Solomon two-control-group research design

Group	Time 1	Time 2	Time 3	Effect formula
Experimental	Pretest	Stimulus	Posttest	Effect = [(posttest$_E$ − pretest$_E$) −
Control 1	Pretest	–	Posttest	(posttest$_{C1}$ − pretest$_{C1}$)] −
				(posttest$_E$ − posttest$_{C2}$)
Control 2	–	Stimulus	Posttest	

test effect. If we are to get an accurate picture of the impact of the stimulus on behaviour, we must be able to remove this test effect from the scores. The **Solomon two-control-group research design** in Table 6.2 allows us to do this.

This design is just like the classic experiment except that a third group is added. The third group (Control 2) receives the stimulus and posttest, but no pretest. Though changes from pretest scores to posttest scores in the experimental group can be due to both the pretest and the stimulus, changes from pretest scores to posttest scores in Control 1 can be due only to the pretest and in Control 2 only to the stimulus. If we can assume that all groups have had essentially the same value on the dependent variable initially and have reacted to the stimulus in the same way, then the difference in the posttest scores of the experimental group and Control 2 represents the test effect. The effect of the independent variable (stimulus) alone can then be gauged by subtracting this test effect from the total effect of the experiment, which is computed by the same formula used to evaluate the results of the classic experimental design. The effect formula in Table 6.2 summarises this logic algebraically.

In addition to the test effect as an alternative explanation of observed changes in subjects' scores, there are other possible causes of change in the groups' scores on the dependent variable (DV) from pretest to posttest. One is the influence of *external factors* not under the control of the experimenter. Another is natural changes in the subjects that proceed independently of the experiment (such as ageing – in long-term experiments – or mental fatigue). The impact of such erroneous factors can be judged (and therefore ruled out as a rival explanation of the experiment's results) by use of the **Solomon three-control-group research design**, depicted in Table 6.3.

This design adds a third control group, which receives neither pretest nor stimulus. Any difference in pretest and posttest scores in this group can be due only to the influence of extraneous factors. If we can subtract this change from the effect of the experiment, we can remove from our results the effects of extraneous factors and changes in the respondents, and can hope to rule out the alternative hypothesis that it is these influences rather than the independent variable that have caused the change in the experimental group's score from Time 1 to Time 3.

Table 6.3 The Solomon three-control-group research design

Group	Time 1	Time 2	Time 3	Effect formula
Experimental	Pretest	Stimulus	Posttest	Effect = [(posttest$_E$ − pretest$_E$) −
Control 1	Pretest	–	Posttest	(posttest$_{C1}$ − pretest$_{C1}$)] −
Control 2	–	Stimulus	Posttest	[(posttest$_E$ − posttest$_{C2}$) +
				(posttest$_{C3}$ − pretest$_E$)]
Control 3	–	–	Posttest	

The difficulty is that Control 3 is not pretested. How can we determine how much these subjects' scores have changed from Time 1 to Time 3? If all of our groups are essentially alike, we can assume that their pretest scores will have been highly similar and simply assign Control 3 a pretest score equal to the average of the scores for the experimental and first two control groups. We can then subtract this score from Control 3's posttest to obtain a measure of the change due to extraneous factors and natural changes in the subjects. With this change removed, we can see more clearly the effects of the independent variable on the dependent variable.

Assigning cases to groups

Each of the experimental designs described above is intended to provide a sound, logical basis for conclusions about the effects of one variable on another. To be successful in this, each design fundamentally depends on the assumption that all groups in the study are essentially the same with respect to those factors that might influence their response to the experiment. If we cannot assume that the groups are essentially the same, there is no logical basis for inferring that observed differences in their scores are the result of differences in the way they have been treated in the experiment (for example, whether or not they have been pretested), and we cannot make sound arguments about the causal influence of our independent variable.

Randomly assigning groups

In **randomisation**, a subject selected from a list of all eligible subjects is assigned to a group by a random process, such as use of a table of random numbers. True randomisation is *not* achieved by chance procedures (such as taking the first thirty people who apply for the experiment as the test group and the next thirty as the control group).

Randomisation has the great advantage of allowing us to feel quite confident that all of our groups are highly similar in *all* respects, not just in terms of the variables we identify as relevant to the experiment, because random assignment ensures that differences in subjects will cancel out *when large numbers of subjects are chosen*. Randomisation, then, allows us to rule out any alternative rival hypothesis that contends that some systematic difference in the groups has produced the observed results. It is *the key to successful laboratory experiments*. In Chapter 7 we discuss detailed procedures for the random selection of cases.

Assigning groups by characteristics

If it is not possible to utilise random assignment, it may be possible to minimise the likelihood of bias through two other systematic case assignment approaches. The first technique utilises **precision matching**. After deciding what characteristics might influence subjects' response to the independent variable, we select a set of subjects for the experiment. For each subject selected, we locate for the control group another subject who has exactly the same combination of relevant characteristics. The result is two groups that are identical in the characteristics that might influence their response to the experiment. Ideally, their pretest scores will be highly similar, and we can use the degree of similarity actually found when pretesting them to judge how well our matching efforts have worked.

There are several problems with this procedure. First, if we need to control for a large number of characteristics, it may be extremely difficult to find subjects who are matched in all the characteristics, as they must be in precision matching. We might, for instance, be able to find people of the same sex, age and race but have difficulty finding people who share those characteristics *and* have the same occupation, educational background and length of residence in the community. In addition, if we want to use a research design calling for more than two groups, it may be difficult to locate three or four subjects with identical characteristics. Unless we have an extremely large pool of potential subjects or a very simple experiment, matching may be impracticable as a means of assigning subjects to experimental groups.

A second method of obtaining similar groups is **frequency distribution control**. Here we do not match each subject with another on all characteristics. Rather, subjects are assigned to groups in such a way as to ensure that the groups have the same average characteristics and the same distribution of each characteristic. There may be no two subjects with the same combination of sex, age, race and occupation, but each group will have the same proportion of males and females, the same average age and so on. Moreover, the groups will have highly similar distributions of these characteristics among their members.

Frequency distribution control is more often practicable than precision matching, but it has two significant defects. First, it allows us to control for only one variable at a time. Frequency distribution assignment may produce, for example, two groups with equal numbers of subjects over forty years of age and equal numbers of women, but there is no guarantee that all the over-forty subjects will not be men in one group and women in the other. If it works out this way, the two groups will not be truly similar. Second, the method offers no control over any factors that influence subjects' reactions but have not been identified by the researcher. If our theory of the phenomenon under study is incomplete (and it almost *always* is), we may have failed to control the frequency distribution of an important variable. If the control and experimental groups happen to differ systematically on this uncontrolled variable, our results may be distorted.

Clearly, each of the techniques for assigning cases by characteristics is inferior to random assignment. Still, they may be useful when we are unable to use a random approach.

Political communication experiments

Political communications researchers are particularly likely to utilise laboratory experiments to study perceptions and effects of media messages. In these experiments subject treatments may include viewing or reading political content ranging from press releases to campaign ads to news broadcasts. The laboratory environment permits controlling exposure, as well as manipulating content message and formatting. Researchers may evaluate major content effects by varying specific text in ads, making the same advertisement carry a positive or negative tone, for example. Production effects may include controlling for male or female advertising voice-overs, evaluating the type of photos or colours of circulars. All of this research assumes that certain types of images or messages may differentially influence citizens.

Field experiments and nonexperimental designs

Political scientists seldom work in laboratories, due to the nature of their subject matter. Rather, these researchers often observe events in natural settings, where they can exercise less control over the factors that might influence the results of the study. In cases where researchers can manipulate the independent variable and control subjects' exposure but cannot control other aspects of the situation, they may conduct **field experiments**.

Field experiments

In recent years, interest in political science field experiments has grown, largely driven by community political mobilisation experiments. Campaigns are increasingly dependent upon electronic communications (i.e., televised ads) and direct-mail circulars, but little research has compared the relative effectiveness of various media. Others are more concerned with attempting to halt the widely noted decline in US voter turnout since the 1960s, using voter mobilisation. Field experiments are a logical means for assessing the general turnout or persuasive effects of mail, e-mail, phone and door-to-door canvassing. In a number of ground-breaking experiments conducted by Green and Gerber (2004), cities and communities were divided into quadrants, and citizens in each area were contacted using different methods (or no method, in the control condition). Not surprisingly, the researchers found that personal contact carried the strongest mobilisation or (candidate-specific) persuasive message.

The field setting makes it more difficult to isolate the effects of the treatment (contact) from other possible causes of changes in subjects' behaviour, but it has the distinct advantage of giving a realistic test of how mobilisation efforts would work in practice. A laboratory experiment, even if it could have been arranged, would not have been as satisfactory, because we cannot be sure that the results obtained in such an artificial environment accurately represent what happens in the outside world. This is a general advantage of field experiments over laboratory studies.

In field experiments, researchers use careful selection of the subjects and random assignment of subjects to the test and control groups to gain some control over background characteristics that may influence results. They also keep a close check on subjects' circumstances throughout the experiment to rule out alternative hypotheses that attribute observed results to outside events that occur during the experiment.

In many cases, political scientists cannot even manipulate the independent variable. You can imagine the difficulty of persuading some nations to have revolutions and others to postpone them in order to conduct a field experiment on the effects of revolutions on political development! The more important the subject under investigation, the less likely it is that we can control it. Under these circumstances, researchers may resort to the use of a nonexperimental design.

Nonexperimental research

In **nonexperimental designs**, the scientists can control neither the assignment of subjects to experimental groups nor the occurrence of the independent variable, and they cannot obtain pretest scores on the dependent variable. They may be forced to use what is referred to as an *after-only* design, in which a single observation is made after the occurrence of the presumed causal event. Sometimes a 'control group' of similar subjects not exposed to the independent variable (IV) can be added and differences in the scores of the two groups attributed to the IV. Such designs, however, provide no basis for sound inferences about the effect of the IV, since they do not allow us to rule out even the most simple of alternative hypotheses. We cannot, for instance, even be sure that the value of the DV we observe after exposure to the IV is any different from the value of the DV before that exposure. Thus, nonexperimental designs are suited only for descriptive or exploratory research, not for explanatory studies.

Quasi-experimental designs

Most of the research schemes employed by political scientists can be classified as **quasi-experimental designs**. In these studies, researchers cannot control exposure to the independent variable or the conditions under which it occurs, but they attempt to simulate an experimental design either by gathering additional data or by data analysis techniques. Properly constructed quasi-experimental designs allow us to proceed *as if* we had exercised all the control characteristic of a true experiment, and they provide a sound, logical basis for causal inferences.

Perhaps the most common type of quasi-experimental design in political science is the ***ex post facto* experiment**. In it researchers make a single observation and collect data about the independent and dependent variables and any other variables they feel should be controlled for. If we want to investigate the effects of college education on voting behaviour, for instance, we may conduct a survey of randomly selected subjects. Then we analyse our data in such a way as to determine whether people who are similar in other regards (for example, race, sex, age and region of residence) but have different educational backgrounds vote differently. There are sophisticated statistical techniques for doing this, but at the simplest level we may sort our respondents into contingency tables so that we can examine the relationship between education and voting in different categories of other variables, looking, for example, only at women who have or have not gone to college or only at men who have or have not gone to college.

This procedure allows us to act *as if* we had set up an experiment years ago in which we had assigned people to experimental groups, had exposed some to college education (the independent variable), and were now testing them to see what impact this had had on their voting.

The members of our sample who have had less than a college education but are similar in other respects to those in our sample who have had a college education serve as a 'control group'. Because there was no pretest, we cannot be sure that it is college education that has created any observed differences in voting, but we can use the additional data gathered in the survey to rule out some plausible rival hypotheses, and we can rely on random selection of the sample to cancel out the effects of variables not controlled for in the data analysis.

There are some situations in which we cannot use random sampling and cannot select comparable control groups. We will find this to be the case if our units of analysis are few in number or unique in many relevant regards. An example is the situation in which a city government wants to know what effect an administrative reorganisation has had on the costs of city services. To fulfil the request, political scientists might use another common research design known as a *time-series design*.

In **time-series designs**, the researcher makes several observations both before and after the introduction of a causal phenomenon and compares values on the dependent variable before and after. In our example, political scientists might use local government records to compare the per capita costs of local public services before and after the administrative reorganisation. (They will have to use per capita costs and control for inflation in order to rule out the possibility that either an increasing population or rising prices have affected the costs of public services independently of the impact of the reorganisation.) Figures 6.1 to 6.3 illustrate some possible results of this study.

In a sense, time-series designs use as a control group the *same* subject or set of subjects, but at an earlier time. If there is a clear trend in the values of the dependent variable prior to introduction of the independent variable, it is assumed that the trend would continue were it not for the independent variable, and as an indicator of the effect of the IV, we use the difference between observed values of the DV and the values that it would have if the trend continued.

Figure 6.1 illustrates this logic. If the data come out as presented in that figure, local public officials will be delighted to learn that not only has the reorganisation reduced the cost of services, but also has reversed the trend towards steadily increasing costs. The effect of the reorganisation in any given year can be measured *by the difference between the value predicted for that year from the original trend line and the observed value.*

If the data come out as in Figure 6.2, the predicted and observed values will be the same, and reorganisation will be judged to have had no effect on costs. Figure 6.3 illustrates a case in which the reorganisation has initially reduced costs but has had no effect on the trend.

Figure 6.1 Hypothetical trend in public service costs showing that reorganisation has reversed the original trend

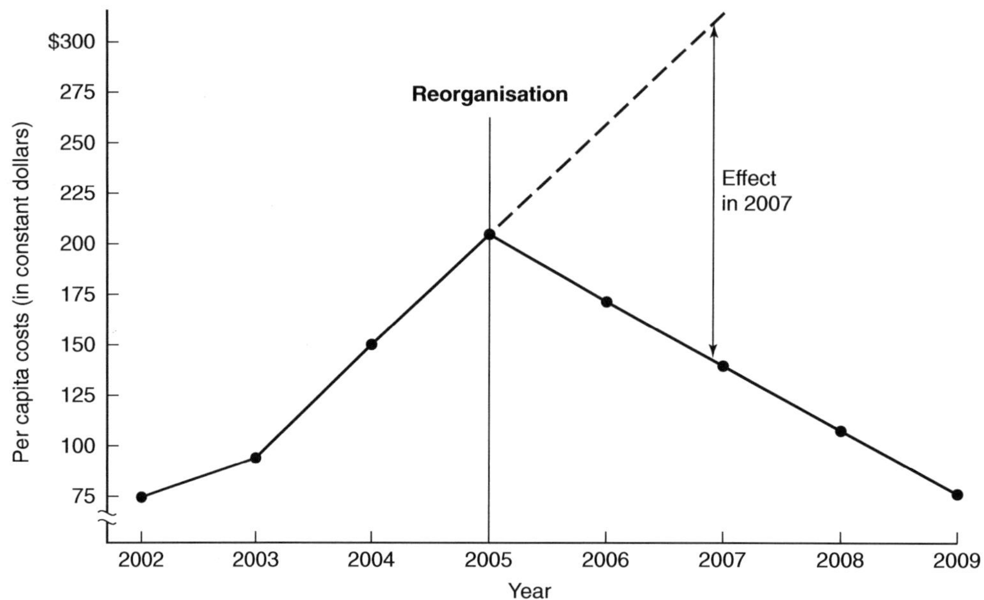

Figure 6.2 Hypothetical trend in public service costs showing no effect from reorganisation

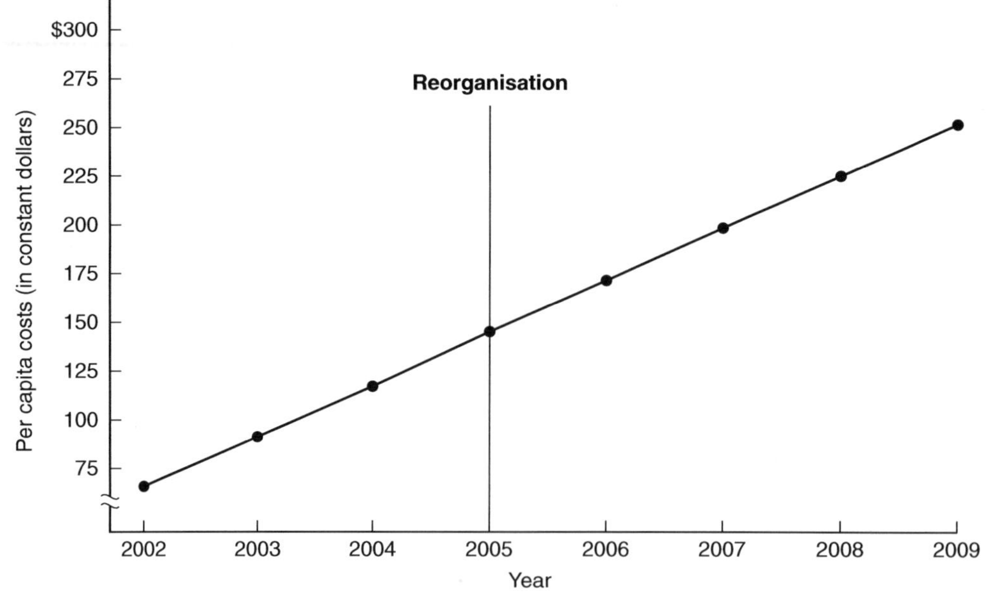

Figure 6.3 Hypothetical trend in public service costs showing that reorganisation has changed the level of costs but has not interrupted the trend

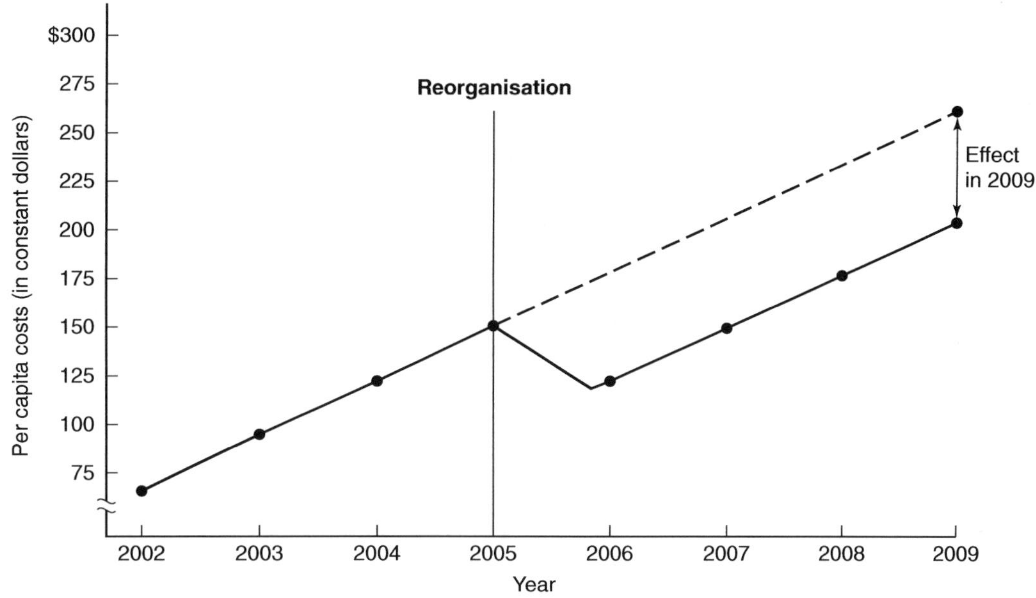

Fluctuating trends: An example

In most instances, the trend we are dealing with is not as clear and steady as in this example. For instance, let us say that one local authority, alarmed by a rise in delinquent court-ordered child support payments to single parents, applies to the government to pilot a programme which will more vigorously collect the owed money from absent parents and subsequently want to know the success rate. Figure 6.4 shows the kind of data that might be collected over a ten-year period. The values of the dependent variable (delinquent child support payments) rise and fall from year to year throughout the period. The researcher's task is to determine whether the *general* post-pilot scheme trend is significantly different from the general pre-pilot scheme trend. One way to do this is to compare the average annual delinquent payment rate prior to the pilot scheme with the average annual rate in post-pilot scheme years. (Both are nine in this example.) Assuming that the original trend would continue without a pilot scheme, we can use any difference between the two averages as an indicator of the impact of the pilot scheme on the *level* of delinquent child support. Another approach is to compare trend lines (represented by a dashed line in Figure 6.4) passed through the pre-pilot and post-pilot scattering of values for the DV to determine whether the general trend differs.

This example illustrates one of the important advantages of time-series designs. If we observe delinquent child support payment rates only in 1999 and 2001, as in a typical before–after study, we may conclude that the local authority pilot scheme has reduced nonpayment of child support. The time-series data, however, allow us to see the 1999–2001 drop in deliquencies as *a normal fluctuation around a general trend* (represented by a dashed line), which remains unaffected by the government action.

Despite this strength, time-series designs have a weakness. In many instances, there is no control group and therefore we cannot be sure what the effects of the IV are because we cannot be sure what the value of the DV would be without the IV; only a guess can be made that the original trend would continue. There are many reasons why this can be a mistake. One of the most important is *regression*

| **Figure 6.4** | Hypothetical trend of delinquent child support payments to single parents, showing no effect from the crackdown |

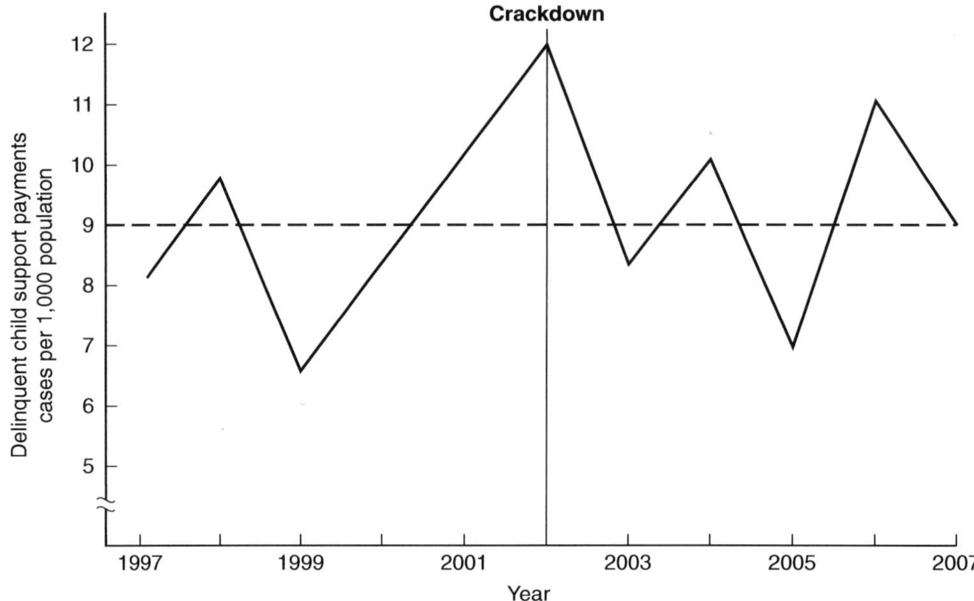

towards the mean. This is a phenomenon that poses a challenge to the validity of conclusions drawn from a variety of research designs.

Regression towards the mean is basically a process by which subjects who have extreme values on a dependent variable at any one time tend naturally to return to a more nearly average value on that variable in subsequent measurements *regardless of any exposure to some hypothesised independent variable*. If this regression towards the mean occurs at the time of a study, the researcher might mistake the natural regression for an effect of the IV. This can be a special problem in cases when subjects are exposed to the independent variable precisely because they have extraordinary values on the dependent variable.

In our last example, the local authority volunteered for the pilot scheme because of an exceptionally high number of cases of nonpayment of child support. This was a deviation from what was normal for the local authority, and it might have corrected itself even if the government had done nothing.

One way to rule out regression towards the mean as an alternative explanation is to employ a *controlled time-series design*. In **controlled time-series designs**, we gather data on a case or set of cases that are as similar as possible to our test case or group in all relevant respects but are not exposed to the IV, and use that case or group as a control in assessing the effects of the IV. In our example, we can select one or more local authorities very similar to the one conducting the pilot scheme that have not changed their policies towards collecting child support payments and observe their delinquency rates in the same years. Figure 6.5 shows some possible results.

By comparing the test (pilot scheme) local authority with a group of similar local authorities, we can see that, although the pre-2000 trend in child support delinquency continues unchanged in the test local authority, the average delinquency rate rises dramatically in the control states. This suggests that while the crackdown has failed to change the trend in the test state, it may be preventing it from being changed by the same events that are driving child support nonpayment rates up in other, similar states. In this case, we use the difference between the test local authority's post-pilot scheme rates and those of the control local authorities in the same year as a measure of the effect of the IV, on the assumption that the test local authority would follow the trend of its companion local authorities were it not for

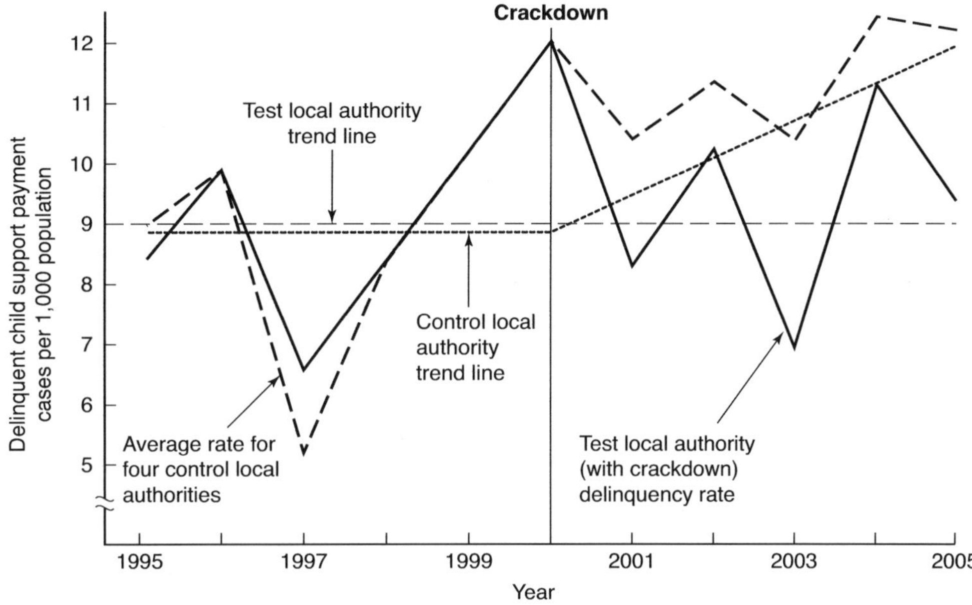

Figure 6.5 Hypothetical trend of delinquent child support payments in a test city and a group of control local authorities

the pilot scheme. In 2005, for example, the effect of the pilot scheme is assessed as three child support delinquencies per 1,000 population (i.e., subtract the trendlines: $12 - 9 = 3$).

Adopting a stronger research design would prevent us, in this example, from reaching the apparently incorrect conclusion that a programme that actually served as an effective deterrent had no impact.

Limitations

No matter how rigorous the research design, politics experiments suffer from significant methodological problems with research which limit the validity of the results. First of all, experiments do not reflect the complexity of real political situations. Precisely because they control for all but the experimental variables, other intervening variables which occur in real situations are not present. Even if a political relationship can be isolated, it is unclear that it will manifest itself in same way in the real situations. Field experiments help solve these problems to a degree, but not completely. It is also often the case that experiments only focus on trivial issues, such as factors which have only a minor impact on voting behaviour or political participation. A full understanding of politics often involves larger scale processes which cannot be tested experimentally. Finally, the results are often limited because the sample sizes involved are so small. Only repeated tests can ultimately confirm the results and this takes time and considerable resources.

Ethical considerations

Before planning a research project, the single overarching consideration in designing research is whether a given project will require a breach of personal or professional ethics. Perceived past abuses of human subjects by researchers in the social sciences include Zimbardo's Stanford (University)

Prison Experiment and Stanley Milgram's work in *Obedience to Authority* (1974). Concerns about long-term harm to people involved with both of these experiments have made them emblematic of some of the potential dangers inherent in conducting social research. A film and a very informative website (www.prisonexp.org) document the former study, and the latter is described in a book of the same name.

Researchers causing what appeared to be unnecessary harm to human subjects led professional organisations to adopt recommended standards of research ethics and promoted guidelines to protect research subjects. Most forms of research that involve deception of human subjects are prohibited. None the less, all research on living human beings inherently manipulates expectations and invades the privacy of those involved to a degree.

Most universities have human subject research guidelines and you must seek approval if your research will involve human subjects. Before making an application, ask yourself: Do the benefits of this research outweigh any possible harm to research subjects? If your answer is not an unequivocal 'yes', then do not pursue your research.

Summary points

■ Laboratory experiments allow direct control of extraneous factors, by comparing groups that are exposed to a treatment to those that are not.

■ The difficulties in controlling the conditions under which politics is studied and the limited conclusions which can normally be drawn from politics experiment suggests that a purely scientific approach to the study of politics is limited.

Suggested reading and examples

Research examples

Results of field experiments comparing the effectiveness of voter mobilisation by mail, e mail, phone and door to-door canvassing are contained in *Get Out the Vote! How to Increase Voter Turnout* (Green and Gerber 2004). In the history of psychological experiments, none is more infamous than Stanley Milgram's 1961 laboratory experiments in which many participants were convinced that they had physically harmed other people or even killed them, after being told to do so by an authority figure. His work is documented in *Obedience to Authority* (1974). Decades after his death, Milgram's work continues to generate controversy, much of which is compiled in a book by Blass (2000). Blass (2004) has also written an engaging biography of Stanley Milgram. In 1971, another controversial research project, the Stanford Prison Experiment, explored people's situational and group behaviour in detention settings (www.prisonexp.org).

Methodological reading

A wide variety of experimental and quasi-experimental designs is described in the *Handbook of Research Design and Social Measurement* (Miller and Salkind 2002). Many applications of experimental designs in political science can be found in *Experimental Foundations of Political Science* (Kinder and Palfrey 1993). A classic text devoted entirely to research design issues is *Quasi-experimentation* (Cook and Campbell 1979). Richard L. Solomon (1949) describes two of the most important and frequently used experimental designs, which he designed.

References

Blass, Thomas. 2000. *Obedience to Authority: Current Perspectives on the Milgram Paradigm*. Mahwah, NJ: Lawrence Erlbaum Associates.

Blass, Thomas. 2004. *The Man Who Shocked the World: The Life and Legacy of Stanley Milgram*. New York: Basic Books.

Cook, Thomas D. and Campbell, Donald T. 1979. *Quasi-experimentation*. Chicago, IL: Rand McNally.

Green, Donald P. and Gerber, Alan S. 2004. *Get Out the Vote! How to Increase Voter Turnout*. Washington, DC: Brookings Institution Press.

Kinder, Donald R. and Palfrey, Thomas R. 1993. *Experimental Foundations of Political Science*. Ann Arbor: University of Michigan Press.

Milgram, Stanley. 1974. *Obedience to Authority: An Experimental View*. New York: Harper & Row.

Miller, Delbert C. and Salkind, Neil. 2002. *Handbook of Research Design and Social Measurement*, 6th edn. Thousand Oaks, CA: Sage.

Solomon, Richard L. 1949. 'Extension of control group design'. *Psychological Bulletin*, vol. 46 (January), pp. 137–50.

Research exercises

1 You want to evaluate the effects of a film about race relations on the levels of racial prejudice held by the film's viewers. Assume that you can select subjects from a pool of 300 college students who have volunteered to take part in scientific experiments. Describe the research design you would use to determine the film's effects on racial prejudice if you wanted to maximise your confidence in the validity of your results.

Key terms

control

control group

controlled time-series designs

experimental design

experimental group

ex post facto experiment

field experiments

frequency distribution control

nonexperimental designs

posttest

precision matching

pretest

quasi-experimental designs

randomisation

regression towards the mean

Solomon three-control-group research design

Solomon two-control-group research design

stimulus

subjects

test effect

time-series designs

Part III

Quantitative data

7 Who, what, where, when: the problem of sampling

- What is a sample?
- What constitutes a representative sample?
- How is a representative sample selected?
- How many cases must be selected before a sample is representative?

Introduction

Every ten years, the Office for National Statistics of the British government conducts a census of England and Wales in an attempt to identify, count and measure certain characteristics of every individual living in the two countries at a given time. In the 2001 census, forms were sent to approximately 60 million people and 24 million households, and it took around ten months to collect all the information. The cost and time expended to carry out a census is enormous.

Needless to say, few politics researchers are able to marshal such vast resources in pursuing their own research interests. Yet the objects of those interests may be, for all practical purposes, equally numerous: 27,000,000 voters, 500,000,000 residents of Western democracies, 100,000 documents – each might be the focus of political research, yet each consists of far too many individual cases to permit a comprehensive analysis. Political scientists and many other researchers find it necessary to employ a *sample*, because it is impossible to collect information on the entire population to be studied.

In this chapter, we examine the uses and the mechanics of sampling – of choosing a relatively small number of cases that may tell us much about the larger population from which they have been selected. In doing so, we are concerned with **generalisability** – the ability to draw general conclusions based on an analysis of relatively few cases.

Defining a representative sample

We begin with three questions: What is a sample? When is it representative? What does it represent?

A **population** is any group of people, organisations, objects or events about which we want to draw conclusions; a *case* is any member of such a population. We should emphasise here that populations may consist not only of people but of anything we wish to study. Thus, we may speak of a population of governments, of decisions or of court documents as readily as of a population of unemployed males living in London. Whenever we refer to a population of any kind, however, all identifying characteristics of that population must be stated, and all members of that population must share them.

A **sample** is any *subgroup* of a population of cases that is identified for analysis. If we want to study and reach conclusions about the decision-making in local authorities, for instance, we might do so by examining such local councils of Nottingham and Birmingham rather than in those of all counties of England, and from these we might *generalise* our findings to the larger population from which the two have been selected. To study the issue preferences of voters in, say, the northeast of England, we might do so by asking questions of fifty call centre workers in Darlington and generalising these results to all voters in the northeast. Similarly, if we wish to measure the intelligence of university

119

students, we might test all members of the rowing team at the University of Cambridge and then generalise our findings to all UK university students. In each instance, our procedure is to identify a subgroup of a larger population; to study that subgroup, or sample, in some detail; and to generalise our results to the population as a whole. These are the basic steps involved in sampling.

It should be quite obvious, however, that each of these samples has a fundamental weakness. Although the legislatures of Nottingham and Birmingham are, for example, indeed part of the population of local councils, they are, for reasons of history, region and political culture, quite likely to operate in a manner very similar to one another and very different from the councils in other areas such as the Vale of Glamorgan and East Sussex. Although the fifty call centre workers in Darlington may indeed be voters in the northeast of England, they are, for reasons of socioeconomic status, education and life experience, quite likely to have different views from those of many other such voters. Similarly, although University of Cambridge rowing team members are indeed university students, they are, for a variety of reasons, likely to be different from other university students. In other words, even though each of these subgroups is, in fact, a sample, the members of each are systematically different from most other members of the population from which they are drawn. As a group, none of these is typical of the distribution of attributes (opinions, behaviours, characteristics) in the larger population with which it is associated. Accordingly, political scientists would say that none of these samples is *representative*.

A **representative sample** is one in which every major attribute of the larger population from which the sample is drawn is present in roughly the proportion or frequency with which those attributes occur in that larger population. Thus, if 50 per cent of all local councils meet only once a month, roughly half the bodies in a representative sample of councils should meet this often. If 30 per cent of the voters in the northeast work in manufacturing, then about 30 per cent of a representative sample of those voters should be manufacturing workers. And if 20 per cent of all university students are involved in sports, roughly the same proportion of a representative sample of university students should be members of sports teams.

In other words, a truly representative sample is a microcosm – a smaller, but accurate, model – of the larger population from which it is taken. To the extent that a sample is truly representative, conclusions based on a study of that sample may be safely regarded as applying to the original population. This extension of findings is what we mean by *generalisability*.

An example

Suppose we want to study patterns of membership in political groups among adults in the United Kingdom. Figure 7.1 shows three circles, each of which has been divided into six equal segments. Figure 7.1(a) represents the population in question. Members of the population have been classified according to the number of political groups (such as parties and interest groups) they belong to. In the example, every adult is assumed to belong to at least one and not more than six groups, and these six levels of membership are equally distributed throughout the population. Suppose that we wish to study people's motivations for membership, choices of groups and patterns of participation, but because of limited resources, we are able to examine only one of every six members of the population. Which individuals should we select for analysis?

The shaded area in Figure 7.1(b) illustrates one possible sample of the size we have specified, but one that is clearly atypical of the population. Were we to generalise from such a sample, we would conclude (1) that all British adults belong to six political groups and (2) that all group-related behaviour of the British is like that of those who belong to precisely six groups. Yet we know that the first conclusion is not accurate, and we may hold suspect the validity of the second as well. The sample illustrated in Figure 7.1(b), then, is not representative, because it does not reflect the distribution of

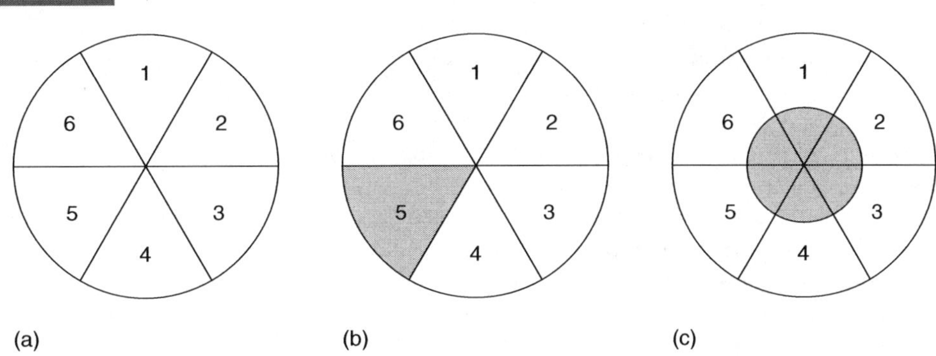

Figure 7.1 Sampling from a population with six population types

(a) (b) (c)

this *population attribute* (often called a **parameter**) roughly in proportion to its actual incidence. Such a sample is said to be *biased towards* members of five groups or *biased against* all other patterns of group membership. Reliance upon such a biased sample will usually lead us to draw erroneous conclusions about the larger population.

The *Literary Digest* Fiasco

The potential problems of biased samples were clearly illustrated in a public opinion polling disaster that befell a magazine called the *Literary Digest* in the 1930s. The *Literary Digest* was a periodical compilation of newspaper editorials and other opinion pieces that enjoyed a wide readership in the early years of the twentieth century. Beginning in 1920, the magazine conducted a large-scale, nationwide straw poll in which postcard ballots were sent to more than a million people asking them to state their candidate preference in the forthcoming presidential election. During a succession of previous election years, the *Digest* poll had proved so accurate that its release in October seemed to make the actual election in November anticlimactic. With such a large sample, how could the poll miss? Yet in 1936, it did just that in predicting a 60 to 40 per cent landslide victory for Republican candidate Alf Landon. In the election, however, Landon lost to incumbent Franklin D. Roosevelt by almost precisely the margin by which he was expected to win. So great was the shock to the credibility of the *Literary Digest* that the magazine was forced to cease publication shortly thereafter.

What went wrong? Quite simply, the *Digest* poll had used a biased sample. The postcards had been issued to persons whose names were drawn from two sources: telephone directories and automobile registration lists. And whereas this method of selection had not made much difference earlier, it did in the Depression year of 1936, when less affluent voters – those most likely to support Roosevelt – could not afford telephones, let alone automobiles. In effect, then, the sample used by the *Digest* poll was biased towards those most likely to be Republicans.

Avoiding bias

Returning to our illustration, compare the sample in Figure 7.l(b) with that in Figure 7.1(c). In the latter, one-sixth of the population is again selected for analysis, but each of the major population types is present in the sample in the same proportion in which it is present in the entire population. Such a sample tells us that one in six American adults belongs to one political group, one in six to two groups and so forth. It will also permit us to recognise other differences among members of our sample that might correspond with their varying numbers of affiliations. The sample illustrated in Figure 7.1(c), then, is a representative sample of the population in question.

This example is, of course, simplified in at least two very important ways. First, most of the populations that political scientists wish to study are more diverse than the one in the illustration. People, documents, governments, organisations, decisions and the like differ from one another on many more than just one attribute. Thus, a representative sample must be one that provides for *each* of the principal areas of difference to be represented in proportion to its share of the population. Second, more often than not the true distribution of the variables or attributes we wish to measure is not known in advance; it may not have been measured previously by a census of the population. Thus, a representative sample must be drawn in such a way that we have confidence in its ability to reflect accurately this distribution, even under circumstances when we cannot directly assess its validity. A sampling procedure must have an internal logic that assures us that if we *were* able to check the sample against a census, the sample would prove to be representative.

In order to provide both the capability to reflect accurately the complexities of a given population and some measure of confidence in their procedures for doing so, researchers draw upon certain techniques developed by statisticians. They do so in two ways. First, they follow certain rules in deciding which specific cases to study, meaning, which to include in a particular sample. Second, they follow still other rules in deciding how many such cases to select. Though we do not examine these various rules in detail here, we do consider their practical implications for political science research. Let us begin by looking at strategies for selecting the cases that make up a representative sample.

Procedures for selecting a representative sample

As we can see from the examples in the preceding section, not all samples are equally representative: Straw polls, in which individuals select themselves as participants and may vote for a favoured position or candidate more than once; street-corner interviews, in which selection of location and lack of control over passersby may strongly influence the findings; questionnaires of MPs, the results of which depend heavily on the views of the more articulate and more politically interested few who are most likely to respond; analysis of the foreign press, of propaganda messages or of some variety of published materials that is restricted to sources available in English, which may be systematically different from other sources of the same type; and blind sampling, in which a researcher simply leaves a stack of questionnaires at a given location with instructions for their completion and surrenders all control over the selection of respondents, all provide common examples of sampling bias. In part, these difficulties may be resolved by a careful definition of the population to which we intend to generalise. In the case of street-corner interviews, for instance, we might want to generalise only to all persons passing a particular location between 10 a.m. and 11 a.m. on 4 March. But in far larger measure, these difficulties may be resolved only by developing a systematic and relatively more sophisticated procedure for selecting the cases to be analysed.

Random samples

The guiding principle underlying such a procedure is that of *randomisation*. A sample is said to be a **random sample** (sometimes referred to as *simple random sample*) if two conditions are met. First, the sample must be chosen in such a manner that each and every individual or case in the entire population has an equal opportunity to be selected for analysis. Second, the sample must be chosen in such a manner that each and every possible combination of *n* cases, where *n* is simply the number of cases in the sample, has an equal opportunity to be selected for analysis.

It sounds a bit complicated and is, in fact, a more rigorous definition of randomness than we use in everyday conversation, but it is at heart a rather simple and straightforward notion. Random selection amounts to little more than selection by lottery. If we have a population of 1,000 persons whose behaviour we wish to examine by studying a representative sample of 100, we might write the names of all 1,000 members of the population on equal-sized pieces of paper, place them in a hopper, mix them well, then draw the names of the 100 persons in our sample. Through such a procedure, each individual has an equal chance of being selected (100 chances in 1,000, or 1 chance in 10), and every possible combination of 100 individuals has an equal chance of selection as well. It is this dual equality that makes the sample a random one.

Often, random samples are employed in studying populations that are too large to permit such a physical lottery procedure. Writing out the names of several hundred thousand cases, entering them in a hopper and drawing out several thousand, after all, would be a very cumbersome process. In these instances, an alternative, but equally valid, approach is employed. Each case in the population is assigned a number. The numbers of the particular cases to be included in the sample are then identified using a *random number table*, a portion of which is reproduced in Figure 7.2. The arrangement of numbers in such tables is usually created by a computer program called a *random number generator*, which, in effect, places a great many numbers in a hopper, draws them randomly and prints them in the order in which they were drawn. In other words, the lottery process still takes place, but the computer, using numbers rather than names, conducts an all-purpose draw. We are able to make use of this draw simply by numbering each of our cases.

A random number table, such as that illustrated in Figure 7.2, may be used in several different ways, each of which involves the combination of three decisions. First, we must decide how many digits we shall use; second, we must develop a decision rule for using them; and third, we must select a starting point and a system for proceeding through the table.

The first decision is simply a function of the number of cases in our population. If the population consists of fewer than 10 cases, we use single digits; 10 to 99 cases, double digits; 100 to 999 cases, three-digit combinations; and so forth. In each instance, we must take care to allow each of our numbered cases a chance to be selected.

Once this has been accomplished, we must devise a rule to relate the numbers in the table to the numbers of our cases. Two choices are available here. The easiest and most straightforward approach, though not necessarily the most correct, is to use only those numbers that fall within the range of our number of cases. Thus, if we have a population of 250 and choose to begin at the top left of the table and work down each column, we will include in our sample those cases numbered, say, 100, 084 and 128, and we will ignore cases numbered, say, 375 and 990, neither of which corresponds to any of our cases. We will continue this procedure until we have identified the number of cases needed for our sample.

A more cumbersome, but technically more correct, procedure arises from the argument that *every* number of a given magnitude (for example, every three-digit number) in the table must be used to

Figure 7.2   Portion of a random number table

10097	32533	76520
37542	04805	64894
08422	68953	19645
99019	02529	09376
12807	99970	80157

preserve the underlying randomness of the table. Following this logic, and again assuming a population of 250, we must break the range of three-digit numbers from 000 to 999 into 250 equal parts. Because there are 1,000 such numbers, we divide 1,000 by 250 and find that each equal part comprises four numbers. Thus, table entries 000 to 003 correspond to case 1, entries 004 to 007 to case 2, and so forth. In order to identify the case number that corresponds to an entry in the table, then, we divide a three-digit table entry by 4 and round to the lower integer. When this method is used the same portion of the table that we used earlier leads us to include in our sample cases 025 (100 ÷ 4), 093 (375 ÷ 4, rounded down, 021 (084 ÷ 4), 247 (990 ÷ 4, rounded down) and 032 (128 ÷ 4) and to ignore none of the entries in the table.

Finally, we must select a point of entry into the table and a system of use. The point of entry might be the upper left-hand corner (as in the previous example), the lower right-hand corner, the left end of the second row or *any* other location. This decision is strictly arbitrary. Once in the table, however, we must proceed systematically. We might select the first three digits of each five-digit set, as in the previous examples; the middle three digits; the last three digits; or even the first, second and fourth digits. (In the first five-digit set, these various procedures yield, respectively, the numbers 100, 009, 097 and 109.) We might work these procedures backward getting 790, 900, 001 and 791. We might work across rows, taking each digit in turn and ignoring the groupings of five (getting 100, 973, 253, 376 and 520 for the first row). The possibilities are many and varied, and each is equally appropriate. Once we have decided upon a pattern of use, however, we must follow it systematically in order to maximise the randomness of the entries in the table.

Variations on random sampling

As you can see from even this brief discussion, the drawing of a simple random sample may be no simple matter. In addition to other problems, which we will discuss, the technique involves a great deal of clerical work, especially when it is employed on a large scale. For this reason, random sampling procedures are often modified to enhance their manageability.

Systematic random samples

One common variation is called the **systematic random sample** and is used when we wish to study a relatively large population whose members are individually listed in some central location, such as a telephone book, a student directory, a list of registered voters, an index or a table of contents, an agenda or a membership roster. The procedure is as follows:

Count (or estimate) the number of cases in the population, and divide this by the desired number of cases in the sample. If we label the result k, we are saying, in effect, that we wish to select one case out of every k; or to put it another way, we wish to select every kth case. A concrete example should help to make this clear. Suppose that from a population of 10,000 public statements issued by the Ministry of Defence we wish to draw a sample of 500, and suppose further that we have a chronological listing that includes all 10,000 documents. To select a systematic random sample:

1   We divide the number of cases in the population by the desired sample size to determine k (in this case, $k = 10,000 ÷ 500 = 20$).
2   With the assistance of a random number table, we select a case number in the range 1 to k (in the example, 1 to 20) to be included in our sample.
3   We proceed through the listing of documents, selecting every kth (20th) case.

Thus, if k is equal to 20 and we use the portion of the random number table illustrated in Figure 7.2, entering at the top left, seeking two-digit numbers (k here lies between 10 and 99), and using only table entries that correspond to actual case numbers (that is, only those in the range from 01 to 20), the first case selected will be 10. We then include in our sample cases 10, 30 (10 + k), 50 (10 + 2k), 70 (10 + 3k) and so forth, all the way up to case 9,990 (10 + 499k). This upper limit of the sample may be stated generally as $j + (n - 1)k$, where j is the randomly drawn first selection and n is the desired sample size. In this way, we can use the random number table in combination with a centralised list to select a sample of 500 documents for analysis.

The technique of systematic random sampling has one major advantage over simple random sampling – ease of application to large populations that meet the criterion of central listing – and it has many potential uses. Still, we must keep in mind that systematic random sampling is less random than is a straight lottery selection, and it may therefore yield a less representative subgroup. We can see this at both the definitional and operational levels.

To begin with, recall that a random sample is one that permits every individual case *and* every possible combination of n cases an equal opportunity of selection. Systematic random sampling meets only one of these criteria. Because we begin to draw such a sample by using a random number table to select the first case, any case in the population has an equal chance of ultimately being included in the sample (though not necessarily on the first draw, because this is limited to the range 1 to k). However, because we then select only additional cases that are k numbers apart from one another, not every possible combination is allowed.

Thus, in the example where $k = 20$, any case from 1 to 20 may be selected to begin with, but once we select case 10, it becomes impossible for us to include, say, cases 11, 237 and 5,724, simply because those cases do not differ from 10 by a multiple of k. A systematic random sample is at best, then, only an approximation of a truly random sample.

Systematic bias

This observation becomes especially important when the list from which we are sampling contains a **systematic bias**. In alphabetical or chronological lists, this is generally not a problem, but in other kinds of lists it may be a significant one. Let us say, for example, that as part of a study of political socialisation, we wish to measure the intelligence level of a sample of students at a particular school where every form consists of twenty children. The school contains 100 forms, or 2,000 students in all. In response to our request, the head teacher of the school provides us with a register of all students in the school, from which we hope to draw a systematic random sample of 100. However, rather than an alphabetical listing, the register consists of a compilation of individual forms listed one after another. Moreover, each form is arranged not alphabetically but in order of the students' academic abilities, with the best students listed first and the lists continuing in order of decreasing accomplishment. In such a circumstance, if we take every 20th (2,000 ÷ 100) case beginning from a randomly drawn case 1, we will have a sample of only the 100 best (and, possibly, most intelligent) students in the school. If we randomly select case 10, we will sample only the middle range of students. And if we begin from case 20, we will sample only the worst students in the school.

In other words, an underlying bias in the list upon which our sample is based will lead to the selection of an unrepresentative sample. Ultimately, this will either preclude our generalising to the larger population or, if the problem escapes notice, will result in our drawing potentially incorrect conclusions. Although this particular example is an extreme one developed for the purpose of illustration, similarly biased lists do exist, and the researcher who employs systematic random sampling procedures must be aware of the potential danger.

Random samples, then, are an ideal to which we aspire and systematic random samples are approximations of that ideal that are often quite useful. Very often, however, a research situation does not readily lend itself to either technique. This is particularly true in the case of survey research. For one thing, centralised lists of the population to be studied are frequently nonexistent (for example, there exists no list of all UK voters or of all residents of a particular city), and even the number – not to mention the identity – of all the cases may not be known in advance. Thus, one of the major preconditions for simple or systematic random sampling – the existence of individual cases that can be identified in advance – may not be met. Moreover, even when this problem can be overcome, logistical difficulties and limited resources may render either of these sampling techniques impractical. This is true because random selection of individual cases requires that *specific individuals*, who may live great distances from one another or who may be very difficult to contact, *must be included in the sample*. In a strictly random process, no substitutions are permissible. These considerations can lead to massive diseconomies of time and money that might even be so great as to preclude conducting the study at all.

Cluster or multistage random area samples

Fortunately, an alternative technique has been developed that preserves the quality of randomness desired while overcoming most of the objections we have just raised. This technique, termed either **cluster sampling** or **multistage random area sampling**, has found wide application in survey research and may, by analogy, be applied elsewhere as well. The idea behind multistage random area sampling is that rather than identifying members of a sample as individuals, we identify them as residents of particular housing units. The reasoning here is that people move from place to place, whereas housing units remain fixed. In addition, the location of virtually every housing unit in the country is known and has been mapped, and each is part of a variety of geographically distinct areas including, among others, estates, census tracts, council districts, parliamentary constituencies, towns, cities and counties.

We shall see that certain types of these areas have characteristics that aid greatly in drawing a representative sample. For the moment, however, the point is that by focusing on the resident of a housing unit, a unit that is always in the same place, rather than on a particular individual, who may be more mobile, we are able to stabilise and localise our sampling procedure. In effect, we are simply redefining our population. Rather than speaking of all persons living in the United Kingdom, we speak of all residents of housing units in the United Kingdom. Because both groups are, for all practical purposes, the same, however, we may sample the latter and generalise to the former. We avail ourselves of the much simpler and, for reasons to be discussed later, much less expensive technique of sampling locations, yet we are able to generalise not to places, but to the people who inhabit them. This is the principal value of multistage random area sampling.

The procedure itself is illustrated in Figure 7.3. For the purpose of illustration, let us assume that we wish to conduct a nationwide sample survey. The same procedures that we set forth here may, of course, be modified for use on smaller-scale projects.

The multistage process

We begin with a map of the United States, which we divide into a large number of equally populated areas (also called primary sampling units, or PSUs). It is less work than it sounds, because the government has already made this division (or at least approximated it) in the form of 435 congressional districts, each populated with somewhat more than half a million people. We assign a number between 1 and 435 to each such district and, using a random number table, select several congressional

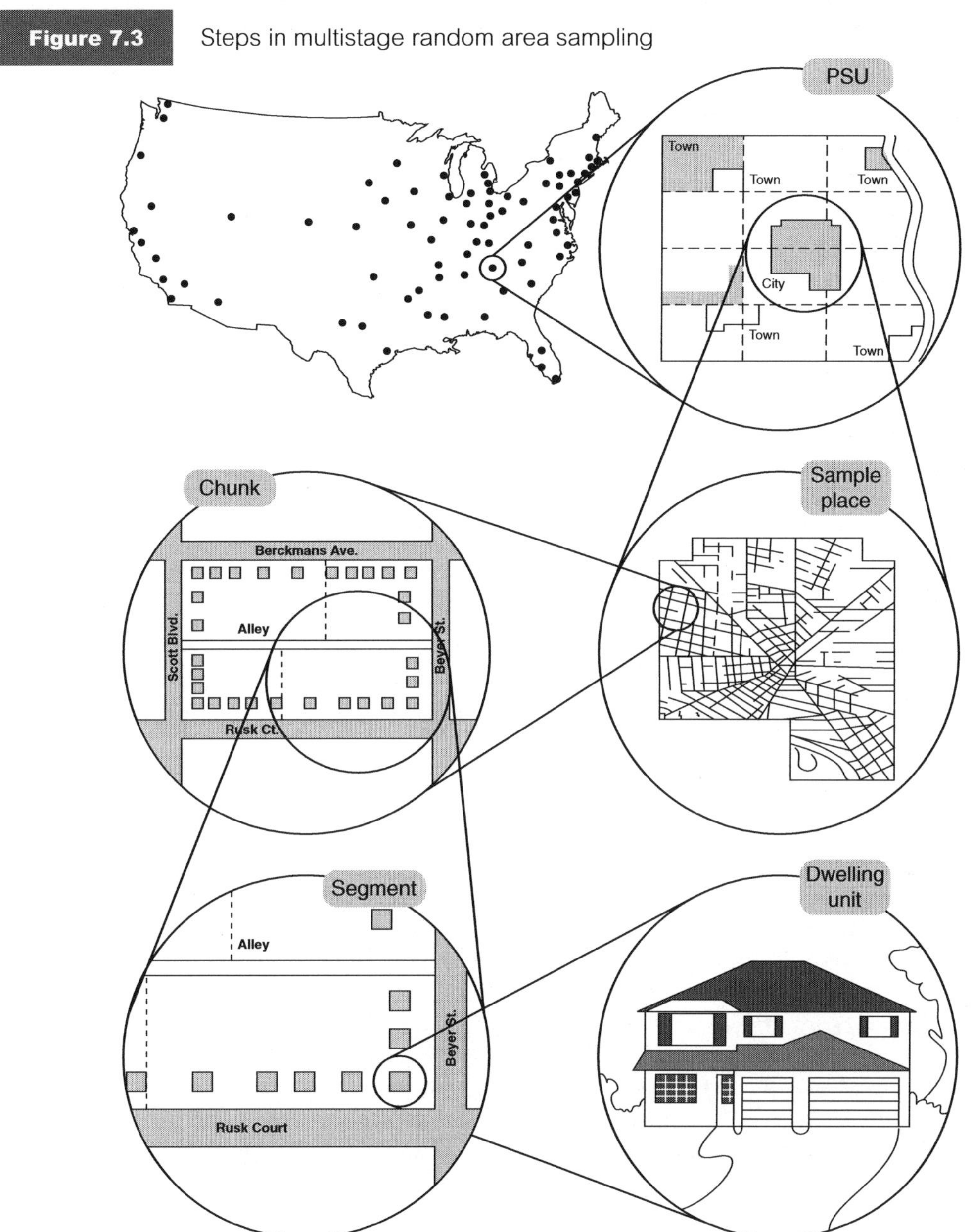

Figure 7.3 Steps in multistage random area sampling

Source: Survey Research Center (1969: 8–12). Reprinted by permission.

districts for analysis. The exact number selected is a function of both the ultimate size of the sample to be drawn and the available resources, but in general, the more districts selected, the better. At this point, the principal cost saving of the multistage random area technique becomes apparent, for rather than having to track down respondents all over the country, we may focus our attention (and money) on relatively few areas, most of which are of manageable size.

Once the subject congressional districts have been identified, each is further divided into still smaller but equally populated areas. In many instances, these may correspond to political boundaries, such as precincts or electoral districts, whereas in others we may find it necessary to create our own divisions. In any event, once these areas have been identified, one or more (depending again on sample size) are randomly selected within each congressional district by the random selection procedures outlined above. These precincts or other areas are then further divided, first into census tracts, then into blocks and finally into dwelling units (houses and individual apartments), with the random selection process employed at each stage of selection. In the end, we shall have identified a number of individual dwelling units that should correspond roughly to our desired sample size. The residents of these dwelling units will become the subjects of the research.

There is, however, one additional complication. Although, for a number of reasons, we generally wish to interview only one person at a given address, more than one person is likely to reside in any particular dwelling unit. Which one do we interview? Most researchers who use sampling procedures of this type provide their interviewers with a series of decision rules to apply at this point, the net effect of which is to create a set of quotas based on the age, sex, and/or family standing of the respondent. In one home, the interviewer might be instructed to seek out the youngest adult male, in another the oldest adult female and so forth.

We can see, then, that the term *multistage random area sampling* is truly descriptive. At each of several stages, equally populated areas are selected at random until, ultimately, individual dwelling units have been identified. In each instance, the geographic location is the subject of the sampling procedure, and at each stage, several clusters of locations are identified (hence the alternative term, *cluster sampling*). Only in the final stage – identifying specific respondents – does the procedure diverge from the principle of randomness, but at so local a level, and with the use of such carefully constructed quotas, that the effects on the representativeness of the sample are probably minimal. In many instances, multistage random area sampling offers a reasonable approximation of a truly random sample at a lower cost in time and resources.

Stratified samples

We should mention one other technique, though it is less a selection procedure than a strategy. This technique is known as **stratified sampling** and is used primarily when we wish to study in detail a population subgroup that is so small that a random sample will include too few members of that subgroup to permit detailed analysis.

Suppose, for example, we wish to study the hypothesis that prime ministers are more open with the news media during the first two months of their government (often termed a *honeymoon period*) than at all later times and that we wish to test the hypothesis by analysing the content of the transcripts of prime ministerial press briefings. Suppose further that we are able to identify 500 such transcripts for a given period, of which only 25 (or 1 in 20) are press briefings from the honeymoon period, and that we wish to sample 100 of these briefings. Using either a simple or a systematic random sample in this instance, we might expect that sample to include approximately 5 honeymoon-period transcripts and approximately 95 post-honeymoon transcripts. The very small number of the former makes a meaningful comparison very difficult, because it may provide too few examples to reflect accurately the range of prime ministerial responses to correspondents' questions.

Under such circumstances, to enhance the importance of a particular subgroup, we may choose to *stratify* our sample. In doing so, we choose not one but *two separate samples*. The first is a simple or systematic random sample of the smaller subgroup (transcripts from the honeymoon period) and is *larger* than the expected frequency of occurrence of the subgroup in the original sample (here, perhaps 15 rather than 5 cases). The second is a simple or systematic random sample of the larger subgroup (transcripts from all subsequent periods) and is *smaller* than its expected frequency of occurrence in the original sample (here, perhaps 85 rather than 95 cases). In the example, our sample can be described as stratified according to the date of the press briefing. The effect is to provide us with relatively more cases of honeymoon-period transcripts for analysis and comparison with those from later periods than we would otherwise select.

Three observations should be made at this point. First, stratification is not a substitute for simple random sampling or some other form of sampling, but an additional step used under particular circumstances. In effect, it is a second-order sampling procedure. In this context, stratification is frequently used, particularly by public opinion pollsters, at the late stages of a sample in order to ensure an appropriate balance of, for example, men and women. It is thus similar in purpose to the quotas that are applied in the final stage of a multistage random area sample.

Second, because it requires the drawing of separate samples, stratification may be used only when we are able to identify the relevant subpopulations *in advance*. In our example, this is not a source of difficulty, because before sampling, we can easily distinguish the honeymoon-period transcripts from those of later periods. In much survey research, however, when we may wish to stratify along less evident variables, serious problems can be encountered.

Third, because stratified sampling uses separate samples and because one can generalise from a sample only to the particular population (or subpopulation) from which it is drawn, we must exercise great care in stating our conclusions from a study based on such a sample. The reason for this is quite clear. In stratifying to increase the number of cases of a particular type in our study, we are, in effect, biasing our total sample in the direction of those cases. To overcome that bias, we must state our conclusions in one of only two ways. First, we may compare with one another our findings for the groups by which we have stratified (for example, comparing our findings for honeymoon-period briefings with those for briefings from later periods). Here we are simply comparing the results of separate samples without drawing any conclusions about press briefings as a whole. Second, we may differentially weight the groups by which we have stratified in proportion to their overall share of the population and then draw general conclusions about the population. In this case, we are taking advantage of our detailed knowledge about the smaller subgroup (honeymoon-period briefings) but are reducing its importance vis-à-vis the population of all press briefings. Under the latter procedure, a stratified sample may be used to approximate a simple random sample while providing more complete information.

Quota and judgemental samples

On occasion, we may find it helpful to select other kinds of samples. One example is the **quota sample**, in which the members of a population are classified according to several relevant characteristics (such as sex, age or party identification) and individuals displaying these traits are selected in proportion to their share of the population. Another example is the **judgemental sample**, in which the observer simply picks out those individual cases believed for some reason to be *typical* or representative of the population from which they are drawn. This is most common in studies of small populations and when only a very small sample can be drawn from a large population. It must be remembered, however, that such samples are in general less likely to be truly representative of their corresponding populations and are therefore usually less desirable.

Determining appropriate sample size

Having defined our terms and considered our selection procedures, we are now left with the question of how many cases to sample. In many ways, an answer to that question draws upon some sophisticated statistical concepts that lie beyond the scope of this text. However, much of the rationale underlying the determination of an appropriate sample size is more readily understood and is worth some attention before proceeding.

Homogeneity

Several factors help us to determine an appropriate sample size. One of the most important of these is **homogeneity**, the degree to which the members of a given population are like one another with regard to the characteristics we are interested in studying. If every individual in a population is *exactly like* every other individual, then by sampling only one individual we can obtain a truly representative sample. If, on the other hand, every individual in the population is *completely unlike* every other individual, we will be required to conduct a census of the entire population before claiming to have a representative group. In the first instance, the population is described as completely *homogeneous*; in the second, as completely *heterogeneous*. In reality, of course, most populations lie between the two extremes.

The closer a particular population is to homogeneity – that is, the fewer the differences among its members – the smaller the sample required to represent it. Conversely, the closer a particular population is to heterogeneity – that is, the more diverse its members are – the larger the sample required to represent it. This has implications in particular for stratified sampling, because by the very act of stratification, we create subgroups that are more homogeneous than the overall population. We can thus use smaller samples within strata than we could for the overall population without a loss of representativeness.

Number of categories

Similarly, the more categories (variables and response options) we wish to study, the larger the sample must be. This is true because increasing the variety and sensitivity of our measures will tend to accentuate the heterogeneity of the population we are studying. In other words, the more questions asked or the more types of answers allowed, the more likely we will be to find differences among our subjects. The more differences examined among our subjects, the more subjects we must examine to claim a representative sample.

Sampling error

Another important consideration is the degree of accuracy required. We use a sample to *estimate* the characteristics of a larger population, but any estimate is likely to include some margin of error. How much of this **sampling error** are we willing to tolerate? The answer is often determined by how we intend to use our results. If we are public opinion pollsters being paid to predict the outcome of a close election, we might be unwilling to accept more than the slightest margin of error. If we are political researchers attempting to spot general trends in attitudes or behaviours, we might tolerate considerably more. In general, the more accuracy we want, the larger our sample must be.

Related to this is a second question, that of just how confident we are that our estimates of the margin of error are correct. Most samples of a given size taken from the same population are very similar to one another and to the population itself, but once in a while a sample is drawn that happens, by chance, to be different. A sample of university, for example, might be far out of proportion to that group's true share of the original population. Thus, while each sample provides us with an estimate of the characteristics of a population, such estimates differ somewhat from one another and from the population as a whole because no two samples are *exactly* alike.

The problem is that in the real world, we do not always know the underlying population parameters our sample is intended to estimate, and we do not draw a great many samples. We draw only one. And though we may be able to check the face validity of our sample by comparing it with those used in other studies of the same or a similar population, *we cannot know for sure* that the sample we have drawn is not the odd one out – an unlikely yet possible unrepresentative sample. We know from a study of statistics, however, that we may reduce the likelihood that ours is the bad apple in the barrel by increasing the size of our sample. The more cases included, the more likely we are to have a truly representative sample – one that does in fact fall within the error range specified.

Confidence interval

We can make this discussion less abstract by considering the summary of sample sizes presented in Table 7.1. The table lists appropriate *minimum* sample sizes for several levels of sampling error and confidence for a *random sample* of a relatively heterogeneous population of more than 100,000 cases.

The table may be used in either of two ways. First, we may wish to specify the particular level of sampling error we are willing to tolerate and the confidence level at which we shall operate. Suppose that these figures are +/– 4 per cent and .99, respectively.

The first tells us that any measurement of our sample we might make is within 4 percentage points above or below the true distribution of the same attribute in the larger population. This range is referred to as a **confidence interval**. If, for example, we find that 43 per cent of our respondents in a survey report identifying with the Labour Party, we will assume that a full census of the population would show the true percentage of Labour identifiers to be 43 per cent +/– 4 per cent, or somewhere in the range from 39 per cent to 47 per cent. The table tells us (reading across at 4 per cent and down at .99) that to achieve that degree of accuracy with 99 per cent confidence, we must select a sample of at least 1,406 cases. To narrow the margin of error (increase our accuracy) to, say, +/– 2 per cent (that is, to refine our estimate to the range from 41 per cent to 45 per cent Labour), we have to increase our sample size to at least 5,625 cases. At both levels of confidence, the table clearly demonstrates that increased accuracy requires an enlarged sample.

Confidence level

The second number that we began with refers to the likelihood that our sample is in fact representative of the larger population within the degree of accuracy we have specified and is called the **confidence level**. In this context, .95 (95 per cent confidence) means that out of 100 samples of a given size that are drawn from the same population, 95 will meet this test for accuracy, and .99 (99 per cent

Table 7.1 Summary of samples sizes

Percentage sampling	Level of confidence	
Error tolerated	.95	.99*
1	10,000	22,500
2	2,500	5,625
3	1,111	2,500
4	625	1,406
5	400	900
10	100	–

*Rounded down from .997 in the source table for purposes of explanation.

confidence) means that 99 out of 100 samples of a given size drawn from the same population will be as accurate as claimed. The chances that any particular sample will achieve the desired accuracy, then, are 95 to 5 and 99 to 1, respectively.

As one might expect, for each level of sampling error the sample size required to attain 99 per cent confidence is substantially larger than that for 95 per cent confidence. Looking again at our Labour identifiers with a margin of error of $+/-4$ per cent, for instance, we find that a sample of 625 cases allows us to say with 95 per cent confidence that somewhere between 39 per cent and 47 per cent of the whole population are Labour identifiers, whereas a sample of at least 1,406 cases is required before we can make the same statement with 99 per cent confidence. In general, the lower the percentage of sampling error and the greater the level of confidence, the better a piece of research will be. By convention, a level of confidence of either .95 or .99 is acceptable in political science research.

This type of table may be used in a reverse manner. If, for example, we encounter a study that employs a sample of 2,500 cases, we may consult the table to ascertain the corresponding sampling error and level of confidence. A glance at Table 7.1 shows that multiple interpretations are possible. We may interpret 2,500 cases to yield a sampling error of $+/-3$ per cent at the .99 level of confidence, or alternatively, to yield a sampling error of $+/-2$ per cent at the .95 level of confidence. Either interpretation is equally appropriate, and the two together help to make clear the trade-off between accuracy and confidence. With the same number of cases, we may be extremely confident of a relatively less precise result or somewhat less confident of a higher order of precision.

Ideally, of course, we always prefer to operate with minimum error and maximum confidence. Unfortunately, practical considerations frequently intervene. A single personal interview in a survey project, for example, may cost as much as £100 or more in labour, transportation and other expenses. This means that at the .99 level of confidence, the cost of reducing our margin of error from $+/-3$ per cent (2,500 interviews) to $+/-2$ per cent (5,625 interviews) may be more than £300,000. In many instances, the difference in the quality of the results is not worth the added expense, and in far more instances, the money is simply not available. Limits on resources thus play an important role in limiting the size of samples. Most national public opinion polls, as well as major political science survey research projects, use samples of approximately 1,200 to 1,600 respondents. Such studies yield results to within 3 to 5 per cent accuracy at the .99 level of confidence and are regarded as both affordable and sufficiently precise.

One other point should be noted before concluding our discussion of sample size, though it is, no doubt, less obvious and less intuitively appealing than others we have raised. As an examination of Tables A.2 and A.3 in Appendix A makes clear, once it reaches a certain limiting point, the size of a population *does not* affect the size of the sample chosen to represent it. And though the proof of this assertion is beyond the scope of this book, its implications are not. In effect, this upper limit on sample sizes means that very nearly the same size sample may be equally representative of the population of Reeth in Swaledale, North Yorkshire; of London; of the United Kingdom; or of the entire western hemisphere, so long as that sample is properly drawn. Only for relatively smaller populations is population size a significant factor in determining sample size.

Ethical considerations

If you are using samples to generalise your findings to the overall population, it is important to remember that you must disclose how you selected your sample and how precise your results might be based on the particular sample used. The goal of such a disclosure is to allow other scholars to evaluate the overall representativeness and relevance of your findings.

The **Code of Professional Ethics and Practices** promoted by the World Association for Public Opinion Research (WAPOR) calls on researchers to disclose the following information about their samples and sampling procedures used: (1) a definition of the population under study, to which the results are to be projected; (2) the method used for sampling the population including type of sample and procedures used; (3) the steps taken to ensure the design was followed; (4) the degree of success in carrying out the survey design including non-response rate and a comparison of actual and anticipated characteristics; (5) the sample size and any procedures used to weight the raw data; (6) a copy of the questionnaire or interview protocol; (7) the training or guidance given to interviewers and coders; (8) the precision of the procedures used including sample error; (9) definition of which data are taken from part of the sample and which from the whole sample; (10) the purpose and sponsorship of the survey; and finally (11) the method, location and dates of data collection. (See the full version of the Code at http://www.unl.edu/wapor/ethics.html.)

Conclusion

An important point that is often overlooked by the novice political researcher is that *any* time you gather data by *any* method from *any* source, if you wish to generalise at all beyond the particular cases examined in the research, then the data set constitutes a *sample* and its constituent cases should be selected with an eye towards the considerations raised in this chapter. Whether the subject of the research is elections, political advertisements, news accounts, political jurisdictions, organisations or anything else, you must be aware of the importance of the selection process and its implications for the meaning and usefulness of your research.

Summary points

- A sample is any subgroup of a population of cases that is identified for analysis.
- A representative sample is one in which every major attribute of the larger population from which the sample is drawn is present in roughly the proportion or frequency with which those attributes occur in that larger population.
- A representative sample is one in which every major attribute of the larger population from which the sample is drawn is present in roughly the proportion or frequency with which those attributes occur in that larger population.
- Representative sampling is based on random sampling procedures, which ensure that (a) each individual or case in the population has an equal chance to be selected and (b) each possible combination of individuals or cases has an equal chance to be selected.
- Sample size depends on the homogeneity of the sample, the number of categories to be analysed and the desired sampling error and level of confidence.

Suggested reading and examples

Research examples

Discussions and examples of sampling procedures appear regularly in the pages of the academic journal *Public Opinion Quarterly*. The 2005 Special Issue (vol. 69, no. 5) of *Public Opinion Quarterly* contains an interesting series of articles on polling politics, the media and election campaigns.

Methodological reading

The statistical procedures underlying the determination of an appropriate sample size are discussed in a number of sources, including Levy and Lemeshow's (2003) *Sampling of Populations: Methods and Applications*, Thompson's (2002) *Sampling* and Lohr's (1998) *Sampling: Design and Analysis*. Several variations on sampling techniques are described, and their respective strengths and weakness summarised, in Miller and Salkind's (2002) *Handbook of Research Design and Social Measurement*.

References

Levy, Paul S. and Lemeshow, Stanley. 2003 *Sampling of Populations: Methods and Applications*, 3rd edn. New York: Wiley-Interscience.

Lohr, Sharon L. 1998. *Sampling: Design and Analysis*. Pacific Grove, CA: Duxbury Press.

Miller, Delbert C. and Salkind, Neil J. 2002 *Handbook of Research Design and Social Measurement*, 6th edn. Newbury Park, CA: Sage.

Survey Research Center. 1969. *Interviewer's Manual*. Ann Arbor, MI: Institute for Social Research, University of Michigan.

Thompson, Steven K. 2002. *Sampling*, 2nd edn. New York: Wiley-Interscience.

Research exercises

1 Using Tables A.2 and A.3 in Appendix A, determine the sample size needed to meet each of the following sets of criteria:

   a per cent sampling error, .95 level of confidence, population of 10,000;

   b per cent sampling error, .95 level of confidence, population of 50,000;

   c per cent sampling error, .99 level of confidence, population of 2,299,999.

2 Locate or construct a map of the parliamentary constituency in your home town showing all principal geographic or political subdivisions, then devise a strategy for a multistage random area sample of 1,000 persons from your parliamentary constituency. What level of confidence and sampling error will such a sample yield?

3 You are planning a study of student politics. Develop practical alternative strategies for sampling the students at your university, using each of the following: simple random sampling, systematic random sampling and stratified sampling (By what characteristic would you stratify? Why?); multistage area sampling; and judgemental sampling (What criteria would you apply? Why?). Summarise the advantages and disadvantages of each approach. Which would you recommend using? Why?

Key terms

cluster sampling	judgemental sample	sample
Code of Professional Ethics and Practices	multistage random area sampling	sampling error
confidence interval	parameter	stratified sampling
confidence level	population	systematic bias
generalisability	quota sample	systematic random sample
homogeneity	random sample	
	representative sample	

8 Survey research

- How is a survey planned?
- How are survey questionnaires designed?
- How do we choose the appropriate survey methodology?
- How is a survey conducted?

Introduction

Often the best (and sometimes the only) way to learn what people think or how they act is to ask them. Acceptance of this fact has made survey research one of the most fully developed and extensively used of social science methods. An understanding of survey research is essential to understanding a great deal of political science since 1930. This chapter provides an overview of what this method involves, when it is appropriate and what its principal strengths and weaknesses are.

Survey research is *a method of data collection in which information is obtained directly from individual persons who are selected so as to provide a basis for making inferences about some larger population.* It is important to note that this definition excludes 'surveys' not based on scientific sampling procedures. Public opinion polls asking for those with an opinion to phone or text their views and 'person-in-the-street' interviews, which are based on chance samples, provide no information other than that particular individuals were motivated to express their views and gave certain answers; there is no reason to believe that others would respond in similar ways.

The information collected in properly conducted surveys is based on careful and rigorous methods of collection. This information may be obtained by direct questioning through *face-to-face* or *telephone interviews* or by having the subjects complete *postal* or *self-administered questionnaires*. Those who answer survey questions are generally referred to as **respondents**.

Surveys provide five types of information about respondents: facts, perceptions, opinions, attitudes and behavioural reports. *Facts* include those background characteristics (age, occupation) and personal history (place of birth, first political involvement) that may be relevant to the interpretation of the other data collected. *Perceptions* are statements of what individuals know (or think they know) about the world, such as the names of public officials or the European Union's current policy towards trade with China. *Opinions* are statements of people's preferences or judgements about events and objects. Such questions as *Do you favour legalisation of marijuana?* and *Whom do you want to win the forthcoming local election?* tap opinions. *Attitudes* are relatively stable evaluations of and orientations towards events, objects and ideas. When we want to know about people's support for civil liberties or government regulation of the economy, for example, we are asking about the attitudes on which specific opinions are often based. *Behavioural reports* are simply statements of how people act (for example, how often they vote or read newspapers).

In survey research, concepts are operationalised through questions, and observation consists of recording respondents' answers to these questions. The method, therefore, is especially suited for studies in which individual persons are the units of analysis and the principal concepts employed pertain to individuals. If our research involves concepts, such as the average daily importation of foreign oil by the United Kingdom or the number of crimes committed with handguns each year, survey research is inappropriate, because average citizens are not likely to have the information we seek. If research focuses on the opinions, attitudes or perceptions of individuals, a survey may well be the best method of data collection. It is, however, a very expensive and time-consuming method. Therefore, researchers should be certain that there is not some other, less expensive way of gathering the necessary data before proceeding with a survey.

Stages of the survey process

Having decided to use a survey as a data collection method, we must now decide what steps to go through. Survey research can be divided into fourteen basic activities. In practice, more than one of these may be going on at any one time, and the researcher may, on occasion, move back and forth between activities as the survey develops. Conceptually, however, the stages of survey research can be described as follows:

1 *Conceptualising.* Specifying the purpose of the research, developing hypotheses, clarifying concepts and operationalising the concepts through survey items.
2 *Survey design.* Establishing the procedures to be used and deciding on the general nature of the sample to be drawn.
3 *Instrumentation.* Drafting the questions and other items that will appear on the survey instrument (the questionnaire or interview schedule) and planning the format of that instrument, as well as designing any visual aids or other devices that will be used.
4 *Planning.* Developing methods of managing the survey and anticipating the materials and personnel that will be needed.
5 *Sampling.* Selecting the persons to be interviewed according to the method that best fits the purposes and resources of a given study.
6 *Training or briefing.* Preparing interviewers, coders, or other personnel to properly contact respondents and administer the instrument to them.
7 *Pretesting.* Administering the instrument to a small sample similar to the larger sample to be contacted so as to ensure that instructions can be correctly interpreted and that items produce the desired type of response.
8 *Surveying.* Administering the instrument (by mail, phone or personal interview) to members of the sample.
9 *Monitoring.* Ensuring that the proper persons are being contacted as respondents both by requiring records of contacts and refusals, and by checking on the administration of instruments.
10 *Verifying.* Using follow-up contacts to make sure that interviews have actually been performed, that mailings have reached potential respondents, and that questionnaires have been returned.
11 *Coding.* Reducing to numerical terms the data collected.
12 *Processing.* Organising the data for analysis.
13 *Analysing.* Working the data with statistical and other tools in order to reach conclusions about their content.
14 *Reporting.* Summarising findings into research reports.

The remainder of this chapter highlights some of the primary points the survey researcher should take into consideration when engaged in each of these activities.

Conceptualising

In this stage, a general research question is reduced to a far more specific set of questions that can be addressed through empirical investigation. Decisions made in the conceptualising stage have important implications for the choices that are available in sampling and survey design. For instance, in deciding to whom our theory applies, we determine what our sampling frame should be. In selecting an operationalisation that requires personal interviewing, we are dictating the level of research support needed. Even when first thinking through the theoretical aspects of the project, then, we have to be sensitive to the issues of resources and accessibility of respondents.

Survey design

Most surveys either are exploratory, descriptive or explanatory in purpose. *Exploratory* surveys help us acquire information that can be helpful in formulating research questions and hypotheses more precisely when we know little about a phenomenon we want to study. *Descriptive* surveys provide precise measurement of variables that may be important in theorising, but provide no basis for making causal inferences. *Explanatory* surveys test causal hypotheses and help us understand observed patterns in terms of a theory. They must be designed so as to allow us to rule out alternative rival hypotheses. Data for each type of survey can be collected through *personal interviews, postal questionnaires, telephone interviews* or *self-administered questionnaires*. Deciding on the objective of the survey and choosing the appropriate data collecting method are the first steps in survey design. The purpose will be dictated largely by our level of theoretical and empirical knowledge of the subject. Which data collection technique is appropriate will be determined by the operationalisations we have chosen and by the resources that are available.

Cross-sectional surveys

We must next select a way to organise the survey. The basic choice is between *cross-sectional* and *longitudinal* designs. In **cross-sectional surveys**, data are collected from respondents only once. If we have a representative sample, this design allows us to describe populations and relationships between variables in those populations at a given time, but it does not allow us to say how the characteristics or relationships have developed or will develop over time. Cross-sectional surveys offer a snapshot of a moving target. They are best suited to exploratory and descriptive studies, but together with a strong theory and proper data analysis, cross-sectional surveys can provide some basis for explanation. For example, in a study of the relationship between personality and political behaviour, we may be willing to assume that a person's level of self-esteem is a relatively stable personality trait that precedes one's level of political involvement. If we find, then, that those with a high level of self-esteem tend to be more politically involved than those with low self-esteem, we might feel safe in arguing that high esteem leads to or causes high political involvement, even though we have data from only one time.

Longitudinal surveys

Longitudinal surveys are those in which data are collected from respondents on more than one occasion. The main types of **longitudinal surveys** are *trend*, *cohort* and *panel* studies.

In **trend studies** samples are drawn from the same population at different times and surveyed. *Different persons* may be included in each survey, but the results will be representative of trends in the *same population*, because, as was explained in Chapter 7, each properly selected sample will be equivalent to every other sample from that population. Thus, if we find different degrees of partisan identification in two samples of the same population surveyed at different times, we may infer that there has been a change in the level of partisan identification *in the population* during the time that separates the surveys. We might also explore changes in the relationship between variables through trend studies. If we find, for instance, that the relationship between gender and political activity is weaker in the second of two surveys of samples from the same population, we might conclude that there is a trend towards the breaking down of sex roles in the political life of that population.

Whereas trend studies are representative of a *general* population at different times, **cohort studies** focus on the same *specific* population over time. Members of the population sampled in trend studies will change with time, but cohort studies draw samples from the *same* population each time even though different members might be included in the samples. For example, we might want to draw a sample among asylum seekers citizens who legally immigrated to the United Kingdom in 2007 and sample that same group again three years later to study their adaptation to life in the UK. Though there may be some loss from this population as members die or move out of the United Kingdom, no new members will be added.

Both trend and cohort studies allow us to document change in a population over time, but because different samples are drawn for each survey, we cannot identify *which* members of the population are changing. This makes it more difficult to discover causal patterns. **Panel studies**, by contrast, use the *same sample at different times*. This allows us to see which members of a population are changing and to identify the characteristics or experiences that are associated with those changes; for example, we might interview the same sample of registered voters before, during and after an election campaign in an effort to determine what aspects of a campaign are most likely to lead people to change their choice of candidates.

This important advantage of panel studies must be weighed against some disadvantages. First, panel studies are very costly, because the expense of keeping track of sample members over time must be added to the costs of conducting several interviews. Second, there can be problems of reactivity of the type discussed in Chapter 6. The very fact that people are being interviewed, perhaps repeatedly, about a subject may cause them to alter their behaviour or attitudes with regard to that subject in ways they would not were they not being interviewed. This creates a kind of test effect that can distort results. At the very least it means there is a risk that the sample will become *unrepresentative of the larger population* by virtue of being included in the study. Third, *attrition* from the sample can compromise the validity of panel studies. Attrition occurs when respondents in the first wave of surveying do not respond in subsequent waves. If those who drop out of the panel share characteristics that are relevant to the study but not shared by those who do not drop out, their withdrawal may create a highly biased sample that both distorts results and prevents generalising to the larger population.

Despite these drawbacks, panel studies are still the strongest design for most explanatory purposes, and they often justify their expense by the additional information yielded.

Instrumentation

Whatever study design is employed, the survey researcher will have to develop a set of questions to use as tools in obtaining measures. This is an extension of the operationalisation process begun in the conceptualisation stage and produces a *survey instrument*, which may be either a **questionnaire**, to be filled in by the respondent, or an **interview schedule**, which guides an interviewer in a personal or telephone interview. When developing these instruments, the researcher must consider (1) the content; (2) the form; (3) the format; (4) the wording; and (5) the order of questions.

The *content* of questions determines what information can be obtained from responses. It is dictated by the hypothesis being tested or the question being studied. What must we know to resolve the research question, and what must we ask to obtain that information? These are the questions that should guide the choice of what to ask. It is essential to be very clear both about what information is expected from responses to each item on a survey instrument and about how that information will be used in data analysis. What will it contribute to our ability to answer the research question?

There are an infinite number of questions to be asked about almost any important subject, but survey instruments must be kept relatively short if respondents are to complete them. Personal interviews should last no longer than 45 minutes under most circumstances, and telephone interviews no longer than 20 minutes. Mail questionnaires should generally be no more than four pages long. The need for brevity, however, must be weighed against the need to obtain all the information necessary to rule out the various rival hypotheses encountered in data analysis or the need to seek explanations for unanticipated results. One way to approach this problem is to follow two general rules. First, keep the number of hypotheses tested or research questions addressed in a survey very limited. This will restrict the number of variables on which information is needed. Second, when selecting items for inclusion, exclude any for which there is no clear and immediate role in the anticipated data analysis.

Surveys usually contain both questions that are specific to the study and general background questions that measure characteristics that past research has shown to be strongly associated with differences in the political behaviour under study. The latter items are included to allow us to rule out rival hypotheses pertaining to background characteristics and to refine our understanding of relationships by seeing how they differ in different **demographic groups**. Questions that seek information on the following characteristics are often at least *considered* for inclusion in any survey instrument:

sex	marital status
age	home ownership
ethnicity	household composition
income	party identification
religion	national origin
education	length of residence
occupation	organisational memberships

Types of questions

Survey questions can be either *open-ended* or *closed-ended*. **Open-ended questions** allow respondents to answer in their own words; no options are imposed on them. For example, *What do you consider to be the most important single issue in this year's local election?* is an open-ended question. Such questions have the advantage of allowing the researcher to discover unanticipated patterns in people's answers. They also prevent the researcher's selection of response options from biasing answers or concealing information. Open-ended questions have some disadvantages, however: They make comparison of respondents' answers extremely difficult, because each person may not use the same frame of reference in answering. In addition, they could encourage long or irrelevant answers, which are often difficult to analyse.

Closed-ended questions force the respondent to choose an answer from a limited number of options and have the advantages of making comparison of responses simple, allowing quick processing and ensuring the relevance of responses. For example, *Do you consider yourself to be a* *conservative, a moderate or a liberal?* is a closed-ended question. The options offered in closed-ended questions should be *exhaustive* (they should include all possible responses that might be expected) and *mutually exclusive* (they should not allow more than one choice as a response to any single question). The options should also allow respondents to express differences in the *intensity* of their response when this might be relevant. A question like *Some people feel that the government should provide free home care for the elderly. Do you agree or disagree with this position?* calls for a more complex set of choices than just agree and disagree. *Strongly agree, agree, neutral, disagree, strongly disagree* and *no opinion* would better reflect the range of opinions people are likely to hold.

However, even when well constructed, closed-ended questions run the risk that the researcher's choice of options may influence responses. A question like *Which of the following would you say is the most important issue facing the United Kingdom today?* assumes that the researcher can list all the issues people will consider the most important. Use of this closed-ended form may prevent our discovering something we have not anticipated about public opinion. The choice between open- and closed-ended questions must be made on the basis of both the resources that will be available for data processing (open-ended requiring more) and the theoretical and empirical knowledge we have of our subject (closed-ended requiring more).

It is also important to think about how a question is presented and answered. Though the straightforward oral or written question-and-answer format is most common, a variety of other techniques is available to help respondents conceptualise choices and understand what is being asked. Many of these involve visual aids, such as charts, photographs or cards that can be sorted into boxes. One example is the 'feeling thermometer' developed at the Survey Research Center of the University of Michigan. Respondents are shown a card with a drawing like that in Figure 8.1 and asked to report how warm or cold they feel towards an object or a person by choosing a temperature reading from the thermometer. This instrument facilitates the ranking of more cases (potential presidential candidates, for example) than respondents could reasonably be expected to rank in an abstract mental exercise. The researcher simply asks about each case individually and compares thermometer readings. The more complex the mental task respondents are being asked to perform, the more useful visual aids and other variations on the question-and-answer format can be.

Figure 8.1 The feeling thermometer is a visual aid for surveying attitudes towards groups or individuals

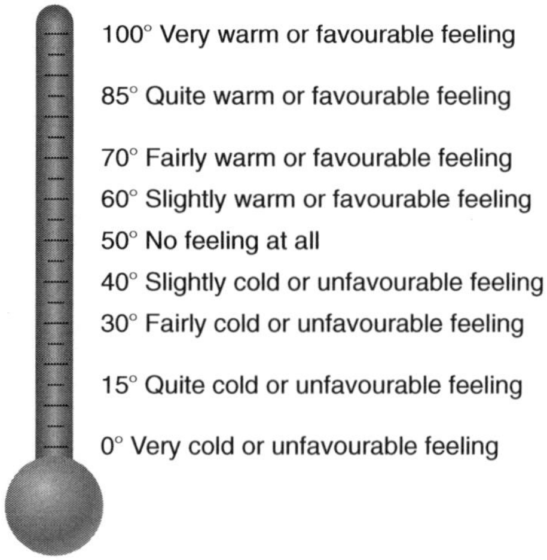

Question wording

Careful and proper **question wording** is crucial to the success of a survey. Researchers can make it easier for an interviewer to do a good job by providing clear instructions and by carefully wording questions. Properly phrased questions can often prevent problems in the field. For example, it is easier for the interviewer to establish a good relationship with the respondent and to avoid the appearance of 'grilling' if questions are phrased so that respondents do not have to admit that they do not know some fact or have given no thought to the subject. A phrase such as . . . *or haven't you had a chance to read about that?* at the end of a question can considerably ease potentially tense situations.

No one can provide precise guidelines for correct wording, because the questions that have to be asked are determined by the subject under study. We can, however, describe some common errors in question wording that should be avoided. Here are some qualities that questions should *avoid*:

1 *Excessive length.* If there is a general rule about question wording, it is to use the shortest form of the question that communicates effectively. Longer questions not only consume more time but are also more likely to lose or confuse respondents. Avoid conditioning phrases and unnecessary adjectives. For example, the question *If an election were to be held at this point in time, rather than at a time that was deemed suitable by the prime minister to dissolve parliament, which of the following parties do you think you would vote for?* can be profitably shortened to *If an election were held today, which party would you vote for?* followed by a list of parties.

2 *Ambiguity.* The quest for brevity should not lead to incomplete or imprecise wording. To be certain that questions contain all the information necessary to elicit an informed response, ask yourself whether the respondent might have to answer the question with a question. For instance, when asked, *Do you ever complain about public services?* a respondent might answer, *Complain to whom? Public officials? Neighbours?* Questions are often ambiguous if they are too general (*Do you feel that people think too much about politics?*) or indefinite about time, location, or point of comparison (*Did you vote in the last election? Do many Asians live here? Do you think Smith is the best candidate?*).

3 *Double-barrelled questions.* These questions are often impossible to answer with a single response because they contain two distinct questions. For example, *Do you feel that we are spending too much on the military, or do you feel it is important to maintain a strong national defence?* cannot be answered with 'yes' or 'no' if the respondent feels that it is important to have a strong defence but also thinks that current expenditures are higher than necessary for that purpose. To avoid double-barrelled questions, examine any question containing *and* or *or* to be certain it does not combine two questions that should be asked separately.

4 *Bias.* Questions can be worded so as to encourage one response rather than another. Such questions are often referred to as *loaded questions.* When asked, *You are opposed to deporting innocent asylum seekers who are fleeing persecution from tyrannical governments, aren't you?* respondents will be far more inclined to agree than if asked, *Do you favour or oppose the provision of refugee status to asylum seekers?* Phrases that evoke social norms (such as, *How often do you fulfil your civic duty by voting?*) clearly bias responses. Phrases that associate a position with authority figures or socially disapproved persons or groups can also distort results. For example, questions that begin with, *Do you agree with the prime minister that . . .* or *Do you share the neo-Nazi view that . . .* will probably produce biased results.

If there are opposing positions on an issue, it is important that questions be worded so as to make each seem legitimate. A useful approach here is to word items as follows: *Some people feel that the government should take control of the nation's water companies and operate them as public utilities. Others think that would be a serious mistake. How do you feel about it? Do you think the government should take control of water companies?*

5 *Response set bias*. People have a tendency to agree with statements, regardless of their own positions. Question items that fail to take this into account are said to exhibit a *response set bias*. We can see the effects of this bias if we measure political conservatism first by using six statements with which we expect conservatives to agree, and then again by using six statements with which we expect them to disagree. The first measure will almost always 'show' that there are significantly more conservatives than will the second, regardless of the actual number of conservatives in the sample. Items should be mixed so that we sometimes expect agreement to reflect a given attitude or position and sometimes expect disagreement to reflect that attitude or position.

6 *Argumentativeness*. Though it is sometimes necessary to provide background for questions, it is a mistake to argue a position. For instance, it is not wise to ask, *Since there are so many dangers associated with the operation of nuclear power plants, some people argue that it is foolish to invest so much in developing nuclear power when we could be devoting resources to the development of safe and inexhaustible energy sources such as solar or wind power. Do you agree that our nation should sharply curtail its investment in nuclear energy?* In addition to being far too long, this question will probably bias responses because it omits alternatives to the position stated.

7 *Encouragement of conditioned responses*. Special problems of wording are posed when questions are asked that touch on sensitive subjects. Most people are reluctant to talk to strangers about such matters as their income, family life, sexual behaviour or even political preferences in some cases. For example, consider the case of questions for which society largely prescribes certain responses. Unless questions are carefully phrased, respondents will tend to give the socially acceptable answer regardless of their own opinions. Racial prejudice is a case in point. Since bigotry is generally condemned in any society, people may be reluctant to express prejudiced views.

We can suggest a couple of tactics to use in getting genuine responses rather than conditioned or socially approved answers. First, we might suggest that socially unacceptable views are widely held or can be viewed as legitimate. For instance, ask, *Many people feel that having Asians in a neighbourhood causes it to go downhill. Others don't think Asians make that much difference in a neighbourhood. Do you agree or disagree with the idea that Asians generally cause neighbourhoods to decline?* A second approach is to word questions so as to appear to assume that respondents engage in socially proscribed behaviour or hold unpopular views so that they are forced to deny it if they do not. This makes it easier for them to 'confess' to socially unapproved opinions. For instance, the question *How much harm do you think it would do to this neighbourhood if Asians began to move in?* makes it easier to express prejudice than a more neutral wording such as, *Do you think it would be harmful to this neighbourhood to have Asians move in?*

8 *Forcing a response*. Many people feel that it is socially undesirable not to have an opinion on political issues and may express opinions on matters to which they have given no thought. This can distort survey results. To avoid such responses, it is generally wise to provide a no-opinion category in response options or to word questions so as to make having no opinion seem acceptable. For instance, try opening a question with wording such as, *Some people consider the national debt to be an important political issue while others are not too concerned with it. Do you think . . . ?*

Questionnaire structure

In addition to constructing individual items, survey researchers must be concerned with the overall format and organisation of the survey instrument. Sound questionnaires or interview schedules generally consist of four main parts: the explanation, some warm-up questions, the substantive questions and the demographic questions.

1 *The explanation* informs respondents of the purpose of the study, and it should convince them that the survey is important enough to warrant their time and attention. This can often be done by

associating the study with a respected authority or with a worthwhile goal. If the survey has a prestigious sponsor, a line such as, *We are conducting a study for the Centre for Survey Research . . .* can have the desired effect. In stating the purpose of a study, the researcher should not use terms beyond the everyday language of respondents. It would be unwise, for example, to say, *We are conducting a study of mass-elite linkages to determine the extent to which formal mechanisms of representation are a façade for social control by political elites,* even if this were the purpose of the study. A more effective statement would be, *We want to know what kind of contact people like you have with their elected representatives, and we hope that the results of this study will help improve the operation of our government.* Though it is never advisable to lie to respondents, the explanation should not reveal study information that would bias responses. If respondents are told that a study focuses on racial prejudice, they may give different answers from those they would give if told only that the study deals with citizens' attitudes or some other neutral term. The explanation can help interviewers establish a good rapport with respondents or encourage respondents to complete a questionnaire by assuring them that the researchers are open about what they are doing and by eliminating any fear that the study might be a front for a sales pitch.

2 *Warm-up questions*, too, can help establish a good relationship with respondents. These are impersonal, nonthreatening items used to initiate an interview or questionnaire. Asking respondents about their length of residence in their present location or what they think are the most important problems in their community or in the nation can be useful warm-ups. Any questions that are selected for this purpose, however, should be relevant to the study and have a definite role in the analysis. Otherwise, they are wasted. Warm-up questions should not be created especially for that purpose but should be selected from questions that are to be asked anyway.

3 *Substantive questions* constitute the bulk of the items on most instruments. The ordering of items within this group is determined principally by the need to achieve a logical flow in the questioning. Question ordering is not always neutral, however. For instance, researchers often want to ask the same question in different ways. When this is done, the different forms of the question should be separated so that respondents do not find the interview repetitive. Similarly, if both general and specific questions about a phenomenon are asked, it is usually best to ask the general questions first in order to get a response that has not been conditioned by a series of specific inquiries. It usually makes sense to place open-ended questions about a subject before closed-ended questions on that same subject in order to prevent the options offered in the closed-ended items from biasing responses to the open-ended items.

4 *Demographic items* seek factual information about respondents that is often regarded as personal or sensitive. They are usually placed at the end of an instrument to prevent having other parts of the interview or questionnaire affected by respondents' being ill at ease or feeling as if the researchers are snooping. Though people are generally willing to provide information on such personal matters as their income or marital status, getting adequate answers to demographic questions requires careful wording.

Placing demographic questions at the end of an instrument has the added advantage of postponing, until more interesting questions have been asked, what some people consider dull questions of the sort they frequently have to answer in filling out official forms. This can be especially important with self-administered questionnaires, because a set of routine questions at the outset can make completing the form seem like work and lead respondents to abandon the questionnaire.

Questionnaire format

Once the principal sections of the instrument have been designed, decisions about how they will be placed must be made. These decisions determine the *format* of the instrument. Earl Babbie (1990; 135) argues:

The format of a questionnaire can be just as important as the nature and wording of the questions asked. An improperly laid out questionnaire can lead respondents to miss questions, confuse them as to the nature of the data desired, and, in the extreme, result in respondents throwing the questionnaire away.

The format of an interview schedule can be just as important. A poorly laid out schedule can confuse interviewers in ways that lead them to skip items, incorrectly record responses and alienate respondents by appearing clumsy. We can offer some guidelines for setting up both questionnaires and interview schedules.

The first rule for both types of instruments is *Do not crowd items.* It is difficult to overstress the harm that can be caused to a survey by crowding print on a page. To prevent errors, leave plenty of white space on each page of the instrument. Especially in self-administered questionnaires, this helps respondents avoid misreading or mismarking and can give them the sense that the questionnaire is easy to complete. It is better to have a few questions on each of a large number of sheets in a questionnaire than to have many questions on each of a few sheets. The total number of pages matters less than the clarity of each page, but a rule of thumb is that it will take approximately 30 minutes to administer an instrument of ten well-spaced pages, and 30 minutes is about as long as researchers can count on to hold their respondents' attention under most circumstances.

Types of surveys

The type of survey required is determined by the research question being addressed, and the type *possible* is dictated by the resources available. But the basic choice is always among four options: *personal interviews, mail surveys, telephone surveys* and *Internet surveys*. In making that choice, the researcher should consider the following features of each type of survey.

Personal interviews

One of the most flexible of survey methods are **personal interviews** because they allow the use of a variety of questioning techniques (visual aids, for example) and give interviewers a chance to pursue questions in order to ensure appropriate responses and prevent respondents from misunderstanding questions or instructions. Personal interviews also provide the largest amount of data per interview, because an interviewer can normally hold a respondent's attention longer in face-to-face interaction than over the phone or through a questionnaire. The response rate is also generally higher for personal interviews.

These interviews are not without disadvantages, however. In the first place, they are very expensive and only the most important of projects can generally command the funds necessary to employ the technique. Second, personal interviews can produce biased data because of the features of the interview process itself. Responses recorded by interviewers may reflect real-world facts or attitudes less than they reflect the effects of the setting in which the interview occurs, the reactions of respondents to a given interviewer, the biases of the interviewer, the liberties the interviewer takes in asking questions, or the interview style employed. In addition, personal interviews are difficult to monitor to ensure quality control. The researcher is unable to observe the interviewers in the field and must rely on a variety of postinterview techniques to ensure that interviews were properly conducted. Though such techniques as contacting respondents to see if they were actually interviewed and comparing the responses reported by different interviewers can be effective, they are not foolproof and are costly and time consuming.

Postal surveys

In cases where personal interviews are impractical, **postal surveys** are a good alternative and offer several advantages:

1 Because postal surveys cost much less to conduct, larger samples can be drawn and a wider distribution of the instrument can be achieved.
2 Many of the biases in distribution of the instrument can be avoided. Among these are biases relating to the reluctance of interviewers to work in certain types of neighbourhoods and their inability to obtain interviews with certain types of individuals.
3 Response biases associated with the interviewer are avoided.
4 There is a greater chance of obtaining truthful responses both because a greater anonymity is implied by a mailed instrument and because the biasing effects of respondent–interviewer interaction are removed.
5 Respondents have more time to give thoughtful replies that may reflect their true feelings more accurately than do the hurried responses given in an interview.
6 Fewer personnel need be involved in the survey. This saves money and time.

Unfortunately, postal surveys have their limitations as well. In the first place, they require a mailing list that can be used as a sample frame and provide a representative sample. No such list exists for many of the populations to which researchers may want to generalise. Second, questionnaires have to be kept short if an adequate response rate is to be obtained. This means that less information can be secured from each contact. Third, the researcher has little control over who responds to the questionnaire. This can pose problems both because someone other than the person to whom it is addressed can complete a questionnaire and because it is difficult to obtain an adequate response rate with a mailed instrument.

The most significant problems associated with mail surveys are low response rates, biased response patterns and improperly completed questionnaires. In general, a response rate of 40 per cent is considered acceptable for mail surveys. A demonstrated lack of bias in responses (which is sometimes imputed through the representativeness of respondents' demographic qualities) is more important than a high response rate, however, because low response rates challenge the value of results chiefly by rendering the sample unrepresentative. The following techniques are available for encouraging better response rates.

The usual procedure for mail surveys is to send a questionnaire, a letter explaining the purpose of the survey, and a return envelope all in one envelope. Research has shown that using *self-mailing questionnaires* increases response rates. Self-mailing questionnaires can be folded, sealed and mailed without an additional envelope. That seems to make it easier for respondents to return the instrument and averts the problem of respondents losing the return envelope.

Follow-up mailings can substantially increase return rates both by reminding respondents of the survey and by locating people who, for some reason, have not received the initial letter. Generally, three mailings (an original and two follow-ups) are best. If individual respondents can be identified from returned questionnaires, then mailing follow-ups only to nonrespondents can save money. If respondents cannot be identified, it is a good idea to do a blanket mailing to all members of the sample, thanking those who have responded and encouraging those who have not to do so. The follow-up mailing should contain both a letter reminding people to send in their completed questionnaire and a second questionnaire in case the first was lost or never arrived.

It is often wise to include in all mailings a phone number that respondents can call to get answers to questions about the survey. This can both increase the response rate and reduce the number of returned questionnaires that were improperly completed. Response rates can also be enhanced by carefully avoiding any marks on the questionnaires (sequence numbers, for instance) that respondents could interpret as a device for identifying their questionnaire. People are generally more likely to cooperate if they feel their responses will be anonymous.

Telephone surveys

The commonly used **telephone surveys** fall between personal and postal surveys in many ways. The number of questions that can be asked is generally larger than for postal instruments, but shorter than for personal interviews. Response rates are usually lower than for personal interviews but higher than for postal surveys. Though interviewer-related sources of bias are not totally removed, a voice over the telephone is normally less likely to create biasing effects than is a person in the respondent's living room. Finally, the personnel requirements of telephone surveys are between those of postal and personal surveys.

The advantages of telephone surveys include the speed of completion, the control provided over who responds, and the flexibility offered in allowing an interviewer to ensure appropriate responses. Their chief limitation arises from the possibility that an unbiased sample cannot be obtained. Those who do not have a telephone or who have an unlisted number may also be distinctive in ways that are relevant to the study. If so, leaving them out of a sample may provide misleading results. For example, many service professionals (doctors and lawyers, for example) have an unlisted home telephone number in some communities, and very poor people often do not have a land line. This can be crucial to a study of the relationship between income and political attitudes.

A sampling technique known as **random-digit dialling (RDD)** has enabled survey researchers to overcome the bias associated with unlisted numbers and inaccurate listings, and has significantly increased the speed with which telephone surveys can be conducted. Surveys conducted with the RDD method rely on random samples of computer-generated telephone numbers. This is usually done by combining the three-digit telephone exchanges (or prefixes) of the geographic area where the survey is to be conducted with randomly generated four-digit root numbers. The advantage of such RDD samples is that they not only guarantee a completely random selection of households to be contacted, but also contain numbers of unlisted households which would be otherwise unreachable.

Internet surveys

The growing popularity of the Internet and the continuing decline of telephone poll response rates have led to the development of surveys that can be distributed through the Internet. In recent years, **Internet surveys**, which usually are administered through e-mail, web pages or a combination of both, have become a standard research tool in government, business, academia and the mass media.

The proliferation of Internet surveys is driven by a number of important advantages this type of survey has over more traditional interviewing methods. First, Internet surveys allow cost-efficient access to potentially millions of national or international respondents. Since Internet surveys are self-administered and distributed online, they eliminate the need for interviewers, long-distance phone charges, or printing and mailing costs. Thus, it is fairly cheap to administer Internet surveys to a large number of respondents regardless of where they live or work. In addition, because in most Internet surveys data are entered directly by the respondents (by clicking on answer choices provided on a survey web page, for example), instantly downloaded and saved by a central computer, there is no need for additional data entry, again saving money.

Second, Internet surveys allow a variety of instrument designs that can be tailored to the specific needs of the research project or the targeted respondents. Questionnaires administered through the Internet can, for example, incorporate images or short video clips – something that is impossible in telephone surveys. This enables researchers to expose respondents to visual cues such as videos or images of different product designs. In addition, to accommodate the needs or preferences of specific respondents, the format of Internet questionnaires can be easily adapted to feature, for example, different colors and designs (appealing to men rather than women, for instance), various languages (for non-English speakers), or larger type fonts (for people who cannot read small print).

Third, Internet surveys permit respondents to complete the questionnaire whenever it is convenient for them – and not when an interviewer calls them or knocks on their door. Since many people are annoyed with the often intrusive and repeated calls by marketing and surveying organisations, surveys delivered through e-mail or the Internet might offer a solution to the declining response rates that have been observed in more traditional telephone surveys.

Although Internet surveys are attractive because of their low cost and simple administration, this survey method has significant drawbacks which severely limit the type of data that can be gathered. The biggest disadvantage of Internet surveys is related to the fact that not everybody has access to the Internet. Although Internet usage has increased in the past few years, many people still do not have access to the Internet. In the United States, for example, only about 7 in 10 people used the Internet in 2007. Moreover, those who are online tend to be younger, more educated and wealthier than those who do not have Internet access (Pew Internet & American Life Project; see www.pewinternet.org). Both of these factors make it extremely difficult to obtain a nationally representative sample of survey respondents. After all, even were we able to obtain a complete list of Internet users in the United States (or anywhere else, for that matter), randomly selecting respondents from such a list would result in strongly biased samples that are not representative of the overall population. Such a sample would not only exclude all those who do not use the Internet, but also would contain more younger, educated and wealthier people than can be found in the general population.

Because of the difficulties associated with drawing representative samples for Internet surveys, it is advisable to verify whether existing Internet surveys rely on self-selected respondents (as many do), or whether they are based on truly representative samples. Many of the online 'polls' that are published by media organisations such as the BBC, for example, are based on responses from people who happen to visit a particular web page at a certain time – and who actually decided to answer the poll questions. It is no surprise then, that Internet surveys that are based on such self-selected respondents provide virtually no information about the opinions or attitudes of any group or population. On the other hand, Internet polls conducted among a self-contained group of people (for example, all employees of *Microsoft*) can be representative if the sample has been drawn from a complete list of possible respondents who have access to the Internet.

It should be noted here that some survey companies have successfully provided access to representative samples of respondents through the Internet. *Knowledge Networks* (www.knowledgenetworks. com), for example, relies on samples of respondents who are first chosen through traditional random-digit dialling procedures (as in telephone surveys) and are then provided with Internet access in return for their cooperation with surveys sent to them via the Internet. Such a methodology is obviously very expensive and requires the periodic replacement of those people in the sample who have become 'professional' survey respondents.

Other survey companies, such as *Harris Interactive* (www.harrisinteractive.com), rely on respondents who have voluntarily agreed to participate in Internet surveys and have provided extensive information about their personal background. In the case of *Harris Poll Online*, for example, this allows researchers to draw speciality samples of respondents who share certain interests or characteristics (for example, people with pets). The problem with such voluntary samples is the fact that they cannot be representative of the overall population – or even people with common characteristics – because of the **self-selection bias** mentioned above. *Harris Poll Online* tries to get around this problem by using a 'propensity weighting' technique that adjusts survey results *ad hoc* by factors such as age and sex in order to match them with their actual proportions in the population of interest. Although such weighting procedures are common in survey research, the question remains whether it is appropriate to rely on samples that exclude large portions of the overall population (in this case, all people who do not use the Internet).

Another big disadvantage of Internet surveys is the lack of control over the administration of the instrument. Since most online polls are self-administered, there is no possibility for interviewers to answer potential questions respondents might have about the survey, or probe any of the respondents' 'don't know' or 'refusal' answers. In addition, the survey administrator has to make sure that the questionnaire is completed by the targeted respondent and not somebody who happens to stumble across the questionnaire while surfing the Internet (this is usually accomplished by using password-protected survey websites).

Finally, researchers interested in using Internet surveys should be aware of the fact that the technology used to access the Internet can differ significantly from one user to the next. For example, although a significant number of people have fast broadband Internet access either at work or at home, some still use the much slower telephone modems to go online. Thus, it might be difficult for respondents with slower Internet connections to receive and answer questionnaires that contain, for example, large video clips or images that cannot be downloaded within a reasonable amount of time. In addition, there are potential technological problems with different browsers or hardware configurations, which can significantly affect the way survey questionnaires are displayed on respondents' computer screens.

Overall then, Internet surveys are most suited to collect data from respondents who belong to finite groups with complete access to the Internet. Research projects that require representative samples of the general population, however, are better served with more traditional forms of surveys, such as personal interviews or telephone surveys based on random-digit dialling procedures.

Training and briefing personnel

The personal interview is simultaneously one of the worst and one of the best data collection tools available to political scientists. The most significant disadvantages of the interview stem from the fact that the interview situation is rich with opportunities for *reactivity* to affect measurement. Respondents' reactions to the appearance or behaviour of the interviewer, to the wording of questions, or to the interview setting can create artificial data that contain less information about the real world than about the interview process itself.

Because respondents react not only to questions but also to the person asking the questions and the manner in which they are asked, characteristics of interviewers that should be totally unrelated to the interview can, in fact, be crucial to its success. In order to minimise error in survey research, the interviews must be standardised. This means that each question should mean the same thing to each respondent, and that each response must mean the same thing when given by different respondents. The presence of an interviewer, ideally, should not affect the respondent's perception of a question, nor the kind of answer that is given. In order to increase response rates and accuracy, interviewers should do what they can to persuade respondents to complete the interview. It is important to interview busy and less cooperative people as well as people who willingly complete the survey.

Interviewer guidelines

The following guidelines should help to reduce interviewer error considerably:

1 Use an informal, conversational style when asking the questions in the survey. You should be matter-of-fact and casual in your approach to questioning, as if there were absolutely no reason to expect people to refuse to answer.

2　You should be sufficiently familiar with the questions so that you sound as if you are not reading them. Do not conduct the interview in a monotonous voice, since this might make you sound disinterested in the respondents' answers. Try to make the respondents feel that you are listening to what they say by using affirmations such as 'I see' or 'Ok'.

3　Do not express your own opinions during an interview by expressing agreement or disagreement with the respondent. Remain neutral and never suggest answers to the respondent even if you think you 'know' what the respondent thinks. Also, do not allow yourself to be drawn into conversations with the respondent about the subject of the survey, because your remarks may bias responses.

4　Let the respondents determine the speed at which you read the survey. It is, however, important to move the interview along as quickly as possible in order to avoid opportunities for the respondent to terminate the interview.

5　Do not intentionally alter the wording or the order of items. All questions should be read exactly as they are written and in the order in which they are presented. Just as survey results can be distorted when questions are reworded, they can also be distorted when questions are asked out of sequence.

6　Do not attempt to interview from memory. Always have the questionnaire before you, and refer to it for question wording and order even if you are so familiar with the instrument that it takes only a glance to remind you of the items.

7　If you are to record respondents' comments, record them in exactly the words the respondents use rather than summarising them.

8　If respondents give indefinite answers, probe for more specific responses. Your probes should be neutral and should not suggest answers. The most effective neutral probe is repeating the original question or response categories. In well-constructed surveys, appropriate probes are indicated on the questionnaire for any question that is likely to require them.

9　Do not accept 'I don't know' or 'no opinion' as a response without at least one probe. Repeat the question and perhaps offer a little encouragement such as 'I know some of the questions might be difficult to answer, but what is your best guess?'

10　If respondents object to question wording or the alternative answers offered, do not defend the survey instrument but merely explain that you must ask the questions as written and that you are not responsible for them.

11　Never tell respondents what others have answered in response to a given question even though respondents may ask.

12　Be prepared to answer any questions the respondent asks you about who is doing the survey and why. Each study should have a sheet prepared by the project manager that provides brief answers to these questions.

Pretesting

Pretesting a survey instrument and all the accompanying procedures of data management is as important to successful survey research as a test-drive is to buying a good used car. Also called a **pilot study**, this trial run helps identify problems that will show up only under actual field conditions.

Pretests are conducted by administering the survey to a small sample of respondents similar to those who will be in the larger sample. The pretest sample need not be representative of the larger population. It is more important to draw the pretest sample in such a way as to ensure that members of all groups of respondents that may react differently to the instrument be included in the pretest than it is to draw a representative sample for the pretest. If, for example, less educated people are likely to have difficulties with the instrument, the researcher should take special pains to include respondents with little education in the pretest, even if they represent only a small portion of the population of interest.

Pretests can serve both to verify the utility of an instrument in which the researcher has a good deal of confidence and to help in the development of an instrument when the researcher knows less about the phenomena under study. In the former case, the instrument should be administered in the pretest in what is expected to be its final form. In the latter case, however, the researcher might want to experiment with different forms in order to learn what works best. A pretest of that type can involve:

1 Different versions of the instrument that test different question wordings or instrument formats.
2 Administering a final questionnaire through actual interviews in order to identify problems in communication.
3 Open-ended questions that help develop response categories for closed-ended questions to be used in the final version.

When these types of devices are used to refine an instrument, the researcher should pretest the instrument that is finally developed, so as to identify any remaining or newly created flaws.

When pretesting an instrument that calls for interviews, researchers often find it useful to conduct a number of the interviews themselves in order to get a feel for the dynamics set up by their instrument and a sense of whether or not it communicates effectively with typical respondents. At the very least, the researcher should meet the interviewers as soon as they return from the field and go over the instrument and accompanying procedures in detail in order to identify any points at which instructions are unclear, specified procedures are awkward, or respondents seem confused by questions.

Often a pretest is as much a test of the sampling technique as it is of the survey instrument. If interviewers using the specified sampling procedure turn up an unusually small number of qualified respondents or an obviously unrepresentative sample in the pretest, the applicability of the sampling technique to that research situation should be re-examined. If personnel find it difficult to record data using the procedures selected for the pretest, then other procedures should be developed for the full-scale survey.

Pretesting is costly and time consuming, but it is an absolutely essential investment, because without it the researcher risks producing useless or misleading data. Think of it as buying insurance against finding yourself with a mountain of very expensive data that are useless because of flaws in the survey – flaws that you could have corrected had you been aware of them.

Surveying

After all these preparations, we are ready to conduct the actual survey. This is the heart of the study, because it is where the data are actually collected. What is done in this stage depends on what type of survey is being conducted.

Most surveys are based either on personal interviews or on telephone interviews. Researchers generally prefer to use face-to-face interviews for longer surveys or questionnaires that contain sensitive topics that respondents might be reluctant to talk about on the telephone. Of course, personal interviews are relatively expensive because interviews have to be conducted at the respondent's home or at a central interviewing facility to which each respondent has to be invited. In addition, surveys that rely on personal interviews can be difficult to conduct in certain areas of the United States (for example in high-crime neighbourhoods or extremely rural areas) and usually take much longer to complete than telephone surveys. Based on the assumption that almost all Americans can be contacted by telephone, a large number of surveys carried out in the United States are conducted by telephone.

Computer-Assisted Telephone Interviewing

Most survey organisations use computers in order to manage and conduct telephone interviews. **Computer-assisted telephone interviewing (CATI)** has mostly replaced the traditional 'pencil-and-paper' method, which forced interviewers to read printed questionnaires to respondents and then manually record their answers.

A typical CATI system consists of twenty or more networked computers that are controlled by a server (or main computer) that functions as a central storage location for the sample and the data. The server controls and displays the interview schedule on each interviewer's computer screen, selects telephone numbers and dials them automatically for the interviewer. As soon as somebody answers the telephone, CATI prompts the interviewer to take the call and then read an introduction to the study ('Hello, my name is . . .'). The introduction typically identifies the survey organisation and the study sponsor, in addition to briefly explaining the purpose of the survey. If respondents agree to participate in the survey, interviewers start to read each question directly from the computer screen and enter responses with their keyboards.

Although most questions require the interviewer to enter only numerical codes for each answer (for example, 1 for *agree* and 2 for *disagree*), interviewers can also record longer responses by typing them into blank boxes displayed on their screens. As soon as the interviewer has entered a response, the CATI system automatically displays the next question until the end of the survey has been reached. After completion of the interview, respondents' data are saved on the server and are available for immediate analysis.

The CATI system offers several advantages over the pencil-and-paper method of conducting telephone interviews. First, it increases the efficiency and accuracy of surveys by displaying question-and-answer categories on the interviewer's computer screen. Since the CATI program automatically guides the interviewer through the questions and records responses as they are entered, the possibility of interviewer error is greatly reduced.

Second, CATI systems allow survey organisations to administer very complex and individualised interview schedules. Based on responses to previous questions, for example, CATI can adjust the interview schedule and skip over questions not intended for certain respondents. This so-called **question branching** would be difficult to implement if an interviewer had to flip through pages of a printed interview schedule in order to get to the next appropriate question. CATI also has the ability to take responses and automatically insert them in subsequent questions, thus allowing the interviewer to ask highly individualised questions that are appropriate to each respondent. In addition, most CATI systems allow multilingual interviews (important for surveys targeting non-English speakers), voice capturing of open-ended question responses (eliminating the need to type them), and the playback of short audio clips (to test commercial jingles, for example).

Third, CATI systems are able to monitor and control interviewers unobtrusively during the interviews. Researchers can listen in on any interview at any time to catch and correct interviewers' mistakes. Interviewers who, for example, mispronounce names or forget to probe 'don't know' answers can then be retrained or pulled entirely from the study.

Finally, because respondents' answers are directly entered into the computer during the interview, researchers can request distributions or tabulations of responses at any point during a survey project. Most CATI systems feature integrated statistical software packages that allow instant analysis of the survey data, thus eliminating the need to reformat and then export data into other statistical programs.

Whereas the introduction of CATI systems has improved and automated the way telephone interviews are conducted, computers have also simplified the administrative functions associated with interviewing, such as scheduling of callbacks, interviewer productivity reporting and sample management. Moreover, integrated text editors enable researchers to write, test and revise questionnaires easily and quickly within CATI, thus reducing the time needed between the development and implementation of new survey schedules.

Monitoring

Surveys are monitored to ensure the validity and generalisability of results. Low or unbalanced response rates can be identified and, perhaps, corrected through careful monitoring. For all types of surveys this involves keeping careful records of completed instruments as they come in.

With postal surveys, returned questionnaires should be opened, checked for proper completion and filed. Each questionnaire should be assigned a serial identification number so that the time of its return can be determined later. The number of questionnaires that is received each day should be logged so that the researcher can keep track of the response rate. If respondents can be identified from the returned questionnaires, the researcher should record incoming questionnaires in a manner that will reveal imbalances in the return as they develop. If a certain geographic or demographic group is making an extremely low response, some extra follow-up mail effort may be called for to keep the sample from becoming unrepresentative. In addition, examination of the incoming questionnaires may reveal mistakes made by respondents, such as overlooking the last page of the instrument or misreading directions about how to mark items. If respondents are identified, a phone call or second mailing can sometimes save questionnaires that otherwise must be discarded.

With personal surveys, monitoring is done principally through a debriefing session as interviewers return from the field. The researcher or a trusted assistant should check the completed interview schedules to determine whether (1) the correct people in the correct households have been interviewed; (2) all completed interview schedules have been returned; (3) each instrument fully identifies the respondent and provides information on the time and date of the interview; (4) each instrument contains an identification number for the respondent and for the interviewer; and (5) all refusals are explained and any outstanding callbacks have been made. All of this helps ensure proper sampling and assists in verification.

Monitoring telephone surveys usually involves the researcher or field director listening in on interviews randomly without being detected. This provides both an incentive for interviewers to be responsible and a means of detecting and subsequently correcting flaws in interviewers' administration of the instrument.

Internet surveys are routinely monitored by checking the received data for possible problems with the sample or the questions themselves. Since most Internet surveys allow 'peeks' at the data even while the survey is in progress, it is relatively simple to get information about who is responding and how questions are answered. Potential problems such as nonresponse, for example, can then be easily addressed by contacting respondents with reminders or sending the survey questionnaires again.

Verifying

Verification is especially important with personal surveys, when unethical interviewers have both an opportunity and an incentive to falsify interviews and when even well-meaning ones can interview the wrong people. Verification procedures allow researchers to catch this type of error and to be sure that the sampling procedure is followed correctly.

Verification of personal interviews usually involves contacting the intended respondent to determine (1) whether the interview has occurred and (2) whether the interviewer has asked and correctly recorded answers to all questions. To do this, ask when the interview occurred and approximately how long it took. If respondents report that the interview has been conducted, ask them to re-answer two simple questions – one from the middle and one from near the end of the questionnaire – under the pretext that the answers were not clearly recorded in the field. Then check their answers against those that were recorded.

In large surveys, verification is done on a spot-check basis because contacting all respondents would be too costly. If spot-checks reveal falsifications or significant errors in any of an interviewer's forms, all of that interviewer's forms should be verified.

Secondary analysis of survey data

It is important to recognise that most political researchers, perhaps even most political scientists who publish books and articles based on survey data, *never conduct a survey*. They do not conduct surveys both because it is difficult to obtain the necessary funding and because it is often possible to answer the research question they want to explore by using survey data others have collected. Studying data collected by someone else is called **secondary analysis**. Such analysis is very common with survey data because they are so expensive to collect.

Secondary analysis is highly desirable for several reasons. In the first place, the results of almost any survey contain data that are never used by the original researchers because they turn out to be only marginally relevant to the particular research question under study. Another researcher may find these data perfectly suited to answering some other research question. Secondary analysis allows fuller use of data and conserves resources by saving the cost of new surveys when sufficient data already exist. Second, surveys run the risk of *contaminating the population*. This means that repeated studies of some subjects among a population may actually cause changes in the phenomena in question or make people reluctant to cooperate with future research. By allowing research to be conducted without yet another survey, secondary analysis minimises the risk of contamination. Third, although there are a great many data analysis techniques available to political scientists, any one researcher is likely to use only a few in a single study. Secondary analysis allows other researchers to apply different techniques that may expand our understanding of the subject or may even produce different answers to the original research question.

The most fruitful approach to secondary analysis is to select a research question, devise hypotheses to be tested, and then seek completed studies that contain the data necessary to test those hypotheses. Working in reverse (locating a sound data set and examining it in the hope of coming up with valuable research questions it can help answer) can sometimes pay off, but it significantly constrains the range of questions that can be investigated.

The first requirement of a useful data set is that it be based on a sample of the *appropriate population*. If we want to generalise to women in the United Kingdom, a study sampling voters in Cumbria will be of no use. The second requirement is that the survey instrument contains *appropriate operationalisations* of the key variables in the hypotheses to be tested. If, for example, differences between African Americans and whites are central to an investigation but the data set has recorded ethnicity only as 'white' and 'nonwhite', it will be of little use, as many ethnic groups will not fit into either of these two categories.

How do we establish whether a study is usable? Good reports of research state what sample has been used and describe the operationalisations of key variables that have been employed.

Consequently, books and journal articles sometimes provide enough information about a data set for us to judge its suitability, and a literature search can turn up a source of data for secondary analysis. Individual political scientists are often willing to share data sets with others when asked, so it is sometimes possible to obtain a data set through a letter to an author.

Data archives

Fortunately, there is a more systematic and reliable way to locate and gain access to data for secondary analysis. There are a number of institutions that collect data sets in the same way that libraries collect books. These institutions are generally referred to as **data archives**. They classify data sets for easy location and put them in a form that facilitates the sets' use by people who were not involved in the original project in which the data were collected. Some of the more important social science data archives are listed here, along with brief descriptions of their holdings.

- The *UK Data Archive (UKDA)* is a repository of data funded by academic institutions in the UK. This includes data archived as a result of studies funded by the Economic and Social Research Council (ESRC) and the Higher Education Funding Councils of England and Wales (HEFCE). One key data set is the *British Election Studies Series* which is a set of electoral related surveys conducted since 1964, the longest running academic national representative sample survey in the world. A list of the types of data available and access links can be found at http://www.data-archive.ac.uk.
- The *European Union (EU)* provides access to European public opinion data including *Eurobarometer* and offers links to other social sciences data archives (ec.europa.eu/public_opinion).
- The International *Social Survey Programme (ISSP)* is an annual programme of cross-national collaboration on surveys covering topics important to social science research (www.issp.org).
- The *American National Election Studies (ANES)* produce data on voting, public opinion and political participation that serve the research needs of social scientists, teachers, students, policy makers and journalists (www.electionstudies.org).
- The *Inter-University Consortium for Political and Social Research (ICPSR)* at the University of Michigan, Ann Arbor, maintains a large collection of surveys conducted in the United States and abroad that stress political variables (www.icpsr.umich.edu).
- The *Roper Center for Public Opinion Research* at the University of Connecticut, Storrs, is one of the nation's largest archives containing data from national and international surveys on a wide variety of subjects (www.ropercenter.uconn.edu).

Each of these institutions publishes a list of the data sets it has and provides a general description of the data. Once a promising-sounding study has been located in a listing of archive holdings, we can determine the actual utility of the study by obtaining the **codebook** for the survey. This lists all questions asked and tells how the responses have been coded, and it will allow us to judge the fit between the study's operationalisations and the hypotheses to be tested

Ethical considerations

There are two main ethical issues involved with surveys. One is the problem of bias in the original instrument. Are the questions being asked sufficiently hermeneutically sensitive to the possible range of interpretations each question might raise? In the process of translating the research problem into specific questions for the survey, the researcher must be aware of shifts in meaning and significance for both the researcher and those being researched. The problems of eliciting biased responses, partly due to how the questions are asked and how they are interpreted by the respondents, can be very subtle and require time to think through the implications.

The other ethical consideration is that the fact that survey researchers ask individuals to talk about their personal attitudes, opinions and beliefs requires them to be especially sensitive to the possible consequences of their questions. In general, researchers need to protect their respondents from harm and ensure that all survey findings are reported accurately. The following ethical considerations should be observed carefully when conducting survey studies:

- *Respondent's right to know*: Survey respondents should provide their permission to be interviewed, affirming that their participation in the survey is voluntary and that they do not have to answer all questions. In addition, respondents should have enough information about the purpose of the study, the sponsor (if any) and the organisation that conducts the survey in order to make an informed decision about their participation.

- *Respondent's right to protection*: Survey researchers have an obligation to ensure that the survey questions do not cause physical or emotional harm to their respondents. This includes practices or methods that may humiliate or mislead survey respondents. Researchers should also consider whether their questions might have any legal consequences for the respondent (for example, workers participating in a survey that was not sanctioned by the employer).

- *Respondent's right to privacy*: Survey respondents have a right to either give or withhold information during an interview. In other words, respondents do not have to answer questions that they consider too personal or private.

- *Respondent's right to confidentiality and anonymity*: Unless waived by the respondent for specified uses, survey researchers are obligated to ensure that the information provided by the respondents will be kept confidential and anonymous. This means that individual survey answers will not be available to people outside the project and that all personal identifiers will be removed from the completed questionnaires in order to ensure that answers cannot be traced to individual participants.

- *Accurate reporting of results*: Survey researchers also should make an effort to fully and accurately represent the results gathered by the survey. Many survey reports do not provide enough information about their data gathering procedures, which might make it difficult to assess the quality of the survey itself. The World Association for Public Opinion Research's (WAPOR's) *Code of Professional Ethics and Practices* specifies that survey reports must include the following information: (1) who sponsored and conducted the survey; (2) the exact wording of questions asked; (3) a definition of the population and the sampling frame; (4) a description of the sample design; (5) sample sizes, eligibility criteria, screening procedures and response rates; (6) estimates of sampling error and a description of any weighting or estimating procedures used; (7) which results are based on only parts of the sample; and (8) method, location and dates of data collection.

Conclusion

Without question, surveys are the most efficient way to collect information about how people think. Technological developments, such as computer-assisted telephone interviewing and online polling, have increased the number of surveys conducted each year. In fact, there are now so many surveys that many people have become annoyed by the seemingly constant intrusion into their private lives. Successful survey studies therefore require a carefully planned design, well-written questions and a representative sample of respondents who are contacted with the most appropriate type of survey (personal, telephone, online etc.).

Summary points

■ Surveys have to be planned carefully to ensure that the data collected will provide enough information to answer research questions or to test hypotheses. In the planning phase of a survey, researchers have to consider the conceptualisation of hypotheses and concepts, the type of survey required, the design of the survey instruments, the required sample and sampling procedures, the interviewer training and the pretesting of the instrument.

■ Survey design focuses on the development of a questionnaire and an interview schedule. Survey questions can be either open-ended or closed-ended and should be worded carefully in order to avoid bias and other related problems. The structure of the questionnaire should encourage respondents' participation.

■ The required survey type (personal interviews, mail, telephone or Internet survey) is determined by the research question and by the resources available. Each survey type has distinct advantages and disadvantages that have to be considered before the start of any research project.

■ Surveys are conducted either by personal interviews, mail, telephone or through the Internet. The surveying process requires monitoring and verification of the conducted interviews, data coding, processing and analysis.

Suggested reading and examples

Research examples

The literature on survey research is one of the largest in the social sciences. Most of it reflects the fact that the method is widely used in sociology and psychology as well as in political science and other fields. The following studies were chosen as examples because they represent a variety of survey methodologies. Mondak *et al.* (2007), for example, rely on a traditional cross-sectional telephone survey to analyse the relationship between people's political knowledge and their attitudes towards Congress. Mattes and Bratton (2007), on the other hand, analysed attitudes towards democracy in Africa with data collected from more than 21,000 face-to-face interviews conducted in twelve sub-Saharan African countries. Shah and Scheufele (2006) use data from a large mail survey to analyse the types of media sources used by opinion leaders in the United States.

Studies based on representative online polls are still the exception. However, good examples of such polls can be found in reports by the Program on International Policy Attitudes (PIPA), which frequently publishes public opinion reports that are based on representative online surveys conducted by Knowledge Networks. You can find their most recent reports at PIPA's website (www.pipa.org).

Methodological readings

A relatively comprehensive overview of survey methods is provided in *Survey Research Methods* (Fowler 2001). Other excellent introductions are found in *An Introduction to Survey Research, Polling, and Data Analysis* (Weisberg *et al.* 1996), *Designing and Conducting Survey Research: A Comprehensive Guide* (Rea and Parker 2005) and *How to Conduct Surveys: A Step by Step Guide* (Fink 2005).

The subjects of question wording and questionnaire design in general are addressed in *Questionnaire Design and Attitude Measurement* (Oppenheim 1999) and *Improving Survey Questions: Design and Evaluation* (Fowler 1995). Interviewer skills are covered in *Standardised Survey Interviewing: Minimising Interviewer-Related Error* (Fowler and Mangione 1990).

A very detailed discussion of how to conduct surveys by mail rather than through personal interviews is found in *Mail Surveys: Improving the Quality* (Mangione 1995). Telephone survey methods are covered in *How to Conduct Interviews by Telephone and in Person* (Frey and Oishi 2004). One of the most widely referenced books on these techniques is Dillman's (2006) *Mail and Internet Surveys: The Tailored Design Method*.

A good introduction to the practical applications of internet surveys is provided in *Internet Data Collection* (Best and Krueger 2004), *Conducting Research Surveys Via E-Mail and the Web* (Schonlau et al. 2002), and *Internet Research Methods: A Practical Guide for the Social and Behavioural Science* (Hewson *et al.* 2002). All three books contain a good selection of references for methodological issues in Internet research.

References

Babbie, Earl R. 1990. *Survey Research Methods.* Belmont, CA: Wadsworth Publishing Co.

Best, Samuel J. and Krueger, Brian S. 2004. *Internet Data Collection.* Thousand Oaks, CA: Sage.

Dillman, Don A. 2006. *Mail and Internet Surveys: The Tailored Design Method,* 2nd edn. New York: Wiley.

Fink, Arlene. 2005. *How to Conduct Surveys: A Step by Step Guide,* 3rd edn. Thousand Oaks, CA: Sage.

Fowler, Floyd J. Jr. 1995. *Improving Survey Questions: Design and Evaluation.* Thousand Oaks, CA: Sage.

Fowler, Floyd J. Jr. 2001. *Survey Research Methods,* 3rd edn. Newbury Park, CA: Sage.

Fowler, Floyd J. Jr. and Mangione, Thomas W. 1990. *Standardised Survey Interviewing: Minimising Interviewer-Related Error.* Newbury Park, CA: Sage.

Frey, James H. and Oishi, Sabine Mertens. 2004. *How to Conduct Interviews by Telephone and in Person.* Newbury Park, CA: Sage.

Hewson, Claire, Yule, Peter, Laurent, Dianna and Vogel, Carl. 2002. *Internet Research Methods: A Practical Guide for the Social and Behavioural Science.* Thousand Oaks, CA: Sage.

Mangione, Thomas W. 1995. *Mail Surveys: Improving the Quality.* Thousand Oaks, CA: Sage.

Mattes, Robert and Bratton, Michael. 2007. 'Learning about democracy in Africa: Awareness, performance, and experience'. *American Journal of Political Science,* vol. 51 (January), pp. 192–217.

Mondak, Jeffery J., Carmines, Edward G., Huckfeldt, Robert, Mitchell, Dona-Gene and Schraufnagel, Scot. 2007. 'Does familiarity breed contempt? The impact of information on mass attitudes toward Congress'. *American Journal of Political Science,* vol. 51 (January), pp. 34–48.

Oppenheim, Abraham N. 1999. *Questionnaire Design and Attitude Measurement.* New York: Continuum International Publishing Group.

Rea, Louis M. and Parker, Richard A. 2005. *Designing and Conducting Survey Research: A Comprehensive Guide,* 3rd edn. San Francisco, CA: Jossey-Bass.

Schonlau, Matthias, Fricker Jr, Ronald D. and Elliot, Marc N. 2002. *Conducting Research Surveys Via E-Mail and the Web.* Thousand Oaks, CA: Sage.

Shah, Shavan V. and Scheufele, Dietram A. 2006. 'Explicating opinion leadership: Nonpolitical dispositions, information consumption, and civic participation'. *Political Communication,* vol. 23, pp. 1–22.

Weisberg, Herbert F., Krosnick, Jon A. and Bowen, Bruce D. 1996. *An Introduction to Survey Research, Polling, and Data Analysis,* 3rd edn. Thousand Oaks, CA: Sage.

Research exercises

1 Write a series of three to five statements with which you might ask respondents to agree or disagree in order to get a measure of each of the following concepts:

> support for the Labour Party
> opposition to the Lisbon Treaty of the EU
> political efficacy
> political activism (participation)
> political liberalism

2 Select a politically relevant topic of interest to you and identify a dependent variable and three independent variables you might want to use in a study of the subject. Design a questionnaire that provides measures of these four variables, and write it out in a form that can be used in interviewing. Include a system of precoding for answers. After you have created the printed questionnaire, use a free Internet survey service (such as www.surveymonkey.com) and create the questionnaire online as well. Think about how a printed survey questionnaire might differ from one designed for the Internet.

3 Write out the theory as a set of testable hypotheses, carefully identifying the variables involved. Now locate an existing survey research data set on the Internet that you can use in a secondary analysis to test these hypotheses. Find some promising-sounding studies, get a copy of the codebook for each so that you can see exactly what questions were asked, and make your selection on that basis.

Key terms

closed-ended questions	interview schedule	questionnaire
codebook	longitudinal surveys	question wording
cohort studies	open-ended questions	random-digit dialling (RDD)
computer-assisted telephone interviewing (CATI)	panel studies	respondents
	personal interviews	secondary analysis
cross-sectional surveys	pilot study	self-selection bias
data archives	postal surveys	survey research
demographic groups	pretests	telephone surveys
Internet surveys	question branching	trend studies

9 Scaling techniques

- What is scaling?
- When are scales used?
- What types of scales are available?

Introduction

One of the most common problems we encounter in designing surveys or other instruments aris- es when we must find a way to assign a single representative value or score to a complex attitude or behaviour. As an example, consider how one might go about measuring the degree of people's prejudice towards university students. Such prejudice can take a number of forms, depending on which attributes of university students a particular individual might focus upon. That is, some people might judge them by their clothing, others by their mannerisms and still others by their behaviour, their social or economic status or even their personal hygiene. Some people might hold stereotypic views based on one or two encounters, either pleasant or unpleasant, with specific university students, and others may barely differentiate between them and other members of the community. These elements of judgement may vary quite widely in sub- stance, direction and degree, but each is, at least potentially, a component of the larger concept *prejudice*.

As researchers hoping to tap these factors, we must design an instrument that is at once sufficiently broad to detect and measure as many of these component elements as possible and sufficiently con- cise to allow us to summarise in some meaningful way the extent to which the more general concept in question is present. Put another way, we need a device that captures or represents a notion such as prejudice in all its complexity *and* tells us how much of it each respondent (or case) has. One impor- tant means by which we can accomplish this is through *scaling*.

The art of scaling

Scaling is a procedure in which we combine a number of relatively narrow indicators (in the example, survey questions about specific perceived traits of university students) into a single, summary measure that we take to represent the broader, underlying concept of which each is a part (prejudice). Thus, we might measure a respondent's attitudes about various behaviours of university students (that they drink too much or have too many loud parties, for example) or about their mannerisms (that they are self-impor- tant or inconsiderate), but we would not take any one of these items *alone* to stand for so broad a concept as prejudice. Rather, we must pull together *several* of these narrow measures in some way that allows us to draw conclusions about the more general point of view to which each may contribute or that each may reflect. And more than that, we must accomplish the task so that we can compare the amount of prejudice (or whatever it is we are measuring) that characterises one respondent with the amount that characterises another, in effect making a judgement (in the example) about which is *more* prejudiced. The unifying measure that represents a given underlying concept is called a **scale**. The individualised assessment of the degree to which any given case manifests that underlying concept is called a **scale score**. Scaling, or scale construction, is simply the procedure by which scales are built and individual scale scores are assigned.

Scale construction: two basic concerns

Scaling, then, seems to be a fairly straightforward process. The task of the researcher is simply to identify several components of the underlying concept, to develop indicators to measure each, to combine those indicators into a summary score by reciting a few magic words or statistical incantations, and – presto – it is done. Unfortunately, this apparent simplicity is deceptive, for there are some potential dangers to which we must be especially sensitive when selecting and interpreting scale components. Most important among these are two with which we are already familiar: the concerns posed by the notions of validity and reliability.

Validity

In the present context, validity questions whether there is reason to believe that each of the individual components (specific questions) in a given scale is actually related directly to the underlying concept and whether, collectively, those components capture the full essence of it. Put another way, we must ask ourselves whether it really makes sense to combine a particular set of indicators *and*, once we have done so, whether it really makes sense to attach to this set of indicators the particular label we have chosen. Thus, in our example, we must ask ourselves first whether persons' attitudes towards student behaviour really have anything in common with their attitudes towards university students' mannerisms or styles of dress, and second, whether all these attitudes together can really be considered to reflect the degree of those persons' prejudice towards university students.

Reliability

In scaling, reliability becomes a concern with whether the various component indicators of a scale are in fact related to one another in a consistent and meaningful manner. In effect, we are asking not whether a particular set of questions or indicators differentiates between apples and oranges, but rather whether, once the apples have been identified, it provides us with consistent standards for sorting them by size, colour and variety. If so, then combining the measures will tell us more about apples than will any single measure. But if our standards are inconsistent or ambiguous, then our observations based upon them may prove misleading.

An example

Consider a scale in which each respondent is instructed to express either agreement or disagreement with each of the following statements:

1 The North Koreans are evil and cannot be trusted.
2 The French are evil and cannot be trusted.
3 The Japanese are evil and cannot be trusted.
4 The Chinese are evil and cannot be trusted.

Let us suppose that this scale is intended to measure *xenophobia* – the fear and distrust of foreigners. Presumably, the more statements with which particular respondents agree, the more xenophobic we may take them to be. But is that really the case? A person who believes only the North Koreans and the Chinese are evil and not to be trusted may, in effect, be expressing anticommunism rather than xenophobia. A person who believes only the Japanese and the Chinese are evil and not to be trusted may, in effect, be expressing racism rather than xenophobia. Even a respondent who regards all four groups as evil and untrustworthy may, upon closer inspection, be expressing not xenophobia but a feeling that *all* people or *all* governments, even the respondent's own, are evil and not to be trusted. Because we cannot say with any assuredness that this scale measures xenophobia per se, the scale lacks validity.

And what of reliability? Even if the scale were measuring xenophobia, could we claim that its components measured consistently? Fear and distrust of the Chinese, for example, may be an indicator of at least two very different characteristics – one ideological and the other racial – and two respondents might give the same answer for very different reasons. Is our anticommunist respondent in some meaningful sense *equally* as xenophobic as our racist respondent? Probably not. To combine these particular items into a single measure by simply adding them together, then, is at best an exercise in futility and at worst a source of erroneous conclusions.

Problems of this type cannot always be overcome easily, and as a result, scaling must be used with great care in some instances and must be forgone in others. Yet the overriding advantages inherent in the ability to develop a single number or score to represent a complex attitude or behaviour provide a substantial incentive to employ scaling techniques in a great many instances. In the remainder of this chapter we discuss four different approaches to the development of meaningful scales. Each of these should be viewed not only in terms of its procedures but also in terms of its strengths and weaknesses in overcoming the problems of validity and reliability.

Likert scaling

The first such technique, and probably the least satisfactory in these terms, is **Likert scaling** – a simple technique by which each respondent is presented with a series of statements requiring a value judgement.

Figure 9.1 illustrates a typical series of such items, which might constitute a measure of prejudice towards university students. In each instance, respondents are asked whether they agree strongly,

| **Figure 9.1** | Typical Likert scale items |

Please indicate whether you *agree strongly, agree, disagree,* or *disagree strongly* with each of the following statements:

1 There may be a few exceptions, but in general university students are pretty much alike.
2 The trouble with letting university students into a nice neighbourhood is that they gradually give it a typical student atmosphere.
3 To end prejudice against university students, the first step is for the students to try sincerely to get rid of their harmful and irritating faults.
4 There is something different and strange about university students; it is hard to tell what they are thinking and planning, and what makes them tick.
5 Most university students would become overbearing and disagreeable if not kept in their place.
6 University students prove that when people of their type have too much money and freedom, they just take advantage and cause trouble.

Source: Adapted from the E (Ethnocentrism) Scale used by Adorno *et al.* (1950).

Note: In this figure statements have been worded in only one direction (that is, all agreements with the items reflect the presence of prejudice) for purposes of illustration. In practice, some items would be reworded so that the negative responses evidence prejudice, and the score values would be reversed accordingly. The goal of such a procedure is to minimise *response set bias* – the tendency of some respondents to give the same answer to every question.

agree, disagree or disagree strongly with the statement. Each such respondent is assigned a numerical score, with 5 representing the strongest agreement and 1 representing the strongest disagreement. A middle or neutral response is assigned the value 3. To obtain the summary measure of prejudice for a particular individual, one adds all the individual scores and divides by the number of statements. Thus, a respondent who has answered questions 1 to 6 as follows:

Item 1: Agree (4)

Item 2: Strongly agree (5)

Item 3: Neutral (3)

Item 4: Agree (4)

Item 5: Disagree (2)

Item 6: Agree (4)

is assigned the summary score 3.67 ([4 + 5 + 3 + 4 + 2 + 4]/6), which might be rounded to 4.

In general, the higher a person's scale score, the more of the measured characteristic (in this case, prejudice towards university students) they are presumed to have. The challenge of interpreting these data are the same as those already noted in our xenophobia scale, which was, in fact, an oversimplified Likert-type scale. For one thing, we know nothing about the relationships among the component items. Each may, in fact, measure different aspects of the same underlying trait, and on its face each appears to do so, but we cannot be sure.

The items that compose a good (or reliable) scale should have high internal consistency – that is, they should be highly correlated with each other. Different statistical models exist for measuring internal consistency. Probably the most commonly used reliability coefficient for items that have three or more answer categories is **Cronbach's alpha**, which is based on the average inter-item correlation. For items with two answer categories (true/false or agree/disagree, for example), the related **Kuder-Richardson 20 (KR20)** coefficient usually is used.

One point that should be clear even now, however, has to do with the way in which the summary (average) score is determined: one simply adds the individual item scores and divides by the number of items. But if we look more closely at the response categories (that is, *strongly agree*, *agree* etc.), we find that they represent measurement at the ordinal level. That is, they distinguish between mutually exclusive categories and rank each relative to the others. They do not, however, establish known and equal intervals (the difference between *strongly agree* and *agree* is not always the same, either from item to item or from one respondent to the next). Accordingly, it is meaningless and misleading to add these numbers together, let alone to average them. A more appropriate procedure, but not a commonly used one, is to calculate a different kind of average, called a *median*, for each respondent's answers and to assign this as the scale score. Determination of the median is discussed in Chapter 16.

Guttman scaling

Many of the problems associated with Likert scaling can be overcome in certain circumstances by using a more sophisticated technique known as Guttman scaling. **Guttman scaling** begins from the assumption that certain attitudes (and behaviours) are related to one another in such a way that holding (or engaging in) one is more difficult or requires more effort than holding (or engaging in) another. Perhaps the best analogy here is to a person standing on a ladder. A person standing on the fifth rung quite likely has climbed there by stepping on the first, second, third, fourth and fifth rungs. It is possible but less likely that the person skipped one or more of the lower rungs on the way up. It is most unlikely that someone would step directly from the ground to the fifth rung of the ladder, at least without enduring some pain. In effect, then, our climber has reached the fifth rung by engaging in a series of progressively higher-order behaviours and can reasonably be *assumed* to have traversed the lower positions to reach the highest one.

Similarly, even if we know that a particular person has voted in an election – an act known from many studies to be one of the most common and least demanding in politics – we cannot assume with any degree of assurance that the same person has also participated actively in some political organisation – a far more demanding and much less common action – or has run for public office – one of the most demanding and least common political acts of all. Yet if, on the other hand, we know that an individual has been active in a political organisation, it *may* be assumed, with some degree of confidence, that that person has also engaged in such lesser political acts as voting, though not that the person has taken the further step of running for office. And by extension, if an individual has been a candidate for office, we have reason to assume that the person has also voted and engaged in organisational activity. These assumptions will not always prove correct, but they will be supported far more often than not.

Certain attitudes may be seen to relate to one another in much the same way. We can see this illustrated in Figure 9.2, which represents an alternative approach to measuring a person's degree of prejudice against university students. In a procedure similar to Likert scaling, respondents are asked whether they agree or disagree with each item in a series of statements. The response that most reflects the trait being measured (for example, prejudice) is scored with a plus (+), and alternative responses are scored with a minus (−). Thus, agreement with item 1 would be scored plus (+) as reflecting prejudice, and agreement with item 2 would be assigned a minus (−), reflecting its absence. The statements themselves may be seen to bear a relationship with one another such that the various responses reflect the degree of one's prejudice or freedom from it. In effect, the closer a perceived threat comes to one's own family or self, the more difficult it presumably is for one to remain free of prejudice. What this means is that there is, at least potentially, a logical, ordinal relationship among the items in the scale – a factor that is missing with the Likert procedure.

Moreover, Guttman scaling provides appropriate procedures not only for summarising the degree of a characteristic possessed by a given respondent, but also for assessing the degree to which a particular set of components meets the assumption of ordinality in the first place. These procedures are illustrated in Table 9.1 on the next page, which reports the responses of 170 hypothetical persons to the statements presented in Figure 9.2.

Figure 9.2　Typical Guttman scale items

Please indicate whether you *agree* or *disagree* with each of the following statements:

1　Given a choice, I would like to see university students kept out of my community.
2　It is okay for university students to visit my community.
3　If a university student wanted to live in my community, that would be okay with me.
4　I would not want to see a university student living in my neighbourhood.
5　I would have no objection to someone in my family bringing home a university student as a guest for dinner.
6　I would be displeased if someone in my famly were to marry a university student.

Source: Adapted from *Social Distance*, Antioch Press (Bogardus, E. 1959).

Note: In this figure, the statements have been arranged in order of their degree of difficulty for purposes of illustration. In practice, their order should be mixed to obscure any implicit ranking.

Table 9.1   Hypothetical distribution of Guttman scale response*

Item	Item	Item	Item	Item	Item		Error		
1	2	3	4	5	6	n	(e)	$n(e)$	Scale Score
+	+	+	+	+	+	10			7
−	+	+	+	+	+	20			6
−	−	+	+	+	+	30			5
−	−	−	+	+	+	30			4
−	−	−	−	+	+	10			3
−	−	−	−	−	+	10			2
−	−	−	−	−	−	5			1
+	−	+	+	+	+	30	1	30	(7) or (5)
+	+	+	+	−	−	5	2	10	(7)
−	+	−	+	+	+	20	1	20	(6) or (4)
45	55	95	145	150	160	170		60	

Marginals (used for ordering items) — Totals

* + indicates a response reflecting prejudice.

Several points in the table are worthy of note. To begin with, the items are ordered on the left-hand side of the table in ascending order according to their number of supportive responses (+). This number is ascertained by summing the number of cases (n) for which a plus (+) has been recorded for a particular item. The assumption here is that the number of agreeing responses will decrease as the difficulty of holding a particular attitude increases. In the example, this ranking happens to correspond with our expectations in that the observed ranking is in the same order as our initial ranking, but this is not always the case.

Each line in the table represents a group of individuals who have given a particular combination of responses to the six items. Thus, the first line represents those ten people ($n = 10$) who have responded to each of the six questions in a manner reflecting prejudice towards university students. The second line represents those twenty respondents whose answers indicate prejudice on items 2 to 6, but not on the more extreme item 1, and so forth. The first seven lines in the table represent those combinations of responses that are wholly consistent with the assumption that the six items are ordinally related with one another. Persons displaying any one of these combinations of responses are termed *perfect scale types*.

In Guttman scaling, there will always be one more perfect scale type than there are items in the scale, because the total absence of the characteristic being measured (*no* prejudice, as in line 7) is regarded as a perfect score. Each perfect score is assigned a number from 1 to $i + 1$, where i is the number of items, with 1 identifying those respondents possessing the lowest level of the trait in question and $i + 1$ those possessing the highest. The appropriate score is then recorded for each respondent. Thus, in the example, each of the ten persons in line 1, whose responses reflect the highest degree of prejudice, are assigned the score 7 ($i + 1 = 6 + 1 = 7$), each person in line 2 the score 6, each in line 3 the score 5, and so on, until the five respondents in line 7 are each assigned the score 1. These scores rank each respondent vis-à-vis every other respondent according to their degree of prejudice.

We have yet to account, however, for the fifty-five respondents represented by lines 8, 9 and 10 in the table. One or more of the responses of these individuals does or do not fit the pattern predicted by our ordering of the items. These are, in effect, people who skipped one or more steps while climbing the ladder. Accordingly, these sets of responses are said to contain one or more *errors*. The term *error* here refers not to a mistake by the respondent, but to a failure of the assumptions of Guttman scaling to apply to these cases. When such errors occur, and they are quite common, we proceed on a line-by-line basis as follows. First, we count the *minimum* number of changes in the line that, if made, would result in a perfect scale score. In line 8, for instance, we can change the plus (+) in column 1 to a minus (−) to obtain a response of 5, or alternatively, we can change the minus (−) in column 2 to a plus (+) to obtain a response of 7. In either event, only one item is changed and so we say line 8 contains one error. This is indicated in the column labelled 'error (e)'. We then multiply the number of errors (1) by the number of cases in which the error occurs (30) and enter our result in the next column. Finally, we assign to each case the scale score it would receive if the error did not occur. Although we have only one error in line 8, we have a choice of two possible corrections, one of which yields a score of 5 and the other a score of 7. Unless there is some compelling reason to choose one of these scores over the other, the standard practice is to assign each of the 30 cases randomly to one or the other scale category.

We move next to line 9 and repeat the procedure. Here we are required to make a minimum of two changes, because we must convert both minus (−) scores to plus (+). Again, we note the number of errors, multiply by the number of cases, and assign a scale score. Here, however, only one score is possible, since we have no options when making our corrections. The procedure is then repeated for line 10, as it is for any additional nonscalar combinations.

In proceeding through lines 8, 9 and 10, we have, of course, assigned scores to each case as if it fitted our scale perfectly, though we know for a fact that it does not. This means that to the extent that we rely upon our scale scores to describe those fifty-five cases, we risk reaching an improper conclusion. How serious is this risk? Fortunately, Guttman scaling procedures suggest an answer.

Recall that we have kept track of the total number of errors in the scale. In effect, an assessment of risk requires us to ask whether this total error is relatively small and therefore unimportant or whether it is so large as to invalidate the scale itself. We may answer this question by calculating a statistic called the *Guttman coefficient of reproducibility* (C_R), the formula for which is as follows:

$$C_R = 1 - \frac{\sum n(e)}{i(N)}$$

where n = the number of cases in lines in which errors occur
e = the number of errors in each line
i = the number of response items
N = the total number of cases

For the example, the coefficient of reproducibility is determined by substituting the appropriate values:

$$C_R = 1 - \frac{30 + 10 + 20}{6(170)} = 1 - \frac{60}{1,020}$$

$$= 1 - 0.06 = .94$$

In this formula, the quantity $\Sigma n(e)$ represents the total number of 'mistakes' in the scale, and the quantity $i(N)$ represents the total number of possible mistakes if *no* items or respondents fit the scale. The fraction

$$\frac{\sum n(e)}{i(N)}$$

thus tells us what proportion of all possible mistakes have in fact been made. By subtracting this proportion of error from one, we ascertain the proportion of scale entries that are error free. As a matter of convention, any Guttman scale with a C_R of .90 or higher is accepted as sound, and any scale with a lower C_R is considered suspect and is generally not used for purposes of analysis.

We can see, then, that for items that meet the criterion of inherent ordering by degree of difficulty, Guttman scaling is a potent technique by which we may bring together a number of indicators into a single summary value that meaningfully represents a more general characteristic of a respondent.

Thurstone scaling

Yet another technique for creating summary measures, though one intended to solve a rather different problem, is the *Thurstone equal-appearing interval scale*. You will recall from our earlier discussion that in phrasing questions to measure such variables as social class, the researcher may choose to measure respondents' characteristics according to some externally imposed criterion, such as income or occupational prestige, or may alternatively permit respondents to apply their own standards of judgement, as by asking them what social class they *identify* with. The first approach enhances the comparability of data from case to case; the second may yield less comparable but more meaningful data. **Thurstone scaling** is a procedure for pursuing the second strategy (but with improved comparability) by letting a few members of the population to be studied actually participate in designing the scales that will be used to measure the characteristics of the population itself. By providing for the internal definition of the meanings of indicators, the Thurstone technique enhances the validity of a scale. By eliminating from consideration all but the most widely agreed-upon scale items, we enhance the reliability of the scale as well. The technique is rather complicated, but once we have these goals clearly in mind, it is not difficult to understand.

In constructing a Thurstone scale, the researcher first gathers a large number of statements, perhaps as many as one hundred, that reflect a variety of attitudes about some object. A number of 'judges' is then selected at random from the population to be studied. These are simply individuals on whom the list of statements will be tried out. The judges usually number at least fifty, and they may include as many as several hundred persons when resources permit. Each judge is presented with an 11-point scale – ranging from *favourable* (11) to *neutral* (6) to *unfavourable* (1) – and with a stack of cards on each of which is printed one of the statements. The judge is asked to examine each statement as it relates to the object in question and to place each card in one of eleven piles corresponding to their evaluation. Thus, those statements a judge regards as most favourable towards some object, such as university students, may be placed in pile 11, those slightly less favourable in pile 10, and so forth. In this manner, the researcher obtains every judge's understanding of the evaluative meaning of each statement.

At this point, each statement is assigned a scale score indicating its relative position on the favourable–unfavourable continuum, with higher scores going to those statements that are seen as more favourable. Many researchers assign these scores by calculating a mean, that is, by summing all of the individual scores for each item and dividing by the number of judges. A more appropriate procedure is to find the median value assigned to each statement (see Chapter 16) and to treat this as the scale score. Those items that are assigned widely divergent scores by different judges (for example, those that are spread over five or six categories) are eliminated at this point. From the remaining list, some fifteen to twenty final items are selected for inclusion in the questionnaire. The items should be those on which the judges most closely agree, and they should collectively cover the full spectrum of evaluations. Figure 9.3 illustrates a few typical statements that might be included in a Thurstone scale of attitudes towards university students.

When these final items reach the interview stage, respondents in the study sample are asked either which of the statements they agree with or, alternatively, which two or three statements are closest to their own view of the object in question, in this case, university students. The median value of the items so designated by each individual is then determined and is assigned as that respondent's scale score, the summary of their views towards the object. When the responses of a given individual are scattered widely over several noncontiguous items, the researcher generally concludes either that the individual has no attitude towards the object in question or that their attitude is organised differently from the structure assumed by the scale. In such cases, no scale score is assigned. But when, as is much more often the case, the responses do cluster tightly in one portion of the continuum, the

Figure 9.3   Typical Thurstone scale items

Please consider each of the following statements and indicate which ones you *agree* with:

1   It may not be widely known, but far more university students have volunteered for the military services than one would expect on the basis of their percentage in the population as a whole.
2   Some university students are definitely much superior in intelligence to other people in this community.
3   Whatever their faults, university students contribute a great deal to the quality of life in this community.
4   There is little in the image of university students in this community as being less ambitious or hard-working on the average than many other groups.
5   Some university students are clean and some are dirty, but the average university student does not differ in any way in his personal habits from the average person.
6   When you come right down to it, university students are just like anybody else in this community; they have their good points and they have their bad points.
7   While there are no doubt a few exceptions, in general university students tend to be especially clannish and to stick together.
8   While every group has a right to get ahead, university students are a little apt to disregard the rights and possessions of other people.
9   University students sometimes try to enter stores, hotels and restaurants where they are just not welcome.
10 Many people in this community would accept university students more easily if there were less drunkenness, self-righteousness and public demonstrations of sexual looseness and immorality among them.
11 It is a fairly well-established fact that university students have a less pleasant body odour than other people in this community.

Source: Adapted from Prejudice and the Norm of Rationality, *Sociometrey*, 27, pp. 353–71 (Schuman, H., Harding, J. 1964).

Note: These statements have been ordered from most favourable through neutral to most unfavourable for purposes of illustration. In practice, their order should be assigned randomly to obscure any systematic relationships. Scale values should not be shown on the questionnaire.

researcher can have reasonable confidence in the validity and reliability of the measure. This is due in no small part to the role of the judges in designing the research instrument.

The semantic differential

The fourth and final scaling procedure we shall discuss is termed the **semantic differential**. This procedure, which is quite different in structure and purpose from those already discussed, relies on a series of adjective pairs to bring out the meaning a given individual attaches to a particular concept. A typical series of these adjective pairs is illustrated in Figure 9.4. Respondents are presented with such a list, usually on a separate card, and are asked to rate a particular object, again in the illustration using university students, on a 7-point scale from one adjective to the other. Measurement of this type allows for variation in both the intensity and the direction of the attitude being measured, with neutrality being represented by the midpoint on the scale. The ordering of adjectives in each pair is determined randomly to prevent response set bias.

Although some researchers do break such scales into various underlying dimensions and sum the responses within each, most agree that semantic differential scales do not readily yield scale scores in the same way as the other techniques we have discussed. Rather, semantic differential scales are useful primarily either for purposes of comparison from object to object (Are ostensibly similar objects viewed by respondents in similar terms?) or for the development of scales measuring more general concepts (For example, what types of actions or views are regarded as either leftist or conservative?). In effect, then, the semantic differential serves a somewhat different and more fundamental purpose in the research process – that of helping to construct and evaluate definitions – than do the Likert, Guttman and Thurstone techniques.

Figure 9.4   Typical semantic differential items

Listed below are several pairs of words that could be used to describe university students. Between the words in each pair are several blanks. Please put an X on the blank for each pair that best describes how you feel about university students.

In general, university students are:

1	Boring	_ _ _ _ _ _ _	Interesting
2	Clean	_ _ _ _ _ _ _	Dirty
3	Emotional	_ _ _ _ _ _ _	Rational
4	Gentle	_ _ _ _ _ _ _	Violent
5	Good	_ _ _ _ _ _ _	Bad
6	Dishonest	_ _ _ _ _ _ _	Honest
7	Serious	_ _ _ _ _ _ _	Humorous
8	Idealistic	_ _ _ _ _ _ _	Realistic
9	Noisy	_ _ _ _ _ _ _	Quiet
10	Pleasant	_ _ _ _ _ _ _	Unpleasant
11	Rich	_ _ _ _ _ _ _	Poor
12	Pleasing	_ _ _ _ _ _ _	Annoying
13	Sincere	_ _ _ _ _ _ _	Insincere
14	Superficial	_ _ _ _ _ _ _	Profound
15	Valuable	_ _ _ _ _ _ _	Worthless

Ethical considerations

The creation of scales provides researchers with a convenient method to combine a number of variables into one overall measure that can reflect a rather abstract concept. Because scales often combine very different measures, it is important to remember that each individual measure must logically relate to the overall concept to be represented. Although such a combination of measures might be perfectly logical to you, others might disagree or have questions about the measures included in your scale. In order for others to be able to evaluate your scale and its components, you must therefore not only list all measures that have been incorporated into your scale, but also explain how these measures were conceptualised and operationalised. This also will allow other scholars to replicate your scale for their own research.

Conclusion

Researchers often use scales to assess 'unmeasurable' constructs such as political participation or social power. Since most complex constructs cannot be measured with a single indicator, one simple solution is to combine a number of related indicators into a single measure that is assumed to represent a broader construct. The scales used most frequently in political science research are Likert, Guttman, Thurstone and semantic differential scales.

There are, we should note, several other scaling techniques that one might employ in survey research. Those we have discussed are the most common and, within the limits noted, among the most useful. Together they should suggest the types of options available, and the criteria one must consider, when it becomes necessary to develop multiple but narrow measures of broad, underlying concepts.

Suggested reading and examples

Research examples

Good examples of scale construction can be found in recent studies on political trust. Mutz and Reeves (2005), for example, examine how incivility in political television programmes affects trust in government. Davis and Silver (2004) investigate how trust in government and perceived personal threat affect people's willingness to trade off civil liberties for security shortly after the 11 September 2001, attacks. Brewer and his colleagues (2004), on the other hand, use people's perceived trust in other nations as a predictor for opinions about world affairs.

Methodological reading

For a comprehensive survey and discussion of many specific scales found in the literature of social science, see *Measures of Political Attitudes* (Robinson *et al.* 1999) and *Measures of Personality and Social Psychological Attitudes* (Robinson *et al.* 1991). Application-oriented introductions to scaling are provided by *Scale Development: Theory and Applications* (DeVellis 2003) and *Scaling Procedures: Issues and Applications* (Netemeyer *et al.* 2003). In the chapter titled 'Undimensional scaling' in *Quantitative Applications in the Social Sciences*, McIver and Carmines (1981) provide succinct overviews of Likert, Guttman and Thurstone scaling at a slightly more sophisticated level than that presented here.

References

Adorno, Theodore W., Frenkel-Brunswik, Else, Levinson, Daniel J. and Nevitt Sanford, R. 1950. *The Authoritarian Personality*. New York: Harper & Row.

Brewer, Paul R., Gross, Kimberly, Aday, Sean and Willnat, Lars. 2004. 'International trust and public opinion about world affairs'. *American Journal of Political Science*, vol. 48 (January), pp. 93–109.

Davis, Darren W. and Silver, Brian D. 2004. 'Civil liberties vs. security: Public opinion in the context of the terrorist attacks on America'. *American Journal of Political Science*, vol. 48 (January), pp. 28–46.

DeVellis, Robert F. 2003. *Scale Development: Theory and Applications*, 2nd edn. Thousand Oaks, CA: Sage.

McIver, John P. and Carmines, Edward G. 1981. *Quantitative Applications in the Social Sciences*. Beverly Hills, CA: Sage.

Mutz, Diana C. and Reeves, Byron. 2005. 'The new videomalaise: Effects of televised incivility on political trust'. *American Political Science Review*, vol. 99 (February), pp. 1–15.

Netemeyer, Richard G., Bearden, William O. and Shama, Subhash. 2003. *Scaling Procedures: Issues and Applications*. Thousand Oaks, CA: Sage.

Robinson, John P., Shaver, Phillip R. and Wrightsman, Lawrence S. eds. 1991. *Measures of Personality and Social Psychological Attitudes*. San Diego, CA: Academic Press.

Robinson, John P., Shaver, Phillip R. and Wrightsman, Lawrence S. eds. 1999. *Measures of Political Attitudes*. San Diego, CA: Academic Press.

Schuman, H. and Harding, J. 1964. 'Prejudice and the norm of rationality', *Sociometry*, vol. 27, pp. 353–71.

Research exercises

1 Select a multifaceted concept (for example, *political alienation*) and identify twenty survey items that might be considered indicators of the concept. Construct both a Thurstone scale and a Likert scale from these items. Administer the survey items to ten friends or classmates and assign each a score on both the Thurstone and the Likert scales. Compare the results.

2 When carrying out Exercise 1, also ask respondents for information on their actual behaviour that can be used to check the validity of the scale scores you obtain as indicators of the concept. (For example, do people who score high on political alienation act as we would expect alienated people to behave, whereas those who score low on alienation exhibit what we would regard as nonalienated behaviour?) Now compare the scale scores with the behavioural reports and write up your findings by comparing the Thurstone and Likert scales for validity.

3 Select a series of adjective pairs to construct a semantic differential scale measuring perceptions of the heads of state of five countries. Prepare an instrument like that in Figure 9.4 and administer it to a sample of your classmates. Compute a summary score for each descriptor pair and each head of state. What have you learned about your classmates? What have you learned about their perceptions of each head of state and of heads of state generally? Which adjective pairs were most useful in drawing meaningful distinctions and conclusions? Why were these most useful?

Key terms

Cronbach's alpha	Likert scaling	scaling
Guttman scaling	scale	semantic differential
Kuder-Richardson 20 (KR20)	scale score	Thurstone scaling

10 Sources and applications of aggregate data

- What is the distinguishing characteristic of aggregate data?
- What is the most common pitfall to avoid when analysing aggregate data?

Introduction

Scientists are interested in individual cases only to the degree that these examples help them to test more general hypotheses. Similarly, political scientists typically observe individuals solely in an effort to learn more about that type of individual. For example, we may study the behaviour of a particular EU commissioner not because we want to know about Commissioner John Bull, but because we think we can better understand or predict the behaviour of commissioners in the European Union from what was observed about Commissioner Bull. Political scientists are usually interested in the study of groups or collections of persons or institutions, such as American migrant workers, South African voters, Japanese bureaucrats or European parliaments.

Defining aggregate data

Sometimes, in order to study these groups, we have to gather information on the individual members of the groups (or a representative sample of them) and combine or *aggregate* that information to obtain information about the group *as a group*. Often, however, there already exists aggregated information about the group. Data on the characteristics of an entire group or aggregate of individuals are referred to as **aggregate data**.

There are two general categories of aggregate data. The first category – **summative indicators** – includes large sets of measures of group characteristics that are created by combining the behaviour of all members of the group. For example, the population of a nation is an aggregate datum derived by adding inhabitants as units. Birth, death, literacy, suicide and crime *rates* are aggregate data created by adding up the number of particular events (births, deaths, crimes etc.) in a group and expressing it in a standardised unit such as *per thousand persons in the population*. In each case, the aggregate datum quantifies some *group* characteristic that individual members of the group cannot possess. Individuals may be born or learn to read and write but cannot have a birth or literacy *rate* in the same sense that a nation does. These data are measures of aggregate characteristics.

A second general category of aggregate data consists of those measures that quantify group characteristics that are derived not from any combination of individual members' characteristics but from qualities of the group *when acting as a group*. They are often referred to as **syntality indicators**. For example, *form of government* is a system-level variable, and a given nation may have a democratic or a nondemocratic form of government regardless of whether its individual citizens hold democratic or nondemocratic values and attitudes.

Types of groups

Data from each category are available on many different kinds of groups from a variety of sources. Such groups may be broadly classified into **areal groups** (those defined by residence within a geographic area, such as a nation, city or census tract) and **demographic groups** (those defined by personal characteristics, such as age, ethnicity or occupation).

In this chapter you will learn that proper use of aggregate data involves solving some challenging methodological problems. The advantages of using such data, however, often far outweigh the costs. Political scientists may find the use of aggregate data necessary or desirable because individual-level data are either unobtainable or too expensive to obtain.

As examples of studies for which individual data might be impossible to obtain, consider the following cases.

1   If we want to do a historical study, at least some of the groups on which we need data (for example, the population of Birmingham in 1901) may be dead.
2   Members of some politically important groups, such as international terrorist organisations, may absolutely refuse to be identified or interviewed.
3   Often, political scientists find themselves in situations in which it is theoretically possible to collect individual level data, but such collection is prohibitively expensive. This is especially likely to be the case when we are interested in comparing nations, because the cost and logistical problems of multinational survey research are enormous.

If you are interested in research questions for which individual-level data are unavailable, you may find it worthwhile to search for aggregate data that contain the basic information needed. In this chapter we introduce you to the types of aggregate data that are available, suggest some sources of these data, discuss some of the methodological problems encountered in using aggregate data and, finally, offer some guidelines for collecting aggregate data. You will soon recognise that the proper use of aggregate data requires the mastery of data collection, processing and analysis techniques. As a student and as a politics researcher, however, you are more likely to work with aggregate data than with data collected through any of the methods described in preceding chapters, because aggregate data are so readily available.

Types of aggregate data

Most of the aggregate data available to political scientists are gathered by nonsocial scientists for reasons unrelated to research. In fact, one of the most challenging aspects of aggregate data analysis is finding a way to use existing data as indicators of concepts of theoretical interest to the researcher. For example, at first glance there is little reason to believe that a politics researcher will be concerned with the percentage of short-wave radios or televisions or how many people have newspaper subscriptions in some nations. As scholars, we are not, after all, marketing agents for the press. But these figures may be useful as partial indicators of the amount of political communication that goes on within a nation or of its level of economic development, and these clearly are appropriate concerns for politics researchers. Similarly, the number of hospital beds per thousand persons in the population takes on political significance when it is viewed as an indicator of, say, the distribution of health care facilities among groups within a city or state.

The point is that aggregate data are often of no intrinsic interest and have to be transformed in some way to be of use. Do not look only for ready-made indicators of concepts, but be alert to the possibility of combining seemingly unrelated measures into useful indicators.

We can identify six types of aggregate data (Merritt 1970). They are explained here in roughly *descending* order of the extent to which they are likely to be valid and reliable.

Census data

Many of the world's nations attempt to survey their entire population (or at least all households) periodically in order to gather information to be used for such purposes as levying taxes and planning public policy. The data commonly collected includes such information as number of people in the family, sex of the head of the household, length of residence, educational levels, family income and condition of housing. Though census data are collected from individuals, by the time they become available to researchers as part of the public record, the data usually appear as summary figures (the total number of persons who own a car in a given geographic area, for instance).

Census data have several desirable characteristics that make them extremely valuable in aggregate data analysis. First, although errors can occur, census data are generally quite reliable. Second, because the variables measured are normally straightforward, census data are usually regarded as highly valid. Third, some nations have been collecting relatively standardised data for many years. Thus, census data provide an opportunity to trace historical trends or to test hypotheses about change over time. Fourth, because census data are generally standardised – that is, they contain responses to the same questions and classify responses in the same categories – within nations and are often comparable between nations, they are useful in comparing different cities, regions or nations. In addition, census data are easily available. Many nations publish reports of both major census projects (generally undertaken once every ten years) and any of a wide variety of specialised surveys undertaken in between. The United Nations (unstats.un.org/unsd/) publishes the annual *Demographic Yearbook,* describing the census data available from various countries. A plethora of UN Statistics Division data is available online, frequently in downloadable, spreadsheet form. In the United Kingdom, the Office for National Statistics (www.statistics.gov.uk) can assist social scientists in gaining access to and working with the wide variety of data available from the agency.

Organisational statistics

In every nation, the various levels of government, businesses and organised groups such as labour unions and professional associations gather data related to their own operations. If these statistics happen to fit the requirements of a particular social scientist's research project, they can be of great value.

Some organisations collect their own data, as does a multinational corporation keeping a record of its capital investments, a hospital recording information on patients, or a local government recording property assessments for tax purposes. Others use data generated by other agencies, such as the United Kingdom Office for National Statistics (www.statistics.gov.uk), to create data in the form of various indices of, for example, economic performance or population shifts.

With either type of official statistics, there can be problems. The first, and perhaps greatest, problem is that of gaining access to the data. Data compiled by government agencies are generally part of the public record and readily available, but data collected by nongovernmental organisations are private property. Some organisations, especially businesses, consider their data sensitive and are most reluctant to share them. Often the problem is less one of gaining access to the data than one of simply learning of their existence. There are no central listings of the statistics collected by the thousands of public and private organisations engaged in such record keeping. Researchers may, therefore, miss major opportunities because of a lack of information about the existence or content of particular statistics.

A second problem is that the content and quality of the data may vary greatly, making comparisons and generalisations difficult. If teachers' unions in Indiana and Ohio do not collect comparable information about their members, we cannot use their statistics to make meaningful comparisons between them. In addition, if we do not know how data have been collected, we may not know how much confidence to place in the figures.

Finally, data may not be in a usable form. A local government's vital statistics (records of births, deaths, marriages, deeds) may be available only in unaggregated form and only in a central location, so that a researcher has to sit for countless hours in a government office tediously hand-recording the data so that they can be converted to a machine-readable (i.e., computerised) form and totalled. This can require an unjustifiable investment of time and money.

These problems are not found in all official statistics, and even when they are encountered, the potential payoff in economical research is generally worth the effort required to solve them.

Sample surveys

Survey research is designed to gather individual-level data. When surveys are based on samples that are representative of a population of interest, it is often possible to use their results as aggregate data. Suppose, for example, we want to compare the political information level of two nations' citizenry. If each nation has a public opinion polling organisation that regularly surveys a national sample (as Gallup and Mori do in the United Kingdom) and that asks questions about such behavioural matters as frequency of watching television news reports or subscriptions to news magazines, we might use the results to construct aggregate measures of our variable. Similar use can sometimes be made of individual surveys conducted for academic purposes. Survey data, if properly collected, have the advantage of being quite reliable, and they can be as valid as the researcher is wise in constructing indicators. Data are also generally available (at least for a price) from the agencies or scholars who have collected them, and they are often in a readily usable form.

Publications' content

In a construction of aggregate data, content analysis can be applied to publications sponsored by or distributed among particular groups. For example, if we are examining political socialisation processes in Great Britain, we might content-analyse the textbooks used in citizenship courses to determine the extent to which they stress democratic values, and we might then use the combined results as one indicator of the nation's democratic orientation. Similarly, we might rely on content analysis of the major newspapers of developing nations to derive an indicator of those nations' relative attention to international and domestic events or of their support for the United Nations. In each case, the product of the content analysis is an indicator of a group characteristic.

This type of aggregate data is generated by the researcher specifically for the purpose of a given research project instead of being collected from a primary source, such as a census report. As a result, access to such data depends on the availability of the publications or databases (such as LexisNexis) needed for a content analysis and on the researcher's having the resources necessary to perform the content analysis. Aggregate data collected through content analysis of publications have the advantage of being adaptable to an individual study but generally provide only highly imperfect indicators of underlying concepts. Ask yourself, for instance, how confident you would feel in making statements about the kind of political values British schoolchildren learn from an analysis of their citizenship texts. It is worth remembering that the reliability and validity of these content-derived aggregate data depend on the skill with which the researcher applies the rules discussed in Chapter 12.

Event data

Often, political scientists are interested in the occurrence of discrete events that are not recorded in census reports or organisational data because they are too infrequent or fall outside the responsibility of any one agency. Riots, revolutions, assassinations, the breaking of diplomatic ties, protest demonstrations, indictments of public officials for crimes in office, *coups d'état*, and the creation of new political parties are all examples. Information on these events can be useful in the construction of indicators of group properties. For instance, we might want to measure a nation's political stability by counting the number of acts of political violence occurring there in a given time period or we might want to compare the level of political corruption in several cities by counting the number of indictments of public officials for bribery.

There are a number of event data sets that may be used for such studies. One of the best known is the *World Handbook of Political and Social Indicators*, into which researchers have been compiling tens of thousands of world events since its inception in 1963 at Yale. Currently it documents political events, coded by country, from the 1940s to the present. These data are available to researchers at member institutions through the Interuniversity Consortium for Political and Social Research (www.icpsr.umich.edu).

If not available from others' research, event data are gathered by a process very similar to content analysis. Guided by our theory and hypotheses, we decide what events are relevant to our study and, carefully operationalising them (for example, deciding what actions constitute a riot), we systematically survey sources such as newspapers, yearbooks and radio broadcast transcripts that are likely to contain reports of them, and we take a tally (being careful to avoid double-counting the same event when it is reported in more than one source). In addition, content-analysis techniques can be used to produce more detailed data about these events. We can, for example, classify terrorist bombings according to their type (e.g., suicide, car etc.), the number of injuries, the number of deaths, the location (e.g., democratic or not, world region etc.), and whether responsibility was claimed in order to develop a taxonomy of terrorist attacks.

Event data can be made relatively reliable by careful training and supervision of those who read and code the source materials, but it is extremely difficult to make event data *valid*. The major challenge to validity is comprehensiveness in reporting. Even when all known sources or reports of some type of event have been reviewed, the researcher cannot be sure that some such events have occurred but have not been reported. In some nations the government carefully controls reports of political events in order to present the preferred image to the world, so that many important happenings, such as the use of troops to break a strike, may not be reported and no valid measure of the events can be constructed. A second and related problem grows from the potential inaccuracy of reports. Even when events are recorded, the details of their occurrence can be distorted intentionally or unintentionally. Such problems are not insurmountable, but researchers must be aware of them in designing their studies around event data, and they must realistically assess their chances of acquiring valid measures by this means.

Judgemental data

Occasionally there simply are no data available to use for construction of measures of particular aggregate properties. In these cases, researchers can sometimes use as data the opinions of experts or persons with special knowledge.

Consider the example of a study of the lobbying efforts by several interest groups for and against environmental protection legislation. There may be no public record on the subject, but researchers can ask key legislators about their judgement of whether and how strongly each group supports or opposes such legislation in its lobbying efforts. Similarly, if researchers are unable to gather data on the force governments employ to stay in power in various nations, they can ask other scholars who have studied those nations' political systems for their judgement about the coerciveness of the governments.

Obviously, judgemental data suffer from serious limitations. In the first place, their accuracy is subject to the biases and limited experiences of the judges. Using many judges and checking their estimates against one another represent one way to avoid relying on false or partial judgements. It is often difficult, however, to find several qualified judges who differ in their background and their experience with the subject matter, so that even using multiple judges is no guarantee against inaccurate data. Second, even when judges provide perfectly accurate information, judgemental data are generally imprecise. We are, after all, asking for opinions and impressions of complex phenomena, not counts of discrete events. It is important that researchers recognise these limitations in designing studies and in analysing judgemental data.

Limitations in the use of aggregate data

From the foregoing discussion you can see that the specific types of problems encountered in aggregate data analysis vary with the types and sources of data being used. There are, however, some general problems that may be confronted in any use of aggregate data analysis. We will discuss two. Our purpose is not to provide solutions but to alert you to the need to be on the lookout for these problems in your research and the research of others.

Ecological fallacy

It is important to consider first the general problem referred to as the **ecological fallacy**, because knowledge of it should guide the design of research and the specification and operationalisation of variables, as well as the very decision to use aggregate data to address a specific research question.

Researchers run the risk of committing one of several types of ecological fallacy anytime they attempt to generalise to one level of analysis from data collected at another. For example, if we collect data on the racial characteristics of individual welfare recipients in each *state* in the United States and find a strong positive relationship between being nonwhite and receiving public assistance, we may be tempted to generalise 'up' to the national level, claiming that this relationship holds for the nation as a whole, or to generalise 'down' by assuming that the relationship found in any given state will also be found in each of its counties. If, however, we actually do aggregate our data at the national or county level, we may find that the relationship is significantly different from that found when data are aggregated at the state level. Empirical studies of the ecological problem have shown that relationships may not only be weaker or stronger at different levels but may even change directions. When researchers generalise from one level of analysis to another, they run the risk of seriously misinterpreting their data and reaching conclusions that are simply wrong.

Does this mean that we must use only data that are aggregated at the level of whatever units of analysis we choose for our studies and can never generalise up or down in research? No. There are techniques of data analysis that, under some conditions, can at least minimise the risks involved in making inferences between levels of analysis. If researchers find that they must use data aggregated at a level other than that with which they are concerned, they should plan to employ one or more of these data analysis techniques outlined by King (1997) or Achen and Shively (1995), and should take care that their data meet the requirements of this type of analysis before investing time and resources in gathering them.

Whenever possible, though, you should avoid selecting indicators that require inferences between levels of analysis. For example, suppose we are studying the relationship between union membership and support for the Labour Party in the United Kingdom, and we discover aggregate data for parliamentary constituency that give the percentage of each district's labour force holding union memberships and the percentage of each district's voters that have voted Labour in recent elections. We will be able to use these data if parliamentary constituencies are our unit of analysis and our goal is to be able to make statements such as, *Those constituencies with proportionately more union members tend to elect Labour candidates.* However, if individual voters are our units of analysis, we will want to be able to make statements such as, *Labour union members tend to support the Labour Party.* In this case we *cannot* use, with any confidence, the aggregate data from parliamentary constituencies, and we will be wise to seek data on *individuals'* union membership and voting behaviour.

Variable precision

A second, and related, set of problems often encountered in aggregate data analysis relates to the difficulties of creating valid indicators from aggregate data. It is rare to find aggregate figures that can be used directly as a measure of some concept of interest to political scientists. Most frequently, we find numbers representing variables that can be viewed as part of the larger phenomena to which our concepts refer. In studying the political impact of modernisation, for instance, researchers may not be able to find aggregate data that directly report the level of modernisation of various nations. They might, however, be able to find information on the proportion of each nation's population that lives in communities of more than 25,000, is engaged in nonagricultural employment, or is literate, all of which can be considered components of modernisation. Such figures are often referred to as **raw data**; they are of no intrinsic interest by themselves but can be used to create indicators of concepts that are of interest.

Developing useful measures

The challenge that aggregate data analysts face is one of finding theoretically and methodologically justifiable ways of converting raw data into useful measures. Two basic approaches to this are the creation of indices and the transformation of data.

Index construction is a means of reducing complex data to a single indicator that more fully captures the meaning of a concept than does any of its components. Three commonly used types of index are additive, multiplicative and weighted. An **additive index** is appropriate when available data represent different measures of the *same* underlying variable. For example, we might want simply to add together reported numbers of exported bushels of wheat, corn and soybeans in order to obtain an indicator of the concept *agricultural exports*.

Often, however, aggregate data represent measures of *different* aspects of a phenomenon and cannot be added. There is, for instance, no mathematical logic by which we can add the number of people involved in a riot to the number of hours it lasts in order to create an index of riot severity. Number of participants and length of duration are nonadditive elements of the phenomenon called *riots*. We can, however, argue that those two elements interact with one another to determine how severe a riot is. By this logic we might *multiply* the number of participants by the number of hours of duration to create an indicator of the severity of the riot by measuring the 'demonstrator hours' devoted to it. Such an indicator is called a **multiplicative index**. Indices of this type are called for anytime we have measures of different aspects of a concept.

In some circumstances, raw data have to be weighted by some standard to become useful indicators of concepts. For example, the *number* of persons attending antigovernment rallies is a useful indicator of the legitimacy accorded a government only when it is expressed as a percentage of the population. By doing this we are weighting one variable (the number attending antigovernment rallies) by a second (the population) to create a **weighted index**. Similarly, we might want to weight the number of anti-government demonstrations by the variable *time* to create an index of demonstrations per year on the assumption that ten demonstrations in one year indicate more political unrest than ten demonstrations spread over ten years. This particular type of weighting is known as *standardisation.*

Weighting is technically simple to do, but it is often conceptually difficult to determine whether a measure should be weighted and by what it should be weighted. For instance, it is not clear whether arms races are triggered by the absolute level of armaments held by nations or by the ratio of one nation's armaments to another's. Should a nation's armament level be weighted by its opponents' armament level before the figure can be used as an indicator in a study of arms races? Answers to such questions are often found in an empirical examination of how the use of weighted and unweighted indicators affects the results of statistical analysis.

Often, in the use of aggregate data, measures are encountered that cannot be made useful simply by combining them with others, but that must be individually modified. Sometimes even indices can be made more useful if they are modified. Such modifications are referred to as **data transformations**. Data are transformed principally in order to meet the requirements of certain statistical procedures that researchers want to employ in data analysis. In general, the justification for transforming data is to avoid having the results of statistical analyses distorted by features of the distribution of the raw data.

There are many techniques of data transformation, and each is designed to correct different flaws in raw data. However, the *logarithmic transformation* can serve as an example of how transformations work. Some of the most useful statistical procedures can legitimately be applied only to data that are normally distributed. (We discuss normal distributions in Chapter 16.) Application of these procedures to data that are not normally distributed can result in serious underestimates of the strength of relationships between variables, as well as other misleading results. Yet raw aggregate data are often not normally distributed. Logarithmic transformations are designed to make data more nearly approximate a normal distribution. The basic procedure is to add a constant to the score for each case on the raw data and then substitute the appropriate logarithm for the original score by using a log table. The effects of such a transformation on data are suggested in Figure 10.1, which shows the results of transforming hypothetical data on the number of people taking part in abortion rights demonstrations in fifty-seven US cities. The distribution of the transformed data in Figure 10.1(b) does not form a normal, or bell-shaped, curve, but it is much more nearly normal than the distribution of the raw data in Figure 10.1(a).

Figure 10.1 Effects of logarithmic transformation on hypothetical data from abortion rights demonstrations in fifty-seven US cities

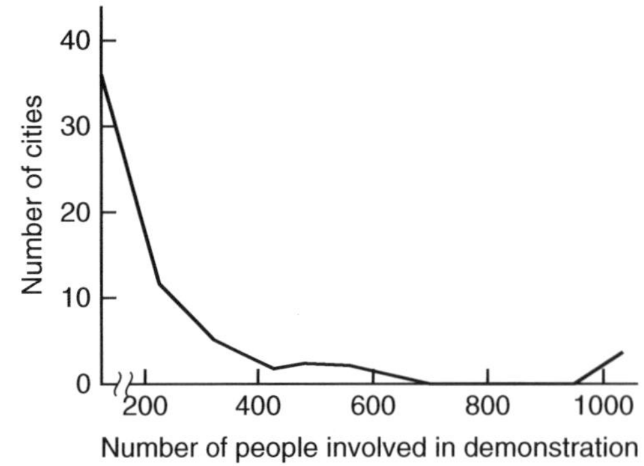

You should not interpret anything we have just said as meaning that having multiple measures of some concept is a problem that must be solved. On the contrary, it is highly desirable to have *multiple indicators* of concepts, and though it is often useful to combine measures into indices, it is usually wise also to record the individual measures and examine them separately at some stage of the data analysis. The reason is that multiple indicators can be used to check the validity of our operationalisation of concepts.

For example, suppose we want to measure the concept *gender discrimination in employment* among the English counties. We might be able to find aggregate data on the following variables:

The ratio of the average salary paid to women to the average salary paid to men.

The proportion of all professionals in the county who are female.

The ratio of the unemployment rate for women to the unemployment rate for men.

We can use all three indicators by scoring each county on each variable and comparing the results. If those counties that appear to have the most discrimination by one measure also rank high on discrimination by the other measures, we will feel more confident that each measure is a valid indicator of the underlying concept *gender discrimination in employment*. If, on the other hand, we find that those counties that rank high on discrimination as measured by two of the indicators rank low on discrimination as measured by the third, we will be reluctant to use the deviant measure as an indicator of our concept.

The more independent indicators we can locate for each concept, the better, for with more indicators we can provide more convincing tests of the validity of each. For instance, in the preceding example, with only three measures, we might not be altogether sure that the deviant measure is not, in fact, the valid one and the other two invalid. It may be its very validity as an indicator of our concept that makes it stand apart from the others in the way it ranks counties. If, however, we have five or ten measures that produce consistent rankings of counties and one that stands apart, we can feel quite confident that it is the deviant measure that is invalid. A variety of techniques is available for using multiple measures to test and enhance the validity of our indicators (see Suggested reading and examples).

There is one additional important issue to consider when using aggregate data. This potential problem stems from the fact that aggregate data are often available in a form that does not allow valid comparisons across units. For example, if we are interested in the degree to which different local authorities in the United Kingdom exhibit a commitment to education, we might find data on how much each local authority spends on education each year. It would be inappropriate, however, to compare the total number of pounds the Isle of Wight spends on education to the total number of pounds Sheffield spends, because the two local authorities differ in size and wealth. The Isle of Wight and may spend only a fraction of the amount Sheffield does and yet exhibit a stronger commitment to education because it is spending far more *per school-age child* or a far greater *portion* of its total budget on schooling. To make a valid comparison among the local authorities, it would be necessary to restate the amount they spend on education in some way that controls for differences in population and wealth. Unless we do this, we will not have a valid indicator of our concept, and our conclusions will be determined by the relative size and wealth of local authorities rather than by their relative commitment to education. Additionally, of course, our research report will have to justify the apparently logical connection between the concept of 'commitment to education' and the variable 'per child state school spending'.

Situations like this require that we *standardise* our measures in some way. A **standardised measure** is one that is stated in a way that, in order to allow valid comparisons, takes into account the differences that might exist among cases on variables other than the one it represents. It is very often necessary to standardise aggregate data prior to making comparisons among units of analysis. This may involve collecting data on variables that are of no direct relevance to the project. For example, in a study of commitment to education, we might need to collect data on the populations and total governmental expenditures of the local authorities in order to standardise their educational expenditures by stating them as pound expenditure per school-age child or a percentage of total expenditures. Similarly, if we wanted to measure the concept *militarisation* by observing the amount of money nations spend on the military, we would need to standardise the measure by stating it as a percentage of a nation's gross national product (the total value of all goods and services produced in the country) before making comparisons. Unless we did this, a wealthy nation might look more militaristic than a poor nation even though it devoted only a tenth as much of its total wealth to the military as a poor nation did.

Whenever you anticipate making comparisons among groups (nations, cities, organisations etc.), you must be alert to the need to standardise your measures and must plan to collect the additional data necessary for this standardisation. Standardisation is generally achieved by stating measures either as a percentage or proportion of some other variable or as so many units per unit of some other variable. This often results in the computation of a *rate* such as a crime rate (crimes per 10,000 persons), literacy rate (literate persons per 1,000 population), or infant mortality rate (infant deaths per 1,000 live births). The additional work of collecting data on the variables on which your key variable must be standardised is *absolutely necessary* for valid comparisons among cases that differ significantly in theoretically relevant ways.

The point of this section is that aggregate data analysts should not only be cautious about using raw data as indicators of concepts but must also be alert to the potential uses of multiple indicators and the possibility of improving indicators by combining, standardising or transforming measures.

Sources of aggregate data

The amount of aggregate data available in the world is so great that one is inclined to believe it possible to find indicators for almost any empirically useful concept. In fact, the very abundance of the available data sometimes poses problems as researchers find themselves having to search scores of sources to find all available indicators. Yet, even with this reservoir of data, researchers are sometimes unable to locate exact indicators of the concept they want to measure, for exactly the right time period and aggregated at exactly the right level.

We cannot begin to list *all* the sources of aggregate data here. We can, however, list those sources of general data that are most likely to be of use for politics research. Whereas some data sources contain data on a variety of subjects and cannot be neatly characterised as a source of one particular type of data, we have classified the sources listed here by the major type of data they are likely to yield. Most university libraries have the publications listed here or are able to help you locate them, and most are easily accessible over the internet.

The key to successful use of any of the documents or data archives described here is knowing precisely what type of measures you are seeking. The hypotheses you are testing, the theory you are working from, or a precise statement of your research question can tell you what type of data, such as a measure of nations' economic productivity or of the size of their military forces, is needed to operationalise the concepts utilised in your research. Simply going to the library with the idea of poking around in available data sources until you run across some indicators that look useful, will almost certainly cause you to meet with failure. If, on the other hand, you approach the task of gathering data with a clearly conceptualised research strategy in mind, you should be able to tell the reference or social science librarian what you need.

1 The *Office for National Statistics* provides access to its own data but also some from government departments and devolved agencies in Scotland, Wales and Northern Ireland. (www.statistics.gov.uk).

The *ONS* not only provides key economic data on the UK but also the *UK Census* which provides aggregate data for the UK for every 10 years up until the most recent census in 2011 (www.statistics.gov.uk/census). Individual level data is only available for historical censuses from 1841 to 1901 at the national archives (www.nationalarchives.gov.uk/census/).

2 The Electoral Commission of the UK maintains a database of registers covering all aspects of political parties including officially registered parties and party finances (including donations and borrowing), some of which can be found on the Commission website: www.electoralcommission.org.uk/party-finance/database-of-registers.

3 A full list of UK parliamentary constituencies is available on Wikipedia at en.wikipedia.org/wiki/List_of_United_Kingdom_Parliament_constituencies, which provides links to particular constituencies, with past voting records and boundaries, but be aware that the Electoral Commission regularly makes changes to constituency boundaries so one needs to consult the Wikipedia pages on possible Constituencies in the next United Kingdom general election as well as the current constituencies (en.wikipedia.org/wiki/Constituencies_in_the_next_United_Kingdom_general_election). An alphabetical List of Constituencies and Members of Parliament often with e-mail, webpage and short biographical links to each MP is available at www.parliament.uk/directories/hciolists/alcm.cfm. A downloadable list in Excel format of parliamentary constituencies with standardised codes for parliamentary constituencies is available from the UK Office for National Statistics at www.statistics.gov.uk/geography/names_codes.asp. Data on individual constituencies can be found at UK Polling Report (ukpollingreport.co.uk) including ethnic composition, educational and social data. Another useful database is The British Parliamentary Constituency Database: 1992–2005 which can be found at wps.pearsoned.co.uk/ema_uk_he_budge_newbritpol_4/67/17308/4430963.cw/-/4430964/index.html.

4 The British Election Study (www.essex.ac.uk/bes) provides a wealth of aggregate data on UK elections drawn from pre and post-election face-to-face interviews with voters and non-voters. The 2010 data are available online.

5 All statistics released by agencies of the United States federal government in the *American Statistical Index*. In addition, statistics on economic and population trends, foreign trade, energy use, and other issues collected for more than 100 federal agencies can be accessed through the Internet at FedStats (www.fedstats.gov). The publications of the Bureau of the Census are indexed in the *Catalogue of United States Census Publications*, which describes the data available from the censuses of housing, population, governments, and agriculture, among others. Many of these data are summarised each year in the publication *Statistical Abstract of the United States*, which presents selected statistical profiles of the United States and its subdivisions and contains an extensive guide to public and private data sources. Many of these tables are also available in downloadable spreadsheets (www.census.gov/compendia/statab/population/). Each of the various censuses of the United States is summarised in *Subject and U.S. Area Reports*.

6 Some frequently used sources of specialised data about the United States are the *Congressional District Data Book*, which provides demographic and economic information and voting records for United States congressional districts and the *County and City Data Book*, which contains demographic and economic data for states, counties, cities, unincorporated places of more than 25,000 in population and urbanised areas in the United States on an annual basis. Similar data are presented in the *State and Metropolitan Area Data Book* from the Bureau of the Census. Voting data are summarised by Congressional Quarterly in the *Guide to U.S. Elections*, which gives returns for presidential, Senate, House and gubernatorial races since 1824.

7 *Demographic and related data on other nations.* Recognising the difficulties in locating comparable measures of any given variable for different countries, a variety of sourcebooks contain data collected by different nations and international bodies. Researchers who use these must be especially sensitive to the need to ensure the comparability of reported figures before basing comparisons on them.

The United Nations Statistics Division (unstats.un.org/unsd/) publishes three especially useful documents: The *Statistical Yearbook* summarises data on population characteristics, economic activity, education, communications and other matters for the world's nations each year; the *Yearbook of National Accounts Statistics* reports detailed information on economic activity; and the *Demographic Yearbook* gives historical data on population characteristics and annually examines a special subject, such as population distributions, mortality rates or ethnic compositions. In addition, the United Nations Educational, Scientific and Cultural Organisation (UNESCO) publishes the *Statistical Yearbook* (www.uis.unesco.org/), which summarises data on education, communication, science and technology in more than 200 countries.

The *Statesman's Yearbook* provides detailed information about nations that has been compiled from a variety of national and international sources. The European Union publishes the *Eurostat Yearbook*, which provides demographic, social, political, and economic data for EU member states and candidate countries for leading EU economic partners (ec.europa.eu/eurostat/). Further summary figures on national characteristics can be found in the *World Almanac* and *Worldmark Encyclopedia of Nations* in well-indexed form. A good deal of economic data can be found in the *Yearbook of International Trade Statistics*.

8 *Event data.* By their nature, event data are not reported in regular, summary form. They have to be discovered in running records of daily events that are not necessarily compiled with the social scientist in mind. In fact, the data recorded will reflect what is considered newsworthy at the time and the prejudices of the journalist and editors who decide to cover the events. It is easier to report on events where access is easy and difficult to cover stories where access is restricted. Care must be taken to make sure that key events have not been ignored or the events that do occur are not exaggerated or biased towards one group or location. Two of the most comprehensive reference sources for events reported in newspapers are the indexes for *The Times* (London) and the *New York Times*. Perhaps the most extensive general news digest is *Keesing's Contemporary Archives: Weekly Diary of World Events*, which contains transcripts of important speeches, some election and statistical data and news summaries, and is indexed by subject and proper name.

9 *Survey data.* Many of the sources named thus far present data in printed form. Using them for large studies requires recording the data and transferring them to machine-readable form. The most useful sources of survey data, by contrast, are electronic data sets. These are available from a variety of data archives, several of which were identified in Chapter 8.

In addition to these sources, it is important to recognise the rich variety of private sources of data. Which of these is appropriate to any given study will be suggested by the subject of the study. For a study of the investment patterns of European firms, for example, useful data may be held by individual banks or by national and international associations of banks.

Collecting aggregate data

If data are not available electronically, researchers face the task of transferring the data from a source to their records in a machine-readable form. The basic challenge is one of systematically coding and recording data.

Though transferring data takes only a fraction of the time required to collect the same data through field research, it can be a very time-consuming task. It is important, then, to do it as efficiently as possible. The way to begin is by carefully thinking through in advance the research design and the data analysis you intend to perform so that you can specify exactly which cases you want data on and what measures you want to record for each. Failure to do this advance preparation will often lead to wasting time recording data for which you ultimately have no use. Moreover, by carefully planning the study, you can list all cases and variables in some order of importance so that if you run short of time or funds in the data collection stage, you can make a rational choice to leave out certain cases or variables in order to terminate data collection in the least harmful manner. Keeping this option open means that you must proceed sequentially, either collecting all data on each case one at a time (if you want to be able to drop cases but need all variables) or collecting data for all cases on each variable one at a time (if you need all cases but want to be able to leave out some variables).

In either event, you need two basic tools for data collection: a set of *data specifications* and a *recording form*. **Data specifications** are simply detailed descriptions of the data that are to be recorded for each case and variable, including any coding instructions. Sometimes a single phrase will serve as a data specification for census data or organisational statistics – for example, *total number of government employees in 1905* or *adult population in 2007*. However, apparently simple pieces of data can require extensive qualifications. For instance, if we want a figure on total state expenditures for public welfare programmes in a given year, we have to identify those programmes that qualify as welfare for purposes of the study. If we want a measure of the number of persons in nations' armed forces, we have to include instructions for excluding domestic police from the count for countries in which the police are formally part of the military. Being able to provide these details in data specifications requires prior study of the subject and the reporting systems of your units of analysis. Even then, unexpected difficulties can arise. You may, for example, discover that budgeted and actual welfare expenditures differ considerably or that corrections for inflation have to be added in time-series studies. The adjustments you make in response to these problems must be both technically correct and consistent with the meaning of the concept operationalised by the measure.

When collecting event data, a coding manual will help to document your data specifications, particularly noting essential distinctions in definitions. You will want, for instance, to be able to distinguish between riots and peaceful demonstrations or between pro-government and antigovernment demonstrations. The most dependable way of doing this is to develop a **coding manual** (or **codebook**) that records the details of those characteristics that distinguish events in which we are interested from one another. (We say more about the use of coding in Chapter 12.)

The coding manual is then used in completing each **recording form**. It is similar to an interview schedule in survey research in that it is a means of systematising and coding observations. You will undoubtedly save considerable time by entering your data directly into an electronic spreadsheet or database. Software bundles frequently include both; for example, Microsoft Office Professional includes Excel and Access. Some time spent learning to use these programs before entering data may well pay handsome dividends when you complete your data collection and you have a data set that is ready to be analysed.

Ethical considerations

There are three principal ethical factors to bear in mind when using aggregate data: (1) you need to document how the data were originally gathered and coded; (2) you should clearly credit the primary sources of the aggregate data; and (3) you will generally want to restrict your analyses to the appropriate group level, using caution if individual-level inferences are desired.

Conclusion

In closing, we want to encourage beginning researchers not to overlook the potential of aggregate data as a *supplement* to other forms of data. There are countless studies that can be based exclusively on aggregate data, but it is also often the case that aggregate data can be used to check the accuracy of results obtained from other forms of data. For example, students of voting behaviour are sometimes faced with the problem created when people who are eager to associate themselves with a winner falsely report, in interviews conducted after the election, that they have voted for the successful candidate. In this case, aggregate voting data can be used to estimate the level of misreporting present in a sample. If responses from a sample show that 75 per cent of a district has voted for the winner of a recent presidential election but voting statistics show that only 25 per cent of that district actually voted for the winner, we have to consider that district's survey responses to be at least potentially an invalid indicator of support for the winner in that district.

In addition to this use, aggregate data can often be relied on to provide additional indicators of concepts so that the multiple indicator approaches to validity discussed earlier can be employed. For instance, in a study of neighbourhood stability, we might ask residents about their commitments to stay in the neighbourhood and, as an additional indicator, seek aggregate data on the frequency of turnover in home ownership in the neighbourhood in recent years. When the findings of a study are confirmed by data collected by such diverse methods, confidence in those findings is greatly enhanced.

Summary points

■ Aggregate data are grouped and lack individual-level information.
■ The ecological fallacy occurs when researchers draw individual-level behavioural connections from grouped data.
■ Aggregate data come in many forms and from many sources, and frequently offer a researcher the best available and least costly data.

Suggested reading and examples

Research examples

Employing a wide range of aggregate economic, demographic and political measures, Poe, Rost and Carey (2006) assess countries' risk of human rights abuses. The country data were collected from a wide range of sources, including Non-Governmental Organisations (NGOs), the United States CIA and the World Bank. In research tracking changes in public opinion towards gay relationships in the United States, Stoutenborough, Haider-Markel and Allen (2006) utilise content analyses of news articles, track aggregate public opinion towards legal gay relationships since 1977 and analyse individual-level data from surveys conducted before and after controversial US Supreme Court gay civil rights decisions.

Methodological reading

A bold and controversial claim for the usefulness of aggregate data in individual-level analyses is made in Gary King's 1997 book. His proposed technique to reduce the likelihood of the ecological fallacy in a *Solution to the Ecological Inference Problem* continues to generate controversy. Difficulties with analysing groups using individual-level data, as well as using aggregate data to study individuals, are addressed by Achen and Shively (1995).

It is rare to find textbooks that are solely devoted to aggregate data analysis. Most of the material is scattered among the literature-reporting studies that have employed the various techniques of aggregate data analysis. Drawn primarily from texts produced many years ago, the best general discussions of how to use aggregate data for beginning political scientists are probably *Politimetrics* (Gurr 1972) and *Systematic Approaches to Comparative Politics*, ch. 2 (Merritt 1970). In *Secondary Research*, Stewart and Kamins (1993) offer some practical tips and an excellent review of the issues surrounding the use of aggregate data in research. More advanced discussions of the problems and techniques of using aggregate data and some examples of its uses are found in *Aggregate Data Analysis* (Taylor 1968). Some valuable hints on data transformation (and on the collection and use of aggregate data generally) are offered in *Unobtrusive Measures* (Webb *et al.* 2000).

References

Achen, Chistopher H. and Shively, W. Philips. 1995. *Cross-Level Inference*. Chicago, IL: University of Chicago Press.

Gurr, Ted Robber. 1972. *Politimetrics*. Englewood Cliffs, NJ: Prentice Hall.

King, Gary. 1997. *A Solution to the Ecological Inference Problem*. Princeton, NJ: Princeton University Press.

Merritt, Richard L. 1970. *Systematic Approaches to Comparative Politics*. Skokie, IL: Rand McNally.

Poe, Steven C., Rost, Nicolas and Carey, Sabine C. 2006. 'Assessing risk and opportunity in conflict studies: A human rights analysis'. *Journal of Conflict Resolution*, vol. 50, no. 4, pp. 484–507.

Stewart, David W. and Michael A. Kamins. 1993. *Secondary Research*, 2nd edn. Newbury Park, CA: Sage.

Stoutenborough, James W., Haider-Markel, Donald P. and Allen, Mahalley D. 2006. 'Reassessing the impact of Supreme Court decisions on public opinion: Gay civil rights cases'. *Political Research Quarterly*, vol. 59 (September), pp. 419–33.

Taylor, Charles L., ed. 1968. *Aggregate Data Analysis*. Paris: Mouton.

Webb, Eugene J., Campbell, Donald T., Schwartz, Richard D. and Sechrest, Lee. 2000, *Unobtrusive Measures*, rev. edn. Thousand Oaks, CA: Sage.

Research exercises

1 Using measures and tools from the UK Office for National Statistics and the websites given above, devise indices to represent (a) the level of party competition in and (b) the socioeconomic status of parliamentary constituencies in the UK. Then use the data reported to assign scores on each of these indicators to every district in one county of the UK (for example, Tyne and Wear in northeast England).

2 Select a research question and state a hypothesis relating to it that you can test using aggregate data. List the variables involved in the hypothesis and identify the units of analysis to which the hypothesis applies. Then use library resources to locate sources for at least three indicators for each variable in the hypothesis. Write a description of each measure, indicating the source in which it is found and the variable it is to represent.

3 Devise a definition for the concept *act of political terrorism* that can be used to identify terrorist acts from newspaper stories. Use the index to *The Times* (London) to obtain a count of the number of acts of political terrorism taking place in Turkey, Germany and Israel for any single year between 1996 and 2006. Which nation suffered the most terrorist acts? Can you devise a means of classifying terrorist acts by their level of violence? By this classification, were the acts in any one nation typically more violent than those in the others?

Key terms

additive index	demographic groups	standardised measure
aggregate data	ecological fallacy	summative indicators
areal groups	index construction	syntality indicators
coding manual (codebook)	multiplicative index	weighted index
data specifications	raw data	
data transformations	recording form	

11 Data preparation and data processing

- Why are proper data coding techniques an important research concern?
- What are the key characteristics of useful data coding formats?

Introduction

We have reached the stage of the research process when we have our data in hand and must decide upon the most efficient and effective strategy for analysing them. It is at this stage that we begin to create a finished record of our effort – in the form of charts and graphs, statistics and other elements of our final research report. These are the products of our research that will be seen and read by others. Yet there remains one far less visible set of operations that we must undertake before analysing our data: the preparation and processing of data. These topics serve as the focus of this chapter.

How do we assign numerical values to the information gathered so that it can be analysed thoroughly? How can we use these numbers to communicate in some meaningful way with our statistics software? What, for that matter, can the software tell us about our data? These and related questions must be resolved before we can proceed to the analysis of data and the reaching and presentation of conclusions.

Coding: what do all those numbers mean?

The process of assigning numerical values to our observations is termed **coding**. Coding is to measurement what the alphabet is to speech: a mechanism for making a precise and lasting record of information. Just as each letter or combination of letters in the alphabet represents a certain sound, each number or combination of numbers in a code represents a particular characteristic or behaviour of a research subject. And just as letters allow those who know the alphabet to communicate complex ideas with one another without speech, numbers allow those who know the codes to communicate complex ideas to one another in a much abbreviated form. However, numerical **codes** allow the researcher to go one step farther, for coded information, precisely because it is in numerical form, can be transformed and manipulated according to the rules of mathematics so that the findings may yield meaningful conclusions that might remain obscure were there no resort to numerical representations. Proper coding, in other words, allows us to learn more from our research than might otherwise be the case.

The role of coding

The codes we assign to each variable's values are determined by level of measurement of each variable, as well as how we plan to analyse the data. Thus, if we measure the educational achievement of members of a given population in which each respondent is scored either as having GCSEs only, as having three good A-levels or the equivalent but not a degree, or as a university graduate, we might assign the numbers 1, 2 and 3, respectively, to represent the three levels of achievement. Alternatively,

Figure 11.1   Coding in research

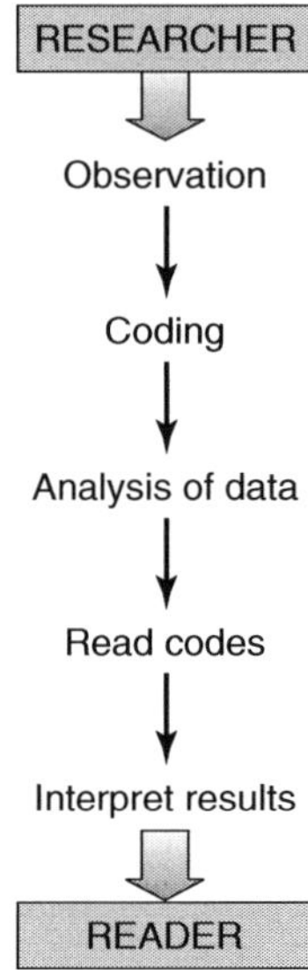

if we wish to score each respondent on the number of years of schooling completed, we might assign to each a numerical code equivalent to that number (for example, the code 7 might represent seven years of schooling). Either coding scheme accurately summarises the findings of our study, though each conveys a meaning different from the other. Once we have assigned one or another set of such numbers, we may process and analyse the data to our heart's content before reconverting our codes into verbal expressions as we prepare our research report. This process of translation can be as shown in Figure 11.1.

The most important thing to keep in mind as we develop data codes is that our numerical representations must always be consistent with the measurement characteristics of the variables we are researching. That is, nominal-level variables should have nominal codes, ordinal-level variables should have ordinal codes and interval/ratio-level variables should have interval/ratio codes. The numbers may *look* very much the same in each instance, but their meanings will differ substantially. Once words or concepts are converted into numbers, we may be tempted to analyse or manipulate our data in ways that simply cannot be supported by their underlying level of measurement (this problem becomes more apparent in later chapters, when we focus more directly on techniques of analysis). Such temptations must be resisted in order to preserve the usefulness of our research, for, as we learned in Chapter 4, not all numbers are created equal, depending upon level of measurement.

Nominal data

The mechanics of encoding (or decoding) data are really quite simple. We begin from the values (categories) of each variable in our study. In the case of *nominal* variables, when our numbers need distinguish only between mutually exclusive categories without respect to rank, we merely assign scores in whatever manner is convenient. If, to choose a relatively typical example, our subjects' religious affiliation is to be classified as Protestant, Catholic, Jewish or Muslim/Islam, we might assign codes according to any of the following schemes:

1 Protestant	1 Jewish	1 Muslim/Islam	43 Catholic
2 Catholic	3 Catholic	2 Protestant	17 Protestant
3 Jewish	5 Muslim/Islam	3 Jewish	27 Muslim/Islam
4 Muslim/Islam	8 Protestant	4 Catholic	07 Jewish

In each instance, a unique numerical value is used to represent one value or category of the variable. Since religious affiliation is a nominal characteristic, the order and magnitude of the codes have no significance whatsoever. We can use one-, three- or even ten-digit numbers in our codes if desired. It is, of course, best to keep the codes as simple and manageable as possible, and we will generally opt for the lowest numbers and the fewest digits possible, but this is a function of our concern for **parsimony** rather than of any mathematical requirement.

It is possible to use slightly more sophisticated nominal coding schemes in order to convey more complete information. Suppose, for instance, that we wish to further categorise our Jewish and Protestant subjects by their specific denominations. Here we might use a two-digit code that builds on our earlier classification. The first digit would be selected as above (for example, 1 representing Protestants; 2, Catholics; and 3, Jews). The second would add the new information. Consider the following scheme:

10 Protestant	20 Catholic
11 Baptist	30 Jewish
12 Methodist	31 Orthodox
13 Presbyterian	32 Conservative
14 Lutheran	33 Reform

Here our codes preserve (in the first column) the gross differences between the categories but allow as well (in the second column) for some fine-tuning. The result is a more complete record of our subjects' characteristics, which still preserves the essence of the less precise variable with which we began.

Were we to list all of the Protestant denominations, of course, the '10' codes (those from 10 through 19) would soon be exhausted and we would be forced to modify our scheme. Either of the following alternatives can easily meet this challenge, though the desirability of choosing one or the other may vary depending on one's analytical requirements.

10 *Protestant*	100
11 Baptist	101
12 Methodist	102
13 Presbyterian	103
14 Lutheran	104
15 Episcopalian	105
16 Church of Christ	106
17 Latter-day Saints	107
18 Church of God	108
19 Christian Science	109
20 Wesleyan	110

21	Assembly of God	111
30	*Catholic*	200
40	*Jewish*	300
41	Orthodox	310 (or 301)
42	Conservative	320 (or 302)
43	Reform	330 (or 303)
50	*Islam/Muslim*	400

In the first instance, we simply expand the number of decades (sets of ten codes) assigned to the Protestants; in the second we add a digit. Again, since the variable in question is nominal, neither the specific numbers nor the number of digits has any significance. As long as our coding system is parsimonious, and as long as the coding categories are mutually exclusive, any numbers will suffice.

Ordinal data

When coding *ordinal* variables, we are a bit more constrained. Because ordinal measurement does not include equal, or even known, intervals between values, we remain free to employ numbers of any magnitude. But because ordinal measurement requires that we preserve in our codes the relative positions (rankings) of these values, we must, at the very least, take care that our numbers are properly ordered. Thus, for the variable *level of political development* or any variable entailing differences of level, degree or likelihood, either of the following coding schemes might be equally correct (and equally meaningful):

1 Lowest	1 Lowest
2 Low	6 Low
3 High	7 High
4 Highest	9 Highest

Each preserves the order inherent in the variable. Neither is in any way more precise than the others, because precision is a function not of the numbers themselves but of the underlying ordinal measurement. As was true earlier, our concern with parsimony might well lead us to select the first of the two schemes, but beyond that, our choice is strictly arbitrary.

In contrast, neither of the following schemes is appropriate:

1 Lowest	1 Highest
9 Low	2 High
6 High	3 Low
7 Highest	4 Lowest

Though the relative magnitude, or ordering, of numerical codes (and therefore the direction of their ordering) has no significance for nominal measurement, it is very important when we work with ordinal data. In the first of the two examples just given, the ranking of the numbers has been mixed; in the second, it has been reversed. As a result, neither coding scheme satisfactorily preserves the relative position and magnitude of the values on the variable. Thus, the codes are an inaccurate translation of our observations. Either they deprive us of the opportunity to rank our cases one against another, or they mislead us about the nature of any ranking we develop. Accordingly, such schemes are to be avoided with ordinal data.

Interval/ratio data

Developing codes for interval/ratio measures may prove the easiest. Here numbers take on more precise meanings, and our options in assigning them are substantially reduced. A dollar is a dollar, a year is a year, and the difference between 47 per cent and 43 per cent is the same as that between 73 per cent and 69 per cent. In interval/ratio measurement, not only are values mutually exclusive and indicative of rank, but also the distances between any two sets of adjacent categories are constant and equal. The coding of interval/ratio variables must preserve these characteristics.

In order to code scores on an interval/ratio, we must find a set of numbers such that each is mutually exclusive of the others, each corresponds to a value of the variable, each is equally distant from its nearest neighbours and the distance between any two adjacent values is known. Finding such numbers is generally an easy task, for unlike most nominal or ordinal scales, for which the researcher must, in effect, invent numerical equivalents for observations, many interval/ratio codes are naturally occurring. That is, interval/ratio codes are far more likely than those at lesser levels of measurement to derive *directly* from the operational definitions of variables. If we define a person's income as the number of dollars earned in a given period, then each specific quantity of dollars earned constitutes not only a value of the variable income but also a code for that value as well. As a result, the emphasis in the coding of interval/ratio data is generally less on *creating* meaningful codes than on recognising and preserving them.

As we pointed out in Chapter 4, situations occur in which the researcher may, in order to enhance the manipulability or the explanatory power of a data set, wish to collapse interval/ratio data into ordinal categories. It may, for example, be both easier and more meaningful for us to compare respondents according to their general level of income than to focus on each dollar of difference. In such instances, it may be that the initial coding of the data will preserve their interval/ratio character and that these categories will subsequently be reaggregated according to the needs of the researcher (for example, we might record the actual number of dollars earned by respondents and then later group these earnings into larger categories), or the design may be to collapse the data at the time of acquisition (as when we simply classify respondents into general income categories [e.g., £20,000–£49,999] and make no record of their specific earnings). Each method entails both advantages and disadvantages, which should be weighed in the context of the research question at hand. Whichever is selected, however, researchers should be sure that their ultimate coding scheme meets the measurement requirements of the indicator in question.

As should be evident by now, the assignment of appropriate codes to data is inseparable from the process of operationalising variables. Indeed, *codes are nothing more than numerical manifestations of our operational definitions.* Decisions about what codes to associate with values on a variable must be made early in the research process. Such decisions are merely one more important part of proper planning. Yet the real usefulness of codes does not become apparent until later in the research process, for it is when we begin to analyse our data that codes come to bear most directly on our enterprise. It is here that coding provides for the transition first from observation to data processing and then from data processing to interpretation. To understand how this transition takes place, let us now consider the structures and uses of several code-related mechanisms.

The codebook and the coding sheet

The first such device we must examine is the codebook. A **codebook** is simply a listing of each variable to be employed in a study, of each value the variable might take on, and of the numerical scores – the codes – associated with each of these values.

An example

Suppose that we are investigating a theory that governments can shape foreign press coverage of them through using public relations firms to manipulate the news. Furthermore, let's say that on 1 July 2003, in reaction to President Bush labelling them the 'Axis of Evil' in his State of the Union address on 29 January 2002, the governments of Iran and North Korea hired public relations firms to improve their images in the US press. (In our example, the other country identified in the speech, Iraq, is not participating in the PR effort.) We wish to design a study to determine the effect these efforts have had on news and editorial content. In such a study we might compare the periods before and after the starting date of these campaigns to see whether, after the contracts took effect, (1) the amount of coverage of each nation increased or decreased significantly and (2) the various nations were presented more or less favourably than they had been in the earlier period. (In reality, we would also have to control for such additional factors as the occurrence of newsworthy events such as political upheavals or natural disasters, but for purposes of illustration let us assume these are not concerns.)

To assess the effects of these image-enhancing efforts, we can turn to any of a number of indexes of news coverage and either analyse the index entries, which will be in the form of either titles or abstracts of various news articles and may, in fact, convey a good deal of information, or use them to identify the actual articles themselves. For purposes of illustration, let us design a project using index entries in Infotrac *Expanded Academic ASAP* (which indexes the contents of a large number of popular magazines) under the headings 'Iran' and 'North Korea'. Our independent variable is the introduction of professional public relations activities or, more correctly, their absence (before 1 July 2003) or presence (after that date).

Following on the two questions identified, we will have two sets of dependent variables. The first set will measure the *quantity* of news coverage and might include the number of index entries each month in the pretest and posttest periods and the proportion of such entries (as evidenced by their titles or index classifications) that refer to the political, economic or social system, respectively, of each country. We might further classify these as focusing on domestic or international concerns. The second set of variables will measure the *quality* of news coverage through judgements on such matters as whether the article (again, as evidenced by its title) suggests progress or decline in the nation's fortunes. Finally, in any such study we should include codes identifying each individual article, the country to which it refers, the date of publication, its length and the specific publication or type of publication in which it appears.

Creating a codebook

An abbreviated codebook for this hypothetical study is illustrated in Table 11.1. As you can see, the codebook summarises the indicators to be used in the study and their associated values. It is, in fact, little more than a formal statement of the operational definitions with which any piece of research begins. Here, however, these definitions are set out in complete detail, including instructions for their interpretation, and are organised not with respect to our hypotheses per se, but with an eye towards facilitating the actual gathering of information. The codebook provides step-by-step guidance to what we are looking for and how to recognise it when we find it.

The codebook identifies the variable names, variable labels, values, and the numerical codes we will assign to each value. It also tells what codes were used to represent nonnumeric data. For example, the codebook depicted in Table 11.1 indicates that a number 1 for *var010* signifies that the type of magazine in which the article in question was found is a news weekly (such as *Time* or *Newsweek*). Having this information in a central location helps researchers correctly record data, and, later, accurately interpret the results of data analysis. It also makes it possible for others who use the data set

Table 11.1 Abbreviated codebook for a hypothetical study of public relations of foreign nations

Variable label *var001*	Variable label Article (Case ID) number	Values	Code
var002	Nation referenced	Iran	1
		North Korea	2
var003	Month of publication	February 2002	01
		March 2002	02
		April 2002	03
		.	
		.	
		.	
		June 2003	17
		July 2003	18
		August 2003	19
		.	
		.	
		.	
		May 2007	64
		June 2007	65
		July 2007	66
var004	Reference to political system in title (including references to government, political leaders or events, political parties, public policies etc.)	No reference Reference present	0 1
var005	Reference to economic system in title (including references to industry, the currency, the workforce, production, markets, trade, economic opportunity etc.)	No reference Reference present	0 1
var006	Reference to social system in title (including references to cultural, religious or social institutions, social events or actors, social structure etc.)	No reference Reference present	0 1
var007	Reference to domestic or international context	Exclusively domestic	1
		Both domestic and international	2
		Exclusively international	3
		Does not apply, NA	9
var008	Reference to progress or decline	Reference exclusively to progress	1
		Reference to both progress and decline	2
		Reference exclusively to decline	3
		Does not apply	9
var009	Number of pages in article		–

Table 11.1 Continued

Variable label *var001*	Variable label Article (Case ID) number	Values	Code
var010	Type of magazine	News weekly (*Newsweek, U.S. News & World Report,* or *Time* only)	1
		Other, primarily political (including opinion magazines and those featuring primarily political news and analysis)	2
		Other, primarily nonpolitical (including general audience magazines and those with specialised but primarily nonpolitical coverage)	3

to see how data are organised and to interpret the results of data analysis without relying exclusively on the original researcher.

Creating a coding sheet

Once the codebook has been prepared, it is a quick and easy step to the next stage of data preparation – the development of a coding sheet. A **coding sheet** is a data recording device whose structure is based on the codebook and whose form will aid in data entry and analysis in our statistics program. It should be noted that we act as if we will be gathering data by hand when creating our coding sheet. This is simply a heuristic to help us develop the most useful electronic form, since manual entry would waste time and increase the opportunity for errors to enter our data. Thus, we will enter our data directly into an electronic coding sheet of our own design. Incidentally, the survey questionnaire described in Chapter 8 is an example of a coding sheet, as is the form presented in Figure 11.2 for our study of coverage of foreign nations in the US press.

In Figure 11.2 the column labels correspond to the indicators developed in the codebook. Each row represents one case, and each numerical entry represents a value on the indicator in question for that particular case. Thus, we see that case number 0001 is an article about Iran that appeared in a news weekly in May 2007, focused exclusively on the political system and made reference to the nation's declining fortunes and to certain weaknesses in its domestic situation. Such scores might derive, for example, from an article in *Time* entitled 'Iran in chaos: leaders unable to halt executions, stability threatened'. In this manner, relevant characteristics of each article title encountered can be recorded on the coding sheet, with each case taking up one row or line. Thus, if we study, or *code*, 821 cases, we can expect to end up with 821 rows of data. In each instance, corresponding data about the various cases will appear in the same column(s) on the coding sheet.

Finally, when printed, all coding sheets should be numbered (to ensure that none has been lost), dated (dates are often useful, for example, if we are forced to alter a definition or add a variable in midstream and must recode or add codes to all previous cases), and signed or initialled by the coder

Figure 11.2 Coding sheet for studying effects of public relations efforts by foreign nations

Identification number				Country	Month of publication		Reference to political system	Reference to economic system	Reference to social system	Domestic/international context	Progress/decline	Number of pages			Type of magazine
0	7	4	2	1	9	4	1	0	0	1	3	0	0	3	1

Coding sheet number ____________________

Date coded   ____________________

Coded by   ____________________

(as a basis for measuring intercoder reliability, as discussed in Chapter 12). If more than one coding sheet is required for each case, as when the number of indicators to be measured is quite large, all sheets for the same group of cases should be both stapled together and numbered identically. This minimises the chances of their being separated and mixed up during processing.

Data entry and data processing

Once the recording of data has been completed, we turn our attention to processing or manipulating our numbers to arrive at our findings. You can well imagine that in a study with large numbers of indicators and cases, the jumble of numbers can be absolutely overwhelming. This demonstrates the value of familiarising yourself with a statistics package. Rather than an additional complication in the research process, correctly employed statistics software will aid in summarising the characteristics of your data and greatly simplify its analysis.

Many software packages are available for performing statistical analysis. Arguably the most common in academic, business and government settings is SPSS. Available for many operating system platforms (for example, Mac OS X, Microsoft Windows and Unix), this software program combines a spreadsheet view of your data with the most common analytic tools you might find useful in testing your hypotheses. Other common statistical programs are, for example, SAS, Statistica, Genstat or Minitab. Software packages with full statistical programming languages like S-Plus, STATA or SHAZAM can provide more flexibility for creating graphics and using new statistical methods. In the end, choosing a program will depend on the analyses you want to do, your statistical background, and which programs are readily available. SPSS and many of these other programs offer student versions at a discount, or your institution may have a site license agreement that reduces the cost of student purchases.

Entering data

All of the most common statistics programs allow the user to enter data directly into a spreadsheet or data-editing screen. When using such a spreadsheet to enter data, you should first define and label one column for each variable of interest. Then you enter the data, with each row representing a different case or observation. If, for example, you would like to analyse ten characteristics (your variables) of 200 newspaper stories (your cases), you would use one line of data for each of the 200 newspaper stories. In this example, each line of data would use ten columns, one for each of the ten variables. In addition to the columns that represent the variables in your analysis, you should also add one column for a case identification number in order to keep track of your data. This should sound familiar, since it is directly analogous to the coding sheet described previously.

Although manual data entry has become easier due to the availability of spreadsheet-like data entry systems, other methods of data entry are available. Optical scan sheets, with which most students probably are familiar ('fill in the bubbles with a number two pencil . . .'), are also popular due to the increased availability of optical scanners and new software that allows the creation and scanning of questionnaires to produce data files. Optical scan sheets are especially useful for recording large amounts of data that have been initially recorded on predesigned, standardised forms, thus avoiding the arduous task of entering this data manually. There are, however, a few disadvantages of using optical scan sheets for data entry. First, scan sheets only allow data to be entered in a predetermined way. Notes in the margins of the scan sheet, for example, will not be recognised by the scanner and therefore will not appear in the final data file. Second, optical scanners often do not recognise markings on scan sheets that do not conform to the predesignated option. Thus, scan sheet bubbles that are not completely filled, or are smudged or wrongly marked, will probably not be recognised correctly by the scanner. Finally, some people may easily lose their place on scan sheets because of the generic layout or the difficulty in identifying the appropriate space for marking the data on the sheet.

Once your data are in the format of your statistics software, the next step is to check them carefully for errors, a process that is also called 'data cleaning'. Manual data entry can easily lead to errors because of typos, incorrect reading of the codes or simply a tired person entering the data. The simplest check for erroneous entries is to print out the distribution for each of the variables in your data set and then look for inappropriate codes. For example, you might have decided to code the variable *party identification* as 1 for Labour, 2 for Conservative, 3 for Liberal Democratic and 4 for Other. If you see in the printed distribution that one of the cases has been coded as 5, it is obvious that an error has been made during the data entry. After identifying an error, simply review the original questionnaire responses and find the correct codes. Unfortunately, erroneous entries within the range of designated values for a given variable can only be found by comparing each entry in the data set to the original data source.

Ethical considerations

A fundamental quality of rigorous research is replicability. That is, can others reproduce a project's research results? An answer of 'yes' to this question is obtained, in part, through careful documentation of data coding by researchers. Replication has such value in the discipline that certain journals publish replication articles, often written by graduate students.

To ensure transparent coding, you should fully document the creation of each variable. Recording each variable's construction in a codebook helps: (1) your instructors to assess your research skills; (2) reviewers to evaluate your analyses; (3) later research to build upon your work; and (4) to supplement your own memory of how each variable was constructed.

Conclusion

Three final points are in order. First, it is not unusual for those without prior statistical software experience to be both overwhelmed and intimidated by these programs. Such feelings are understandable, but they should not be allowed to stand in the way of learning, since all programs include help menus.

Second, do not be ashamed if you make mistakes. Careful data entry and proofreading eliminate many errors, but as with any new skill you will invent ways to make more. This is a common pattern and should not trouble you. When you think about it, making and correcting mistakes represent two of the most important ways that we learn. Track down your own errors when you can, get help when you must, and keep trying.

Finally, do not get carried away. Computers are inherently stupid; they process information and they follow instructions precisely, but they do not think. By using the software packages we have described here, you can easily get a computer to perform the most elaborate statistical analyses imaginable on data of such low quality that the results, though impressive-looking, are meaningless. Accordingly, it is important that you think through and understand the statistical and analytical procedures that you call upon the computer to perform, and that you select only those that fit your needs and your data. Those procedures are the subjects of the next several chapters.

Summary points

- The type of data analysis you may perform is governed by your data's measurement and coding format.
- The most useful data coding schemes are detailed and highly systematic.

Suggested reading and examples

Research examples

Examples of coding schemes, and their authors' rationale, may be found in the appendices of the quantitative data analysis articles in the current issues of the political science journals listed in Chapter 3.

In recent years, several massive projects have coded large numbers of factors linked to international conflicts. The Correlates of War project covers the breadth of history, while the International Crisis Behaviour Project is a more temporally constrained study that analyses conflict in the twentieth century. The website for the former study (www.correlatesofwar.org/) includes exceedingly detailed codebooks, which offer numerous examples of coding techniques.

An example of an automated coding technique is offered by King and Lowe (2003). These authors advocate using coding formulas for very large data collection projects, suggesting that automation permits researchers to utilise data that would be impractical with hand coding.

Methodological reading

Although from another era, a still-relevant discussion of coding procedures is found in *Data Processing: Applications to Political Research* (Janda 1969).

References

Janda, Kenneth. 1969. *Data Processing: Applications to Political Research,* 2nd edn. Evanston, IL: Northwestern University Press.

King, Gary and Lowe, Will. 2003. 'An automated information extraction tool for international conflict data with performance as good as human coders: a rare events evaluation design.' *International Organization*, vol. 57 (July), pp. 617–42.

Research exercises

1 a Prepare a codebook for a hypothetical study using survey research or content analysis.
   b Develop a coding sheet to correspond to your codebook.
   c Either gather data on twenty-five cases or make up imaginary data on twenty-five hypothetical cases. Enter these data on your coding sheet.
   d Find out what software packages are available at your computer laboratory. Obtain and peruse the manual for at least one of these packages.
   e Enter your data into the computer, using the rules stated in the manual. Be sure to proofread and correct any errors.
   f Experiment with writing a set of instructions to analyse the data you have entered.

2 Go to the website of the Inter-university Consortium for Political and Social Research (ICPSR) at the University of Michigan (www.icpsr.umich.edu) and access its online archive of social science data. Choose one of the listed topics and examine the available abstract and codebook. (Note: The codebook is listed together with the data set.)

Key terms

codebook	coding sheet
codes	parsimony
coding	

Part IV

Quantitative analysis

12 Content analysis

- What is content analysis?
- What is the research process for content analysis?

Introduction

Politics researchers may learn a great deal about individuals, groups, institutions or even nations through a careful examination of their communications. How much do campaign advertising and election year news reports tell us about candidates' attitudes and how close observers perceive them? Do the internal memoranda of a large corporation reveal a systematic plan on the part of management to bribe representatives of foreign governments with whom they wish to deal? What does the *Congressional Record* tell us about the relative influence or importance of each US senator? Do diplomatic communiqués between the United States and Russia reflect the public perception of a lack of conflict between these two nations?

These questions and others like them may best be answered by a direct examination of various items of communication. In general, these items fall into one of three classes, depending upon the source and intended audience of the material: (1) those that are internally generated and internally directed by the individual, organisation or government we are studying (such communications as corporate memoranda, which represent or reflect the decision-making process itself); (2) those that are internally generated and externally directed (such publications as the *Congressional Record*, which are purposefully moulded to create a particular image for the source among outsiders and which may reflect or obscure the process and outcome of decision making); and (3) those that are externally generated and externally directed (such as campaign news stories that are read by potential voters). Each class of communication may be different in purpose or effect, as well as in accessibility and usefulness for research, but each provides potential opportunities to further our understanding of political behaviour.

Defining content analysis

In each instance, the most appropriate technique for pursuing these opportunities is **content analysis** – the systematic counting, assessing and interpreting of the form and substance of communication. Content analysis provides us with a method – really a set of methods – by which we may summarise fairly rigorously certain direct physical evidence of the behaviours of, and the relationships between, various types of political actors.

In this chapter we shall discuss when it is appropriate to use content analysis, how the technique is applied and how the results of content analysis should be interpreted, as well as certain limits of content analytic procedures.

Preparing to use content analysis

Content analysis may be used to answer research questions whenever there is a physical record of communications by, to, within or among the political actors that interest us, as long as the researcher has access to that record. Examples of such a record include books, pamphlets, magazines, newspapers, CDs, audiotape, videotape or DVD recordings, photographs, web pages, transcripts of meetings or proceedings, government documents, memoranda, films, diplomatic communiqués and instructions, political posters and cartoons, political advertising, speeches and even letters and diaries. Some of these records may be extremely detailed and precise (as is a verbatim transcript of a congressional hearing), whereas others are much less so (for example, the agenda for the same hearing). Many will have been created independently of the research process (as are newspaper articles by or about the person or group we wish to study), whereas others must be created by the researchers themselves (for example, videotapes of television news programmes). However, all sources of data for content analysis will have in common one principal characteristic: the existence of a physical record of communication. Whenever such a record exists or can be created, content analysis may serve as an appropriate research method.

Choosing a population

The first step in preparing to undertake a content analysis is to define the population of communications we want to study. Here we have a number of options. Which is the best that will be determined by our particular research question? For example, if we are interested in studying the development of political themes in post-9/11 US novels, we might define our population as all novels (the type of communication) written by Americans (the type of communicator) and published in the United States (the location of communication) between 1 January 2002 and 1 July 2007 (the time period of communication). If we wish to study newspaper coverage of a congressional campaign conducted in the shadow of a presidential campaign, we might define our population as all campaign-related newspaper articles (the type of communication) of two column inches or more in length (the size of the communication) published in daily newspapers (the frequency of communication) that are home delivered (the distribution of the communication) in the Sixth, Seventh and Eighth Congressional Districts of Ohio (the location of the communication) during the period 1 September to 3 November of the election year (the time period of communication). Or, similarly, if we want to study the level of tension between the leaders of the United States and those of Serbia, we might define our population as all diplomatic messages (the type of communication) passed between the governments of the United States and Serbia (the parties to the communication) during a given time period.

In each instance, we define the population of messages to be studied by establishing sets of criteria to be met by each item. In the examples, these criteria include the type of communication (novels, newspaper articles or diplomatic notes); the type of communicator; the parties to the communication (the sender or the receiver or both); and the location, frequency, minimum size or length, distribution and time period of the communication. Although other criteria may be used on occasion, some or all of those listed here will be found in most studies that employ content analysis. The first task in preparing for a content analysis is to choose those criteria that relate most directly to the research question at hand.

Once the population is defined, we are faced with the problem of deciding which particular cases we shall examine in detail. Because the cases to be analysed are often limited in number and relatively accessible and because content analysis is generally less expensive per case than other methods (most notably survey research), we are sometimes able to examine every case in a given population – to conduct a census of the material. Indeed, the opportunities it offers for the examination of large numbers of cases is one of the major attractions of content analysis as a research technique. More often than not, however, even content analysis must be based on a more limited sample drawn from the larger population. Since documents, newspaper articles and the like are frequently indexed or otherwise listed in a central location and since such indexes or lists may easily be created by the researcher, the most common sampling procedures used in content analytic studies are the simple random and systematic random techniques. Even when sampling is required, however, the accessibility and relatively low cost of researching messages of various types come into play, and the sample sizes drawn for content analysis may be substantially larger than those employed in other types of research. The result, of course, is a reduction in sampling error and an increased level of confidence in generalising from our results.

Choosing a unit of analysis

Finally, in preparing to undertake a content analysis, we must decide on our unit of measure, or, as it is more commonly termed, our *unit of analysis*. The **unit of analysis** for content analysis is simply the particular element or characteristic of a given communication that we shall examine, count or assess. The most basic element of a communication, for example, is the *word*, and it may be employed in a fairly straightforward manner. For example, in speeches before the United Nations during the period 1975 to 2005, which country was most conciliatory on questions of eliminating conflict in the Middle East: Israel, Egypt, Syria or Saudi Arabia? We might simply examine the record of all such speeches and count references to such words as *peace*, *brotherhood* and *compromise*. In each instance, we identify certain important words and count the frequency with which they appear.

Even in so simple a procedure, however, we must take care to avoid at least two pitfalls. First, we must remember that nonstandardised measures can lead to biased results. If over the years in question, the Israelis have uttered a total of 100,000 words, including fifty salient references (to the words we wish to count), and the Egyptians have uttered some 200,000 words, including 100 salient references, we might reach either of two conclusions from a study of these speeches, depending on whether or not we have chosen to standardise our indicator. If we simply count salient references, we will conclude that the Egyptians have been twice as concerned as the Israelis with procuring a settlement. If, however, our measure is standardised to obtain the *proportion of* all words that are in fact salient (for example, salient references *per 1,000 words*), we will conclude that both sides have shared an equal concern about settling their differences. Which approach is better? This is a fundamental problem in operationalising variables, and the answer is best determined by looking closely at how we have conceptualised the research question initially. The point here is that the use of even such a seemingly concrete indicator as *number of salient words spoken* can entail some ambiguity. The researcher must recognise and deal with that ambiguity, because the decisions made (or overlooked) can have a substantial impact upon the conclusions one draws.

A second potential pitfall in a reliance upon raw word counts arises because any word may have different meanings, depending upon how it is used: 'We seek peace, *but* . . .'; 'The Arab brotherhood *can never allow* . . .'; 'There will be *no* compromise.' In the absence of any sort of control, references such as these to peace, brotherhood and compromise will be included as positive references and will, at the very least, inflate our assessment of the interest on the part of one or both sides in reaching an accommodation. If such usages are sufficiently common, they may well mislead us altogether. For this reason, if we choose to count words, we should in most instances choose to count them in context.

To assess word meanings, we may either (1) read each passage and interpret it; or (2) broaden the unit of analysis. First, we may use *judges* or **coders** – people who are part of the research team or are employed by it – to read each salient reference *in context* and to judge that context as positive, neutral or negative. This contextual judgement can then be used to enrich our data by allowing us to count and interrelate not only all references to the words on which we are focusing, but also the proportions of positive and negative references. Typically, more than one coder reads each reference, and a relatively high level of agreement among coders should be required before a final determination is reached. (We say more on this point later in this chapter.) Along with introducing additional subjectivity, using interpretive coders may increase the cost of our analysis, and require additional training time.

A second unit of analysis, the *theme*, may also partially address the problem of interpreting individual words in context. A theme is a particular combination of words or ideas, such as a phrase, a sentence or even a paragraph. In effect, when counting themes, we search for recurring subjects in a text, as, for example, the expressions *cold war*, *refugee problem*, *national health insurance* or *faith-based politics*. The procedure is similar to that for counting words and represents an improvement to the extent that themes incorporate the modifiers (adverbs, adjectives) and explanatory text that both accompany usage of a particular word and help to establish its meaning.

Unfortunately, although analysis at the thematic level makes clear the context in which individual words are used, it does so at the cost of much added complexity. This is true in that the same theme may be referenced in very different ways and by very different sets of words. Sometimes these references may be very subtle, displaying few or none of the overt characteristics we are looking for. References to immigration issues, for example, may be veiled in conciliatory words about political asylum, whereas those applied to religion in politics may be cloaked in nationalistic rhetoric. Do such words and rhetoric constitute salient references? Is the theme present, or is it not? These questions do not have simple answers. To the contrary, they generally require us to arrive at some clearly stated but potentially limiting definitions and to develop a series of highly formalised decision-making rules (for example, allowing only overt references that contain one or more words or phrases from a given list to be counted), which may make our findings more reliable but at the same time less meaningful.

A third unit of analysis commonly used in content analysis research is the *item* – the communication itself taken as a whole. What proportion of *books* published in the United Kingdom in 1935 advocated socialism? Which UK party leader in 2010 was the subject of the greatest number of negative newspaper *articles*? How did *letters* written by Tony Blair after he left government differ from those written earlier? In each instance, we treat the item of communication as a unit and examine its *overall* characteristics. Does it or does it not deal with a particular issue? Does it or does it not reflect a certain set of values or preferences? Such questions lose some of the subtlety of judgement required by lesser units of analysis and they necessitate the making of summary evaluations. For precisely these reasons, however, their analysis is generally more manageable than is that of words or themes, in a sense making fewer demands of the researcher. This is true because variables may be operationalised at a less specific level, one on which events (that is, occurrences of a salient reference) are often more apparent and on which measurement is often more reliable.

An example

In recent years, item-based studies of the use of words and themes have become much easier to perform due to the availability of online, searchable databases such as LexisNexis, which was introduced in Chapter 3. Suppose, for example, we wanted to know how often George W. Bush referred to Saddam Hussein as 'evil' during the months leading up to the Second Gulf War, with troops entering Iraq in March 2003. Using LexisNexis, we could request both a full-text search to count all of the articles in the *New York Times* (or any of a large number of other newspapers, magazines, newswires or broadcast transcripts) in which the words *George Bush*, *Saddam Hussein* and *evil* appeared for each given month of the period under review. Once in the relevant file, and depending on the interface one uses for access, the instruction might look something like this:

((George Bush) OR (President Bush)) AND ((Saddam Hussein) w/10 evil) AND (Date = 1/1/2003 to 2/28/2003)

This string of terms would identify any article published during January or February 2003 in which Mr Bush's named appeared *and* in which Mr Hussein's name also appeared *within ten words in either direction* from the word *evil*. Similar searches also could be conducted to test (1) whether Mr Bush was referred to more often by title rather than by first name as the crisis moved more clearly towards military conflict (as might be the case, for instance, if the media were subtly enhancing his stature as the nation approached war); (2) whether Mr Bush led or lagged behind other political leaders in his use of the 'evil' terminology (and *which* leaders used the term more); or (3) numerous other hypotheses related to the framing of public perceptions of the conflict.

The results of item analysis may be at least as meaningful as those of component analysis in many instances. Is it more important that the Egyptians have made, say, seven conciliatory references in a given speech at the United Nations, or simply that they have made a conciliatory speech? Is it more important that the United States has sent a note to Iraq with four overt references to military intervention, three veiled references to the failure to disarm and two sharply critical references to the possible presence of weapons of mass destruction, or that the United States has issued a note that can be characterised as contentious in tone? In content analysis we always risk losing sight of the forest for the trees or, more precisely, of the overall significance of a communication for its component parts. Thus, we must use great care in selecting the unit of analysis. We should choose the unit that best tests our hypothesised relationship(s), given the content we are using.

Computer-based content analysis

Whereas LexisNexis provides basic word counts for text within its own database, those who are interested in analysing text from other sources (for example, transcripts of speeches, e-mail messages, or web pages) have to use more specific software packages written for content analysis of digital documents. Among some of the better-known programs for sale are, for example, *Concordance* (www. concordancesoftware.co.uk), *Diction 5.0* (www.dictionsoftware.com) and *WordStat* (www.provalis research.com/wordstat/wordstat.html). Other programs are free for academic use; these include the popular *General Inquirer* (www.wjh.harvard.edu/~inquirer).

All of these content analysis programs provide basic text analysis functions such as *word frequency counts* and *category frequency counts*. **Word frequency counts** provide a list of all the words that occur in a text and the number of times they occur. In most of these programs, text can be split into subparts and then compared either visually or statistically to see if there are significantly more mentions of particular words in one part or the other. Another advantage of these software packages is that they often make use of synonym lists in order to merge word counts. Thus, instead of counting all words in a given document, the program first removes the grammatical structure and then counts as identical those words that share the same stem. In such a frequency count, for example, 'politics' and 'political' would be counted as the same word. In **category frequency counts**, on the other hand, a set of words or phrases are first grouped into categories, then the program shows how many times each category occurs in the document. For example, the category 'election' might consist of the words *voting, vote, voter, election, electorate, choice, participation, ballot, poll* and *survey*, which would then be counted as part of one category only. Thus, category counts allow a slightly more sophisticated text analysis, because users can define more specific or complex models of content.

Some of the programs also allow the user to generate so-called concordances (or KWIC, as in 'keywords in context'), which basically analyse the context in which certain keywords appear in the text. For example, a concordance analysis of the keyword *liberal* might provide some important insights about how often this term has been used to describe either a politician or a policy. Concordances also are useful for finding lists of words that co-occur reliably in a particular text that then can be combined and used in the category frequency counts described above.

The main advantage of such computer-based content analyses is the fact that as long as the unit of content is short, simple and well-defined (such as words or small group of words), it is relatively easy to analyse a lot of information. Thus, as long as the text is available in digital form, even documents spanning many thousands of text pages can be analysed in only seconds. In addition, since the drudgery of content analysis is done by the computer, there is no need to train and employ human coders.

A disadvantage of software-aided content analysis is that computers cannot easily code and analyse latent content, such as meaning or bias. An analysis of whether Deputy Prime Minister Nick Clegg has been portrayed by the *Daily Telegraph* in a more positive or negative light, for example, still requires the input of the researchers (defining the codes for 'positive' and 'negative') and human coders (evaluating the text as positive or negative).

Undertaking a substantive content analysis

Once we have settled upon a population, a suitable sample and an appropriate unit of analysis, we are ready to get under way. **Substantive content analysis** is based on a study of words, themes and items that focuses on the *substantive content* of a given communication. Thus, in preparing to analyse these elements, we must anticipate their substance and define each possible observation in accordance with our expectations.

Creating a dictionary

What this means, in effect, is that as the first step in undertaking a content analysis of this type, we must create a sort of dictionary in which we define each and every observation we might make according to the particular category it fits. Suppose, for example, we are interested in studying all of the sixth-grade schoolbooks used in Havana, Cuba, last year and in identifying in them all references to Americans and the United States? Before proceeding with such an analysis, we must define just what constitutes a salient reference. Do we look only for the words *American* and *United States*? In doing so, we may miss a great many salient references using such derogatory terms as *Yankee aggressors, northern imperialists, gringos, invading forces at Guantanamo* and *the outlaw regime in Washington.*

A parallel but more difficult problem arises when the *absence* of a word or phrase has substantive meaning and must be captured. For example, in a twelfth-grade civics text published in 2006 for use in Palestinian schools, the maps either failed to label Israel, or portrayed Palestine territory as covering the entire area (Lackner 2007). These omissions are meaningful and significant, and a content analysis scheme for studying such books must capture them.

The point is that we must anticipate not only the references likely to be encountered but also the contextual elements of their use, and we must devise a thorough and systematic set of decision rules for judging each usage as it occurs. This problem is usually resolved by a combination of pretesting the population of communications to be analysed (that is, reading through a selection of items to identify the types of salient references most likely to be encountered in a subsequent and more thorough

| **Figure 12.1** | Sample phrases in newspaper editorials endorsing a candidate (random order) |

Best of a bad lot	Best available
Better than the opponent	Our first choice
Urge you to vote for	Finest candidate in a crowded field
Everything the people of this state could ask for	Woman (man) of the hour
An outstanding leader	Promising
One of the nation's best	Lesser of two evils
Best the selection process could produce	Our perennial favourite
Acceptable	Most acceptable
Recommend with reservations	Recommend without reservations
Wholeheartedly endorse	Warmly recommend
Offer our support	Enthusiastically commend to your attention

analysis) and developing informed judgements about the contexts and uses of terms. Here, as in the later formal analysis, the observations of several researchers are preferred over those of one.

A more difficult problem arises when we must assign *evaluations* to salient references – when we must decide whether a particular reference is good or bad, favourable or unfavourable, pro or anti and so forth – and when a series of such references must be ranked according to their intensity (which is most favourable, which is next most favourable and so forth). Here we are concerned with developing and applying indicators that are sufficiently refined to tell us not only how the political actor feels but also how strongly the actor feels that way. A situation of this type is illustrated in Figure 12.1. The figure summarises a number of ways in which a newspaper might endorse a candidate. If our goal is to determine which of several newspapers most strongly supports that candidate, then our immediate task is to decide how to rank these statements according to the intensity of support that each reflects.

Pair-comparing

Several techniques are available to assist us in making these decisions. One of the most prominent of these ranking techniques is **pair-comparison scaling**. Like the Thurstone scaling technique described in Chapter 9, it relies upon the decision of a group of judges about the meaning or intensity of a term, though here the judges may be drawn from the issuers of the communication, the receivers of the communication, a group of scholars familiar with the general subject area under study, the general population or the researchers themselves.

The goal of pair-comparison scaling is the same as Thurstone scaling, but the procedure itself is rather different. Each item to be evaluated by the judges is paired with *every* other item, in a series of comparisons, and each judge is asked to decide which word or phrase in each pair is the stronger or more intense. Thus, if we have five statements for comparison, each judge compares item 1 against items 2, 3, 4 and 5; item 2 against items 3, 4 and 5; and so forth – in each instance designating one or the other as more intense. By counting the number of times each statement is so designated by each judge, by totalling these numbers for each item for all judges and by dividing by the number of judges (that is, by calculating the average score the judges as a group have assigned to a particular statement), we are able to arrive at a quantitative ranking of the intensity of each item. The higher its mean score, the stronger the judges consider a statement.

One of the problems associated with the pair-comparison procedure is the fact that it relies entirely on the decisions of judges whose criteria for judgement may or may not be appropriate or consistent. The standards for expertise in such undertakings are not always clear, or at least are not always clearly stated, and as a consequence, the judgements themselves are open to question. Indeed, it is not uncommon for a single judge to assign different scores to the same statement in a series of identical tests. Because we are sampling content and not humans here, there is neither a clear reference population, as there is in Thurstone scaling, nor a set of underlying parameters to be approximated. The selections made by judges are necessarily arbitrary. Consequently, the reliability of results derived by depending upon such judges may be minimal.

Undertaking a structural content analysis

In addition to, or in lieu of, words, themes or other elements that denote the substantive content of a communication, several units of analysis are available that allow **structural content analysis**. Here we are less concerned with *what* is said than with *how* it is said, and while we must retain a concern with the subject matter, we measure something else.

We may be concerned, for example, with the amount of space or time devoted to a given subject in a particular source. How many words or column inches of newspaper coverage have been accorded each candidate in a particular election campaign? How many articles or pages in political science journals published in the United States are devoted each year to an analysis of governments and politics in Africa? Has the number changed or has it remained constant over the past three decades?

Alternatively, we might be concerned with other, and perhaps more subtle, aspects of the communication format. Is a particular news item accompanied by a photograph or illustration of some sort? Those with an illustration have been found to attract more attention from readers than those that do not. How large a headline accompanies a news item? Does coverage of a particular subject receive front-page prominence, or is it buried somewhere in the small ads section? In answering questions like these, we are less concerned with subtleties of meaning than with styles of presentation. We watch for the presence or absence, the prominence and the extent of treatment of general themes rather than for substantive nuance. The result in many cases is an analysis whose measurements are much more reliable than those employed in a more substance-oriented study (since there is less ambiguity built into the indicators), but one whose lessons may, as a direct consequence, be less rich.

Figure 12.2 illustrates a typical coding sheet for recording data from a structural analysis of content. Drawn from a study of newspaper coverage of congressional elections (Manheim 1974), the unit

Figure 12.2 Typical coding sheet for structural content analysis

ID Number	Article type	Publication date	Candidate	Newspaper	Preference	Prominence	Graphics	Headline	Content	Total	Column	Inches	Candidate	Column	Inches

of analysis for this particular study was the *candidate insertion*, which was defined as any newspaper item that mentioned by name or implication any candidate for Congress in the district in which the newspaper was distributed. Thus, each row on the coding sheet summarises the characteristics of a single candidate insertion. After each item was assigned a unique identification number, it was classified according to type (news story, feature article, editorial, letter to the editor), the date of publication, the candidate it referred to, the newspaper in which it appeared, the general preferences expressed in the item (if any), its prominence of placement (front page, inside page), the presence or absence of accompanying photographs or drawings, reference to the candidate in the headline of the item, the primary content of the item (news of a campaign event, content of a speech, endorsement), the overall size of the insertion and the proportion of the insertion actually relating to the candidate in question.

Structural versus substantive content analysis

Identifying the frequency of occurrence of a name or other item requires only a general concern with the actual substance of each insertion rather than the highly detailed and specific judgement necessary in the substantive approach discussed earlier. As a result, structural content analysis is usually easier to design and carry out, and therefore less expensive and often more reliable, than is substantive content analysis. And though its results may be less satisfying in that they provide us with what amounts to a sketch of a communication rather than a finished portrait, those results often prove entirely adequate in answering a particular research question.

Special problems in the use of content analysis

Although content analysis is a relatively inexpensive technique that draws on a relatively accessible database, and although there are few special ethical dilemmas that are likely to be encountered in undertaking it (unless we are analysing confidential or classified communications), we must still be careful to avoid several potential difficulties when using this method.

Biased content

We must be aware that communications are issued, and may be specifically designed, for a purpose, whether it be description, persuasion, exhortation, direction, self-protection or even obfuscation. In analysing such communications, therefore, we must attempt to interpret their content in the context of their apparent purpose. For example, it is common to find in the Chinese press statements of the type, '*All of the Chinese people believe* that membership in the World Trade Organization is a major step forward in the progress toward social revolution.' Taken at face value, such statements are demonstrably false, since not every one of many millions of people would be aware of, let alone agree upon the value of, any single policy. From this perspective, we might be inclined to view these statements as the most blatant form of propaganda. We have learned from studying the Chinese press, however, that statements of this type are not printed for purposes of external propaganda at all, but rather are intended to suggest to the Chinese people themselves the beliefs that their government wishes them to hold. In other words, the purpose of such statements of consensus is not descriptive, but directive. Knowing this, we may interpret them as useful indicators of the policy interests of the Chinese leaders rather than as meaningless items of propaganda, and we may employ them to some advantage. The purpose of a communication, then, can provide an important context for understanding its content, and we must attempt, when possible, to ferret out this information.

Intended audience

The distribution that is accorded a particular item of communication can have significant implications for its meaning. A pamphlet that circulates only among Chinese dissidents, a letter from a parliamentary candidate or special-interest group that reaches only those people on a particular mailing list, a document that circulates only among a small group of persons – each is an example of a communication with a limited or specialised distribution. Even a newspaper that is generally available may have a limited or specialised clientele. *The Guardian*, for example, has a readership that is generally more affluent and better educated than that of the *The Sun*, yet both are readily available to all of the city's newspaper readers. The *Financial Times* has nationwide distribution, but its readership does not extend equally to all socioeconomic classes. Very often, in order to assess properly the significance of a communication, we must know whom it reaches. Whether by judgement (rendered, for example, by knowledgeable experts, as might be the case in studying communication among Chinese dissidents), by inquiry (as when we ask a candidate or group which mailing lists were used), by self-evidence (which we have when a document is accompanied by a routing slip listing, and perhaps initialled by, all who have read it, or when a web page includes a counter showing the number of visitors) or by reliance on an audience survey (such as the kind usually taken by newspapers to document their circulation claims), we must attempt to measure or to estimate how widely a message has been disseminated and to whom. Having this information enables us to judge the value or the importance of the material we analyse.

Representative sample

We must try to gauge the degree of our own access to the items at issue. Have we been provided with free choice over the materials to be analysed? Are those materials available in an unbiased manner (that is, do we have access to *all* of them), or has some external control been imposed by someone other than the researcher? Do we, for instance, have access only to documents that have been declassified, only to Chinese newspapers that are published for and distributed primarily to foreigners, only to records of *formal* meetings of a government commission? The issue here is one of generalisability, and the question is whether the research population itself, not to mention the sample, is truly representative. If it is not, the researcher may, if not exercising care, at the very least be misled and at the worst be manipulated.

The difficulty in overcoming these challenges to a successful content analysis is that the information we require in order to make informed judgements may simply be unavailable. We may not know, and may be unable to ascertain, the purpose of a communication, its distribution or the degree of access to it that we have been accorded. The dangers here are manifold, and the content analyst must be sensitive to them. We must not allow appearances to cloud our judgement, but must maintain a healthy scepticism regarding our data as long as these questions remain unanswered. That is not necessarily to say that we should not undertake content analysis under conditions of uncertainty, but merely that we should not lose sight of the uncertainty itself once the analysis is under way.

Intercoder reliability

We should say a few words about *intercoder reliability*. With the exception of raw word counts and other content analysis procedures that have been thoroughly computerised (several programs embodying concept dictionaries and search or count procedures have been developed), all content analysis depends on human judgements about communication content. Messages, after all, do not analyse themselves. They are poked and prodded, counted and classified by *Homo sapiens* in the form of the researcher. Therefore, individual researchers may differ from one another in their understanding of the content of a given communication. Indeed, only when some degree of consensus can be reached about that meaning can we have real confidence in our measurements. **Intercoder reliability** is the term political scientists use to describe the degree of that consensus. The higher it is, the better. In general, intercoder reliability may be promoted by taking three basic steps:

1   Operationalise all variables carefully and thoroughly. Make sure that all meanings have been clearly stated and as many ambiguities as possible have been eliminated. In effect, this will create *common standards of judgement* that can be used consistently in classifying and measuring content.
2   Use as many observers (coders) as possible. The larger the number of subscribers to the consensus, the more confidence we can have in it. This may, of course, mean more work and considerable duplication of effort (and, if proper training is not provided, it carries a risk of increased measurement error), but the payoff can be substantial. The limiting factor here is usually cost.
3   Maximise the interaction among the observers. Hold common practice sessions and argue out all differences of interpretation so that ultimately the consensus extends not only to the data but also to the real meanings of the operational definitions themselves.

Calculating reliability

The success of this process can be measured in either of two ways, both of which draw upon statistical concepts that we develop more fully in Chapters 16–18. One approach, used primarily in substantive content analysis, is to have all observers who are working on a given project analyse and code independently (assign their own numerical values to) the same communication, then to calculate a statistic called a correlation coefficient (Pearson's *r*) among the codes recorded by each pair of observers. This coefficient (discussed in detail in Chapter 17) measures the degree of correspondence in the judgements of the researchers on whether and how often a particular word or theme is present. The coefficient ranges from -1 to $+1$, and readings of $+.90$ or better are usually interpreted as indicating a high degree of intercoder reliability. Unfortunately, the correlation coefficient only measures the degree of directional agreement between the coders; in other words, if one coder's values were always the same amount greater than the others, they would rate an *r* of 1.0.

An alternative measure may be more useful for structural content analysis, in which we are less concerned with the treatment of themes than with their presence or absence, and in which duplicated measurement is less necessary. Here the differences between observers are treated as a variable in their own right, and we ask whether that variable is associated with systematic differences in any other variable we have measured. In other words, we are concerned with the possibility that one or more observers have recorded results consistently differently from the others. If it can be assumed that all cases have been distributed to the observers in an unbiased manner (some effort is generally made to distribute them *randomly*), any systematic differences we observe are more likely to be the result of differences between coders than of underlying differences in the cases that happen to have been assigned to the aberrant observer. The coefficient of intercoder reliability here takes the form $(1 - \eta^2)$, where η^2 is a measure of the variance in each subject variable that is accounted for by differences between coders (Freeman 1965: 120–9). By subtracting this 'observer error' from 1, we obtain the proportion of error-free observations. The coefficient is calculated separately for each variable and should exceed $+.90$ if we are to have confidence in the reliability of our measures.

This brief treatment of intercoder reliability is intended to suggest that the subject is quite complex, and a thorough examination requires more space than is available here. An excellent overview of the most popular methods for measuring intercoder reliability, including computational equations and examples, can be found in Neuendorf (2002: ch. 7).

Ethical considerations

Although humans are not being directly studied in content analysis, a human product is being examined. This indirect source of information limits explanations from those producing the communications, at least at the time they were recorded, making accuracy a paramount concern.

You, the researcher, must ensure that the communications are being fairly represented by the research design, coding, data analysis and interpretation. Since all humans have biases, you should utilise a manifest and transparent coding process. The veracity of the results is elevated (for you and your readers) by using outside coders who do not know the purpose of the research. The documentation you use to instruct these coders, or the software commands you use, should become part of your research record and be included in your written research report.

Conclusion

In sum, content analysis is a widely applicable technique with advantages in cost, sample size and, often, access to data. Perhaps more than any other technique, however, it demands careful operationalisation of all variables and constant monitoring of the process of observation. Its results may be highly informative, but they must be understood in a context that it is often beyond the scope of the content analysis technique itself to describe. For this reason, content analysis is often used to best effect in combination with other data gathering methods (surveys, direct observation) in what are termed *multimethod designs*.

Summary points

■ Content analysis assesses written or textual information that people receive, whether in visual or auditory form.

■ Before conducting a content analysis, you need to determine the population of interest, select a sample of documents, choose a unit of analysis and decide whether computerised or human coders are most appropriate.

Suggested reading and examples

Research examples

Content analysis can only identify the frequency of concepts, not their meaning. The best analyses find ways to substantively interpret these concepts' meaning to their readers, listeners or viewers. In their article studying news coverage of the debate over the future of Social Security, Jerit and Barabas (2006) used an innovative experiment to learn readers' interpretation of Associated Press wire service articles on this programme's financial outlook. Governmental strategies to shape minority groups' impression of opposition parties were identified in

Hoddie's (2006) research on the Chinese press. This study reported the simple percentage of intercoder reliability, based upon a 10 per cent sample of the articles coded for topical focus.

Methodological reading

The two most thorough and accessible content analysis texts available today are written by communications professors: Kimberly A. Neuendorf (2002) and Klaus Krippendorff (2004). Neuendorf also offers a website, featuring updated information and an extensive flowchart describing an entire content analysis project (academic.csuohio.edu/kneuendorf/content/). Krippendorff's website (www.asc.upenn.edu/usr/krippendorff/) includes links to his content analysis work and documents explaining the computations for his reliability measure, *Krippendorff's Alpha*.

References

Freeman, Linton C. 1965. *Elementary Applied Statistics: For Students of Behavioural Science*. New York: Wiley.

Hoddie, Matthew. 2006. 'Minorities in the official media: determinants of state attention to ethnic minorities in the People's Republic of China'. *Harvard International Journal of Press/Politics*, vol. 11 (Fall), pp. 3–21.

Jerit, Jennifer and Barabas, Jason. 2006. 'Bankrupt rhetoric: how misleading information affects knowledge about social security'. *Public Opinion Quarterly*, vol. 70 (Fall), pp. 278–303.

Krippendorff, Klaus. 2004. *Content Analysis: An Introduction to Its Methodology*, 2nd edn. Thousand Oaks, CA: Sage.

Lackner, Chris. 2007. 'Palestinian textbooks biased: study: Grade 12 book depicts Israeli conflict as 'Religious Battle', not land dispute'. *Ottawa Citizen* (9 February), p. A11.

Manheim, Jarol B. 1974. 'Urbanization and differential press coverage of the Congressional campaign'. *Journalism Quarterly*, vol. 51, pp. 649–53, 669.

Neuendorf, Kimberly A. 2002. *The Content Analysis Guidebook*. Thousand Oaks, CA: Sage.

Research exercises

1. List as many words or phrases as you can that might constitute references to human rights abuses in news stories about China, Indonesia, Mexico, Sudan, the United Kingdom and the United States. Using a pair-comparison procedure, rank these terms in order of intensity. Compare the countries' rankings.

2. Design a study using *structural* content analysis to answer this question: Is *The Guardian* biased in its coverage of the Middle East? What are the principal variables to be measured in such a study? Next, design a *substantive* content analysis to answer the same question. Will the principal variables in this second study differ from those in the first? In what ways? If you had to choose, which method would you pick as most appropriate to answer the research question? Why?

3. The journal *Political Communication* publishes many research articles that employ content analysis. Locate and read one such article, then summarise and evaluate the content analysis procedures employed by the author(s).

Key terms

category frequency counts	intercoder reliability	substantive content analysis
coders	pair-comparison scaling	unit of analysis
content analysis	structural content analysis	word frequency counts

13 Quantitative comparative research

- Why should we use comparative research?
- How are quantitative comparative studies designed?
- What kind of data can be used in comparative research?

Introduction

All of the research strategies we have dealt with thus far could easily be carried out without ever setting foot outside our country. On most questions we can obtain more than enough data from our own nation's experience to help us explain political life. But an exclusive focus on one nation has some limitations. If we want to improve our ability to explain and predict political events, then one way is to take a comparative approach. This offers a broader range of information about the issues we want to study and, in fact, allows us to pose some kinds of questions that data from a single country might not answer. Thus, whether the question is about the causes of political violence, the reasons people become alienated from government, the effects of different kinds of political organisation on public policy or something else, comparative research can increase our chances of reaching valid conclusions.

Research across borders

Why comparative research?

You might ask yourself why there should be any limitations in studying only one country. First, our results are likely to be *country specific*. That is, each nation has certain unique traits that can bias the findings. Suppose, for example, we want to explore the connection between socioeconomic class and voting choice. Looking only at data from the United States,[1] we are likely both to conclude that class and voting are only modestly related and to question the notion that political preferences are shaped by the socioeconomic conditions in which voters must live and work. If, on the other hand, we expand our sample to include other Western countries – say, Britain, France, or Germany – we are likely to find a far stronger link, partly because of differences in the historical development of social classes in those countries. Thus, the United States might not be a representative example.

To take another case, suppose that we focus on voter turnout in national elections. For the United States, we will find that close to half of all eligible voters simply stay home on Election Day. We may explain this by arguing that democratic elections, especially at the national level, tend to discourage voter participation because the large number of voters makes any individual ballot almost meaningless. But that conclusion, too, will be quite different if our sample includes other nations. Electoral turnout at parliamentary elections averaged 86 per cent of eligible voters in Sweden since 1945, and almost 90 per cent in Italy during the same period (International IDEA 2004). Thus, there must be other reasons for the lower rate of participation within the United States, and these come

---

[1]The US political system dominates political research journals, hence its prevalence in this work.

into sharper focus when we add data from other nations. A comparative analysis shows that electoral competitiveness, and institutional features such as electoral laws and the existence of a two-party or multiparty system go a long way towards explaining different rates of voter turnout (Jackman 1987). These examples suggest that there are specific features in the US system – or in any system – that can distort our conclusions about political relationships. This is a serious problem because much of the politics research is written by US scholars about the US political system. This tends to distort our knowledge of politics.

Focusing on only one country also limits us in another way: it prevents our drawing conclusions about **system-level traits**. In other words, there are some variables, such as type of political system or type of territorial organisation, that describe whole countries, and their effects can be studied only by comparing two or more nations. Consider, for example, the impact of federalism. We might argue that federal arrangements – in which power is shared between two or more levels of government – make for an inequitable distribution of public funds among localities. When regions or localities have power independent of the national government, they are likely to have different views about how much public money to spend and how to spend it.

In order to test this, we need to study at least one unitary system (in which regions and localities have no formal power independent of the national government) as a standard of comparison. Only if we found significant differences between nations with federal systems and those with unitary systems could we conclude that federalism was an important variable influencing the distribution of public funds. Similarly, we might make a case that economic growth in newly industrialising countries hinges on a government's ability to coerce and control the labour force. Our test of this proposition requires a sample that includes countries with varying degrees of control over labour. Of necessity, then, any concern with system-level attributes implies a cross-national study.

Cross-national research can also be a valuable tool for those committed to political reform. Studying other nations can offer insight into the advantages and disadvantages of alternative political 'rules of the game'. It thus helps to pinpoint the potential costs and benefits of political reform at home. Some analysts in the United States, for example, advocated reforms in the 1950s along the lines of the British system in order to encourage more unity within each major political party and a clearer choice between parties for the average voter. Others have been intrigued by proportional representation (as in France), giving out legislative seats to each party in proportion to the number of votes it receives, so that many different parties and groups have a legislative voice equal to their electoral support. In each case, the experience of other countries speaks volumes about both the benefits and the problems that flow from such political arrangements.

Requirements in comparative research

Comparative analysis is an important part of political research because it allows us to generalise beyond the sometimes narrow confines of a single culture and because it permits us to test for the effects of system-wide characteristics. Needless to say, it should meet all the standards for good research that we have discussed in other chapters. But cross-national studies also require sensitivity to some additional issues. The first lies in conceptualising what we want to address: *We need to ensure that the questions we pose actually permit cross-national study.* The second lies in operationalisation: *Each variable we use must be an equivalent measure of the same concept for every country in our sample.* The choice of a sample raises a third issue: *Countries should be chosen to minimise biases that can affect our conclusions.* Finally, the sample must also satisfy another rule: *Observations must be independent from one country to another.*

The following sections explain each of these requirements in turn, describing how they can influence the results we obtain and offering examples of questions that invite comparative analysis.

Finding questions that 'travel'

The first requirement in cross-cultural research is to pose questions that *apply* from one country to another. Stated so bluntly, this might seem too obvious to require comment. But its simplicity can be deceptive, because many of the questions we raise in political studies are applicable only to a very select group of countries. Take, for example, the case of explaining electoral behaviour – one of the mainstays of political science research. Our long-standing interest in the reasons why people cast a ballot and in the factors that influence their choices has produced a rich body of theory and a set of sophisticated methods that should be applicable in any setting, domestic or otherwise.

Yet questions about why and how people vote do not 'travel' well, because they restrict us to studying countries that have regular, competitive, free and fair elections – a qualification that automatically eliminates many of the world's nations. We would, for example, be likely to exclude consideration of single-candidate or single-party elections, since there would be little variation in electoral behaviour and basically no choice other than to abstain. Without variation, there is not much to explain. The factors that lead people to cast a ballot in a certain way in a country with competitive voting appear to make no difference in a noncompetitive election.

Thus, by choosing to analyse elections, we have set up a research question in terms that are specific to certain countries. This in itself might not seem too big a drawback, because we still have a large number of countries in our potential sample. But there is a second problem, one that relates to our ability to draw more general conclusions from voting data. If we assume, as many researchers do, that ballots reflect support for, or alienation from, the political system or reflect a preference for a certain candidate, party or policy, then we have, in effect, equated elections with political expression. We are treating votes as measures of the more general concept of political participation. Almost by definition, this excludes the possibility that countries without regular and competitive elections provide their populations with a way to express satisfaction with, alienation from or preferences for the government. Do they? Or are we unnecessarily limiting ourselves by framing our research around competitive electoral behaviour? Will we come to different conclusions by redefining what we want to study?

An example

We might want to explore the patterns of court cases among different countries as a means to test for the connections between democratic political institutions, the frequency of litigation and the outcomes of court decisions. However, the question of courts and litigation might not travel well, because societies can have very different modes of resolving disputes. In some countries, the emphasis may be on mediating conflicts through local notables rather than bringing them before a formal court, and such countries would be omitted from our analysis of formal court activities. *If, like most politics researchers, we are interested in drawing valid conclusions that are not country specific, then our initial research question must be phrased to allow us to generalise beyond one or a few countries.*

Our initial question must also be appropriate to the countries included in the study. Suppose that we are studying the development of women's rights. One approach might be to explore how workplace grievances are resolved, since questions about pay equity and working conditions are a central concern for many women's groups. Yet, if we focus on jobs alone, we overlook a critical issue. In some countries, especially those with strong traditions of social democracy, campaigns for women's rights may focus much more on social policies – parental leave, child care or other benefits – rather than on individuals at work. Thus, the more appropriate question for us to pose is, *What kinds of women's rights issues are on each nation's political agenda?* Our original question needs to be recast in terms that are appropriate to the countries we study.

In this brief discussion, we have not touched on all the possible biases that might colour our initial research questions. We have, for example, dealt only with cases involving advanced industrial societies, in which government is embodied in the work of large, highly specialised bureaucracies. Clearly, the modes of political expression, and the provision of public goods and services take quite different forms in societies without such institutions, such as many of the developing countries, and these are things we need to consider when forming the questions that will guide our research. Whatever the issue, and whatever countries are studied, we need to be sure that our research is constructed in a way that permits us to generalise about our conclusions and in a way that fits the context of the countries we want to explore. In effect, our design should be able to travel and to focus on questions appropriate to the sample we ultimately choose.

Using equivalent measures

Once we have settled on a question that allows cross-national study, we will need **equivalent measures** in each country we observe. In other words, comparative research should measure the same concept from one culture to another. There are two ways we can do this: (1) by using the same variable everywhere; and (2) by choosing variables that are specific to each country. At first glance, this might appear to be a lopsided choice, for nothing should ensure equivalence between countries better than using the same variable in each one. But this is true only if our 'identical' variable means the same thing in every country we study.

Using identical variables

Suppose that we want to compare levels of tolerance for minority rights across nations. We might adopt one of two approaches. In one, we might compare the degree to which people in each nation are willing to grant political rights to particular groups, such as a religious sect. Based on this measure, we are likely to conclude that citizens of some nations are more tolerant than others. However, if people in the nations under study are more or less hostile to the specific group in question, this measure might reveal how the group under study is perceived by people in different nations and *not* how tolerant they are of minority rights. This means that our 'identical' measure of tolerance does not have the same meaning in each nation.

Alternatively, we might ask people about their willingness to grant political rights to the groups *they most dislike.* This would allow us to control for differences in the acceptance of different groups across nations. This raises another question, however. In some nations, the most disliked groups are larger and more powerful than in other nations, where they may be tiny minorities with little power. If so, the degree to which people are willing to grant political rights to a group may reflect the degree of threat the group poses to the majority. In that case, our measure might reflect fear of a given group rather than citizens' general level of political tolerance. Thus, for comparisons to be valid, *we need measures that tap the same underlying concept,* whatever countries are included in our sample.

Similar problems may arise no matter what question we take up or what countries we study. Suppose, for example, we want to compare the relative commitment to social welfare between nations at different levels of development. We might predict that the more developed a country, the more resources it will commit to social programmes. Our measure of commitment to welfare should be relatively easy to define: we can look at expenditures on social welfare programmes (such as pensions and aid to the disabled and poor) as a share of a country's total government spending or a share of all the goods and services it produces (as measured by its gross national product). With this measure, we are likely to discover that our prediction holds true: more developed countries devote a greater share of resources to welfare.

Yet here, too, our measure may not be equivalent for all the countries we might want to study. By defining it in terms of formal programmes, such as government pensions and aid to the disabled and poor, we may be underestimating the degree of noninstitutional, local effort that aids the most needy in countries where formal government programmes either do not exist or are limited in scope. If farmers and local villagers in less developed countries organise to contribute food, shelter and other kinds of assistance to their indigent relatives and neighbours, then they are, in effect, redistributing community resources in the same basic sense that welfare programmes do in more developed systems. Thus, different communities may rely on different methods of providing for the needy, so that a measure based only on formal programmes may well exclude informal but significant redistribution. If this is the case, then our measure of welfare provision is more a reflection of a society's degree of institutionalisation than of its commitment to aiding the indigent.

Using country-specific variables

Both examples illustrate how the use of identical measures in all countries can lead to serious problems when our variables take on different meanings from one country to another. As an alternative, we may decide on measures that are *country specific*; that is, we may use a different variable for each nation studied, with the choice depending on the local culture. In this case, we need to be sure that every indicator reflects the same underlying concept. As with the selection of identical or common indicators, this can create a problem, since there is no guarantee that our choices will, in fact, be equivalent.

As evidence of this, consider the issue of political protest. Clearly, if each political system has somewhat different rules governing political life, then protest against the system may take different forms from one country to another. Although one government may permit open dissent or demonstrations, another may impose severe penalties for the same behaviour, forcing people to vent their dissatisfaction by other means. Thus, where open dissent is costly, we may anticipate that people protest through indirect methods, such as evasion of government demands and regulations. The discontented may avoid overt ways of expressing antisystem attitudes and may turn instead to beating the system by misappropriating funds, evading taxes or bending bureaucratic rules. Thus, in order to compare the extent of antisystem activity between countries, we may look at open dissent in one place and noncompliance or evasion (assuming that we can measure it) in another.

We can thus make a plausible case that the two are equivalent measures of protest, but we cannot prove it conclusively. Another researcher may argue that the two activities really reflect different things: Open dissent may actually be a good barometer of our underlying concept, whereas white-collar crime is not. People may misappropriate funds, evade taxes or bend bureaucratic rules for any number of reasons, none of them directly related to protest against, or dissatisfaction with, the political system. If this is the case, then our two measures are not equivalent, and we are not really tapping the same thing in each country. In other words, white-collar crime may not be a valid indicator here, because it may not reflect what we want to measure. Our use of country-specific variables, then, is not necessarily a guarantee that we have comparable data for all the nations included in our sample.

This suggests that both of our options for choosing variables – the use of identical or country-specific indicators – have their limitations. Neither guarantees equivalence. But we can offer some ways to minimise the problem. First, we clearly need a good, basic knowledge of the nature of politics of each country we study, so that we can determine when a given measure is appropriate. Second, we need multiple measures or indicators. If we can define several different ways of measuring protest, for example, and if those ways tend to produce the same conclusions, then we can have some confidence that we are in fact tapping the right dimension. Using these strategies can help to give us equivalent or comparable data for all the countries studied.

Choosing cases to study

Given an appropriate question and a sensitivity to the problem of equivalence, we also need to be sensitive to the problems involved in selecting a sample. Ideally, we should not have to choose among countries: the best way to keep our results from being culture-bound is to include data from every possible nation. But in practice, our range of options is much narrower, because the data available to us are limited. If, for instance, we rely on data provided by each individual country, we are limited by the fact that many nations publish little or no information about the issues we want to study. In some countries, accurate and timely publication of political, economic and social data remains a luxury; and even where resources are available, some topics may be considered too sensitive (such as data on political unrest) or not salient (such as statistics on domestic violence) to warrant publication. Countries that do provide information often use different ways of defining and reporting data, so that published information might not really be useful for comparison. If, on the other hand, we want to collect our own data – for example with a survey – the costs of research abroad can be prohibitive and the amount of data collected will be limited.

Most-similar-systems design

These constraints mean that for most questions studied, we have to work with a sample of a few select countries chosen expressly to minimise bias. Our choice thus has to be made with some care, because it can have a significant effect on what we find. We might follow one of two strategies common in comparative research. The first, called a **most-similar-systems design**, focuses on countries that are very similar, on the grounds that the characteristics they share can thus be held constant. Then, if the countries differ in some other trait, we can eliminate the shared characteristics as explanations for the variation.

To picture how this might work, imagine that we have decided to explore differences between countries in the scope of government activity. Why do governments play a much larger role in the economic and social life of some nations than of others? There are several possible explanations, ranging from differences in levels of economic development to differences in political practices and norms. Practices and norms, however, are sometimes difficult to measure precisely. Accordingly, we might control for their effects by looking at variations in the scope of government action among countries with similar practices and norms, such as the United States and Britain. Whatever differences we find in the reach of political institutions cannot be attributed to cultural factors, because such factors are, in effect, roughly constant across our sample. To put it another way, focusing on countries that have similar traits means that we can safely rule out these specific factors in explaining the differences we find.

Most-different-systems design

Alternatively, we might adopt the opposite strategy: choosing countries that are different in as many ways as possible. This is referred to as a **most-different-systems design**. In this case, if we find a common characteristic across our sample, we can rule out the differences between countries as explanations. As an example, consider our earlier question about social welfare. We might choose a set of countries at different levels of economic development and with different types of political systems but, using an equivalent measure for each, discover that they devote roughly the same share of resources to welfare. If so, the differences between them must not affect what each country spends to help needy citizens. Thus, choosing countries that differ on several characteristics allows us to eliminate these characteristics while explaining some shared trait.

Which of the two options should we choose? The answer depends in part on how well we have developed the theory that guides our research. For example, the most-similar-systems approach is appropriate when we can identify all of the important factors that might influence our findings and can locate a set of countries that share them. However, because few countries are likely to be so well matched, it is normally much easier to find a sample that differs on the important dimensions. In that case, the most-different-systems design is likely to be more suitable. This design also makes it less likely that we will find a common pattern between widely different countries. It thus gives more credibility to the results when we do find a common pattern. In effect, a most-different-systems approach offers us somewhat better control over the factors that might influence or bias what we find, as well as more assurance that our results are valid.

Finding independent observations

In choosing a sample, we are usually guided by the notion that the more countries included, the more confidence we can have in our results. A large sample increases the chance that we have included a representative range of values for key variables and lends more weight to whatever statistical procedures we might employ. This is true, however, only when each observation is *independent*. The advantages of a large sample hold only when data from one country are not influenced by events in another. If the two are not independent, then we really do not have two separate pieces of information backing up our results.

The process whereby events in one country affect the life of another is referred to as **diffusion**, and testing for its effects on cross-national research is referred to as **Galton's problem** after the author who first described it. It suggests that we may see a strong causal connection between two variables – such as a country's reaching a certain stage of development and its experiencing shifts in policies – where none really exists, all because several countries in our sample are jointly influenced by another country. If so, having a large sample is of no real value because all the extra observations really add no new information.

Actually, we would be hard-pressed to find a sample in which all of the data are completely independent. It is almost inevitable that some degree of diffusion influences virtually everything we study in cross-national research. If this is true, we need strategies that can minimise diffusion's effects. One, of course, is to look for explicit signs that one country in our sample has been influenced by another and to exclude it from our analysis. Another is to adopt a most-different-systems design, choosing countries that are as divergent as possible and choosing observations from different time periods. If it can be assumed that diffusion effects diminish with distance and time, this strategy can help to increase the chance that each piece of data in our sample is independent of the others.

Finding data

Each issue that we have discussed corresponds to a stage in comparative research, from developing the appropriate question to deciding how best to choose measures and select a sample. In theory, at least, the last stage is to locate the actual data (though sometimes the whole sequence is reversed). If our goal is to find consistent and comparable information, we will need to take several issues into account.

Aggregate data

There are substantial variations in the scope and quality of aggregate information from one country to another, and even more variation in the availability of data on different topics. Not surprisingly, more developed countries generally have better infrastructure and resources for assembling and publishing national data. They are also likely to face more domestic demand for such information. Thus, comparable aggregate data are far easier to find on the United States, Europe and other developed states than on poorer countries. The CIA's *World Factbook* (www.cia.gov/library/publications/the-world-factbook), for example, offers comprehensive country-by-country overviews of political structures and economic conditions such as GDP per capita and percentage of the population living in poverty. But the data are much more complete for wealthier states than for poor ones. Even for wealthier countries, we are likely to encounter differences in definitions and coverage of ostensibly identical data. To take our earlier example of public spending on social welfare programmes, each country may include different types of expenses or programmes in its national statistics, and some may include state and local spending, whereas others may not.

Data availability also differs by topic. Data on election results, for example, have become increasingly easy to locate and are accessible online (one good source is the *International Foundation for Electoral Systems* at www.ifes.org). Other types of information can be more difficult to collect. As one example, consider the question of whether democratisation breeds greater income equality. To answer it, we would need data on the timing of democratisation and on the distribution of incomes during and after the shift from authoritarian rule. For measures of democratisation, we might tap data from *Polity IV* (www.cidcm.umd.edu/polity), a data set housed at the University of Maryland with country-by-country evidence on regime changes extending back to the 1800s, or *Freedom House*'s annual ratings of civil liberties and political rights (www.freedomhouse.org). However, comparable measures of income inequality are far harder to locate. Even if the data exist, they may be issued sporadically, making it difficult to determine how inequities respond to changes in the political system.

Survey data

Limitations arise in using survey data. Such data are generally far easier to find for wealthier countries, where resources, logistics and political stability facilitate individual interviews. Many major cross-national survey projects have thus focused predominantly on more developed states. And, as with aggregate data, coverage varies by topic. It can be much easier to find cross-national surveys on elections and partisan choice, or on core attitudes and values than on individual political behaviour, or on interethnic relations. Thus, we are generally limited to the topic and questions defined by other researchers.

The alternative, collecting new survey data, does give us control over the choice of sample and variables employed. But, as with aggregate data, the more countries and time periods we include, the more difficult it becomes to guarantee that we are measuring the same thing in each one. In fact, collecting data on individuals in other cultures can be an extremely complicated task. Assuming that we have the resources to carry out a cross-national study – say, a survey of political alienation or of participation – and that we have the cooperation of the government in each of our sample countries (which should not be taken for granted), we need to consider several issues.

First, we need to be confident that our survey ensures **linguistic equivalence** – that is, questions we use in one language are translated accurately into others. This clearly requires fluency (or translators who are fluent) in the language of each individual we interview, as well as back-translations to ensure that the questions are indeed equivalent. Even the most fluent researcher, however, may still have some difficulty in expressing some concepts. Certain ideas or terms derived from one culture may simply have no counterpart in another. Take, for example, the notion of an interest group (that is, a collection of like-minded individuals who attempt to influence government policy) and the notion of pluralism (a political order in which different groups compete and cooperate to influence the government's actions). Because the two notions are products of Western democratic theory, both may have equivalents in Western democratic systems. But in other cultures, neither idea may even exist because each derives from the experience of highly institutionalised political systems that give rise to formally organised groups. When such differences occur, our survey questions will have to be rewritten in terms that allow equivalent translations between cultures.

In addition to the possibility of differences in concepts and language from one country to another, there is the possibility that beliefs specific to the country or region may influence the way people respond. Thus, for example, respondents in some countries may view the survey as a threat to their privacy so simply string along an interviewer, whether their answers are accurate or not. Others may place a high value on cooperation or deference to authority and thus may be inclined to give the responses they think the interviewer wants to hear. Finally, some may not acknowledge having certain reactions or values, because they go against what local society prescribes (for example, racial or ethnic stereotyping). In each case, these types of responses constitute a bias that influences the responses obtained.

As with other aspects of the equivalence problem, part of the solution lies in in-depth research on each country to help identify factors that might influence the way people answer. Another lies in the use of multiple measures of what we want to study. If other types of evidence support our survey results, then we have more reason to believe that our findings are valid.

Ethical considerations

Comparative research involves the same ethical considerations that are present in other types of research. However, because cross-national studies often bring together scholars with very different cultural, social or political backgrounds, ethical standards might differ greatly between those who work together on such projects. As a consequence, comparative researchers need to be aware of the social, cultural and political differences that might exist between the subjects or communities under study.

In general, it is best not to assume that scholars from different countries share the same ethical principles, such as the rights of study participants or the ethical conduct of research. Scholars who conduct studies in other countries or cultures should therefore discuss the ethical principles of all participating researchers at an early stage in the project in order to ensure that all research is consistent with the ethical standards of both the home and the host country.

Comparative researchers also need to be aware of, and comply with, the requirements of data protection laws and other relevant legislation that might differ from country to country. Particular attention should be paid to different legal standards that might be applied to issues such as privacy, informed consent or confidentiality of records. Ignoring these differences in national legislation can cause unforeseen problems later in the research process, either during the data collection, the analysis or the interpretation.

Finally, as in any other research project, comparative scholars must carefully consider the risks and benefits of their studies, especially when they involve human subjects. As a general rule, researchers should limit their intrusion into the lives of the individuals or communities they study and protect them from any potentially harmful effects of participating in their studies.

Conclusion

This very short overview of comparative research identifies neither all of the data sources available for cross-national research nor all of the problems we might encounter in using them. It does suggest, however, that each source has different strengths and weaknesses, and these are factors that we need to recognise in any comparative study.

Given the state of our theories about politics and our access to information, we obviously do not have perfect solutions for each of the problems that comparative research might raise. Yet we still need to take each one into account when designing a study and interpreting its results. The more clearly we recognise and control for possible biases, the more confidence we can have that our conclusions are accurate.

Summary points

- Comparative analyses are necessary if we want to develop generalisations that apply beyond national borders and if we want to study system-level traits.
- Cross-national research must be designed in accordance with several considerations, including the framing of truly comparative questions, the use of equivalent measures, the choice of an appropriate sample and the inclusion of observations that are independent from one country to another.
- The availability and accessibility of comparative data differ from country to country. Generally, it is easier to find data for industrialised rather than developing nations. Increasingly, however, international organisations provide access to comprehensive country-by-country overviews through the Internet.

Suggested reading and examples

Research examples

Cross-national analyses allow us to evaluate political issues or systems with a comparative perspective, thus avoiding a narrow understanding of 'how things work'. One recent study of public opinion regarding globalisation conducted in seventeen developed and developing countries (Edwards 2006), for example, found that views of cultural globalisation are mostly influenced by attitudes towards the free market, consumerism and modern life – thus indicating that attitudes towards certain issues might not be that different in the developed and the developing world. Iversen and Rosenbluth (2006), on the other hand, found that labour market opportunities for women explain much of the cross-country variation in the gender division of labour as well as the gender gap in political preferences. Comparative studies also have been useful for pointing out national differences in political news coverage. For example, a study of the news coverage of the 2002 and 2004 US election campaigns in the United States and Sweden (Strömbäck and Dimitrova 2006), found that US newspapers were more likely to frame the elections as a strategic game, whereas Swedish newspapers were more likely to emphasise political issues. If you are interested in reading other examples of research on comparative politics, a good source is the academic journal *Comparative Political Studies*.

Methodological reading

For a general discussion of comparative methods, consult *Innovative Comparative Methods for Policy Analysis: Beyond the Quantitative–Qualitative Divide* (Grimm and Rihoux 2006), *The Logic of Comparative Social Inquiry* (Przeworski and Teune 2000), *Issues and Methods in Comparative Politics: An Introduction* (Landman 2000) or *Comparative Politics: Theory and Methods* (Peters 1998).

References

Edwards, Martin S. 2006. 'Public opinion regarding economic and cultural globalisation: evidence from a cross-national Survey'. *Comparative Political Studies*, vol. 39, pp. 1133–56.

Grimm, Heike and Rihoux, Benoit, eds. 2006. *Innovative Comparative Methods for Policy Analysis: Beyond the Quantitative–Qualitative Divide*. New York: Springer.

International IDEA. 2004. *Voter Turnout in Western Europe Since 1945: A Regional Report*. Stockholm: International IDEA.

Iversen, Torben and Rosenbluth, Frances. 2006. 'The political economy of gender: explaining cross-national variation in the gender division of labour and the gender voting gap'. *American Journal of Political Science*, vol. 50, pp. 1–19.

Jackman, Robert W. 1987. 'Political institutions and voter turnout in the industrial democracies'. *American Political Science Review*, vol. 81 (June), pp. 405–24.

Landman, Todd. 2000. *Issues and Methods in Comparative Politics: An Introduction*. London: Routledge.

Peters, B. Guy. 1998. *Comparative Politics: Theory and Methods*. New York: New York University Press.

Przeworski, Adam and Teune, Henry. 2000. *The Logic of Comparative Social Inquiry*. Melbourne, FL: Krieger Publishing Co.

Strömbäck, Jesper and Dimitrova, Daniela V. 2006. 'Political and media systems matter: a comparison of election news coverage in Sweden and the United States'. *Harvard International Journal of Press/Politics*, vol. 11, pp. 131–47.

Research exercises

1 Choose four countries to include in a *most-similar-systems design* to study each of the issues listed below and explain why you would choose each. Choose four countries to include in a *most-different-systems design* for each issue and explain your choices.

   a The relationship between poverty and extent of protest against the government.

   b The effect of economic development on political democratisation.

2 To get a sense of the types of information that different countries make available, you might examine a United Nations publication such as the *Statistical Yearbook*. Do all countries provide data in all categories listed in the yearbook? Answer the following questions:

   a How does the level of economic development or the type of political system influence the amount of information that some countries report?

   b Does each country's definition of a category match others, say, for the percentage of the population living in urban areas or the percentage unemployed? What effect might differences in definitions have on comparative analysis?

3 Imagine that you are about to set up a study to explain why the scope of government varies from one country to another. Select three possible indicators you might use to measure the extent of government activity. Would these necessarily be equivalent measures in a study that includes countries at different levels of development and with different types of political systems?

Key terms

diffusion	most-different-systems design
equivalent measures	most-similar-systems design
Galton's problem	system-level traits
linguistic equivalence	

14 Social network analysis: finding structure in a complex world

- What are social networks?
- What are the principal facets of social networks?
- What are the basic techniques for analysing social networks?
- What types of data are useful in social network analysis?
- What different forms can social networks take?

A concept of social networks

A **social network** is a group of actors – people, organisations, governments – who are linked together by some common actions, common membership, shared communication or some other form of exchange.

An example

The world is filled with social networks, some highly visible and others hidden. The directors of corporations, for example, often are members of the same trade or business organisations, such as the National Association of Corporate Directors, or read the same magazines, such as *Corporate Board Member* – patterns that might increase their cohesiveness as a group. At the same time, many corporate directors serve on the boards of more than one company, which can produce communication flows and even perhaps common perspectives across those companies.

Similarly, those who may be at odds with business leaders also form organisations with overlapping memberships. Environmental and other activist groups participate in coalitions with overlapping membership and frequently share directors or advisers with other organisations. The result can be information sharing, commonality of perspective or even coordinated action. Networks of donors to political campaigns often give to the same candidates, political action committees or advocacy organisations. Activist foundations of the left and right contribute funds to advocacy groups that may, themselves, form activist networks.

Participants in criminal conspiracies are, by definition, members of a network, and demonstrating the nature of that network is often an important part of prosecuting them. Even terrorist organisations such as Al-Qaeda are constructed in the form of networks through which resources such as money, plans and instruction flow.

The key facet of networks

Not all of these networks have the same structure and not all function in the same ways. However, at their core is a common fact: they are based on patterns of exchange – money, information, influence, leadership, programmatic objectives and the like – that can be usefully summarised in the form of maps of these various relationships. Social network analysis is the method by which such maps are produced and analysed.

This chapter provides some very basic information about the development and analysis of social network maps. The introductory treatment here is restricted to some very basic graphic and generally nonmathematical applications of the technique. In point of fact, social network analysis is a highly developed quantitative methodology that is based, among other things, on the analysis of matrices. If you are interested in more sophisticated applications of social network analysis, the bibliography at the end of this chapter includes references to several keyworks.

Social network data

The data employed in social network analysis consist of two types: nodes and links. **Nodes** are the actors or participants in a network. For example, if we are studying networking structures associated with the Republican Party in the United States, our nodes might include the Republican National Committee (RNC), the Senate and House Republican Caucuses, the Republican Governors' Conference, the Ripon Society (a group of moderate to liberal Republicans), the Federalist Society (an influential conservative group with ties to the Republican Party) and the Log Cabin Republicans (an organisation of gay and lesbian Republicans). Nodes can be of different types. The RNC, for example, is a direct arm of the party itself, whereas the Federalist Society is not.

Links are the connections among the actors. In the present example, this might include such elements as shared members or leaders, the flow of funds to or from each organisation and the sources and movement of policy proposals.

Links may also have different intensities. The ties between the Republican Governors' Conference and the RNC, for example, are likely to be much stronger than those between the RNC and the Log Cabin Republicans. Strength can be measured in a variety of ways, such as the number of personnel interlocks, the value of dollar flows between the nodes, and the number of messages or policy proposals. When constructing a map of such a network, then, we have a number of choices to make: *which nodes we want to include* (all? only those that share a particular characteristic?); *which resource flows do we want to include* (money? information? interlocking directorships? direct membership?); *the extent or intensity of the flows* (we can represent this in our map by the size or number or colour of the links); and *the direction in which those resources flow* (only towards one or another key participant? only from that participant? both? or do we simply ignore the direction of flow?). As we make each of these choices, we begin to develop the appearance of our network map and, in the process, shape both the information it conveys and the analysis it supports.

Social network matrices

All social network analysis begins with a data matrix that represents both the nodes of the network and the relationships, or links, among them. Although these tables contain detailed information, the data will also be placed into more intuitive figures. Examples of matrices are provided in Tables 14.1(a), and 14.1(b). In the tables, the letters represent the nodes in a five-member network. Where the nodes have some form of relationship with one another, the corresponding cell in the table shows where there is no connection, the cell shows a '0'.

The matrix in Table 14.1(a) is known as a **symmetrical matrix**, which means that the relationships represented in the table are reciprocal – if A is linked with B, then B is also linked with A. For example, if the connection between Company A and Company B is provided by Jane Smith, who serves on the board of directors of each company, then Ms Smith also provides a linkage in the opposite direction, (i.e., between Company B and Company A). In the table, this means that if there is a '1' in cell AB (row A, column B), there must also be a '1' in cell BA (row B, column A). In a basic symmetrical matrix, the direction of exchange is not an important consideration.

Table 14.1
(a) Matrix of symmetrical relationships

	A	B	C	D	E
A		1	1	1	1
B	1		0	0	1
C	1	0		1	1
D	1	0	1		1
E	1	1	1	1	

(b) Matrix of asymmetrical relationships

	A	B	C	D	E
A		1	1	1	1
B	0		0	0	1
C	0	0		1	1
D	0	0	1		1
E	0	1	1	1	

(c) Matrix of symmetrical relationships showing intensity

	A	B	C	D	E
A		1	3	1	5
B	1		0	0	1
C	3	0		1	1
D	1	0	1		4
E	5	1	1	4	

The matrix in Table 14.1(b) is known as an **asymmetrical matrix**. Here the relationships are not necessarily reciprocal, though some of them may be. For example, if the Progressive Policies Foundation gives money to Environmentalists to Save the World, but the environmental group does not give money to the foundation, then the flow of money is in one direction only, which is to say nonreciprocal. In this instance, if the foundation were represented in the matrix by 'A' and the environmental group by 'B', then the table would have a '1' in cell AB, but a '0' in cell BA. In a basic asymmetrical matrix, the direction of exchange is an important consideration.

Finally, consider the matrix in Table 14.1(c). This is a symmetrical matrix that is similar to that in Table 14.1(a) in all ways but one – the entries in the cells are not all equal to '1'. Rather, they take on different values that represent the amount or intensity of the connection between each pair of nodes. Suppose, for example, that A and C are activist organisations that share five members in common, D and E share four members, A and C share three members and the other combinations of activist groups share either one or no members in common. If our objective is to analyse patterns of political activism, that information might be well worth capturing. Table 14.1(c) captures it by assigning

Figure 14.1 Sample network maps of relationships

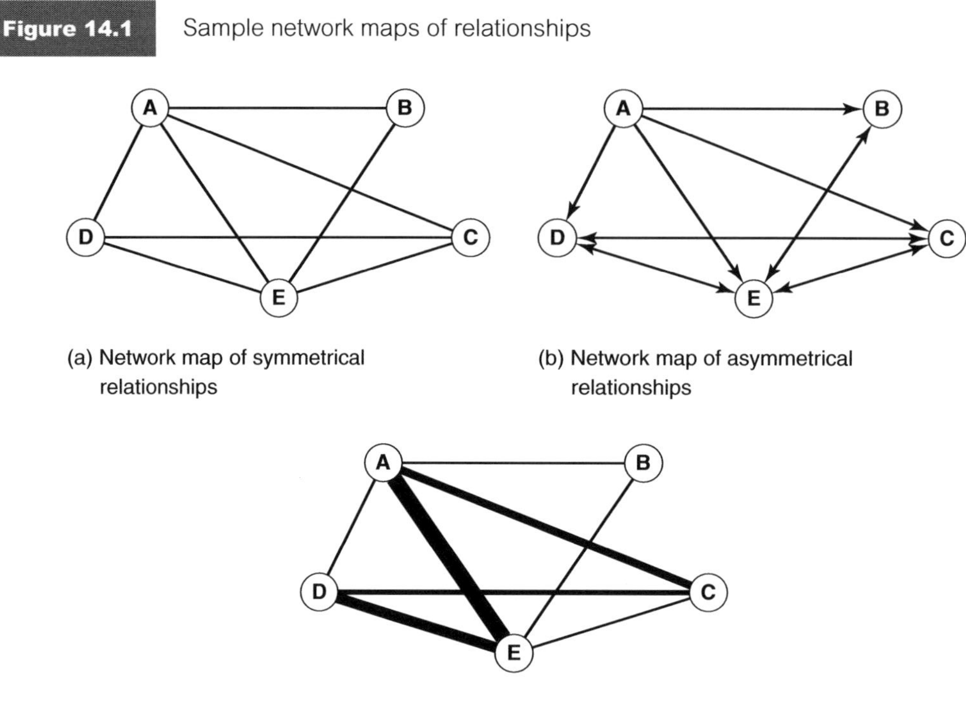

(a) Network map of symmetrical
relationships

(b) Network map of asymmetrical
relationships

(c) Network map of symmetrical
relationships of varying intensity

different values to the cells depending on the number of shared members. These entries could be actual counts of members in common (and, hence, interval data) or simply a ranking from lowest to highest overlap (and, hence, ordinal data). Though not illustrated here, asymmetrical matrices can also capture variable degrees of interconnectedness among the nodes.

Mapping a network

Working from a matrix like those we have just constructed, it is then a simple matter to draw a map of a given network. As specified in the matrix, the nodes are represented as points in space and the links as lines that connect them. Figure 14.1 illustrates network maps that correspond, respectively, with the matrices in Table 14.1.

Notice that in Figure 14.1(a) there are five nodes, corresponding to the five participants in the network, and that lines have been included to connect each pair for which a '1' appeared in the matrix in Table 14.1(a). So, for instance, A is shown as being connected with each of the other participants, while B is connected – or *linked* – only with A and E.

In Figure 14.1(b), we have the same five nodes, but rather than using simple lines to represent the relationships among the nodes, we have employed arrows.[1] Recall that in the asymmetrical matrix in Table 14.1(b) the exchanges were in one direction only. The arrows capture that additional directional information.

---

[1] Often symmetrical networks are shown with arrows in both directions rather than with simple lines. We have chosen not to do so here in the interests of clarifying the basic dynamics of network analysis.

Finally, in Figure 14.1(c), we return to a symmetrical network, but one in which some relationships are stronger (or larger and more important) than others. In this instance, we capture the additional information by increasing the thickness of the connecting lines, or links. If the links were of different types – say, money, common programmes and interlocking directors – we could also capture their variations by using multiple lines (in different forms, e.g., solid, dashed or dotted), each of which could vary in thickness.

Types of networks

Networks can be very simple and straightforward, or they can be very complex and convoluted. The more members (nodes) included, the more types of linkages we incorporate and the further out we extend our notions of connectivity (e.g., including other networks in which our principal nodes may participate), the more complicated things become. At the same time, however, networks tend to display certain structural characteristics that can help us to analyse and understand them. Figure 14.2 illustrates some of these basic configurations.

The first type of network structure shown in Figure 14.2(a) is the **chain** or **linear network**. In this structure, each participant has contact with only two others. Typically, this would be an asymmetrical arrangement in which one participant passes resources or instructions to another (hence the arrows). Although Participant A has a natural power advantage here as the initiator of all exchanges, a network of this type is highly decentralised – indeed, there is no central, controlling authority – and the members do not actually know who their co-members are at more than one degree of separation. And because Participant A has no direct links to any participants beyond B, and thus has no way to monitor or adjust subsequent exchanges, even A's power is limited.

As an example, consider a terrorist network in which plans and goals are set by A and sent into the network. By the time D and E have their exchange, both plans and goals may have been modified in ways unknown to, and inconsistent with the wishes of, Participant A. At the same time, should some portion of the network be compromised, the fact that no participant can identify more than two other participants – if certain precautions have been taken in communicating (e.g., through blind drops), each participant may actually only know the identity of the next participant downstream – provides a measure of security against the network being fully dismembered.

A variant on the chain network is the **circle network** shown in Figure 14.2(b). Here the flow remains asymmetrical, but Participant E closes the loop with Participant A. This structure can provide some measure of feedback to A, who can then make adjustments as necessary. But in the previous example, because it requires that E possesses some means of exchanging with A, it can also compromise the security of the network at the highest level.

Figure 14.2 Basic network configurations

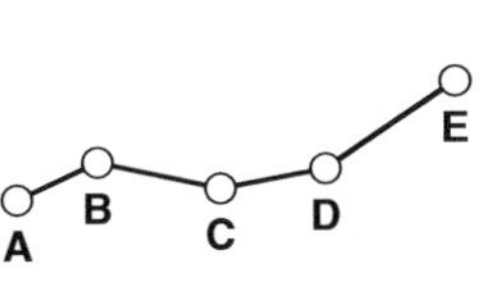

(a) Chain network

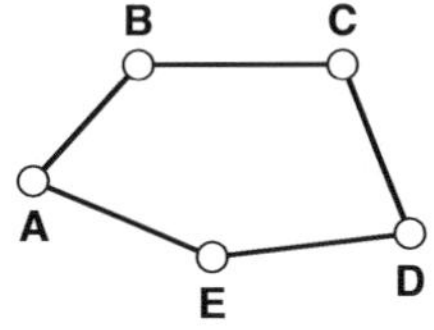

(b) Circle network

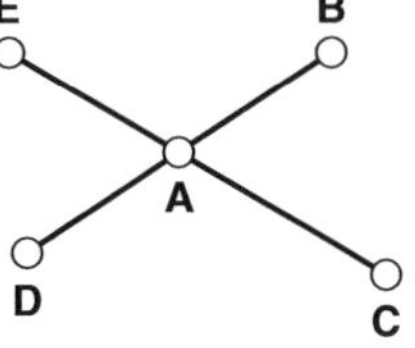

(c) Star network

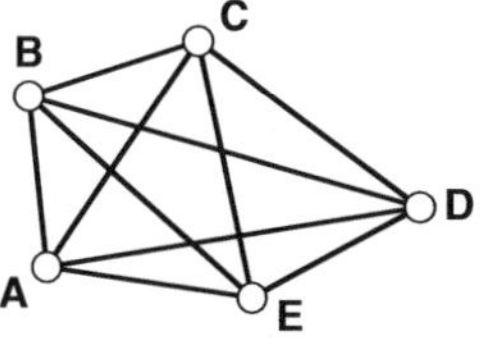

(d) All-channel network

A **star network** shown in Figure 14.2(c) is one in which a central actor – Participant A – is linked with every other actor, but none of the other actors is linked with one another. This is very much the opposite of the chain network, because here there is a single, centrally located participant who controls, and is a party to, every exchange that takes place. In fact, in a star network the identities of the other participants may be entirely unknown to any of them. Each deals only with A. Modifying the previous example, a terrorist network organised in a star pattern would have substantial security at its periphery because no individual cell has any contact of any kind with other cells. Such a network could be easily and effectively controlled because each cell depends on the central participant for its resources and instructions. But, should Participant A ever be compromised, the entire network would be destroyed for the simple reason that no combination of other participants could communicate with one another because each participant other than A operates in virtual isolation.

Finally, there is the **all-channel network** shown in Figure 14.2(d). Here, every participant is linked with every other participant in a thoroughly decentralised structure. In this form of networking, rather than limiting, masking or controlling exchanges, every member interacts more or less openly and more or less extensively with every other member.

Consider the previous example using the Republican Party. Broadening the range of connections to include not only common membership but also communication between organisations, support for common policies, campaign contributions and other types of financial support, you can see that the organisations in question have a variety of contacts with one another. Some contacts are stronger or more frequent than others. Some are of one type, some of another. But the participants in the Republican network know and engage in exchanges with one another more or less independently of any central authority. Similarly, we can think of the nations of the world as participants in an all-channel network. They all belong to international organisations like the United Nations, but also retain direct diplomatic relations with one another. Not all of these channels will be equally important, but together they do very closely resemble a large-scale version of an all-channel network.

Roles of participants

In addition to documenting the overall structure and functioning of the network per se, researchers are often interested in the functions of individual participants. The most basic question, of course, is which individuals, organisations or other kinds of entities are members of a given network and, conversely – but also often equally as interesting – which ones are not. This is important, for example, in determining which actors are likely to have an influence on the actions of others within the network and which are not.

Analysing influences

Similarly, an examination of the particular role(s) played by a participant within a social network can often help us to understand the behaviours and influence possessed by that particular actor. In the star network depicted in Figure 14.2(c), for instance, there is a clear difference between the roles of Participants A and D. Participant A is more centrally located, more influential and presumably more important in determining the actions of the network.

In the circle network depicted in Figure 14.2(b) and the all-channel network in Figure 14.2(d), on the other hand, every participant appears to have roughly co-equal influence. Factors determining a particular participant's role and influence would be such things as the participant's number of network links relative to other nodes, the types of exchanges in which the participant engages (e.g., a participant may be involved in exchanges of money but not information), and the direction in which resources flow (e.g., whether a given participant is a major source of funds for the network or, alternatively, a major recipient of funds from others; whether a participant originates most of the plans for the network or receives direction from others). In effect, then, social network analysis provides a tool for gauging and characterising the relative power of each participant.

Outside links

It may also be worth noting which nodes in a network provide links to other networks. Some participants may be relatively isolated, interacting only with other members of the original network. Others may provide connections to outside sources of money, information or other resources. And some may be highly integrated into a large number of networks, which would permit them to serve as conduits through which networks might exchange resources with one another, in effect creating a network of networks. Participants that perform this external integrative function may not be powerful within the structure of any given network, yet may exercise considerable power through their ability to control the flow of exchanges *between* networks.

An example: Networking for the environment

We can illustrate the use of social network analysis by examining some of the relationships among environmental activists, social responsibility investors (those who invest based on the social policies of companies as well as their financial prospects) and religious organisations. This is accomplished in Figures 14.3–14.5. For purposes of this example, we will not show the underlying matrix of relationships. It is important to note, however, that compiling such a matrix was the first step in the analysis.

We begin by examining three organisations, the Coalition of Environmentally Responsible Economies (CERES), the Social Investment Forum (SIF) and Co-op America. CERES is a prominent group of environmental organisations and others that has created a set of environmental business practices that its members ask companies to follow. Searching websites to research CERES (see Chapter 4 for Internet research techniques), we can easily learn that CERES was established in 1988 and was originally begun at the initiative of another group, SIF. SIF, in turn, is a part or project of yet another

Figure 14.3   Origins of CERES

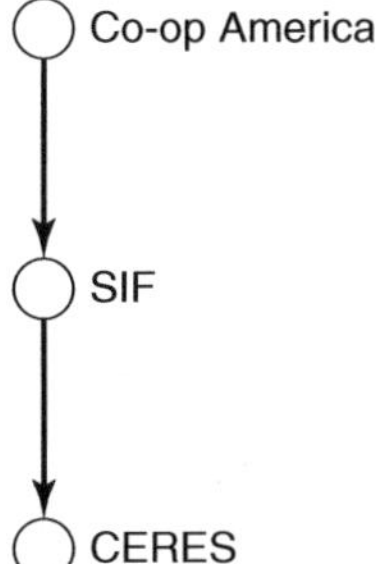

Figure 14.4   CERES members

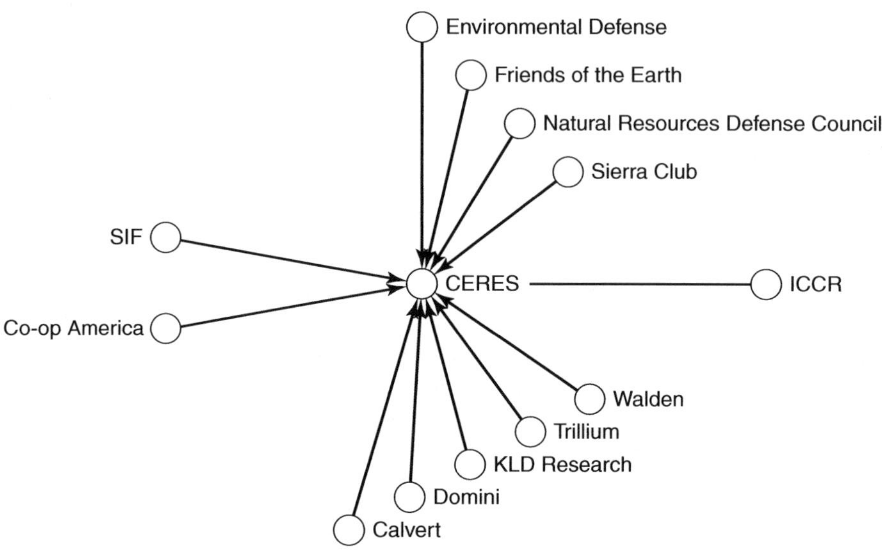

organisation, Co-op America, a relatively little-known environmental group. Applying this information, Figure 14.3 illustrates the networking origins of CERES. The network is directional because each group acted in turn to create the next. Figure 14.3 is a basic chain network.

Next, let us consider the membership of CERES itself. CERES is a coalition of more than eighty organisations, including well-known environmental advocates, social responsibility investment companies and others. You will find these members listed on the group's website. The star network illustrated in Figure 14.4 shows a few of these members. Since all are members of CERES rather than the reverse, we have, again, included directional links. To help facilitate the analysis, we have organised the network into clusters. On the left are the two companion organisations (Co-op America and SIF) that founded CERES. On the bottom are several of the more prominent social responsibility research and investment companies. At the top are several of the better known environmental activist groups. To the right is yet another organisation, the Interfaith Center for Corporate Responsibility (ICCR). Organising the network in this manner helps us begin to understand the nature and role of CERES, about which we will say more.

Figure 14.5 adds two new sets of information, both, again, based on readily available information from the Internet. ICCR is a coalition of approximately 275 faith-based organisations and others that tries to influence corporate policies. We have included a few of the organisation's church-based members to represent its membership, and we have also added links from three of the social investment companies to the Social Investment Forum. Each of these three companies is represented on the organisation's board of directors. (Because the network is now becoming more complex, we have eliminated the arrows to reduce visual clutter.)

What can be discerned from Figure 14.5? We can see that CERES has been constructed as a diverse coalition that includes policy-oriented environmental groups, investors who value environment-friendly business practices, and faith-based activists who share an interest in corporate policies. As political scientists, this might suggest to us that the group relies on the environmentalists for its policies, on faith-based activists for its moral authority, and on social responsibility investors for its financial clout. If we were to take such additional steps as including more members of each coalition in the

Figure 14.5 Network interlocks including CERES, ICCR and SIF

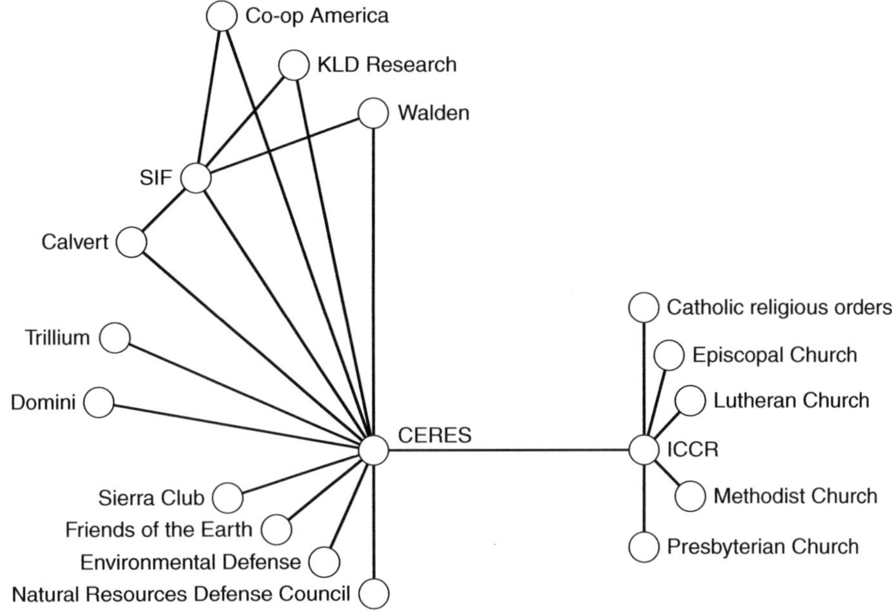

network, examining patterns of cross-membership (one group belonging to two or more coalitions) more extensively, examining different kinds of links (money, leadership and so forth), and examining other affiliations of the members of this particular network (that is, links to other outside networks), we could learn a great deal more still.

Ethical considerations

Some networks are openly observable, whereas others may be closely concealed. Following the flow of money or tracing overlapping boards of directors between organisations is substantially simpler and less ethically challenging than recruiting and interviewing confidential informers who reveal the presence of alliances between politicians or internal agency policies that skirt administrative rules or laws.

Civil servants and potential sources in private organisations may welcome your research in much the same way they would react to the scrutiny of an investigative reporter. If your research involves personal contacts, be honest in your interviews about the amount of confidentiality you will be able to guarantee. Recall that most of your research will be publicly available (whether as a thesis or a book or article), and other insiders may be able to identify your (even unnamed) sources simply by *what* they know.

Conclusion

To the extent that power relationships drive politics, a set of techniques that systematically characterises patterns of exchange among groups of political actors clarifies these relationships. Social network analysis advances political science research by focusing on the structure and character of political relationships.

This form of analysis addresses such research questions as:

1 Does a network exist among some group of political actors, be they individuals, organisations or governments? Who are the members? What do they have in common?
2 What form does the network take? What resources flow through it? How extensive is it?
3 What is the respective role of each participant? Which participants, if any, are positioned to have greater influence within the network? How and why?
4 What does the network's structure indicate about the relative and absolute relationships among the participants?
5 Which key actors have been excluded from the network? What, if any, light does this shed on the nature of the relationships?
6 Does the presence of actors holding membership in multiple networks effectively link the networks to one another? How many (and which) members have such dual linkages? What are the implications of either the isolation of individual networks or their linkage one to another?

The examples in the preceding discussion have only begun to suggest the types of networks that could be explored using this analytic approach. Networks of activists of various stripes, funding networks, terrorist or criminal networks, governmental networks in the international system, networks of political organisations with governments or political parties, networks of parties and interest groups, networks of citizens joined together through memberships in organisations or through their exposure to the same television broadcasts or magazines – these are but a few of the potential sets of relationships that can be studied using social network analysis.

Summary points

- Social networks are linkages connecting individual actors or groups.
- Networks may involve individual citizens, interest or advocacy groups, party organisations, agencies of government or even national governments.
- Relationships or exchanges between the participants in a network may be described using a network matrix and transformed into maps that convey the linkages' direction, extent and significance.
- In addition to the value of the network dynamic itself in contributing to our understanding of the behaviours of various political actors, the individual networking roles of the actors themselves – including their possible connections to still other networks – can yield important insights.

Suggested readings and examples

Research examples

Trying to understand terrorist organisations' decision framework when planning attacks by suicide bombers, Pedahzur and Perliger (2006) map the hubs of several organisations in the Middle East. Surprisingly, they find that most suicide bomber attacks are the result of local decisions. They also identify a number of predictors that might be used in 'dealing with suicide attacks'.

Turning to the small arms trade in Africa, Kinsella (2006) offers exceedingly detailed network maps of both the markets for arms on the continent and the outside sources of the illicit arms trade. This analysis concludes that small arms smuggling should be studied as a network rather than as a market, which yields important guidance for those wishing to control it.

Through a careful analysis of the interrelationships between a wide range of left-leaning organisations, Manheim (2004) studies why so many progressives are politically marginalised. His network analysis maps many links between organisations, including those connecting the 'anti-business' foundations and the recipients of their funding.

Methodological reading

A thorough and concise conceptual overview of social network analysis is provided by Monge and Contractor in *Theories of Communication Networks* (2003). Castells (2000) offers a sweeping, even visionary, account of the increasing importance of networks in *The Rise of the Network Society*. An early and influential work on political networks is *Political Networks: The Structural Perspective* (Knoke 1990). Those interested in understanding the mathematics associated with social network analysis will want to consider Pattison (1993) *Algebraic Models for Social Networks*.

Software

An example of the specialised software that facilitates large-scale and complex social network analysis is UCINET 6, a package developed by Steve Borgatti, Martin Everett and Linton C. Freeman. UCINET is available online from Analytic Technologies (www.analytictech.com), which offers student pricing. Accompanying the software is an excellent introduction to the technique, *Introduction to Social Network Methods* (Hanneman and Riddle 2005). The text is also available at the website: www.faculty.ucr.edu/~hanneman/. In this chapter, Figures 14.3–14.5 were prepared using the UCINET software.

References

Castells, Manuel. 2000. *The Rise of the Network Society*, 2nd edn. Oxford: Blackwell.

Hanneman, Robert A. and Riddle, Mark. 2005. *Introduction to Social Network Methods*. Riverside, CA: University of California, Riverside (published in digital form [www.faculty.ucr.edu/~hanneman/]).

Kinsella, David. 2006. 'The black market in small arms: Examining a social network'. *Contemporary Security Policy*, vol. 27 (April), pp. 100–17.

Knoke, David. 1990. *Political Networks: The Structural Perspective*. New York: Cambridge University Press.

Manheim, Jarol B. 2004. *Biz-War and the Out-of-Power Elite: The Progressive Left and the Attack on the Corporation*. Mahwah, NJ: Lawrence Erlbaum Associates.

Monge, Peter R. and Contractor, Noshir S. 2003. *Theories of Communication Networks*. New York: Oxford University Press.

Pattison, Philippa. 1993. *Algebraic Models for Social Networks*. New York: Cambridge University Press.

Pedahzur, Ami and Perliger, Arie. 2006. 'The changing nature of suicide attacks: a social network perspective'. *Social Forces*, vol. 84 (June), pp. 1987–2008.

Research exercises

1 Identify five to ten popular authors, all of whom are generally considered either liberal or conservative in their views. Go to www.amazon.com and find the page devoted to the most recent book written by each author. Further down on the page, you will find references to other authors whose books are being purchased by customers who purchased the book you have selected. Make note of these for each author. Then develop a matrix and network map of the reading habits of liberals or conservatives. Which authors appear to be the most influential?

2 Identify the members of the following international organisations: NATO, the European Union and the Group of Eight. Draw a network map of the organisations and their members. Can you draw any conclusions about the world role of the United States? Russia? France?

3   Gather news stories about the terrorist organisation Al-Qaeda from the last six months. You can do this by using indexes at the library or, if your university provides access to the service, using search procedures on LexisNexis. Using the techniques of content analysis, identify all references to ties or linkages between any two individual members, or between Al-Qaeda and other organisations (including governments). Use these references to build a matrix of relationships and to prepare a map of the Al-Qaeda network. Can you identify two or three individuals whose capture might significantly disrupt the network?

4   Examine the network illustrated in Figure 14.5. Using the Internet research skills you learned in Chapter 4, locate the information on which this network diagram was based. How would the network change if you included other members of CERES, such as the AFL-CIO? Other members of ICCR? What do these changes tell you?

Key terms

all-channel network	circle network	social network
asymmetrical matrix	links	star network
chain or linear network	nodes	symmetrical matrix

15 Describing the data: the construction of tables and charts

- How may information be visually communicated?
- What are the standard guidelines for visual information presentation?

Introduction

The problem we face at this point in the research process is how best to share with others the results of our work. We seek a style of presentation that is clear, precise, concise and, above all, true to our data. Yet at the same time, we must help others to understand the meaning or significance of what we have found. That is, we must present our results so they may be readily interpreted. In part, the successful presentation of data involves statistical analyses, which we shall discuss in the next chapter. But in large measure, the effective communication and interpretation of research data depend on the quality of tabular and graphic presentation, on the tables and charts that one chooses, and on the appropriateness and clarity of their construction.

The simple table

We begin our discussion of these issues by looking at a device with which you are probably already familiar – the simple table. A **simple table** is little more than a tabular presentation of research data in what is essentially the form of a list.

An example

Table 15.1, for example, summarises the US Democratic Party presidential vote and its gender components for the period 1980 to 2004.[1] Each column in the table represents a different variable (there are four variables in all). The fact that the table is ordered by the variable year, which appears in the first column, provides a cue for the interpretation of the data. It suggests that the table has been constructed to answer the question, *How has the Democratic presidential vote varied from year to year?*

Although the findings reported in Table 15.1 are easy to digest, you should not expect such clearly distilled results directly from a statistics program such as SPSS or even Excel. For example, the data in this table came from ten separate crosstabulations, drawing on five different surveys. That is to say, after obtaining your data analysis, often you will need to compile new summary tables that condense data from several sources into a simple presentation. When combining, however, great care must be used to accurately represent your data.

A close examination of Table 15.1 reveals a number of points about the proper format for tabular presentation. As in the example, all tables should be numbered consecutively. In a lengthy paper with

---

[1] Just as gender is commonly used in the literature to denote differential partisan voting by females in the term *gender gap*, sex and gender are used interchangeably here, although sex is a biological characteristic and gender a social construct.

Table 15.1 Size and gender composition of the US Democratic vote, 1980–2004[*]

Year	Democratic vote (%)	Male democratic vote (%)	Female democratic vote (%)
1980	44	39	47
1984	42	37	45
1988	47	44	50
1992	58	55	61
1996	58	51	64
2000	53[†]	47	57
2004	49	46	52

Source: Data reported in this table are computed from the quadrennial surveys of the American National Election Studies (ANES), available at www.electionstudies.org. Any opinions, findings and conclusions or recommendations expressed in these tables are those of the authors and do not necessarily reflect the views of the ANES funding organisations.

[*]Data on minor party voting have been excluded from the present analysis.

[†]In the regionally divided electorate of 2000, this national survey somewhat overstates the Democratic vote percentage.

several numbered sections (or in a thesis or book with several chapters), these numbers may take the form of Table 3.1, Table 3.2 and so forth, or Table III:1, Table III:2, and so forth. In a shorter or more simply structured paper, single-numbered listings (Table 1, Table 2) are quite sufficient. When tables appear in the same work with charts, graphs or other illustrations, they are usually numbered separately. Graphic presentations are generally referred to as, for example, Figure 1 or Figure 3.1.

Titling tables

Each table should have a title that accurately summarises the nature of the data it reports. This title should give the reader enough information to decide whether to examine the table in detail, but it should not go so far as to save the reader the trouble of doing so. Thus, a title for Table 15.1 such as 'Data showing that Democrats polled more than half of the votes three times in 1980–2004 and did better among women than men' would be inappropriate. In general, a title should simply indicate the major variables for which data are reported in a given table. When, as in Table 15.1, these data represent a geographic or political subdivision (e.g., the United States) or cover a particular time period, those characteristics should be incorporated into the title as well. When a table is drawn in whole or in part from another source, the reference should be placed immediately below the table (e.g., the American National Election Study). Explanatory references pertaining to the table as a whole (the first footnote in the example) should be indicated with superscript lowercase letters or other symbols following the title. Those pertaining to parts of the table (the second footnote in the example) should be placed appropriately within the table. The footnotes themselves should be located immediately below the table and should follow a source identification when one is present.

Other points to keep in mind when preparing tables:

1   The table number and title should be separated from both the preceding text and the table itself by open space. Place each table on a separate page at the end of the research report, after the list of references. At the point in the text where the table is discussed, skip a line, type [Table 1 about here] in the centre of the page, skip another line and continue the text.

2   Normally we avoid drawing vertical lines to separate cells within the table. The Table function available in most graphics, word processing or database programs simplifies the creation and

editing of tables. Microsoft Word, for example, allows you to create tables quickly and automatically format them with a variety of borders, fonts and shading. This feature is especially useful for 'hiding' vertical lines in tables and giving all of your tables a consistent look.

3   Labels and data within the table should be double-spaced to facilitate reading, except that titles and category labels that will not fit on one line may be single-spaced. Category labels should describe as briefly as possible the variables or values in question, but they should always be sufficiently complete to clarify the meaning of the data simply by reading the table.

Tables should only be included if they advance the analysis presented in the research report. The key finding(s) of each table should be discussed in the text, but your reader should be able to fully interpret the findings of each table without looking at the description in the report. Avoid overloading the discussion with percentages or other quantitative terms, though these can be used sparingly. Rather, the discussion of a table should make clear any relationships demonstrated in the table and should focus the reader's attention on the highlights and particularly noteworthy findings. The discussion may also be used to report the results of any statistical tests one has performed on the data in the table (see Chapters 16–18).

An example

A discussion of Table 15.1, for example, would probably touch on the overall level of and changes in the Democratic vote during the period in question and on the relative contributions of male and female voters to that vote. Additionally, the discussion of alternative explanations for this gender-based vote disparity might lead to the next table or chart that explores other hypotheses. Specific points to be discussed might include the range of variation and the consistency (if any) in the pattern of variation for the variables, any notable inconsistencies in the data and even the reliability of the source from which the data have been obtained.

The line graph

Sometimes we may wish to augment or replace tabular presentations with visually simpler graphics. This may be done either to clarify the presentation (consider the difficulty of interpreting Table 15.1 if it covered the period of 1896 to 2004) or to illustrate a particular aspect of the data.

An example

One of the simplest graphical presentation formats is the line graph, as illustrated in Figure 15.1. A **line graph** connects with a continuous line all the data points for a given indicator and provides for a comparison of data points across indicators by representing each in a separate corresponding line, often in a contrasting style. Line graphs are especially useful for representing trends.

The chart in Figure 15.1 reports the same data as does Table 15.1, but in graphic form. In contrast to the table, which requires a thorough reading, a quick glance at Figure 15.1 is sufficient to tell us that between 1980 and 2004 Democrats polled, in general, between 40 and about 60 per cent of the vote in presidential elections; that they did better in 1992, 1996 and 2000 than in 1980, 1984, 1988 or 2004; that the pattern of male and female voters' support for the party followed very much the same path as its overall fortunes (males and females deserted the party in 1980 and 1984, but returned strongly in

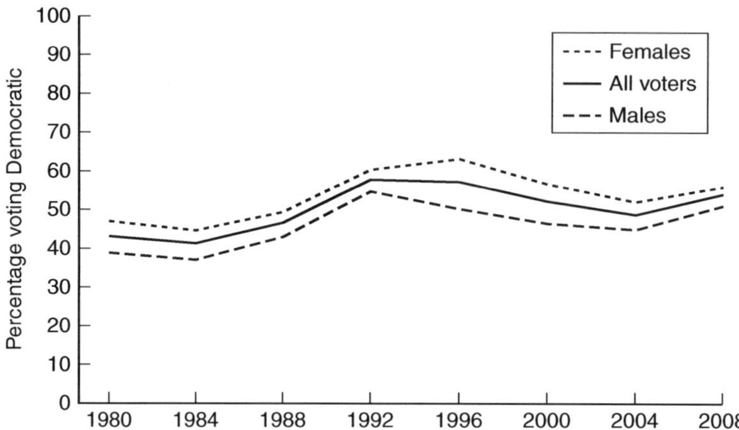

Figure 15.1 Line graph: size and gender composition of the Democratic vote, 1980–2008

1992); and that support for the Democratic Party among female voters was consistently higher than among males. The fine detail available in Table 15.1 is less evident in Figure 15.1, but the overall lessons of the data emerge much more readily.

In general, graphs should be formatted similarly to tables. Each figure should be numbered separately and titled appropriately. Both the vertical and horizontal axes, when present, should be labelled. Vertical-scale labels should be placed to the left of the vertical scale numbers. Horizontal-scale labels should be placed below the figure. If the horizontal-scale numerals are years (as in the example), further labelling is optional. In the case of a complex line drawing, a **key** (an itemised explanation) to the lines should be placed below the figure. Alternatively, explanatory labels can be placed on the graph.

Just as great care should be exercised to ensure that each figure you create is properly and consistently scaled, attention should also be given to scaling when reading others' charts. Improperly or inconsistently scaled axes can confuse the reader, or even the researcher, by either overstating or understating orders of magnitude or degrees of change. Indeed, truncated graphs (those on which lower values are not included) or stretched graphs (those on which the scale is smaller for one range of values and larger for another) may be deliberately employed to misinform a careless reader. Fortunately, use of these devices is less common in the academic research literature than in advertisements or commentaries.

The pie chart and the bar chart

Both the simple table and the line graph are useful primarily for describing and summarising information. With some slight transformation of the data, however, it is possible to use graphic techniques to analyse or interpret these numbers as well. Suppose, for example, we are interested in highlighting the relative importance of women and men voters to the fortunes of Democratic presidential candidates. In particular, we might be interested in such questions as whether females' or males' support is more crucial to Democratic victories and whether (as was widely argued at the time) women voters put Bill Clinton in the White House in 1992, and why Democratic candidates did not win again until 2008. Let us suppose further, to keep our argument simple, that in each of the six election years we are considering, 47 per cent of all voters were males and 53 per cent females. In reality, since the 1980s, women typically do account for roughly 53 per cent of voters, but turnout rates vary from one election to the next (Center for American Women and Politics 2006). Combining this pattern of turnout with the data presented in Table 15.1, we can identify the components of the Democratic vote in each election in terms of their proportional support.

In 1992, for example, we know that 55 per cent of male voters supported the Democrats and that 47 per cent of all voters were male. Taking 55 per cent of 47 per cent, we find that 25.85 per cent of all voters were males who voted Democratic. Similarly, we know that 61 per cent of women voters supported the Democrats and that 53 per cent of all voters were female. Taking 61 per cent of 53 per cent, we find that 32.43 per cent of all voters were women who voted Democratic. Together these figures account for the roughly 58 per cent of all voters who went Democratic in 1992. (*Note:* The total figure is actually 58.28; these numbers are fractionally different from those in Table 15.1, because of rounding error and because the actual turnout rates that underlie the data in the table only approximate 53 per cent for women and 47 per cent for men.)

Let us carry this calculation a step further. We know that these male and female voters constituted around 58 per cent of the two-party vote in 1992. What proportion of its support did each contribute to the Democratic Party? To ascertain this we simply divide each individual figure by 58 per cent (25.85 ÷ 58 and 32.43 ÷ 58) to find that in 1992 around 44 per cent of Democratic votes came from males and around 56 per cent from females. Similar calculations for each of the five other elections show females have contributed 58 per cent, 58 per cent, 56 per cent, 58 per cent, 58 per cent and 57 per cent of all Democratic votes in 1980, 1984, 1988, 1996, 2000 and 2004, respectively; males contributed 42 per cent, 42 per cent, 44 per cent, 42 per cent, 42 per cent and 43 per cent. These figures may be illustrated graphically by a pie chart, as shown in Figure 15.2.

Using pie charts

A **pie chart** is a figure in which a circle (or in this case, a series of circles) representing a given population has been segmented to show the distribution of particular attributes. In Figure 15.2, each circle represents 100 per cent of the Democratic presidential vote in a given year. The shaded area represents the proportion of that vote provided by women voters. Note that the title and key to the figure are similar in style and placement to those in Figure 15.1 and that each circle, or pie, is labelled individually at the bottom of the figure. Percentages of the pie taken up by each segment may be labelled either within the graph, as in Figure 15.2(a), or outside it, as in Figure 15.2(h), whichever is clearer. Alphabetic labels (a, b, c and so on) for separate elements within the figure often make it easier for the researcher to discuss the chart in the text and for the reader to follow the discussion.

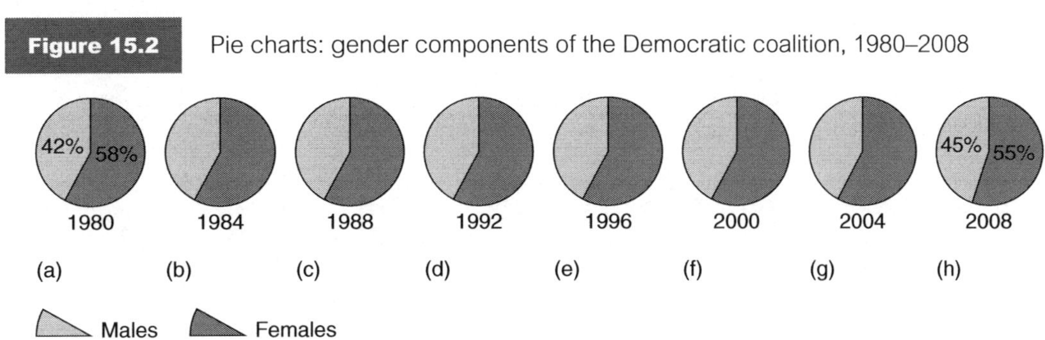

Figure 15.2 Pie charts: gender components of the Democratic coalition, 1980–2008

Limitations of pie charts

Looking at Figure 15.2, one may be struck by the seeming lack of change in the proportion of Democratic votes contributed by women between 1980 and 2004, which is consistently about 58 per cent. Using Figure 15.2 (and assuming the accuracy of the underlying data), one might thus be tempted to argue in answer to one of the questions posed earlier that in fact Bill Clinton was not put into office by women's votes. Indeed, substantiation for this argument is apparent from even the most cursory inspection of the pie charts. Unfortunately, in the present instance, the pie charts, although quite accurate, offer evidence that is incomplete and that consequently may prove misleading. This is true because the size of the Democratic vote varied from election to election (47 per cent one year, 58 per cent the next), whereas the size of the circles in the chart – representing 100 per cent of that vote regardless of size – remains constant. Thus, for accuracy and completeness the pies themselves should vary in size to account for variations in the overall Democratic vote. Unfortunately, few people are good at visually judging the relative size of changing pie chart circles.

Using bar charts

An alternative graphic device that can illustrate the proportion of women's votes for the Democrats in a given year while at the same time making clear the fluctuations in the overall level of Democratic votes is a segmented bar chart like that illustrated in Figure 15.3. A **bar chart** is a graphic representation in which the height, and occasionally the width, of a series of bars illustrate a set of observations on one or more variables. In a **segmented bar chart**, each individual bar is subdivided to illustrate an additional set of observations relating to the distribution of attributes among the population represented by the bar itself. Note once again that the format is similar to those of Figures 15.1 and 15.2 except that in a bar chart, the key is typically found *above* rather than *below* the chart itself. (Occasionally, bar charts are drawn horizontally beginning at the left margin rather than vertically as in Figure 15.3. In such instances, the key should be placed either below the chart or to the right.)

In Figure 15.3, the female vote is again represented by the shaded area of the chart. The bars, however, vary in size according to the overall percentage of the Democratic vote. This percentage is evident both in the scale along the left-hand margin of the chart and in the labels atop each individual

Figure 15.3 Bar chart: gender components of the Democratic vote, 1980–2008

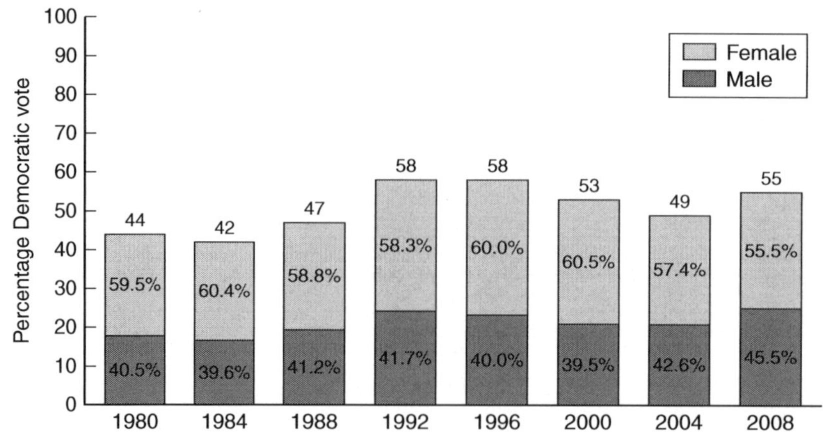

bar. As a result, the impression one gets from the figure is rather different from that suggested by the pie charts, for here we see that although the female Democratic vote did shift up and down a bit, it did so within a relatively narrow range. Instead, it was the overall Democratic vote that proved most volatile, expanding and contracting in concert with the party's fortunes. Returning to our research question of whether female or male support is more crucial to the Democrats, we are now able to answer that the party wins when both genders are mobilised. The data used to arrive at this conclusion are essentially the same as those reported in Figure 15.2, but they are more complete. As a result, the conclusions drawn from them are both more sophisticated and more satisfying.

The bilateral bar chart

Another type of chart commonly found in the research literature of political science is the **bilateral bar chart** – a two-directional figure that is used to illustrate variation above or below some norm as represented by a centre line. Two typical bilateral bar charts are illustrated in Figure 15.4. In Figure 15.4(a), the centre line represents the average (mean) percentage of males who voted Democratic in presidential elections from 1980 to 2008 (46 per cent). The bars represent variations around that average in each of the six elections, with bars to the right of the line signifying above-average support among male voters for the Democrats and those to the left signifying below-average support. The length of the bars represents the degree of variation from the average, and the numerals indicate the precise degree of difference. For example, the average of 46 per cent minus the variation of 6 per cent in 1980 yields the 40 per cent support by men noted in that year in Table 15.1. Figure 15.4(b) presents a similar analysis of women's votes, based on an average level of Democratic support of 54 per cent.

These figures add yet another dimension to our analysis of the data reported in Table 15.1; taken together, they suggest that Democrats can only win the presidency with both men's and women's

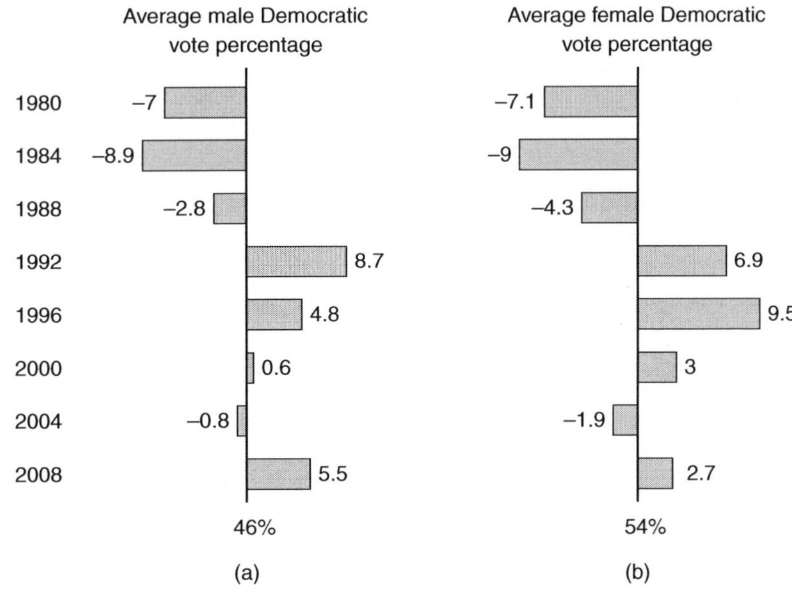

Figure 15.4 Bilateral bar chart: variations in presidential voting by gender, 1980–2008

support. In 1992, a majority of both males and females supported Bill Clinton, the Democratic presidential candidate. In 1996, women maintained strong support, whereas men drifted away from the Democrats. Between 2000 and 2004, on the other hand, women's support for Democrats slipped by 5 percentage points, whereas men's support for Democrats slipped only 2 percentage points. However, support from both men and women increased in 2008 to elect Barak Obama. We can see that the type of information available from a bilateral bar chart complements and supplements that which can be developed by using other graphic devices.

The cross tabulation

One other form of tabular presentation deserves attention before we move on to a discussion of statistics. Indeed, it is perhaps the single most common form of table used in contemporary political science research and provides the basis for a number of the statistical calculations we examine in the next chapter. This form of presentation is known as the **cross tabulation** (or **crosstab**) and is illustrated in Tables 15.2 and 15.3

In format and structure, the crosstabulation resembles the simple table presented earlier, but its substance is different. Crosstabs are based more directly upon hypotheses and are structured to facilitate an examination of the relationships between variables. Table 15.2, for example, summarises the relationship between gender and the presidential vote for 1980; Table 15.3 summarises the comparable data for 2004. In each instance, the data are drawn from the National Election Study, and the sample sizes are noted in the table. These tables are organised so as to permit us to examine the

Table 15.2   Crosstab: Gender differences in presidential voting, 1980

Presidential vote	Gender		
	Male (%)	Female (%)	All voters (%)
Democratic	39	47	44
Republican	61	53	56
Total	100	100	100
Number of cases	(394)	(483)	(877)

Source: Warren E. Miller and the National Election Study, 1980.

Table 15.3   Crosstab: Gender differences in presidential voting, 2004

Presidential vote	Gender		
	Male (%)	Female (%)	All voters (%)
Democratic	46	52	49
Republican	55	48	51
Total	101	100	100
Number of cases	(374)	(437)	(811)

Source: The National Election Study, 2005.

hypothesis that women, for one reason or another, are more likely than men to vote Democratic in any given year.

Each entry (exclusive of totals) in each table is termed a *cell*. The tables may be described by the number of rows and columns that they contain, where each row represents a particular value on one variable and each column a particular value on the other. Thus, Tables 15.2 and 15.3 are each referred to as a 2 × 2 (two-by-two) table, since each table has two rows of cells and two columns of cells, excluding totals.

Crosstabs are always arranged so that the data total on the independent or explanatory variable's column or row. In the present instance, that variable is gender (in the columns). This means that if the table contains percentages, they will be based upon and sum to 100 per cent along the independent variable. Thus, Table 15.2 tells us that in 1980, 39 per cent of males voted Democratic – not that 39 per cent of all Democrats were male. The columns for gender total 100 per cent, indicating that gender is the independent variable, since one's party preference *invariably* is acquired later than one's gender (Table 15.3 totals 101 per cent for males due to rounding error). The sum of all of the percentages in column 1 of the table accounts for all (100 per cent) male voters, in column 2 for all female voters, and in column 3 for all voters. The row labelled 'number of cases' reports the number of respondents to our survey who were classified as members of each group. These numbers constitute a *frequency distribution* (discussed in Chapter 16) and, because of their position in the table, are often referred to as the *marginals*.

In examining tables such as these, it is often possible to tell in general terms whether or not your hypothesis is supported by the data. In both Table 15.2 and Table 15.3, for instance, it is evident that women did vote consistently more Democratic than males. Although a majority of women voted Republican in 1980, even in that year female voters were 8 percentage points more likely to vote Democratic (47 minus 39). The data demonstrate that George W. Bush was able to somewhat narrow the gender gap in 2004, when women were only 6 percentage points more likely to support candidate John Kerry (52 minus 46). Still, such simple measurements only give us a rough idea of basic relationships, and may be unreliable. In Chapter 16 we consider some statistics that enable us to state more precisely the degree of harmony between hypotheses and data.

Creating tables and charts

Now that you have a sense of how you can present your results, how do you make the charts or tables? Given the capabilities of the analytic software available today, this process is much easier than you may think.

Available software

A tremendous variety of tabular and graphic presentations may be created using standard software packages. Common programs such as Microsoft Word, Excel or PowerPoint, for example, all have interactive tools and templates to produce a wide range of presentation-quality tables and charts. Similarly, statistical programs such as SPSS make it very easy to display data in the form of bar or pie charts, histograms or scatterplots, to name but a few options. In most of these programs you must first enter the data for the table or chart into a worksheet or spreadsheet and then build the table or graph through a graphical menu or 'wizard' tool. Once your chart or table is created, modifications can be made interactively by changing the data or the graph or table itself. For example, you can insert or delete graphical elements, change colours and textures, rotate three-dimensional graphs and adjust lines and surfaces.

Interactive tables

A substantial benefit of interactive table and chart tools is that they allow you to identify visually the clearest presentation format by changing the order of the variables or the way the data are displayed. The fact that data can now be examined so easily by reorganising the layout of a graph or viewing different levels of detail has added a new dimension to the art of data analysis that should not be underestimated. Whereas graphs might be useful to display complex information in a simple and easy-to-understand way, the introduction of interactive graphs has created an entirely new technique for exploratory data analysis.

In the limited space available here, we are unable to describe in any depth even the most common software packages that allow the tabular or graphical presentation of data. Rather, by examining a few typical examples, we suggest the kinds of concerns you need to take into account when either reading or preparing tables, graphs and the like. In the process, we deal with such questions as: When should you employ a graphic representation? Which is better, a table or a chart? What should tables and charts look like (what is their structure)? How can tabular and graphic presentations help you to better understand your findings?

Ethical considerations

Tabular and graphical devices must be used appropriately. As should be evident from this chapter's brief treatment, it is quite easy to present research results deceptively. Misleading presentation of findings is harmful, whether accomplished through the subtle abuse of these techniques, or through careless misuse.

You have an ethical obligation to report your findings accurately and fairly. Your colleagues have an intellectual obligation to examine your research rigorously. Together, these obligations are the cornerstones upon which to build your research.

Conclusion

In conclusion, remember these three important points about the use of tabular and graphic presentations.

First, these devices should be used both imaginatively and constructively. As part of the research process itself, they can be extremely helpful in developing your concepts to the fullest and in bringing you to a firm understanding of what the data really mean. Flexibility and an openness to new forms of analysis can contribute greatly to expanding your knowledge of political phenomena, and techniques as simple as those discussed here can help you shape your discoveries.

Second, in the presentation of research, tables and graphics should be used parsimoniously. Too many such materials in a research report clutter the text and detract from its readability. Your decision to include a table or chart is taken by the reader as an indication of the importance attached to the particular information contained therein. You must make those choices deliberately, rather than simply offering your reader a smorgasbord of information. Such discretion not only enhances your report, but forces you to think more clearly and decide what is important, thus contributing directly to the quality of your research.

Finally, the best way to learn data presentation is through hands-on use and experimentation. Tackling unfamiliar software may be daunting, but it is the best way to add weapons to your research arsenal. If you run into difficulty, programs such as Excel or SPSS have useful help functions, offering step-by-step instructions for constructing charts and tables.

Summary points

- Different facets of your data are revealed by using photographs, charts and tables or text.
- Your audience's understanding of visual information will be improved by simplification, enlargement and using methods appropriate to the data type.

Suggested reading and examples

Research examples

The uses of graphical data are endless, and often visual data can summarise a great deal of information. In introducing a topic about which there is great diversity of opinion, one might plot a bar chart showing the number of respondents predicting a given percentage of gay population in their own community (Overby and Barth 2006). Alternatively, an interest in understanding the voting dynamics in smaller groups might lead one to graph each state's overall position in the roll-call votes at the US Constitutional Convention (Dougherty and Heckelman 2006). Graphical tools are even used in multivariate analysis, through Loess smoothing techniques (Jacoby 2000). Quantitative analyses typically include tables, which range from very complex to quite simple. Opening the most recent issue of any political science journal will yield a variety of such tables.

Methodological reading

More theoretical discussions of the use of graphics can be found in William Jacoby's works on univariate and bivariate data presentation (1997) and multivariate presentation techniques (1998). The second edition of Tufte's (2001) classic *The Visual Display of Quantitative Information* is a lovely book, moving beyond simply presenting data to design and aesthetics. For insights into the subtleties and potential abuse of graphic presentation, see *How to Lie with Charts* (Jones 2006).

References

Center for American Women and Politics (CAWP). 2006. *Fact Sheet: Sex Differences in Voter Turnout.* Eagleton Institute of Politics, Rutgers University, NJ.

Dougherty, Keith L. and Heckelman, Jac C. 2006. 'A pivotal voter from a pivotal state: Roger Sherman at the constitutional convention'. *American Political Science Review*, vol. 100 (May), pp. 297–302.

Jacoby, William G. 1997. *Statistical Graphics for Visualizing Univariate and Bivariate Data.* Newbury Park, CA: Sage.

Jacoby, William G. 1998. *Statistical Graphics for Visualizing Multivariate Data.* Newbury Park, CA: Sage.

Jacoby, William G. 2000. 'Loess: A nonparametric, graphical tool for depicting relationships between variables'. *Electoral Studies*, vol. 19 (December), pp. 577–613.

Jones, Gerald E. 2006. *How to Lie with Charts*, 2nd edn. Sedona, AZ: La Puerta.

Miller, Warren E. and the National Election Studies. 1980. *The 1980 National Election Study* (dataset). Ann Arbor, MI: University of Michigan, Center for Political Studies (producer and distributor).

Overby, L. Marvin and Barth, Jay. 2006. 'Numeracy about minority populations: Americans' estimations of local gay population size'. *Polity*, vol. 38 (April), pp. 194–210.

The National Election Studies (www.electionstudies.org). 2005. *The 2004 National Election Study* (dataset). Ann Arbor, MI: University of Michigan, Center for Political Studies (producer and distributor).

Tufte, Edward R. 2001. *The Visual Display of Quantitative Information,* 2nd edn. Cheshire, CI: Graphics Press.

Research exercises

1 Using the list of political science journals presented in Chapter 3, find three examples of graphic presentations from three separate articles. Reproduce each and write a brief summary of the information it conveys.

2 Using the list of political science journals presented in Chapter 3, find three examples of crosstabulations from three separate articles. Reproduce each and write a brief summary of the information it conveys.

3 Consult the most recent editions of the *State and Metropolitan Area Data Book* (published by the US Census Bureau online at: www.census.gov), and the *UNESCO Statistical Yearbook* (online resource at: www.uis.unesco.org). Examine and compare the structures of the tables in these sources. Are these simple tables or crosstabs?

4 Using data from the *State and Metropolitan Area Data Book,* arrange the fifty states of the United States into three groups according to their population ranking in the 2000 census. Prepare a crosstab comparing the three groups of states according to their respective per capita income levels in the same year. This will require that you develop ordinal categories of per capita income, determine which is your independent variable, count the number of cases in each cell of the resulting table and calculate the appropriate percentages. In doing so, you may wish to use as a worksheet a grid similar to the one shown in Table 15.4.

Table 15.4 Crosstab format

	I	II	III	IV
I				
II				
III				

Key terms

bar chart	key	segmented bar chart
bilateral bar chart	line graph	simple table
cross tabulation (or crosstab)	pie chart	

Part V

Statistical techniques

16 Statistics I: summarising distributions on one variable

- What are the three measures of central tendency?
- Which level of measurement is most associated with each?
- How is a variable's dispersion measured?

Introduction

Often in politics research, charts and tables alone do not tell us enough about our data to permit a satisfactory answer to our research question. In part this is a problem of complexity (our variables may have either too many values or too many cases – or there may even be too many variables involved – to lend themselves to ready analysis) and in part a question of precision (degrees of difference or subtle variations among variables may be important, and they are often difficult to assess accurately by simply eyeballing a table or chart). In instances such as these, as well as others that call for highly sophisticated analysis, politics researchers employ *statistics.*

In this context, **statistics** are numbers that summarise either the distributions of values on, or the relationships between, variables. They are a form of mathematical shorthand capable of telling us at a glance and with great precision what our data show (or, in many cases, what they do not show). What is the political ideology of the typical university student? Do white voters differ systematically in their party preferences from non-white voters? What kinds of actions or situations in the world community are most likely to give rise to armed conflict? If the proper data are applied for analysis, statistics can answer these questions and many more.

Statistics can be extremely complex. It is equally true, however, that many of the primary concepts and techniques of statistical analysis are extremely simple, can be learned in a short time, and can get you a good deal further into the subject than you might imagine. In fact, your knowledge of GCSE mathematics arms you with just about all the background you will need, and you may be surprised at how intuitive many statistical concepts really are.

We should make clear that this chapter and the two that follow will not teach you all there is to know about statistics, nor even all there is to know about the particular statistical measures we discuss. Still, upon completion of these chapters, you should have a good sense of what statistics are and of how to use them, you should have some understanding of the concepts that lie behind the numbers and the calculations and you should have a reasonable facility in the use of several specific statistics. Together, these skills will enable you both to employ statistical analysis in your own research and to comprehend more fully and more critically what you read in scholarly journals and other reports of political research.

In this chapter we examine statistics that answer the following types of questions about a given set of data: How are the cases distributed among the values of each of our variables? What does the typical case look like? How typical is it?

Statistics and level of measurement

In each instance, we examine a different statistic for each level of measurement: nominal, ordinal and interval/ratio. You will recall from Chapter 4 that these levels differ from one another in that the first merely differentiates categories, the second ranks them and the third assumes constant degrees of difference between them. In effect, then, *nominal*, *ordinal* and *interval/ratio* numbers are different kinds of numbers with different qualities. In a sense, nominal numbers are soft numbers; they do not tell us very much. Because they merely separate objects into groups and serve as no more than labels for those groups, nominal numbers cannot even be added or subtracted. Accordingly, we cannot use very sophisticated statistical methods in analysing nominal data. On the other hand, interval/ratio numbers are much harder, or more concrete, in that these values convey a great deal more information about the data they represent. They can be added, subtracted, squared and variously transformed. As a result, they offer much more flexibility and an opportunity for far more sophisticated analysis. It is for this reason that different techniques are applied to different levels of measurement. For the same reason, of course, one must take care to use each technique appropriately.

Measures of central tendency and dispersion

Two types of statistics are used to describe the distribution of cases over the values of a single variable. The first – the measure of **central tendency** – helps us to identify the most typical value: the one value or score that best represents the entire set of cases on that variable. Suppose we were told that the average UK female employee is an office worker, has three A-levels or equivalent qualifications and has 1.86 children. Clearly not every UK woman fits these categories, but when we look at all British females in a summary manner, this set of characteristics might well come closest to a general description of the findings. It is this same notion of an average, or typical, case that we employ in calculating a measure of central tendency. Indeed, it was precisely such measures that identified these particular traits of British females in the first place.

As we have noted, however, not every member of the female population fits this description. Many are manual or professional workers or perhaps even unemployed, some have finished only GCSEs whereas others hold advanced degrees, and some may have five or more children whereas others are unmarried and childless. In other words, the 'typical' British female may well represent the *tendencies* within the population, but she does not accurately reflect each individual case. For this reason, once we have identified such a typical case, we must ask follow-up questions: How typical is it? How good a job does this average score do of summarising the distribution of scores for all the cases on a given variable? We answer these questions by using a second type of statistic – the measure of dispersion. The measure of **dispersion** tells us whether the variation around the average value identified is limited, in which case we can have confidence that our average is a meaningful one, or whether that variation is so great that the most typical case is not really representative of the population after all.

This raises an important point, which should be explained before we proceed any further. Statistics are powerful tools of analysis; they can tell us a great deal about our data that we could not otherwise ascertain. But statistics, on their own, are mindless. One can calculate and report *any* statistic on *any* set of numbers and in the process appear to be wringing the last drop of knowledge from one's data. For two reasons, however, many of these 'results' may be meaningless. The first reason is one we have discussed already and whose logic should become more evident as we proceed. Put most simply, the level of sophistication of our statistics may exceed the level of sophistication of our data. If our statistic requires us to add two numbers, but our data are based on nominal-level measures for which the whole concept of addition is inappropriate, we could, in fact, go through the mechanical process of combining the coded values, but the result would be worthless. Thus, if the score 1 represented office workers; 2, manual workers; and 3, professional workers, we could add 1 and 2 and get 3, but would we really want to argue that one manual worker plus one office worker *equals* one professional? Certainly not.

The second reason that statistical results may be less than meaningful is that one statistic, by itself, often cannot tell the whole story. If the single *most* typical level of education of British females is three A-levels or the equivalent, but only 30.5 per cent of women have both reached that level and stopped there, how much does this average really tell us? Not much. And how many people do you know who actually have an average of 1.86 children? Thus, although we can calculate and report these figures accurately, they should not be allowed to stand alone. Each measure of central tendency should be qualified or evaluated with an accompanying measure of dispersion. And similarly, as we shall argue later, whenever we are dealing with a sample, each measure of association between two variables should be accompanied by a measure of statistical significance, which is an indication of how likely that finding is to represent a substantive relationship between the variables in question. Thus, statistics must be not only appropriate to the level of measurement of the data but substantively meaningful as well if they are to prove of much value.

All measures of central tendency and dispersion are based on a summary of values and cases termed a *frequency distribution*. A **frequency distribution** is simply an ordered count of the number of cases that take on each value of a variable. For example, suppose we ask 100 people to tell us their present occupation and then classify their responses according to type. For the variable *type of occupation*, we might arrive at the frequency distribution shown in Table 16.1. The frequency distribution

Table 16.1 Frequency distribution: Type of occupation of respondents

Code	Value	Number of cases
1	Blue-collar	25
2	White-collar	23
3	Professional	22
4	Farm	20
5	Unemployed	10

Figure 16.1 Histogram: Type of occupation of respondents

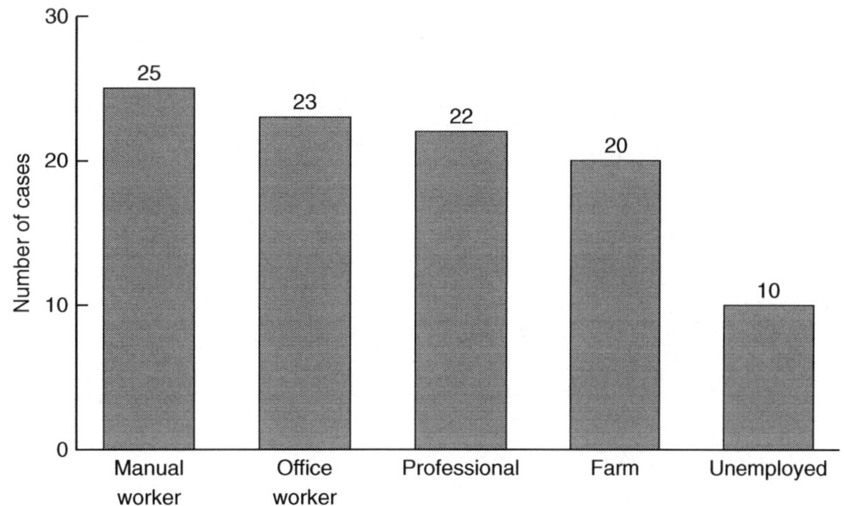

simply lists each value on the variable and reports the number of cases that take on that value. The same information may be communicated by a bar graph, which, when used for this particular purpose, is often called a **histogram**, as illustrated in Figure 16.1. Using this information, we may identify the most typical case and determine its descriptiveness.

Measures for nominal variables

As we suggested earlier, different measures of central tendency and dispersion are appropriate for different levels of measurement. Since *type of occupation* is a nominal variable, let us begin to examine these calculations by focusing on statistics appropriate for nominal-level measures.

The mode

At this level, where numbers represent merely category labels without regard to order, the only available measure of central tendency is the mode. The **mode** is simply *the most frequently occurring value* – the one which is taken on by the greatest number of cases. In the example, this is category 1, or the value *manual labour*. We refer to this as either the mode or the modal category. (A distribution in which two categories tie for the greatest number of cases is said to have two modes, or to be *bimodal*, and it is possible to have a tie between even more than two categories.) Manual employment, then, is the single most typical type of occupation among our sample of 100 persons.

Clearly, however, most people in this sample (in fact, fully 75 per cent) are not manual workers, so even though we can identify the most typical value in this distribution, that information may not be very meaningful. We can be more precise in judging just how meaningful it is by calculating the appropriate nominal-level measure of dispersion – the **variation ratio** – the formula for which is as follows:

$$v = \frac{\sum f_{\text{nonmodal}}}{N} \quad or \quad v = 1 - \frac{f_{\text{modal}}}{N}$$

where $\sum f_{\text{nonmodal}}$ = the sum of all cases *not* falling into the modal category

f_{modal} = the number of cases in the modal category

N = the total number of cases.

In effect, this statistic tells us the *percentage of all cases that do not fit into the modal category.* In the example,

$$v = \frac{23 + 22 + 20 + 10}{100} = .75$$

or, in the simplified form,

$$v = 1 - \frac{25}{100} = .75$$

The variation ratio ranges between 0 (when all cases take on the same value) and $1 - 1/N$ (when each case takes on a different value). In general, the lower the variation ratio, the more typical or more meaningful the mode. In the case of bimodal or multimodal distributions, one modal value is arbitrarily selected for purposes of calculation and N is determined precisely as above.

Measures for ordinal variables

When dealing with ordinal-level data, we have a bit more information, since our codes represent not only categorisation but relative position or ranking as well. Our selection of measures of central tendency and dispersion should both reflect and take advantage of this fact.

The median

The appropriate measure of central tendency for ordinal data – the median – does precisely this. The **median** is simply *the value of the middle case in a distribution* – the case above and below which an equal number of other cases lie. Obtaining the median, then, requires only that we count from either end of the distribution towards the centre until finding the middle case and then ascertaining the value associated with that case. When we have an odd number of cases, we will be able to locate one middle case (for example, for 99 cases, the 50th case from either end of the frequency distribution will have 49 cases both above and below it). The value of this case is the median. When N (the number of cases) is an even number, two middle cases will emerge (for example, for 100 cases, the 50th and 51st cases from either end together constitute the midpoint of the distribution). If both of these cases take on the same value, that value is the median. If they take on different values, the median is the midpoint between those two values.

An example may help to make this clear. Let us consider the distribution of educational achievement in three samples (Table 16.2). In the first, we identify the middle case (the 50th from either end), note its value, and determine the median level of education to be 3, or *three A-levels or the equivalent*. In the second, we identify two middle cases (the 50th and 51st from either end), note that each takes on the same value, and determine the median once again to be a score of 3. In the third sample, however, the middle cases split between the *less than three A-levels or the equivalent* and *three A-levels or the equivalent* categories. Here the median is the midpoint between the two values in question, or $(2 + 3)/2 = 2.5$. Because fractional values have no meaning in ordinal measurement, this figure merely tells us that the midpoint of the distribution lies somewhere between 2 and 3.

Using quantiles

Any of several measures of dispersion for ordinal variables, termed **quantile ranges**, tells us how tightly the various cases cluster around the median or, again, how typical or representative the median is of the whole distribution. A **quantile** is a measure of position within a distribution. For example, a percentile divides a distribution into 100 equal parts such that the first percentile is the point or value

Table 16.2 Educational achievement in three samples

Code	Value	Sample 1(n)	Sample 2(n)	Sample 3(n)
1	GCSE only	25	25	10
2	< Three A-levels	23	23	40
3	> Three A-levels	22	22	35
4	University degree	20	20	10
5	Advanced degree	29	210	225
Total n		9	100	100

in that distribution (counting from the lowest score up) below which 1 per cent of all the cases lie, the second percentile that point or value below which 2 per cent of all the cases lie and so forth. This is used most notably in the main university entrance examination used in the United States called the Standardised Aptitude Test (SAT) which is based on the notion of percentiles. A prospective university student who scores in the 85th percentile on the SAT has achieved a test score that is higher than the scores of 85 per cent of all who took the test. Similar to a percentile, a decile divides the distribution into tenths (for example, the third decile would be the point below which 30 per cent of all the cases lie), a quintile into fifths, a quartile into fourths. Any of these can be used to indicate dispersion around the median, though the decile and quintile ranges are most commonly found in the literature.

An example

Let us use the quintile range to illustrate the procedure. The quintile range (q) is defined as follows:

$$q = q_4 - q_1$$

where q_4 = the fourth quintile (the value below which 4/5, or 80 per cent, of the cases lie)

q_1 = the first quintile (the value below which 1/5, or 20 per cent, of the cases lie).

The narrower the range of values separating these two points in the distribution, the more tightly clustered the cases are about the median and the more truly representative of the distribution the median will be. In sample 2 in Table 16.2, for instance, where $n = 100$, we calculate q by locating the 81st case (below which 80 per cent of the cases lie) and the 21st case (below which 20 per cent of the cases lie), starting our count within the frequency distribution from the lowest scores. We then subtract the value associated with the 21st case from that associated with the 81st ($q = q_4 - q_1 = 4 - 1 = 3$) to obtain the quintile range. In sample 3, the equivalent computation yields a quintile range of 1 ($q = 3 - 2 = 1$), suggesting by comparison that this distribution is better typified by its median of 2.5 than is sample 2 by its median of 3. An examination of the two frequency distributions will confirm the validity of this conclusion.

One difficulty in interpreting quantile ranges is that they are extremely sensitive to variation in the number of categories on a given variable. The more categories there are, the greater the range is likely to be. For this reason, quantile ranges can prove difficult to interpret for comparison between variables that differ in their number of categories. For similarly coded variables, for longitudinal or cross-sectional comparisons of the values of any single variable, or for some absolute indication of variability around the median, however, they are generally quite adequate.

Measures for interval/ratio variables

Interval/ratio data, of course, provide us with the most complete information of all, including categorisation, rank and distance. Interval/ratio values can be subjected to any arithmetic manipulation. Consequently, our measures of central tendency and dispersion for interval/ratio data can and should take this added information and capability into account.

The mean

The measure of central tendency for interval/ratio data is the **mean** – a measure that locates *the central point of a distribution* in terms of both the number of cases on either side of that point and their

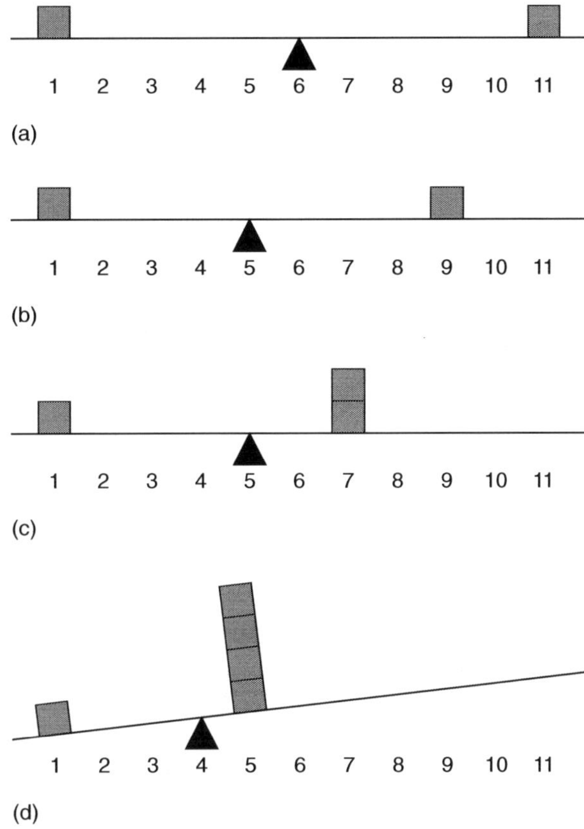

Figure 16.2 The mean as a point of balance

distance from it. The mean of a distribution is the statistic many people commonly associate with the term *average*.

Let us visualise the nature of the mean by using Figure 16.2. If all the cases in a distribution are represented by equal weights, and if they are arranged on a board at fixed intervals so that those with the most extreme values are furthest from the centre in one or the other direction and those with equal values are placed at the same point on the board, the mean value of the distribution will be the fulcrum point – the value at which the combined weights and distances to one side precisely balance those to the other. As illustrated in the figure, both weight (number of cases) and distance (extremity of the scores) are important in ascertaining the mean.

The mean of a distribution, designated $\overline{X}$, (or X–bar) is calculated by taking the sum of the values of the individual cases and dividing by the number of cases. This procedure is summarised in the following equation:

$$\overline{X} = \frac{\sum_{i=1}^{N} X_i}{N}$$

where X_i = the value of each individual case

N = the number of cases

$\sum_{i=1}^{N}$ = an instruction to take the sum of all the individual values of cases 1 to N.

Note, too, however, as illustrated in Figure 16.2(d), that precisely because it is sensitive to distance, the mean is subject to distortion in a distribution that has a few, or even one, very extreme case(s). That is, a small number of cases with very extreme scores can cause the mean to be less than a truly typical value. Let us see how this might occur.

Consider a group of 11 persons, 10 of whom earn £10,000 a year and 1 of whom earns £1 million. The mean income for this group equals £100,000, but 10 of the 11 members of the group actually earn one-tenth of that amount. Thus, the mean, although correctly calculated, is not as representative as, say, the median, which in this case is £10,000.

$$\frac{(10*\$10,000) + \$1,000,000}{11}$$

It would seem at first glance that to determine how typical of a distribution a given mean is, all we need do is measure the distances of all cases from that point (taking account of direction), add these together and divide by N (the number of cases). In effect, we would calculate the mean of the distances around the mean as in the formula

$$\text{Dispersion} = \frac{\sum_{i=1}^{N}(X_i - \overline{X})}{N}$$

The greater the dispersion for a given distribution, then, the *less* typical the mean; and the less the dispersion, the *more* typical the mean.

But when we try this with, for example, the three cases illustrated in Figure 16.2(c), a problem emerges. Applying the formula to the example, we find

$$\text{Dispersion} = \frac{(1-5) + (7-5) + (7-5)}{3}$$

$$= \frac{-4 + 2 + 2}{3} = 0$$

Even in a distribution with such clear divergence as our income example, we find

$$\text{Dispersion} = \frac{10(10,000 - 100,000) + (1,000,000 - 100,000)}{11}$$

$$= \frac{-900,000 + 900,000}{11} = 0$$

Indeed, for *any* mean in any distribution the result is the same. The reason is a simple one. We have, in effect, *defined* the mean as precisely that point where these weights and distances cancel out, or the point or value about which all variations are balanced. Therefore, after calculating the mean, we should hardly be surprised to find exactly the effect we have intended. Yet the notion that we ought to be able to measure dispersion by comparing the closeness of cases to, or their remoteness from, the mean retains its appeal. Enter the standard deviation.

Calculating the standard deviation

The **standard deviation** (*s*) employs a mathematical device to accomplish our purpose. In effect, it is a procedure that eliminates the tendency of opposing distances to cancel one another out by the simple expedient of squaring those distances (thereby eliminating all negative signs), averaging the *squares* of the distances around the mean, and then taking the square root of the result so as to return to the original units of distance. The formula by which all of this is accomplished resembles the rejected formula except for the use of the squared distances and the square root of the result. That formula is

$$s = \sqrt{\frac{\sum_{i=1}^{N}(X_i - \overline{X})^2}{N}}$$

where X_i = the value of each individual case

$\overline{X}$ = the mean

N = the number of cases

$\sum_{i=1}^{N}$ = an instruction to take the sum of the individual values for cases

Thus, in the example from Figure 16.2(c),

$$s = \sqrt{\frac{(1-5)^2 + (7-5)^2 + (7-5)^2}{3}}$$

1 to N.

$$= \sqrt{\frac{16 + 4 + 4}{3}} = \sqrt{\frac{24}{3}} = \sqrt{8} = 2.8$$

It is expressed in the same units as the original data.

When two variables are measured by the same or comparable scales, the standard deviation provides a basis for comparing the representativeness of the means: the greater the standard deviation, the less representative the mean. However, when scales differ substantially or when a single variable is being analysed, the interpretation of the standard deviation is less clear.

The normal distribution

One exception to this applies to variables whose values closely approximate a **normal distribution**, or one in which there is *a single mode in the very centre of the distribution and in which the frequencies decline symmetrically as the values become more extreme in each direction.* (The bell-shaped curve with which you may be familiar is simply a graphic representation of a normal distribution, and appears in Chapter 17.) In these cases, we know that 68.3 per cent of all cases will lie within +1 and −1 standard deviation from the mean, 95.5 per cent will lie within +2 and −2 standard deviations from the mean and 99.7 per cent will lie within +3 and −3 standard deviations from the mean. (The derivation of these mathematical properties lies beyond the scope of the present discussion.) In fact, for such distributions, we can locate the exact number of standard deviation units any particular value lies above or below the mean, then use this information for comparing the relative position of two cases on the same variable or, alternatively, the relative scores on two variables for the same case. The measure that allows us to do this is called the **standard score** (or **z-score**), and it is calculated by simply subtracting the mean $(\overline{X})$ from the score (X) and then dividing by the standard deviation (s):

$$z = \frac{(X_i - \overline{X})}{s}$$

What makes the standard scores so useful is the fact that they allow us to compare scores that are based on very different units of measurements (for example, age measured in number of years and height measured in inches). Since z-scores all have a mean of 0 and a standard deviation of 1, each score simply tells us how many standard deviation units a variable (age, height etc.) is above or below the mean[1]

Suppose, for example, that we have data showing the per capita spending by each Local Education Authority (LEA) for education, the number of teachers per 1,000 students each LEA employs and the number of A-levels or equivalent per 100,000 population awarded by each LEA in a given year; and that values on these variables are distributed among the LEA in a manner approximating the normal curve. Suppose further that we wish to use these data to examine educational policy in, say, Aberdeen and Cardiff. We first calculate the mean $(\overline{X})$ and standard deviation (s) for each variable for all LEAs and then determine the respective standard scores (z) on each variable for the two LEAs of interest. The result will be two sets of scores in standard units (no longer pounds sterling, teachers and certificates, but the number of standard deviations about the mean) that can be used to construct indices of educational policy, determine an average position for Aberdeen or Cardiff among the LEAs or provide for standardised comparisons across substantively different measures. As the basis for the standard score, then, the standard deviation may be an especially useful statistic.

Ethical considerations

Each researcher's duty to utilise the proper techniques is the primary ethical responsibility that will be emphasised in the three chapters on data analysis. Of course, which techniques are most appropriate depends upon the nature of the research and the variables' qualities. For example, you are only likely to use the univariate statistics described in this chapter to initially describe and evaluate each of your variables. Assessing relationships between variables requires the type of tools described in the next two chapters.

Conclusion

In this chapter we have focused on statistics that summarise the distribution of scores on one variable. Because these statistics describe the characteristics of individual variables, they are often called **univariate statistics**. We have seen that different univariate statistics are appropriate for variables with different levels of measurement: nominal, ordinal and interval/ratio. In the next chapter we examine what are termed **bivariate statistics** – those that summarise the relationship between *two* variables.

Summary points

- Central tendency may be measured with the mode, median or mean.
- The mode is typically used with nominal variables.
- The median is most appropriate with ordinal data.
- The mean works best with interval/ratio information.
- The standard deviation measures the dispersion of interval/ratio variables – literally, the deviation of the values from the mean.

---

[1] Table A.6 in Appendix A summarises the area between the mean and z, as well as the area beyond z in the distribution, for standard scores between 0 and 4, which is to say, for all values between the mean and a distance of four standard deviations in either direction around it. The values in the table can be used to locate (for purposes of comparison) any number of cases relative to the means on different variables.

Suggested reading and examples

Research examples

Finding examples of political science research using the mean is difficult, because most research focuses on hypothesis testing. These studies, by definition, examine relationships rather than calculating univariate statistics. Thus, researchers are more likely to report mean values as a precursor to more formal comparisons.

For example, in preparing to explore the association between democracy and equality of educational achievement by both sexes, Brown (2004: 142) calculates a ratio between the years of schooling for males and females, by country. He reports the mean gender inequality ratio by continent, giving the reader some perspective on these trends throughout the world.

Methodological reading

At the end of Chapter 18 we suggest several books you might read to begin learning about statistics in more detail. At this point, though, it might be more useful to start with books that can put you at ease about using statistics and at the same time help you grasp some important basic concepts. These books are somewhat dated, but the information is still relevant and the writing is often more engaging than the writing in other works. For this purpose, we suggest *How to Lie with Statistics* (Huff and Geis 1993), a classic and lighthearted examination of the uses and abuses of statistics, or what the authors term 'statisticulation'. For those who prefer to absorb their statistics through the medium of cartoon drawings, we recommend *The Cartoon Guide to Statistics* (Gonick and Smith 1993).

References

Brown, David S. 2004. 'Democracy and gender inequality in education: a cross-national examination'. *British Journal of Political Science*, vol. 34 (January), pp. 137–52.
Gonick, Larry and Smith, Woollcott. 1993. *The Cartoon Guide to Statistics*. New York: HarperPerennial.
Huff, Darrell and Geis, Irving. 1993. *How to Lie with Statistics*. New York: Norton.

Research exercises

1 For each of the following frequency distributions, determine the mode and variation ratio, the median and quintile range and the mean and standard deviation. Think about your results.

Value	Sample 1	Sample 2	Sample 3
1	0	50	14
2	0	0	14
3	0	0	14
4	100	0	16
5	0	0	14
6	0	0	14
7	0	50	14

2 Both of the following frequency distributions approximate the normal (bell-shaped) curve. For each one, calculate the mode, median and mean.

Value	Sample 1	Sample 2
1	5	0
2	10	5
3	20	20
4	30	50
5	20	20
6	10	5
7	5	0

3 Consider again the frequency distributions in Exercise 2. Both have the same mean, and both approximate a normal curve.

a Draw a bar graph summarising each of these distributions. Which would you expect to have the smaller standard deviation? Why?

b Calculate the standard deviation for each of these distributions. Did you find what you expected?

Key terms

statistics	variation ratio	normal distribution
central tendency	median	standard score (z-score)
dispersion	quantile ranges	univariate statistics
frequency distribution	quantile	bivariate statistics
histogram	mean	
mode	standard deviation (s)	

17 Statistics II: examining relationships between two variables

- How is association defined?
- What does chi-square represent?
- How does one know which measure of association is most appropriate when comparing variables with different levels of measurement?

Introduction

In political science research, we are generally less concerned with describing distributions on single variables than we are with determining whether, how and to what extent two or more variables may be related to one another. It is these bivariate (two-variable) and multivariate (more-than-two-variable) relationships that usually cast light on the more interesting research questions.

When examining the relationship between two variables, we typically ask three important questions. The first is whether and to what extent changes or differences in the values of one variable – generally the independent variable – are associated with changes or differences in the values of the second, or dependent, variable. The second question examines the direction and form of any association that might exist. The third considers the likelihood that any association observed among cases sampled from a larger population is in fact a characteristic of that population and not merely an artefact of the smaller and potentially unrepresentative sample. In this chapter we introduce some of the statistics that are most commonly used to answer these questions, and we explain when it is appropriate to use them and what they tell us about relationships.

Measures of association and statistical significance

An **association** is said to exist between two variables when knowing the value of one for a given case improves the odds of our guessing correctly the corresponding value of the second. If, for example, we examine the relationship between the size of a country's population and the proportion of its adults who are university educated, we may variously find (1) that larger countries generally have a greater proportion of university-educated adults than smaller ones; (2) that smaller countries generally have a greater proportion of university-educated adults than larger ones; or (3) that there is no systematic difference between the two – that some countries from each group have relatively high proportions of such people, but that some from each group have low proportions as well. If our research shows that either case 1 or case 2 holds, we can use our knowledge of values on the independent variable, *size of population*, to guess or predict values on the dependent variable, *proportion of adults who are university educated*, for any given country. In the first instance, for any heavily populated country, we predict a relatively high proportion of university-educated adults, and for a less populous nation, we predict a lower proportion. In the second, our prediction is precisely reversed. In either event, although we may not guess every case correctly, we will be right fairly often because of the underlying *association* between the two variables. Indeed, the stronger the association between the two variables (the more the individual countries' educational level values tend to align on each in precisely the same order), the more likely we are to guess correctly in any particular instance. If there is total correspondence in the alignments on the two variables, high scores with high scores or, alternatively, high scores on one with low on the other, we can predict one from the other with perfect accuracy. This contrasts sharply with the third possibility, which permits no improved prediction of values on the education variable based on our knowledge of populations. In such instances, when cases are, in effect, randomly distributed on the two variables, there is said to be no association.

To get a mental picture of what a strong association might look like, consider the two maps presented in Figure 17.1, which relate to the murder rate in Washington, DC, during the 'crack wars' of

Figure 17.1   Drug markets and homicide locations, Washington, DC, 1988

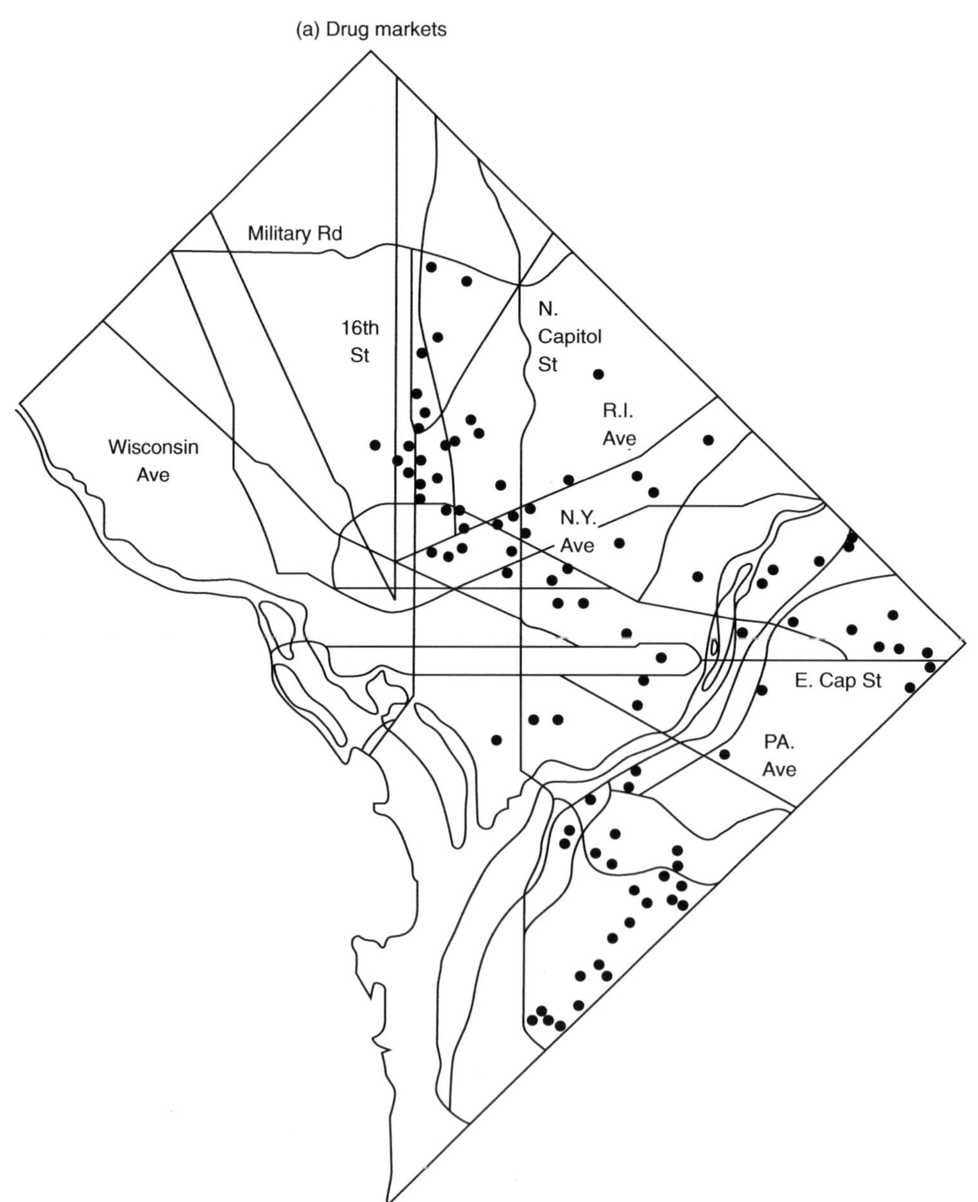

Figure 17.1   (*Continued*)

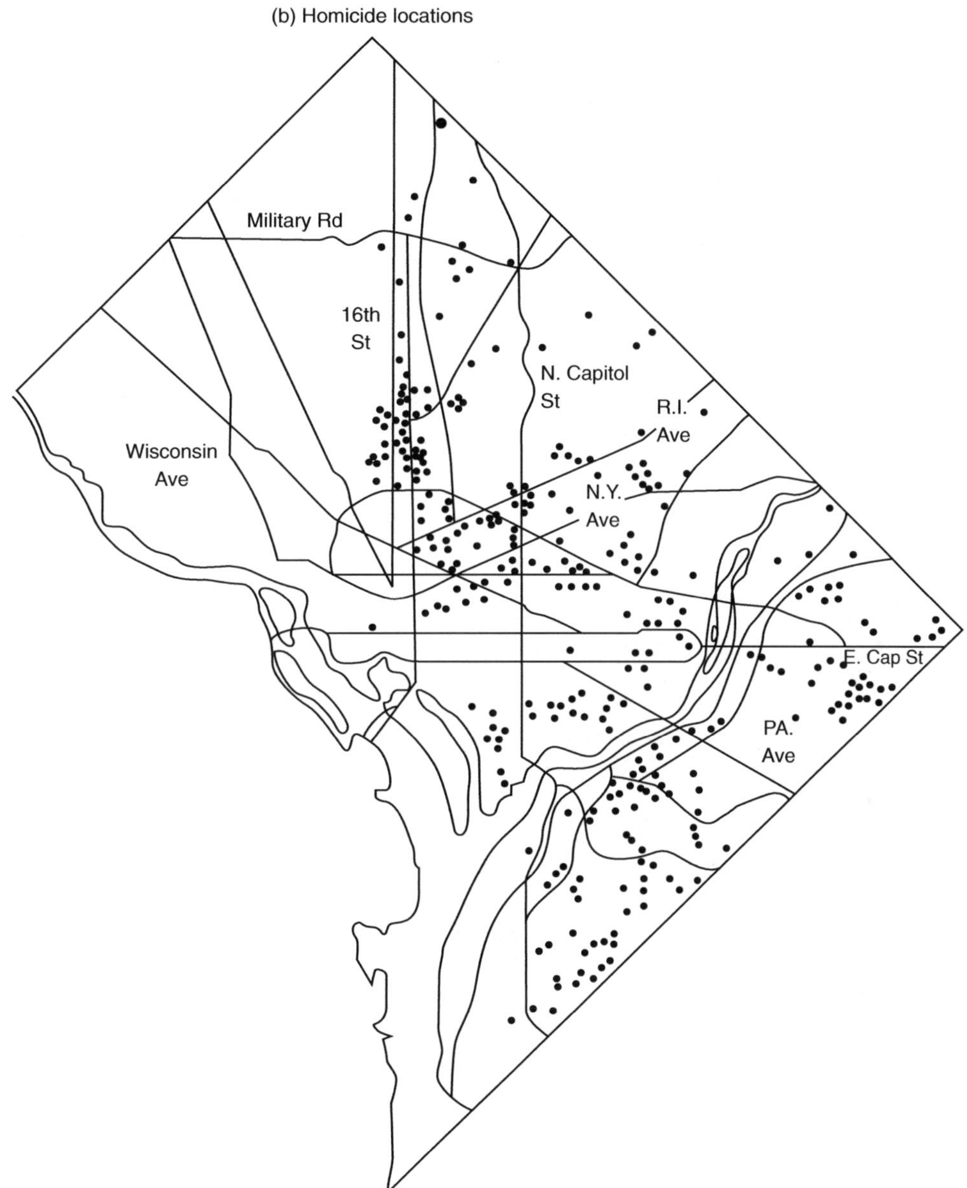

Source: Reprinted from the *Washington Post*, 13 January 1989, p. E1, with permission of the publisher.

the 1980s. Figure 17.1(a) shows the location of known drug markets in the US capital; Figure 17.1(b) shows the location of homicides. Both are based on information provided by the DC Metropolitan Police Department. The apparent similarity in the locations of clusters of drug dealing and murders suggests an *association* between the two phenomena.

Measuring association

Clearly there can be more or less association between any two variables. The question in each instance then becomes, *Just how much association is there?* The answer is provided by a set of statistics known as coefficients of association. A **coefficient of association** is a number that summarises the amount of improvement in guessing values on one variable for any case based on knowledge of the values of a second. In the example, for instance, such a measure would tell us *how much* our knowledge of a country's population size helps us in guessing its proportion of university-educated adults. The higher the coefficient, the stronger the association and, by extension, the better our predictive or explanatory ability. In general, coefficients of association range from 0 to 1 or –1 to 1, with the values closest to unity indicating a relatively strong association and those closest to 0 a relatively weak one.

In addition to the magnitude of association, it is also useful to know the direction or form of the relationship between two variables. Take another look at the earlier example about level of education of a nation's adults, and most particularly at options 1 and 2. We have already suggested that the closer we get to either case, the higher will be our coefficient of association and the better our chances of guessing a particular country's proportion of university-educated adults based on our knowledge of its population size. It should be obvious, however, that our predictions in the cases are precisely opposite. In the first instance, higher values of one variable tend to be associated with higher values of the other, and in the latter instance, higher values of one tend to be associated with *lower* values of the other. Such relationships are said to display differences in *direction*. Those like the first, in which both variables rise and fall together, are termed *direct*, or *positive* associations. Those like the second, in which scores move systematically in opposing directions, are termed *inverse* or *negative* associations. This additional bit of information, which is represented by a plus or a minus sign accompanying the coefficient of association, makes our guessing even more effective. Thus, a coefficient of –.87 (negative and relatively close to 1) might describe a relatively strong relationship in which the values on the two variables in question are inversely related (moving in opposite directions), whereas a coefficient of .20 (positive – the plus sign is usually omitted – and rather close to zero) might describe a weak direct association.

Defining statistical significance

Finally, we should say a word about tests of *statistical significance*, though our discussion of the topic will be purposely limited.[1] You will recall from our discussion of levels of confidence and sampling error in Chapter 7 that when we draw a presumably representative sample and use that sample to develop conclusions about the larger population from which it is drawn, we run some risk of coming to incorrect conclusions. This is true because there is a chance that the sample is not in fact representative and that the actual error in our measurement exceeds that specified for a given sample size (Tables A.2 and A.3 in Appendix A). The *chance* of such improper generalising is known, but we cannot tell whether or not it has occurred in any particular instance. For a level of confidence of .95, that chance is .05, or 1–.95. For a level of confidence of .99, it is .01. These values represent the likelihood that any generalisation from our sample to the larger population, even allowing for the estimated range of sampling error, is simply wrong.

Tests of **statistical significance** perform the same function in evaluating measures of association. They tell us just how likely it is that the association we have measured between two variables in a sample might or might not exist in the whole population. Let us see if we can clarify this point.

---

[1] A full explanation of statistical significance is beyond the scope of this text; to pursue a deeper understanding of significance testing, you are encouraged to consult one of the statistics texts listed at the end of Chapter 18.

An example

Suppose, to continue our example, we have a population of 200 nations for which we *know for a fact* that the coefficient of association between population size and the proportion of adults with a university education is 0. There is, in reality, no relationship between the two variables. But suppose further that we take a sample of only 30 of these countries and calculate the association between these two variables. It might come out as 0, but this is actually unlikely, because the strength of association is now based not on all the countries but on only 30 and will probably reflect their particular idiosyncrasies. In other words, the coefficient itself is determined by *which* 30 countries we pick. If, by chance, we pick 30 countries that are truly representative of all 200, we will in fact find no association. But chance might also lead us to pick 30 countries for which the association between population size and education level is unusually high, say, .60. In that case, our coefficient of association measures a characteristic of the particular sample in question, but if we generalise to the larger population, our conclusions will be incorrect. Knowing this, of course, we reject our measure of association based on this particular sample.

The problem is that in the real world we seldom know the underlying population parameter, which is the true degree of association in the whole population (as defined in Chapter 7). Indeed, the reason to draw samples in the first place is exactly because we often simply *cannot* study whole populations. It follows, then, that more often than not the *only* tests of association we will have will be those based on our sampling. Moreover, these calculations will usually be based on only *one* sample. Thus, the question becomes one of how confident we can be that a test of association based on a single subgroup of a population accurately reflects an underlying population characteristic. The job of the test of statistical significance is to pin a number on that confidence – that is, to measure the probability or likelihood that we are making an appropriate, or, conversely, an inappropriate, generalisation.

To see how this works, let us continue our example. Suppose that we draw not one sample of 30 nations from our population of 200, but 1,000 separate and independent samples of the same size and that for each we calculate the coefficient of association. Because the true coefficient for the entire population is in fact 0, most of the coefficients for our 1,000 samples will also be at or relatively near 0. Some particular combinations of 30 countries may yield relatively higher values (that is, we might by chance happen to pick only countries scoring either high–high or low–low on the two variables), but the majority will be nearer to the population parameter. Indeed, the closer one gets to the true value, the more samples one finds represented. These distributions, in fact, often resemble the normal curve mentioned earlier. This is illustrated in Figure 17.2, where the height of the curve at any given point represents the number of samples for which the coefficient of association noted along the baseline has been calculated. As you can see, most of the sample coefficients cluster around the true population parameter.

Figure 17.2   Normal distribution of coefficients of association for samples of 30 cases

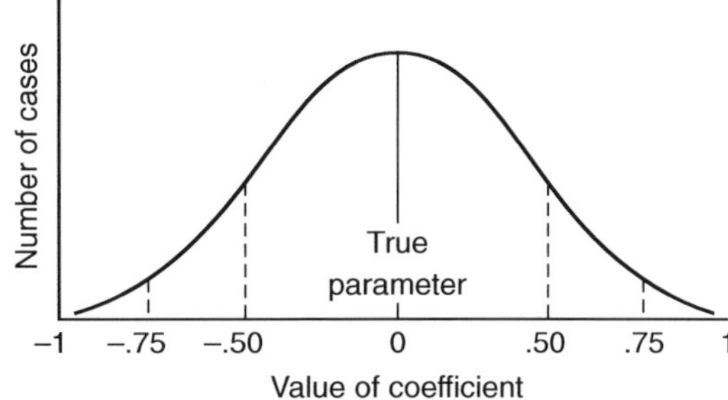

What, then, is the likelihood that any particular coefficient is simply a chance variation around a true parameter of 0? Or, in other words, if we take a sample from some population and find in that sample a strong association, what are the chances that we will be wrong in generalising so strong a relationship from the sample to the population? The normal curve has certain properties which enable us to answer this question with considerable precision.

Suppose, for example, we draw from our 200 nations a sample of 30 for which the coefficient of association is −.75. How likely is it that the corresponding coefficient for the population as a whole is 0? From Figure 17.2, the answer must be a resounding *Not very!* The area under the curve represents all 1,000 (actually any number of) sample coefficients when the true parameter is 0. The much smaller area at and to the left of −.75 represents the proportion of such coefficients that are negative in direction and .75 or stronger in magnitude. Such cases constitute a very small proportion of the many sample coefficients. For this reason, the odds of drawing such a sample in any given try are quite slim. If 5 per cent of all samples lies in this area, for instance, then only one time in twenty will we be likely to encounter a sample from a population with a true coefficient of 0 for which we find a coefficient in our sample of −.75. Yet that is precisely what we have found in this instance.

In other words, we have just drawn a sample with a characteristic that has a 5 per cent likelihood of being an erroneous representation of a population in which the two variables in question are not associated with each other. Thus, if we claim on the basis of our sample that the two variables are in fact associated in the larger population (that is, if generalising our results from the sample), we can expect to be wrong 5 per cent of the time. That means, of course, that we will be right 95 per cent of the time, and those are not bad odds. Indeed, levels of statistical significance of .05 (a 5 per cent chance of erroneous generalisation), .01 (a 1 per cent chance of such error) and .001 (a 1/10 of 1 per cent chance of such error) are commonly accepted standards in social science research.

If we look again at Figure 17.2, it should be apparent that more extreme values such as −.75 are less likely to give rise to this kind of error in generalisation than are those closer to the centre (for example, a greater proportion of samples from such a population will, by chance, show coefficients of −.50 or stronger and so forth). It seems, then, that we can never be very confident of the trustworthiness of weaker associations, since we can never eliminate the heavy odds that they are simply chance occurrences in a population with a true coefficient of 0.

We can increase our confidence in our sample simply by increasing our sample size. If instead of 30 cases per sample we draw 100 or 150, each will be more likely to cluster around 0. In effect, the normal curve will be progressively squeezed towards the middle, as illustrated in Figure 17.3, until ultimately there is only one possible outcome – the true parameter. In the process, with a set of sufficiently large samples, even a coefficient of association of .10 or .01 can be shown to have acceptable levels of statistical significance. We can conclude, then, that some combination of sufficiently

Figure 17.3 Sampling distribution for differing numbers of cases in a population of 200

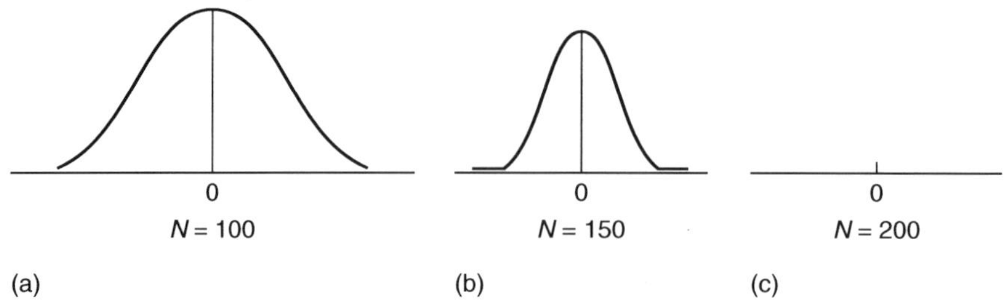

extreme scores and sufficiently large samples allows us to reduce to tolerable levels the likelihood of incorrectly generalising from our data.

In the balance of this chapter we present a brief discussion of the most common measures of association and significance for each of the three levels of measurement. Although the procedures employed in calculating each of these measures differ, the purpose in each case, as well as the interpretation of the result, will remain relatively consistent, for each coefficient of association is designed to tell us to what extent our guessing of values on one variable is improved by knowledge of the corresponding values on another. Each test of significance tells us *the probability that any observed relationships in a sample result from bias in the sample rather than from an underlying relationship in the base population.*

The examples we use to illustrate these statistics involve comparisons of variables that are operationalised at the same level of measurement. However, researchers often want to look for relationships between variables that are at *different* levels of measurement (as in the case of an ordinal-level independent variable such as socioeconomic status and a nominal-level dependent variable such as party identification). To select the correct statistic in these situations, you need to be aware of a simple rule: You can use a statistic designed for a lower level of measurement with data at a higher level of measurement, but you may *not* do the reverse – doing so would produce statistically meaningless results. It would, for example, be legitimate to use a statistic designed for the nominal level with ordinal-level data, but illegitimate to use an ordinal-level statistic with nominal-level data. This means that when comparing variables that are measured at different levels of measurement, *you must choose a statistic suitable to the lower of the two levels.*

Measures of association and significance for nominal variables: lambda

A widely used coefficient of association for two nominal variables where one is treated as independent and the other dependent is λ (lambda).[2] **Lambda** measures the *percentage of improvement* in guessing values on the dependent variable on the basis of knowledge of values on the independent variable when both variables consist of categories with neither rank, distance nor direction.

An example

Suppose we measure the party identification of 100 respondents and uncover the following frequency distribution:

Labour	50
Conservatives	30
Liberal Democrat	20

Suppose further that we want to guess the party identification of each individual respondent, that we must make the same guess for all individuals, and that we want to make as few mistakes as

---

[2]Actually, the statistic we shall describe here is λ_a, or lambda asymmetrical, a measure that tests association in only one direction (from the independent to the dependent variable). A test of mutual association, the true λ, is also available.

possible. The obvious strategy is simply to guess the mode (the most populous category), or Labour, every time. We will be correct 50 times (for the 50 Labour supporters) and incorrect 50 times (for the 30 Conservatives and 20 Lib-Dems), not an especially noteworthy record but still the best we can do. For if we guess Conservative each time, we will be wrong 70 times, and a guess of Liberal Democratic will lead to 80 incorrect predictions. The mode, then, provides the best guess based on the available information.

But suppose we have a second piece of information – the party identification of each respondent's father – with the following frequency distribution:

Labour	60
Conservative	30
Liberal Democrat	10

If these two variables are related to each other – that is, if one is likely to have the same party identification as one's father – then knowing the party preference of each respondent's father should help us to improve our guessing of that respondent's own preference. This will be the case if, by guessing for each respondent not the mode of the overall distribution, as we did before, but simply that person's father's party preference, we can reduce our incorrect predictions to fewer than the 50 cases we originally guessed wrongly.

To examine a possible association between these variables, we construct a crosstab summarising the distribution of cases on these two variables. In Table 17.1, the independent, or predictor, variable (father's party identification) is the row variable, and its overall distribution is summarised to the right of the table. The dependent variable (respondent's party identification) is the column variable, and its overall distribution is summarised below the table. The numbers in the cells have been assigned arbitrarily, although in the real world they would, of course, be determined by the research itself.

With this table we can use parental preference to predict respondent's preference. To do this, we use the mode just as before, but apply it *within each category on the independent variable* rather than to the whole set of cases. Thus, for those respondents whose father is identified as Labour, we guess a preference for the same party. We are correct 45 times and incorrect 15 (for the 5 Conservatives and 10 Lib-Dems). For those whose father is identified as a Conservative, we guess Conservative. We are correct 23 times and incorrect 7. And for those whose father is identified as a Liberal Democrat, we guess a similar preference and are correct 5 out of 10 times. Combining these results, we find that we are now able to guess correctly 73 times and are still wrong 27 times. Thus, knowledge of the second variable has clearly improved our guessing. To

Table 17.1 Paternal basis for party identification

	Respondent's party identification			
Father's party identification	*Lab.*	*Con.*	*Lib-Dem.*	*Totals*
Labour	45	5	10	60
Conservative	2	23	5	30
Liberal Democrat	3	2	5	10
Total	50	30	20	100

ascertain the precise percentage of that improvement, we use *the general formula for a coefficient of association:*

$$\text{Association} = \frac{\text{Reduction in error in guessing}}{\text{Amount of original error}}$$

$$= \frac{\text{Amount of original error} - \text{Amount of remaining error}}{\text{Amount of original error}}$$

In the present instance, this is

$$\text{Association} = \frac{50 - (15 + 7 + 5)}{50}$$

$$= \frac{23}{50} = .46$$

By using father's party identification as a predictor of respondent's party identification, we are able to improve (reduce the error in) our guessing by some 46 per cent.

The formula for calculating λ, which will bring us to the same result though by a slightly different route, is

$$\lambda = \frac{\sum f_i - F_d}{N - F_d}$$

where f_i = the maximum frequency *within each subclass or category* of the *independent* variable

F_d = the maximum frequency in the *totals* of the *dependent* variable

N = the number of cases.

Lambda ranges from 0 to 1, with higher values (those closer to 1) indicating a stronger association. Because nominal variables have no direction, λ will always be positive.

Our next step is to decide whether the relationship summarised by λ arises from a true population parameter or from mere chance. That is, we must decide whether the relationship is statistically significant.

Chi-square

The test of statistical significance for nominal variables is χ^2 (**chi-square**). This coefficient tells us whether an apparent nominal-level association between two variables, such as the one we have just observed, is likely to result from chance. It does so by comparing the results actually observed with those that would be expected if no real relationship existed. Calculating χ^2, too, begins from a cross-tab. Consider Table 17.2, which resembles Table 17.1 in that the marginals for each variable are the same as those of Table 17.1, but Table 17.2 does not include any distribution of cases within the cells.

To begin the determination of χ^2, we ask ourselves what value is *expected* in each cell, given these overall totals, if there is *no association* between the two variables. Of the 60 cases whose father was a Labour supporter, for instance, we might expect half (50/100) to be Labour supporters, almost a third (30/100) to be Conservatives and one in five (20/100) to be Liberal Democrats, or, in other words, 30 Labour supporters, 18 Conservatives and 12 Liberal Democrats. Similarly, we might arrive at expected values for those with a Conservative or Liberal Democratic father. These expected values are summarised in Table 17.3.

Table 17.2 Paternal basis for party identification: marginal values

Father's party identification	Lab.	Con.	Lib-Dem	Totals
Respondent's party identification				
Labour				60
Conservative				30
Liberal Democrat				10
Total	50	30	20	100

Table 17.3 Paternal basis for party identification: expected values

Father's party identification	Lab.	Con.	Lib-Dem	Totals
Respondent's party identification				
Labour	30	18	12	60
Conservative	15	9	6	30
Liberal Democrat	5	3	2	10
Total	50	30	20	100

The question then becomes, are the values we have actually observed in Table 17.1 so different (so extreme) from those that Table 17.3 would lead us to expect if there were, in reality, no relationship between the two variables that we can be reasonably confident of the validity of our result? Chi-square is a device for comparing the two tables to find an answer to this question. The equation for χ^2 is

$$\chi^2 = \sum \frac{(f_o - f_e)^2}{f_e}$$

where f_o = the frequency *observed* in each cell (Table 17.1)

f_e = the frequency *expected* in each cell (Table 17.3)

We calculate χ^2 by filling in the values in Table 17.4 for each cell in a given table. The ordering of the cells in the table is of no importance, but f_o from Table 17.1 and f_e from Table 17.3 for any particular line must refer to the same cell. The rationale for first squaring the differences between f_o and f_e and then dividing by f_e is essentially the same as that for the treatment of variations around the mean in determining the standard deviation. Chi-square is determined by adding together all the numbers in the last column. In the example, this yields a value of 56.07.

Degrees of freedom

Before interpreting this number, we must make one further calculation, that of the so-called degrees of freedom. The **degrees of freedom** (*df*) in a table simply consist of the number of cells of that table that can be filled with numbers before the entries in all remaining cells are fixed and unchangeable. The formula for determining the degrees of freedom in any particular table is

$$df = (r - 1)(c - 1)$$

where r = the number of categories of the row variable

c = the number of categories of the column variable.

In the example, $df = (3-1)(3-1) = 4$.

Table 17.4   Values used in deriving χ^2

f_o	f_e	$f_o - f_e$	$(f_o - f_e)^2$	$\dfrac{(f_o - f_e)^2}{f_e}$
45	30	15	225	7.50
5	18	−13	169	9.39
10	12	−2	4	.33
2	15	−13	169	11.27
23	9	14	196	21.78
5	6	−1	1	.17
3	5	−2	4	.80
2	3	−1	1	.33
5	2	3	9	4.50

We are now ready to evaluate the statistical significance of our data. Table A.4 in Appendix A summarises the significant values of χ^2 for different degrees of freedom at the .001, .01 and .05 levels. If the value of χ^2 we have calculated (56.07) exceeds that listed in the table at any of these levels for a table with the specified degrees of freedom (4), the relationship we have observed is statistically significant at that level. In the present instance, for example, in order to be significant at the .001 level – that is, if when we accept the observed association as representative of the larger population we run a risk of being wrong one time in 1,000 – our observed χ^2 must exceed 18.467. Since it does so, we are quite confident in our result.

Measures of association and significance for ordinal variables: gamma

A widely used coefficient of association for ordinal variables is G, or **gamma**, which works according to the same principle of error reduction as λ, but focuses on predicting the ranking or relative position of cases rather than simply their membership in a particular class or category. The question treated by G is that of the degree to which the ranking of a case on one ordinal variable may be predicted if we know its ranking on a second ordinal variable.

When examining two such variables, there are two possible conditions of perfect predictability. The first, in which individual cases are ranked in exactly the same order on both variables (high scores with high scores, low scores with low), is termed *perfect agreement*. The second, in which cases are ranked in precisely the opposite order (highest scores on one variable with lowest on the other and the reverse), is termed *perfect inversion*. Therefore, predictability is a function of how close the rankings on these variables come to either perfect agreement (in which case G is positive and approaches 1) or perfect inversion (where G is negative and approaches −1). A value of G equal to 0 indicates the absence of association. The formula for calculating G is

$$G = \frac{f_a - f_i}{f_a + f_i}$$

where f_a = the frequency of agreements in the rankings of the two variables

f_i = the frequency of inversions in the rankings of the two variables.

Table 17.5 Centralised crosstabulation

	Dependent Variable		
Independent Variable	*Low*	*Medium*	*High*
Low	*a*	*b*	*c*
Medium	*d*	*e*	*f*
High	*g*	*h*	*i*

G is based on the relative positions of a set of cases on two variables. The cases are first arranged in ascending order on the independent variable. Their rankings on the dependent variable are then compared. Those for which the original ordering is preserved are said to be in agreement, and those for which the original order is altered are said to be in inversion. Limitations of space do not permit us to consider this procedure in detail or to discuss the calculations of G when the number of cases is relatively small and/or no ties are present in the rankings. Rather, we shall focus on the procedures for calculating G under the more common circumstances, when ties (more than one case with the same rank) are present and the number of cases is large.[3] Here, as before, we work from a crosstab, as shown in Table 17.5.

To measure the association between these two variables, we determine the number of agreements and inversions relative to each cell in the table. An agreement occurs in any cell *below* (higher in its score on the independent variable) and to the *right* (higher in its score on the dependent variable) of the particular cell in question. Thus, agreements with those cases in cell a include all cases in cells e, f, h and i, since these cases rank higher than those in cell a on *both* variables. An inversion occurs in any cell *below* (higher in its score on the independent variable) and to the *left* (lower in its score on the dependent variable) of the particular cell in question. Thus, inversions with those cases in cell c include all cases in cells d, e, g and h, since these cases rank higher on one variable than those in cell c, but lower on the other. The frequency of agreements (f_a in the equation), then, is the sum for each cell of the number of cases in that cell multiplied by the number of cases in all cells below and to the right ($a[e + f + h + i] + b[f + i] + d[h + i] + e[i]$). The frequency of inversions (f_i in the equation) is the sum for each cell of the number of cases in that cell multiplied by the number of cases in all cells below and to the left ($b[d + g] + c[d + e + g + h] + e[g] + f[g + h]$). The resulting totals are simply substituted in to the equation.

If, for example, the variables in Table 17.1 were ordinal, we could calculate G as follows:

$$f_a = 45(23 + 5 + 2 + 5) + 5(5 + 5) + 2(2 + 5) + 23(5)$$
$$= 1{,}575 + 50 + 14 + 115 = 1{,}754$$

$$f_i = 5(2 + 3) + 10(2 + 23 + 3 + 2) + 23(3) + 5(3 + 2)$$
$$= 25 + 300 + 69 + 25 = 419$$

$$G = \frac{f_a - f_i}{f_a + f_i} = \frac{1754 - 419}{1754 + 419} = \frac{1335}{2173} = .61$$

---

[3]In such applications, G may be unreliable, but it is included here to facilitate the discussion of association as a concept. A related statistic, Kendall's *tau*, may be more reliable, but its determination may be less intuitive to the beginning political scientist.

This tells us that there is 61 per cent more agreement than disagreement in the rankings of the cases on the two variables. If f_i exceeded f_a, the sign of G would be negative, in order to indicate the existence of an inverse relationship.

The test of the statistical significance of G is based on the fact that the sampling distribution of G is approximately normal for a population with no true association, as was the sampling distribution of the hypothetical coefficient of association discussed earlier. Since this is so, we can determine the probability that any particular value of G has occurred by chance by calculating its standard score (z), locating its position under the normal curve, and assessing the probabilities. The actual calculation of z_G (**standard score of gamma**) will not be presented here, because the formula is complex and its understanding requires a more detailed knowledge of statistics than we have provided. Suffice it to say that when z_G exceeds ± 1.645 (when G lies at least 1.645 standard deviation units above or below the mean), G is sufficiently extreme to merit a significance level of .05, and that when z_G exceeds ± 2.326 (when G lies at least 2.326 standard deviation units above or below the mean), G achieves significance at the .01 level. The interpretation of these results is precisely the same as that in the earlier and more general example.

Measures of association and significance for interval/ratio variables: correlation

The measure of association between two interval variables is the Pearson product-moment correlation (r), also known as the **correlation coefficient**. This coefficient summarises the strength and direction of a relationship using the same notion we have already presented – about proportionate reduction in error in guessing values on one variable on the basis of known values of another – though the procedure, like the data for which it is designed, is more sophisticated than others we have discussed to this point. Here, rather than using the mean of the dependent variable (usually designated Y) to predict the values of individual cases, we use its geometric relationship with the independent variable (usually designated X) for this purpose. More particularly, we focus on the degree to which the equation of a particular straight line can help us to predict values of Y based on knowledge of corresponding values of X.

Graphing the variables

The determination of r begins with the examination of a **scatter plot**, which is a graphic summary of the distribution of cases on two variables, in which the base line, or X-axis, is denoted in units of the independent variable; the vertical line, or Y-axis, is denoted in units of the dependent variable; and each dot represents observations of one case on both variables. Such a plot is presented in Figure 17.4, in which the independent variable is age, the dependent variable is years of schooling completed, and the number of cases is twenty-five. The circled dot thus represents one case – a person thirty years old with ten years of schooling. The values in the figure have been arbitrarily assigned but would in reality be ascertained by the research itself.

The next step is to draw a straight line, called a **regression line**, through this field of dots so that no other line comes closer to touching all of the dots. This *line of best fit* for the relationship between two variables is analogous to the mean in univariate descriptive statistics. Just as the mean represents a most typical case in a frequency distribution, the regression line represents a most typical association between two variables. Just as we might use the mean to guess values of a variable in the absence of additional information, we can use the regression line to guess values of one variable on the basis of our knowledge of the values of another. If, for example, we know the value of X for a given case, we

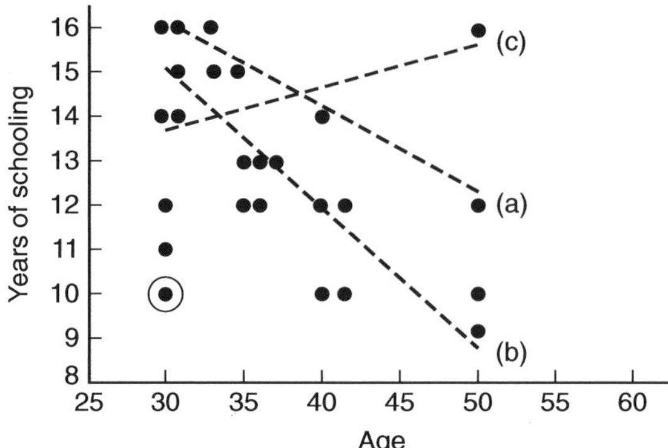

Figure 17.4 Scatter diagram showing relationship between age and years of schooling

can project a vertical line from that point on the *X*-axis to the regression line, then a horizontal line from there to the *Y*-axis. The point of contact on the *Y*-axis gives us a predicted value of *Y*.

But just as a mean may be the single most typical value yet not be a good summary of a particular distribution, a regression line may be the best possible summary of a relationship between two variables yet not be a very useful summary. Accordingly, just as we use the standard deviation (*s*) as a measure of dispersion or goodness of fit around the mean, we use the correlation coefficient (*r*), or, more correctly, for purposes of interpretation, the square of that coefficient (r^2), as a measure of the *goodness of fit* of the various data points around the regression line. It is, in effect, a measure of how typical that line is of the *joint* distribution of values of the two variables.

Closeness of association

Where all points actually fall directly on the line, as in Figure 17.5(a) and (e), the line provides a perfect description of the relationship between the two variables. Where the points are generally organised in the direction indicated by the line but do not all fall upon it, as in Figure 17.5(b) and (d), the line provides an approximation of the relationship between the two variables. And where, as in Figure 17.5(c), no one line is closer to the data points than any other, no association exists between the two variables. The problem, then, is twofold: First, what does this line of best fit look like? Second, how good a fit to the data does it in fact provide?

Figure 17.5 Summary of regression lines and values of *r*

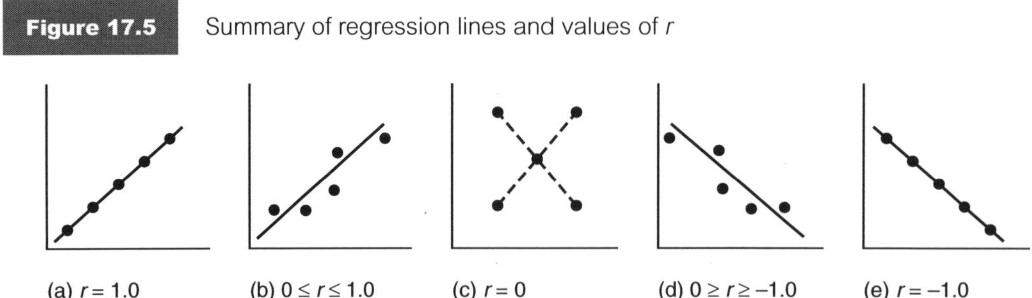

(a) $r = 1.0$ (b) $0 \leq r \leq 1.0$ (c) $r = 0$ (d) $0 \geq r \geq -1.0$ (e) $r = -1.0$

You may recall from your study of algebra that any straight line takes the form

$$Y_i = a + bX_i$$

where a = the value of Y when $X = 0$

b = the slope of the line

X_i = the value of a given case on the independent variable.

The regression line is simply the one set of guessed values of this form that provides for the most accurate prediction of values of Y based on knowledge of values of X.

For reasons we shall not explore here, the slope b of that line will always take the form

$$b = \frac{\sum_{i=1}^{N}(X_i - \overline{X})(Y_i - \overline{Y})}{\sum_{i=1}^{N}(X_i - \overline{X})^2}$$

where X_i and Y_i are the corresponding values of the independent and dependent variables for case i, and $\overline{X}$ and $\overline{Y}$ are the respective means. Applying this formula and using a chart similar to the one we used in computing χ^2, we are able to ascertain the slope of any particular relationship between two interval variables. This process is illustrated in Table 17.6 for the data reported in Figure 17.4. For these data, $\overline{X} = 37.08$ and $\overline{Y} = 12.88$. Substituting these values in the equation, we find

$$b = \frac{-136.79}{1,151.93} = -.12$$

In a **linear relationship** – one described or summarised by a straight line – a particular change in the value of the independent variable X is always accompanied by a particular change in the value of the dependent variable Y. Moreover, in such a relationship the rate of change is constant; that is, no matter what the particular values of X and Y, each change of one unit in X will be accompanied by a change in Y of some fixed size determined by the slope of the regression line. Relationships in which slight changes in X are accompanied by relatively large changes in Y are summarised by lines that have a relatively steep slope ($b.1$). Relationships in which large changes in X are accompanied by smaller changes in Y are summarised by lines that have a relatively flat slope ($b,1$). Relationships in which one unit of change in X is accompanied by one unit of change in Y are summarised by lines for which b is equal to 1. Lines that slope upward from left to right, such as those in Figure 17.5(a) and (b), have a positive slope and represent relationships in which increases in X are accompanied by increases in Y. Those sloping downward from left to right, such as the lines in Figure 17.5(d) and (e), have a negative slope and represent relationships in which increases in X are accompanied by *decreases* in Y. Indeed, the slope of the line is simply the rate of change in Y for each unit of change in X. In our example, then, where b is equal to $-.12$, we know that the regression line will slope downward from left to right and will, if the two variables are drawn to the same scale, be relatively flat.

To arrive at the formula we used to compute the slope of the regression line, we had to assume that the line passes through the intersection of $\overline{X}$ and $\overline{Y}$ – the means of the respective variables. This is a reasonable assumption, because the means represent the central tendencies of these variables and because we are, in effect, seeking a joint or combined central tendency. Because we know both

Table 17.6 Values used in deriving the equation of the regression line

X_1	$(X_1 - \bar{X})$	$(X_1 - \bar{X})^2$	Y_1	$(Y_1 - \bar{Y})$	$(X_1 - \bar{Y})(Y_1 - \bar{X})$
30	−7.08	50.13	10	−2.88	20.39
30	−7.08	50.13	11	−1.88	13.31
30	−7.08	50.13	12	−.88	6.23
30	−7.08	50.13	14	1.22	−7.93
30	−7.08	50.13	16	3.12	−22.09
31	−6.08	36.97	14	1.12	−6.81
31	−6.08	36.97	15	2.12	−12.89
31	−6.08	36.97	16	3.12	−18.99
33	−4.08	16.15	15	2.12	−8.65
33	−4.08	16.15	16	3.12	−12.73
35	−2.08	4.33	12	−.88	1.83
35	−2.08	4.33	13	.12	−.25
35	−2.08	4.33	15	2.12	−4.41
36	−1.08	1.17	12	−.88	.95
36	−1.08	1.17	13	.12	−.13
37	−.08	.01	13	.12	−.01
40	−2.92	8.53	10	−2.88	−8.41
40	−2.92	8.53	12	−.88	−2.57
40	−2.92	8.53	14	1.12	3.27
42	−4.92	24.21	10	−2.88	−14.17
42	−4.92	24.21	12	−.88	−4.33
50	−12.92	166.93	9	−3.88	−50.13
50	−12.92	166.93	10	−2.88	−37.12
50	−12.92	166.93	12	−.88	−11.37
50	−12.92	166.93	16	3.12	40.31
Totals	0	1,151.93		0	−136.79

means and have now determined the value of b, we can easily find the value of a (the point at which the regression line intercepts the Y-axis) and solve the equation. The general equation of the regression line is

$$Y' = a + bX_i$$

and at the point where the line passes through the intersection of the two means

$$\bar{Y} = a + b\bar{X}$$

It must then follow that

$$a = \bar{Y} + b\bar{X}$$

Because all of these values are now known, we can determine that

$$a = 12.88 - (-.12)(37.08)$$
$$= 12.88 + 4.45 = 17.33$$

Thus, the equation of the regression line – the single best-fitting line – for the data reported in Figure 17.4 would be

$$Y' = 17.33 - .12X$$

Using this equation, we can predict the value of Y for any given value of X.

Once this equation has been determined, we may use the correlation coefficient (r) to assess the utility of the regression line. The formula for r_{XY} (the coefficient of correlation between X and Y) is

$$r_{XY} = \frac{N\sum XY - \sum X\sum Y}{\sqrt{\left[N\sum X^2 - \left(\sum X\right)^2\right]\left[N\sum Y^2 - \left(\sum Y\right)^2\right]}}$$

where

X = each value of the independent variable (the subscript i has been omitted here to simplify the presentation)

Y = each value of the dependent variable

N = the number of cases

Although the assertion is certainly not obvious and although its algebraic proof lies beyond our present discussion, this working formula is derived from a comparison of the original error in guessing values of Y by using Y (the mean of the frequency distribution) with the error remaining when one guesses values of Y using Y' (the equation of the regression line). Thus, the procedure for computing r is analogous to that for computing both λ and G. It may best be accomplished by setting up a chart of the type with which we are now familiar in which the columns include X, Y, XY, X^2 and Y^2. The sums required by the equation are then provided by the column totals. Thus, for the data represented in Figure 17.4, whose regression line we have already determined, the chart is completed as in Table 17.7.

We substitute these totals in the equation

$$r = \frac{25(11,803) - (927)(322)}{\sqrt{[25(35,525) - (927)^2][25(4,260) - (322)^2]}}$$

$$= \frac{295,075 - 298,494}{\sqrt{(888,125 - 859,329)(106,500 - 103,684)}}$$

$$= \frac{-3,419}{\sqrt{(28,796)(2,816)}}$$

$$= \frac{-3,419}{\sqrt{81,089,536}}$$

$$= \frac{-3,419}{9,005}$$

$$= -.38$$

This tells us that the slope of the regression line is negative and that the points cluster weakly to moderately around it (because r ranges from $+1$ to -1, with the weakest association at 0).

Table 17.7 Values used in deriving the correlation coefficient (r)

X	Y	XY	X^2	Y^2
30	10	300	900	100
30	11	330	900	121
30	12	360	900	144
30	14	420	900	196
30	16	480	900	256
31	14	434	961	196
31	15	465	961	225
31	16	496	961	256
33	15	495	1,089	225
33	16	528	1,089	256
35	12	420	1,225	144
35	13	455	1,225	169
35	15	525	1,225	225
36	12	432	1,296	144
36	13	468	1,296	169
37	13	481	1,369	169
40	10	400	1,600	100
40	12	480	1,600	144
40	14	560	1,600	196
42	10	420	1,764	100
42	12	504	1,764	144
50	9	450	2,500	81
50	10	500	2,500	100
50	12	600	2,500	144
50	16	800	2,500	256
Totals 927	322	11,803	32,525	4,260

Explained variance

Although r itself is not easily interpreted, r^2 may be interpreted as *the proportion of reduction in the variance of Y attributable to our knowledge of X*. In other words, r^2 is the proportion of variation in Y that is predictable (or explainable) on the basis of X. The quantity r^2 is often referred to as the percentage of *explained variance*, and the quantity $1 - r^2$ is often termed the percentage of *unexplained variance*. Thus, in our example, the r of $-.38$ means that differences on the independent variable *age* account for some 14 per cent, or $(-.38)^2$, of the variance in the dependent variable *years of schooling* for the cases under analysis.

Computing statistical significance

For reasons that lie beyond the scope of the present discussion, we are able to specify the statistical significance of r only when *both* the independent *and* dependent variables are normally distributed. This is accomplished by using Table A.5 in Appendix A, for which purpose two pieces of information are needed. The first is r itself, which, of course, is known. The second, analogous to the χ^2 test, is the number of degrees of freedom of the regression line because two points determine a line (in this case, the intersection of $\overline{X}$ and $\overline{Y}$ was the first and the intercept with the Y-axis the second), all other data points may fall freely, so df will always equal $(N - 2)$, where N is the number of cases. To use the table, then, we locate the appropriate degrees of freedom (in the example, $N - 2 = 25 - 2 = 23$) and the desired level of significance (for example, .05), just as we did for χ^2; identify the threshold value of r necessary to achieve that level of significance; and evaluate our actual observation. In the present instance, this requires interpolating values in the table between $df = 20$ and $df = 25$. For $df = 23$, these values would be .3379, .3976, .5069 and .6194, respectively. Thus, our r of $-.38$ is statistically significant at the .10 level (it exceeds .3379), but not at the .05 level (it does not exceed .3976). The interpretation of this result is the same as those for other measures of statistical significance.

Ethical considerations

In doing initial bivariate analysis of your data, you need to always keep level of measurement in mind. One of your most important duties as a researcher is to employ the proper analytic techniques (e.g., statistical measures), while maintaining close attention to each variable's level of measurement as you evaluate whether or not a hypothesised relationship achieves statistical significance.

Conclusion

In this chapter we have introduced some of the more common statistics that are used to summarise the relationship between two variables. As in Chapter 16, we found that differing measures of association and statistical significance were appropriate, depending on the level of measurement that characterised the data being analysed. Together with the techniques presented earlier, these various coefficients provide the researcher with some very useful basic tools with which to summarise research results. In Chapter 18 we outline some more sophisticated statistical techniques, which can further enrich our ability to analyse and understand what we have discovered.

Summary points

- If knowledge of the values of a given variable improves your ability to predict the values of a second variable, the variables are associated.
- In a crosstab, chi-square (χ^2) numerically assesses the deviation of cell counts from expected values – that is, the values that are expected if there were no association between the variables.
- When comparing two variables that have different levels of measurement, the most appropriate measure of association is the one indicated for the lower level of measurement. For example, if comparing a nominal to an ordinal variable, you may choose lambda.

Suggested reading and examples

Research examples

Given the complexity of political science research questions, it is unsurprising that few current articles employ simple two-way crosstabs or bivariate correlations. Although excellent learning tools, these bivariate procedures have given way to more sophisticated techniques that simultaneously control for multiple factors. Thus, we lack current research examples for this chapter.

Methodological reading

A bibliography on statistics and related topics is found at the end of Chapter 18.

Research exercises

1 Find a recent report of a Gallup poll or some other public opinion poll (try your local newspaper or a nationally daily newspaper such as *The Independent,* the *Daily Telegraph* or *The Guardian*) in which a bivariate relationship is presented. What statistics might the pollsters have used to evaluate their findings? If sufficient information is present, construct a crosstab for the two variables in question, and then calculate and interpret the appropriate coefficient of association.

2 Recalculate r and r^2 for the data in Figure 17.4, eliminating the data points at $X = 30$, $Y = 10$; $X = 30$, $Y = 11$; $X = 30$, $Y = 12$; and $X = 50$, $Y = 16$. How do you account for the difference in explained variance between this and our earlier result? Is the new value of r statistically significant?

Key terms

association	lambda (λ)
chi-square (χ^2)	linear relationship
coefficient of association	regression line
correlation coefficient (r)	scatter plot
degrees of freedom (*df*)	standard score of gamma (Z_G)
gamma (G)	statistical significance

18 Statistics III: examining relationships among several variables

- What is the primary analytic advantage of multiple regression techniques?
- What limits the type of variables upon which regression analysis may be performed?

Introduction

The univariate and bivariate statistics described in the preceding chapters often help us to understand the subjects we are researching. However, univariate and bivariate analyses rarely can provide convincing tests of hypotheses or the theories from which they were derived. To test a hypothesis convincingly, we must be able to rule out major alternative rival hypotheses. Although a sound research design can sometimes allow us to dismiss alternative rival hypotheses, social scientists commonly find that they must rely on data analysis rather than research design to examine the validity of rival hypotheses. This requires the use of **multivariate analysis**, which is analysis of the simultaneous relationship among three or more variables.

Tabular analysis

Many of the statistical tools we have already discussed can be employed in multivariate analysis. To illustrate, we can use a highly simplified example to suggest the way in which crosstabs and bivariate statistics can be adapted in order to conduct a multivariate analysis.

An example

Suppose we want to explore the relationship between political ideology and attending university. Reasoning that going to university gives people a stake in maintaining the status quo by preparing them to do relatively well within the existing socioeconomic system, we might begin with the hypothesis that those who have completed university will be more conservative than those who have not. To test this hypothesis, we might interview a sample of fifty people who have completed university and fifty people who have not.

Imagine that we obtained the results shown in Table 18.1. The diagonal 'loading' or trend in the cases in this table indicates that those who have attended university are more likely to be classified as conservative than those who have not. By calculating a chi-square for this table, we find that the relationship between university and political ideology is statistically significant at the .01 level. All of these findings are consistent with our original hypothesis.

Before we rush to submit this finding to *American Political Science Review*, however, we need to test some alternative rival hypotheses to be sure that our result is valid. One approach is to extend our bivariate analysis into a multivariate analysis that will allow us to 'control for' the effects of other variables on the relationship between university and ideology. For example, one alternative rival

Table 18.1 Hypothetical relationship between university education
and political ideology

	Ideology		
Education	*Centre-Left*	*Conservative*	*Totals*
College	40% (20)	60% (30)	(50)
No college	60% (30)	40% (20)	(50)
Totals	100% (50)	100% (50)	(100)

hypothesis that merits examination derives from the observation that men are more likely to be conservative than women. If, by chance, more of the people in our sample who went to university were male than female, the results shown in Table 18.1 may reflect gender differences rather than an actual effect of university attendance on political opinions.

Controlling for other factors

To explore this possibility, we could examine the relationship between university and ideology separately for men and for women by constructing two crosstabs such as Tables 18.2 and 18.3. If the alternative rival hypothesis is valid, the statistical relationship between university and ideology shown in Table 18.1 will *not* show up in these new tables because the effect of gender on that relationship will be eliminated. This process of holding constant the influence of a third variable on the relationship between two other variables is referred to as **controlling**, and is a major step in all forms of multivariate data analysis.

In this case, Tables 18.2 and 18.3 actually show that the relationship between university and ideology is essentially the same for men and women. Although the women in our sample are, as predicted, less likely than the men to be classified as conservative, the 'loadings' in these two tables

Table 18.2 Hypothetical relationship between university education
and political ideology for males

	Ideology		
Education	*Centre-Left*	*Conservative*	*Totals*
College	33% (5)	57% (20)	(25)
No college	67% (10)	43% (15)	(25)
Totals	100% (15)	100% (35)	(50)

Table 18.3 Hypothetical relationship between university education
and political ideology for females

	Ideology		
Education	*Centre-Left*	*Conservative*	*Totals*
College	43% (15)	67% (10)	(25)
No college	57% (20)	33% (5)	(25)
Totals	100% (35)	100% (15)	(50)

are highly similar to each other, and calculation of the chi-square for each table shows that the relationships they represent are statistically significant. In such a situation, researchers say that the original relationship has 'survived control' and that an alternative rival hypothesis can be 'ruled out' as an explanation of the original findings. If a relationship survives enough such controls, it will be accepted as valid.

We have thus conducted a very simple multivariate analysis using techniques designed for bivariate analysis. We could extend this logic to evaluate more alternative rival hypotheses by controlling for two or more additional variables *at the same time*. To illustrate, one of our alternative rival hypotheses might contend that racial differences between whites and nonwhites in terms of both political values and the likelihood of attending university created the apparent relationship between university and ideology shown in Table 18.1. To hold constant the effects of both race and gender on the relationship between university and ideology, we would have to set up four crosstabs tables showing the relationship between university and ideology: one for white males, one for white females, one for nonwhite males and one for nonwhite females.

Limitations of tabular multivariate analysis

Under many circumstances, generating separate tables can be quite a useful multivariate approach to evaluating hypotheses. However, it has important limitations. First, tables become very cumbersome to use and the results become difficult to interpret if the variables involved have many possible values. This makes it impractical for analysis of interval/ratio-level data and difficult to use with many nominal and ordinal variables. For instance, to compare an independent and dependent variable each having five values while controlling for a third variable with ten values would require an analysis of ten tables with twenty-five cells each. In that situation, unless we have an exceptionally large and diverse sample, many of the cells in the tables will have no cases in them, which can make it impossible to calculate some measures of association and significance. We might try to avoid this by collapsing certain categories of the variables in order to create fewer values and hold down the number of tables and cells needed (as when we reduce the measure 'years of education' to a dichotomy of 'fewer than 12 years' and '12 years or more'). However, it would mean giving up potentially important information contained in our original measures and may produce misleading results. Moreover, the same problem will appear, even after collapsing categories, if we tried to apply several control variables at once in order to examine the *combined effects* of different variables. Second, even if we can complete such an analysis, its results may be difficult to report because the patterns are likely to be complex and there are no overall statistics with which to summarise the results.

Fortunately, there is a variety of statistical procedures designed specifically for multivariate analyses, that can be used in a wide range of situations, and that provide easily interpretable results. The procedures are important because of their value in hypothesis testing (allowing us to examine the relationship between two variables while holding the effects of other variables on each constant), but their greatest value may come from the ways in which they help us understand the complex and subtle networks of relationships within which social phenomena are usually embedded. In this chapter we introduce you to two of the most commonly used multivariate techniques so that you can know when and how to apply them in your research and can judge the skill with which others have applied them when you are reading research reports. We selected these techniques from among the many that are available because (1) they are very widely applicable, (2) they illustrate many basic principles of multivariate analysis and (3) they are based on the same basic mathematical techniques and can therefore be explained more quickly than techniques that rest on different mathematical foundations.

Multiple regression

The bivariate correlation and regression procedures described in Chapter 17 can be extended to cases in which you want to explore the relationship between one dependent variable (DV) and several independent variables (IVs). The purpose of **multiple regression** is to (1) yield an estimate of the *independent* effect of a change in the value of *each* IV on the value of the DV and (2) provide an empirical basis for predicting values of the DV from knowledge of the joint values of the IVs.

Analysis begins with your statement of an equation that you feel accurately describes the causal influences being investigated. Because this equation can be viewed as a **model** of the process in which you are interested, this step is referred to as **model specification**. It involves translating your verbal theory of the phenomenon into a mathematical equation. The general form for a **multiple regression equation** is

$$Y' = a_0 + b_1X_1 + b_2X_2 + b_3X_3 \ldots b_nX_n + e$$

which you should recognise as an extension of the bivariate regression equation explained in Chapter 17. Understanding this equation is simplified by the introduction of a concrete example.

An example

Let us say that we are interested in assessing the validity of the theory that election to the US Senate can be 'bought' by heavy spending on a media campaign, because advertising messages reach voters not already predisposed by partisanship to vote for either candidate. We might begin by analysing hypotheses that explain the percentage of the vote that candidates get as a function of (1) the amount they spend on media advertising and (2) the percentage of the electorate in their state that has the same party identification as the candidate. These hypotheses yield this simple model of the electoral process:

$$Y' = a_0 + b_1X_1 + b_2X_2 + e$$

where

Y' = the predicted percentage of the vote received by the candidate

a_0 = the average value of Y when each IV equals 0

b_1 = the average change in Y associated with a unit change in X_1 (the amount spent on advertising), *when the effects of other variables are held constant*

X_1 = the amount the candidate spends on advertising (in units of $1,000)

b_2 = the average change in Y' associated with a unit change in X_2 (the percentage of the electorate that shared the candidate's party identification), *when the effects of other variables are held constant*

X_2 = the percentage of the electorate that shares the candidate's party identification

e = an 'error term' representing any variance in Y that is not accounted for by variance in the IVs in the model.

We might test the accuracy of this model by collecting appropriate data on 100 races for US Senate seats. Before analysing the data, however, we need to ensure that our model does not violate the assumptions inherent to regression analysis.

Regression assumptions

Successful application of multiple regression techniques to any task requires that our model and the data with which we hope to test it conform to five assumptions that underlie the regression procedure:

1   The model is *accurately specified* (it accurately describes the actual relationships in question). This includes the assumptions that (a) the relationship among variables is linear, (b) no important IVs have been excluded and (c) no irrelevant IVs have been included.
2   There is *no error in measurement* of the variables.
3   Variables are measured at the *interval/ratio level.*
4   The following are true of the error term, *e:*

   a   Its mean (the expected value for any given observation) is 0.
   b   The error terms for each observation are *un*correlated.
   c   The IVs are *un*correlated with the error term.
   d   The variance for the error term is constant for all values of the IVs.
   e   The error term has a *normal distribution.*

5   None of the IVs is perfectly correlated with any of the other IVs or with any linear combination of other IVs. If this is true, there is *no perfect multicollinearity.*[1]

If our study comes *close enough* to meeting these assumptions,[2] we can substitute actual values from our research for Y', X_1 and X_2 and solve the regression equation representing our theory for the unknown terms a, b_1 and b_2 using the logic of least squares estimation. One hypothetical result of such a solution could be

$$Y' = 10 + .1X_1 + 1X_2$$

Interpreting multiple regressions results

The *least squares procedure* for multiple regression works in a manner similar to bivariate regression in that it passes a line through a plotting of the values of cases on several variables in such a way as to minimise the sum of the squared distance of each point from that line. The difference is that the 'line' in the case of multiple regression is a set of mathematically estimated points on a plane that cannot be represented in a two-dimensional scatterplot. The a or intercept term is generally of little practical interest, because the values of the IVs are rarely 0. However, the substantive interpretation of an a of 10 in the equation is that even if the candidate spent no money on advertising and 0 per cent of the voters in the state shared the candidate's party identification, the candidate would receive 10 per cent of the vote just by being on the ballot.

---

[1] For an explanation of these assumptions and an extended general discussion of multiple regression, see Pedhazur (1997).

[2] Studies seldom meet these requirements fully, and it is often impossible to know in advance of analysis whether or not they are met in a given data set. In this context, 'close enough' means that the effect of any violation of assumptions can be corrected for or at least estimated and taken into account in drawing conclusions. For further clarification, see Pedhazur (1997).

Interpreting coefficients

The key to interpreting multiple regression analyses is to understand the meaning of the b_i terms. They are referred to as **partial regression coefficients** and describe the unique contribution of each IV to the determination of the DV. In our electoral example, a b_1 of .1 would be substantively interpreted as meaning that every additional \$1,000 spent on advertising increases the candidate's portion of the vote by one-tenth of a percentage point, and a b_2 of 1 would indicate that for every 1 per cent increase in the percentage of voters that share the candidate's party identification there is a corresponding 1 per cent increase in the share of the vote that goes to that candidate. In calculating these coefficients, regression statistically holds constant the effect of any variables that influence both the individual IV and the DV through use of the formula

$$b_i = \frac{\sum (X_n - X_n')(Y - Y')}{\sum (X_n - X_n')^2}$$

This statistical control simulates the control we might have obtained in an experimental setting and is thus valuable in two important respects. First, as we will explore shortly, it allows us to assess the *relative* importance of different IVs in determining the value of the DV. Second, it allows us to rule out the alternative hypothesis that the relationship between the DV and any given IV is spurious. If we are willing to assume that we have included all important causes of change in the DV in our model and find that the partial regression coefficient for any given IV is significantly different from 0, we can conclude that the relationship between that IV and the DV is *not* spurious. If, however, the b is near 0 or statistically insignificant, we must conclude that there is no independent relationship between that IV and the DV. In that case, we would drop the IV from our model in order to make it conform more closely to observed reality. Clearly, then, multiple regression can be a valuable tool in refining and improving our theories of political phenomena.

Interpreting R^2

We can assess the completeness of our theory by calculating a **coefficient of determination**, or R^2 (sometimes referred to as the *multiple R*), using the formula

$$R^2 = \frac{\sum (Y' - \overline{Y})^2}{\sum (X' - \overline{Y})^2} = \frac{\text{Regression sum of squares}}{\text{Total sum of squares}}$$

This coefficient tells us how close all the data plots came to touching the 'line' projected by our model and is commonly interpreted as the *proportion of the variation in the DV that is 'explained'* (accounted for) *by variation in all of the IVs*. For example, an R^2 of 0.57 would be interpreted as showing that the IVs in the model from which it was calculated explain 57 per cent of the variance in the DV. R^2 can range between 0 and 1; the closer it is to 1, the more complete the model is. The size of R^2 can almost always be increased by adding additional IVs to the model, but the researcher must ask if additional variables make the model too complex or add anything of value to our understanding of the phenomenon in question. In the case of our electoral example, for instance, we might marginally increase the R^2 by adding a variable to the equation that coded the number of letters in the candidate's last name. We will not do this for two reasons: (1) this variable violates the assumption that the regression contains no irrelevant variables; and (2) we only wish to include variables that our theory suggests – to do otherwise would rob our model of its potential predictive benefit.

Solving common problems in multiple regression

Returning to the regression assumptions for a moment, we need to acknowledge that neither data nor reality always conforms to the conceptual model underlying multiple regression analysis. Relationships are not always linear, measurement error is almost always present, and so on. Fortunately, statisticians have devised ways for us to adapt multiple regression in order to compensate for some of these problems. In this section we discuss adaptations to three of the most commonly encountered problems so that you can (1) learn how to cope with these issues in your applications of multiple regression and (2) get a sense of the flexibility of multiple regression as an analytic technique.

Noninterval data

In the social sciences, important variables often are not (and sometimes cannot be) measured at the interval/ratio level, thus violating the assumption of interval-level measurement. Noninterval data can, however, be used in multiple regression under two conditions.

First, if the measure is (or can be converted into) a *dichotomy*, it can be entered directly into the regression by simply coding the value of the dichotomy as 1 and the other as 0. For example, in a study of international trade, goods might be classified as 'foreign' or 'domestic', with a code of 1 being assigned to the value 'foreign' and a code of 0 assigned to the value 'domestic'. Regression would treat this scheme as if it were interval because dichotomies have special mathematical properties. As a result, we can interpret the partial regression coefficient computed for any variable coded as a dichotomy just as if it were measured at the interval level.

Second, noninterval variables that have multiple categories can be incorporated into multiple regression by use of a system of *dummy variables*. For example, consider the case in which occupational status is measured only as 'high', 'medium', or 'low' in a study that seeks to predict the number of political organisations to which a person belongs as a function of education (number of years of schooling) and occupational status. We can use the ordinal data on status in a multiple regression if we create two dichotomous dummy variables to represent the variable occupational status. The equation would be:

$$Y' = a + b_1X_1 + b_2X_2 + b_3X_3 + e$$

where

$Y^{a\prime}$ = the number of organisational memberships

X_1 = the number of years of schooling

X_2 = a dummy variable scored 1 if occupational status = 'low' and 0 otherwise

X_3 = a dummy variable scored 1 if occupational status = 'medium' and 0 otherwise.

Why use only two dummy variables to represent a noninterval variable with three categories? Because the value of the third dummy variable would be an exact linear function of the values of the other two, thus violating the assumption of no perfect multicollinearity and making it impossible to obtain a unique estimate of the various coefficients.

Whenever using dummy variables, we must follow the rule of creating *one fewer dummy variables than there are categories in the noninterval variable* being represented. In practice, it is usually advisable to leave out the category in which you expect the fewest cases. In our example, the 'high' category was not represented by a dummy variable because there are relatively few high-status jobs.

Interaction effects

Conventional least squares regression assumes that the effects of different IVs on the DV are independent of one another and can be added together to determine the total effect of a set of variables. In practice, the effects of many variables reinforce or amplify the effects of another variable. Whenever the impact of one IV depends on the value of another IV, an *interaction effect* exists. To return to the electoral example used earlier in this chapter, we might argue that the effect of advertising expenditures is different for incumbents (who tend to be well known) and challengers (who need to make voters aware of their qualifications).

Multiple regression can be adapted to this situation by including the interaction between advertising and incumbent status as a separate variable. Letting incumbent status be represented by a dummy variable (X_3) coded 1 for challengers and 0 for incumbents, the new regression model would be:

$$Y' = a + b_1X_1 + b_2X_2 + b_3(X_1X_3) + e$$

where X_1X_3 is an interaction variable created by multiplying X_1 by X_3. This procedure allows us to interpret b_1 as the unique contribution of advertising expenditures to vote percentage by breaking off the *joint* effects of advertising and incumbency into b_3, and it can yield more accurate predictions of Y.

Multicollinearity

Regression analysis requires that no IV be perfectly correlated with any other IV or any linear combination of other IVs. It is usually easy to meet this strict requirement because few social science variables can be perfectly predicted from knowledge of any other variable or set of variables. However, many important variables are highly correlated with each other. (Consider urbanisation and industrialisation, education and income or party and ideology in western Europe.) This condition is referred to as **multicollinearity**. If the correlations among IVs in a regression model are high enough, estimations of the coefficients become inaccurate and we cannot place any confidence in the results of the regression analysis. Significant multicollinearity can cause such large variances in the estimation of partial regression coefficients that it becomes impossible to compare the relative effects of different IVs on the DV. In addition, coefficients may fail to attain statistical significance even where there is a substantial relationship, leading us to falsely identify bivariate relationships as spurious.

It is therefore essential that researchers make a serious effort to determine if multicollinearity is present and to make the adjustments necessary to correct for it. Multicollinearity is usually indicated by one or more of the following symptoms:

1   A high R^2 for the equation but statistically insignificant regression coefficients (b's).
2   Dramatic changes in regression coefficients (b's) for given variables when other IVs are dropped from or added to the equation.
3   Regression coefficients that are *far* larger or smaller (either in absolute terms or in relation to the coefficients for other IVs) than theory and knowledge of other research results would lead us to expect.
4   Regression coefficients that have the wrong sign – that are negative when we have good reason to expect them to be positive or positive when we have good reason to expect them to be negative.

When any of these symptoms is noted in a regression analysis, it is important to test for multicollinearity. This is done by *regressing each IV on all other IVs*. We would, for example, test the equation

$$Y' = a + b_1X_1 + b_2X_2 + b_3(X_3) + e$$

by running the following equations:

$$X_1 = a + b_2X_2 + b_3X_3$$

$$X_2 = a + b_1X_1 + b_3X_3$$

$$X_3 = a + b_1X_1 + b_2X_2$$

If the R^2 for any of these equations were higher than, say, .8, we could conclude that substantial multicollinearity existed.

There are several possible approaches to correcting for multicollinearity. If we have the option of adding cases to our sample (as when we are collecting data from published records and can simply go back and resample), then increasing the sample size will sometimes eliminate multicollinearity. A second strategy would be to determine *which* of the IVs are highly related to each other and then combine them into a single indicator. If, for example, we had originally measured expenditures on radio, television and newspaper advertising separately in our study of senatorial elections and found these three indicators to be highly correlated, we could combine the three into a single measure called *media expenditures* in order to eliminate the destabilising effects of multicollinearity. Clearly, any such combining of variables works only when it is theoretically justified. We could not, for instance, solve a problem of multicollinearity by combining the incumbent status of the candidate with the regional location of the state because these are theoretically distinct concepts. Finally, we can attempt to cope with multicollinearity by discarding one or more of the highly intercorrelated variables. This can produce specification error, but by dropping first one and then the other correlated IV and comparing the results of different regressions, we can at least get a firm estimate of the damage done by both multicollinearity and misspecification.

Comparing IVs

It is often important to know which of several IVs exerts the most influence on a DV. If we wanted to encourage people to wear seat belts, for instance, we might want to know which of several factors that could lead to this behaviour actually has the most impact on the decision to buckle up in order to invest our resources in the most efficient way. Multiple regression analysis is well-suited for this purpose since it provides estimates of the unique contribution of each IV to variance in the DV in the form of its partial regression coefficients. Unfortunately, determining the relative effects of different IVs is not a simple matter of comparing the size of their regression coefficients.

When IVs are measured in different units (number of dollars versus percentage of voters, for instance), regression coefficients do not reflect the relative influence of IVs on the DV. One way to cope with this is to *standardise* the variables – so that they are measured in the same units – and obtain new estimates of the regression coefficients. Standardisation of a case's score is achieved by converting the raw score into units of standard deviation from the mean value of the variable using the formula

$$X* = \frac{X - \overline{X}}{s_X}$$

where the * indicates that the variable is standardised, X is the score for a given case, $\overline{X}$ is the mean score on that variable for all cases, and s is the standard deviation of the distribution of values on variable X (see Chapter 16).

When standardised scores are substituted for raw scores in the regression equation, the a term drops out because standardisation forces it to 0, and the equation takes the general form

$$Y'* = \beta_1X_1* + \beta_2X_2* \cdots \beta_nX_n + e$$

where β represents a *standardised partial regression coefficient*, referred to as a **beta weight** or **beta coefficient**. A beta weight corrects the unstandardised partial regression coefficient by the ratio of the standard deviation of the IV to the standard deviation of the DV and can be calculated by the formula

$$\beta_i = b_i \frac{S_{Xi}}{S_Y}$$

A beta weight can be interpreted as representing *the average standard deviation change in Y associated with a standard deviation change in X* when the effects of other IVs are held constant. Thus, a β of .5 would indicate that one standard deviation change in the value of an IV would be associated with a change of one-half standard deviation in the DV.

Standardising thus allows us to compare the influence of different IVs *within a single sample*. However, when seeking to compare the influence of variables *across samples*, it can be misleading. If we wanted to compare the effects of campaign spending on the electoral success of candidates in the United States and Mexico, for example, we would find that there were substantial differences in the variance (and thus the standard deviation) of key variables because media campaigns cost more in the United States and election outcomes are usually significantly closer in one nation than in the other. Since the size of β is a function of variance (the larger the variance, the larger the β, other things being equal), we could be misled into thinking that spending had more of an effect in one nation than in the other simply because of mathematically determined differences in β. To avoid this error, it is important to use the *un*standardised partial regression slopes (b's) for a variable whenever we are seeking to compare the effects of an IV in different samples *if the variance for that variable differs considerably from sample to sample.*

Path analysis

Regression analysis can be quite useful in testing specific hypotheses and assessing the relative impacts of different IVs. However, regression assumes a model of causation that does not always reflect the complexities of the real world – it assumes that all IVs *directly* affect the DV. In reality, variables often act indirectly through other variables.

An example

If we wanted to investigate the determinants of racial segregation in UK state school systems, for instance, we could hypothesise that school segregation was caused by segregation in housing (since most schools draw on a given geographic area), which was in turn caused by racial differences in income. A causal diagram or model of these relationships developed according to the advice given in Chapter 2 is shown in Model 1.

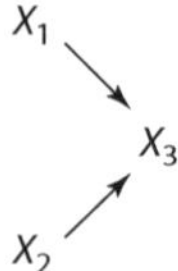

Model 1

(X_1 = *racial differences in income*; X_2 = *housing segregation*, and X_3 = *school segregation*)

This simple diagram is typical of the causal model assumed by conventional regression analysis because it indicates that the IVs exert their influence on the DV independently. In real social situations, however, IVs often influence *one another* as well as the DV. To return to our example, the least bit of knowledge about our subject would suggest that income differentials affect housing segregation as well as school segregation, because more and less expensive houses each tend to be geographically clustered. Taking this into account would require us to revise our model. We might propose a developmental sequence in which one IV exercises its influence on the DV exclusively by causing changes in another IV. This would be diagrammed as in Model 2:

$$X_1 \rightarrow X_2 \rightarrow X_3$$

Model 2

A more sophisticated understanding of our subject might lead us to realise that racial differentials in income affect school segregation directly as well as through housing segregation, because more affluent people can place their children in private schools. This information would be incorporated into the model by creating an arrow directly from X_1 to X_2, as in Model 3:

Model 3

Path analysis is a statistical technique by which we can evaluate the accuracy of such models by empirically testing the direct *and indirect* effects of one variable on another. It has been widely used in the social sciences because it is applicable to a great many research questions and has the advantage of allowing us to test large pieces of a theory at once rather than one hypothesis at a time. Our objective in this section is to introduce you to the basic procedures of path analysis and to teach you to read the path diagrams you are likely to encounter in the literature. We do not attempt to address the many issues involved in more sophisticated applications of the technique, so you would be wise to do additional reading before attempting to apply path analysis to complicated research questions.

Recursive and nonrecursive models

Path analysis begins with a conceptual model that specifies the causal relationships the researcher thinks are at work in the world. For purposes of path analysis, Model 3 would be redrawn as Model 4, where the R's represent the variance in the variable with which they are associated that is *un*explained by variance in other variables in the model:

Model 4

The model is then stated as mathematical equations. However, any model in which the IVs are not independent of each other (as they are in Model 1) cannot be represented in a single equation, but must be described by a set of *structural equations*. Model 4 would be represented by the following set of equations:

$$X_1 = p_{1u}R_u$$

$$X_2 = p_{21}X_1 + p_{2v}R_v$$

$$X_3 = p_{32}X_2 + p_{31}X_1 + p_{3w}R_w$$

The *p*'s in these equations represent *path coefficients* that summarise the amount of influence one variable has on another when the effects of all other variables are held constant. The standard way of writing path coefficients is as p_{ij}, which indicates the path *to* variable *i from* variable *j*. The set of equations just given, then, tells us that X_1 is caused entirely by factors outside the model, X_2 is caused by X_1 and factors outside the model and X_3 is caused by X_1, X_2 and factors outside the model. Variables like X_2 and X_3 that are determined at least partially by other variables in the model are referred to as *endogenous*, and variables that are determined entirely by factors that are left out of the model are called *exogenous*.

Models are classified as *recursive* or *nonrecursive*. A model is **recursive** if all of its variables can be ordered so that the first one is determined only by factors outside the model, the second is determined only by factors outside the model and the first variable, the third is determined only by factors outside the model and the first and second variables, and so on. In essence, this means that *all causal influence must flow in one direction*, with no 'feedback'. Model 4 is an example of a *recursive model*.

If there is feedback (reciprocal causation) among any of the variables in the model, it is referred to as **nonrecursive**. For example, we might add the variable 'occupation' (X_4) to our model of school segregation and argue that segregated schooling leads to racial differences in occupational attainment that in turn cause income differentials, so that the model would look like Model 5. The model no longer contains any variable that is determined entirely by factors outside the model and is now nonrecursive. Such models require special analysis techniques that are well beyond the scope of this book. Recursive models, however, can be successfully examined by using the ordinary least squares regression techniques described earlier in this chapter. When variables are stated in standardised form, the path coefficients can be estimated as the *standardised regression coefficients* produced by regression.

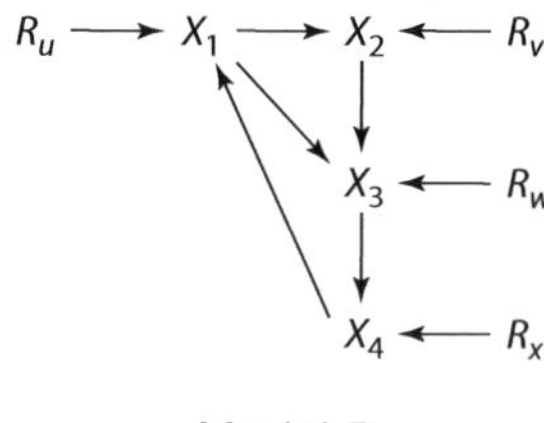

Model 5

Using path analysis

We can test the empirical accuracy of the predictions implied in a model by running a series of regressions in which each endogenous variable is regressed on all variables that are theorised to influence it. To take a purely hypothetical example, we might work with the five-variable recursive model in Model 6 (eliminating the residual terms for simplicity of presentation). To test this model, we would regress X_5 on X_1 through X_4; X_4 on X_1 through X_3; and X_2 on X_1. X_1 and X_3 are considered exogenous. If any of the path coefficients (standardised regression coefficients) produced by this process approaches a value of 0 or is statistically insignificant, we know that we have misspecified the model by anticipating a relationship that is not actually found in the data.

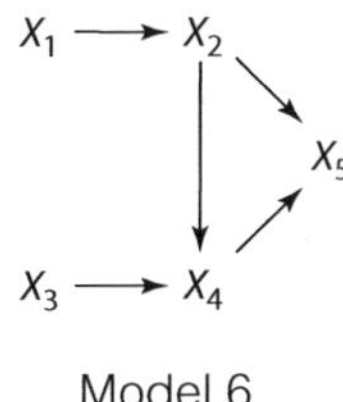

Model 6

In addition, we would test the validity of our assumptions about the *absence* of effects by regressing endogenous variables on others to which they are *not* supposed to be related. For example, in testing Model 6, we would regress both X_3 and X_4 on X_1 to see if the arrows we omitted should have been drawn in. If the resulting path coefficients are substantially different from 0 ($\geqslant.2$, for instance) and statistically significant, we would conclude that the model (and our theory about the events it represents) should be modified by adding a path.

One of the major advantages of path analysis is that it facilitates *theory elaboration* by bringing theory and data analysis into a fruitful interaction in which each informs the other. A path analysis of this type will tell us not only whether or not the variables in our model are related in the way we hypothesise but also *what relative influence each variable has on other variables in the model*. The *total effects* of one variable on another are equal to the value of the direct path between the two plus the indirect paths by which they are linked. An indirect path is equal to the products of the direct paths of which it is composed. For example, in Model 6, the total effect of X_2 on X_5 is equal to

$$p_{52} + (p_{42} \cdot p_{54})$$

and the total effect of X_1 on X_5 would be

$$(p_{21} \cdot p_{52}) + (p_{21} \cdot p_{42} \cdot p_{54})$$

As long as we are using *standardised* regression coefficients, we can use this procedure to compare the total effects of different variables in the system. Such knowledge can be of great practical significance because it can help citizens and policy makers to focus their energies where they will be most effective. For instance, if we were trying to encourage students to resist drugs, we could find out if one of several factors that contribute to that decision has a disproportionate impact and invest our resources in changing that variable.

Path analysis can also be used to compare the effects of variables in different settings. To return to the school segregation example, we might gather data on, say, Birmingham, Milton Keynes and London and test the accuracy of Model 4 in each city. If we do not standardise our data and we use *unstandardised regression coefficients*, we can compare the effects of, say, housing segregation on school segregation in each of these cities to see if the causal processes we are interested in differ from city to city. It is necessary to use the unstandardised coefficients because standardising makes the size of the path coefficient dependent on the variance of the variable in the sample. If, for example, there is a great deal more school segregation in one city than another, the relative size of the standardised regression coefficients will reflect that difference in variance rather than reflect any real difference in the relative strength of the influence of variables in the different cities.

The general rule is to use *standardised* coefficients when comparing the effects of different variables in the same sample and to use *unstandardised* coefficients when comparing the effects of the same variable in different samples. It is the unstandardised coefficients that are viewed as representing the 'causal laws' that drive social processes.

Ethical considerations

Now that you have read three chapters on data analysis, you may feel well prepared to load your data set into a statistics program (e.g., SPSS) and point-and-click your way through a multiple regression analysis. Temper your statistical enthusiasm by evaluating your data in light of the procedure's basic assumptions. Including hastily computed results in your essay, thesis, conference presentation, dissertation or published work tempts fate. If you rush into statistical analysis without fully assessing the qualities of your data, your future may well include an embarrassing public retraction of your research findings.

Conclusion

We end this chapter with two notes of caution. First, it is important to recognise that we have discussed only a fraction of the many multivariate statistics that are available for the analysis of both interval and noninterval data. Each of these techniques is applicable to different analytical tasks. Among the most important, commonly used techniques that we have *not* discussed here are *logit regression*, which allows the use of a dichotomous dependent variable, a common condition for voter turnout and other simple decision variables; *analysis of variance (ANOVA)*, which is used to test hypotheses about differences of multiple means in various groups and can be especially valuable in identifying the effects of some 'treatment' or intervention on the degree to which cases manifest a concept; and *factor analysis*, which is used to identify common factors that reflect the relatedness of apparently independent indicators. Explanations of when and how to use these and other techniques may be found in the 'Suggested reading' section at the end of this chapter.

With such a wide variety of statistical techniques to choose from, the task of selecting the statistical procedure that is most appropriate to your data and research question can be quite challenging. Your lecturer can help you in choosing which statistical techniques are most appropriate for your research, given your data. Ultimately, however, the best way to learn which technique is most useful for your data is through hands-on experimentation.

The second caution to bear in mind is that the overview of statistical techniques in this text has only introduced you to data analysis – it has not prepared you to actually execute more sophisticated data analysis techniques. Fortunately, you need not be a statistician to learn about and use the most common methods, since statistical analysis programs such as SPSS or SAS will carry out the calculations for you if the analysis is correctly set up. These programs have 'help' functions that will enable you to learn both the statistics and the analytic requirements. Still, it is your responsibility to ensure that you are employing the correct procedure, and that you are correctly interpreting your analyses.

Summary points

- Multiple regression permits the use of additional independent variables as controls.
- To successfully perform regression analysis, the interval or ratio variables and error terms must satisfy a set of assumptions.

Suggested reading and examples

Research examples

Examining the influence of political institutions on a government's level of corruption, Tavits (2007) studies the countries of the OECD and eastern Europe. Using ordinary least squares multiple regression, she finds that a government's clarity of responsibility (which includes majority status, cabinet duration, opposition influence and effective number of parties) has a tremendous independent effect on government corruption level.

Although examples of political science research using multivariate analysis are found in nearly every issue of the major journals listed in Chapter 3, path analysis is less common. The continued utility of path analysis in public opinion and news media framing analysis is demonstrated by Druckman's Figure 2 (2001: 1060), which models the different weights given to free speech, safety concerns and opposing racism, depending upon whether one was reading the *National Enquirer* or the *New York Times*.

Methodological reading

Among the many texts that provide a general introduction to statistics appropriate to the social sciences are *Statistics for Social Data Analysis* (Bohrnstedt and Knoke 1994) and *Statistics*, 9th edn. (McClave and Sincich 2003).

A highly-regarded, comprehensive examination of regression techniques is provided by *Applied Linear Regression* (Weisberg 2005). A detailed introduction to the types of statistics most often used in hypothesis testing is found in *Using Multivariate Statistics* (Tabachnick and Fidell 2001). Procedures for analysing noninterval data are covered in detail in *Nonparametric Methods in Quantitative Analysis* (Gibbons 1997). A highly readable introduction to path analysis, as well as a graduate-level examination of the procedure, is found in chapters 5 and 6 of *Principles and Practice of Structural Equation Modeling* (Kline 2005).

Detailed and generally quite readable explanations of many specific analysis techniques can be obtained in the Sage series: *Quantitative Applications in the Social Sciences*. There are dozens of these monographs, each focusing on a specific social science quantitative procedure. Each analytic procedure is taught using concrete examples from the literature.

A useful introduction to SPSS, complete with step-by-step instructions for carrying out commands is *An SPSS Companion to Political Analysis, 3rd edn* (Pollock 2008).

References

Bohrnstedt, George W. and Knoke, David. 1994. *Statistics for Social Data Analysis*, 3rd edn. Itasca, IL: F. E. Peacock.

Druckman, James N. 2001. 'On the limits of framing effects: who can frame?', *Journal of Politics*, vol. 63 (November), pp. 1041–66.

Gibbons, Jean Dickinson. 1997. *Nonparametric Methods in Quantitative Analysis*, 3rd edn. Columbus, OH: American Sciences Press.

Kline, Rex B. 2005. *Principles and Practice of Structural Equation Modeling*, 2nd edn. New York: Guilford.

McClave, James T. and Sincich, Terry. 2003. *Statistics*, 9th edn. Upper Saddle River, NJ: Prentice Hall.

Pedhazur, Elazar J. 1997. *Multiple Regression in Behavioral Research: Explanation and Prediction*, 3rd edn. Fort Worth, TX: Harcourt Brace.

Pollock, Philip H. 2008. *An SPSS Companion to Political Analysis*, 3rd edn. Washington, DC: Congressional Quarterly.

Tabachnick, Barbara G. and Fidell, Linda S. 2001. *Using Multivariate Statistics*, 4th edn. Needham Heights, MA: Allyn & Bacon.

Tavits, Margit. 2007. 'Clarity of responsibility and corruption'. *American Journal of Political Science*, vol. 51 (January), pp. 218–29.

Weisberg, Sanford. 2005. *Applied Linear Regression*, 3rd edn. New York: John Wiley.

Research exercises

1 Does spending more on public education reduce the amount of poverty? Select a sample of thirty Local Education Authorities (LEAs) in the United Kingdom and gather data on three variables for each LEA: (1) whether it is above or below the national average on the amount it spends on education per student; (2) whether it is above or below the national average on the percentage of its population that is defined as poor; and (3) the political party that controls the local council. Set up a crosstabulation to show the relationship between variables 1 and 2. Set up a crosstab to show the same relationship *controlling for variable 3*. Use the formulas given in Chapter 17 to compute lambda and chi-square for each of the tables. Write an interpretation of your findings.

2 Devise a theory to explain differences in the rate of growth in the gross national product of Third World nations that includes four IVs. Write a single multiple regression equation that summarises this theory, and explain what each term in the equation represents.

3 Draw a path diagram illustrating the theory you developed for Exercise 2, being sure that at least two of the IVs are endogenous. Then write the structural equations necessary to represent this model in a path analysis, explaining what each term in the equations represents.

Key terms

beta weight (β) or beta
   coefficient (b)
coefficient of
   determination (R^2)
controlling
model

model specification
multicollinearity
multiple regression
multiple regression
   equation
multivariate analysis

nonrecursive
partial regression
   coefficients
path analysis
recursive

Part VI

Qualitative methods

19 Elite and specialised interviewing

- How can we study organisations and events that involve relatively small numbers of people?
- How can we study groups and individuals who are outside the political mainstream?
- What challenges are presented by elite and specialised interviewing?
- How can we ensure the validity of information obtained in personal interviews?
- In what ways do qualitative interview methods differ from quantitative methods?

Introduction

Intensive interviewing techniques involving in-depth, one-on-one conversations with respondents are a primary instrument of qualitative research. They are used as a means of gaining *in-depth understanding* of a phenomenon and discovering aspects of that phenomenon that researchers did not anticipate.

As you read this chapter about elite and specialised interviewing, be alert to the ways in which effective use of this technique requires attention to a different set of concerns from those encountered in survey interviewing or any other quantitative data collection method. Pay special attention to the distinct 'mind-set' required for qualitative inquiry. In some cases you will find that you will be less concerned with carrying out a precisely planned research design and measuring process than you are when conducting quantitative research, and more concerned with being open to learning what your subjects can uniquely teach you about the subject.

Elite interviewing

Many important research questions in politics can be answered only if we can learn how certain individuals or types of individuals think and act. For example, whereas we can always speculate about reasons for the passage of a specific piece of legislation, we can learn the actual reasons only by finding out what the legislators thought. Answering these types of questions requires **elite interviewing** rather than surveys of the general population.

Defining elites

In this context, people are referred to as *elite* if they have knowledge that, for the purposes of a given research project, requires that they be given individualised treatment in an interview. Their elite status depends not on their role in society but on their access to information that can help answer a given research question. Although people who get elite treatment in research *are* often persons of political,

"

social or economic importance, this is not a requirement. In a study of 'extremist' groups like the Ku Klux Klan, for example, 'elite' respondents (those with special knowledge of the organisation), may not be persons of wealth or public notoriety.

Elite interviewing versus surveying

A central difference between sample survey interviewing and elite interviewing is the degree to which the interview is *standardised*. In sample surveys, each respondent is treated as much like every other respondent as possible. This is because the purpose of the interview is to obtain specific information that can be used to make quantitative comparisons between respondents in an effort to generalise to some larger population. In elite interviewing, each respondent is treated differently to the extent that obtaining the information possessed by that individual alone requires unique treatment. The purpose of elite interviewing is generally not the collection of prespecified data but the gathering of information to assist in reconstructing some event or discerning a pattern in specific behaviours.

A second major difference between elite interviewing and survey interviewing is that, whereas survey interviews are generally highly **scheduled interviews**, elite interviews are largely **unscheduled interviews**. An interview is highly *scheduled* if the questions to be asked and the order of their appearance are predetermined and inflexible. Highly scheduled interviews produce standardised data because they require that all respondents answer the same questions and select from the same options in answering. This has the advantage of allowing comparisons between respondents and facilitates data processing. Strict scheduling, however, has the disadvantage of restricting the information obtained from interviews to that which the researcher has already decided is necessary for understanding the phenomena under study. Scheduling limits the researcher's opportunities to learn what respondents consider relevant or important and to gain new theoretical insights.

In a totally *unscheduled* interview, the interviewer is guided only by a general objective (for example, to find out how a given decision was made in a particular state agency) and has no predetermined set of questions to ask. Unscheduled interviews produce data that are difficult to condense and summarise and that may not allow precise comparisons among respondents. The asset accompanying this liability is a greater opportunity to learn from respondents and to acquire unexpected information that can lead to truly new ways of understanding the events being studied.

Unscheduled interviews are especially suited to elite interviewing, because in elite interviewing the researcher is interested in learning what the respondent perceives as important and relevant to the research and lets the respondent's observations suggest what questions should be asked in order to obtain useful information. The interviewer is concerned with discovering facts and patterns rather than with measuring pre-selected phenomena.

Elite interviews can provide crucial information about political events that is otherwise unavailable. Elite interviewing involves some very real risks, however. It generally means asking people who are deeply involved in a political process to shape the researcher's definition of the process. This may threaten the validity of the information obtained if respondents (1) have so narrow a view of the events in question that they do not understand which aspects are important in explaining them; (2) have inaccurate information (either because they misperceived events in the first place or because they have forgotten important elements); (3) have convinced themselves, in order to rationalise their own actions, that things are one way when they are actually another; or (4) intentionally lie in order to protect themselves or others. For example, interviews with high ranking members of George W. Bush's administration about the timing of their knowledge of the torture or prisoner abuse in Guantanamo Bay might produce instances of invalid information for each of these reasons.

Seeking validity

Though researchers cannot control what respondents say, they can guard against drawing invalid conclusions from elite interviews by following some general guidelines. First, never treat what interviewees say as factual data, but rather *treat the fact that they said it as data*. For an understanding of political behaviour, it is often as important to know what people believe or claim to be true as it is to know what is true. For example, if you want to know why residents of a given community have got together to demand the closing of a nearby chemical plant, finding out how much of a safety hazard the plant actually poses may be less useful than finding out how much of a safety hazard residents *believe* the plant poses.

Second, never rely on a single respondent for information about any event, but obtain information about each event from as many respondents as possible before drawing conclusions.

Third, always seek ways of verifying information from elite interviews by comparing it with information from outside sources. If we interview party leaders to learn why a given candidate has been selected as the party's nominee in an election and respondents refer to 'the obvious public support for the candidate' as their reason for supporting that candidate, we will want to look for public opinion polls that supply evidence of the degree to which the public actually did support them.

Fourth, learn enough about the subject to be able to recognise incorrect statements or to analyse responses perceptively for possible sources of invalidity. We should be able to answer questions such as the following before engaging in elite interviewing: Is there any reason why respondents might want to believe something other than the truth or want to have others believe something other than the truth? Do they stand to gain economically or politically from given statements? What answers are plausible given the facts we know about the subject from other, reliable sources?

Despite these possible complications, elite interviewing has tremendous potential for shedding light on important political phenomena and can often be a valuable supplement to studies relying principally on other data collection techniques, as well as, on occasion, providing the sole basis for important conclusions. It is crucial to remember, however, that information from people with inside knowledge is no substitute for a sound theoretical understanding of the subject. In order to reach valuable conclusions, politics researchers must construct their own analytic categories and conceptual schemes based on theory and avoid being overly influenced by the information gathered from elites.

Techniques of elite interviewing

One of the first questions faced in elite interviewing is whom to interview. In survey interviewing, all of the respondents are treated as equally able to contribute information that can be used in answering the research question, and sampling methods determine whom to interview. Elite interviewers have to assume that potential respondents differ in how much they can contribute to the study and that each respondent has something unique to offer. Often, background research will identify the entire population of those likely to have relevant information. If we are studying the decisions of the US presidential commission created to investigate the terrorist attacks of 11 September 2001, for instance, background research would identify the members of the commission, their staff personnel and the people called to testify. By contrast, if we are doing a 'community power study' to determine who controls public policy in a certain city, we will not find any official list of people who exercise political influence in the city. Finding out whom to interview in this case is one of the objectives of the interviews themselves.

Once a group of potential interviewees has been identified, the question of the order in which to see them arises. It is tempting to see first those people who should be most willing to talk and most sympathetic, or to want to see first the person believed to have the most information. Two things should be kept in mind, however. First, elite interviewing is a process of discovery. We seldom come to the interviews knowing everything important to ask. Early interviews may teach us things that help us get the most useful information from subsequent interviews. Often it is best to interview the most central figures late in the study.

Second, in elite interviewing, we are generally not dealing with isolated and uninvolved individuals. Each respondent is likely to have a unique (perhaps self-interested) view of the situation under study and may intentionally or unintentionally give inaccurate advice about whom should be interviewed. Under no circumstances should the researcher let early interviewees' suggestions *determine* the choice or order of subsequent interviews, although those suggestions can provide partial data on which to base such decisions. Sometimes, the fact that early interviewees have suggested certain other persons is evidence in itself, as it may reveal alliances, communication patterns or shared perceptions.

In addition, because elite respondents are likely to know one another and be involved with the subject matter, the researcher must be cautious that early interviews do not jeopardise the study by identifying it with a particular group among the potential respondents. If possible, it is best to avoid interviewing the most unusual persons first – the mavericks, opposition leaders, persons thought to have extreme views or leaders of any dominant coalition. If word is passed to other interviewees that you have already spoken with those perceived to be outside the norms or in positions of power, it may bias your other interviews.

Considering all this, researchers may find that the best initial interviews may be with people who are somewhat marginal to the situation, but who are viewed as neutral or 'mainstream' by most participants. In a study of politics in a legislature, for example, it may be best to interview members of the legislative staff (such as general service officials used by all members of the legislature) first, rather than starting with key legislators. It is also wise to explain to the first respondents that the interview is preliminary and exploratory and that you may want to see them again. This is because you may learn what other questions to ask or how to interpret answers only after subsequent conversations.

Arranging interviews

It may be difficult to schedule interviews with elites because such individuals are often busy people and this type of interview generally demands large amounts of their time (an hour or more is common). The following tips will generally help in securing interviews, *though it will sometimes be impossible or inadvisable to follow them in particular situations.*

1   Always call or write in advance to arrange for the interview rather than simply showing up, as is done in survey interviewing.
2   Be sure to request the interview by speaking with *the person to be interviewed* rather than a secretary or aide. You want to be certain the respondent understands the purpose of the meeting so they will not feel you are being deceitful.
3   Avoid highly detailed explanations of the purpose of the interview because these can bias responses or cause potential respondents to refer you to a staff person who has 'expert' knowledge of the subject.
4   Always try to determine the reasons for refusals and try to see whether you can remove the cause. For example, if scheduling is a problem, you may offer to interview after work hours; if confidence is a problem, you may be able to secure references from people the potential respondent trusts, or agree to have a third party sit in on the interview as insurance against subsequent false claims.

5 Always have on hand materials that identify you and the sponsor of the research, in case questions arise. If possible, give contact information for someone who can verify the purpose and legitimacy of your study.

Conducting elite interviews

Once an interview has been arranged, it should *not* proceed by the rules given for survey interviewing. Elite interviewers have to be more flexible and have a wider range of interviewing styles than survey interviewers, but there are some general guidelines that will fit most situations:

1 Always introduce yourself and restate the broad purpose of the study at the beginning of each interview rather than assuming that the respondent remembers these facts from a letter of introduction, phone call or even a prior interview session.
2 The setting of an interview can be crucial. It is generally best to arrange a private interview away from potential distractions. Interviews over meals in restaurants or in the presence of the respondent's family usually do not go well. Occasionally, however, it is useful to have an interview in an unorthodox place (a city park, a bus, a logged forest) if it serves to put respondents at ease or jog their memory of past events.
3 Though group interviews can sometimes help produce a consensus on facts or reveal personal relationships, it is normally best to interview only one person at a time.
4 The tone of the interview should be reflective and conversational. Avoid firing questions in rapid succession. Do not be afraid of pauses as you or the respondent process information and collect thoughts.
5 Plan initial questions carefully. Though the bulk of the interview will be unscheduled, the first few questions are important in focusing respondents' attention, stimulating their memory and clarifying their perception of what you want. Initial questions should be: (a) clearly related to the stated purpose of the study; (b) likely to be answered with ease so that no ego-threat arises; (c) phrased to show the respondent that the interviewer has knowledge about the subject of the study; and (d) conducive to the kind of free-flowing answers that the researcher hopes to receive in the interview rather than to flat, factual answers. (If you need background information on the respondent, it can be obtained later in the interview.) Questions that stress the respondent's feelings about or definition of a situation can be especially useful opening questions.
6 In contrast to survey research, questions should often be subject to multiple interpretations. Remember that the objective is to learn how *respondents* see the situation and what they feel is relevant.
7 Comments, as well as questions, can be used to evoke a response. A remark like, 'that is not the way it is usually done', for example, can lead to revelations about how respondents believe things do work.
8 Always maintain eye contact when possible (unless interviewees seem uncomfortable with this), and make it clear that you are listening intently and sympathetically. Phrases like 'I see' or 'Of course' or simply a thoughtful 'Yes' can encourage respondents and keep them talking.
9 Remember that one of the chief rewards respondents get from granting in-depth interviews is the chance to 'teach' someone who is knowledgeable about and genuinely interested in a subject of great importance to them. It can be important to let them realise that they are, in fact, helping and informing you.
10 It is generally best to appear to accept whatever comments respondents make. Do not appear to reject their opinions or challenge their statements of fact.

11 An exception to rule 10 occurs when respondents are reluctant to reveal information you feel sure they have. In that situation, it may be necessary to employ what is often referred to as the **Nadel technique** (Nadel 1939). Here you play the role of critic or antagonist, questioning and challenging respondents' remarks in the hope of forcing them to reveal information in order to defend their views or prove a point.

12 Respondents who are reluctant to divulge information because they fear the way it may be used can sometimes be reassured by a reminder that the information will be kept confidential or that the researcher is really not in any position to affect the situation in any way.

13 Note-taking can be used as a tool to improve interviews. In elite interviewing, respondents can often be encouraged to give more information or stay on a given subject by the way an interviewer takes notes. Intense recording can serve as a cue that you find comments useful, and putting the pencil down altogether can signal that the respondent has ventured off the central topic. Because you have to take such extensive notes that it is probably impossible to be inconspicuous, you may as well use note-taking for all it is worth.

14 Always be sensitive to the interviewee's personality and personal style, and adapt your tactics to it. Some people are highly formal and others are very casual. Some deal in ideas almost exclusively, and others tend to personalise everything. Some people are accustomed to interacting mainly with superiors, and others mainly with subordinates. You may be able to get more information by adopting one of these roles. Never enter an interview with a fixed idea of the style you will use, but decide what is necessary when talking with the respondent.

15 Always review your interview notes as soon as possible after the interview to elaborate at points where you could get only an outline and to make comments about your interpretation of the interview. This may mean sitting in a cold parking lot or buying an unwanted cup of coffee in order to have a place to write, but it is important to trust to memory as little as possible.

16 Type up handwritten notes as soon as possible. Make several hard or electronic copies and store them in separate places to insure against loss.

Voice recorders are controversial tools in interviewing. Obviously they can help avoid mistakes about what is actually said, and they can capture subtle facts about the *way* in which things are said. Recorders can also help interviewers learn how they sound to respondents. This is useful because the way in which a question is asked can be an important consideration in interpreting a response. A drawback to recording interviews is that respondents are often inhibited by a recorder, because it denies them the chance of claiming that they have not made some remark if it later proves embarrassing. Sometimes they fear that the recording can be edited to make it appear as if they had said things they have not. Moreover, the mechanics of working the recorder can distract from the interview.

Researchers must decide about the use of recorders on the basis of the type of question they are investigating, the nature of the interviews they expect and the character of the respondents. If the subject matter is highly sensitive or respondents are likely to be inhibited by recorders, the drawbacks of using them probably outweigh the advantages. If lengthy, detailed and technical interviews are necessary and specific facts are crucial to the study, recorders may be necessary.

If a recorder is used, the researcher should ask permission to use it and should place the device in full view of the respondent. Pretest the recorder to ensure that it is suitable for the kind of interview anticipated (sufficiently sensitive, simple to operate, able to record long enough). *Never depend exclusively on a recorder.* It can malfunction and cause the loss of an irreplaceable interview. Always take written notes as well.

A final issue in elite interviewing is confidentiality. This can be more important with elite interviews than with surveys, because elites are often asked for information that, if revealed or misused, may have considerable public impact or personal consequences. If confidentiality is promised, and it generally must be, *researchers should make every reasonable effort to safeguard information.* This is often easier than in survey research, because large numbers of personnel are not generally required in elite studies, but interviewers can buy a little insurance by storing records in secure places and keeping the purpose of the study from becoming general knowledge, if possible. One threat to confidentiality occurs when a typist is used to type handwritten notes or transcribe recorded interviews. If researchers absolutely cannot do this work themselves, they should only employ dependable people to do it and conceal from the typist the identity of respondents when possible. Remember never to make interview records available to people not involved in the project.

Specialised interviewing

In some studies, a politics researcher does not want to obtain information from specific individuals, as in the case of elite interviewing, or from respondents who are representative of the general population, as in surveys, but needs information from persons who are *representative or typical of some particular group*. This often calls for **specialised interviewing**.

A specialised interview is any interview in which the characteristics of respondents demand procedures different from those employed in standardised survey interviewing. Interviews with children, prison inmates, homeless persons, non-English-speaking migrant workers, mental patients and members of a religious cult are all examples.

Specialised versus survey interviewing

Specialised interviewing is called for when researchers cannot assume that they and their respondents share a *common vocabulary*. Words that researchers use frequently may not be understood by respondents. Similarly, respondents may use terms or slang with which the researcher is not familiar or may use conventional words in special ways the researcher does not understand. In addition, specialised interview situations often involve distinctive relationships between respondents and interviewers. Whereas ordinary respondents regard interviewers largely as equals who can be trusted to a degree and treated cordially, specialised subjects may view interviewers as authority figures or 'outsiders' and may be hostile and suspicious. In these circumstances, communication can be difficult and the validity of responses can suffer.

All of these features of specialised interviews combine to create settings in which researchers cannot take communication for granted. Rather, interviewers have to carefully establish a basis for communication and then check to be sure that effective communication is occurring.

An example

If we want to know the degree to which young people living on council estates are alienated from the political system, we first need to define the concept of alienation and be sure that potential respondents know what we mean when we speak of the political system. Once we have developed a common understanding of the concepts and have asked our central questions, we need to ask additional questions to determine whether the young people's responses have the same meaning for them as we interpret them to mean. One way to do this is first to give our respondents examples of young people stating beliefs or acting in ways that suggest alienation from the political system, then to ask our respondents to interpret the actions described as showing either high or low levels of respect for the political system, and then to tell us whether or not they would be likely to take these same actions.

If the young adults being interviewed frequently misinterpret the fictitious actions or say they would take actions that are inconsistent with the level of alienation they have told us they feel towards the political system, it will not be safe to assume that the respondents understand our questions or their answers in the same way we do.

Ethical considerations

As in other types of research, in elite interviews you are obligated to explain to the participants the nature, the risks (if any) and the purpose of the research project. In addition, you should be absolutely sure that the interview will not cause physical or emotional harm to your subjects. For example, some findings obtained in elite interviews might be so sensitive that they could compromise the interviewee. It is, therefore, important to consider carefully the timing and the context of your study. Ask yourself whether the information you collected might have any negative consequences for the interviewee, for example, getting fired for divulging 'privileged' information, being ostracised from the community for speaking with outsiders or getting arrested for speaking out in a nation that does not entirely support the idea of free speech.

The interviewees also should be aware that their participation is entirely voluntary and that they can refuse to answer any of your questions. They should also know how the information gathered during the interviews will be used (for example, will it be used in an internal report only, or will it be published in an academic journal).

Although surveys and other types of research studies are usually conducted under the assumption that the findings are anonymous, elite interviews often cannot guarantee anonymity. In interviews with high-level officials, for example, it might be difficult to hide their true identity simply because they are the only (or most likely) person responsible for a particular aspect of your research. However, if it is possible to ensure anonymity, you should explain to the participants how you will keep what is being said during the interviews confidential and anonymous – such a pledge will make it much easier for your participants to be frank and open with you.

When reporting your findings, it is important to represent accurately what you observed or were told in the interview. Be sure to avoid personal biases and opinions that might influence the way your research findings are explained. Also, remember not to take interview responses out of context by discussing only selected or 'most appropriate' parts of the whole interview.

Finally, if your interviews are conducted in order to be used in institutional research (particularly if you are a student or a faculty member), your research has to be approved by the ethics review board of your university to ensure that you are not violating any of the above-mentioned ethical considerations. In most of these cases, you also need to ask the subjects to agree to participate in your study by signing a consent form, which must explain the purpose of the study and the way the gathered information will be handled (guarantee of anonymity, use of data etc.).

Conclusion

Intensive interviewing techniques offer access to information about the world that cannot be obtained through other methods. When properly conducted, these interviews can yield valuable insights leading to further research, help us more fully develop our theories of some phenomenon, and let us discover *why* things happened as they did to a greater degree than more 'detached' methods can.

Like other qualitative methods, however, they also place special demands on the abilities and discipline of the researcher(s). They should never be the only approach used in answering a research question because you cannot be assured of access to the right people or of being able to validate the information you collect in this way in advance of actually doing the study. Documentary evidence must also be used to compare and consider competing evidence from interviews. It is also important to be especially diligent in planning and training for your interviews, and careful to enlist the help of others in verifying your interpretations of the discussions.

When reading research based on elite or specialised interviewing you will want to pay special attention to the details of the description of the methods used. This will be necessary in judging accurately the degree to which bias might have been introduced into the findings by the unique challenges of intensive interviewing.

Intensive interviews can be an enormously rich source of data for politics researchers, but they require the development of almost artistic skills to be used effectively. In developing this skill, no amount of reading about in-depth interviews can substitute for experience with them.

Summary points

- Intensive interviewing can let us learn about events that only a few people know about and can be used to study people who are outside the norms of society.
- Intensive interviewing of 'elites' – persons with unique knowledge – is a special skill and has to be done in a manner appropriate to individual respondents and situations.
- Intensive interviewing of 'special' respondents, who are unlikely to respond to questions the same way as 'average' citizens, requires great sensitivity and in-depth knowledge of the circumstances of the respondents.
- Ensuring the validity of conclusions drawn from elite and specialised interviewing poses special challenges that require both cross-checking of the researcher's reasoning and detailed reporting of observations so that others can draw their own conclusions.
- Research designs employing intensive interviewing must be far more flexible than most quantitative research designs, and are aimed at developing theory and gaining in-depth and unexpected knowledge. In addition, the information produced by intensive interviewing methods is almost never quantitative and must be analysed with techniques other than standard statistical analyses.

Suggested reading and examples

Research examples

Although studies based on elite interviews are not common in political science journals, they are frequently used in more intensive research published in book form. These provide more depth and context than quantitative-focused journal articles. Some interview-based research is published in journals but it is less common. Chen (1999), for example, uses elite interviews to compare attitudes and opinions of ordinary citizens living in Beijing with those of political officials. Similarly, Miller *et al.* (1995) employ elite interviews to compare the policy preferences and political attitudes of parliamentary representatives and ordinary citizens in Russia and the Ukraine six months after the collapse of the Soviet Union. The potential pitfalls of interviewing elites in politically divided societies are discussed in a recent study by McEvoy (2006), who interviewed former ministers from Northern Ireland's power-sharing government.

Methodological readings

Two texts that explain intensive interviewing in detail are *Interviews: An Introduction to Qualitative Research Interviewing* (Kvale 2007) and *Qualitative Research Interviewing: Biographic Narrative and Semi-Structured Methods* (Wengraf 2001). For an examination of the role of interviewing in the larger context of qualitative methodologies, see *Analyzing Social Settings: A Guide to Qualitative Observation and Analysis* (Lofland *et al.* 2005).

References

Chen, Jie. 1999. 'Comparing mass and elite subjective orientations in urban China'. *Public Opinion Quarterly*, vol. 63 (Summer), pp. 193–219.

Kvale, Steinar. 2007. *Interviews: An Introduction to Qualitative Research Interviewing*, 2nd edn. Thousand Oaks, CA: Sage.

Lofland, John, Snow, David A., Anderson, Leon and Lofland, Lyn H. 2005. *Analyzing Social Settings: A Guide to Qualitative Observation and Analysis*, 4th edn. Belmont, CA: Wadsworth.

McEvoy, Joanne. 2006. 'Elite interviewing in a divided society: lessons from Northern Ireland'. *Politics*, vol. 26, no. 3, pp. 184–91.

Miller, Arthur H., Hesli, Vicki L. and Reisinger, William M. 1995. 'Comparing citizen and elite belief systems in post-soviet Russia and Ukraine'. *Public Opinion Quarterly*, vol. 59 (Spring), pp. 1–40.

Nadel, S. F. 1939. 'The interview technique in social anthropology' in F. C. Bartlett, M. Ginsberg, E. J. Lindgren and R. H. Thouless, eds. *The Study of Society* (pp. 317–27). London: Kegan Paul, Trench, Trubner & Co.

Wengraf, Tom. 2001. *Qualitative Research Interviewing: Biographic Narrative and Semi-Structured Methods*. Thousand Oaks, CA: Sage.

Research exercises

1   State a research question that can be answered through elite interviewing. List the types of information needed in order to answer the question and identify, either by name or by official position, (for example, all federal district court judges in the eleven southern states) the people you would expect to interview in gathering that information. Describe what steps you would take to ensure the validity of your conclusions. How would you check the accuracy of what respondents tell you?

2   (Note: Do not undertake this exercise without permission from your instructor.)

   a   State a research question dealing with the local government of your community or with decision making in your university that can be studied through elite interviewing. List the types of information you will be seeking and the specific persons you will have to interview to acquire that information.

   b   After the project has been approved by your instructor, arrange and conduct interviews with three of the persons you need to interview. (*Remember*: You need to tell these people that this is part of a class assignment, so do not set your sights too high. You may well be unable to see the mayor of a large city or the president of a large university. Also, make certain to do enough background research to ask intelligent questions on the subject selected.)

   Type up the notes from the interviews along with all of your observations about the significance and interpretation of different remarks. Explain what you have learned about the subject from these interviews, state what else you need to know, and say how you would proceed if you were going to carry the research further. Also identify any steps you feel could be used to verify the information gained in the three interviews.

Key terms

elite interviewing	Nadel technique	specialised interviewing
intensive interviewing	scheduled interviews	unscheduled interviews

20 Focus group methodologies

- What is focus group methodology and when should it be used?
- What are the advantages and limitations of focus groups?
- How are focus groups conducted and how are the data analysed?
- How can focus group methodology be used with other methods?

Introduction

Researchers sometimes want to study questions that others have not investigated, or they may want to gain a fresh perspective in an area where past research has failed to resolve major questions. In such cases, they will be unable to rely on prior theories or empirical studies to guide their efforts. If the phenomenon in question is new (or at least new to social science researchers), there may not even be firsthand knowledge of the events in question. In these situations, scholars may need to gather information through the use of focus groups.

At the most basic level, **focus group** methods involve bringing together small groups of carefully selected individuals for an in-depth discussion of some topic, guided by a **moderator**, in order to learn how people think about that topic. Focus groups can be used for different purposes at different stages of the research process. They can help formulate hypotheses for future studies, develop indicators to be used in data collection, improve the interpretation of data collected by other means or produce data that are directly useful in answering a research question.

This chapter explains why and when researchers might use focus group methods either as their primary methodology or in support of other data collection methods. It then describes some of the basic rules for conducting focus groups and using the information they produce.

Why use focus groups?

Focus group methods were developed in the 1940s by researchers who wanted to get as realistic a view of people's thinking as possible. Government agencies, political advisers and social scientists have been making more use of focus groups in recent years, but the approach has been used most extensively in *market research* to help businesses explore aspects of consumer behaviour as part of their effort to develop and sell products. Businesses often use focus groups to gain insights into such questions as how consumers will react to a new product, how effective a proposed advertising campaign might be and why consumers prefer one product over another.

Limitations of surveys

Survey research or individual interviews can often be used for these purposes, but early researchers recognised at least five limitations to survey-based methods:

1   Respondents can give us only the information we know to ask for, and many problems may have aspects that researchers will not think to ask about. For example, in a survey, we might ask a

random sample of voters to rate two opposing candidates on each of five dimensions that we feel will determine how voters decide among candidates. We might then be surprised to find that the candidate who earned the higher rating did not win the election because voters used a different set of criteria in making their actual choice. Even if voters answered our questions honestly, we had asked the wrong questions.

2 Even if one uses open-ended questions, respondents may be influenced by the style in which questions are asked or by subtle aspects of their interaction with the interviewer and may not give valid answers.

3 Surveys are very expensive and time-consuming. If we do not have a clear understanding of what we want to know and how to ask questions in order to get that information from respondents, we run the risk of making a large investment to obtain useless data.

4 Survey results are not always 'self-explanatory' because it is always possible that respondents interpreted questions differently from the interpretations the researchers intended and that respondents' answers meant something different to them than they meant to the researchers.

5 People do not make decisions in isolation but are influenced by others' opinions and reactions. A survey interview, however, asks people to act in isolation from their social context in expressing opinions or making judgements. As a result, the data produced by a survey or interview may not accurately reflect social reality.

Limitations of direct observations

To avoid these limitations of interview-based data collection, researchers could turn to direct observation. Whereas that approach may be very valuable for certain research questions, it may be inappropriate for others. Scholars who are interested in a fairly narrow subject may face several problems with direct observation.

An example

To illustrate the challenges of direct observations, let us use the subject of how heterosexuals perceive the goals of the gay rights movement. First, it may be difficult to find a site at which to observe interaction on this topic. Where can researchers go to be sure they will hear a discussion of the gay rights movement by nongays? Second, in a natural setting, it may be necessary to observe *many* hours of discussion of other topics in order to hear a few minutes of conversation about gay rights. Third, even if the subject comes up, the discussion may not address the aspects of the issue that are of interest to researchers since, in direct observation, researchers have no way to guide the discussion. Finally, even in natural settings, discussion may be artificially constrained. For example, people who work together may avoid expressing political disagreement for fear that they will damage relationships in the workplace. Properly designed and executed focus groups can help overcome all of these problems.

Advantages of focus groups

The central feature of focus group methods is that they *rely on interaction among the participants to generate insights into the subject under study*. As you will see when we describe the technique, focus groups enable their members to interact in a 'safe' environment with very little direction from the researcher. As a result, participants have a chance to express their true feelings on the topic under study and can bring up any aspect of that topic that they feel is important. The group process may also allow them to come to understandings about the topic that none of them could have achieved alone.

This means that focus groups have three substantive advantages: (1) they *may* provide more accurate insights into what people actually think than do other techniques that involve more influence from the researcher; (2) they can produce results that reflect social realities more accurately than methods that ask people to act in isolation; and (3) they give us the ability to study *group dynamics* in ways that other techniques do not. In addition, focus groups offer some practical advantages. First, though they are *not* inexpensive, focus groups typically cost far less than a large survey and take far less time than direct observation. Second, because focus groups do not require elaborate measuring instruments and procedures, they can usually be conducted with far less preparation than interview-based research or even direct observation. This saves time and money.

Limitations of focus groups

Like other methods, focus group research has its potential drawbacks. We will describe four common limitations and suggest ways to cope with them. Each of the limitations may affect any given focus group session, but they do not all affect every focus group project equally. This is because there are many different ways to structure focus groups and because focus groups are held for many different purposes. If recognised and properly addressed, the limitations of focus groups need not damage the usefulness of the method.

First, focus group research may yield *subjective interpretations*. The primary product of a focus group is a transcript of what was said. To contribute to our understanding, this transcript must be interpreted by someone. Since the transcript does not consist of numerical data that can be subjected to statistical tests, its interpretation inevitably involves more subjectivity than do the analyses associated with other methods. As a result of differences in their own background or values, different observers may reach different conclusions about what 'lessons' are to be learned from the focus group.

Remember that the interpretation of quantitative data can also be subject to debate. We are saying only that focus groups are more prone to the interpretation problem than some other methods are, and *not* that focus groups have this problem when other approaches do not.

Since subjectivity is inherent in the interpretation of focus group sessions, the only protection against being misled by it is some combination of the following steps: Researchers must be honest with themselves about their biases and try to be as objective as possible. They can bring in disinterested but qualified persons to do independent interpretations of the focus group results. Researchers can also share their work with other scholars who can judge the validity of their interpretation and suggest alternatives before considering their conclusions final. In addition, when writing up the study, researchers can faithfully describe enough of what was said to allow others to draw their own conclusions.

A second limitation is that the small number of people that can be involved in any focus group offers *limited representativeness* of any larger population. As a result, we cannot generalise to the larger population with the same precision or confidence that we can when larger samples are used. Additionally, there is always the chance that even carefully selected groups may be atypical of the population and thereby lead us to incorrect conclusions. Moreover, even if the focus groups are quite typical of the larger population, we have no objective measures to tell us this is the case in advance (as we do with probability sampling). We must wait until we can verify focus group results through some other method.

The appropriate responses to this problem consist of the researcher's awareness of the potentially unrepresentative nature of the results of focus groups and the researcher's avoidance of making unwarranted generalisations. Clearly it would be unwise to attempt very precise predictions of popular behaviour on the basis of focus group results. For example, one could not, on the basis of focus group results, justifiably claim that '68.6 per cent of citizens will vote against higher taxes to be used to retrain defense industry workers for civilian jobs'. However, by observing focus groups, scholars might be able to reach conclusions like, 'the participants tend to see the retraining of defense industry workers as a personal rather than a public responsibility'.

A third limitation is that the *artificial setting* of a focus group may unpredictably affect subjects' behaviour. The major purpose of focus groups is to get people to express themselves freely and reveal their true thinking without the restrictions imposed by a survey or interview. They often do this very well. However, we must recognise that the focus group is *not* a natural setting. Even if the moderator succeeds in creating a 'permissive environment' that encourages self-expression, responses may be sincere but still unlike what they would have been in a different setting. As a result, we may not be able to generalise from the results of the focus group to the way people will behave in other social settings.

For example, the composition of the group may be unlike that of any group with which the participants are likely to interact on a regular basis. If we have intentionally selected participants of mixed socioeconomic backgrounds but who seldom cross socioeconomic lines in their daily life, the group dynamic that develops may not be typical of any that would occur in the real world. Similarly, the permissive environment of the focus group may allow people to express ideas they would never verbalise in naturally occurring groups that have more restrictive norms. As a result, a consensus may emerge that is unlike any that would be produced by a real-world interaction.

In addition, each focus group develops its own dynamic as a result of some chance factors such as who happens to express an opinion first or the direction or tone of the first set of comments. The same members might behave differently on another evening or if placed in another group. As a consequence, the results of any given focus group may be unrepresentative both of real-world outcomes and of the thinking of the group participants as individuals.

In short, even a carefully designed and well-run focus group may create false impressions because it is not itself a natural setting. There are two main avenues to coping with these issues. First, researchers can run a number of groups and form conclusions based on *patterns* rather than isolated results. Second, they must be sensitive to both the ways in which focus groups may differ from natural settings and the effects these differences may have on the outcome of the sessions, and they must incorporate that awareness into their analysis of the focus group observations.

A fourth limitation is that this technique may produce *method effects*. Most observational research methods carry the risk of influencing subjects' responses in some way. (Recall, for example, our discussion in Chapter 8 of biased question wording and resulting survey responses.) Focus groups are no exception. *Method effects* can arise from biases introduced by the behaviour of the moderator, who could have preconceived notions about what the focus group will or 'should' reveal and who may unconsciously steer the discussion in that direction. Moderators who conduct several focus groups on the same subject may have had early experiences that cause them to lead discussions in subsequent groups in the direction of being consistent with the early groups. Similarly, unintentional cues given to participants before the group session (through a description of the purpose of the group or simply the naming of its sponsor, for example) may shape the outcome.

When are focus groups useful?

Researchers must weigh the strengths and weaknesses of focus groups in the context of specific research situations and tasks. Focus groups can be of great value under some conditions and of little use under others. Here is a nonexhaustive list of some general situations in which focus groups' research is an advantageous method.

Conducting exploratory research

When researchers venture into an area that is so completely unexplored that they do not even know how to go about studying it or when they want a fresh perspective on an old but unresolved research question, focus groups can help them formulate ideas about both what questions to ask and what methods to use. An example of this can be found in study of the transformation of eastern European nations from authoritarian to democratic political systems following the fall of communism after 1989. Researchers might want to know how citizens who have been denied any opportunity for meaningful participation in politics approach the tasks of democratic citizenship when they are given the chance. Because the transition from communism to democracy has never happened before, we have no prior theories or studies to guide us. Moreover, Western scholars have generally been unable to conduct surveys in those nations for decades and have little knowledge of how their citizens thought about politics before the transition. In this case, focus groups consisting of citizens of the changing nations could help researchers discover what is to be explained and develop hypotheses to guide research.

Refining data collection instruments

Even when researchers know enough about an area to formulate hypotheses, they may be unsure about the best way to operationalise concepts. For example, standard question wording on a survey may not communicate effectively with unusual respondents. In the case of the eastern European nations, we cannot even be sure that their citizens think about politics in the same terms as citizens of Western nations do. A series of focus groups could provide information that would assist in the development of appropriate wording for survey questions to be used with this population. Alternatively, researchers who plan to use direct observation to study political participation in eastern European nations could use focus groups to learn the meaning of different expressions or actions so that they would know what significance the people being observed attached to their own words and deeds.

Interpreting quantitative findings

When researchers have used other methods to collect data that show clear patterns, they may still be unsure about how those patterns developed or what the patterns mean to the people who exhibit them. Again, focus groups can often provide answers. For example, many studies of environmental politics have found that women are far more likely than men to express concern about environmental hazards and to regard technologies as risky. Focus groups in which men and women discuss environmental issues may help researchers understand differences in the way the sexes tend to judge environmental hazards: what standards they use, how they process information, whom they trust as an authority and so on. Scholars could then make more sense of the statistical relationships observed in their data.

Studying group processes

Whether they are legislative committees, juries, military units, law enforcement task forces, workplace teams, street gangs or any of dozens of other collections of people, small groups make many of the decisions in our society. Understanding the processes by which groups influence their members' perceptions and reach decisions can, therefore, help us understand social phenomena or formulate public policies. Social scientists have long recognised that one behaves differently when in a group than when alone, and that the only way to understand *group* behaviour is to study *group dynamics*. If our interest is in some aspect of group dynamics, then focus group methods offer an excellent way to observe efficiently and to avoid raising some of the ethical issues involved in direct observation.

Designing and evaluating public policy

Focus groups can often help public officials and policy analysts gain an understanding of how citizens see problems, evaluate services and are likely to react to new programmes. Such insight can then be used to create new policies that address problems or to evaluate how well existing policies are working. To illustrate, public housing officials could conduct focus groups to help them anticipate how residents of a public housing development would react to a system of tenant management that gave the residents a voice in running the housing project. Based on what they learn, they could try to build into the tenant management programme a realistic set of incentives for participation, rather than guess at what might motivate residents to take part.

An even more practice-oriented use of focus groups is to design and evaluate specific communication materials and strategies. To illustrate, imagine that public health officials want to convey to an immigrant community that has its own distinctive subculture certain information on a serious health hazard. The officials might use focus groups composed of members of the immigrant population to determine such things as what channels of communication would be most effective in reaching those residents and whether or not a given message would successfully capture residents' attention and be properly interpreted.

This use of social science methods to achieve very practical ends is commonly referred to as **applied research**, and focus groups constitute one of the most commonly used methods in 'applied' settings. Such groups have, for example, proven especially valuable in designing election campaigns because they help campaign managers identify voters' most powerful concerns, thus enabling managers to get a feel for the ways that different appeals will be interpreted by voters.

Planning and conducting focus groups

Once researchers have decided that focus groups are an appropriate method to use in a given study, they will confront several basic choices in planning and conducting the focus group sessions. We can explore these choices as responses to a series of questions.

The role of goals

The first step is to determine exactly what is to be learned from the focus groups. Objectives can range from the very general to the very specific. A relatively general goal might be 'to gain insight into the impact of a localised environmental hazard on the lives of residents in order to formulate hypotheses about what determines how residents respond to the hazard'. A more specific goal might be 'to find out which of five possible sources of information about the hazard citizens are most likely to trust in order to devise a plan for conveying believable information to the public'.

It is only when you are clear about what you hope to learn that you will know what to listen for in the focus group discussions. From a practical standpoint there are at least three reasons to identify goals as clearly as possible:

1 The goals will affect *the selection of participants and composition of groups*. If, for instance, you wanted to find out how the controversies surrounding a local environmental hazard had affected social relations within the community, you would want to be sure to include in the groups people on both sides of any issues. The statement of goals should help researchers identify important characteristics to be considered in recruiting participants and assigning them to groups.

2 The goals will influence *the degree of moderator involvement*. Some goals will require that members of the focus group perform a task while others do not. You may, for example, want the group to reach a formal consensus, solve a hypothetical problem, or make a recommendation about how to address some issue. If so, you will need to have the moderator be more active in guiding the discussion to be sure that the task is completed. If the goals are very general, moderator involvement can be minimised. Selecting goals is therefore the first step in the planning of focus group sessions and the instructing of the moderator.

3 The goals will direct *the development of a 'guide' for the moderator*. Even in largely unstructured focus groups, researchers will want the moderator to have a **guide** which sets forth some rules for the discussion and provides a very general outline of how the session should proceed in order to be sure that all of the important points are raised and addressed. A focus group guide is not as detailed as an interview schedule in survey research or even an observational schedule in direct observation. Each guide will be different and will reflect the objectives of the study. Most will cue the moderator to step in at appropriate times to move the discussion along or bring it back to the main issue if it strays too far. Most guides list the main points to be addressed in some appropriate order, suggest phrases to use in making the transition from one subtopic to another, and may even set time limits for the discussion of subtopics or lay out procedures to be used in performing tasks (for example, 'Have the group break into three subgroups of equal size . . . ').

Choosing how many sessions

It is almost always necessary to conduct more than one focus group session to rule out the possibility that there was something atypical about the participants or the group dynamic that developed in any one group. If similar patterns appear in more than one group, we can have more confidence that those patterns accurately reflect reality. Since two groups may give exactly opposite impressions or reach opposing conclusions, many practitioners consider *three* to be the minimum number of group sessions that should be held. Two other considerations, however, will weigh heavily in the choice of the number of sessions.

First, on the substantive side, your research objectives may dictate that you hold separate sessions for different subgroups within a general population or in different geographic locations. In the environmental contamination example, you may want to have separate sessions for citizens who choose to move away and for those who will stay in the contaminated community, or you may want to hold groups in various towns facing different types of environmental hazards so you can compare the groups' reactions. You would need to hold several sessions *for each subgroup* to have confidence in the results. These design considerations may dictate a larger minimum number of sessions.

Second, from a practical standpoint, focus groups are expensive and time-consuming to plan, arrange, conduct and analyse. The amount of time and money and the number of personnel available for the project may impose a limit on the number of sessions that can be held. The costs of *each* focus group session generally vary from £1,000 to £3,000 depending on such variables as whether a professional firm is hired to conduct the sessions, how much money participants must be paid, how transcription is done and transportation costs.

Choosing an appropriate number of participants

Experience has shown that focus groups rarely work well with fewer than six or more than ten participants. With smaller numbers of participants, especially strong personalities tend to exert too much influence on the outcomes, and individuals may feel too much pressure to carry a share of the conversation. With larger numbers, it is both difficult to give all members enough time to express their thoughts and hard to keep the discussion focused.

Again, the time and money available for the project will play some role in determining how many participants to include, given the decision to hold a certain number of sessions. One reason this is true is that it is frequently necessary to pay participants. The appropriate fee varies with the prevailing wage scale in a given area and with the characteristics of the participants. A group of, say, physicians or business executives may require far higher compensation than those who earn less. Occasionally, people can be persuaded to volunteer their time if the purpose of the research is one they value or if the sponsor of the research is one that commands respect and support. Local public health officials, for example, may be willing to take part in a study sponsored by their professional association and conducted for the purpose of improving public health services in the community.

Selecting participants

Once the number of participants has been determined, the task of recruiting them begins. The first issue here is what kind of people you want to attract. The key is that you want people who are typical of the population group under study. Depending on the focus of the study, you may be able to work from a telephone book if any of the residents of a given community will do, or you may need more specialised lists of people such as welfare recipients, public school teachers or members of local civic organisations. Once you have a list to work from, it is common to conduct a **screening interview** to determine whether specific individuals are suited for the study and are willing to take part. This is usually done by phone and followed with a written invitation and a follow-up call to confirm prospective participants' acceptance.

In the recruiting process, researchers must be alert to several additional issues. First, there is a tendency for people with unusually strong feelings about a subject to be more willing to participate than those with less emotional involvement in the issue. To keep this from distorting results, researchers should make a conscious effort to recruit some people with little initial interest in the subject. Second, unless friendship ties, work relationships or family roles are a specific part of the research focus, it is usually better to recruit people who do not know one another. Strangers are usually less inhibited in their responses. Finally, researchers need to consider the effects of placing people who have different *social roles* in the same focus group. If the topic to be discussed relates to the expectations and interests associated with different social roles, participants in 'mixed' groups may change their behaviour as a result. Generally, it is unwise to put into the same focus group people with significantly different but interacting roles (like managers and workers or regulatory agency officials and members of the regulated industry) if those roles are relevant to the topic of the discussion. Unless interaction between people in different social roles is specifically part of the research objectives, it is better to select *relatively homogeneous groups* in order to have a sufficient basis for communication among the participants.

Selecting a physical setting

Since the main product of a focus group session is a transcript of what was said, it is important to arrange a high-quality audio recording of the event for later transcription. Audio equipment should be tested in advance to be sure it picks up comments from all positions in the room, and the moderator should have a backup system on hand in case the primary recording equipment fails. In some cases, it may also be desirable to videotape the sessions in order to capture the nonverbal communication that may occur. This advantage has to be weighed against the possibility that video cameras may make respondents self-conscious and that hidden cameras can seldom be positioned properly so as to pick up all the action.

In any case, it is important both to tell participants they are being recorded and to get their permission. Professional ethics require that such recordings and any transcripts made from them be kept strictly confidential by the project staff and not be used for any purpose beyond the research.

Focus groups are best conducted in a room large enough to allow participants to sit around a single table (or at least in a circle) but small enough to feel intimate. The room should be furnished and decorated in a manner that puts people at ease. Sometimes researchers want to observe the sessions in person and need a place to sit to the side. Other times they may not want to be seen and thus need a room with a one-way glass so they can observe without affecting the dynamics of the group. Actual discussions usually last about one and a half hours, but it is wise to allow two hours per session in case participants are late arriving, technical problems arise or the discussion simply runs longer than anticipated.

Working with the moderator

No single factor is more important to the success of a focus group than the competence of the moderator. The moderator is responsible for putting participants at ease, ensuring that all relevant topics are covered in the discussion, keeping more aggressive speakers from dominating the conversation, and helping to characterise the results of the session in a set of notes for the researchers. Accordingly, it is important to hire an experienced and skilled moderator if the budget allows or to invest substantial time in training someone to serve as moderator if an experienced one cannot be hired. It is generally unwise for a researcher to serve as the moderator because a researcher may unintentionally bias the results.

Moderators should share enough characteristics with focus group participants to help participants feel free to talk and to understand well enough what they *mean* by their remarks so as to respond properly. This is especially true with distinctive groups (for example, farmers, unemployed industrial workers or female state legislators) and when the topic is one that touches on tensions between social groups.

An *assistant moderator* is almost always necessary. The assistant sits to the side and takes more detailed notes on the session than the moderator can take while interacting with the participants. The assistant may handle mechanical tasks such as greeting participants when they first arrive or distributing any written materials to be used in the session. Assistants can also serve as a backup since they often are familiar enough with the focus group process to step in if for some reason the moderator cannot attend a session. The assistant's most important function, however, may be to serve as a check on the moderator's perception of the sessions. The assistant works with the moderator in writing up an accurate set of notes after the session. If the two disagree on an event, both opinions should be included in the notes for the researcher to consider.

Once moderators are hired or trained, they must be instructed. As explained earlier, much of the moderator's role is dictated by the objectives of the project and outlined in the focus group guide.

Even in those cases when moderators are expected to take a fairly active role in moving the discussion along, it is vital that they do not influence the outcome. Doing this requires that they strike the proper balance between empathy and detachment, being accepting of all opinions expressed but not rewarding any particular type of statement. The emphasis must be on *having the participants express their opinions.*

At the end of the session, the moderator should write up a set of **field notes** summarising themes or conclusions that emerged from the discussion, and pointing out any facts about the session that might influence the researcher's interpretation of the transcript. The moderator might note such issues as a high level of tension in the group, the exceptional influence of one or more participants over the group, or an apparent reluctance of some participants to express opinions. Moderators might also compare the results of different sessions they have conducted.

This raises the issue of whether to use *one or more than one main moderator.* Using the same moderator for all sessions offers more consistency in the way the sessions are run and provides a better basis for comparing sessions. It also allows a moderator to develop some insight into the topic and may help a moderator to anticipate problems and do a better job of running sessions subsequent to the first one or two.

However, researchers may want to use more than one moderator in several circumstances. One is the situation in which very different social groups are represented in different sessions and it is necessary to use different moderators to match participants' characteristics. For instance, if race relations is the topic and groups are racially homogeneous, it would be wise to select a moderator of the same race as the participants in each session. A second situation that calls for more than one moderator is one in which researchers want the results of each session or group of sessions to be totally independent of each other and there is some fear that a moderator might influence the outcomes on the basis of expectations developed in early sessions. Finally, logistical considerations such as geographically separated research sites or the need to conduct several sessions at once in order to meet a deadline or avoid 'contamination' of the groups by news reports appearing between sessions might dictate the need for multiple moderators.

Conducting sessions

Focus group meetings usually open with the moderator explaining the general purpose and the ground rules for the discussion. This is commonly followed by an opening statement by each participant. Such statements usually tell a few basic facts about the individual. Having each person speak helps participants feel as if they have been introduced and makes the discussion more relaxed. It also encourages less outgoing individuals to speak up later in the session. The key objective of the opening moments of a session is to make it clear that the moderator wants to hear each member's story in their own words and that the purpose of the exercise is for the moderator and the session's sponsors to learn from the participants. Thereafter, the moderator should ask general questions like, 'How do you feel about X?' 'Has anyone had any experience with Y?' and 'Does anyone want to respond to that?' This keeps things focused and moving. Most of the discussion will involve the participants reacting to one another.

One variation on this procedure is to ask participants to complete a questionnaire before and/or after the session. Such questionnaires can be used to gather background information on the participants that might not be evident from the discussion, but that influences interpretation of participants' comments. They also show how participants' views changed as a result of the focus group discussion if the same questions are asked both before and after the session. Finally, they elicit from participants their assessments of the focus group process in order to improve the running of subsequent sessions. Pre-session questionnaires must be very carefully constructed so as not to influence the direction of the session by asking questions that suggest positions on issues or set up expectations about how the session will go. As a result, pre-session questionnaires should be used only if the benefits outweigh any threat of distorting the results of the sessions.

Analysing focus group results

As a qualitative method, focus groups do not produce numerical data that can be analysed using statistics to identify patterns and relationships. Focus groups produce a very large volume of verbal data in the form of transcripts, recordings of sessions and moderators' field notes. The tasks of reducing all of this information to a readable summary and of drawing some justifiable conclusions from it can be daunting. We can provide no step-by-step guide for focus group analysis both because there is so much variation in project objectives and focus group procedures and because qualitative analysis relies heavily on insight and creativity. We can, however, suggest some general guidelines that will help you recognise a good analysis.

The first principle of focus group analysis is that researchers should always begin with a clear picture of what they hope to learn from the data. This step should have been taken in the identification of the purpose for the study as the first step in designing the project. Returning to that objective helps identify relevant information from the sessions and eliminate marginal information. It provides a benchmark as to how detailed the analysis must be. For example, if the purpose was largely descriptive (such as finding out what terms ordinary people use to discuss some political issue), only a summary may be needed. If the purpose was more analytical (such as determining why people were opposed to nuclear power), the analysis would have to be much more complex, and certain subtle features of the discussions might take on importance.

Once the objective has been established, researchers face the task of organising the data for analysis. One approach is to read through the transcripts and literally cut out sections addressing specific topics. Researchers can then physically reassemble the sections so that all the comments relevant to a given subtopic are together. This approach can help reveal themes more clearly and can reduce the volume of data to be considered at any one time. It must be done skilfully to avoid taking comments out of their context and, thereby, concealing their *actual meaning*.

In analytical studies, it is especially important to listen to the recordings of the sessions in order to be sure that the context of members' comments is taken into account and their *meaning* understood. Transcripts can be produced so as to reflect some of the subtle texture of oral communication by means of certain conventions such as typing in all capitals those words that speakers stressed or putting interpretive comments in parentheses. For example: 'Oh, I *never* believe what *my* mayor says' (*laughing*). However, even these practices may conceal subtle differences in meaning that only listening to the tape can reveal. Taken in context, for instance, the comment about the mayor may have been sarcastic, indicating that the speaker *does* believe the mayor. Researchers therefore rely on moderators to report significant *nonverbal communication* (body language) that went on in the group and that may influence the interpretation of verbal comments.

One potentially productive approach to interpreting focus group data is to use *content analysis* to help identify themes in the discussions. For example, if focus group participants were asked their reasons for opposing a hazardous waste incinerator, they would probably offer many different answers. A sophisticated content analysis of the transcripts might help by grouping those answers into a smaller set of related arguments that identified themes in the responses and indicated which occurred most often.

In all this, the researcher's job is to form an impression of how the participants felt about the topic and to produce a summary statement of their expressions. The object is not to explain why participants feel as they do in the scientific sense of explanation discussed in Chapters 2 and 6. Analysts might, however, draw on existing theories or their knowledge of the subject in order to offer interpretations of what participants meant by various comments, why participants said what they did in the manner in which they said it, or even how they developed these attitudes. Often the most useful insights derived from analyses of focus group results come from linking what was observed to larger theories or processes in order to highlight the *larger significance* of what was said in the focus groups. For instance, if focus groups reveal that residents of racially divided communities are denying the problem, a researcher may turn to theories of social psychology to interpret those residents' remarks as examples of coping mechanisms.

Reporting focus group results

Reporting focus group results can be as challenging as analysing them. Whereas quantitative data can be reduced to measures of association and presented in tables, it is difficult to reproduce the richness of qualitative data for simple presentation. It is worth putting a good deal of time into meeting this challenge because the report is very important to the success of a project.

Krueger and Casey (2005) suggest that reports perform three primary functions. First, and most obvious, a report communicates to a given audience information about the results of a study. Only if it is easy for the intended audience to understand, and clear in its message, will it actually have an impact on how that audience sees the topic of the study and thereby influence scholarship or public policy. Second, the act of writing a report assists researchers in developing their own personal understanding of a project and the subject it was designed to address. Third, a report provides a usable historical record of the results of a project. Because focus group data are so complex, it is especially important to have a compact summary if the results are ever to be used as background for future studies.

Researchers usually choose among three basic approaches for reporting focus group results:

1 They can *present enough carefully selected quotations* from the participants to convey an accurate picture of the discussions. This amounts to providing a representative sampling of what was said so readers can draw their own conclusions.
2 They can *summarise statements* by participants to point out major themes, using quotes only for illustrative purposes. This is a descriptive approach in which researchers assume responsibility for deciding what is important enough to report but also in which they offer little analysis.
3 They can *interpret what was said* so as to provide understanding, using description and quotes only to support their conclusions or illustrate points. Which strategy is appropriate depends on the purpose of the focus group project and the nature of the intended audience for the report.

To know what kind of report is called for, researchers must ask who will receive it and what use will be made of it. To understand the significance of this, recall the list of conditions under which focus groups are useful that was presented earlier in this chapter. If the focus groups were used to supplement another data collection technique, then the primary users of the report will be the researchers themselves. They will use understandings gained from the focus groups to formulate hypotheses, develop indicators or assess their interpretation of data gathered by other means. Others may never see any more about the focus groups than a brief statement in a subsequent report to the effect that focus groups were used to frame the research question, design the project or verify interpretations. In those cases, the report on the focus group results may be closer to the representative sampling of quotes just described, because the intended audience has the capability to draw informed conclusions from raw data.

If the focus groups were used to evaluate some aspect of public policy, assist in policy development or design a campaign strategy, the audience for the report is likely to be persons who are less interested in the details of the sessions and more interested in the lessons to be learned from them.

Such persons are, however, still also likely to want a strong sense of the thrust of the sessions. In this case, the report will probably rely heavily on summarised statements and a description of the key themes. Finally, if focus groups were used as a primary source of data collection (as in a study of small-group dynamics) and the results will appear in an academic publication, the report will have to be briefer and will have to stress interpretation of the sessions.

Ethical considerations

Ethical considerations for focus groups are basically the same as for the other methods of social research mentioned in this book. For example, researchers must ensure that all participants are fully informed about the purpose of the focus group session and that the research procedures do not harm participants physically or psychologically. Participants should also be aware that they cannot be pressured to speak during the group sessions and that they may decline to answer any questions with which they are not comfortable. Most importantly, all participants must know that their identity and responses will be kept strictly confidential and that the final transcripts and reports will not identify participants or anyone mentioned during the group sessions.

Of course, assuring confidentiality in focus groups is somewhat problematic because once something is said during a group session, it is instantly known to everyone else in the group. For that reason, at the beginning of each session your moderator needs to encourage participants to keep confidential what they hear or learn during the group session. In order to ensure complete understanding of and agreement with these ethical principles, you should require a signed consent form from all focus group participants.

At the conclusion of your focus group session, you will have a short 'debriefing' component, which should provide a short explanation of the purpose of the session and a quick summary of what has been discussed. This will allow participants to talk about their reactions to the research topic and the conversations in which they have participated, and allow you, the researcher, to reiterate the confidential nature of the focus group conversation.

Finally, focus groups are very limited in academic and practical value. They may provide an insight into a limited set of issues, but focus groups suffer many disadvantages. They are carried out in an artifical environment which may not reflect how ideas are perceived in more natural settings. They are also limited by the small size of the samples involved. They can also be overused. In its early days between 1997 and 2000, Tony Blair's New Labour government was accused of being overly reliant on focus groups to test and determine policy. Without a clear sense of purpose and sense of perspective as to the limitations of focus groups, the result of such studies can be misleading and unhelpful to researchers and policy makers alike.

Conclusion

We want to highlight the point we made at the outset of this chapter. Focus groups can make a contribution at several stages of the research process. Not only can they serve as the primary data collection method for more qualitative studies, but they can also be integrated with quantitative methods. In the early stages of research, they can help clarify research questions or suggest new approaches to old problems. Once under way, they can help design measuring instruments to be used in interviews or direct observation. In the analysis stage, focus groups can improve our interpretation of quantitative data by shedding light on the meanings people attach to responses or actions. They have limitations, however, which should not be ignored, and must always be used selectively and wisely.

Summary points

- Focus group methodologies are a form of qualitative research that relies on brief but intense observation of carefully selected small groups of people to gain insights into social phenomena.
- Focus groups are especially appropriate for studying new subjects and for formulating new theories. Additionally, this method may provide insights that more structured methods cannot, as well as allowing researchers to explore people's thinking in detail.
- Focus groups are not statistically representative of larger populations, and produce data that must be analysed subjectively.
- Focus groups are brought together in a room and guided through a recorded discussion of a subject by a trained moderator. The transcripts and other records of focus groups are analysed, along with the report of the moderator, by researchers seeking to identify patterns, themes and new insights.
- Focus group methodologies can be used to develop research designs using other methods and to verify the results of studies done with other methods.

Suggested reading and examples

Research examples

Manheim's (2005) *Strategic Public Diplomacy & American Foreign Policy* illustrates the use of focus groups in politics by providing an account of their use to design the presentation to the American public of the George H. W. Bush administration's rationale for US involvement in the first Gulf War. Bates (2005), on the other hand, uses twenty-five focus groups to investigate how the news and entertainment media affect the public's understanding of genetics.

The novel idea that online focus groups might one day replace or supplement traditional face-to-face focus groups is pursued in a study by Price, Nir and Cappella (2006), who investigate the impact of such online group discussions on people's willingness to express their opinions during the 2000 presidential election campaign.

Methodological reading

Two general introductions to focus group methods are Edmunds' (2000) *Focus Group Research Handbook* and Bader and Rossi's (2002) *Focus Groups: A Step-by-Step Guide*. Three books that explain the use of focus groups in social science research are *Focus Groups in Social Research* (Bloor *et al.* 2001), *Using Focus Groups in Research* (Litosseliti 2003) and *Focus Groups: A Practical Guide for Applied Research* (Krueger and Casey 2005).

References

Bader, Gloria E. and Rossi, Catherine A. 2002. *Focus Groups: A Step-by-Step Guide*, 3rd edn. San Diego, CA: The Bader Group.

Bates, Benjamin R. 2005. 'Public culture and public understanding of genetics: a focus group study'. *Public Understanding of Science*, vol. 14, no. 1, pp. 47–65.

Bloor, Michael, Frankland, Jane, Thomas, Michelle and Stewart, Kate. 2001. *Focus Groups in Social Research*. Thousand Oaks, CA: Sage.

Edmunds, Holly. 2000. *Focus Group Research Handbook*. New York: McGraw-Hill.

Krueger, Richard and Casey, Mary Anne. 2005. *Focus Groups: A Practical Guide for Applied Research*, 3rd edn. Thousand Oaks, CA: Sage.

Litosseliti, Lia. 2003. *Using Focus Groups in Research*. London: Continuum International Publishing Group.

Manheim, Jarol B. 2005. *Strategic Public Diplomacy and American Foreign Policy*. New York: Oxford University Press.

Price, Vincent, Nir, Lilach and Cappella, Joseph N. 2006. 'Normative and informational influences in online political discussions'. *Communication Theory*, vol. 16, no. 1, pp. 47–74.

Research exercises

Note: Before conducting any of these exercises, ensure with your instructor's assistance that your university's research committee will authorise a waiver for this type of educational illustration of human subject research.

1 Much attention has recently been focused on the idea that the words we use to discuss people and events reflect our attitudes about the subjects of those discussions and help determine the status of those people and events in society. By that reasoning, means of expression are political and can be judged as more or less consistent with some set of values and, therefore, as 'correct' or 'incorrect'.

   Some commentators are worried that political correctness is being so strongly enforced that it threatens to stifle meaningful discussion of ideas, especially on university campuses. Others argue that there is no such danger and that advocates of 'politically correct' language are simply calling attention to the biases inherent in much of what has come to be accepted as everyday speech. Who is right?

   Form teams within your class to conduct a focus group to learn how university students perceive and are affected by the issue of 'political correctness'. First, write a statement of objectives for a focus group, stating what you hope to learn about political correctness from the group. Develop a 'guide' to the focused discussion, in which you identify some questions about political correctness that you want explored in a focus group composed of university students. You may want to know, for example, whether students are even aware of the issues raised by the idea of political correctness, whether they are receptive or hostile to the idea of politically correct language, whether they feel pressured to be politically correct, or how political correctness might be enforced (if at all) in their social circles. Then devise a set of standards by which you would select participants for such a focus group.

   Recruit six to ten students who are not in your research methods class to take part in the group. Conduct the group using one of your team as the moderator and having the other members observe and take notes. Video-record the session if possible. After the group leaves, go over the notes as a team, come to an agreement about what was observed and write a summary of the session. Analyse the discussion and ask yourself if it offered answers to the questions around which you designed the focus group.

   Ideally, you can divide your entire class into several teams, have all the teams conduct focus groups with different students and then compare results at the end to see how input from several groups may change the conclusions drawn from one group alone.

2 This exercise shows how focus groups can be used to enrich the information gathered through other means. It is also best done by a team.

Part A

Draw on what you learned from Exercise 1 above and from Chapter 8 on survey research to devise a brief questionnaire designed to measure people's opinions about *political correctness*. Write an explanation of the ways in which the things you learned in Exercise 1 influenced the questions you chose and the way you phrased those questions.

Part B
Administer the questionnaire to at least ten students from diverse backgrounds. Total the responses and look for simple patterns (for example, different answers from men and women or from people studying different subjects). Shortly after that, get at least six of those students to participate in a focus group that will review their reactions to the questionnaire. Try to find out what they thought was being asked with each question, how they chose their answer, what other issues they felt each question was related to and how responding to the questionnaire made them feel. Review the notes from this focus group and make a list of all the things that surprised you – things that were revealed by the focus group that you had not thought of when you devised the questionnaire or that might affect your interpretation of the responses you received.

Key terms

applied research	focus group	moderator
field notes	guide	screening interview

21 Direct observation and political ethnography

- When might researchers need to observe political events directly as they occur?
- Can this be accomplished with validity and rigour?
- What are the advantages and limitations of direct observation?
- What ethical issues are posed by direct observation and how might they be addressed?

Introduction

In the other data collection techniques we have discussed in this text, researchers must rely to some degree on others' experience with the political events they are seeking to understand. For example, with aggregate data, we usually rely on information collected by public or private agencies to represent the events we are studying; we do not actually observe coups, agricultural production, the distribution of income or any of the other phenomena represented by the figures with which we work. Even when conducting surveys, we are relying on respondents' memories of their experiences or perceptions of their surroundings – we do not actually observe their actions nor the setting in which those actions occurred. Although there is a great deal to be learned through these data collection methods, there are times when researchers need to see and hear events for themselves in order to gain a full understanding of them.

New phenomena may best be studied directly. For example, the alternative political parties that developed in the former communist states of eastern Europe in the 1990s were a new phenomenon: political parties seeking to gain power through elections in previously nondemocratic Soviet bloc nations. To understand their functioning, we could try to apply theories of political party behaviour that have been developed by observation of parties in democratic nations of the West. However, there are good reasons to suspect that these new parties will operate according to very different rules because they exist in a dramatically different context from, say, Canadian or French political parties. To formulate theories about their operation, we may need to observe them firsthand.

A second situation calling for direct contact with the subject of research is one in which we cannot be confident of the usefulness of others' reports of some ongoing behaviour. In some cases, even though we could interview participants in the events that interest us, we may feel they would be unable to give us the understanding we need because they do not share our conceptual framework. We might, for instance, be looking for the effects of institutionalised ideology on the decisions of US embassy personnel in handling requests for political asylum. If we ask the officials how they make decisions, they will quite sincerely cite the written rules they follow. If we see for ourselves the procedures followed, however, we might be able to identify unofficial ideological criteria at work.

Another situation in which we might not be willing to rely on others' accounts of events is one in which those who can supply the information might have an interest in misleading us. Estate agents, for example, would have legal and professional reasons for giving the impression that they always comply with equal housing opportunity laws even if they knew that some practices often did not satisfy the requirements of such legislation.

In these and other circumstances, researchers may need to turn to **direct observation** or, as it is sometimes called, **political ethnography**. When we collect data through personal contact with the organisations and events, we are studying *as they unfold naturally*, we are employing direct observation.

Direct observation/political ethnography as a research method

Political ethnology originated in anthropology, has been widely used by sociologists and has spread to education research and management studies. Political anthropologists and political sociologists are most likely to use this method, but it is easy to forget that two of the classics of political research were based on a similar approach. Robert Dahl's study of local government in New Haven, Connecticut, *Who Governs?* (1961), used interviews and observational methods to argue that 'pluralism' – the situation where competition for influence means that no one group dominates – characterises democratic decision making. His work is seen as a response to Floyd Hunter's (1953) *Community Power Structure* which argued that even nominally democratic Atlanta, Georgia was effectively ruled by a political elite. The debate between elite theory and pluralism has raged ever since. Both of these works relied on both interviews and direct observation. Hunter's method of asking interviewees for their views of the power structure also allowed him to use the data to construct an understanding of power hierarchies. Such approaches are not unlike direct observation and political ethnography.

Direct observation and political ethnography are most appropriate to small-scale political environments. However, these can reveal patterns of interaction which are replicated in various forms across a political system. For example, Gerald Curtis followed a candidate during his election campaign for the Japanese parliament and his analysis, *Election Campaigning Japanese Style* (1971), became required reading for anyone studying Japanese party organisation. His observations depicted a pattern of electoral and constituency organisation which, while unknown in the political research literature, accurately described key features of Japanese party organisation across Japan. This use of the technique in Japan might suggest that the method is only appropriate for 'exotic' non-Western cultures, but it has also been used by Richard Fenno Jr to discuss how US Congressmembers interact with constituents and interest groups in their home district. Such research is part of any good research programme and is not limited to 'exotic' cultures or the political margins.

Direct observation and political ethnology can provide insights into the richer context in which political decisions are made and political acts are carried out. It is not impossible for such research to be used for model testing or refining case studies, but political ethnology promises more than that. It can pick up hidden relationships, adaptations and inconsistencies. When done well, it enables the researcher to be open to new models and modes of thinking. Political ethnography claims to be more holistic and phenomenological than quantitative approaches to politics in that it argues that it does not reduce data produced by political life to simple discrete categories. That is, it is not reductive. Ethnography has a more flexible notion of categories that permits the emergence of new concepts or provides fresh insights into patterns of interaction behind existing categories. It reveals that unexamined, but often 'natural', behaviour has deeper meaning and significance than obvious at first glance. Geertz (1973) has called the method 'thick description' but it might be more accurately considered 'thick or rich with meaning'.

Direct observation and political ethnology can also complement and extend other types of research, even if it also has distinct attributes. For example, interviews with politicians can be complemented with ethnographic research to determine whether their behaviour is consistent with espoused views.

These methods are particularly useful for studying organisations and institutions, such as interest groups, political parties and government agencies, and the focus of such studies can range from elite bureaucrats to extremist groups. Direct observation may even be better than conventional methods for research into subjects that are difficult to examine openly such as corruption, racism, political alienation and other areas where transparency is a problem.

Despite its rich potential for providing insight, the use of direct observation is relatively uncommon in political research. One reason for this is that many of the subjects of academic political research are too large in scale to allow direct observation. Elections, for example, happen all over a nation simultaneously and therefore cannot be physically observed directly as complete events. Individual researchers must rely on indirect observation for an overview of large events.

A second reason for the infrequent use of direct observation in political science is that we often do not have access to events that could be fruitfully studied using this method. Spontaneous popular uprisings, for example, such as those that unseated the Milošević government in Serbia in 2000, occur too rapidly to allow us to plan a research project. Similarly, even ongoing phenomena may be inaccessible to us, for instance, we would be unlikely to get permission to observe the White House staff making national security decisions.

A third set of reasons why we do not see more use of direct observation relates to the nature of the method. First, it is usually a very time-consuming technique that may take months or even years to produce results and can be quite expensive to carry out. Second, it often demands a great deal of the researcher, who may have to become immersed in the study to the exclusion of other activities, and it can seldom be carried out by assistants.

There are at least five reasons why these concerns should not deter politics researchers from using direct observation under the right conditions.

1   Research has different purposes at different stages of the study of a topic and, as discussed in Chapters 1 and 5, the requirements differ with the purpose of research. Direct observation is especially well suited to the exploratory and descriptive stages of research, when we are seeking to *develop* theories rather than to test them, or to test the micro-foundations of political relationships. Descriptive research can be crucial to the research process in that it can provide an accurate picture of how a social or political process unfolds. A description of how relationships unfold in small-scale environments can serve as a foundation for using inductive logic to devise testable theories. When used at the proper stage of the research process, direct observation is not only adequate to the task but often far superior to other methods of data collection.

2   Many of the fears about subjectivity in reporting results can be overcome by proper execution of direct observation. If researchers follow correct procedures in making and recording observations, it is possible for others to verify their conclusions or at least judge the degree of confidence that should be placed in them.

3   Qualitative data can be analysed rigorously and objectively if the analyst employs the right techniques. The fact that direct observation may produce primarily qualitative data need not be taken as a major limitation in terms of its applicability.

4   Under the right conditions and with the right approach, direct observation can be used to *test* theories and should not be ruled out as a potential data-gathering technique in explanatory research.

5   Against any of the limitations associated with the method, we must weigh the fact that direct observation has the distinct advantage of providing a very high level of *external validity* for our research. Because we observe *actual behaviour* (not oral reports, written accounts or simulations of it) and observe it *in the context in which it naturally occurs*, we can obtain a realistic view of events and can get highly valid measures of our concepts. Moreover, in some types of direct observation, *reactivity may be less of a problem than with more obvious data-gathering techniques, such as surveys.*

In the rest of this chapter, we explore the potential of direct observation and suggest some methods for using it to its full potential.

Degree of obtrusiveness

Direct observation can take several forms. First, we can distinguish between *obtrusive* and *unobtrusive* approaches. **Obtrusive research** occurs any time the persons being studied are aware of being observed. It always carries some risk of provoking reactivity and, thus, producing at least partially invalid results. In **unobtrusive research**, subjects are unaware of being observed and, therefore, unlikely to alter their natural behaviours in response to the research itself. This has the advantage of increasing the chances of obtaining valid data.

Obtrusive observation

In *obtrusive* observation, the researchers or trained assistants request permission to observe subjects and are identified as observers at the time of the data collection. An example of this approach is the case in which an investigator attends meetings of a committee of a local council and observes its decision-making processes. Committee members are aware of the observer and know the general purpose of the study.

Unobtrusive observation

In *unobtrusive* observation, whether the researcher is concealed from those being studied or visible to them, the purpose of the observation is unknown to the subjects of the study. In the first type of study, the observer might be concealed from view or might use a hidden camera. An example would be a project in which the researcher is given permission to study the behaviour of public personnel by observing the interaction of welfare clients and welfare agency caseworkers from behind a two-way mirror when neither the caseworkers nor the clients know they are being observed. In the second type, the observer may be in full view, but the purpose of the study is concealed. There are two versions of this type of unobtrusive observation.

The first is **passive observation**. It can be exemplified by a case in which a researcher attends all public meetings of a city council and openly sits with other citizens in the audience but carefully watches the debate to analyse patterns of influence on the council *without the knowledge of the council members*. A second form of unobtrusive observation is known as *participant observation*. When researchers actually become part of the events under study, they are engaging in **participant observation**. The researcher studying a given political organisation who joined that group as any other citizen might, attended its meetings, served on its committees, took part in its fund-raising efforts, voted on its policies and otherwise acted as a member *without the other members of the organisation knowing that they were being observed as part of a study* would be using unobtrusive participant observation.

The obvious advantage of unobtrusive observation is that it virtually eliminates the possibility that subjects will alter their behaviour in reaction to being studied so that it can yield highly valid information. However, unobtrusive observations can be very difficult to arrange and conduct and, as we discuss later in this chapter, often pose serious ethical questions for the scholar.

Degree of structure

A second division among approaches to direct observation is made between *structured* and *unstructured studies*. This distinction is made on the basis of the degree to which the researcher organises or *structures* the process of observation by imposing a preconceived set of concepts and categories.

Structured observation

In a **structured observation**, we use our understanding of the events under scrutiny to construct an **observation protocol** to guide the observer. The protocol tells the observer what to look for, the order in which to make observations and the way to record the results. This approach is especially suitable for obtaining accurate descriptions of events.

As an illustration, we might want to study the ways in which members of parliament use debate on the floor of the House of Commons to gain support from interest groups and constituents. If we have a strong enough theory of how this is done, a checksheet could be developed listing the techniques that we expect to be used. We could then observe floor debates and use the checksheet to record whether or not each MP used the given techniques to send messages to potential supporters. The protocol would restrict our attention to a limited range of what was happening when MPs made public statements, but would provide more objective data than a survey and would facilitate comparisons of the behaviour of different House members.

Unstructured observation

By contrast, if we were in an earlier stage of our study of this subject, we might be unwilling to restrict our observations to a list of items on a protocol. Such a situation would call for the use of **unstructured observation**, in which we attempt to pay attention to all that goes on in a debate, take careful notes and then analyse those notes in an effort to discover patterns that can provide a basis for theorising about how MPs use floor debate to influence potential supporters.

Structured and unstructured observation can be combined in a single research project. In fact, it is quite common for researchers using direct observation to mix the two approaches. A study may start with unstructured observation to gain a broad understanding of an event and formulate concepts with which to analyse it. The researcher may then use these insights to structure subsequent observations of the same phenomenon in order to test the utility of the conceptualisations. Alternatively, the two approaches may be combined by structuring portions of the observational task while leaving other parts unstructured.

It is important to recognise that the distinction between structured and unstructured observations is *not* a true dichotomy, with 'pure' types of observation on either side. It is a continuum ranging from the least structured to the most structured methods of observation. Even the least formally structured observation involves an element of structure in that the researcher approaches the task with a set of questions about the event under study and with perceptions of how the event might work. Similarly, even in a highly structured observation, an alert researcher often notices unexpected qualities of the phenomena under study and may learn more than what is anticipated by the observation protocol. In this sense, the two approaches to observation are almost always blended to some degree.

We can offer some guidelines for the effective use of structured and unstructured techniques in both obtrusive and unobtrusive research.

Techniques of unstructured observation

Unstructured observation is used to develop a full understanding of the behaviours and relationships under study. It requires that investigators be open to discovering new dimensions to the behaviour and willing to devise new ways of thinking about the topic. Observers are seeking to be taught by the world and want to get as close to the reality of the events as possible without being so constrained by preconceived notions of how things work that they overlook some important patterns.

The procedure for unstructured observation begins with identifying the set of behaviours that have to be observed in order to acquire a full understanding of the events in question. Refining the research question so that it provides a better guide to observation may require doing some background reading, talking with others who have had contact with the subject and engaging in some very preliminary theorising about what processes might be at work.

Next, the researcher needs to gain access to the subjects for purposes of observation. How this is done depends on whether the researcher is using obtrusive or unobtrusive methods, and varies with the details of the project. It can be one of the most challenging portions of the work. Clearly, some subjects will be less willing to be observed than others, and most subjects will find some objectives in the study to be more acceptable than others. For example, revolutionaries conducting a guerrilla war will not be open to outsiders under almost any circumstances. By contrast, bureaucrats who may be willing to cooperate with research described as 'a study of chains of command in public agencies' may be quite unwilling to participate in 'a study of corruption in the management of public agencies'.

This early step in the research process may very well present an ethical dilemma: Do you tell people they are being observed and, if so, do you tell them the real purpose of the study, even if doing so risks losing their cooperation or at least creating a serious problem of reactivity? We address this and other ethical issues of direct observation later in this chapter. For now, assume that the ethical questions are resolved in favour of taking an obtrusive approach so that we can move to the third stage in the process.

The primary activity here is to observe and take careful notes on all that is seen and heard. The *written record of observations* is referred to as **field notes**. Although field notes are not as structured as interview notes, there are definite general rules for the proper taking of field notes.

1 You should *clearly define the objectives of the research* so that you know what you want to learn about the events under observation. From that you can develop a list of the types of things you are looking for, in order to focus your attention on those features of the events that are most important to observe. Having such a list is not inconsistent with keeping an open mind and being willing to change your focus as you gain a better understanding of the behaviours in question. It merely simplifies the task of reducing all that you will observe to a manageable number of entries for your notes.

This list will be nothing more than a set of broad categories of information you hope to obtain about the events observed. For example, in observing meetings of opposing teams of negotiators who represented two sides of a civil war, you might want to note such things as (1) how often each side initiates proposals; (2) how eager each side seems to be to continue the talks as opposed to breaking them off; (3) how willing each side is to make concessions; and (4) whether each negotiating team is united or seems divided into factions. As you learn more about the process, you will want to refine these broad, overlapping categories into a more focused list of things to note, with each observation building on what you learned in the prior one.

2 *Avoid taking detailed notes in the presence of those who are being observed.* The primary reason for this is that open note-taking can make your subjects even more aware of your presence and cause them to alter their normal behaviour. Your objective is to put the subjects so at ease that they act exactly as they would if you were not present. This requires developing the skill of making *mental notes* of all that you see that is relevant to the study so that you can write up detailed notes later. This

is a difficult task, so prior to going into the field, it is wise to practise mental note-taking by observing activities similar to those you are to study and then trying to re-create the events on paper later. If the practice subjects agree and you have the necessary equipment and setting, you can check on your accuracy by recording or filming the events observed and comparing the recordings of the events with the impressions conveyed by your field notes.

Though you should not take detailed notes in the presence of subjects, it is sometimes possible to keep a small note pad concealed so you can inconspicuously jot down keywords or phrases that will later serve to jog your memory of events when writing up field notes.

3 *Always write up field notes as soon as possible after actual observation* so that your memory of the events is clear. This is often difficult, because you may be tired at the end of several hours of observations and there may not be a convenient place to sit to write your notes. However, it is *essential* that you find a way to get the observations on paper as soon as possible so that you have a detailed and accurate record. Some investigators expedite this process by using a tape recorder to record their field notes verbally and then transcribe them later. If you choose this approach, it is crucial to check the tape immediately to ensure that it worked properly; in that way, you will avoid discovering several days later, when you may find it difficult to re-create them from memory, that notes from an observation session have been lost.

It may take up to half as much time to make notes on observations as it took to actually make the observations, but this is time well spent because *field notes are the foundation of a direct observation project.*

4 *Make field notes as complete and detailed as possible.* Especially in the early stages of a project, it is important to put in almost everything that was observed. Facts that at first seemed unimportant may turn out to be crucial as you acquire a fuller understanding of the topic.

5 *Always distinguish clearly in your notes between descriptions of actual behaviour and your speculation about the meaning or importance of that behaviour.* It should be clear to you, even after your memory of the events has faded, what was actually said and done by the subjects and what you *inferred* from their behaviour at the time.

Because the content of field notes is dictated by the objectives of an individual project, it is difficult to state rules for what to include. In general, however, it is better to include too much than to risk leaving out useful information. Excessive detail in field notes may complicate the task of analysing them, but this problem can be handled. There is no way to remedy the problem of not having information if you failed to put it in at the time of the observation. Remember that one of the major objectives of direct observation is the creation of a complete and accurate description of a political phenomenon. More detail, therefore, is usually preferable to less.

Figure 21.1 provides an example of the kind of information that is recorded in field notes. It presents observations from a hypothetical study of several community organisations in which the investigator is seeking to understand how leaders of these organisations persuade residents of a neighbourhood to join and remain in the group. Note the detail in which events are recorded. Notice also how notes on actual events are set off from interpretations or analysis of those events.

The next stage in the direct observation project is to analyse the field notes. With other methods there is a clear distinction between data collection and data analysis. This is not true of direct observation because the process of making field notes blends both data collection (writing down descriptions of what happened) and analysis (noting your impressions about the reasons for or importance of what happened). *Data analysis begins with the making of field notes.* Moreover, in direct observation, the researcher must *not* wait until all the data are in to begin analysis. It is vital that investigators review field notes from time to time during the period in which they are making observations. The purpose of this is to begin to look for patterns in what has been observed so as to be alert to the most important aspects of events in the next observation session.

Figure 21.1 Example of transcribed field notes from a hypothetical study of community organisations

24 June 2009. Observation of a demonstration by members of the Waterside Neighbourhood Improvement Association to protest the announcement by the city government of plans to open a landfill on some abandoned property in the Waterside neighbourhood.

Background: The Waterside community is composed of large old homes that were left behind as members of the middle class abandoned the terraced houses for detached houses further out from the city centre in the 1950s and 1960s. Today it is a fairly poor area with few remaining local businesses and inhabited almost exclusively by lower income families. The neighbourhood organisation was formed in 1985 to combat problems of crime, unemployment and poor access to public services in the area.

Observations: The demonstration was held on the steps of city hall during the noon hour, when a large number of people were entering and leaving the building. The organisation had obtained a permit from the police department, and all members remained on a grassy area beside the main entrance so that they did not block pedestrian traffic. Thirty-three members of the Waterside Association took part in the demonstration. In addition, there were activists from trade unions, the local leader of a major environmental group and a member of the city council, who represents the neighbourhood. The event was covered by two reporters from the local paper, a camera crew and reporter from each of the two local TV stations and a reporter from BBC Radio.

The demonstration began promptly at noon and consisted of the following activities: (1) Throughout the demonstration, twelve of the participants waved handmade signs with slogans condemning the landfill. They were careful to face the TV cameras at all times. (2) The association president, the city council member and the environmental group leader (in that order) each stood on an old oil drum the demonstrators had brought to the site to make speeches lasting about ten minutes each. (3) Between each speech, a very energetic member of the group used a megaphone to lead chants about the injustice of the landfill decision. The chants were defiant in tone (e.g., 'We won't take your rubbish!'), and one accused the city council of 'selling out'. All members of the association who attended the demonstration were very active during the action, shouting, cheering, clapping, calling out to passersby and appealing directly to the cameras. The signs were skilfully written and the chants seemed to have been rehearsed. Each speaker referred at least once to the fact that Waterside was a lower income community. Each asked at least once why the landfill was not put in Carlton (an affluent neighbourhood at the edge of the city that had been recommended by a consultant's study as the most logical site).

When she was not speaking, the president of the Waterside Association was moving among the demonstrators, encouraging them to wave their signs, shout and otherwise show their feelings. She pulled reporters into the middle of the group on three occasions and coached the camera crews on what to shoot. Comments made by the other speakers revealed she had personally invited them to attend and speak. While the group was returning to the neighbourhood on a bus borrowed for the occasion, the president made a statement about how she was sure that the event had made a difference and how important it was for poorer people to stand up for their rights. She then went down the aisle and personally thanked everyone on the bus for taking part in the demonstration, using a lot of handshaking and sympathetic listening. Everyone else had carried out the tasks assigned to them, but no one seemed to share responsibility for making the demonstration work.

Comments: This group has a well-organised, highly disciplined core of active members and a good deal of support from other community institutions. The president, however, appears to be the main moving force. She seems to come up with most of the ideas and to mobilise others with her energy. The members seem to be motivated by a growing sense of neighbourhood solidarity, but each one carries on partly because they do not want to let the others down. The president apparently encourages both of these tendencies – perhaps because she knows that she cannot promise the members much in the way of material rewards. I cannot help but wonder how the organisation would survive if she stepped down. She takes on so much responsibility that no one else seems to be getting any leadership training. Her strength may be the organisation's weakness.

Once all observation has been completed, you will formally shift to data analysis. With direct observation data, this means *using inductive reasoning to discover patterns among the many discrete facts recorded in the field notes.* The first step is usually to review the notes in order to find some meaningful categories to use in distinguishing among the events observed.

An example

Consider a hypothetical study of parliamentary committees designed to investigate the degree to which they are subject to influence by organised interest groups. You might observe the meetings of several committees and then ask: Are there any systematic differences in the way these groups function? After examining your notes, you may decide that the groups differ along two important dimensions: the degree to which power is centralised in the formal leaders versus being widely shared among the members, and the degree to which the groups are businesslike and rule-driven in transacting their business versus being more collegial and relying on personal interaction. If we break these two dimensions in the middle and juxtapose them, we get the typology of committee operating styles presented in Figure 21.2, and we have a way of classifying committees for analysis.

Figure 21.2 Hypothetical typology of congressional committees

Style of operation	Power configuration	
	Decentralised	**Centralised**
Collegial	Populist	Machine
Rule-driven	Democratic	Authoritarian

The next step in analysis is to examine the field notes for evidence of differences *between* and *within* categories or types. For example, we might ask if committees of different types responded differently to interest groups and if the same type of committee treated different types of interest groups differently. We might ask if it seems to be easier for interest groups to gain access to some types of committees than to others or if the ease of access depends more on the characteristics of the interest group (such as how well financed it is, how professional its lobbying staff is or how politically active it is in the MPs' home constituencies).

The major challenge in both taking and analysing field notes is to avoid the natural tendency to see only what you expect to see. If you are to gain a truly accurate understanding of these events, it is crucial to be open to the possibility that things do not work as expected and *to avoid imposing patterns* that are not there. One technique for keeping an open mind about your subject and ensuring that you are not overlooking important relationships is to occasionally ask trusted colleagues who are *not* involved with your research project to read over portions of your field notes and share with you their impressions of what is happening. They may be able to see patterns that your preconceived theory of the events has hidden from you.

Techniques of structured observation

If unstructured observation is used to gain a more refined and accurate understanding of political behaviour so that we can develop theories of it, structured observation is used to verify the utility of our understandings and to test hypotheses derived from our theories. Conducting a structured observation requires a clear idea of what we expect to see when we observe and what specific behaviours we are looking for. We are interested primarily in *recording specific behaviours,* not in finding the meaning our subjects attach to their behaviours or patterns in those behaviours. It is similar to carrying out a survey or a content analysis in that we are guided by an instrument that makes our observation very systematic and facilitates recording what we see in ways that make comparing cases easier. In direct observation, this instrument is known as an *observation schedule.*

Designing an observation schedule

An **observation schedule** is a detailed list of specific things to be observed and a system for recording them. The content and design of observation schedules depend on the nature of the research project and can vary widely, so that it is difficult to provide firm guidelines for their construction. Our objective here is merely to suggest some very general rules to follow and techniques to use in designing useful observation schedules.

Before we turn to a discussion of those rules, it is important to mention three features of structured observation that set the context for development of an observation schedule. First, recall that structured observations may be either obtrusive or unobtrusive. Because the observer must pay attention to a great many details and is most concerned with precision in recording events, *it is essential that observations be recorded as they are made.* As a result, structured observations run a greater risk of creating reactivity than unstructured ones do when they are done obtrusively. Subjects who see an observer busily taking notes on their actions are very likely to be keenly aware that they are being studied and may alter their behaviour as a result. Structured techniques, then, are probably most effective when used unobtrusively.

An additional implication of the need in structured observation to record events as they happen is that *it is almost never possible to use structured techniques in a participant observation.* It would be virtually impossible to keep detailed records of behaviours while acting as a participant and would almost certainly give away your purpose in being there.

The second contextual feature of structured methods to consider before discussing the construction of observation schedules is that structured observations are often made by someone *other than the principal investigator.* Because the observations are more routine and often more numerous than those involved in unstructured methods, researchers commonly hire assistants to carry out the observations. This means that the observation schedule must be detailed and informative enough that it (1) can be used by an assistant *as the researcher intends it to be used* and (2) leaves very little discretion to the observer, so that the observations recorded by different assistants can legitimately be compared.

Finally, it is important to recognise the basic design of a structured observation in order to understand what is needed in an observation schedule. This design involves first identifying a *unit of analysis* for the study. In direct observation, units of analysis usually consist of recurring events. Examples include reaching a compromise at a negotiating session, debating a motion before the UN Security Council and arguing between members of opposing groups at a demonstration which might turn violent.

After identification of a unit of analysis, the next step is to *designate the aspects of that event to be observed.* Here is where the observation schedule comes in. An observation schedule is far more than a simple checklist in several ways:

1 It often provides more than simple *yes* or *no* options for recording behaviours. Observers are usually asked to record events in degrees or frequencies.
2 It usually contains instructions on *how* to conduct the observations by telling the observer what procedures to follow.
3 It generally includes some fairly detailed definitions of the behaviours to be observed so that observers know what to look for.

This last feature is vitally important. An observation schedule *is always based on operational definitions of the behaviours in question*. If it is to be useful, it must reduce a set of potentially complex events or behaviours to basic elements, so that the observer can be sure when it has been observed and can distinguish it from other, similar behaviours or events. To do this, an observation schedule breaks behaviours and/or events into discrete variables, gives the observer an operational definition of each and provides a scheme for recording observations of each variable.

An example

Returning to the example of the study of the operating styles of US congressional committees, one unit of analysis for such a study might be a public disagreement among members of the committee. The researcher would need to define what constitutes a disagreement and then identify the features of the event (the variables) to be observed – that is, the dimensions along which to classify each disagreement. These dimensions can be highly specific or quite broad. In the committee study, we might want to know something as specific as how often the parties to the disagreement interrupted each other, whether or not certain words were used by either side and who spoke last. Alternatively, the dimensions may be as broad as whether the tone of the argument was hostile or cordial, whether or not it seemed to be conducted within mutually accepted norms or what role the committee chair played in mediating the argument.

Which approach is better depends on the specific research project. However, *the broader the dimensions to be observed, the greater the discretion the observer has in classifying events*. Narrower dimensions may seem to trivialise the subject, but they have the advantage of limiting observers' discretion and, thereby, producing data that are more standardised and more comparable from observation to observation. Researchers are usually well advised to be *as specific as possible* in constructing an observation schedule.

A major reason for this is that one of the most important rules for designing an observation schedule is that *the categories used to classify events must be exhaustive and mutually exclusive*. It must be possible to place all observed events in some category. However, it must not be logically possible to place any single observation in more than one category. The best way to achieve this mutual exclusivity of categories is to be very specific – to break larger variables down into smaller ones. For example, rather than asking the general question about whether or not a disagreement seemed to be governed by mutually accepted norms, we might ask if the parties to the argument interrupted one another, raised their voices or yielded the floor promptly when asked to do so by the chair.

Figure 21.3 is a segment of a hypothetical study of community organisations in which the meeting is the unit of analysis. Note that some items require only that the observer record objectively verifiable information about the meeting (when it started, how many people were in attendance etc.), whereas other items require a judgement on the part of the observer (whether the members paid attention to the chair when he or she spoke, if the members were cordial and friendly to each other before the opening of the meeting etc.). This mix is almost inevitable, but the investigator should provide observers with clear instructions on how to make a judgement about those matters that require judgement. It is wise to check their understanding of these instructions by having the assistant record observations of an event that the researcher also observes and then comparing the assistant's classification of events with those of the investigator.

Assessing reliability and validity

Those who use structured observation to gather data have to be just as concerned with the validity and reliability of their measurements as those who use other data collection techniques. It is, therefore,

Figure 21.3   Partial observation schedule for a hypothetical study of community organisations

COMMUNITY ORGANISATION OBSERVATION SCHEDULE

1. a. Name of organisation ____
   b. Date and time of meeting ____
   c. Location of meeting ____
   d. Nature of meeting: *(1) regular business*
                            (2) annual meeting
                            (3) special or emergency
                            (8) other_______________________________________
   e. Purpose of meeting: *(1) routine business*
                            (2) to elect officers
                            (3) to discuss a problem
                            (4) social gathering
                            (5) to recognise members/accomplishments
                            (8) other_______________________________________
2. Pre-meeting socialising: *(1) less than half participated*
                             (2) about half participated
                             (3) most members participated
3. a. Was there a written agenda for the meeting?   YES   NO
   b. If yes, was it distributed to the members?   YES   NO
   c. If yes, when was it distributed? *(1) before the day of the meeting*
                                      (2) just prior to the meeting
                                      (3) after the meeting
4. How many people attended the meeting?___________________________________
5. a. Was the meeting open to the public?   YES   NO
   b. How many persons who were apparently not members attended? ___________
   c. Were any non-members on the formal programme?   YES   NO
   d. If yes, who (city council member, police officer etc.)?___________________
6. Who presided at the meeting (by office)?___________________________________
7. What other persons had a formal role in the meeting (made a presentation, gave a report etc.)?

   ____

   ____

8. Did the presiding officer say that members were encouraged to speak during the meeting?   YES   NO
9. How many members made comments or asked questions during the meeting? [Use tic marks to keep track.]

   ____

10. How closely were parliamentary procedures followed in managing the meeting?
    _________ (1) not at all
    _________ (2) loosely
    _________ (3) fairly closely
    _________ (4) strictly

11. What were the main topics discussed during the programme?
    a. ____
    b. ____
    c. ____
    d. ____
    e. ____

(continued)

| **Figure 21.3** | (*Continued*) |

12. a. How many formal votes were taken? [Use tic marks to keep track.]
    b. How was voting done? *(1) show of hands*
                               (2) voice vote
                               (3) paper ballot
                               (8) other _____________________________
    c. What was the issue and outcome on each vote taken?
           ISSUE   OUTCOME
    Vote 1: ____
    Vote 2: ____
    Vote 3: ____
    Vote 4: ____
    Vote 5: ____

important to build into the data collection effort ways to check on this. When data from an observation schedule are quantitative, they can be analysed with standard statistical techniques and are subject to the same tests of validity and reliability discussed in Chapter 4.

However, the observation schedule almost always gives observers some degree of discretion about how to record events. Therefore, if more than one observer is used, it is also especially important to pay attention to **interobserver reliability** – the degree to which different observers classify similar events in the same way on the observation schedule. This is essentially the same as the problem of intercoder reliability in content analysis and can be verified by procedures similar to those discussed in Chapter 12. It is crucial, however, that investigators build into the instrument and data collection procedure the means of collecting the information they will need to verify the validity and reliability of their measures.

It is also a good idea to *pretest the observation schedule and procedure* before beginning actual fieldwork. A pretest involves the researcher and/or assistants using the schedule to record an event like the one they are studying to be sure that the categories are exhaustive and mutually exclusive, that the instructions on the form are easy to follow and that the explanations of how to classify are clear enough that different observers can agree on the coding for the same or highly similar behaviours and events.

Sampling procedures in direct observation

After identifying a set of behaviours to treat as a unit of analysis, we must decide which of these units to study. Because we cannot observe all instances of the behaviours that serve as our units of analysis, we are forced to select a sample of them.

Representative sampling

The objective of this sampling – as in survey research or other methods of data collection – is *to examine a representative group of cases*. We want to understand how the events in question *usually* happen and do not want to be misled by observing atypical episodes. However, what we are sampling is not people or nations or publications, but events and behaviours. The important point about this is that we can seldom predict in advance when (and sometimes where) these events will take place. As a result, it is often impossible to apply standard random sampling procedures to the type of events that are most often studied through direct observation.

The sampling procedure that *is* used depends on the nature of the study. If the events recur on a regular basis and occur frequently enough, it may be possible to take a random sample of these events to study. For instance, if we were studying the way a large administrative agency processes citizens' complaints, and we knew that formal complaints were accepted in a specific office every workday between the hours of 2 p.m. and 5 p.m., and that the agency heard an average of fifteen complaints a day, we could set up rules for drawing a random sample of the anticipated complaints. In the room where complaints were received, we could station observers on random days with instructions to record the details of the handling of the eighth complaint brought each day until some statistically determined minimum number had been observed. We could have a good deal of confidence in the representativeness of this sample because of the number and regularity of the events.

However, if there are far fewer instances of our units of analysis or if we cannot predict when or where they will occur, then standard sampling procedures cannot be relied on to yield a good sample. To illustrate this, let us change the preceding example to say that the agency scheduled the hearing of complaints *only once a month* at a regular time and heard an average of only four complaints at each session. We could sample by way of the procedure just described, but would have to observe the organisation over *many* months before our random procedure had produced a representative sample (because random procedures are not dependable with small numbers of cases). We may not be able to stretch our research out over such a long period.

To modify the example again, assume that the agency accepted complaints at a window in its offices *at any time of any workday.* Because we cannot predict when citizens will show up with complaints, it is impossible to apply standard sampling procedures to select complaints. However, if we had reason to believe that complaints were fairly evenly spaced throughout the day and the week, we could divide the workweek into hours and sample certain *time periods.* Observers could watch the window at preselected hours of specified days of the week and record any complaints filed at those times. With a sufficiently large number of complaints, this could provide a representative sample. However, if the number of complaints is small (only one or two each day, for instance), most observation periods would not include a complaint, and it would again take a *very* long time to observe enough complaints to have confidence in our sample. This would be both time-consuming and extremely expensive.

When we turn from events that occur with some regularity to more sporadic events, sampling problems become even greater. To stay with our administrative example, say that we are concerned with complaints made only by certain types of citizens (elderly persons, minority-group members etc.) or only with a certain type of complaint (like those that involve allegations of nonenforcement of a specific rule, or gender discrimination in service delivery). We have no way of knowing when and if such complaints will arise and cannot effectively sample them using some variant of random sampling.

Judgemental sampling

When we are studying a behaviour that occurs infrequently or without warning, we almost always have to rely on a *judgemental sample* as described in Chapter 7. We use what we know about the nature of the event to select a set of occurrences that will be *typical* of the behaviour of interest if not representative in a strictly statistical sense. The task in judgemental sampling is to select for observation events that informed readers of the research can be persuaded are likely to be representative.

To illustrate, say that our study of complaint-handling was focused entirely on complaints about nonenforcement of agency rules and that we knew from agency records or prior research that complaints of this type came almost exclusively from low-income communities. We might choose to observe only complaints filed at those agency offices serving low-income neighbourhoods in the hope of locating enough complaints of the desired type. If background research makes it possible to build a statistical profile of the events we want to study (when and where they happen most often, what types of people participate, how long they last etc.), this information can assist in the judgemental selection of typical cases.

Coping with method effects in direct observation

In Chapter 1, using the example of the Hawthorne Effect, we pointed out that researchers must always be alert to the possibility that their data collection efforts have, in some way, influenced the data that are obtained and have produced an inaccurate picture of the reality they hope to understand. For example, because people tend to give what they feel are socially acceptable answers to survey questions regardless of their true feelings, one effect of using the personal interview to gather data is a tendency to *understate* the occurrence of behaviours and attitudes that are contrary to dominant social norms. This impact is referred to as a **method effect**.

Minimising reactivity

The possibility of a method effect is especially high in direct observation for at least two reasons. First, in most direct observations, researchers are in closer and more extended contact with the subjects than with other methods, so there are more opportunities for the observer's actions or presence to influence subjects' behaviour. We call this effect *reactivity*. Second, because observers exercise so much discretion in determining what to record and how to record it, direct-observation data are heavily influenced by observers' values and expectations. We call this effect *bias*. If we fail to minimise these method effects, we lose the main advantage of direct observation – the high degree of external validity it provides our research.

Which strategies are appropriate for minimising method effects depends on the character of the specific project. We can, however, offer some general guidelines. The most effective means of coping with reactivity is to employ *unobtrusive observation*, because subjects who are not aware they are being observed do not react to being studied. Investigators should always consider the possibility of arranging an unobtrusive observation. However, as explained earlier, it is often impossible to use unobtrusive methods and, as will soon be discussed, it may sometimes be judged unethical to do so.

Moreover, one particular technique of unobtrusive study – participant observation – may not get around reactivity problems even when it is possible. Even if the observer's identity and purpose are concealed from members of the group, the observer's actions *as a member of the group* can cause other members to act differently from ways they otherwise would. If a researcher posing as a member of a political organisation takes part in the group's debate about what action to take in response to some new threat to its interest, for example, that participation may sway the decision. Similarly, the researcher's work on one of the organisation's projects may lead to its success when it otherwise would have failed or to its failure when it otherwise would have succeeded.

This sort of effect is difficult to avoid if the investigator is to retain credibility as a devoted member of the organisation, but observers have to be very sensitive to it and attempt to strike the delicate balance between losing credibility and actually shaping the events they are trying to study. It is also important to attempt to judge the degree to which researcher participation influences outcomes, so that this effect can be discounted in attempting to form an accurate picture of the processes under investigation.

When obtrusive methods are the only possibility, researchers can still take steps to minimise reactivity. Here, the key to success lies in investigators' ability to *control their relationship to the subjects and the subjects' perception of the researcher.* Researchers must consciously manipulate subjects' perception of their character, values and purpose in order to put the subjects so at ease that they behave as they normally would. Subjects must come either to ignore the observer as harmless, or to trust the observer enough to reveal their true feelings and behaviour patterns. To accomplish the former, observers must blend in; to accomplish the latter, they must fit in.

Blending in

When **blending in**, observers can use several tactics:

1 They can physically stay in the background or at the margins of any action they are observing so that subjects easily forget their presence when focusing on the activity. (This practice often has the added advantage of placing observers in a location that provides a good vantage point from which to view the entire scene at once.)

2 Observers can adopt a passive manner, which makes it easy for others to overlook them or to consider them unthreatening. In this mode, they will certainly want to avoid commenting on what they see or confronting subjects in any way.

3 Observers can exercise patience and perseverance by showing up again and again so that they become commonplace and subjects begin to relax in their presence. The objective is to make the process of observation seem normal to the subjects – part of everyday life. This can take a great deal of time to accomplish.

4 Observers can blend into the group physically by grooming themselves and dressing in a manner that is inconspicuous under the circumstances. Wear what the subjects wear, but be careful to avoid violating any dress codes that may exist in the group by, for instance, wearing something recognised as a symbol of rank in the group or something reserved for persons with special status in the group.

5 Researchers can blend in socially by learning to converse comfortably with the subjects. This involves talking about things that are common topics of conversation among the subjects, using a personal style that is appropriate to the norms of the group (loud and outgoing or reserved and introspective, openly sharing feelings or putting up a front, frequently touching the subject or keeping your hands to yourself etc.), and respecting any clear role definitions within the group such as a norm that says that women do not talk about politics or that younger members do not volunteer information about themselves unless asked by an elder. It is important not to carry this too far by trying to imitate subjects' speech patterns, mannerisms or dress if it seems unnatural for the observer to act that way. An observer with a strong public school accent probably should *not* dress like a young black man in an effort to study the political views of inner London housing estates. Unnatural behaviour will only attract attention and may be seen as an insult to those being studied.

Fitting in

Observers can *fit in* by using some of these same tactics. However, **fitting in** demands much more interaction between observer and subjects than blending in. It is a much greater concern in participant observation than in nonparticipant observation. Fitting in requires that the researcher consciously project an image as one of the group. This is done primarily by expressing values consistent with those of the subjects (perhaps a disregard for authority, prejudice towards some other group or acceptance of a given political ideology). Behaving like one of the subject group may be necessary to build trust, but it has its dangers.

There is sometimes a risk that adopting the identity of a group member will make observers lose their objectivity about the study. Coming to see the world as subjects see it is known as **going native**. Investigators must be alert to this prospect because going native can cause researchers to lose sight of the goals of their research. This is not a simple matter, because there is a fine line between going native and 'getting inside' subjects to understand their motivations, values and the like. Successful researchers are able to get close to subjects without losing sight of their objectives. At the same time, the interpretive framework for a study might be improved by interaction with others and coming to understand new conceptual categories and problems.

Observers who seek to fit in also face ethical problems if they find that they must deceive subjects. They are very likely to have to lie about how they feel, what they have done, how they live, their background and so on. We address this problem in the last section of this chapter.

Avoiding personal bias

Another method effect (when the method used distorts the responses of the research subjects) associated with direct observation is the bias that can result when observers' values or expectations influence their perception and interpretation of what they see. Direct observation is especially subject to this danger because, with this method, *the observer is the primary instrument of measurement*. Bias can result from a researcher's rigid adherence to preconceptions about the phenomena under study or from a researcher's uncritically accepting the perspective and interpretations of the subjects (going native). Avoiding bias requires being both open-minded about and detached from the subject of our studies. Several strategies can help achieve this end.

First, in obtrusive research, when observer and subjects can interact, observers can avoid letting their preconceptions lead them to wrong conclusions by periodically *checking their interpretations of what they see with the subjects*. For example, rather than simply assuming we know what motivates subjects to take a particular action, we can ask subjects why they did what they did. Their understandings of the situation or their values may be so different from the researcher's that their motivations are just the opposite of what the researcher had thought. Someone from a politically tolerant society with free speech might think that popular support for harsh punishment of isolated acts of political dissent is motivated by political views shared with those in authority. In fact, the population may publically support suppression of political dissent because dissent may lead to wider repression of society as a whole. Similarly, researchers may assign meaning to events that subjects do not. An example would be the case in which an observer interprets as a danger signal a group of teenagers 'hanging out' on a block, but a local resident knows the youths and views them as protecting the block from intruders by their presence.

It is wise to ask subjects how they interpret events before making assumptions. However, it is important to be subtle in asking these questions, phrasing them in terms familiar to the subjects, and presenting them as concerned inquiries, not demands for explanations. After observing a heated verbal exchange, for example, an observer should not ask, 'Why were you so hostile towards her?' but may ask, 'Do you think she will be angry about this?' to find out if the actor saw the exchange in the same terms as the observer. This does *not* mean that observers should let subjects determine their analysis of events, but only that they should check to see if subjects are thinking what the observers believe they are thinking.

Second, observers can avoid the mistake of seeing events too much as subjects see them by (1) periodically discussing with someone outside the study what they have seen and how they interpret it and (2) soliciting the views of persons who are marginal to the group, such as the lone environmentalist on a city planning commission generally unconcerned about environmental issues, or people who have recently moved back into a community after living elsewhere. Such persons can be a valuable resource for researchers, because they have the insight born of close association with the events in question but can still take a critical perspective on those events.

Third, it is often useful to blend direct observation with some other form of data collection so the other data can be used to verify impressions formed from direct observation. A direct observation study of the effect of crime on citizens' behaviours might be augmented by a survey in which the same people who had been observed are asked direct questions about how fearful they are and how their behaviour has changed as a result of their fear. The survey would not provide as much detailed data as the direct observation and may have less external validity. It could, however, be used to verify impressions gained from direct observation by asking such questions as, 'Do respondents see the actions that observers attributed to fear (e.g., staying off the streets at night) as being motivated by fear of crime or do they have other explanations for this?' A wide variety of data sources (content analysis, public records etc.) can serve this verification function.

These and other means of *cross-validating* the conclusions drawn from observation can reduce the degree of subjectivity involved in the method and add significantly to the degree to which results are accepted as valid.

Ethical considerations

Direct observation provides a powerful research tool for political researchers. At best, this method may unlock political and social attitudes that are otherwise inaccessible, but it may also involve a potentially challenging ethical balancing act. Researchers' deep immersion in research subjects' lives and in issues that subjects personally value inherently increases the value of qualitative research, but may also raise substantial ethical challenges. Any research project can raise questions of what is ethically right or fair. The often close researcher–subject relationships that form in qualitative research may conspire to make it even more likely that researchers will confront questions of ethics. The two areas in which ethical issues are most likely to arise are *the relationship of the researcher to the subjects* and *the reactions of the researcher to what is observed.*

Ethics in relationships

Problems can arise in the relationship of the observer to the observed, because there is often a fundamental tension between being honest and obtaining scientifically valid information. If subjects know they are being studied or know why they are being studied, they may refuse to cooperate or may alter their behaviour in ways that make it impossible to secure a valid answer to a research question. Yet getting around these problems by using unobtrusive observation or by concealing the true purpose of the study from subjects involves some degree of deception. Investigators are most likely to face choices about whether or not to use deception with regard to (1) *the grounds on which they gain access to opportunities to observe* and (2) *the development of trust between themselves and their subjects.* We can examine these issues in turn.

If it is possible to observe subjects without their knowledge, observers first face the question of whether or not to tell subjects they are being studied. The issue here is whether the researcher has a right to watch and possibly report people's actions when they have not given their consent and cannot control what the observer sees or reports. Researchers confront a similar situation when telling subjects they are being studied but deceive them as to the purpose of the study. Are such actions an invasion of privacy and a denial of the fundamental human right to control of our lives?

It is often possible to argue *in favour* of deception in a given qualitative project for any of several reasons:

1   Subjects will not be harmed in any way by being observed, given the purposes of the study.
2   Researchers will keep subjects' identity secret in any reports from the study, so no one will be hurt.
3   Subjects would agree to the study if they were given the opportunity to do so but cannot be asked in advance without risking reactivity.
4   The good that will come from the findings of the study outweighs any harm that may be done to subjects through the deception.

Researchers, funding agencies, sponsoring agencies and critics must decide whether these are valid arguments in any given case by careful examination of the facts of the situation.

Ethical questions can arise with respect to the issue of trust between observer and observed. First, in order to gain subjects' trust, observers may have to lie about who they are, why they are there, how they feel about events and so forth. Moreover, once trust is established, do researchers have the right to use what is told them in confidence to advance the purposes of the research or to report such information in a write-up of the project? Can deception be justified in the name of science when we abhor its use for personal, political or financial gain? Deception at this stage can sometimes be justified by the same kind of arguments previously cited.

Ethics in personal feelings

Another arena in which ethical issues may arise deals with the researcher's reactions to what is observed or learned through contact with subjects. Those who investigate behaviours that are potentially illegal or unethical in society put themselves in situations in which they may witness actions that outrage or disgust them. Some actions may impose a moral obligation to report the events to some authority. At other times, observers may witness actions in which their own moral code demands that they intervene to stop.

Each type of qualitative research poses unique ethical challenges, but direct observation often puts the researcher in the most difficult situation. Although we might find it repugnant to listen to focus group participants discuss their visceral disgust that women would even attempt to run for high political office or it may irritate our law-abiding nature when a captain of industry brags in an interview about his success in skirting environmental regulations, these examples pale beside the challenges of direct observation.

Consider the example of a researcher engaged in participant observation of the politics of Neo-Nazi skinheads. What if the skinheads shout insults at and spit on minority children? What if they vandalise a synagogue? What if they beat up an elderly Jewish man? Researchers who react as their value system dictates would 'blow their cover' and put an end to the project. (To keep the case as simple as possible, assume that such reactions would not endanger the researcher.) What are the researcher's obligations in this situation? Can the need to understand what motivates people to join such groups and how the groups function outweigh the obligation to express personal moral outrage? Can it negate the obligation to report violations of the law? Can it possibly justify allowing someone to be physically harmed? How do we balance long-term objectives against the short-term need for justice? How do we balance benefits to society (in this case, added knowledge about how to control a problem) against the welfare of individuals who may be harmed if we do not act?

Each ethical question must be answered in the context of a specific research project and situation. The value of some projects will justify actions that could not be justified by others. On rare occasions it is possible to come up with creative arrangements that allow researchers to minimise ethical dilemmas. For instance, it may be possible to observe without informing subjects but to tell them later, show them how the observations of their behaviour will be used, and give them the right to veto use of the data. In most cases, however, investigators must confront ethical questions head-on and make hard choices between unattractive alternatives.

The important point is that it is vital that those who plan to use direct observation consider *in advance* the ethical implications of their decision. Before putting themselves in situations that pose ethical dilemmas, researchers should think through the problems that are likely to arise, and they should weigh the relative value of the good of the project against the rights of subjects or social and moral obligations. Most important, they must *be very clear about their own values* and, if at all possible, *decide in advance where they will draw the line in cases of ethical conflict.*

For example, in conducting an unobtrusive observation, you may feel compelled to build a close relationship based upon a false identity. How certain can you be that when you reveal yourself to your subject (as required by research standards), they will not experience a long-lasting emotional pain that exceeds the possible benefit of your research findings? Although this is a particularly dramatic example, this caveat to balance potential for harm versus benefit strongly applies to all qualitative research, and requires substantial forethought by researchers.

The political ethnographer should also consider the possibility of engaging in **critical ethnography**. Critical ethnography challenges the implicit assumptions of academic political research. Rather than attempting to gather and report research findings in a disengaged way, it attempts to look for perspectives that open up alternatives to conventional ways of thinking about politics. This critical approach has much in common with critical discourse analysis and hermeneutics, which are the subjects of the next two chapters. By application of critical approaches to political ethnography, direct observation can reveal new ways of thinking about politics. Critical ethnography is sensitive to issues of power and culture where societal norms are reinforced in social interactions related to politics. For example, in much recent research a critical understanding of gender roles and how they are defined in political life has revealed much about the subtle ways in which political socialisation and interaction occurs.

Critical ways of thinking may be more sympathetic to the orientations and values of the persons being researched without 'going native'. In doing so, the critical ethnographer takes an ethical position, but by making this explicit and engaging in rigorous data collection, research results can be just as revealing and informative as those from conventional research, if not more so. It is not a 'bias' in favour of a particular type of power relationship or special ideal gender roles, but without a critical perspective to raise your awareness of such issues, many nuances of interaction and their impact on political behaviour would be lost. Sometimes by listening carefully to the concerns and frustrations of those you are observing, you can learn more about politics than by imposing some grand theory from the academic literature on your observations.

Conclusion

Direct observation techniques of information gathering and political ethnography are important approaches to political research. They can offer unique access to aspects of interesting phenomena that cannot effectively be studied using other methods. Both quantitative and qualitative researchers should actively consider these methods as a possible way of seeking answers to the questions they are investigating. However, direct observation must not be undertaken without a full understanding of its processes, serious consideration of its potential drawbacks and careful planning and preparation. In most cases, this will require consideration by a research ethics panel of your university, so it is crucial to check with relevant members of staff before undertaking this type of research.

This is true because direct observation techniques place field researchers in situations that can be both professionally and personally risky. Such techniques rely to a greater degree than most other methods on the judgement and skills of individual researchers, and can, in some circumstances, cause researchers to confront directly the most difficult questions of personal and professional ethics. Against these risks, researchers must balance the exceptional potential for gaining valid insights that direct observation can offer and the personal and professional growth that can result from meeting its unique challenges.

As you read research reports based on direct observation, you should keep all dimensions of this method in mind. In order to look carefully for evidence that biases have been introduced into the findings of the research by the peculiar features of direct observation, you will need to know as much about the research design and its implementation as possible. Always ask what steps the researchers(s) took to get around the potential pitfalls described in this chapter, and be cautious about accepting its conclusions until you are satisfied.

Summary points

- When researchers are seeking to develop a theory or gain a complex and subtle understanding of a phenomenon, they may use direct observation techniques.
- Direct observation makes special demands on the researcher if it is to reach valid, intersubjective conclusions, but it can produce empirical analyses.
- The major advantage of direct observation is that it can provide a very high level of external validity by observing events in 'real-world' settings and it (potentially) minimises research reactivity.
- The disadvantages of direct observation include the intensive demands it makes on the researcher, the time and resources it requires, and an enhanced risk that subjective factors will affect the validity of conclusions.
- Direct observation methods are divided into obtrusive and unobtrusive, structured and unstructured, and passive and participant observation techniques.
- Because it requires intensive contact with subjects in 'real world' settings, direct observation can pose numerous ethical challenges for researchers. To meet these challenges, researchers need to be clear about their own values, weigh the importance of the research against other values, and try to anticipate ethical issues they may confront in specific projects.

Suggested reading and examples

Research examples

Studying the relationship between law enforcement and protestors, Steinhoff (2006) personally observed and recorded Japanese police patterns of behaviour when confronted with anti-Emperor protests. She identified three distinct approaches the police used and noted protestors' strategies to skirt them and participate in street demonstrations against the government.

In more mainstream settings, LeBlanc has used political ethnography to study the political world of the Japanese housewife in *Bicycle Citizens* (1999) and the problem of masculine identity among Japanese politicians in *The Art of the Gut* (2009). Both of these works demonstrate a sensitivity to gender issues which reflects a critical approach to ethnography.

The lack of truth in the Truth and Reconciliation Commissions in Sierra Leona was studied by Kelsall (2005) using ethnographic method to demonstrate that the ritual aspects of reconciliation were more important that the public truth telling to the participants in the process.

Examining the decision-making processes in the forests of Latin America, Mitchell (2006) directly observed indigenous groups as a participant. He identified key themes that emerged from these observations and his semi-structured interviews in two Mexican communities.

Methodological reading

Many of the texts guiding direct observation are written by anthropologists and sociologists, home fields for this qualitative method. General introductions to direct observation methods include *Qualitative Researching* (Mason 2002) and *Learning in the Field: An Introduction to Qualitative Research* (Rossman and Rallis 2003). Close-contact participant-observation techniques are explained in considerable detail in *Participant Observation* (Dewalt and Dewalt 2002). Glasser (1996) has provided 'Seven Lessons of Participant-Observation Research' building on the campaign watching techniques of Fenno (1978, 1986). *New Perspectives in Political Ethnography* (Joseph *et al.* eds. 2007) provides examples of a range of cases and issues in political ethnography. For a discussion of the problems and potential of approaches which challenge the orthodoxy of being 'objective' see *Engaging Contraditions: Theory, Politics and Methods of Activist Scholarship* (Charles Hale ed. 2008) and Tilly (2006) 'Afterward: Political Ethnography as Art and Science' in *Qualitative Sociology*.

References

Curtis, Gerald. 1971. *Election Campaigning Japanese Style*. New York: Columbia University Press.

Dahl, Robert. 1961. *Who Governs?* New Haven, CT: Yale University Press.

Dewalt, Kathleen Musante and Dewalt, Billie R. 2002. *Participant Observation*. Lanham, MD: Rowman & Littlefield.

Fenno, Richard, Jr. 1978. *Home Style: House Members in their Districts*. Little, Brown.

Fenno, Richard, Jr. 1986. 'Observation, context and sequence in the study of politics'. *American Political Science Review*, vol. 80, no. 1 (March), pp. 3–15.

Geertz, Clifford. 1973. 'Description: toward an interpretive theory of culture', *The Interpretation of Culture*. New York: Basic Books, pp. 3–30.

Glasser, James M. 1996. 'The challenge of campaign watching: seven lessons of participant-observation research'. *PS: Political Science and Politics*, vol. 29, no. 3 (September), pp. 533–37.

Hale, Charles. ed. 2008. *Engaging Contradictions: Theory, Politics and Methods of Activist Scholarship*. Berkeley, CA: University of California Press.

Hunter, Floyd. 1953. *Community Power Structure: A Study of Decision Makers*. Chapel Hill: University of North Carolina Press.

Joseph, Lauren, Mahler, Matthew and Auyero, Javier. eds. 2007. *New Perspectives in Political Ethnography*. New York: Springer.

Kelsall, Tim. 2005. 'Truth, lies, ritual: preliminary reflections on the Truth and Reconciliation Commmission in Sierra Leone'. *Human Rights Quarterly*, vol. 27, no. 2 (May), pp. 361–91.

LeBlanc, Robin M. 1999. *Bicycle Citizens: The Political World of the Japanese Housewife*. Berkeley: University of California Press.

LeBlanc, Robin M. 2009. *The Art of the Gut: Manhood, Power and Ethics in Japanese Politics*. Berkeley: University of California Press.

Mason, Jennifer. 2002. *Qualitative Researching*, 2nd edn. Thousand Oaks, CA: Sage.

Mitchell, Ross E. 2006. 'Environmental governance in Mexico: two case studies of Oaxaca's community forest sector'. *Journal of Latin American Studies*, vol. 38 (August), pp. 519–48.

Rossman, Gretchen and Rallis, Sharon. 2003. *Learning in the Field: An Introduction to Qualitative Research*. Thousand Oaks, CA: Sage.

Steinhoff, Patricia G. 2006. 'Racial outcasts versus three kinds of police: constructing limits in Japanese anti-Emperor protests'. *Qualitative Sociology*, vol. 29 (Fall), pp. 386–408.

Tilly, Charles 2006. 'Afterward: political ethnography as art and science'. *Qualitative Sociology*, vol. 29 (Fall), pp. 409–12.

Research exercises

1 Develop a research question that can be answered through direct observation about one of the politically oriented student groups on your campus – groups like Young Labour, Liberal Youth and Conservative Future. (For example, you might ask if the role of female members is different in left and conservative groups or what common values members of the group share beyond their political ideals.) Write out a list of the things you would have to observe in the group to answer this question.

2 Attend a meeting of the student group and observe it according to the list you developed for the previous exercise. Keep mental notes and write up formal field notes immediately afterward. Then write a short essay on what you learned that you had not expected. How did what you saw and heard differ from the way you thought things would work? How would you modify your list of things to look for in light of what you actually observed?

   As an extension of this exercise, have another student in your class observe the same meeting and write up a set of field notes independently. Then compare your notes with the other student's and write a description of the ways in which they differ and the points on which they agree.

3 Devise a simple prediction about the operation of your city council. (For example, 'Economic issues will produce more serious disagreements than social issues.') Develop an observational schedule that fully operationalises the concepts involved in the prediction and any strong rival interpretations you feel you would have to be able to rule out before having confidence in the original prediction. Observe at least two meetings of the council and use the observation schedule to record what you see. Write an essay both on what you concluded about your prediction and on how you would change the observation schedule after having had some experience with it. What shortcomings did you find?

Key terms

direct observation	structured observation	method effect
political ethnography	observation protocol	blending in
obtrusive research	unstructured observation	fitting in
unobtrusive research	field notes	going native
passive observation	observation schedule	critical ethnography
participant observation	interobserver reliability	

22 Revealing political understanding: discourse analysis

- How is discourse analysis different from content analysis and what are its advantages?
- In what way can key political relationships be revealed through discourse analysis?
- What are the main types of discourse analysis? How do functional and critical approaches differ?
- How does the notion of the social construction of reality relate to discourse analysis?
- What are the potential problems with discourse analysis and how can these pitfalls be overcome?

Introduction

Discourse analysis focuses on the use of language in politics. All qualitative approaches use discourse analysis to some extent: focus groups, political ethnography, interviews and the analysis of texts (written word), speech and even images which 'say a thousand words'. Quantitative approaches also use language, for example, the wording and assumptions of a survey can contain a worldview which is implicit in its **discourse**, that is, the way questions are framed and asked. Even the way in which a political subject is approached, quantitatively or qualitatively, makes certain assumptions about political reality as revealed in the ways we talk (discourse) about the political world.

Despite similarities in the way it looks at the political use of language, discourse analysis is not the same as content analysis. Content analysis, as we have seen in Chapter 12, focuses on the quantitative analysis of words and, in its more sophisticated forms, on the quantitative analysis of grammatical constructions and phraseology used in political texts. Discourse analysis focuses not only on the text but also on the overall strategy and impact of words as they are used, in order to understand how language can shape political understanding. In so doing, it attempts to reveal symbolic or latent meanings, which content analysis might miss, or can help to explain the significance of patterns revealed in content analysis. One might argue that discourse analysis examines not just the 'text' but the 'subtext' as well. In this sense, discourse analysis also looks at what is not said or what is implied as well as what is written. Indeed, it is not enough to know that an individual holds an opinion or how many times a word or phrase is repeated in a text. One must also know how words and concepts are associated with sets of views and the political implications of these interrelationships.

Discourse analysis can examine the way concepts are expressed, including the emotive and pejorative context. Again, in comparison to content analysis, discourse analysis is an intensive approach which focuses on a small number of key texts and would be inappropriate for large amounts of textual data. At the same time, discourse analysis and content analysis can complement each other. Exploratory discourse analysis might suggest categories for content analysis. Similarly, terms and relationships between words that repeatedly appear in content analysis can be explained as part of an overall mode of communication by discourse analysis. For discourse analysis, it is not just what is said but how it is said and how different views interrelate with one another. The linguistic evidence of how individuals and groups interact with each other in the political system can enhance our understanding of the nature of politics.

The social construction of reality

Discourse analysis, in its most sophisticated forms, is predicated on a notion of social constructionism, that is, discourse is used to construct social reality and individuals are compelled to deal with this reality. However, you will find that the notion of **social construction** is often difficult to define. Terms such as **constructivism** and **constructionism** are often used and can be easily confused. Table 22.1 provides a rough guide to distinguish the terms. Only in its most radical and constructivist forms could one argue that there is little relationship between political reality and discourse about politics.

There is little doubt that our understanding of the world is influenced by social relationships and by the power relationships behind them. These influences can be subtle and so deeply embedded in a social order we consider natural that the construction of the relationships is not always apparent. It can be difficult to notice the implications of power structures, and social relations are inherent in the very language we use to interact. Often it is only after a set of relationships and their underlying assumptions have been made explicit that the nature of the situation becomes clear.

This is not new. For example, the notion that only certain types of political elites can rule effectively, due to their innate characteristics, has been consistently challenged over the centuries. It has been alleged in the past that women, certain ethnic groups and those who paid little or no taxes or owned no land were unfit to vote or participate in public life. The arguments against participation in these cases were based less on external realities than on an interconnected set of beliefs about natural capabilities and limitations. It has taken centuries to unpick and challenge these beliefs, some of which stubbornly remain in the minds of a few.

Table 22.1 Definitions of types of constructivism and constructionism

> *Radical constructivism*: This is a rationalist position that argues that knowledge is not passively received by the senses, but is instead built up by an individual so the world is organised by the individual and not merely a reflection of external objective reality. Each individual's knowledge of the world is unique and cannot be compared to others.
>
> *Constructivism*: Like the radical version, this argues that the individual mind constructs reality, but in the moderate view there is a systematic relationship between the mind and external reality, so there is some basis for comparison.
>
> *Social constructivism*: Argues that the individual mind constructs reality in its relationship to the world based on strong influences from social relationships.
>
> *Social constructionism*: Focuses on discourse as the vehicle through which the self and the world are articulated. This discourse manifests itself in social relationships.
>
> *Sociological constructionism*: Focuses on the way understanding is influenced by power relationships. This includes both informal social power and institutionalised governmental power.

Adapted from Gergen 1999: 60.

It is only in retrospect that such notions, such as the idea that women are unfit for political life, seem absurd. None the less, in the context in which such beliefs are held, the socialisation and education of women, their role in the household and relationships with society could be so arranged as to reinforce the view that women are unfit for politics. The discourse opposing the involvement of women in politics has argued, for example, that females are too emotional, illogical and weak to withstand the rigours of political debate and competition or would produce poor decisions based on these alleged defects. These alleged deficiencies might even appear to be empirically correct given the limitations of women in society at certain periods in history or in specific societies from the position of male researchers who would have observed it. It is only in the context of understanding how the position of women in politics is socially constructed that the nature of the limitations has been made clear.

At the same time, there may be limits to the notion that all social reality is socially constructed. For example, is the view that children are incapable of independent political involvement socially constructed? The answer would be yes, but it is founded in the very real issue of the social and emotional maturity of children. The fact that such arguments were used to exclude women or the poor from politics does not mean that they are not valid for children. A case could be made for additional involvement of children in political life, but it would have to consider the differences between adults and children. One might reasonably argue it is a mistake to dismiss such differences as socially constructed, even if that is true to a large degree.

The concept of social construction is most useful when we consider all interaction, not just speaking and writing, as communicating our understanding of the world in interaction with others. All of us 'construct' reality, political and otherwise, through these assumptions and interactions. 'Reading' these interactions, and decoding the assumptions which might lie behind them, is a crucial aspect of discourse analysis.

An example

Consider the following typical interaction at a protest march:

Passerby: Why are you protesting?

Protester: It is important to make a stand.

Passerby: It will not do any good.

Protester: Yes it will.

This situation represents a clash between two views of protest activity. Additional research would be required to examine the underlying complexities of the attitudes represented by this simple exchange:

- The protester might believe the passerby is trying to discourage them by denying the efficacy of the protest action. Therefore, it is essential to demonstrate that she is not discouraged or wavering.
- The passerby might believe in the aims of the protest but could feel that there are more effective ways of bringing about change or could have once been a protester herself but came to think that protest action is futile.

Both standpoints would be part of a set of interrelated ideas and beliefs. These beliefs reflect larger worldviews which can only be examined by interviews, further observation or reading and discussing the views of individuals and groups of individuals. It is only then that discourse can be analysed and understood.

One typical aspect of the interaction outlined above is the view of the individuals towards others. The protester may hold the view that anyone questioning the protest is opposed to it, in that those who do not wholeheartedly agree must be opponents. In this context, it is a clear sense of a defined 'us' against 'them' (others who are not us). The passerby may hold the belief that protest is ineffective because the political system is biased in favour of a small elite. This apathy may reflect a **hegemonic** outlook (overarching and controlling set of views) which, for example, discourages all but the most conventional forms of political participation, such as voting. The protester, in contrast, may display the attitudes of an individual who has developed a philosophy of **resistance** which challenges this hegemonic outlook and believes a broader range of political action is valuable.

Hegemonic views of what is right and wrong in a society can be so ubiquitous that we tend not to notice them in our daily lives. It is often only when something goes wrong or we are forced to challenge some of these unstated assumptions about correct behaviour or beliefs that these overarching and implicit values in a society become clear and are questioned. In this sense, discourse is often deeply **embedded** in the day-to-day interactions of a society, including its political interactions and assumptions.

Embedded discourse

Key political relationships can be revealed by analysis of discourse. It is not just directly political subjects which are important. Embedded socio-political structures, such as social class, are often expressed as differences in the way people communicate with each other and the subjects they choose to talk about. Looking at the types of relationships individuals and groups stress as important or the ideas they fear or hold dear will say much on their worldview as political actors.

A strategy of discourse analysis might, for example, look at the following four features of embedded political discourse:

1 **Structures**. This is the set of beliefs which enable political actors to place themselves in context. This includes beliefs about class, religion, community, citizenship etc.
2 **Identities**. These place the individual within a set of beliefs which underpin identification with a position within a structure, for example, statements such as 'I am a conservative', 'I am working-class', 'I am a freedom fighter', 'I do not care much for politics' etc.
3 **Dynamics**. This is the set of relationships which political actors believe connect them to others. It incorporates notions of how they relate to others and how others might frustrate or facilitate their political goals, for example, the belief that 'the upper classes try to keep the working classes in their place' or that 'there is no point in trying to change the political system because it is corrupt' etc.
4 **Agency**. This is the set of actions that political actors believe must be taken to deal with others and achieve their goals, for example, 'we must fight for our rights', 'only a strong political leader can save the country', or 'only traditional values will solve social problems' etc.

Discourse analysis looks at the way language is used and manipulated in politics. For example, discourse can be used to divide opponents and unify or mobilise one's allies ('Us' against 'them', 'Why we fail' and 'Why they succeed'). The protester in the example above might divide the world into the activists, such as herself, who want change (or the good 'us'), and entrenched interests which oppose fundamental change to the political system (or the bad 'them'). Those critical of protest or simply apathetic might be viewed as bad as the 'them' because they too do nothing to promote change. Any discourse which questions the need for or extent of change can be seen to undermine meaningful political progress.

Furthermore, it is not just the content but also the mode of expression. Discourse can be confrontational or accommodating. In fact, it is how others are viewed and treated that will tell you a lot about the political orientation of those speaking or writing. This can be as obvious as how the views are expressed or more subtle, such as how many times one speaker tries to interrupt or talk over another or cynical comments on behaviour, language and dress sense. There will be differences in how the discourse unfolds, depending on gender, personal background, political experience and other attributes. Part of discourse analysis involves teasing out the patterns to these interactions as much as analysing the content of the speech or written words. All these aspects of discourse, most of which go beyond simply the words used, can be part of the research. These are also the aspects of discourse likely to be missed in conventional content analysis.

Approaches to discourse analysis

There are a bewildering variety of approaches to discourse analysis and this chapter can only provide some sense of the overall features. One key is how the researcher views **epistemology**, that is, how human beings understand or 'know' what is happening in the world around them. This is why the concept of the **social construction of reality**, or how we put together our knowledge of our world, is sufficiently important to be discussed at some length above. In this context, discourse is crucial because our understanding of our world, especially the social and political aspects of our world, is constructed by our language.

Since language is so central, discourse analysis often focuses on linguistic issues such as grammar and rhetoric. At the same time, it is essential that the focus of research into politics does not stray too much from politics to minor problems of linguistic theory. Psychological aspects of discourse can also be fruitfully used to gain insights to political discourse since our fears, hopes and desires impact on political interactions. However, once again, it is unhelpful if the analysis is so overwhelmed with psychoanalysis that the politics of the discourse becomes secondary. The same can be said of anthropological and sociological approaches. The practices and experience of discourse analysis in other academic fields should inform and enhance political analysis but not obscure it. Discourse analysis also relies heavily on interpretation, which is why any researcher considering using this analysis should also carefully read Chapter 23 on 'Hermeneutics'.

Discourse analysis can, and often should, be connected to theoretical understandings of politics. For example, a Marxist might look not only at how discourse within and between classes had kept the working class 'in its place' and preserved a privileged position for the middle and upper classes, but also at the latent contradictions which undermine this dominance. In another context, it might be used to examine how political extremists are able to recruit supporters. This can be used to test and refine theories of extreme right-wing or left-wing movements or religious fundamentalism.

It is worth pausing here to make a distinction between ideology and discourse. Discourse analysis is not the analysis of ideology. The term ideology usually refers to/means a system of beliefs with a logical structure and comprehensive vision of how the world works. You may have studied socialism, communism, conservatism, anarchism or other ideologies including the major theorists. In contrast, discourse is how individuals and organisations articulate their beliefs and understanding of the world. The logic and assumptions of ideology are often distinct from the discourse of individuals who hold an ideology, because discourse is more interactive and focused on the accommodation of beliefs to actual situations. Few individuals are driven purely by ideology so that their discourse is perfectly consistent with their ideology. In fact, there are always compromises and contradictions in ideologically framed beliefs held by individuals in real-world politics. A study of ideology can provide background to discourse analysis, but ideology is generally more coherent and explicit than discourse. When discourse is pointedly non-ideological ('I am not political, but . . .'), then understanding the implicit structure of belief systems is even more important.

Functional discourse analysis

The simplest and crudest approach to discourse analysis can be termed *functional discourse analysis*. This approach most often relies on a predetermined set of categories and concepts through which discourse is analysed. A **functional** approach would note that certain types of beliefs seem to correlate with other beliefs and specific sets of political behaviour. It relates discourse to specific roles and institutional settings. Some instrumentalist uses of Marxism can be functionalist in this sense so that events, institutions and individuals are seen as either serving the interests of capitalism or the working class.

Functionalism is no longer as explicit in the social sciences as it once was, but many theories of politics still retain a functional understanding of politics. For example, political research into political participation may look at the degree to which an individual is integrated or alienated from the political system. Sites of political socialisation will be examined, such as the family, school, peer groups etc., to determine the degree to which each facilitates integration with the political system or fosters alienation. Analysis in these cases is simply a matter of finding discourse that is consistent with the predetermined categories which are theoretically assumed to exist. Functional discourse analysis is most similar to content analysis, though there will be differences in the depth and sophistication of analysis. It attempts to find discourse that fits the concepts and categories, usually derived from a theoretical research programme.

Critical discourse analysis

In contrast to functionalism we have *critical discourse analysis*. It has been used for many years in anthropology and sociology but is also found in political studies. **Critical** discourse analysis focuses on discourse in order to reveal power relations which oppress and control. By examining how discourse reproduces social and political inequality, power abuse or domination, it can reveal the processes of control and identify or foster effective strategies of resistance and change to combat these problems. That is, critical discourse analysis goes beyond a purely functional approach to discourse by systematically considering the complexities and consequences of structures of discourse. The focus is not neutrality. It is a conscious attempt to reveal problems and address them. Unlike functional approaches to discourse analysis, the categories are not necessarily derived theoretically. More important is a critical frame of mind for looking at how political and power relations are expressed and reinforced in subtle and unexpected ways. You will be familiar with this approach from the discussion of critical ethnography in Chapter 21, but it is also connected to radical hermeneutics discussed in Chapter 23.

For example, it might make sense to examine how particular groups are isolated or excluded based on the discourse used to discuss them. This usually involves a set of stereotypes such as racist, right-wing discourse on the role of Muslims in British society. These stereotypes used to exclude groups are very resilient and may have a long tradition. The beliefs that Muslims are violent, lust after Western women and are religious fanatics might seem new, but such views have existed in the West since the Middle Ages (Karim 1997: 153–82). Even though the lives and behaviour of most Muslims would not justify such beliefs, discourse on Islam is used to highlight differences between Muslims and Christians and to selectively point to specific incidents to support the stereotypes. An examination of average Muslims throughout history would reveal them as peaceful, chaste and humbly pious. However, even mainstream political leaders can find it useful to use negative images of Islam and Muslims to promote their own policies and political careers. It is also easy to sell such stereotypes because they create a sense of urgency and fear. This creates solidarity among political followers in opposition to a clear enemy. Discourse analysis can look at how exclusion is used and its consequences for those who seek advantages from it as well as those who are harmed by it.

The problem with critical discourse analysis is that it would seem to violate the need for objectivity in research. After all, if a researcher has already decided to look for oppression and control, for example, then that research is likely to find it or interpret the discourse to support that point of view. Some might believe that the results of any such research will be tainted. Objectivity, however, is not straightforward. Even those using a functionalist approach to discourse or content analysis have made prior decisions about which categories to use for analysis. Even if these categories are drawn from theoretical expectations, they are still assumptions. The problem, therefore, is not the objective truth of categories. No categories are objectively valid. The problem of biased research approaches arises when researchers are not explicit about how the categories used are constructed, and are not open to the possibility the categories are incorrect or need modification.

One might approach research on political socialisation in families from a gender critical perspective, for example, but find that it is not simply gender but also social-economic factors that play a role. Gender may be a factor in ways that were not anticipated. An approach critical of patriarchy might be expecting the father to directly discourage daughters' involvement in politics, but find that it is more likely that other male relatives can play a larger role or that female relatives are also important. An approach focused only on a narrow conception of patriarchy would fail to understand the complexity of the gendered discourse in family political socialisation. Openness and willingness to see alternatives and modify your approach to a problem is crucial in any type of research. If this is done explicitly, consistently and systematically in research, then the problem of bias can be partially addressed.

Application of discourse analysis to politics

In the section which follows are two applications of discourse analysis to politics. The first, and the most formal example below, examines aspects of democratic theory. The second uses critical discourse theory. Each approach is slightly different, but the nature of applied discourse analysis should be clearer after reviewing these examples.

The politics of accommodation

Steiner *et al.* (2004) have undertaken a very sophisticated analysis of parliamentary discourse in order to reveal the extent to which the quality of discourse is a factor in deliberative politics. They contrast the assumption in much of political science that politicians and groups only pursue their narrowly defined interests with the fact that a 'politics of accommodation' is often needed to make democracy work. In a democracy, debate must be undertaken with the aim of persuading opponents and modifying views to reach a mutually acceptable solution. Even when one group or another forces through its own views, it is usually not the end of the debate. Continuous exchange of views and compromise is essential to preserve democracy. In those societies in which there is a significant minority population with interests divergent from the majority, this spirit of accommodation is even more important. Therefore, they searched for a discourse of accommodation which might underpin this crucial aspect of democracy.

They created their categories for analysis from a wide range of literature from comparative politics and the political philosophy. These ideas were tested against actual parliamentary discourse in western Europe. This discourse is coded, much along the lines of content analysis, to determine the level of participation (i.e. was the speaker interrupted or given an opportunity to speak?); the level of justification (i.e. was there no justification of the speaker's position, a weak justification, qualified justification or a sophisticated justification?); content of justifications (i.e. explicit use of group interest, neutral statements, explicit on common good in utilitarian terms, and explicit on common good in terms of the difference principle?); was respect shown for opponents (i.e. no respect, neutral, explicit respect, and to what degree were counter-arguments of opponents ignored, included and valued?); and how constructive political dialogue was (i.e. was the original position retained, or were alternative or mediating proposals created?). These categories were coded based on a clear and explicit set of rules (which are set out in an appendix on the Discourse Quality Index) (Steiner *et al.* 2004: 170–79)

They found that not all aspects of discourse quality were important at all times or in all settings (parliamentary debates versus committee deliberations), but that overall the quality of the discourse of accommodation did have an influence on the ability of democratic institutions to reach compromises. This research is a more formal version of discourse analysis, again closest to content analysis, and hypotheses are derived from a wide range of politics literature.

Critical discourse analysis

The critical approach to discourse analysis has been used by Fairclough (1995) in examining how 'enterprise' discourse and 'business' discourse have crept into public service organisations with the implicit argument that such thinking is inappropriate and to the disadvantage of the individuals working in the sector. He examined the possible meanings of enterprise and business discourse and how it has been used or transformed into a dominant mode of public discourse, including in universities. These new forms of discourse pose a challenge to traditional understanding of work but also constrain the ways in which traditions can be defended, particularly if they seem to deny economic rationales of efficiency and utility. Once business discourse takes hold in a public service institution, it tends to colonise key posts so that subsequent recruitment and promotion depends on sharing the identity of those who believe and accept the intellectual rational of the business approach. In this way, Fairclough demonstrates the process by which new forms of domination take hold and advance their interests, and why it is often difficult to resist them.

Engaging in discourse analysis

Theoretical or critical perspective

As the discussion above suggests, theoretical literature is just as important in discourse analysis as it is in other forms of research. The role of literature is clearest in functional approaches where analysis of discourse is aimed at revealing structures and relationships which are expected by the theory. In doing so, the nature of these structures and relationships must be made explicit and hypotheses can be formulated in advance of the analysis. Critical discourse analysis also often has a critical perspective which can and should be made explicit, such as a focus on gender, race, class, exclusion, repression, resistance etc. drawn from insights provided by the literature. Identifying the theoretical framework can be a problem if the literature related to the subject is limited and the research is exploratory along the lines of political ethnography where no assumptions are made going into the research. None the less, as in critical discourse analysis, the orientation of the researcher can and should be made explicit at the outset of the research, including the works of literature which inform the critical perspective, and a record made of how it was modified in interaction with others.

Identifying the individuals or groups

Since structures and relationships in discourse analysis can be complex, analysis usually focuses on specific individuals or groups who can reveal the nature of the discourse in their usage and interaction with others. In functional discourse analysis, identification of individuals and groups should flow from the theory. For example, you will need to look for members of a specific social class, oppressed group, political elite etc. In critical theory, it should be clear whether the research is focused on relations of domination or resistance or both. Again, in ethnographic methods of data collection for critical discourse analysis, the perspective of the researcher in relation to these individuals and groups is important.

Selecting appropriate 'texts'

The term 'texts' here refers to the data collected in order to be analysed. You must take care to ensure that the discourse identified and collected is truly representative of the individuals and groups you plan to study. An effort must be made to collect discourse which is appropriate to make the claim that it reflects the beliefs and orientations of those being studied. Things said and written in moments of crisis are interesting, but they cannot be said to be representative of everyday normal discourse. Crisis and stress may reveal hidden anxieties and wishes, but cannot be taken as representative of all beliefs at all times. The context of collection and the range of possible discourse must be considered to provide a complete picture of where the discourse fits into the lives of those studied.

Refining versus building models

Functional uses of discourse analysis focus on testing and refining models of relationships and orientations. If the theory specifies that individuals are integrated into the political system through family socialisation, then the collection of discourse in this case will be aimed at refining our understanding of the process by which this is done. Critical analysis, in particular, will be aimed at building models of interaction based on observation and analysis of relationships identified in discourse. In both cases, it is crucial that you state your models clearly so that they can be understood and tested by others in similar situations.

Collecting and reporting the results

Discourse analysis inevitably must be more selective in the texts it considers compared to content analysis. None the less, large of amounts of discourse must be collected and analysed for patterns to emerge and relationships to be confirmed. The amount of data collected can be unwieldy. It is important to summarise key beliefs and relationships with quotations of discourse to serve as examples. This evidence must be summarised and used in support of a model carefully. Where it appears that the meaning of a text has been twisted to fit the model, the argument made will be much less persuasive. For the extent to which meaning might be contested, you need to refer to Chapter 23 on hermeneutics.

Ethical considerations

In its most conventional forms discourse analysis, like content analysis, often starts with predetermined categories into which the data are to be placed. It does tend to privilege pre-existing assumptions about the nature of the discourse. The words and ideas of those being studied can be unreasonably forced into a theoretical scheme that is inappropriate. In doing so, the analysis itself just becomes part of the political discourse with its own interpretation of the world (for example, post-colonialism).

This notion of discourse can be used to analyse the discourse of politics academic research as much as politics itself. For example, it is easier to get government research grants and publication outlets for research that engages in a discourse focused on radical Islamic terrorist groups rather than on peaceful, democratic Islamic communities. Of course, governments and the general population perceive the danger of Islamic fundamentalist terrorism as immediate and demand research to understand the nature of the threat. However, an excessive focus on extremist Islam, even as part of an 'objective' research programme, will tend to reinforce societal stereotypes and can aid and abet politicians who manipulate these images. In this way, the discourse of academic research on Islam can have an impact on the overall political discourse of a community. This suggests that you must think about the consequences of research beyond the narrow focus of a particular study.

The mode of analysis and communication of ideas in discourse analysis can also be problematic. The approach draws from other disciplines such as linguistics and semiotics, so it is not unusual for technical terms from disciplines outside politics to be incorporated into discourse research. In addition, academics who engage in discourse analysis use new terms which can be difficult to understand, such as 'the structure of discursive formations' and 'relations of domination'. When these are defined, then there is not usually a problem, but the usage of terms such as 'discursive' in discourse analysis can be significantly different from its normal dictionary definition. Excessive use of specialist jargon in this approach, as in any other method, can obscure rather than inform. This is a problem to the extent that discourse analysis creates its own discourse which is inaccessible or only open to the privileged few who share a belief in the assumption, implicit in the vocabulary.

Discourse analysis must also deal with the problem of how the text is selected and the validity of the inferences which can be drawn from the text. Texts selected from speeches by individuals who hold extreme views may not be representative of the entire group of which they are part. A case must be made for the selection of the text or individuals studied and the attribution of patterns of thinking to groups from individual cases.

Finally, critical discourse analysis challenges conventional approaches to objectivity and reality, but must still address the problems of bias and empirical validity. When research diverges from standard norms of objectivity, then the advantages of critical approaches must be demonstrated and in all cases the potential drawbacks acknowledged.

Conclusion

All political analysis uses language in some form, so discourse analysis aids us in understanding how language is used to structure interactions in political contexts. Since some of the structures and interaction are not immediately apparent, critical discourse is useful in exploring potential assumptions about the nature of political relationships and our understanding of the political world.

Summary points

■ Discourse analysis shares some of the attributes of content analysis but it focuses on much more complex and implicit relationships which would be missed by content analysis.

■ Empirical political analysis often focuses on simple political relationships which are easy to study. Discourse analysis reveals hidden orientations which are embedded in complex and large-scale political relationships. Making sense of these embedded beliefs and constraints will produce more nuanced and thoughtful political research.

- Functional approaches to discourse analysis start with an existing theory or an assumed set of relationships. It is then just a matter of using the discourse to determine whether these relationships are manifest in discourse and how they reveal themselves. Critical approaches focus much more on relations of domination and resistance. Because techniques of domination and reactions to control can evolve and vary overtime, it is more difficult to specify set relationships and the discourse which would reveal them.

- Although discourse analysis does not depend on the notion of the social construction of reality, there is a strong assumption that discourse shapes social understanding of reality and that individuals and groups act on this understanding. Changes in discourse indicate a change in understanding and will be reflected in beliefs and interactions.

- As with any method, the key is to provide a theoretical context for the research, select representative data and conduct analysis in a way that is transparent, coherent and consistent. The validity of text selection is a key issue in discourse analysis and considerable effort is required to demonstrate that discourse data represents the beliefs and relationships identified by the researcher.

Suggested reading and examples

Research examples

Discourse theory is increasingly used to study politics in Europe, for example, Steiner *et al.* (2004) *Deliberative Politics in Action*. On British politics there are works such as *New Labour, New Language*? (Fairclough 2000) whose work was noted above, and a study by Jordan 'The Europeanization of national government and policy' in the *British Journal of Political Science* (2003). The approach is probably most widely used in international relations, including security studies such as Campbell (1998) *Writing Security: United States Foreign Policy and the Politics of Identity*, Hansen (2006) *Security as Practice: Discourse Analysis and the Bosnian War* and Jackson (2005) *Writing the War on Terrorism: Language, Politics and Counter-terrorism*; gender in international relations theory, Hooper (2001) *Manly States: Masculinities, International Relations and Gender Politics*; *The Politics of Famine Relief,* Edkins (2000) *Whose Hunger? Concepts of Famine, Practices of Aid*; and environmental protection, Dalby (2002) *Environmental Security*.

Methodological reading

There are numerous books promising to explain how to engage in discourse analysis. Most are heavy on theory and light on clear rules for analysis. Part of the problem is that discourse analysis can quickly be overwhelmed by linguistic theory and particularly semiotic theory. The following are a few of the more practical guides, but even they cannot completely escape from lingusitic issues: Jørgensen and Phillips (2002) *Discourse Analysis as Theory and Method*; Johnstone (2008) *Discourse Analysis*; McHoul and Rapley (2001) *How to Analyse Talk in Institutional Settings*.

References

Campbell, David. 1998. *Writing Security: United States Foreign Policy and the Politics of Identity*, Manchester: Manchester University Press.

Dalby, Simon. 2002. *Environmental Security*, Minneapolis: University of Minnesota Press.

Edkins, Jenny. 2000. *Whose Hunger? Concepts of Famine, Practices of Aid*. Minneapolis: University of Minnesota Press.

Fairclough, Norman. 1995. *Critical Discourse Analysis: The Critical Study of Language*. London: Longman.

Fairclough, Norman. 2000. *New Labour, New Language*? London: Routledge.

Gergen, K. 1999. *An Invitation to Social Construction*. London: Sage.

Hansen, Lene. 2006. *Security as Practice: Discourse Analysis and the Bosnian War*. London: Routledge.

Hooper, Charlotte. 2001. *Manly States: Masculinities, International Relations and Gender Politics*. New York: Columbia University Press.

Jackson, Richard. 2005. *Writing the War on Terrorism: Language, Politics and Counter-terrorism*. Manchester: Manchester University Press.

Johnstone, B. 2008. *Discourse Analysis*, 2nd edn. Oxford: Blackwell.

Jordan, Andrew. 2003. 'The Europeanization of National Government and Policy'. *British Journal of Political Science*, vol. 33, no. 2 (April), pp. 261–82.

Jørgensen, M. and Phillips, L. 2002. *Discourse Analysis as Theory and Method*. London: Sage.

Karim, H. Karim 1997. 'The historical resilience of primary stereotypes: core images of the Muslim other' in Stephen Riggins, ed. *The Language and Politics of Exclusion: Others In Discourse*. Thousand Oaks, CA: Sage.

McHoul, A. and Rapley, M. eds. 2001. *How to Analyse Talk in Institutional Settings: A Casebook of Methods*. New York: Continuum.

Steiner, J., Bächtiger, A., Spörndli, M. and Steenbergen, M. R. (2004). *Deliberative Politics in Action: Analyzing Parliamentary Discourse*. Cambridge: Cambridge University Press.

Research exercises

1 Organise a group discussion with 6–7 students on a controversial and topical political subject. The students should be a mixed group with both male and female and from varied backgrounds (state/ private school, geographical origins etc.). Indicate that you are interested in their views but for the purposes of this exercise focus more on how these views are expressed. Who is more likely to speak or interrupt others? How are views expressed? Is strong language or slang used and by whom? Who tends to agree with others or solicit the views of the rest of the group? Who insists that they are right or tries the hardest to persuade others? Note differences in gender, background, experience and other attributes. Is there a set pattern to the ways political discourse is performed based on differences in gender, educational background etc.?

2 Examine the websites of 30 or more major corporations in which they discuss corporate responsibility in such areas as environmental protection. Are there patterns to how the role of the company is presented? Are certain keywords used repeatedly in most of the web pages accessed? Is the tone idealistic or realistic, friendly or serious, simple to understand or technically sophisticated? To whom is the text attributed: the public relations section or one of the executives or is it anonymous? Compare the texts with critiques made by relevant non-profit organisations (such as environmental protest groups) of corporate attitudes towards these issues and the corporate counter-arguments. What are the key differences between the non-profit organisation and corporate discourse on the same issues?

3 Collect the party conference keynote speeches of the leaders of one political party for the past thirty years and compare the discourse within the speeches. Exclude references to topical issues of the day and focus instead on key themes repeated through two or more conferences. Do issues shift in terms of the context and timing of their appearance in the speech? Does the meaning of keywords remain the same or change over time? Does the style and content of the discourse indicate the type of audience the leader is trying to reach? How would one describe the potential audience and how it changes from year to year?

Key terms

agency	dynamics	identities
constructionism	embedded	resistance
constructivism	epistemology	social construction
critical	functional	social construction of reality
discourse	hegemonic	structures

23 Hermeneutics and interpretation in pol itical research

- What is hermeneutics and how can it help to develop a better understanding of the nuances of meaning in political research?
- How do the main types of approaches to hermeneutics differ?
- What are the advantages and drawbacks of each approach?
- How can inter-subjectivity and reflexivity help to deal with the problems of interpretation?

Introduction

This chapter is aimed at bringing together arguments that are implicit or underdeveloped in previous chapters. The concept of hermeneutics was mentioned in the first chapter as was the notion of reflexivity. The previous chapter on discourse analysis raised similar issues, but now it is essential that we consider the fundamental problems of interpretation. Most of these problems involve the relationship of the researcher as an interpreter. In the end, these also have implications for the ethics of the relationship between the researcher and researched.

Hermeneutics is probably a new term to you but it is just a fancy word for interpretation. As we have seen, all the chapters of this book require the investigator to engage in some degree of interpretation. Quantitative research requires one to interpret the nature of the problem and the best categories for data collection. The results of quantitative research might be numerical but one should not ignore the need for interpretation in making sense of the results as well. When the focus of research is comparative or qualitative methods are used, interpretation is even more important.

It is true that a discussion of hermeneutics moves us away from traditional political analysis. Hermeneutics does not aim at explanation but can enhance understanding.

One might ask: How are explanation and understanding different? In examining a political event, such as the terrorist attacks on New York and Washington on 11 September 2001, it is not enough to simply ask 'What happened?' (an empirical question), one is also compelled to ask 'What did it mean?' (a question of interpretation). Even if we explain the 'facts' of the events leading to 11 September and the reaction of political leaders afterward, we still need to consider the significance of the events and how others have interpreted them. Thus, there is clearly a difference between explanation – defined as an empirically demonstrated causal explanation of an event, and interpretation – which involves ways of attempting to understand the significance of an event. Hermeneutics is especially useful when no definitive explanation is possible or existing explanations are highly contentious.

This chapter explains the nature of hermeneutics and its relationship to political research. It provides a background to various strategies of interpretation and the problems with each approach, as well as some partial solutions. It also discusses in more detail the key notion of 'reflexivity', which is the idea that the researcher must be aware of their relationship to the subject being researched. The aim is to produce not only more sensitive researchers but also ones who can carry out rigorous and engaging research.

Therefore, this chapter ends by discussing the ethical issues raised in each of the chapters of this book. There is no one correct interpretation of the nature of politics. This textbook should help you pursue politics research with a high degree of sophistication and care, but even the most rigorous researcher must engage the problem of interpretation. It is essential that a politics researcher be open-minded and make an effort to understand other perspectives on, approaches to and interpretations of politics.

The nature of hermeneutics

Hermeneutics is not new. Its origins lie in biblical interpretation and it is still commonly used in this context today. It emerged because the Reformation challenged the authority of the established Catholic Church in Europe and suggested that Christians should develop their own personal relationship with God. In order for this to happen, the Bible was translated into the local languages and widely read without the guidance of the clergy. However, the meaning of the Bible is not always clear and the context in which it was written was very different from the world in which it was subsequently being read, so it was often difficult for readers to apply the scripture to their own lives. As a result, there emerged a need for strategies to interpret biblical texts.

Simply put, hermeneutics are strategies for assessing the meaning of a **text**. It is now applied to understanding all 'texts', sacred and secular, and the idea of a 'text' has been broadened to include all things (cultural artefacts) produced by human beings. Of course, political data, images and events are included in this broader definition of a 'text'. Hermeneutics, in this sense, is very important in cutting-edge research in politics.

There are a few key elements of a hermeneutic strategy. Not all are given equal weight and there is considerable disagreement among scholars over which element or elements are most important. The basic ones are as follows:

1   *'Authorial' intention.* What did the person or persons who created the text or object or engaged in an action intend to convey when they created it or acted? How can we know what the author really intended?
2   *Nature or genre of the 'text'.* What was the purpose of the text or action? Was it intended to have a specific impact (such as party political platform or a revolutionary proclamation or terrorist attack)?
3   *Context.* When was it created? How did the historical, social and political context of the time have an impact on the meaning and significance of the text or event?
4   *Role of the 'reader'.* What was the audience at which the text or event was aimed and could that have an influence on its meaning? If a text or event became important or retained importance long after it was created, what was it about the text that made people later view it as important?

Approaches to interpretation

Depending on the weighting given to each of the above elements there are differing strategies to approaching a text or event.

Conventional

The conventional approach to hermeneutics tries to reconstruct the meaning of a text or event from the available evidence. What is the evidence based on the documentary record to indicate the meaning of a

Table 23.1 Narratives of governance

	Traditions			
	Tory	**Liberal**	**Whig**	**Socialist**
Narrative of governance	Wrecked intermediate institutions.	Building networks of communities.	Return to the organic constitution.	Joining-up government.
Storyline	Preserving traditional authority.	Restoring markets and combating state overload.	Evolutionary change.	Redefining the bureaucratic state.

Source: Bevir and Rhodes: (2004: 131).

text or political event? This record is usually based on interviews and documents directly related to the event. This can be supplemented by contextual information – what else was happening at the time – to help make sense of beliefs and actions, but the documentary record is the main basis of interpretation.

Authorial intention is often given priority here. That is, it is argued that a text or event means what the author or actor meant it to be. For example, Bevir and Rhodes (2003) have identified 'Narratives of governance' (Table 23.1) based on the beliefs of British higher civil servants. These beliefs and preferences, they argue, supplement and supplant the formal authority of government so must be studied for a clearer picture of British governance to emerge. They argue that their interviews and analysis of civil servants' beliefs provides more detail and nuance than conventional accounts, and that focusing on the meanings of main characters in the policy-making process allows for a special kind of authenticity. This approach, as one critic put it, seems 'to privilege (indeed almost exclusively entail) the actor's own contemporary interpretations of their own actions' (Dowding 2004: 137), so is an extreme case of intentionalism which seems to rely almost entirely on interviews. In fact, it points to the dangers of relying on interviews alone.

Studies focused on authorial intention or the meaning of events as interpreted by the participants themselves are normally supplemented with the corpus of writing by the individual or individuals involved, including autobiographical material and their correspondence with others. In the case of historical subjects, where interviews are no longer possible, this other evidence is the main focus of reconstructing authorial intention. Less reliable, but also essential material focuses on what others believe that the author or political actors meant. This might involve interviews, writings or correspondence of family members, colleagues, friends and even enemies. The danger of this information is that hearsay regarding what others have reported them to have said is not as reliable as direct interviews or documents written by the person or persons themselves.

Contextual information is often necessary to put authorial intentions and actors' beliefs into perspective. The position of the individual or group is essential in making sense of intentions and beliefs. Orientations can vary according to that individual's or group's place in an organisation, institution, society or political system. Looking only at the perspective of the person or persons involved in an event is often too narrow. Contemporary newspaper articles can tell you what else was happening at the time and how a particular individual or group view was reported at the time. For more recent political actors and events, there is a wealth of information from public opinion surveys, interviews with other relevant individuals and related documentary evidence to put the focus of your study in context. This information can be used to compare your case with similar ones to suggest possible patterns or contrasts. Even secondary sources, including biographies, provide a more comprehensive background to an individual, group or event to help put them into perspective.

Table 23.2 Historicist approaches

> ***Strong historicism***: There is a logic to history and understanding it will reveal the 'true' interpretation. This has both idealist (for example, Hegelian) and materialist (for example, Marxist) forms. History is interpreted as part of this 'grand design'.
>
> ***Historicist determinism***: Historical context explains the production of ideas embodied in texts and other artefacts of the period. The production of ideas, genre and theories are related to the presence of identifiable types of social classes, institutional arrangements, external threats etc. which are part of the historical period to which they belong.
>
> ***Weak historicism***: Interpretation must rely on knowing the historical context of the text, event etc. to be interpreted. Greater historical understanding allows one to get closer to the correct interpretation.
>
> ***Radical historicism***: Only the original audience at the time a work was produced can truly appreciate it, so valid interpretation is impossible.

In conventional studies of texts, the genre of a text is also important. In literary theory, this focuses on whether a piece of work is a play or a novel or a short story. Each has its own structure and purpose, though these vary over time. In politics there are also genre, such as a party manifesto, political speech and even a terrorist act. The last case also involves a specific type of act intended to elicit a relatively defined reaction. In this way, audience reception can also play a role here. The reception of the speech or terrorist act is part of the interpretation of the meaning of a political event.

This focus on historical context can be problematic. There is a danger with historicism. **Historicism** takes many forms and Table 23.2 provides a rough guide to key types. If history or political context is assumed to have structured or determined the beliefs and actions of individuals and groups, then it suggests that there is no autonomy on the part of individuals. Thus the intention of an author of a text or act almost becomes irrelevant. Since conventional approaches tend to rely on intentionalism, only weak forms of historicism usually play a role.

One argument in favour of the conventional approach is that it reflects standard validity arguments. It collects empirical evidence connected to an individual or event and bases the interpretation primarily on an assessment of this evidence. In reality, however, there are rarely enough pieces of evidence to reconstruct meaning completely from the available evidence. Even if we had full access to the person who created a text, it is not clear that that person knows all the meanings, some of which might be subconscious or unintentional but still significant. Rather than focus only on authorial intention or historical context, it may be that other information is needed to make sense of the significance of the text.

The biggest problem with the conventional approach is the relationship of the text to the reader and readers in general (**readership/audience**). The conventional approach would have us stick to the facts of authorial intention and historical context. They would argue that the problem of the reader is a separate issue which should not be confused with the text itself. They tend to resist the notion that interpreters can find new meanings for a text. For example, Betti does not deny subjectivity in interpretation, but there is a meaning of a text which is independent of any one interpreter. He insists that 'an object remains an object and an objectively valid interpretation can reasonably be striven for and accomplished' (Betti 1999: 56). He believes that although it may be difficult to achieve in some cases, it is an ideal worth pursuit.

For Betti, the main aim is for the subjective interpreter to engage the 'otherness' of the object or it would merely be a reflection of the interpreter's initial subjective views. Although we read and understand texts in the context of what interests us from our own experiences, we are pulled away from our own, and vicariously gain new experiences by trying to understand another viewpoint. From the point of view of conventional hermeneutics, we should not interpret in a way that merely confirms our own beliefs by imposing our interpretation on a text.

Hirsch argues that the significance of the text for the interpreter is not the point. It is only through trying to understand the 'meaning' of the text through understanding such things as the genre, similar texts from the place and time it was written, philology of the terms and usage of linguistic symbols or conventions, that we can obtain a valid understanding of a text. He makes a distinction between 'the meaning of a text (which does not change) and the meaning of a text to us today (which changes)' (1967: 255). However, Hirsch assumes that 'the meaning' in the first sense was and can be made clear.

Evolution of tradition

A very different approach to interpretation can be found in the work of Georg Gadamer. Gadamer was one of the most important philosophers of hermeneutics in the twentieth century and, in contrast to the conventional approach, he focused firmly on the reader as central to interpretation. The author of a text and the reader of a text are most often connected by language. We should note that Gadamer does not see language merely as a tool. It is a medium between individuals and the rest of being (existence), past, present and future (Scheibler 2000: 136–7). He maintains a holism that seems to oppose the analytical tradition of separating communication into parts without considering the whole (which includes the present).

From this perspective, the conventional focus on historical context or author intention misses the point. There are two aspects to interpretation from Gadamer's point of view: **reconstruction** and **integration**. The conventional approach focuses entirely on reconstruction; that is, trying to understand a work by reconstructing all elements of the context in which it was created: the author, historical context and maybe the original audience and purpose of a work. These are important, but must be viewed in the context of the need for integration; that is, allowing us to bring the work to life in a way that a mere knowledge of the context cannot do. For Gadamer, it is not just a case of reconstruction (of the intended or original contextual meaning) but also integration (making it meaningful for the current reader).

Gadamer goes on to suggest that this process of integration is mediated by previous readings, which he refers to as tradition, as an essential part of the context in which a work can be made sensible to (integrated with) us. Gadamer prefers to accept the reasoned arguments of traditions of interpretation (just as a jury verdict is accepted) in preference to a single rational observer's conclusions. He also suggests that dialogue and questioning of ideas is important as well as reconstructing original meaning. There must be a dialogue between reasoned tradition and the challenge of other perspectives (based on their own traditions and prejudices). Gadamer recognises that there are traditions which have negative implications, especially in the eyes of later observers. One example is the dominance of the male perspective in political history and political theory. Still, he believes that there must be a sense in which knowledge is held together to make it intelligible, and that role is played by tradition. To some degree we can reconstruct a less gender-biased understanding of the past from a variety of sources including letters, diaries and even works of art which can reveal the views of women. At the same time, we cannot ignore the political tradition as transmitted because it is also part of our understanding. In fact, existing political tradition might be reinterpreted in light of new perspectives. The way the male-dominated perspective on political history or theory portrayed, and sometimes revealed, a significant role for women tells us much. It can reveal the fears, hopes and contradictions are the foundation of a society and its politics.

Even so, we can never become another person to truly understand their intentions and interpretations, but we can reach out to attempt a **'fusion of horizons'** as Gadamer calls it (1989: 306–07). This implies two horizons: the one of the interpreter, the other of the author or person being interpreted. Interpreters have limited horizons based on the traditions in which they operate but the text, person or event has a different horizon which pulls the reader away from familiar understanding towards new ideas and understandings. Gadamer recognises the pull of the 'Other' as Betti put it, but also wants to recognise the role of the reader as co-equal.

One word often used by Gadamerians is dialogue. We are in a dialogue with a work or a research subject. We can say what we like about it, but we must be prepared to listen to what it has to say. What it CAN say is not just what the author intended to say but also what it has said (meant) to people in the past and to others in other times and contexts since. We must constantly return to the work itself to make sure that we have not twisted the meaning unreasonably or to make sense of where traditional meanings may diverge from new readings, but new readings are part of the context you should consider. For example, Hannah Pitkin has examined the key concept of fortune or luck in Machiavelli which is anthropomorphised as a woman (1984/1999). Although she does not consciously use a Gadamerian perspective, her close reading of Machiavelli's use of the concept reveals a disturbingly misogynistic side to his writing. This adds to our understanding of his thought. At the same time, it is essential that this new reading is discussed in the context of the existing literature on Machiavelli and the historical context in which he lived, thus not ignoring the tradition from which it springs.

This is why feminist readings of political theory have been such important new developments in politics literature in recent decades, but other approaches are also possible, including disabled, gay, religious, secular or other perspectives. A dialogue with a text will prompt new questions about a thinker. Just as it is legitimate to critique an unacceptable view of a key thinker, it is also essential that we make an attempt to understand why it might be the case and how it relates to the rest of the system of thought in question. One problematic view in a thinker should not lead us to reject all of that thinker's ideas, but it should enable us to understand better the implications of this thought for us today.

This approach is said to be historical without historicism. It is interpretation constrained by understanding of the historical context of the original text and subsequent interpretation, including that of the current interpreter. To paraphrase Gadamer: 'The past is in the present and the present is in the past.' This suggests that while the historical context of the author is important, so is the historical context of the reader. It is not just being aware of what the author (or informant) is trying to say but also an awareness of what the reader (listener) wants out of it as well. This is not a relativist position which rejects older or alternative interpretations. It merely seeks to put each of the interpretations into context with the others.

Gadamer argues that we inevitably approach a text or event with certain 'baggage'. We are inevitably prejudiced in this sense because we have prejudgements that determine our interest in and approach to a problem. It might be more neutral to term this our **'structure of fore-understanding'** as he sometimes calls it, but Gadamer seems to want us to accept that we have prejudices and need to confront these in our approach to a text. This is not just a case of realising that one might have bias and trying to avoid it. One must also realise that you and your audience (peers, British academics, native English speakers) come from a specific tradition which has its concerns and you are expected to address those concerns. Not only is it pointless trying to ignore the tradition in which one works when trying to understand a text or event, that tradition is part of the understanding process.

The best example is the problem of 'going native' as noted in Chapter 21. If you use political ethnography, it is natural to begin to adopt the concerns of the people you study. However, you should remember that you are not necessarily one of those you are studying and that you have approached your subject, at least initially, from an academic point of view. Indeed, there is often little point in your becoming a spokesperson for the subjects of your research. The reason for your interaction with the people you study is to learn about them and advance academic research. Inevitably, if you are going to communicate with academics, you have to use the terms and techniques of your own academic community. Even if one does take the side of research subject, and it is perfectly legitimate to do so, it must be couched in terms that make it possible for other scholars to understand where your work fits in the existing academic traditions.

A large part of the problem of mediating traditions is bound up with the language we use. In fact, the main impact of tradition arises through the very language we use: 'Tradition is not a process that we learn to master but a transmitted language in which we live' (Habermas 1970: 359). Gadamer seems to argue for a more flexible view of language based on a constantly evolving language with changing traditions and with potential to draw on these traditions for more change. There is no system because humans create and recreate language. However, one problem with Gadamer is that the 'politics' behind the process of language and tradition creation and destruction is left unclear.

Radical hermeneutics

The final approach considered here is radical hermeneutics. This can often overlap with critical discourse analysis even though there are distinct attributes to both. The distinctive nature of radical hermeneutics becomes clearer when we look at the work of the literary philosopher Jacques Derrida. Derrida goes one step further than Gadamer by pointing out that language, and even the words and sentences constructed which make up a language, are unstable and unreliable as foundations for knowledge. If language is unstable, it will be difficult to pin down the meaning of texts and events constructed from language.

For example, how would you respond, if I were to ask you, 'Do you know what a political party is?' Everyone has a notion in their mind of a political party, but when confronted with a concrete example, it becomes necessary to move from the vague notion in your head and articulate what you meant clearly. Real political parties are always less perfect than the ideal concept in our heads. Eventually, there is a tendency to settle on a contextual definition. The definition will change depending on those aspects that can be quantitatively measured (as in number of members, votes and MPs), qualitatively measured (as in the organisational and ideological aspects of the party), or conceptually measured (as in the history of the idea of a political party and how the idea has changed over time). If we look historically, we can even find groups called parties which were not at all like modern parties. The term party was originally a negative term similar to the word faction today. Recently, political parties seem to be in decline, but they are still significant political organisations in most countries. The point is that there is often a big gap between the *signifier* (word or term such as 'party') and the *signified* (the things called 'party') when one tries to pin down the relationship precisely. If meaning is so unstable, then knowledge of authorial intention, context and even traditions are largely irrelevant. The current reader is sovereign in radical hermeneutics. Text and events can be interpreted in a variety of ways and the process of teasing out interpretations is the focus here, not the objective meaning of the text.

Since language is used in all aspects of politics and political research, a politics researcher must be aware of how language is used and manipulated. This use and manipulation may be conscious or unconscious. As we have seen in the chapter on discourse analysis, the meaning of language can be so deeply embedded into our understanding of the world that it takes considerable effort to untangle. One method used to untangle the complex relationship between the symbolic meaning of words and their referents is called **deconstruction**.

Deconstruction as [not] method

As with most hermeneutic approaches, it is often claimed that deconstruction is not a research method. It might be more accurately called a set of tactics for analysing texts, but there can never be an exhaustive list of tactics of deconstruction because there are myriad ways to test the relationship between symbols, such as words, and human understanding.

Perhaps the easiest and most common approach to deconstruction is to focus on **binary oppositions**. Interpretation often relies on discrete oppositions between contrary concepts such as 'good' and 'evil'. It may seem natural to use such categories, but they are fraught with difficulty. The relevance of these ideas to political ethnography or discourse analysis is clear as these two approaches take as central the idea that terms are contested, and meaning emerges only in the context of political and social interaction. However, there are lessons for quantitative political analysis as well.

For example, if the notion of gender is not fixed, then there may be circumstances in which simply asking the question 'Are you male or female?' may be inadequate. Since conventional notions of the identity of male and female are deeply rooted in most societies, the question will have a meaning to most respondents and they will respond accordingly. The problem is that it is unclear what the question is asking. What is it about gender differences that is important to the research project? It is most likely not the simple biological/chromosonal differences between male and female that are the focus of attention. Most studies examining gender differences assume or suggest a set of values and dispositions. For example that women are more empathetic, non-violent, nurturing etc., while men are purposive, aggressive, domineering etc. Therefore, if we look at gender distinctions in attitudes to foreign policy or support for particular political parties or politicians, then it is not the brute fact of gender that is in question, but the set of values and attitudes it is believed to embody. If we question the construction of these gender categories (for example, 'Does this series of dichotomies really neatly map onto specific gender identities?'), then we can see that the usage of gender in research is not so straightforward.

In fact, you might want to look at the construction of gender first and then at the political correlates of specific values and dispositions. By deconstructing the notion of gender, the sophistication and validity of the research is enhanced. It does not stop you from using gender or other terms in quantitative research, but at least it will be done knowingly and with an increased degree of nuance and humility. By using standard notions of gender, you may unknowingly reinforce existing gender stereotypes. The same can be said for other concepts such as race, religion, class etc., which are commonly coded simply into quantitative databases.

In addition to questioning oppositions, another key radical hermeneutic tactic is to reveal the hidden **trace** or **supplement** behind a narrative or argument. For example, when an author argues in favour of natural rights, a radical hermeneutist might ask what does this mean exactly? What is nature in this sense? How can nature bestow rights? How would we know if nature did it? The trace is the use of language to create a set of assumptions which rest on uncertain foundations. Sometimes the trace is deeply hidden and takes considerable reading between the lines to reveal. It is a hidden supplementary logic which is deeply embedded in a text.

An example used by Derrida, a key figure identified with deconstruction, is the American Declaration of Independence where, in the preamble, it states:

> We, therefore, the representatives of the United States of America in General Congress assembled . . . do in the Name and by the Authority of the good People of these Colonies solemnly publish and declare, that these united colonies are and of right ought to be free and independent states.

You might ask: Why should we accept that the authors of this text are 'representatives'? They were not elected. Also, what makes this declaration 'solemn' and how does this legitimate the declaration? The authors of this proclamation could have used the word 'joyfully' rather than solemn but that would have not given the appropriate amount of gravity necessary to make the event serious and profound. One might also point out that the use of the word 'good' in this context is also contentious, but a more empirically accurate statement, such as 'most of the people, most of the time trying to be good' would again not be as impressive or rhetorically effective. There is also a shift in the text from 'is' to 'ought', but it is not clear how they are free and independent just by this statement or why they ought to be by extension. By questioning the ways in which language is used in such passages, it undermines the attempt of the authors to create a sense of firm foundations.

The point is not to attack the Declaration of Independence. One can take these words at face value as a self-enacting statement of liberal-democratic faith or a patriotic declaration of autonomy, as most Americans do. However, it is possible to see that this language is the same sort of foundationless and grandiose hypocrisy behind any *coup d'état* or revolution – not all of which are seen as legitimate. Such a statement gains its force from the performative act of asserting a position. The meaning of such texts is not in the logic or empirical basis of the words and phrases used, it is in the impact that the text has on those who are guided by and act on it.

Any text which sets itself up as foundational (for at nation or a political group), can be deconstructed in this manner. It is also true with important speeches and declarations of war on poverty, terrorism, global warming and other campaigns of politicians. Such texts are clearly aimed at setting a grand and eloquent tone, but should we accept the logic of the language? How does it lead others to act? Derrida's main aim, it seems, is the deflation of the grand pretentions of the author. Language is used to build grand structures of meaning, but the substance of the meaning can be shown to be invented. It is not based on eternal truths. It is based on the manipulation of language to make a point.

The problem with deconstruction is that it seems only to undermine and question the foundational logic of political discourse and texts. It usually is not used to put forward a positive programme. We sometimes need to use oppositions to support a position we think is correct and attack a position with which we disagree. In addition, it is sometimes necessary to create a presence to support a particular argument. If foundational rhetorical devices are always called into question, it will be difficult to say anything at all. From this point of view, deconstruction can be accused of promoting relativism and obfuscation. Defenders of deconstruction consistently make great efforts to refute these charges but doubts remain.

The main obstacle appears to be the fact that any position put forward could itself be deconstructed. There are no doubt implicit beliefs and orientations behind the work of many deconstructionists. However, these are not explicitly stated even when they motivate and guide their analysis. In some ways, deconstruction takes the position of the neutral observer as it deconstructs and assumes a privileged position that it denies to other approaches.

A hermeneutic checklist

Hermeneutic techniques are often only implicitly used and not well developed methodologically. It does not help that the major theorists reject the idea of a hermeneutic method. None the less, the following points are relevant both to the analysis of specific historical texts and to data collected via surveys, interviews, archival research or direct observation. All political data is potentially a text with an author, context etc.

Introduction and conclusion

Write a clear introduction and conclusion for your analysis. The introduction sets out the overall structure and focus of the analysis so is crucial. It should state why the text being examined is significant and what your hermeneutic approach adds to our understanding of it. This point should be reinforced in the conclusion.

Identify the author(s) and text(s)

There should be a full discussion of the life and work of the author(s). It is not essential to dwell entirely on the personal life stories, but if it is significant to what they wrote, make note of the key ways in which it is relevant. Some hermeneutic analyses will focus almost exclusively on the author, particularly those involving psychological analysis. Where the focus is not on the author or authors (and in some cases very little information may be available), you must also focus on the text in relation to the larger textual context. Since this technique necessarily requires a focus on sections of text rather than complete works, the passage used must be related back to the rest of the text in a long work or set of texts from which it was drawn. This is tricky because the passage given may not be representative of the rest of the text, or, more likely, will only make sense if you understand what is being argued in the rest of the text. What is the overall point of the text and how does the particular passage being analysed fit into it? How does this fit into the corpus of work by the author(s)?

Comparison

Identify other key figures working at the time of the author who might have written similar and/or contrasting work. Is it part of a widespread genre? Was the source the text is drawn from famous or infamous? Was the work criticised as a whole by others? How and why? Is it from a book, speech, official government document etc.? How distinctive are the ideas of the author? Do they clash with or reinforce others? Are they the ultimate expression of a trend or counter-argument to the trends? Much analysis can hinge on these contrasts and similarities. The key is to keep it coherent, i.e. focus on two (or at most three) key arguments or 'schools of thought' if they exist. Be explicit about any criteria you are using to assess the relative merits of the different texts and schools.

Historical context

Identify the historical context of the text. What was happening in the historical period and specific location in which the author was working? Does this text express the dilemmas, ideas, prejudices, solutions etc. of the age? Is it a reaction to the age or is it a contrast (undercurrent) to the period? Did they change the nature of thinking at the time? Do they typify the approach in a period to a specific issue or does it challenge thinking at the time?

Subsequent traditions

Traditions of reading the text inform how it was transmitted over time and preserved for our current reading. Relevant traditions can be either academic or popular or both. Explain the significance of these ideas over time. Did they later have an impact but were ignored in the period they were written (spoken etc.)? This type of analysis requires reference to secondary literature (books and articles) to provide substance to the various readings of a text. Look in particular for ways in which key sections or arguments were ignored or explained away by later commentators, and consider why certain ideas are highlighted and preserved.

Radical hermeneutic techniques

Radical hermeneutic techniques are unlimited in theory. The simplest have been noted above. Identifying binary oppositions is the most obvious because often creating and insisting on mutually exclusive categories does violence to the complexity of real politics. The use of metaphors in an argument can play a similar role. You should also look for key arguments in a text where a rhetorical flourish insists that the argument rests on immutable or timeless foundations. The use of verbs such as 'must', 'require' and 'mandate' often mark these passages.

The limits of hermeneutics

On the practical level, one of the biggest problems with hermeneutics, as in discourse analysis, is text selection. Those who use the approach often take particular texts as implicitly 'representative' of the approach of an author or set of authors, but how do we know that a particular text demonstrates, for example, the flaws of liberalism, the nature of US foreign policy, problems with ethnic identity or patriarchal thinking? No matter which hermeneutic approach is used, you should present evidence that the texts you are interpreting can be shown to be amenable to the interpretation you have put forward and are representative of the subject you claim to be analysing.

Another problem is that hermeneutics could be seen to undermine the notion of 'objectivity'. As Gadamer suggests, however, no one is objective. Instead of striving for the unattainable goal of objectivity or assuming that it is inherent in quantitative or scientific approaches to the study of politics, the problems caused by bias should be made explicit. Approaches and interpretations are problematic if they are created by a process that does not involve dialogue and critical thinking about categories.

Intersubjectivity

It is true that the point of view of each individual is subjective, but even if we accept that fact (that is, no one is objective), we should share and discuss research findings in order to identify common ground for understanding. This is called **intersubjectivity** because it is founded in a shared understanding of subjective observers. The problem of bias is still not entirely addressed by this approach because researchers, as in any group of individuals, might share mistaken assumptions and unexamined prejudices. Intersubjectivity deals with individual bias but not group bias. None the less, discussing and circulating research widely among one's peers and experts in the field is a useful process. Through scholarly exchange and even the involvement of research subjects themselves in reviewing and refining one's research, the problem of bias on an individual level can be addressed to a degree.

Reflexivity

Another solution to the problem of potential bias is called **reflexivity**. It is the conscious 'taking of a position' in relation to one's research. That is, one considers and openly states potential sources of bias in the context of the research. One of the biggest problems with 'reflexivity' is that it can be done badly. In its worst form it is a self-indulgent confessional statement in the preface or introduction to a piece of research, such as, 'As a middle-class, white male, it has been difficult for me to research poor women in ethnic communities . . . '. Indeed, poorly considered applications of reflexivity have undermined initiatives to get researchers to adopt the approach.

The key point is to be aware of differences between oneself as a researcher and the people (subject) you are researching. It is not adequate to make it one throwaway line at the beginning of a research report. These issues need to be addressed consistently in the formation of the theoretical framework, the collection and interpretation of data, and the drawing of conclusions. This must be done in a consistent but nuanced manner. Most importantly, a researcher must take care not to make the reflexivity exclusively personal. Sometimes the assumptions that cause problems are inherent in the field of research or widespread social and political assumptions, especially in well-known situations which are rarely examined. The key to reflexivity is the relationship between the research subject and both the researcher and the research community of which the researcher is a part. This needs to be made explicit and considered carefully.

Ethical considerations

Following on from the above discussion of hermeneutics and reflexivity, we can see how Gadamer in particular helps deal with the problem of bias by making bias explicit and always assuming that some interpretative 'fore-understanding' (bias) is present. Bias should be confronted and not assumed away. This approach is useful for all forms of political analysis including quantitative. A good politics researcher must constantly ask: Do the concepts and categories only work because they fit existing preconceptions? Is this the best way to think about this problem and the data produced? What are the alternatives and how would they change understanding of the problem?

At the same time, we must also take care to realise hermeneutics is not a neutral tool. On the one hand, it can be used to defend or support interpretations which are harmful or limit understanding, while, on the other hand, radical 'playful' deconstructive critiques can be damaging as well as liberating.

Reflexivity is essential to research but it also has its dangers. It can reinforce fixed notions of identity and opposition. The danger here is making the relationship between groups a matter of 'us' versus 'them', especially where it appears to be making too much of the differences between the researcher and the researched. In fact, reflexivity can be applied too mechanically and as a form of demonstrating that one is 'politically correct'. It needs to be used with nuance, sincerity and depth of conviction.

One must also be aware that acceptability of reflexive discourse varies by field and subfield and even by individual. Some readers, including politics instructors, will find too much focus on reflexivity a distraction from the research itself. You should take care to introduce reflexivity when it seems especially appropriate and to an extent that enhances the understanding of your potential audience. This is not to say that it should be ignored, but it does require careful application in a context where it might encounter hostility or derision.

Conclusion

The key term in hermeneutic approaches to political research is dialogue: openness to discussion and willingness to learn from others. This is also a good basis to an overall ethical approach to political research.

Summary points

- Hermeneutics is another word for interpretation, but it is also a set of techniques to enable a researcher to explore the meaning of a text, speech, image or event. Skill in interpretation is required by all politics researchers no matter what method they use.
- This chapter has identified three broad types of hermeneutics. The conventional approach focuses on the author and the original context to provide clues to meaning. Gadamerian hermeneutics emphasises a dialogue between the reader and original author as mediated by tradition. Radical hermeneutics challenges the assumptions underlying the apparent meaning to reveal hidden relationships and foundations. All three aid our understanding of the nature of interpretation.
- What are the advantages and drawbacks of each approach? Conventional hermeneutics can be too limited in its approach, especially if focused solely on authorial intention. However, those approaches which focus on the reader, whether through the traditional readings or the current reader, must take care not to ignore the author and historical context entirely.
- Intersubjectivity helps anchor interpretation because it provides a shared experience and wider standard for interpretation. Reflexivity situates the interpreter so others can make sense of a particular interpretation of a text or situation.

Suggested reading and examples

Research examples

Hermeneutics is relatively new to political analysis and not all of the uses of hermeneutics in political studies are empirical in nature. The self-proclaimed interpretist approach of Bevir and Rhodes *Interpreting British Governance* (2003) is a very narrow example of conventional hermeneutics. A special issue of the *British Journal of Politics and International Relations* (2004, vol. 6, no. 2) takes up the approach in some detail. Gibb's (2006) 'Hermeneutics, political inquiry, and practical reason: an evolving challenge to political science', provides a considered basis for incorporating a Gadamerian approach into political research. The problem is that it is a theoretical and not an empirical study. Shapcott's *Justice, Community and Dialogue in International Relations* (2001) directly applies a Gadamerian perspective to international politics but it is focused on theories of communitarianism and justice which are the remit of political theory and not as amenable to empirical political analysis. Radical approaches to hermeneutics are well represented in international relations, including the work of David Campbell, such as his *National Deconstruction: Identity, Violence and Justice in Bosnia* (1998). The work of Campbell and others also shares features with critical discourse analysis, and it is common for critical discourse and radical hermeneutics to be intertwined in this way. They have only been separated in this textbook in order to highlight specific issues. As with all categories and distinctions, it is a matter of interpretation.

Methodological readings

Christopher Norris has provided two accessible introductions to radical hermeneutics in his *Deconstruction* (1982) and *Derrida* (1987). The concept of radical hermeneutics itself can be credited to Caputo's *Radical Hermeneutics* (1987) which can be profitably read to understand the methodological issues raised on a political and philosophical level. *Gadamer: Hermeneutics, Tradition and Reason* (Warnke 1987) and *Gadamer and Hermeneutics* (Silverman 1991) are the two best introductory works on Gadamer and his approach to hermeneutics.

References

Betti, E. 1999. *A General Theory of Interpretation*. S. Noakes, trans. & ed. Aldine de Gruyter.

Bevir, M. and Rhodes, R. A. W. 2003. *Interpreting British Governance*. London: Routledge.

Bevir, M. and Rhodes, R. A. W. 2004. 'Interpreting British governance', *Journal of Politics and International Relations,* vol. 6, pp. 130–36.

Campbell, David. 1998. *National Deconstruction: Identity, Violence and Justice in Bosnia*. Minneapolis: University of Minnesota Press.

Caputo, John. 1987. *Radical Hermeneutics*. Bloomington: Indiana University Press.

Dowding, Keith. 2004. 'Interpretation, truth and investigation: comments on Bevir and Rhodes,' *British Journal of Politics and International Relations*, vol. 6, no. 2, pp. 136–42.

Gadamer, H.-G. 1989. *Truth and Method*. London: Sheed & Ward.

Gibb, Michael T. 2006. 'Hermeneutics, political inquiry, and practical reason: an evolving challenge to political science'. *American Political Science Review*, vol. 100, no. 4, pp. 563–71.

Habermas, J. 1970. 'A review of truth and method' in F. Dallmayr and T. McCathy (1977) *Understanding and Social Inquiry*. London: University of Notre Dame Press.

Hirsch, E. D. 1967. *Validity in Interpretation*. London: Yale University Press.

Norris, Christopher. 1982. *Deconstruction*. London: Routledge.

Norris, Christopher. 1987. *Derrida*. London: Fontana Press.

Pitkin, Hannah Fenichel. 1984. *Fortune is a Woman: Gender and Politics in the Thought of Niccolò Machiavelli: With a New Afterword*. Chicago, IL: University of Chicago Press.

Scheibler, I. 2000. *Gadamer: Between Heidegger and Habermas*. Oxford: Rowman & Littlefield.

Shapcott, Richard. 2001. *Justice, Community and Dialogue in International Relations*. Cambridge: Cambridge University Press.

Silverman, H. 1991. *Gadamer and Hermeneutics*. London: Routledge.

Warnke, Georgia. 1987. *Gadamer: Hermeneutics, Tradition and Reason*. Cambridge: Polity Press.

Research exercises

1 Apply conventional, Gadamerian and deconstructive approaches to a text, such as a famous speech, policy statement, preamble to key legislation etc.
2 Which of the hermeneutic approaches do you believe is best? List five points for and against each approach, and then argue, on balance, which position you favour. Is it possible to be neutral? Are interpretations arbitrary?

Key terms

authorial intention
binary oppositions
deconstruction
fusion of horizons
hermeneutics

historicism
intersubjectivity
readership/audience
reconstruction/integration
reflexivity

structure of fore-understanding
text
trace/supplement

Part VII

Reporting the results

24 Writing (and reading) the research report

- When does the planning for the research report begin?
- What are the main components of a research report?

Introduction

If the purpose of research is to discover or understand the world we live in, then the purpose of the research paper must be to communicate our discoveries or understandings to others in as effective a manner as possible. Just as good research itself must be explicit, systematic and controlled, the descriptions and assessments of research findings must be clear, complete and – most especially – well organised. Because it often constitutes the first statement of discovery, and because it provides a primary means for developing a shared understanding, the research report is one of the most important, and potentially most effective, instruments of academic communication.

Good research reports do not simply emerge, unassisted, from good research. Rather, the writing of a solid report requires every bit as much craftsmanship, and every bit as much practice, as any other stage of the research process. It requires the same planning, careful organisation, clarity of thought and expression, and attention to detail exercised all along the way. Although it is true that good research eases the writing of a good research report, it is equally true that a poorly written report can obscure the value of even the best research effort. After all, the research report is the *only* means we have to telling others of our work, and, conversely, it is the *only* means by which those others can learn what we have accomplished. If we fail to communicate fully and effectively, the value of our research itself is greatly lessened.

In general, considerations of style, organisation, proper grammar and usage, and other elements of effective writing lie well beyond the scope of this book. There are, however, a number of practical concerns that have a particular bearing on the writing of the research report and that do deserve some comment. In this chapter we examine several of these very briefly and present an annotated example of research reporting to help illustrate applications. Although the chapter itself is oriented towards writing a research report, the points presented also provide a basis for the *critical reading* of research reports prepared by others.

The plan

Planning a research report should begin at the earliest stages of the research process. Recall that the six steps of the research process are: (1) the selection of a research problem; (2) the systematic examination of related literature; (3) the formulation of a theory and hypotheses; (4) the determination of what type of evidence is required and (5) how it is to be obtained; and (6) the decision about how the resulting data are to be analysed. Each of these actions contributes in an important way to the writing of the research report, and each should be undertaken with that fact in mind. Indeed, one of the greatest dangers the beginning researcher can confront is the tendency to compartmentalise the work, to treat each stage in the research process as if it were virtually independent of every other stage. In point of fact, the reverse is true. No stage of research, from problem formulation to the reporting of results, stands alone. Not only is each stage dependent on every other stage, but each must also be carried out with the others in mind. We may speak of six stages of the research process, but we speak of only one unified *process*.

Nowhere is this interdependence of parts clearer than in the writing of a research report, for it is in that report that we must join the pieces of our work together. We must precisely state our concepts and definitions; demonstrate the linkage between concept and research; describe, summarise and evaluate our procedures and results; and assess our findings as they relate back to our concepts. In reality, then, the planning of a research report is inseparable from the planning of the research itself, and the writing of a report is inseparable from the conduct of our inquiry.

The structure

Because different subjects and different approaches to research can give rise to many different forms of research report, it is neither possible nor desirable to set forth hard-and-fast rules for the structure of these communications. We can, however, suggest the basic elements that should be present in any such report and point out the most commonly accepted way of organising them. Those elements are: (1) the introduction; (2) the literature review; (3) the statement of research methods; (4) the statement of findings; and (5) the conclusion.

The introduction

The introduction to a research report should state clearly the theme or purpose of the research, the principal hypotheses (work that is primarily descriptive may not include hypotheses) and the rationale underlying both conducting the research and writing the report. In general, the purpose of the introduction is to set forth the *goals* of the work, to defend them and to put them into what the author regards as the proper perspective.

It is at this point, too, that we alert readers to what we see as the major significance (the main contribution) of the research being reported. Only if the purpose of the work is stated clearly at the outset can readers judge the relevance to the central point of each argument or piece of data analysis presented. Surprise endings may be appropriate for short stories, but in a research report they only create extra work and confusion for readers.

The literature review

The literature review in a research report is closely linked to, and builds upon, the introduction. A review of the relevant literature should cite and describe the research and the theories of those who have worked on related problems in the past. Our new theory may challenge or discount the existing literature, but we need to specifically identify (1) what we are improving upon in the current research and (2) why our work constitutes an improvement.

In sum, the literature review places our research into a broader context within the discipline, substantiates the importance of your original research and establishes the plausibility of your theory.

How much attention others will pay to your research findings may be determined by the quality of the review of the literature: a literature review that precisely identifies the body of literature within political science to which you are contributing, allows others to more easily incorporate your findings into later research. The literature review establishes the distinct contribution that your research will make to the existing body of research. Since no research stands completely on its own authority, reviewing the literature related to your research initially establishes the plausibility of your theory.

The methods

The methods section should answer several questions. What was the source of data for the research? How were data gathered? Was there a sample? How was it selected? How many cases were included? How were the principal variables operationalised? Did the study encounter any special problems or develop any special instruments (for example, a new scale for measuring a particular attitude or behaviour) worthy of note? The object here is to make a complete and precise statement of the steps taken in performing the research. As we pointed out in the introductory chapters, one important benefit of science as a way of knowing is that the findings of science are replicable, that the scientific method provides a way for sharing and evaluating both knowledge and the way to knowledge. Only by stating explicitly what we have done during the undertaking of our research can the results of our work be judged fully and critically by others. *The statement of the method of our study is the component of the research report that contributes most directly to such sharing.* For that reason, it must be written with honesty, thoroughness, care and precision.

The findings

The presentation of findings may include tables, graphs or charts that help to summarise the results of our work, together with statistical or other analyses that prove germane. Researchers may be tempted at this point in their writing to include every shred of evidence and every table or chart that they examined when analysing the data. The result is often a presentation that overwhelms the reader with unedited facts, some of which may be only marginally useful. It amounts to something of a *laissez-faire* approach to writing: here are the facts – decipher them however you wish. Remember that no one is better positioned than you to identify and assess the meaning of your research results. Indeed, it is an obligation of the researcher to present in as clear a manner as possible only those results that speak most pointedly to the issues at hand.

Two suggestions, one general and one more specific, may offer some guidance here. First, the presentation of findings should be organised so as to illustrate the principal variables, hypotheses or arguments set forth in the introduction to the report. Results not relating directly and importantly to these foci should not be included. By keeping this in mind, the researcher not only can eliminate a great deal of trivia from the report but also can present those findings that are included in a logical and meaningful manner. Second, it is a general rule of thumb that any table, chart or graph included in a research report should be accompanied by at least two paragraphs of text in which the points are illustrated and their significance discussed. If the researcher cannot generate enough points of discussion to fill two paragraphs, it is quite likely that the particular table, chart or graph in question is not sufficiently important to warrant inclusion in the report.

We also should emphasise that the researcher should not be reluctant to report either unexpected results or 'nonfindings'. The fact that a hypothesis is not supported by one's data may be just as important and interesting as the fact that it is. Thus, the criterion for including or excluding a piece of evidence in writing a research report is not whether or not it shows what was predicted, but, rather, whether what it shows is of any importance or interest.

The conclusion

Finally, a research report generally concludes with a summary of findings, a discussion of the relationships between those findings and the theory in which the research was grounded, and, in some cases, an evaluation of the method of the study. Have we found anything of significance? If so, why is it significant, and what does it tell us? If not, why not? Were our hypotheses simply incorrect, or did we make some error or encounter some problem in designing or carrying out our research that prevented us from finding supporting evidence? Where do we go from here? This section of the report is, in effect, retrospective towards both the research paper and the research process. It presents the researcher with an opportunity to place the work in proper perspective between past and future research effort.

The placement of these several elements can vary somewhat depending on the development of a particular research report, but all or most will usually be present. In fact, these components can serve as an outline or organising basis for most research reports, and the beginning researcher should take some care to see that each component is represented where appropriate and also that the relationship between them in the body of the report is both straightforward and logical.

The style

Research reports are not written like novels or blogs. Unlike those writing for others' recreation, researchers often must communicate very complex technical information to a specialised audience in a relatively small space. Still, research reports should be neither stodgy and heavy-handed nor overburdened with jargon. Our goal is to produce a report that balances readability with precision and clarity with thoroughness. The following guidelines should help you to achieve these goals:

1 Work from an *outline*. Be sure the logic of your writing is clear to the reader.
2 Use words and phrases with which you are comfortable. Do not use big words just because they sound impressive. Use the word that most precisely defines your terms.
3 Reread, revise and rewrite. Reading your work aloud to see if it sounds right can help to identify and smooth out obvious rough spots. First drafts are *never* final drafts.
4 Seek others' opinions when possible. Have 'new eyes' view your work; ask a roommate, friend or colleague to read a draft of the report. They can alert you to errors that countless readings on your own will not reveal. Others' unfamiliarity with your field or methods is no hindrance to their proofreading; it may, in fact, be an asset. The best research is easily interpretable by an intelligent layperson.
5 Be sure to differentiate between observations and opinion; research reports rarely rest on one's own opinion (see the next point).
6 Fully document all of the research or popular work you reference in conducting your research and writing your report.

Continuing with the final point, clear citation of others' work is essential to the academic enterprise. Documentation is ethically required as it keeps us intellectually honest by preventing the fabrication of convenient evidence. It also provides a basis on which others can judge the validity of our arguments. By drawing evidence from dependable sources or relying on the opinions of informed authorities in reaching our own conclusions, the persuasiveness of our argument is increased.

Citations must be used *whenever* we borrow facts or ideas from another author. Not only direct quotations, but *any* data or ideas we draw from the work of others must be accompanied by references. Information on the form and placement of citations and construction of a bibliography is best obtained from a style guide which most academic departments in the UK require their students to follow. If there is none for your department, use a style manual, several of which are listed at the end of this chapter or adopt the citation style of a major journal, such as the *American Political Science Review* or the *Journal of Politics*. Consistent form and complete information are the keys to documenting a research report correctly.

The title and abstract

The title of a research report should be descriptive and complete, but it should not be overly detailed. It should give readers a good idea of what the report discusses, but not so good an idea that one need not read the paper. Compare, for example, the following alternative titles for the same research:

1 *Politics on the Day That Hell Freezes Over*
2 *Control over the Distribution of Scarce Resources at Such Time as the Temperature of Certain Regions Remains below 0° Celsius throughout the Month of July, as Measured on a Mercury Thermometer and through the Use of Pretested Survey Instruments, Including Guttman Scales, on a Small Population of Residents of Stonehaven, Scotland: An Experiment*
3 *The Effects of Climate on the Distribution of Political Resources*

Title 1 is short and to the point but not sufficiently descriptive to give the reader much idea of the article's content. Title 2 is so comprehensive as to be unwieldy. Only title 3 conveys the content of the report without undue attention to detail. The point is that the title should tell the reader the general topic of the report, but should not itself substitute for the sections of the report that deal with methods and findings.

Often, we find it useful to follow the title page of a report with an **abstract**, a brief statement, usually not more than 150 words and often no more than one or two sentences, in which we briefly summarise the contents of our report. The summary usually includes, in barest outline, a statement of what we have found, how we found it and why it is important. Consider the following example:

Abstract: The effects of climate on the distribution of political resources

Using both temperature and survey data from a study of Stonehaven, Scotland, the author concludes that resource allocations vary systematically with changes in the weather. More particularly, the data suggest that the poor are more adequately cared for and the downtrodden raised higher on the proverbial cold day in July than at other times. This finding offers considerable support for the hypotheses of Marx, Weber and others.

By giving readers a concise summary of the accompanying report, the abstract tells one whether the material is likely to be of sufficient interest to warrant a close reading and thereby obviates the need for an extended title.

Ethical considerations

The research project culminates in writing your research report. Likewise, the ethical challenges discussed throughout this book come together as you write and submit your research to your professor or for publication.

Asking yourself a series of questions may help you maintain a high ethical standard. Have you carefully paraphrased and fully documented others' work in your citations? Have you clearly explained your research design, data gathering and coding procedures so others may replicate your work, based solely upon your research report? Have you utilised the proper analytic tools, given the characteristics of your qualitative or quantitative data? Have you impartially explicated your research findings and limitations, as well as the broader implications of your work?

Conclusion

One final question about research reports that often arises is that of length. How long should a report be? There is no simple answer to this question. Most journals in political science prefer manuscripts of some twenty-five to thirty pages typed and double-spaced. A master's dissertation may run to 100 or 150 pages, and a doctoral thesis may take up to several hundred. Student research reports may run anywhere from ten to fifty pages, though fifteen to twenty is probably more common.

It is important to remember that the scope of your research project determines the report's length. Thus, if your outline threatens to exceed the paper's page limit, then you need to more tightly constrain your research. Similarly, if from the outset you struggle to fill the outline, you may need to enlarge your research focus. Therefore, the material itself determines the length of the report. The argument should be adequately developed and the appropriate literature adequately reviewed. The method of the study should be fully expounded and the results fully but judiciously reported. The conclusions should be both well developed and properly supported. Yet the length of each portion will vary from one report to the next. How long, then, should a research report be? As long as it needs to be to cover the subject, but brief enough to maintain interest.

Summary points

- The groundwork for producing an effective research report begins at the initial stages of the research project and should be part of the project.
- The five parts of a research report are: introduction, literature review, methods used, research findings and the conclusion.

A CASE IN POINT

The remainder of this chapter is devoted to an annotated example of a research report. The example illustrates most of the elements we have described, and it should suggest to you the ways in which these components can be combined to produce an informative research report. The source of this report is Craig Leonard Brians and Steven Greene. 2004. 'Elections: voter support and partisans' (mis)perceptions of presidential candidates' abortion views in 2000,' *Presidential Studies Quarterly*, vol. 34, pp. 412–19; reprinted by permission of the publisher.

Elections: voter support and partisans' (mis)perceptions of presidential candidates' abortion views in 2000[*]

Title

CRAIG LEONARD BRIANS AND STEVEN GREENE

Although the 2000 Republican and Democratic national party platforms show the parties at opposite poles on abortion policy, Governor George W. Bush publicly supported a vaguely defined 'culture of life', rather than the constitutional amendment barring abortion that was advocated by his party. In light of Bush's campaign strategy, this article uses national survey data to examine the accuracy of citizens' knowledge of the candidates' abortion policy positions. Interestingly, pro-choice Republican voters were much less likely to defect from their party in 2000 than in 1996, suggesting that the Bush campaign's efforts to avoid public opposition to his abortion position were successful.

Abstract

In August of 2000, a self-avowed fundamentalist Christian who had publicly pledged to 'do everything in my power to restrict abortion' earned the Republican presidential nomination in Philadelphia.[1] In an apparent attempt to diffuse this controversial issue, throughout the nomination and presidential campaign Governor George W. Bush obscured his abortion views and avoided discussing the topic. His official position is that abortion should be outlawed except in cases of rape, incest or to save the life of the mother.

In a debate with Senator John McCain on *Larry King Live*, Governor Bush simultaneously maintained that he completely endorsed and agreed with the Republican Party platform (which calls for a constitutional amendment barring all abortions) and he supported the above-noted exceptions. Senator McCain apparently found it so frustrating to attempt to force Governor Bush to clarify these mutually exclusive positions that he eventually quit discussing abortion (*Larry King Live* 2000).

Introduction

Statement of
research assertion

Source citation

---

[*]Authors' note: The data used in this article were made available by the Inter-University Consortium for Political and Social Research. Neither the collector of the original data nor the consortium bears any responsibility for the analyses or interpretations presented here.

[1]Quoted in the 22 October 1994, *Dallas Morning News*.

The Bush campaign's efforts to obscure the candidate's abortion position reached their height during the first presidential debate when Bush refused to verify his previously stated plan to try to overturn the FDA's approval of the RU-486 abortion drug, saying he was only interested in doing whatever would protect women's health. He then linked his position on abortion to promoting a 'culture of life', saying that while 'abortions ought to be more rare in America', this culture would also lead to fighting laws that 'allow doctors to take the lives of our seniors' and change the culture to discourage 'youngsters who feel like they can take a neighbour's life with a gun' (Commission on Presidential Debates 2000). It would be difficult to find anyone who actively favours more abortions and more killing of older people and neighbours by teenagers. In the same debate, Vice President Al Gore clearly stated his support for a woman's right to choose abortion and RU-486, although he said he did not favour late-term or partial birth abortions (Commission on Presidential Debates 2000).

During the campaign, disguising the Republican Party's long-standing strong opposition to legal abortions could have advantaged Bush in several ways. First, only a small minority of Americans shares the Republican Party's official position – only 17 per cent in the most recent Gallup poll (Gallup Organization and *USA Today* 2003). Publicly supporting an unpopular policy is not likely to increase one's broad-based general election support.[2] Second, even within the Republican Party, the abortion issue has generated tremendous conflict. The last several conventions have been characterised by a certain amount of rancour over abortion, although these disagreements are most visible when the platform is written before the convention. Third, Bush's campaign may have been trying to avoid having an abortion controversy attach itself to the candidate and increase the attention paid to this issue by voters.

It seems reasonably clear that Bush attempted to obscure his abortion position to broaden his appeal to pro-choice voters, but on an issue as salient as abortion, how effective was this strategy? Was it, in fact, any more effective at preventing defection of pro-choice Republicans than Gore's clear statement of his abortion position was effective at preventing defection of pro-life Democrats? Because there are a roughly equal number of pro-life Democrats and pro-choice Republicans (Greene and Brians 2001), the most effective test may be to determine how many of each party's adherents defected in presidential voting. This comparison is facilitated by the fact that there are only small differences in the issue importance between those in the minority in either party – that is, pro-life Democrats or pro-choice Republicans (Greene and Brians 2001).

Those holding minority abortion policy views in a given political party may not defect and vote for the candidate closer to their view because the voters may not see the issue as that important, they may choose to ignore their party's and candidate's views on the issue, or they may not realise they do not hold the dominant view in the party. While candidates' actions and statements may facilitate each of these possibilities by making their issue position less obvious,

---

[2]Although Al Gore's issue positions were closer to more voters, the vice president often seemed unable to communicate his shared ideas with voters during this campaign, leading to a widespread lack of accurate issue knowledge about the candidates in 2000 (Waldman and Jamieson 2003).

voters who attribute their own position to their favoured candidate – or at least 'move' their favoured candidate's attitudes closer to their own position – find it easier to vote for that candidate (Wilson and Gronke 2000; Krosnick 1990; Martinez 1988). The tendency of some voters to project policy positions onto candidates to rationalise their vote choice was empirically identified in the 1948 presidential election (Berelson *et al.* 1954: 219–23), the 1968 election (Brody and Page 1972; Page and Brody 1972), and the 1980 election (Wattenberg 1991: 111–16).[3]

Quantitatively testing an apparent campaign strategy, such as the obfuscation of an abortion policy position, poses serious challenges, because one cannot know what other outcomes might have occurred in the absence of the strategy. On the one hand, Governor Bush would seem to be successful if he did not do worse than Vice President Gore at preventing defections by abortion opinion minorities in his party through projection. On the other hand, an identical outcome could suggest that Gore was more successful, because he achieved no worse defections without obfuscating his abortion position. Alternatively, if abortion has been a more contentious issue for Republicans, Bush simply holding his defections equal to Gore's may connote success. Ultimately, it is not possible to know for certain what voters would have done if Bush had more clearly stated his abortion stance. Still, it would be instructive to compare the 2000 election data to 1996, when the Democratic nominee held Gore's position, but the Republican presidential nominee had been identified as open to a pro-choice position. This was particularly highlighted when Senator Bob Dole chose pro-choice New York Representative Susan Molinari to be the 1996 Republican National Convention keynote speaker, and proposed including language that tolerated alternative points of view on abortion in the party platform. Thus, to gain perspective, at several points in the analysis, 2000 data will be compared and contrasted with the 1996 results.

Assessment of strengths and weakness of the design

Use of a control

Data

We primarily use data from the 2000 National Election Studies (NES), as well as the 1996 NES, in order to assess the role that abortion played in the 2000 campaign. Our analyses rely principally on several key variables: respondent's position on abortion, respondent's placement of the presidential candidates on abortion, respondent's partisanship and respondent's two-party vote choice. The analyses are conducted by placing respondents into four groups based upon their partisanship and abortion position: pro-choice Democrats, pro-life Democrats, pro-choice Republicans and pro-life Republicans.

Method of study

Secondary analysis of data

Identification of the (independent and dependent) variables

The standard NES abortion question ranges from 1 to 4, with 1 being 'abortion should never be permitted', 2 stating that 'abortion should be permitted in case of rape, incest, and threat to mother's life', 3 indicating that 'only after the need for the abortion has clearly been established', and 4 holding that 'by law, a woman should always be able to obtain an abortion as a matter of personal

Discussion of question wording

Coding procedure

---

[3]While Reagan benefited from rationalisations that citizens used to vote against Carter in 1980, voters seemed more comfortable acknowledging their policy differences with Reagan in 1984 while still supporting him at the polls (Wattenberg 1991: 116).

choice.' Respondents place themselves, as well as each candidate, on this scale. In order to categorise our respondents, we place those who indicated that their own position was 1 or 2 as pro-life and those indicating 4 as pro-choice. Unfortunately, the 'clear need' category proves so problematic that we choose not to group respondents based upon this belief.[4] As for the partisanship basis of our group categorisations, because we are interested in how the supporters of each party stand on abortion, leaners may reasonably be grouped with self-identified party supporters (Greene 2000). We use these four categories to analyse respondent vote choice and respondent placement of candidates' abortion position in both 1996 and 2000.

Data analysis

Our analyses examine general voting patterns depending upon abortion attitudes and partisanship and evaluate more specific tests of the possibility that voters projected their own attitudes onto candidates. Although our main focus is the 2000 election, we include 1996 data as well, to provide a relative baseline for the 2000 candidates' performance. The primary goal of these analyses is to determine which candidate benefited most from his campaign's approach to abortion policy: whether it was Gore's more plainly stated position, or Bush's less clear abortion position. The secondary and related goal is to assess the relative impact of projection for the candidacies of Bush and Gore.

The initial examination of projection on the abortion issue indicates similar levels of misperception about both candidates by both Republicans and Democrats, regardless of abortion attitude. In Figure 1, we see that as Democrats become more liberal on abortion, the distance they see between Bush and Gore on the issue increases dramatically. Likewise, as Republicans become more conservative on abortion, the distance between Gore and Bush increases in a similarly pronounced fashion. In general, as respondents move in the direction of their party's core position, they are not only more in line with their party's candidate on the abortion issue but are more distant from the opposition party candidate as well. These figures thus further demonstrate the potentially important role for projection of abortion positions to play in voter decision making.

Comparing the two-party vote with partisans' abortion stances, it is apparent that Bush held the Republican Party together much better in 2000 than did Dole in 1996. Table 1 presents the percentage of voters in each of our four categories (pro-life Democrat, pro-choice Democrat, pro-life Republican, pro-choice Republican) who voted for each of the major party candidates in 1996 and 2000. This crosstabulation of the two-party vote by a four-level combined measure of abortion stance and partisanship demonstrates that the Republican Party lost

---

[4]When exploring how people with this attitude characterise 'supporters of abortion' and 'opponents of abortion' on the 1990 NES feeling thermometer measures, the mean values are close – 45 and 55, respectively (on a 0 to 100 scale) – and the distribution of scores has large numbers at the extreme ends of both measures. This group seems to contain persons holding a range of moderate and situational abortion views, making it impossible to accurately place them into either a pro-life or pro-choice category.

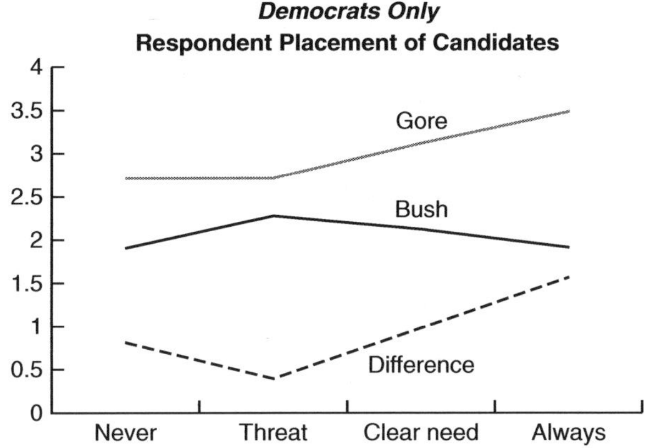

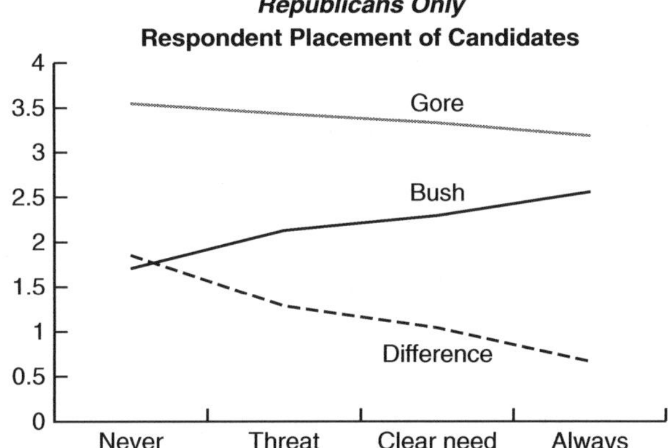

Figure 1 Presidential candidates' abortion position as rated by voters depending upon citizen abortion position — **Graphic presentation**

Source: 2000 National Election Study.

Note: The *X*-axis represents respondents' positions on when abortion should be legal, and the *Y*-axis tracks respondents' perceptions of each candidate's abortion view. On the *X*-axis, *never* means 'by law, abortion should never be permitted', *threat* indicates that 'the law should permit abortion only in case of rape, incest, or when the woman's life is in danger', *clear need* means that 'abortion should be permitted only after the need for the abortion has clearly been established', and *always* indicates that 'by law, a woman should always be able to obtain an abortion as a matter of personal choice'.

substantially more pro-choice Republican votes (29 versus 18 per cent) in 1996 as opposed to 2000, and even saw 8 per cent of the pro-life Republicans defect in 1996. On the other hand, even though Gore held onto pro-choice Democratic votes at a rate almost equal to Clinton (93 versus 95 per cent), he lost 15 per cent of pro-life Democrats, in contrast to only 8 per cent for Clinton. Thus, even though the Democratic Party appeared to have an absolute advantage on the abortion issue in 2000, its position was weakened relative to 1996.

Table   **Table 1**   Vote per cent by partisanship and abortion attitude in 1996 and 2000

	1996		2000	
	Dole	**Clinton**	**Bush**	**Gore**
Pro-choice Democrats	5	95	7	93
	(15)	(266)	(22)	(273)
Pro-life Democrats	8	92	15	85
	(13)	(156)	(26)	(148)
Pro-choice Republicans	71	29	82	18
	(93)	(38)	(118)	(26)
Pro-life Republicans	92	8	96	4
	(217)	(18)	(226)	(10)

Source: 1996 and 2000 National Election Studies.
Note: The numbers in parentheses are cell frequencies.

Discussion of the table

Given the political salience and personal importance attached to the abortion issue, one might ask why there are not more defections in vote choice, especially among pro-life Democrats. Tables 2a and 2b present analyses demonstrating the high levels of projection taking place on the abortion issue. The projection on abortion is most evident in the pro-life Democrats' ratings of Gore and Clinton and pro-choice Republicans' ratings of Bush and Dole. One can clearly see that these groups are, in fact, dramatic outliers. Pro-life Democrats place Gore at 2.76, when objectively, his true position would have to be close to 4. Likewise, pro-choice Republicans place Bush at 2.70, when his actual position could objectively not be considered more than 2 – which is almost exactly where the other groups placed him. The results follow a very similar pattern in 1996. The notable difference is that Bush is seen as more pro-choice, 2.70, by pro-choice Republicans, than is Dole, 2.46, who was actually the more liberal of the two on abortion. At least relative to Dole, Bush's strategy on abortion was clearly more effective.

Assessment of the correspondence between predictions based on theory and actual observations

Additionally, Tables 2a and 2b provide strong evidence as to why the Democratic candidates are more effective at holding their party's minority abortion position voters. In both 1996 and 2000, pro-life Democrats saw themselves as 1.12 away from the Democratic candidate. In contrast, Bush was seen as 1.43 away from pro-choice Republicans. In sum, the results in Tables 2a and 2b suggest that Democratic candidates benefit from projection on the abortion issue more than Republicans. Crucially, in 2000's razor-thin outcome, Bush was much more successful in keeping pro-choice Republicans loyal, clearly in part from a campaign that allowed very substantial projection of their own abortion issue position onto him.[5]

---

[5]In an analysis not reported here, we found that abortion is not the only issue where Governor Bush benefited from voter projection in 2000. More voters projected their government spending views onto Bush in 2000 than had done the same with Dole in 1996.

Table 2a Projection of abortion attitudes on 2000 presidential candidates

	Pro-choice Democrat	Pro-life Democrat	Pro-choice Republican	Pro-life Republican
Abortion rating for Gore	3.56	2.76	3.34	3.54
Abortion rating for Bush	2.02	2.30	2.70	2.07
Respondent–Gore abortion distance	0.48	1.12	0.78	1.84
Respondent–Bush abortion distance	2.07	0.76	1.43	1.22

Source: 2000 National Election Study.

Note: Gore's and Bush's abortion positions were rated by respondents on a scale ranging from 1 to 4, with 1 barring all legal abortions and 4 leaving the choice entirely to the woman. Respondent–Gore and Respondent–Bush distance shows the relative distance between the respondent's own abortion placement and where he placed Bush and where he placed Gore. The lower this number, the closer the respondent's own abortion position is to the candidate's perceived position.

Table 2b Projection of abortion attitudes on 1996 presidential candidates

	Pro-choice Democrat	Pro-life Democrat	Pro-choice Republican	Pro-life Republican
Abortion rating for Clinton	3.56	2.76	3.26	3.59
Abortion rating for Dole	1.99	2.26	2.45	2.12
Respondent–Clinton abortion distance	0.44	1.12	0.74	1.86
Respondent–Dole abortion distance	2.00	0.94	1.55	0.47

Source: 1996 National Election Study.

Note: Clinton's and Dole's abortion positions were rated by respondents on a 1 to 4 abortion scale, where 1 bars all legal abortions and 4 leaves the choice entirely to the woman.

Conclusion

This study indicates that campaigns may be able to influence voters' level of misinformation about candidates' issue positions. These preliminary results suggest that Governor Bush was more successful in obscuring his, and his party's, abortion policy position among voters in 2000, than was Senator Dole in 1996. Vice President Gore's more straightforward approach may have cost him some support, when compared to President Bill Clinton in 1996.

The salience of abortion will most likely only increase in upcoming elections. With recent controversies over 'partial-birth' abortion and anticipation already building over what are likely to be among the most contentious Supreme Court appointments ever made – largely due to concerns over the continued legality of abortion – the ability of presidential candidates to strategically campaign on the abortion issue and take advantage of voter's predilections toward projection

Conclusion

Implication of the research

will become even more important. The Democrats seem to have an advantage on the issue, for the time being, but Bush's 2000 performance suggests that this advantage can be dramatically diminished.

Addressing possible ethical concerns with others' use of the findings

Some may be concerned by this article's findings and the potential for future manipulation of public opinion by campaigns. Clearly, the degree to which candidates will be able to increase voters' misperceptions of their issue stances in the 2004 presidential election largely depends upon the news media's attention to the campaign. The substantially greater care most campaigns have used in preparing and documenting their advertising following the intense press attention to ads in the 1988 campaign demonstrates that candidates can regulate their own behaviour when they know that the watchdogs are on duty. Thus, it is reasonable to conclude that if the press closely watches the candidates in 2004, the projection seen among voters in 2000 is less likely to be repeated.

References

Bibliography

Berelson, Bernard, Lazarsfeld, Paul F. and McPhee, William N. 1954. *Voting: A Study of Opinion Formation in a Presidential Campaign*. Chicago, IL: University of Chicago Press.

Brody, Richard A. and Page, Benjamin I. 1972. 'Comment: the assessment of policy voting'. *American Political Science Review*, vol. 66 (June), pp. 450–58.

Commission on Presidential Debates. 2000. *General Election Presidential Debates, October 3*. University of Massachusetts, Boston, MA. Available from www.debates.org/pages/debhis2000.html.

Gallup Organization and *USA Today*. 2003. 24–26 October 2003. *National Survey of 1006 Adults*. Storrs, CT: Roper Center at the University of Connecticut.

Greene, Steven. 2000. 'The psychological sources of partisan-leaning independence'. *American Politics Quarterly*, vol. 28 (October), pp. 511–37.

Greene, Steven and Brians, Craig Leonard. 2001. 'Elite versus popular views on abortion within American political Parties'. Paper prepared for presentation at the Annual Meeting of the Midwest Political Science Association, 19 22 April Chicago, IL.

Krosnick, Jon A. 1990. 'Americans' perceptions of presidential candidates: a test of the projection hypothesis'. *Journal of Social Issues*, vol. 46 (Summer), pp. 159–82.

Larry King Live. 2000. GOP Debate with Senator John McCain and Governor George W. Bush. *CNN*, 15 February.

Martinez, Michael D. 1988. 'Political involvement and the projection process'. *Political Behavior*, vol. 10 (Spring), pp. 151–67.

National Election Studies (www.electionstudies.org). *The 1996 and 2000 National Election Studies [datasets]*. Ann Arbor, MI: University of Michigan, Center for Political Studies [producer and distributor].

Page, Benjamin I. and Brody, Richard A. 1972. 'Policy voting and the electoral process: the Vietnam War issue'. *American Political Science Review*, vol. 66 (September), pp. 979–95.

Waldman, Paul and Hall Jamieson, Kathleen. 2003. 'Rhetorical convergence and issue knowledge in the 2000 presidential election', *Presidential Studies Quarterly*, vol. 33 (March), pp. 145–63.

Wattenberg, Martin P. 1991. *The Rise of Candidate-Centered Politics*. Cambridge, MA: Harvard University Press.

Wilson, J. Matthew and Gronke, Paul. 2000. 'Concordance and projection in citizen perceptions of congressional roll-call voting'. *Legislative Studies Quarterly*, vol. 25 (August), pp. 445–67.

Suggested reading and examples

Research examples

The best place to find sample research reports is in the journals of political science and related disciplines that are described in Chapter 3. Excerpts from articles that illustrate many of the principles of research discussed in this text are found in *The Political Research Experience: Readings and Analysis* (Ethridge 2002).

Methodological reading

A book that addresses all facets of writing political analyses is *Writing in Political Science: A Practical Guide* (Schmidt 2005). For excellent suggestions on ways to improve your writing style, see the classic, Strunk and White *The Elements of Style* (2000). *Bartlett's Roget's Thesaurus* (1996) can contribute much to the clarity and variety of your presentation and can, on occasion, offer direction for reducing your reliance on jargon. For guidance on the proper form and placement of footnotes and bibliography, consult *The Style Manual for Political Science* (American Political Science Association 2001). A revised version of the classic by Kate Turabian, *A Manual for Writers of Term Papers, Theses, and Dissertations* (2007), is now available.

References

American Political Science Association. 2001. *The Style Manual for Political Science*, rev. edn. Washington, DC: American Political Science Association.

Bartlett's. 1996. *Bartlett's Roget's Thesaurus*. Boston, MA: Little, Brown.

Brians, C. L. and Greene, S. 2004. 'Elections: Voter support and partisans' (mis)perceptions of presidential candidates' abortion views in 2000'. *Presidential Studies Quarterly*, vol. 34, pp. 412–19.

Ethridge, Marcus E. 2002. *The Political Research: Readings and Analysis*, 3rd edn. Armonk, NY: M.E. Sharpe.

Schmidt, Diane E. 2005. *Writing in Political Science: A Practical Guide*, 3rd edn. New York: Pearson Longman.

Strunk Jr., William with White, E. B. 2000. *The Elements of Style*, 4th edn. Boston: Allyn & Bacon.

Turabian, Kate L. 2007. *A Manual for Writers of Research Papers, Theses, and Dissertations*, 7th edn. Revised by Wayne C. Booth, Gregory G. Colomb, Joseph M. Williams and University of Chicago Press Staff. Chicago, IL: University of Chicago Press.

Research exercises

1 Read and *outline* three research articles in political science journals. Decide whether all the necessary elements of a research report are present in each case.

2 Read and *evaluate* the writing of three research articles in political science journals. Pay attention both to the method of the study and to the structure of the research report.

3 Read and *abstract* three research articles in political science journals. Where possible, compare your abstract with that prepared by the author of the article (which you should not read until you have finished your abstract).

Key term

abstract

25 Overview

Introduction

We have now presented the basic information you need to plan and execute a complete research project. In Figure 4.6 in Chapter 4 we provided an overview of the research process. We have explored the components of that process at length in the remainder of the text. In this closing chapter we review the research process as an integrated whole. We stress the ways in which the steps you have seen separated by chapter boundaries are, in practice, interwoven and interdependent. Our purpose is to facilitate your attacking research questions with a full understanding of the research process rather than a disjointed focus on each stage as it is reached. The value of an integrated understanding, of course, is that *many research problems can be avoided if the researcher is aware of the implications of decisions made at one stage of a project for subsequent stages.*

Developing hypotheses, measures and a research design

Research begins with a research question that asks why things are as we observe them to be. We are generally seeking an explanation for observed events. The place to start looking for this explanation is in the social science literature pertaining to our general subject. If we are fortunate, a literature search will turn up a ready-made explanation in the form of a theory that others have developed to explain events like the one that interests us. More often, however, we have to use the literature more creatively to *devise* the best theory possible, given existing information about the subject. The remainder of the research process is then devoted to testing this explanation to see how much it adds to our understanding of the events in question.

Stating hypotheses

The first step in this testing is to state some hypotheses that logic tells us must be accurate if our proposed answer to the research question is valid. These hypotheses serve several key functions. In the first place, they identify the units of analysis that must be observed in order to assess our explanation. Second, they isolate the variables for which we must develop indicators. Finally, hypotheses suggest ways in which our observations must be organised in order to provide useful evidence of the validity of our explanation. In stating hypotheses we also need to consider two questions. Can we observe the stated relationship? Can we locate the necessary data, or do we have the resources required to collect them for ourselves? It is essential that we select hypotheses that can be adequately tested with the time, skills and resources available to us. To do otherwise is to ensure failure.

Operationalising hypotheses

Next, the variables identified in the hypotheses must be operationalised so that we can obtain measures to compare in reaching a conclusion about the accuracy of our predictions. In selecting operationalisations or measurement procedures, we must be acutely sensitive to the resources required to apply them. If we do not have the necessary time, money or cooperation of subjects, we cannot use the measuring procedure. In addition, it is necessary to ask whether we are altering the meaning of any of the concepts included in our explanation when we let the results of any given measuring procedure represent them in our research. Though validity can often be assessed in data analysis, the question of validity must be faced well in advance of data collection, for no amount of clever data analysis can make invalid measures useful.

Choosing measurements

When creating measures, we must already be thinking ahead to the data analysis stage of the research. Researchers should examine their hypotheses to determine the statistical comparisons necessary to test their accuracy. First, we must be sure that the measuring procedures we have selected will yield data at the level of measurement required by the statistical procedures that will be used to test the hypotheses. For example, those who plan to use a measure of association that requires ordinal-level measurement must be certain that their measuring process yields at least ordinal data. A second consideration here is the similarity between the distribution of the values obtained with a measurement procedure and the distribution assumed by the statistical procedures that will be applied. Those who plan to use a test of statistical significance that requires a normal distribution should be certain their measuring procedure does not preclude obtaining a near normal distribution.

Selecting a research design

The next step is the development of a research design to guide the application of our measuring procedures. The central purpose of a research design is to ensure that we can feel confident that any relationships observed are the result of the processes described in our explanation and not of some other set of processes. Research designs provide this confidence by allowing us to rule out alternative rival hypotheses. A good research design, then, begins with a review of the literature. That review (along with logical analysis of situations) can suggest the major alternative rival hypotheses that must be ruled out before we can place confidence in our central explanation of observed events.

Research designs are developed by: (1) identifying the comparisons that must be made in order to test a hypothesis; (2) deciding what observations must be made (of whom or what, in what order, by what means, under what conditions) before those comparisons can be made; (3) anticipating all results that might be obtained from making the comparisons (no relationship, a positive relationship, a negative relationship and so forth); (4) identifying the major alternative rival hypotheses that can explain each possible result; and (5) organising a set of observations that will allow the additional comparisons necessary to test the validity of the most important of these alternative rival hypotheses as explanations of whatever results are observed.

Choosing data analysis

It is essential that we know what statistical analyses to perform when developing a research design, for it is the design that determines what data will be available for analysis. For example, if we anticipate controlling for many variables in the data analysis stage, we must be certain that our research design will yield enough cases to allow for such a complex breakdown of the sample. If we want to hold party affiliation constant by examining measures of association between two key variables for members of each party separately, we must include enough members of each party for computation of valid measures of association and we must plan to obtain information on subjects' party affiliation. If we plan to use time-series analysis in a study employing aggregate data, we must be sure that data on values of our independent variable come from a period prior to the time at which data on the dependent variable are collected if we have theoretical reasons to believe that there is a lag in the impact of the IV on the DV.

In the design of research, as in the selection of hypotheses and the devising of measures, it is essential to ask whether we are setting ourselves too ambitious a task. The best research design in the world is useless if the researcher lacks the resources to execute it. One must give careful consideration to the costs and logistics of data collection in designing research projects.

Data collection and analysis

As we have presented the research process, data collection and analysis are carried out in order to test hypotheses. We have discussed the primary rules to be observed in using various methods of data collection and analysis and, in Chapter 2, described the process of reasoning from empirical results to theory, thereby completing the research circle. There is no need to repeat those discussions here. We would, however, like to make two points that may not have come through our sequential presentation as clearly as they should.

Using multiple methods

The first point is that although we have presented the various data collection techniques separately, they need not be kept separate in the research process. In fact, there are good reasons for *mixing* methods of data collection in a study. In the first place, different methods can serve different purposes. Researchers may, for example, use focus groups to determine the breadth and nature of people's concerns about a set of political issues, then use survey research to estimate the *distribution* of those same views among the general population. In addition, it is often useful to employ a variety of methods in the data collection stage of a study because of the added confidence *multiple methods of measurement* can give us in the validity of results, as discussed in Chapters 4 and 11. For example, in studying variations in the quality of public services among a city's neighbourhoods, one will find it useful to confirm assessments of service quality obtained from survey research by means of aggregate data, official records, interviews with public officials and the judgements of trained observers. If all these methods of measurement produce a similar ranking of neighbourhoods, researchers can feel quite confident that they have accurately measured service quality.

Exploring your topic

A second point is that empirical research can be exploratory in nature. Rather than using it to test hypotheses derived from explanations, we can use it to provide data for use in devising explanations in the first place. Each research project generally raises new questions, suggests new explanations and leads to new research. Looking back at Figure 4.6, you will see a shortcut from *generalisation of observed relationships to hypotheses* and back to *data analysis*. This shortcut is the result of applying inductive logic in data analysis. A feedback loop serves an important function in empirical inquiry, for it suggests new data analyses that allow researchers to refine and elaborate explanations in ways they did not anticipate when designing a project, or to test explanations they did not anticipate.

A checklist for judging research

In an evaluation of others' research or in the design of your own, it is often helpful to step back from the details of each stage and try to get an overview of the research, asking whether it meets certain general but clearly stated requirements of sound empirical inquiry. To facilitate doing this, we have provided at the end of this chapter, in Figure 25.1, a list of things to look for. The questions are listed in approximately the sequence in which you might expect to encounter different problems in a report of research or in the execution of a project. The rules suggested by these questions are broad, and a project that 'checks out' on all these items may still contain subtle or highly technical errors. None the less, if you can answer 'yes' to each of the questions in the figure, the research being assessed is probably free of any error that this book has prepared you to identify and exhibits the basics of sound research.

Use the checklist carefully

In using the checklist, be aware of three cautions. First, not all questions will apply to any one research project. Exploratory research, for example, will not be designed to test hypotheses, and research based on elite interviews will probably not require a random sample. Second, the questions refer to technical rather than substantive aspects of research. A researcher may do everything

Figure 25.1   Checklist

A CHECKLIST FOR EVALUATING EMPIRICAL RESEARCH

☐ 1. Is the research question clearly stated? Do we know what the objectives of the research are so that we can assess the overall project? Is the research clearly related to some larger political issue or problem? Is this an important subject to study?

☐ 2. Are the units of analysis clearly identified, correctly chosen and consistently used throughout the project?

☐ 3. Are the concepts employed in the research clearly specified and adequately developed? Do the concepts have identifiable referents?

☐ 4. Is it clear what explanations are being tested? If a theory is used, is it logically correct? Do the concepts have identifiable empirical referents?

☐ 5. Is the theory or explanation consistent with existing literature on the subject? Is there evidence of a thorough literature review? Is the relationship of this research to prior research and larger political issues made clear?

☐ 6. Are hypotheses to be tested identified clearly and stated correctly? Do they logically follow from the explanation or theory being examined? Are they empirically testable?

☐ 7. If more than one hypothesis is being tested, are the relationships between them specified? Are all hypotheses clearly related to the theory, and their role in testing it made explicit?

☐ 8. Are the variables under investigation clearly identified and their status (independent, dependent, intervening, antecedent) specified in the hypotheses?

☐ 9. Are variables that might be expected to modify predicted relationships included in the study? (For example, can we expect relationships to hold for both men and women, or, in both industrialised and nonindustrialised nations?)

☐ 10. Are operationalisations of concepts stated clearly and measurement procedures specified in sufficient detail that others can replicate them? Have others used these operationalisations?

☐ 11. Are the measures likely to be valid and reliable? Are tests of validity and reliability anticipated? Are threats to validity and reliability recognised and provisions made to control them?

☐ 12. Is the research design clearly stated and appropriate for testing the hypotheses being examined? Are major alternative rival hypotheses recognised and provision made in the research design for examining these hypotheses as alternative explanations? Will the design provide a logically sound basis for causal inferences?

☐ 13. Is the population of interest to the researcher identified clearly? Is the sample used representative of that population? If not, does the researcher recognise the limitations this places on how results can be generalised? Are sampling procedures adequately described?

☐ 14. Is the data collection technique employed (survey research, content analysis and so forth) appropriate to the study given its units of analysis and the type of information being sought? Are all procedural rules observed that pertain to the particular method of data collection?

☐ 15. Is the data collection fully described? Are outside primary data sources fully identified so others can locate them?

☐ 16. Are coding systems that might affect measurement (such as collapsing various income groups into broad categories or treating certain types of responses as supportive or nonsupportive) fully described and justified?

☐ 17. Is the construction of any indices or scales fully described? Do these summary measures preserve the meaning of the concepts? Do they seem to be unidimensional (to reflect a single underlying concept or pattern)?

☐ 18. Have instruments been pretested?

☐ 19. Have efforts been made to verify results? (For example, have follow-up calls been made to survey respondents, or have alternative sources of aggregate data been sought?)

☐ 20. In presenting the data, are the tables and figures appropriate for illustrating the point they are intended to make? Are they fully discussed in the text and their central significance pointed out? Do they represent the results accurately?

☐ 21. Are the tables and figures clearly and completely labelled so that they can be easily interpreted?

☐ 22. Are the interpretations of the tables and figures offered correct, or do they suggest a misreading of the data?

☐ 23. Are appropriate descriptive statistics (such as mean and standard deviation) used to summarise the data and supplement tables and figures?

☐ 24. In examining relationships between variables, do the researchers provide evidence of the strength, direction, form and significance of relationships?

☐ 25. Do the researchers explore the possible effects of antecedent, intervening and suppressor variables? Do they attempt to control these effects in the data analysis?

☐ 26. Are all statistics or other methods used appropriate for the level at which variables are measured, and are they suited to the purpose for which they are used?

☐ 27. Do the data conform to the assumptions (random sampling, normal distribution and so forth) involved in legitimate application of the statistics or other method used? Have the researchers investigated the degree to which their data fit these assumptions?

☐ 28. Are measures of statistical significance applied only where appropriate and correctly interpreted? Have the researchers avoided confusing statistical significance with substantive significance?

☐ 29. Are major alternative rival hypotheses statistically explored and the results both reported and correctly interpreted?

☐ 30. Is each piece of data analysis clearly related to the major conclusions drawn from the study? Are the interpretations consistent with the data and with the theory or explanation being tested?

☐ 31. Does the research report:
    a. contain a precise statement of the purpose of the study?
    b. review enough of the relevant literature to demonstrate the contribution of this study?
    c. adequately describe the research design, data and methods used?
    d. follow a clear and appropriate organisation in presenting findings?
    e. state conclusions clearly?

☐ 32. Are the conclusions reached actually warranted by the data presented and the research design used? Does the study make the kind of contribution to the literature the authors claim it does, or have the authors generalised too far beyond the limits of their research?

☐ 33. Have the authors been sensitive to ethical issues raised by the research? Have they satisfactorily resolved these issues?

correctly and still be investigating a trivial subject. *Valuable research is both technically correct and substantively important*. In judging research, ask whether its proper execution will add useful knowledge to our attempts to understand significant political events. Sometimes, lower levels of technical sophistication are justified by the complexity and magnitude of an important subject. On the whole, the project that adds a little to our knowledge of an important subject is more valuable than a project that adds a lot to our knowledge of a trivial matter. Third, few projects can be free of limitations. For instance, it may be impossible to obtain a representative sample of an entire large population within the resource limits of a given study. It may be necessary to sample only one sub-group (as when a study of UK political behaviour is conducted with a sample from one city only). Such limitations become errors only when the researcher fails to recognise them and modify accordingly the conclusions drawn from the study.

The checklist can be used to assess others' research as well as to evaluate your own. As a research exercise, you may want to locate an article reporting the results of a research project and evaluate it using the checklist in Figure 25.1, identifying any errors you may find and explaining why they are errors.

Ethical considerations

In every chapter, this book has promoted ethical research in each facet of research. For political scientists, ethical responsibilities can not be overemphasised, because we conduct our research on people's behaviour, for people. This charge carries with it a substantial responsibility to care for the subjects of our research throughout the process.

For example, whereas most of the standards in Figure 25.1 focus on technical considerations, the final standard explicitly focuses on ethics. Yet, all thirty-three research standards implicitly call for ethical behaviour by researchers. The questions in Figure 25.1 and the professional guidelines in Appendix B should offer concrete means to answer the myriad of ethical issues that are raised in research, ranging from the necessity of protecting research subjects from harm, to presenting analyses that fairly represent the underlying data.

Never forget, it is immaterial whether anyone else ever realises the lengths to which you have gone to conduct your research and your life ethically. As the aphorism states, your personal ethics are most accurately measured when you do not think anyone is watching you. As fellow politics scholars, we hope that ethically you measure up.

Conclusion

Armed only with the information contained in this book, you could successfully carry out a wide range of empirical investigations. You should recognise, however, that this text has just scratched the surface of the huge subject of empirical political research. The dozens of other books listed in our suggestions for further reading should convince you that there is much more to be said and much you cannot learn from this book.

In the process of research, you may discover the importance of the things you do *not* know. Even if you carefully and properly follow every guideline and rule presented in this text, you may find yourself either (1) unable to complete some research projects or (2) producing a set of research results that more experienced social scientists recognise as seriously flawed because you have made errors we did not warn you against. If you follow the suggestions presented in the first five chapters, you should make very few errors in stating hypotheses, operationalising concepts, searching the literature or devising a research design. Our chapters on sampling and data management probably provide less complete guides, however, because those processes are both more technical and more closely tied to the situations encountered in individual research projects. Similarly, we have only been able to provide you with a partial guide to the various data collection and data analysis techniques because of the scope and technical nature of these subjects; you would be well advised to study them further before claiming expertise in empirical analysis. The research examples and methodological readings at the ends of chapters provide good *starting places* for acquiring genuine expertise.

We have provided a sound foundation on which you can build your competence as a political scientist. We hope you find that task as exciting and rewarding as we have and that in the future you will agree that getting there was half the fun.

Appendix

Statistical tables

Table A.1 Random digits

10097	32533	76520	13586	34673	54876	80959	09117	39292	74945
37542	04805	64894	74296	24805	24037	20636	10402	00822	91665
08422	68953	19645	09303	23209	02560	15953	34764	35080	33606
99019	02529	09376	70715	38311	31165	88676	74397	04436	27659
12807	99970	80157	36147	64032	36653	98951	16877	12171	76833
66065	74717	34072	76850	36697	36170	65813	39885	11199	29170
31060	10805	45571	82406	35303	42614	86799	07439	23403	09732
85269	77602	02051	65692	68665	74818	73053	85247	18623	88579
63573	32135	05325	47048	90553	57548	28468	28709	83491	25624
73796	45753	03529	64778	35808	34282	60935	20344	35273	88435
98520	17767	14905	68607	22109	40558	60970	93433	50500	73998
11805	05431	39808	27732	50725	68248	29405	24201	52775	67851
83452	99634	06288	98083	13746	70078	18475	40610	68711	77817
88685	40200	86507	58401	36766	67951	90364	76493	29609	11062
99594	67348	87517	64969	91826	08928	93785	61368	23478	34113
65481	17674	17468	50950	58047	76974	73039	57186	40218	16544
80124	35635	17727	08015	45318	22374	21115	78253	14385	53763
74350	99817	77402	77214	43236	00201	45521	64237	96286	02655
69916	26803	66252	29148	36936	87203	76621	13990	94400	56418
09893	20505	14225	68514	46427	56788	96297	78822	54382	14598
91499	14523	68479	27686	46162	83554	94750	89923	37089	20048
80336	94598	26490	36858	70297	34135	53140	33340	42050	82341
44104	81949	85157	47954	32979	26575	57600	40881	22222	06413
12550	73742	11100	02040	12860	74697	96644	89439	28707	25815
63606	49329	16505	34484	40219	52563	43651	77082	07207	31790
61196	90446	26457	47774	51924	33729	65394	59593	42582	60527
5474	45266	95270	79953	59367	83848	82396	10118	33211	59466
94557	28573	67897	54387	54622	44431	91190	42592	92927	45973
42481	16213	97344	08721	16868	48767	03071	12059	25701	46670
23523	78317	73208	89837	68935	91416	26252	29663	05522	82562

(Continued)

Table A.1 (*Continued*)

04493	52494	75246	33824	45826	51025	61962	79335	65337	12472
00549	97654	64501	88159	96119	63896	54692	82391	23287	29529
35963	15307	26898	09354	33351	35462	77974	50024	90103	39333
59808	08391	45427	26842	83609	49700	13021	24892	78565	20106
46058	85236	01390	92286	77281	44077	93910	83647	70617	42941
32179	00597	87379	25241	05567	07007	86743	17157	85394	11838
69234	61406	20117	45204	15956	60000	18743	92423	97118	96338
19565	41430	01758	75379	40419	21585	66674	36806	84962	85207
45155	14938	19476	07246	43667	94543	59047	90033	20826	69541
94864	31994	36168	10851	81553	34888	01540	35456	05014	51176
98086	24826	45240	28404	44999	08896	39094	73407	35441	31880
33185	16232	41941	50949	89435	48581	88695	41994	37548	73043
80951	00406	96382	70774	20151	23387	25016	25298	94624	61171
79752	49140	71961	28296	69861	02591	74852	20539	00387	59579
18633	32537	98145	06571	31010	24674	05455	61427	77938	91936
74029	43902	77557	32270	97790	17119	52527	58021	80814	51748
54178	45611	80993	37143	05335	12969	56127	19255	36040	90324
11664	49883	52079	84827	59381	71539	09973	33440	88461	23356
48324	77928	31249	64710	02295	36870	32307	57546	15020	09994
69074	94138	87637	91976	35584	04401	10518	21615	01848	76938

Source: The RAND Corporation. *A Million Random Digits with 100,000 Normal Deviates* (New York: Free Press, 1966), p. 1. Reprinted with permission.

Table A.2 Sample size for sampling attributes at specified levels of precision (in per cent with a 95% confidence interval, p = .05)[*]

Population size	Sample size for precision of					
	±1%	±2%	±3%	±4%	±5%	±10%
500	†	†	†	†	222	83
1,000	†	†	†	385	286	91
1,500	†	†	638	441	316	94
2,000	†	†	714	476	333	95
2,500	†	1,250	769	500	345	96
3,000	†	1,364	811	517	353	97
3,500	†	1,458	843	530	359	97
4,000	†	1,538	870	541	364	98
4,500	†	1,607	891	549	367	98
5,000	†	1,667	909	556	370	98
6,000	†	1,765	938	566	375	98
7,000	†	1,842	959	574	378	99
8,000	†	1,905	976	580	381	99
9,000	†	1,957	989	584	383	99
10,000	5,000	2,000	1,000	588	385	99
15,000	6,000	2,143	1,034	600	390	99
20,000	6,667	2,222	1,053	606	392	100
25,000	7,143	2,273	1,064	610	394	100
50,000	8,333	2,381	1,087	617	397	100
100,000	9,091	2,439	1,099	621	398	100
→ ∞	10,000	2,500	1,111	625	400	100

Source: Taro Yamane, *Elementary Sampling Theory* (Englewood Cliffs, NJ: Prentice Hall, 1967), p. 398. Adapted and reprinted with permission of the publisher.

[*]Proportion of units in the sample possessing the characteristic being measured; for other values of p, the required sample size will be smaller.

[†]In these cases, 50% of the universe in the sample will give more than the required accuracy. Since the formal distribution is a poor approximation of the hypergeometrical distribution when n is more than 50% of N, the formula used in this calculation does not apply.

Table A.3 Sample size for sampling attributes at specified levels of precision (in per cent with a 99% confidence interval, p = .01)[*]

Population size	Sample size for precision of				
	±1%	±2%	±3%	±4%	±5%
500	†	†	†	†	†
1,000	†	†	†	†	474
1,500	†	†	†	726	563
2,000	†	†	†	826	621
2,500	†	†	†	900	662
3,000	†	†	1,364	958	692
3,500	†	†	1,458	1,003	716
4,000	†	†	1,539	1,041	735
4,500	†	†	1,607	1,071	750
5,000	†	†	1,667	1,098	763
6,000	†	2,903	1,765	1,139	783
7,000	†	3,119	1,842	1,171	798
8,000	†	3,303	1,905	1,196	809
9,000	†	3,462	1,957	1,216	818
10,000	†	3,600	2,000	1,233	826
15,000	†	4,091	2,143	1,286	849
20,000	†	4,390	2.222	1,314	861
25,000	11,842	4,592	2,273	1,331	869
50,000	15,517	5,056	2,381	1,368	884
100,000	18,367	5,325	2,439	1,387	892
→ ∞	22,500	5,625	2,500	1,406	900

Source: Taro Yamane, *Elementary Sampling Theory* (Englewood Cliffs, NJ: Prentice Hall, 1967), p. 399. Adapted and reprinted with permission of the publisher.

[*]Proportion of units in the sample possessing the characteristic being measured; for other values of p, the required sample size will be smaller.

[†]In these cases 50% of the universe in the sample will give more than the required accuracy. Since the formal distribution is a poor approximation of the hypergeometrical distribution when n is more than 50% of N, the formula used in this calculation does not apply.

Table A.4 Distribution of χ^2

df	.05	.01	.001	df	.05	.01	.001
1	3.841	6.635	10.827	26	38.885	45.642	54.052
2	5.991	9.210	13.815	27	40.113	46.963	55.476
3	7.815	11.345	16.266	28	41.337	48.278	56.893
4	9.488	13.277	18.467	29	42.557	49.588	58.302
5	11.070	15.086	20.515	30	43.773	50.892	59.703
6	12.592	16.812	22.457	32	46.194	53.486	62.487
7	14.067	18.475	24.322	34	48.602	56.061	65.247
8	15.507	20.090	26.125	36	50.999	58.619	67.985
9	16.919	21.666	27.877	38	53.384	61.162	70.703
10	18.307	23.209	29.588	40	55.759	63.691	73.402
11	19.675	24.725	31.264	42	58.124	66.206	76.084
12	21.026	26.217	32.909	44	60.481	68.710	78.750
13	22.362	27.688	34.528	46	62.830	71.201	81.400
14	23.685	29.141	36.123	48	65.171	73.683	84.037
15	24.996	30.578	37.697	50	67.505	76.154	86.661
16	26.296	32.000	39.252	52	69.832	78.616	89.272
17	27.587	33.409	40.790	54	72.153	81.069	91.872
18	28.869	34.805	42.312	56	74.468	83.513	94.461
19	30.144	36.191	43.820	58	76.778	85.950	97.039
20	31.410	37.566	45.315	60	79.082	88.379	99.607
21	32.671	38.932	46.797	62	81.381	90.802	102.166
22	33.924	40.289	48.268	64	83.675	93.217	104.716
23	35.172	41.638	49.728	66	85.965	95.626	107.258
24	36.415	42.980	51.179	68	88.250	98.028	109.791
25	37.652	44.314	52.620	70	90.531	100.425	112.317

Source: From Table IV of Ronald A. Fisher and Frank Yates, *Statistical Tables for Biological, Agricultural and Medical Research*, 6th edn, published by Longman Group, Ltd, London (previously published by Oliver & Boyd, Edinburgh). Reprinted with permission of the authors and the publisher.

Note: For odd values of n between 30 and 70, the mean of the tabular values for $df - 1$ and $df + 1$ may be taken. For larger values of n, the expression $\sqrt{2x^2} - \sqrt{2df - 1}$ may be used as a normal deviate with unit variance, remembering that the probability for χ^2 corresponds with that of a single tail of the normal curve.

Table A.5 Values of the correlation coefficient for different levels of significance

df	.1	.05	.01	.001	df	.1	.05	.01	.001
1	.98769	.99692	.999877	.9999988	16	.4000	.4683	.5897	.7084
2	.90000	.95000	.990000	.99900	17	.3887	.4555	.5751	.6932
3	.8054	.878	.9587	.99116	18	.3783	.4438	.5614	.6787
4	.7293	.8114	.91720	.97406	19	.3687	.4329	.5487	.6652
5	.6694	.7545	.8745	.95274	20	.3598	.4227	.5368	.6524
6	.6215	.7067	.8343	.92493	25	.3233	.3809	.4869	.5974
7	.5822	.6664	.7977	.8982	30	.2960	.3494	.4487	.5541
8	.5494	.6319	.7646	.8721	35	.2746	.3246	.4182	.5189
9	.5214	.6021	.7348	.8471	40	.2573	.3044	.3932	.4896
10	.4973	.5760	.7079	.8233	45	.2428	.2875	.3721	.4648
11	.4762	.5529	.6835	.8010	50	.2306	.2732	.3541	.4433
12	.4575	.5324	.6614	.7800	60	.2108	.2500	.3248	.4078
13	.4409	.5139	.6411	.7603	70	.1954	.2319	.3017	.3799
14	.4259	.497	.6226	.7420	80	.1829	.2172	.2830	.3568
15	.4124	.482	.6055	.7246	90	.1726	.2050	.2673	.3375
					100	.1638	.1946	.2540	.3211

Source: From Table VII of Ronald A. Fisher and Frank Yates, *Statistical Tables for Biological, Agricultural and Medical Research*, 6th edn, published by Longman Group, Ltd, London (previously published by Oliver & Boyd, Edinburgh). Reprinted with permission of the authors and the publishers.

Table A.6 Portions of area under the normal curve

(A) z	(B) Area between mean and z	(C) Area beyond z	(A) z	(B) Area between mean and z	(C) Area beyond z	(A) z	(B) Area between mean and z	(C) Area beyond z
0.00	.0000	.5000	0.37	.1443	.3557	0.74	.2704	.2296
0.01	.0040	.4960	0.38	.1480	.3520	0.75	.2734	.2266
0.02	.0080	.4920	0.39	.1517	.3483	0.76	.2764	.2236
0.03	.0120	.4880	0.40	.1554	.3446	0.77	.2794	.2206
0.04	.0160	.4840	0 41	.1591	.3409	0.78	.2823	.2177
0.05	.0199	.4801	0.42	.1628	.3372	0.79	.2852	.2148
0.06	.0239	.4761	0.43	.1664	.3336	0.80	.2881	.2119
0.07	.0279	.4721	0.44	.1700	.3300	0.81	.2910	.2090
0.08	.0319	.4681	0.45	.1736	.3264	0.82	.2936	.2061
0.09	.0359	.4641	0.46	.1772	.3228	0.83	.2967	.2033
0.10	.0398	.4602	0.47	.1808	.3192	0.84	.2995	.2005
0.11	.0438	.4562	0.48	.1844	.3156	0.85	.3023	.1977
0.12	.0478	.4522	0.49	.1879	.3121	0.86	.3051	.1949
0.13	.0517	.4483	0.50	.1915	.3085	0.87	.3078	.1922
0.14	.0557	.4443	0.51	.1950	.3050	0.88	.3106	.1894
0.15	.0596	.4404	0.52	.1985	.3015	0.89	.3133	.1867
0.16	.0636	.4364	0.53	.2019	.2981	0.90	.3159	.1841
0.17	.0675	.4325	0.54	.2054	.2946	0.91	.3186	.1814
0.18	.0714	.4286	0.55	.2088	.2912	0.92	.3212	.1788
0.19	.0753	.4247	0.56	.2123	.2877	0.93	.3238	.1788
0.20	.0793	.4207	0.57	.2157	.2843	0.94	.3264	.1736
0.21	.0832	.4168	0.58	.2190	.2810	0.95	.3289	.1711
0.22	.0871	.4129	0.59	.2224	.2776	0.96	.3315	.1685
0.23	.0910	.4090	0.60	.2257	.2743	0.97	.3340	.1660
0.24	.0948	.4052	0.61	.2291	.2709	0.98	.3365	.1635
0.25	.0987	.4013	0.62	.2324	.2676	0.99	.3389	.1611
0.26	.1026	.3974	0.63	.2357	.2643	1.00	.3413	.1587
0.27	.1064	.3936	0.64	.2389	.2611	1.01	.3438	.1562
0.28	.1103	.3897	0.65	.2422	.2578	1.02	.3461	.1539
0.29	.1141	.3859	0.66	.2454	.2546	1.03	.3485	.1515
0.30	.1179	.3821	0.67	.2486	.2514	1.04	.3508	.1492
0.31	.1217	.3783	0.68	.2517	.2483	1.05	.3531	.1469
0.32	.1255	.3745	0.69	.2549	.2451	1.06	.3554	.1446
0.33	.1293	.3707	0.70	.2580	.2420	1.07	.3577	.1423
0.34	.1331	.3669	0.71	.2611	.2389	1.08	.3599	.1401
0.35	.1368	.3632	0.72	.2642	.2358	1.09	.3621	.1379
0.36	.1406	.3594	0.73	.2673	.2327	1.10	.3643	.1357

(Continued)

Table A.6 (*Continued*)

(A) z	(B) Area between mean and z	(C) Area beyond z	(A) z	(B) Area between mean and z	(C) Area beyond z	(A) z	(B) Area between mean and z	(C) Area beyond z
1.11	.3665	.1335	1.49	.4319	.0681	1.87	.4693	.0307
1.12	.3686	.1314	1.50	.4332	.0668	1.88	.4699	.0301
1.13	.3708	.1292	1.51	.4345	.0655	1.89	.4706	.0294
1.14	.3729	.1271	1.52	.4357	.0643	1.90	.4713	.0287
1.15	.3748	.1251	1.53	.4370	.0630	1.91	.4719	.0281
1.16	.3770	.1230	1.54	.4382	.0618	1.92	.4726	.0274
1.17	.3790	.1210	1.55	.4394	.0606	1.93	.4732	.0268
1.18	.3810	.1190	1.56	.4406	.0594	1.94	.4738	.0262
1.19	.3830	.1170	1.57	.4418	.0582	1.95	.4744	.0256
1.20	.3849	.1151	1.58	.4429	.0571	1.96	.4750	.0250
1.21	.3869	.1131	1.59	.4441	.0559	1.97	.4556	.0244
1.22	.3888	.1112	1.60	.4452	.0548	1.98	.4761	.0239
1.23	.3907	.1093	1.61	.4463	.0537	1.99	.4767	.0233
1.24	.3925	.1075	1.62	.4474	.0526	2.00	.4772	.0228
1.25	.3944	.1056	1.63	.4484	.0516	2.01	.4778	.0222
1.26	.3962	.1038	1.64	.4495	.0505	2.02	.4783	.0217
1.27	.3980	.1020	1.65	.4505	.0495	2.03	.4788	.0212
1.28	.3997	.1003	1.66	.4515	.0485	2.04	.4793	.0207
1.29	.4015	.0985	1.67	.4525	.0475	2.05	.4798	.0202
1.30	.4032	.0968	1.68	.4535	.0465	2.06	.4803	.0197
1.31	.4049	.0951	1.69	.4545	.0455	2.07	.4808	.0192
1.32	.4066	.0934	1.70	.4554	.0446	2.08	.4812	.0188
1.33	.4082	.0918	1.71	.4564	.0436	2.09	.4817	.0183
1.34	.4099	.0901	1.72	.4573	.0427	2.10	.4821	.0179
1.35	.4115	.0885	1.73	.4582	.0418	2.11	.4826	.0174
1.36	.4131	.0869	1.74	.4591	.0409	2.12	.4830	.0170
1.37	.4147	.0853	1.75	.4599	.0401	2.13	.4834	.0166
1.38	.4162	.0838	1.76	.4608	.0392	2.14	.4838	.0162
1.39	.4177	.0823	1.77	.4616	.0384	2.15	.4842	.0158
1.40	.4192	.0808	1.78	.4625	.0375	2.16	.4846	.0154
1.41	.4207	.0793	1.79	.4633	.0367	2.17	.4850	.0150
1.42	.4222	.0778	1.80	.4641	.0359	2.18	.4854	.0146
1.43	.4236	.0764	1.81	.4649	.0351	2.19	.4857	.0143
1.44	.4251	.0749	1.82	.4656	.0344	2.20	.4861	.0139
1.45	.4265	.0735	1.83	.4664	.0336	2.21	.4864	.0136
1.46	.4279	.0721	1.84	.4671	.0329	2.22	.4868	.0132
1.47	.4292	.0708	1.85	.4678	.0322	2.23	.4871	.0129
1.48	.4306	.0694	1.86	.4686	.0314	2.24	.4875	.0125

Table A.6 (*continued*)

(A) z	(B) Area between mean and z	(C) Area beyond z	(A) z	(B) Area between mean and z	(C) Area beyond z	(A) z	(B) Area between mean and z	(C) Area beyond z
2.25	.4878	.0122	2.62	.4956	.0044	2.99	.4986	.0014
2.26	.4881	.0119	2.63	.4957	.0043	3.00	.4987	.0013
2.27	.4884	.0116	2.64	.4959	.0041	3.01	.4987	.0013
2.28	.4887	.0113	2.65	.4960	.0040	3.02	.4987	.0013
2.29	.4890	.0110	2.66	.4961	.0039	3.03	.4988	.0012
2.30	.4893	.0107	2.67	.4962	.0038	3.04	.4988	.0012
2.31	.4896	.0104	2.68	.4963	.0037	3.05	.4989	.0011
2.32	.4898	.0102	2.69	.4964	.0036	3.06	.4989	.0011
2.33	.4901	.0099	2.70	.4965	.0035	3.07	.4989	.0011
2.34	.4904	.0096	2.71	.4966	.0034	3.08	.4990	.0010
2.35	.4906	.0094	2.72	.4967	.0033	3.09	.4990	.0010
2.36	.4909	.0091	2.73	.4968	.0032	3.10	.4990	.0010
2.37	.4911	.0089	2.74	.4969	.0031	3.11	.4991	.0009
2.38	.4913	.0087	2.75	.4970	.0030	3.12	.4991	.0009
2.39	.4916	.0084	2.76	.4971	.0029	3.13	.4991	.0009
2.40	.4918	.0082	2.77	.4972	.0028	3.14	.4992	.0008
2.41	.4920	.0080	2.78	.4973	.0027	3.15	.4992	.0008
2.42	.4922	.0078	2.79	.4974	.0026	3.16	.4992	.0008
2.43	.4925	.0075	2.80	.4974	.0026	3.17	.4992	.0008
2.44	.4927	.0073	2.81	.4975	.0025	3.18	.4993	.0007
2.45	.4929	.0071	2.82	.4976	.0024	3.19	.4993	.0007
2.46	.4931	.0069	2.83	.4977	.0023	3.20	.4993	.0007
2.47	.4932	.0068	2.84	.4977	.0023	3.21	.4993	.0007
2.48	.4934	.0064	2.85	.4978	.0022	3.22	.4994	.0006
2.49	.4936	.0064	2.86	.4979	.0021	3.23	.4994	.0006
2.50	.4938	.0064	2.87	.4979	.0021	3.24	.4994	.0006
2.51	.4940	.0064	2.88	.4980	.0020	3.25	.4994	.0006
2.52	.4941	.0054	2.89	.4981	.0019	3.30	.4995	.0005
2.53	.4943	.0057	2.90	.4981	.0019	3.35	.4996	.0004
2.54	.4945	.0055	2.91	.4982	.0018	3.40	.4997	.0003
2.55	.4946	.0054	2.92	.4982	.0018	3.45	.4997	.0003
2.56	.4948	.0052	2.93	.4983	.0017	3.50	.4998	.0002
2.57	.4949	.0051	2.94	.4984	.0016	3.60	.4998	.0002
2.58	.4951	.0049	2.95	.4984	.0016	3.70	.4999	.0001
2.59	.4952	.0048	2.96	.4985	.0015	3.80	.4999	.0001
2.60	.4953	.0047	2.97	.4985	.0015	3.90	.49995	.00005
2.61	.4955	.0045	2.98	.4986	.0014	4.00	.49997	.00003

Source: Richard P. Runyon and Audrey Haber, *Fundamentals of Behavioral Statistics*, 3rd edn. (Reading, MA; Addison-Wesley, 1976), pp. 378–79.

B Ethical standards in empirical research

American Political Science Association

The American Political Science Association has adopted a set of 'Principles of Professional Conduct.' The following rules are excerpted from the section on ethical research practices.[1]

1. Openness concerning material support of research is a basic principle of scholarship....

3. In applying for research funds, the individual researcher should:

    3.1 clearly state the reasons for applying for support and not resort to stratagems of ambiguity to make the research more acceptable to a funding agency;

    3.2 indicate clearly the actual amount of time the researcher personally plans to spend on the research;

    3.3 indicate other sources of support of the research, if any; and

    3.4 refuse to accept terms and conditions that the researcher believes will undermine his or her freedom and integrity as a scholar.

4. In conducting research so supported, the individual bears sole responsibility for the procedures, methods, and content of research. The researcher:

    4.1 must avoid any deception or misrepresentation concerning his or her personal involvement or the involvement of respondents or subjects, and must avoid use of research as a cover for intelligence work or for partisan political purposes;

    4.2 must refrain from using his or her professional status to obtain data and research materials for purposes other than scholarship;

    4.3 with respect to research abroad, should not concurrently accept any additional support from agencies of the government for purposes that cannot be disclosed;

    4.4 should carefully comply with the time, reporting, accounting, and other requirements set forth in the project instrument, and cooperate with institutional grant administrators in meeting these requirements; and

    4.5 should avoid commingling project funds with personal funds, or funds of one project with those of another.

5. With respect to any public scholarly activity including publication of the results of research, the individual researcher:

    5.1 bears sole responsibility for publication;

    5.2 should disclose all relevant sources of financial support;

    5.3 should indicate any condition imposed by financial sponsors or others on research publication, or other scholarly activities; and

    5.4 should conscientiously acknowledge any assistance received in conducting research.

    5.5 Authors are obliged to reveal the bases of any of their statements that are challenged specifically, except where confidentiality is involved.

---

[1] Reproduced with the permission of the American Political Science Association. The full text of *A Guide to Professional Ethics in Political Science*, 2nd edition (2008) is available from www.apsanet.org/imgtest/ethicsguideweb.pdf

6. Scholars have an ethical obligation to make a full and complete disclosure of all nonconfidential sources involved in their research so that their work can be tested or replicated.

   6.1 As citizens they have an obligation to cooperate with grand juries, other law enforcement agencies, and institutional officials.

   6.2 Conversely, scholars also have a professional duty not to divulge the identity of confidential sources of information or data developed in the course of research, whether to governmental or nongovernmental officials or bodies, even though in the present state of American law they run the risk of suffering an applicable penalty.

   6.3 Scholars must, however, exercise appropriate restraint in making claims as to the confidential nature of their sources, and resolve all reasonable doubts in favour of full disclosure.

7. Political scientists, like all scholars, are expected to practice intellectual honesty and to uphold the scholarly standards of their discipline.

   7.1 Plagiarism, the deliberate appropriation of the work of others represented as one's own, not only may constitute a violation of the civil law but represents a serious breach of professional ethics.

American Association for Public Opinion Research

The American Association for Public Opinion Research has adopted the following Code of Professional Ethics and Practices.[2]

I. Principles of professional practice in the conduct of our work

   A. We shall exercise due care in developing research designs and survey instruments, and in collecting, processing, and analyzing data, taking all reasonable steps to assure the reliability and validity of results.

      1. We shall recommend and employ only those tools of analysis which . . . are well suited to the research problem at hand.

      2. We shall not select research tools and methods of analysis because of their capacity to yield misleading conclusions.

      3. We shall not knowingly make interpretations of research results, nor shall we tacitly permit interpretations that are inconsistent with the data available.

      4. We shall not knowingly imply that interpretations should be accorded greater confidence than the data actually warrant.

   B. We shall describe our methods and findings accurately and in appropriate detail in all research reports, adhering to the standards for minimal disclosure specified in Section III below. . . .

II. Principles of professional responsibility in our dealings with people

   A. The public

      1. If we become aware of the appearance in public of serious distortions of our research, we shall publicly disclose what is required to correct these distortions. . . .

   D. The respondent

      1. We shall strive to avoid the use of practices or methods that may harm, humiliate, or seriously mislead survey respondents.

---

[2]*Code of Professional Ethics and Practices* (2005), courtesy of the American Association for Public Opinion Research. The full text is available from www.aapor.org/AAPOR_Code.htm

2. Unless the respondent waives confidentiality for specified uses, we shall hold as privileged and confidential all information that might identify a respondent with his or her responses. We shall also not disclose or use the names of respondents for nonresearch purposes unless the respondents grant us permission to do so.

III. Standard for minimal disclosure

1. Who sponsored the survey, and who conducted it.
2. The exact wording of questions asked, including the text of any preceding instruction or explanation to the interviewer or respondent that might reasonably be expected to affect the response.
3. A definition of the population under study, and a description of the sampling frame used to identify this population.
4. A description of the sample selection procedure, giving a clear indication of the method by which the respondents were selected by the researcher, or whether the respondents were entirely self-selected.
5. Size of sample and, if applicable, completion rates and information on eligibility criteria and screening procedures.
6. A discussion of the precision of the findings, including, if appropriate, estimates of sampling error, and a description of any weighting or estimating procedures used.
7. Which results are based on parts of the sample, rather than on the total sample.
8. Method, location, and dates of data collection.

Glossary

abstract a brief statement summarising the contents of a report

actors individuals and groups which act and interact

additive index a measure created by combining indicators of different aspects of the same concept

agency the actor or actors responsible for a set of actions or conditions

aggregate data data pertaining to groups of cases or to collectivities

alternative rival hypothesis an alternative explanation for obtained results that logically cannot be accurate if the initial hypothesis is accurate

antecedent variable a variable that causes variation in the variable that, for purposes of a given hypothesis, is regarded as the independent variable

applied research research, the primary purpose of which is to examine or resolve particular policy problems

areal group a group defined by residence within a particular geographic area

association a relationship in which two (or more) variables covary

assumption (also axiom or postulate) an abstract assertion about relationships that serves as a foundation for theoretical reasoning but is not subject to empirical test

authorial intention the motives of the author of a text in creating the text

bar chart a graphic device in which bars are used to represent observations

basic research research, the primary purpose of which is to develop or test a scientific theory

beta weight (β) or beta coefficient (b) a standardised partial regression coefficient used to compare the relative effects of independent variables on a dependent variable

bibliographic sources systematic listings of publications organised to assist in literature reviews

bibliography a compilation of books, articles and other materials on a given topic

bilateral bar chart a two-directional graphic device in which bars are used to represent variation above or below some norm

binary opposition a tendency to place actors or actions in contrasting categories; contrasting categories may seem mutually exclusive but actors and actions often do not fit the categories so completely

bivariate statistics statistics summarising the relationship between two variables

Boolean operators words such as 'and', 'or', or 'not' that provide linkages among concepts during a computerised literature search

case study   an intensive exploration of the detailed causal linkages in a single case or small number of cases

causal model   a model that graphically specifies a set of relationships between concepts or variables such that change in one or more precedes and gives rise to change in another

causal relationship   a relationship in which change in one or more concepts or variables leads to or 'forces' changes in one or more other concepts or variables

central tendency (measure of)   device for determining the value or score that best represents a set of cases on a given variable

chi-square (χ^2)   a test of the statistical significance of the association between two nominal variables

closed-ended question   a question that forces respondents to choose an answer from a limited number of options

cluster sampling   *see* **multistage random area sample**

codebook   a listing of variables and values indicating how they are coded in a study

coder   a person who assigns scores to cases or responses, usually with reference to content analysis coded in a study

codes   numbers assigned to represent different values on variables for purposes of data analysis

coding   the process of assigning numerical values to represent values on variables

coding manual   *see* **codebook**

coding sheet   a structured form for recording data

coefficient of association   a measure of the degree and direction of association between two variables

coefficient of determination (R^2)   the multiple regression coefficient tells how much of the variance in the values on a dependent variable is 'explained' by variance in a set of independent variables

cohort study   a study based on repeated surveys of a specific group (for example, persons born in a given year) at different points in time

collectively exhaustive   a characteristic of measures by which all cases can be assigned to at least one category

computer-assisted telephone interviewing (CATI)   interviewing using computer display of instrument, usually includes continual calculation of summary statistics

concept   a word or phrase that symbolises some idea or phenomenon

concurrent validation   the characteristic of a measure that allows accurate sorting of cases on the basis of related concurrent traits

confidence interval   an indicator of the accuracy with which a population parameter can be predicted from a sample statistic stated in terms of the range of values above or below the sample statistic the population parameter is likely to fall

confidence level   an indicator of the likelihood that a sample is representative stated in terms of the probability that a sample statistic is within a given confidence interval of a population parameter

construct validity   the characteristic of a measure by which it behaves as we would expect on the basis of theory

constructivism   the theory that the world is purely a mental construct and there is no objective material reality

content analysis   a technique used in the study of communication-related materials and behaviours

contingency question   a filtering device used in survey research to ascertain the appropriateness of asking a subsequent question

control   in experimental design, to limit the factors influencing a variable under observation; in data analysis, to hold the values of one variable constant while examining the relationship(s) between two or more other variables

control group subjects   in an experiment not exposed to the independent variable (experimental event)

controlled time-series design   a research design that uses control groups to assess the impact of an event

controlling   holding constant the effect of one variable on the relationship between two other variables in order to obtain an accurate measure of that relationship

convergent validation   *see* **internal validity**

convergent validity   a characteristic whereby several measures of a common concept provide essentially the same result

correlation coefficient (*r*)   the coefficient of association between two interval variables measuring the closeness of fit of data points around the regression line

covariational relationship   a relationship in which two or more concepts or variables tend to change together for unspecified reasons

critical   looking for patterns of interaction or interpretation, often empowering or disempowering, which go beyond the assumptions of theories or the conventional views of the actors themselves

cross-sectional survey   a survey that compares data from different cases at a single point in time

cross tabulation   a tabular presentation summarising the relationship(s) between two or more variables

data   observations of or information arising from the research process

data archives   collections of the results of previous research

data specifications   detailed descriptions of the data that are to be recorded for each case and variable

data transformation   modification of data to meet the requirements of a particular analysis technique

deconstruction   revealing the latent structures of texts to expose them to critical analysis

deduction   reasoning that moves from abstract statements about general relationships to concrete statements about specific behaviours

degrees of freedom (*df*)   the number of cells in a table or points along a regression line that may be entered without being determined by prior entries

demographic group   a group defined by some personal characteristic(s) of its members

dependent variable   a variable whose value changes in response to changes in the value of some other variable

descriptive research   research concerned primarily with measuring some aspect of reality for its own sake rather than with developing or testing some theory

direct observation   a technique used primarily in the study of group norms and behaviours where the investigator(s) directly observe behaviour in its natural setting

discourse   patterns of expression in texts used by actors

discriminant validation   a characteristic whereby a measure is valid for one concept alone as opposed to several concepts

dispersion (measure of)   an indicator of variation around the measure of central tendency, that is, an indicator of its representativeness

dynamics   interactions which support and reinforce structures

ecological fallacy   the improper use of aggregate data to draw conclusions about the characteristics of individual cases or groups

elite interviewing   gathering data through interviews designed to tap the unique knowledge of the respondents

empirical   pertaining to or characterised by observations or descriptions of reality

empirically grounded   a type of theory that is based on induction from actual observation

empirical referent   an observable object or event that corresponds to a concept

enumerative table   a simple tabular listing of research data

epistemology   the study of knowledge; how we know what we know

equivalent measures   indicators that measure the same phenomena in more than one system

experimental design   a research strategy in which the relationship between a given stimulus, event, or other variable and some observable behaviour is isolated

experimental group subjects   exposed to the independent variable (experimental stimulus)

explanatory research   research that uses observations of reality to test hypotheses and to help identify or develop an understanding of patterns of behaviour in the context of a theory

exploratory research   research designed to discover factors that should be included in theorising and research on a subject

***ex post facto* experiment**   a research design in which experimental controls are simulated in data analysis

external validity   *see also* **generalisability**, pertains to the degree to which a given study relates to other populations

face validity   a characteristic of a measure that gives it intuitive appeal

field experiment   a partial application of experimental design in a real-world setting, as distinct from a laboratory

field notes   written records made during direct observation

focus group   a small group used for in-depth study of a subject through directed discussion

frequency distribution   an ordered count of the number of cases that take on each value of a variable

frequency distribution control   a procedure by which experimental and control groups can be made equivalent by selection of combinations of subjects with comparable aggregate characteristics

functional   related to a set of preset functions and processes which are assumed to exist

Galton's problem   the task of testing for the effects of diffusion in comparative research

gamma (*G*)   a coefficient of association between two ordinal variables

generalisability   the characteristic that permits the results of research on a limited set of cases to be extended to the population from which those cases are drawn

going native   the situation in which a researcher involved in participant observation adopts the values and mind-set of those being observed and loses objectivity

guide   a set of instructions to guide a moderator in conducting a focus group

Guttman scaling   a method of scale creation that provides internal criteria for determining the degree to which a set of items exhibit unidimensionality (measure a single concept)

hegemonic   dominant and pervasive in influence

hermeneutics   simply, interpretation; issues involved in the process of interpretation when standards and evidence are contested

histogram   a bar chart showing the distribution of values on a variable

historicism   the view that a text can only be understood in historical context

homogeneity   the degree to which members of a given population are like one another

hypothesis   a statement predicting the relationship(s) between variables

identity   the ways in which an actor views themself in relation to others

independent variable   a variable whose own value changes influence the value of some other variable

in-depth interviewing   a technique for gathering information by interviewing subjects at length while being highly flexible in the structure and content of the questions asked in order to discover unexpected facts

index construction   combining two or more related indicators into a single, more comprehensive indicator

indicator   a specific measure of a variable

indirect causation   the phenomenon by which one variable exerts causal influence on another only by changing the value of other variables that directly affect it

induction   reasoning that generalises from what has been observed to what has not – that is, in which an abstract theory is developed from concrete evidence

inference   reasoning from either observation or a logical system to reach conclusions not already apparent

in-person interview   a survey interview in which the interviewer questions the respondent face-to-face

instrument   a device or procedure used for taking a measurement

instrumentation   the specification of steps to take in making observations; the creation of measurement devices

intercoder reliability   agreement in the values assigned to the same or similar cases by independent observers

internal validity   a form of construct validity evaluating if the measures are accurately evaluating the theoretical concepts

interobserver reliability   the degree to which two or more individuals agree on the details of an event they have observed as part of a research project

intersubjectivity   the notion that even if objectivity is impossible, it is possible to reach a concensus within a community of subjective observers who maintain a shared standard for the collection and interpretation of evidence

interval measurement   measurement that classifies and rank orders cases so that the distance between cases is known by using a standard unit of measurement

intervening variable   a variable that influences the effect of an independent variable on a dependent variable

interview schedule   the questionnaire used with in-person interviews

judgemental sample   a sample in which specific cases are purposely selected

key   the explanation of symbols used in a graphic presentation

keyword or key phrase   a word or phrase that is meaningfully related to a given concept, used for bibliographic search

lambda (λ)   a coefficient of association between two nominal variables

least-likely case study   a case least likely to fit with a theory but does so is explored to see why, in detail, the theory fails in this case

level of measurement   the amount of information provided by a set of instruments

Likert scaling   a method of scale creation based on asking respondents to report the degree to which they agree or disagree with a series of statements selected to represent a trait

linear relationship   a relationship between two variables that can be graphically represented as a straight line

line graph   a graphic device using lines to connect points representing observations so as to suggest trends or other relationships

longitudinal survey   a survey that compares the attributes or behaviours of a given set of cases at different points in time

marginal   the frequency distribution as it appears in the row and column totals of a contingency table

mean   a measure of central tendency for interval variables

measurement   the application of an instrument to count or in some other way quantify observations of reality

measurement error   inaccuracies in the observation of reality; differences between reality and recorded observations of it

measurement theory   a statement of why one expects values on an indicator to change when the value of the variable it represents changes

median   a measure of central tendency for ordinal variables

method effect   any misleading impact of the particular method used to study a subject on the results of that study

mode   a measure of central tendency for nominal variables

model   a simplified representation of reality

model specification   the process of selecting the variables to be included in a regression model and specifying their relationship to one another

moderator   the person who directs discussion in a focus group and reports on its results

most-different-systems design   a strategy for comparative research in which characteristics that differ between units of analysis can be ruled out as explanations for others that are shared

most-likely case study   a case most likely to prove a theory but does not so is explored to see why, in detail, the theory fails in this case

most-similar-systems design   a strategy for comparative research that focuses on units of analysis that are very similar, on the theory that shared characteristics can be held constant when differences between the units are examined

multicollinearity   the condition in which one or more of the independent variables in a regression equation are perfect linear functions of one or more other independent variables in the equation

multidimensional   having several facets or elements

multiple causation   the common situation in the social sciences in which an effect is the result of more than one cause

multiple indicators   more than one measure of the same variable, especially useful for enhancing the validity of indicators

multiple regression   a statistical procedure for examining the relationship among a dependent variable and several independent variables

multiple regression equation   the mathematical equation that represents the conceptual process described by a regression model and is used as a basis for multiple regression analysis

multiplicative index   a single measure constructed from a combination of measures of different but related concepts

multistage random area sample   a sample in which geographic units or their analogues rather than individuals are selected for analysis

multivariate analysis   any statistical analysis examining the relationship between *more than two* variables simultaneously

multivariate statistics   statistics relating to the relationships among more than two variables

mutually exclusive   characteristic of measures by which a given case can be assigned to only one category

negative relationship   the relationship said to exist when corresponding values on two variables change in opposite directions

nominal measurement   measurement that merely classifies cases without regard to rank or distances between cases

nonexperimental studies   studies in which there is no research design to provide a logical basis for causal inference

nonrecursive   the term describing a causal model in which at least one variable influences another variable that occurs earlier in the model

normal distribution   a distribution that is unimodal and symmetrical, with the peak at the centre, and in which the mode, median, and mean take on the same value

normative   pertaining to or characterised by preferences or value judgements

observation   the application of an instrument to assign values to cases on indicators

observation point   the time of observation or measurement

observation schedule   a form facilitating systematic recording of data observations

obtrusive measure   a measurement that is evident to the research subjects

obtrusive research   research which is carried out openly and obvious to those being studied

open-ended questions   questions that allow respondents to answer in their own words

operational definition   set of observations that represent abstract concepts

operationalisation   the process of designating sets of observations to represent abstract concepts

ordinal measurement   measurement that classifies and ranks cases without regard to the distance between them

pair-comparison scaling   a technique employed in content analysis to measure the intensity of evaluative statements

panel study   a study that employs the same group of subjects for a series of observations at different points in time

parameter   any characteristic of a population, as distinct from a characteristic of a sample

parsimony   the presentation of material in as efficient a manner as possible; simplicity in a theory

partial regression coefficient   a statistic that indicates the effect of an independent variable on a dependent variable when the effects of all other variables in a model are controlled

participant observation   a form of direct observation in which the researcher becomes more or less actively involved in the behaviours of the group that is being studied

path analysis   a statistical technique for assessing the relative influence of variables in a causal model

periodical indexes   systematic listings of journals and other periodicals used in literature reviews

pie chart   a graphic device in which sectored circles are used to represent observations

pilot study   a small-scale trial of measures and procedures used to identify in advance any weaknesses in the research plan or instrumentation

population   a set of cases about which one wishes to draw some conclusions

positive relationship   the relationship said to exist when corresponding values on two variables change in the same direction

postal surveys   surveys conducted by mailing questionnaires to respondents and asking that they complete and return them

posttest   in an experiment, a measurement taken after the introduction of the experimental event

pragmatic validation   the process of determining the pragmatic (practical) validity of an indicator

pragmatic validity   the validity of an indicator as a measure of a concept that is demonstrated by the ability to use it to predict the values of indicators of other concepts

precision matching   a procedure by which experimental and control groups may be made equivalent through the selection of comparable individuals

predictive validity   a characteristic of a measure that allows the accurate prediction of future events

pretest   in an experiment, a measurement taken before the introduction of the experimental event

process tracing   finding evidence of specific causal links at the micro-level between independent and dependent variables

proposition   a statement of the relationship between concepts that is logically derived from the assumptions of a theory; a component of a theory

q-sort   a technique employed in content analysis to measure the intensity of evaluative statements

qualitative   research based on systematic and detailed description and analysis of data but not involving assigning mathematical values to data or statistical analysis of cases

qualitative methods   research strategies designed to gather qualitative information, usually in narrative form, in order to describe or understand people and events, often in their natural setting

quantile   a measure of position within a distribution

quantile range   a measure of dispersion for ordinal variables

quantitative   research based on statistical analysis of the characteristics of the numerical measured representative cases being studied

quasi-experimental design   research in which data analysis techniques or data-gathering strategies are used to approximate the degree of control associated with experimental research

question branching   ordering survey questions based on responses to earlier questions

question format   the technique by which survey questions are presented and answered

questionnaire   a survey instrument intended for use in mailed or self-administered surveys

quota sample   a sample in which cases are selected to fill a predesignated distribution of attributes

random errors   nonsystematic measurement errors that render indicators invalid and unreliable as measures of a concept

randomisation a procedure for selecting cases for study (or for obtaining equivalence in experiments) in which each case in a population, and every combination of cases of a given size, has an equal chance of selection

random sample a sample in which cases are selected from a population in accordance with the principle of randomisation

ratio measurement *see* **interval measurement**

raw data the product of unstandardised or otherwise unprocessed observations

reactivity the circumstance in which persons under study modify their behaviour in reaction to the research itself

readership includes both the original readership of a text or audience as well as subsequent readers or audiences in different historical and cultural contexts who may appreciate or interpret differently from the original audience and/or authorial intention

recording form the form used to transfer aggregate data from a source document to machine-readable form

recursive the term describing a causal model in which no variable influences any variable that occurs before it in the model and thus contains no 'feedback'

reflexivity ability of the research to position themselves critically in relation to their research and research subjects

regression line the line that best summarises the distribution of data points on a scatter diagram and the slope of which characterises the relationship in units of change between two internal variables

regression towards the mean the natural tendency for extreme values to move towards more typical values over time

reliability the consistency with which a measuring instrument allows assignment of values to cases

representativeness the degree to which a relatively small number of cases resemble the larger number of cases from which they are drawn

representative sample a sample in which all major traits of the population being sampled are present in the same proportion as in the population itself

research design the plan of a study that organises observations in such a way as to establish a sound logical basis for causal inference

research question a question identifying the basic information we are seeking in a research project

resistance not necessarily overt confrontation because it is most often takes the form of avoidance, passivity and refusal to engage as strategies in response to undesirable situations (conditions, interactions, demands etc.)

respondents persons who respond to an interview or questionnaire

sample a small group of cases drawn from and used to represent some larger group

sampling error differences between the attributes of a sample and those of the population from which the sample is drawn

scale   a series of indicators that can be ordered so as to rank cases according to the degree to which they manifest a concept

scale score   a single measure of how much a subject has of a given attribute measured by a scale

scaling   the process of combining several indicators of a given concept into a single complex indicator of that concept

scatter plot   a graphic summary of the distribution of cases on two variables, using dots to represent observations

scheduled interviews   elite or specialised interviews that are guided by an interview schedule specifying the questions to be asked

screening interview   an interview conducted to select participants for a focus group

secondary analysis   analysis of data that have been gathered previously, usually by another researcher

segmented bar chart   a graphic display of data with bars divided into segments to show the distribution of a second characteristic in the population represented by the bar

small-n problem   the difficulty of finding reliable patterns when the population of cases is small

social construction   the theory that actors participate in the construction of their social reality; it does not deny physical reality but argues social reality is an interactive human construct

Solomon three-control-group research design   a variation on the classic experimental design intended to allow researchers to identify any influence of maturation on the results of an experiment

Solomon two-control-group research design   a variation on the classic experimental design intended to allow researchers to identify any test effect present in the experiment

specialised interviewing   interviews with respondents who require nonstandard procedures to ensure communication

spurious relationship   a relationship in which two variables covary but only because of chance or because of the action of some other variable

standard deviation   the measure of dispersion for interval variables

standardised measures   indicators adjusted so as to allow valid comparisons among units of different sizes in the analysis of aggregate data

standard score   the measure of location in an interval distribution based on standard deviation units about the mean

standard score of gamma (Z_G)   a test of the statistical significance of an association between two ordinal variables

statistical significance   the likelihood that an association noted between two variables, based on analysis of a sample, might have occurred by chance and might not exist in the larger population

statistics   numbers that summarise either the distributions of values on or the relationships between or among variables; in sampling, the characteristics of a sample that correspond to the parameters of a population

stimulus the independent variable in an experiment

stratified sampling a procedure in which subgroups are selected on the basis of one or more shared characteristics and then sampled separately

structural content analysis analysis focusing on the format of a communication

structured observation direct observation using a prepared schedule or protocol to record data

structures fixed patterns which are difficult to modify due to frequent repetition by large numbers of actors

subjects those who are being studied in a research project

substantive content analysis analysis focusing on the meaning of a communication

summative indicator a measure of group characteristics created by combining the individual characteristics of group members

survey research a technique used in the study of individual attitudes, attributes or behaviours

syntality indicator a measure of some quality or characteristic of a group as a whole

systematic errors measurement errors that affect all applications of an instrument and render indicators invalid as measures of a concept

systematic random sample a sample in which cases are drawn from a master list by random selection of the first case and application of a selection interval for choosing subsequent cases

telephone surveys surveys in which interviews are conducted over the telephone

test effect any difference in the pretest and posttest scores of a subject due exclusively to a response to the pretest

text any type of human behaviour or artefact which can be interpreted; original meaning of written material has expanded to include speech, behaviour, images and all other forms of human expression and interaction

theoretical import the degree to which a concept plays an important part in a conceptual explanation of an event

theorising the process of stating conceptual explanations for real-world events by asserting systems of relationships among concepts

theory a possible explanation for events, often a set of logically related assumptions and propositions

theory elaboration the result of theory testing that refines a theory rather than confirming or refuting the theory

theory testing an effort to demonstrate the utility of a theory through research

Thurston scaling a technique of scale construction in which some members of the group being studied are asked to act as 'judges' to assign values to items to be used in a scale in order to increase its validity as a measure of some underlying concept

time-series analysis a data analysis technique based on regression that seeks to establish causal relationships through temporal ordering

time-series design a research design that seeks to establish causal relationships through analysis across time

trend study analysis based on a comparison of the same general population (such as persons of voting age in a certain state) at different times

unit of analysis the smallest component or element about which generalisations are to be made

univariate statistics relating to or describing one variable

unobtrusive research or measure a measurement that intentionally avoids influencing the behaviour of research subjects

unscheduled free-form, without a specific format or instrument; said of interviews, observations etc.

unscheduled interviews elite or specialised interviews that are *not* guided by an interview schedule listing questions to be asked

unstructured observation direct observation using notes but not a prepared schedule or protocol, to record data

validation the process of assessing the degree to which an indicator accurately reflects the concept it is intended to measure

validity the extent to which measures correspond to the concepts they are intended to reflect

value the characteristic or score of a particular case on a given variable

variable a characteristic that takes on different values from one case to another or, for a given case, from one time to another

variation ratio the measure of dispersion for nominal variables

weight to alter the relative importance of items in an index or cases in a sample; the differential value assigned to a particular item or case to accomplish this

weighted index an index in which scores on one variable have been standardised by reference to scores on some other variable in order to facilitate valid comparison of index scores for different cases

working hypothesis a statement predicting a relationship between indicators

Index